W9-AGX-595

The Library of
Southern Civilization

*The
Diary of
Miss Emma Holmes
1861–1866*

Emma Holmes in 1900

The Diary of Miss Emma Holmes

1861 ∽ 1866

Edited, with an Introduction and Notes, by
JOHN F. MARSZALEK

Louisiana State University Press
Baton Rouge and London

Copyright © 1979 by Louisiana State University Press
All rights reserved
Manufactured in the United States of America

Designer: Patricia Douglas Crowder
Type face: VIP Baskerville
Typesetter: G&S Typesetters, Inc.
Printer: Thomson-Shore, Inc.
Binder: John Dekker & Sons, Inc.

LIBRARY OF CONGRESS CATALOGING IN PUBLICATION DATA

Holmes, Emma, 1838–1910.
    The diary of Miss Emma Holmes, 1861–1866.

    (Library of Southern civilization)
    Includes index.
    1. Holmes, Emma, 1838–1910.   2. Charleston, S.C.—History—
Civil War, 1861–1865—Sources.   3. Charleston, S.C.—Biography.
4. United States—History—Civil War, 1861–1865—Personal narra-
tives—Confederate side.
I. Marszalek, John F.   II. Title.
F279.C453H643   975.7′915′03   78–25924
ISBN 0–8071–0386–1

CANISIUS COLLEGE LIBRARY
BUFFALO, NY 14208

For Alester Garden Holmes, Jr.

Contents

Illustrations

Acknowledgments

There are numerous people whose assistance has made the editing of this diary possible. I can only hope that this brief mention expresses my gratitude to each of them: Lyell C. Behr, dean of the College of Arts and Sciences, Mississippi State University, who first suggested I edit this diary; John K. Bettersworth, vice-president for Academic Affairs, and James D. McComas, president, Mississippi State University, for their encouragement, advice, and support; J. Chester McKee, vice-president for Research and Graduate Studies, and Marion T. Loftin, dean of the Graduate School, Mississippi State University, for their support in preparing the manuscript; Donald J. Mabry, Glover Moore, Clifford G. Ryan, and Harold Snellgrove of the History Department, Mississippi State University, for advice, suggestions, and encouragement; E. L. Inabinett and William Stokes of the South Caroliniana Library, University of South Carolina; R. Nicholas Olsberg and Mrs. Craig Carson of the South Carolina Department of Archives and History, for providing research aid; Carolyn Wallace of the Southern Historical Collection, University of North Carolina, for information on the Wilmot Stuart Holmes Collection; Mrs. Granville T. Prior of the South Carolina Historical Society for aid in locating information on Civil War Charleston; Martha Irby of the Mitchell Memorial Library, Mississippi State University, for her efficient processing of interlibrary loan materials; Carol Combs for her excellent preparation of the final manuscript; Ronald Otis and Julie Dean of the Mississippi Cooperative Extension Service for their photography assistance; George Wilson of the Geology and Geography Department, Mississippi State University, for providing the map of Charleston; Mississippi State University Development Foundation for permission to publish this diary and for a grant to aid in the final preparation of the manuscript; Edith Holmes for providing information on the Holmes family; Caroline Holmes Bivins for her generous sharing of her vast knowledge of the Holmes family genealogy.

Six people in particular have shared in the editing of this diary. My wife, Jeanne Kozmer Marszalek, helped with proofreading and tolerated my many hours with "another woman" —Emma Holmes. Helen Thompson, my student assistant for three years, worked long hours tracking down bits of information, offering suggestions, indexing, and completing those time-consuming but necessary tasks I assigned her. She was followed by Cathryn T. Goree and Charles J. Morris, who saw the project through to its conclusion. Linda Schexnaydre was my editor at Louisiana State University Press. Alester Garden Holmes, Jr., professor emeritus, Mississippi State University, initiated the idea of publishing this diary and throughout the work was a constant source of information, inspiration, and encouragement. He gave support but never once tried to direct the work. His only instructions were to make it accurate. No historian could quibble with such a caveat, and I hope I have met it. For all his kindness and support, I owe him much gratitude.

All these people share in the credit for this diary's publication; I alone am responsible for any errors.

Introduction

It was February 13, 1861, and a twenty-two-year-old Charlestonian began keeping a record of the events swirling about her. Passionately discussing the turmoil of the recent past, she described how the election of a Republican president had propelled South Carolina into leading the parade of southern states seceding from the Union. She started her diary two months before the Civil War began; and she finished it after the fighting was over, the Republican president had been assassinated, and the seceding states had begun to grope their way back into the Union.

Emma Edwards Holmes kept a detailed diary of the years 1861 to 1866. A woman of intelligence, she possessed an intense intellectual curiosity about contemporary events. The information in her diary comes from situations that she herself witnessed, through wide reading of Charleston newspapers, and through letters from far-flung friends and relatives in and out of the Confederate army. The result is an intelligent young Confederate's penetrating—and partisan—insight into the Civil War South.

Any Civil War diary, and certainly one written by a South Carolina woman, will inevitably be compared with Mary B. Chesnut's *A Diary from Dixie*. The comparison is even more appropriate here. Mrs. Chesnut and Miss Holmes both spent part of the war in Camden, South Carolina. They knew one another and had mutual acquaintances. Unfortunately, in her diary Mrs. Chesnut made no reference to Miss Holmes, and Miss Holmes's diary mentioned Mrs. Chesnut only in passing. In a number of instances, however, both women discussed the same people and events. Mrs. Chesnut was a much wittier, much livelier writer, sometimes cynical about contemporary events, while Miss Holmes was more detailed, much more serious minded, and unabashedly chauvinistic. One learns different things from the diarists because of their distinct personalities and war situations. Mrs. Chesnut was the wife of a wealthy plantation owner-politician-aide to Jefferson Davis, and her diary provided information about wartime life at the highest Confederate echelons. Miss Holmes, a member of an important South Carolina family, described the impact of war on the old-line southern elite. She also discussed the results of the war, its impact on whites and blacks, and the beginnings of Reconstruction, subjects Mary Chesnut did not discuss in similar depth. The Emma Holmes diary is a valuable supplement to the justly famous *A Diary from Dixie* and provides information and insights not contained in that classic.

To understand the Emma Holmes diary and the many names it contains, it is necessary to comprehend something of the genealogical background of its author. Emma Edwards Holmes was born on December 17, 1838, the daughter of Dr. Henry McCall and Eliza Ford Gibbes Holmes. There was much intermarriage between leading South Carolinians during the eighteenth and nineteenth centuries, and thus Miss Emma Holmes was related to many of the leading families of the Palmetto State.[1] The three families in her line that are the most famous are the DeSaussure, the Gibbes, and the Holmes families. The DeSaussure line has been traced as far back as 1440 in France to "deSaussure, Lord of Dommartin and Monteuil near the village of Amance." In 1556 the family became a leading French Huguenot force. Six generations later, in the person of Henry DeSaussure (Henry of Lausanne), the DeSaussures came to America, settled in the Beaufort dis-

---

1 A Holmes descendant of today wrote recently that a Gibbes descendant wrote her that "his family tried to make him kin to everybody in S.C. and he was about right." Caroline Holmes Bivins to editor, March 31, 1974.

trict of what today is South Carolina, and became one of the state's leading families.[2]

The most famous American DeSaussure was Henry William (1763–1839), lawyer, director of the United States Mint (1795), and chancellor of South Carolina. According to the *Dictionary of American Biography*, his codification of South Carolina law was so significant that "he was to South Carolina what Kent was to New York." In 1785 Henry William DeSaussure married Eliza Ford of Morristown, New Jersey, and they produced a large family including Miss Holmes's grandmother, Anna Frances. Henry William DeSaussure's children mentioned in the diary include: Henry Alexander (Uncle Des), William Ford (Uncle William), Louis McPherson (Uncle Louis), John McPherson (Uncle John), Mary Caroline (Aunt Carrie Blanding) and Anna Frances, who married Wilmot G. Gibbes in 1806.

The Gibbes family was another prominent South Carolina institution. Research has traced the Gibbeses back to England during the reign of Richard II (1377–1400).[3] The founder of the American line was Robert Gibbes (1644–1715), one of the key figures in the settlement of the Carolinas, later becoming governor and chief justice of South Carolina. His descendants included Dr. Robert W. Gibbes, a leading physician, author, and scientist. In the diary, Miss Holmes mentioned many Gibbeses including Octavius Theodosius Gibbes (Uncle Ta), Susan Adelaide Gibbes (Aunt Sue), and Henry DeSaussure Gibbes (Uncle Henry).

On her paternal side, Miss Holmes's ancestors have been traced back to 1702, to a leading "Charles Town" merchant, Isaac Holmes.[4] His grandson, John Bee Holmes, married Elizabeth Edwards, and they had twelve children including Miss Holmes's father, Dr. Henry McCall Holmes. Other off-

---

2 DeSaussure Family Genealogy, drawn by F. G. DeSaussure, Meadville, Pa., June 25, 1925–June, 1927, in possession of Alester G. Holmes, Jr., Starkville, Miss.

3 H. S. Holmes (comp.), "Robert Gibbes, Governor of South Carolina and Some of His Descendants," *South Carolina Historical and Genealogical Magazine*, XII (April, 1914), 78–105; Robert Wilson, "Genealogy of Gibbes Family of South Carolina" (MS in South Carolina Historical Society, Charleston).

4 Caroline Holmes Bivins, "Holmes Family Genealogy" (Microfilm copy in William R. Perkins Library, Duke University).

spring of this marriage were several persons who figure prominently in this diary: antebellum South Carolina congressman Isaac Edward Holmes (Uncle Edward), James Gadsden Holmes (Uncle James), and Arthur Fisher Holmes (Uncle Arthur). Hosts of cousins, the sons and daughters of these uncles, also appear frequently. These include Charles Rutledge Holmes, Cousin Willie Holmes, and Cousin Beck Holmes. Rutledge was a particular favorite of Miss Holmes, and his name becomes very familiar to the diary reader.

Miss Holmes's immediate family during the period of the diary (1861–1866) consisted of her widowed mother, Eliza Ford Gibbes Holmes, and nine brothers and sisters. Some of the children were married; others married during the war. Some of Miss Holmes's brothers were often not at home because of military service. The oldest member of the family was Frances DeSaussure Holmes (Sister Fanny, 1830–1875). Fanny never married and, according to the diary, apparently suffered from some sort of emotional disturbance. Susan Boone Holmes (Sue, 1833–1872) was the second child, and she too never married. She attended many social events with Miss Holmes during this period. Henry McCall Holmes (Brother Henry, 1834–1899) married Sidney Pasteur (Chick) in 1858, and a family quickly followed. He was a physician and served in the Confederate army.[5] Wilmot Gibbes Holmes (Willie, 1837–1899) also served in the army, but much of his service was in South Carolina so he was often at home. During the war he married Maria B. Scriven, a widow with five children. Next in the family came Miss Holmes (1838–1910) and after her, Caroline Octavia Holmes (Carrie, 1841–1915). Carrie married Isaac DuBose White and delivered two children during the war. All three events are described in the diary. Edward Isaac Holmes (1844–1898) was a teenager during part of the war. For a time he was a student at the Citadel and later entered the army. He did not marry until 1880. Eliza Ford Holmes (Lila, 1845–1899) was also very young during the war. She lived at home and was Miss Holmes's frequent social companion. Alester Garden Holmes (Allie, 1847–1868), though quite young, served some time in

5 Alester G. Holmes, Jr. (ed.), *Diary of Henry McCall Holmes, Army of Tennessee, Assistant Surgeon, Florida Troops* (State College, Miss.: privately printed, 1968).

the army but was usually home. John Bee Holmes (Johnnie, 1848–1896) was the youngest child, and his Civil War years were filled with books and schools. By the end of the conflict, however, family needs forced him to find work.

Emma Edwards Holmes was thus a member of a large family of distinguished heritage. Her family ties and her attachment to Charleston and the Palmetto State were deep, and her life revolved around her large immediate family, relatives, and many close friends. Her father died in the 1850s, so her mother was family head during the war, morally supported by the DeSaussures, the Holmeses and Gibbeses. Fortunately, Dr. Holmes, a physician and plantation owner, had provided well for his widow and family. Until the 1861 Charleston fire destroyed their home and the Civil War–Reconstruction dislocation took its toll, the Holmes family was financially secure. They lived graciously, complete with comfortable home, close friends, and attending slaves. They exemplified the qualities nineteenth-century Charlestonians revered. They loved family, church, and state and remained intensely loyal to each.

Circumstances permitted Miss Holmes to view the war from several perspectives. She lived in Charleston during the April, 1861, bombardment of Fort Sumter and was visiting there during the 1863 Union shelling of the city. She experienced the great fire of December, 1861, which leveled a large part of the city including her family home. She visited army camps in the coastal area and described the ever-expanding ring of fortifications circling the once peaceful seaport city. She spent extended periods on plantations, but she preferred city life, specifically Charleston. When the loss of her family home forced a move to Camden, South Carolina, she experienced life as a refugee in a small up-country town and was able to contrast it with life in the larger, more cosmopolitan Charleston. At Camden, too, she came face to face with Union forces: first Sherman's army, then black troops, and finally the small Reconstruction "occupation" garrison.

In presenting her picture of the wartime South, Miss Holmes discussed a host of varied institutions, topics, and individuals. She knew and commented on leading figures of the South Carolina Episcopal church, including Bishop Thomas F. Davis and later Bishop W. B. W. Howe and described the religious life of that denomination during the war years. She provided insight into the social life of the day with her descriptions of the Citadel orations, the dinner parties, sailing in Charleston harbor, and "frolics" in general. She discussed the role women played in the war with their flagmaking, their societies to aid the troops, and their attitude toward their men in the war effort. She detailed courting habits, engagements, and war weddings of the time. She showed that fighting and disease took a heavy toll on the military and civilian populations and that death seemed to hover over every family. She gave the reader a perspective on the relationship of white owners and black slaves and documented the changed situation for both in the early days of Reconstruction. She commented on the books she read during the war and described contemporary education. She taught in an organized institution and later was a governess for a large family.

In this diary, Emma Holmes described the war feelings of an intelligent southern woman. Her knowledge of what was happening—more thorough than that of the average Confederate—is a good indication of how southern nonofficials reacted to the burdens of war. For example, there are scant diary references to Confederate military reversals. In some cases, Miss Holmes simply refused to acknowledge defeat; for example, when she claimed victory for Lee at Gettysburg and insisted he was falling back for strategic or tactical reasons. When a Union victory was obvious, such as Sherman's capture of Savannah, she rationalized it as unimportant and even of benefit to the Confederacy. The reader can surmise that the people of the Confederacy, even those who made a real effort to stay informed, did not have accurate intelligence on the war's progress.

Another obvious theme of the diary is Miss Holmes's hatred for the North in general and "Black Republicans" in particular. She castigated northerners, except when she felt they embraced a southern position (for example, Clement L. Vallandigham). She viewed Abraham Lincoln as a power-hungry perverter of the presidency who was purposely running roughshod over civil liberties. Union officers and men were either cowards, who ran at the first sign of Confederate gray, or brutes. They were particularly cruel to Confederate prisoners of war. At one point she opined that "the horrors of the slave ship have been out-rivaled" by the sufferings of Confederate soldiers on crowded Federal POW ships.[6]

By the same token, although she finally concluded that southern selfishness had doomed the Confederate war effort, for most of the war she attributed total virtue to the southern cause. She idolized General P. G. T. Beauregard and Confederate cavalry raider John Hunt Morgan. She defended Jefferson Davis against all criticism and was a supporter of Braxton Bragg, the much maligned, unsuccessful commander of Confederate troops in the western theater. After the Battle of Bull Run, her exuberance for the Confederate army caused her to exclaim: "Every Southerner was a hero on that battlefield."[7] These pro-Confederate, antinorthern attitudes peaked in 1865, when she contemplated the probable future: "To go back into the Union!!! No words can describe all the horrors contained in these few words. Our souls recoiled shuddering at the bare idea. . . . Our Southern blood rose in stronger rebellion than ever and we all determined that, if obliged to submit, never could they *subdue* us."[8] Since this statement was written just a few lines after her mention of Lincoln's assassination, it indicates the depth of her antinorthern feeling. Rejoining the Union would not come easily for Emma Holmes; Reconstruction would obviously be a difficult time for the re-united states.

As a young woman (twenty-two to twenty-eight years of age during this period), Miss Holmes enjoyed the companionship of her contemporaries; she relished parties and social gatherings of all sorts; she was exhilarated by the events she was experiencing. The war was a source of southern glory and an opportunity for personal adventure and new experiences. She had confidence in the South's truth and justice and never doubted that ultimately God would grant the success of Confederate arms (after inflicting a necessary amount of purifying trial). Still she recognized the horror of war. As time wore on, a repugnance to continued suffering replaced her initial exuberance.

A believer in aristocracy, Miss Holmes felt that people could be classed as betters or inferiors; and she often spoke

6 November 12, 1864.
7 July 29, 1861.
8 April 22, 1865.

of the "mobocracy." She accepted slavery without question, matter of factly viewing blacks as an intellectually and morally deficient people. She classified poor whites as individuals beneath her friends and relatives, and she had as little contact with them as possible. She was a woman of considerable intellect and curiosity. She read widely in both the classics and contemporary literature and read the newspaper regularly. Her intellectual bent drew her to the teaching profession, but her native intelligence and wide interests made her intolerant of the lack of similar academic enthusiasm in her students. Consequently, she suffered pedagogical frustrations. Still she remained a teacher most of her life.

Throughout the diary, much of Miss Holmes's life revolved around men, both friends and relatives. Her attitude toward males, however, was ambivalent; she enjoyed their company yet was wary of them, fearing they would not live up to her expectations. This attitude, which she referred to as her "high standards," convinced her she would become an old maid. At one point, she even hoped she would die young to avoid this fate. She felt this sense of marital hopelessness so intensely that she was saddened whenever friends or relatives became engaged. Such tidings meant her social circle was being dislocated and her range of unmarried acquaintants narrowed. Still, she associated with many men and became infatuated with several of them. Each time she was disappointed, however, because they did not feel the same way about her. She never received a marriage proposal—not even during the marriage-filled war years—and fulfilled her self-prophecy. She remained unmarried all her life.

Throughout the war, Miss Holmes suffered from a number of physical maladies. In 1861 she hurt her foot so badly that the doctor considered amputation. Fortunately a long convalescence prevented the necessity of surgery, but the foot remained a constant physical and emotional problem from that time on. Often she felt too tired or too sick to carry on her duties or enjoy recreation, and she blamed these apparent depressions on the pressures of war, her home situation, and her desire to be independent. Hot weather brought on lethargy and added to her woes. In a postwar statement, Miss Holmes's mother, with the love and exasperation only a parent can feel toward a child, succinctly analyzed her daughter.

"I am too sorry to see Emma so depressed and wished she could go somewhere when I get funds in June—but she [is] so provokingly fussy & notional that she must not be indebted to me for anything, that it takes all my love to bear up under her ways—yet if I am sick she is very attentive to me—she certainly is her own enemy in her dictatorial character & prejudiced views."[9]

Miss Holmes kept this diary from February 13, 1861, to April 7, 1866—from secession, through Civil War, to early Reconstruction. At one point in this diary, she mentioned old journals, indicating that she may have kept another diary earlier. Perhaps too she kept chronicles in later years. Unfortunately, no such diaries have been discovered. The original diary manuscript consists of three volumes. The first volume covers the period from February 13, 1861, to August 19, 1861; the second volume includes August 20, 1861, to April 2, 1862; and the third contains April 3, 1862, to April 7, 1866. The first two volumes are in the possession of the William R. Perkins Library, Duke University, while the third is in the South Caroliniana Library, University of South Carolina. Literary rights for the entire diary remained with the family until 1973 when Alester Garden Holmes, Jr., grandson of Miss Holmes's brother Henry and professor emeritus at Mississippi State University, arranged to have them assigned to the Mississippi State University Development Foundation. It is with the foundation's permission that the diary is now being published.

The reasons for the diffused disposition of the diary are, unfortunately, known only in outline. Before she died, Miss Holmes apparently gave the diary's first two volumes to a cousin. The third volume was not discovered until some time after her death in 1910, by which time the first two had already been sold to Duke University. An attempt was made to reunite the three volumes, but when this failed, the third volume was given to the South Caroliniana Library.[10] During the 1930s, typed copies of the entire diary (generally accurate

9 Eliza Ford Gibbes Holmes to Henry M. Holmes, April 27, 1875, in Eliza Ford Gibbes Holmes Papers, South Caroliniana Library, University of South Carolina; *ibid.*, March 13, May 7, 1874.
10 Edith Holmes to Caroline Holmes Bivins, February 7, 1971 (Microfilm copy in William R. Perkins Library, Duke University).

but with some errors and omissions) were made and given to the Duke Library, South Caroliniana Library, and several family members. Later, the Southern Historical Collection, University of North Carolina (which possesses a substantial body of family papers in the Wilmot Stuart Holmes Collection) had a microfilm made of the typed copy. A daughter of Carrie Holmes White, Julie Wilson, identified some of the family members among the diary's innumerable names but left most unidentified.[11] Later an attempt was made to have the diary edited for publication, but this never went beyond the preliminary stage.

The diary itself was written using the poor quality ink and pens available at the time (Miss Holmes often complaining about the latter). Fortunately, her handwriting is clear, and the diary is readable. Still there are problems. Most of the time she did not indent paragraphs, and, as the war progressed, the script became smaller and the sentences longer. Early in the third volume, she began to write two lines to every one line of her ruled paper. Paragraphing became less and less frequent, and in places, a space of from one inch to three inches between the end of one sentence and the beginning of another served as indentation. Near the end of the third volume, she wrote from the very top of the page to the very bottom and even used the end leaves.

In order to clarify meaning in this edition, I have indented paragraphs, broken up many long sentences, eliminated a host of dashes, and made necessary grammatical changes. Ship names and book titles have been uniformly italicized, as have the dates heading each day's entry. These changes are not noted in the text unless they are major ones, because to have done so would have encumbered the text and made it unreadable. No words have been eliminated nor any added, however, unless this fact is noted by the use of ellipses or brackets. Miss Holmes, following nineteenth-century practice, did not capitalize the word *negro*. I have let this stand without comment.

This edited diary represents about three-fourths of the original. I have eliminated passages that merely cataloged names or that went into great detail (often erroneous) on

11 Caroline Holmes Bivins to editor, April 10, 1974.

military skirmishes and battles. Miss Holmes was very inaccurate in her presentation of war news, and the elimination of these sections detracts little from the edited diary's value. It still contains many military references, however, emphasizing the war's impact on Miss Holmes's life and on the lives of her contemporaries. This diary is most valuable as a commentary on the social aspects of the war, and this fact served as the guiding editorial principle.

I have identified the many persons mentioned in the diary, when possible. In some cases this has meant supplying a last name, in other cases supplying a first name. Place names are identified by state unless they are well known (*e.g.*, Savannah) or unless they are located in South Carolina. To help the reader keep track of the many family names appearing in the diary, I have prepared a chart for easy reference (see page xxvii). When a person or term is sufficiently unclear or particularly important or when an incorrect statement of fact appears, I have included an annotation. This auxiliary information has been added to aid reader comprehension without unduly cluttering the text.

I have not attempted to debate the Civil War with Emma Holmes. A diary, after all, is valuable for what the writer says in it, not for what a later editor adds to it. The reader should clearly recognize that any characterization of an individual or statement of opinion is Miss Holmes's assessment and is not necessarily accurate. Miss Holmes did not consciously distort information, but, like any diarist, she could only write what she felt and what she knew based on her sources of information. She was a Confederate partisan and her diary expresses this partisanship. This diary, like any other, should be read for its opinions and commentary and should not be treated as a textbook on the Civil War and Reconstruction. When read critically, it provides a valuable insight into both of these periods.

Frequently Mentioned Names

NICKNAME	FULL NAME AND RELATIONSHIP TO MISS HOLMES
Allie (Alester)	Alester Garden Holmes, brother
Aunt Carrie	Caroline DeSaussure Blanding, maternal aunt
Aunt Des	Sarah Boone DeSaussure, wife of Henry Alexander DeSaussure (Uncle Des)
Aunt Sue	Sue Adelaide Gibbes, maternal aunt
Brother Henry	Henry McCall Holmes
Carrie	Caroline Octavia Holmes White, sister and wife of Isaac DuBose White
Chick	Sidney Pasteur Holmes, Brother Henry's wife
Edward	Edward Isaac Holmes, brother
Dora	Dora Furman, close friend
Dan (Dr. Dan)	Dr. Daniel DeSaussure, maternal cousin
Emily	Emily Ford, friend
Fanny	Frances DeSaussure Holmes, sister
Father	Dr. Henry McCall Holmes
Grandmother	Anna Frances DeSaussure Gibbes, maternal grandmother
Isaac	Isaac DuBose Holmes, Carrie's husband
John (Johnnie)	John Bee Holmes, brother

Lila	Eliza Ford Holmes, sister
Maria	Maria Broughton Scriven Holmes, Brother Willie's wife
Mother	Eliza Ford Gibbes Holmes
Rosa	Rosa Bull Guerard, close friend
Rutledge	Charles Rutledge Holmes, favorite cousin
Sidney	*See* Chick
Sue	Susan Boone Holmes, sister
Sims	Sims Walter White, Isaac and Carrie's son
Sims (Big Sims)	Sims Edward White, Isaac's brother
Uncle Arthur	Arthur Fisher Holmes, paternal uncle
Uncle Des	Henry Alexander DeSaussure, maternal uncle
Uncle Edward	Isaac Edward Holmes, paternal uncle
Uncle Henry	Henry DeSaussure Gibbes, maternal uncle
Uncle James	James Gadsden Holmes, paternal uncle
Uncle John	John McPherson DeSaussure, maternal uncle
Uncle Louis	Louis DeSaussure, maternal uncle
Uncle Ta	Octavius Theodosius Gibbes, maternal uncle
Uncle William	William Ford DeSaussure, maternal uncle
Willie	Willie Guerard, Rosa's husband
Willie (Brother Willie)	Wilmot Gibbes Holmes, brother

The
Diary of
Miss Emma Holmes

1861–1866

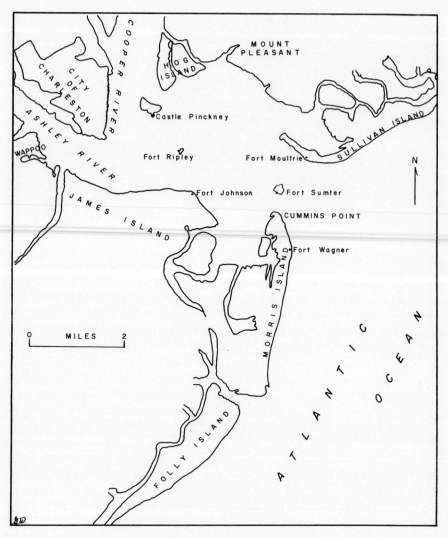

Charleston, South Carolina, and vicinity

February
13
ᗒᗊ
May
24, 1861

Preparation for War

H ow I wish I had kept a journal during the last three months of great political changes. A revolution, wonderful in the rapidity with which it has swept across the country, from the Atlantic almost to the Pacific, convulsing the whole of what was once our pride and boast "The United States," now alas broken into fragments through the malignity and fanaticism of the Black Republicans. Even England herself, wrapped in her mantle of pride, is thrilled to the core and trembles for the future, depending as she does on "King Cotton" the ruler of the world. Doubly proud am I of my native state, that she should be the first to arise and shake off the hated chain which linked us with Black Republicans and Abolitionists. "Secession," said a gentleman, was born in the hearts of Carolina women.

On the 17th of December, 1860, delegates elected by the people of South Carolina met in solemn Convention in Columbia to withdraw our state from the Union. Small pox was so prevalent there that they as well as the Legislature adjourned to Charleston, and, on the 20th, The Ordinance of Secession, declaring South Carolina a free and Independent Republic, was passed *unanimously* at quarter past one P.M., and that evening the two Bodies met and marched in procession to Secession Hall, where it was signed amidst an immense throng. But few ladies were present, as it was so late before it was determined to sign it the same evening, instead of the next day as had been at first proposed, that very few persons knew it until too late to come back for them. The news flew upon the wings of the wind, carrying dismay among the Black Republicans, who did not believe it until the deed was accomplished. Commissioners[1] were sent to Washington to treat with the Federal Government respecting the Forts and other government property, and all seemed going well, when on the morning of [December] the 27th, [1860] we were startled and almost stunned by the intelligence that [Major Robert] Anderson had evacuated Fort Moultrie and set it on fire, then taken possession of Fort Sumter in direct violation of the President's promise that the "relative military status in Charleston Harbor should be preserved." Fort Sumter could have been taken at any time previous by the Carolinians, for it had no garrison, only a keeper and his wife staying there, but they trusted the *honor* of the Federal Government and were thus repaid. The evacuation took place during the night of the 26th, [Anderson] stealing away in the darkness like a thief after cutting the flagstaff, [and] to add insult to injury, spiking the guns and burning the carriages. The Governor [Francis W. Pickens] immediately ordered several companies to Fort Moultrie, under cousin Wilmot DeSaussure's command, and others to Castle Pinckney.[2] As the latter only contained a half dozen Federal soldiers, they quietly surrendered, and in a few days the damages at Fort Moultrie were prepared [*sic*] and both forts put into excellent order. On Friday, the 28th, [December, 1860] the Custom House, which had been closed for several days, was re-opened under the Palmetto Flag. On Sunday, 30th, the Arsenal was taken possession of by the Palmetto Guard, and, as it was thought that Fort Moultrie might be attacked and no cartridge bags were ready, the ladies immediately went to work to supply the demand and during the

1 Martin J. Crawford, John Forsyth, A. B. Roman.
2 Wilmot G. DeSaussure (1822–18?), the son of Henry Alexander and Sarah Boone DeSaussure and grandson of Chancellor Henry William DeSaussure, was a lawyer, writer, legislator, and soldier. He was a member of the state legislature from 1848 to 1850 and from 1854 to 1864 and a leader in the state militia. He played an active role in the South Carolina Civil War effort, reaching the position of state adjutant general. After the war, he returned to his successful law practice and was an active civic leader.

rest of the week our fingers were busily employed making
them. That same afternoon, Maj. [P. F.] Stevens, with fifty
[Citadel] cadets[3] and two hundred negroes and several cannons, went to work to construct Fort Morris, which commands the Ship Channel.

The city seemed suddenly turned into a camp. Nothing was
heard but preparations for war, and all hands were employed
in the good cause. Our Commissioners immediately left
Washington, after such a breach of trust, especially as the
President [James Buchanan], though declaring he had not
ordered Anderson's move, sanctioned it by refusing to order
him back or to withdraw the troops from our harbor. On the
ninth of January [1861], Mississippi seceded from the Union,
and Alabama and Florida on the eleventh, Georgia on the
19th, Louisiana on the twenty-fifth or sixth. March 11th
Texas, or rather the Convention, passed the Ordinance of
Secession about the first of February, but it was not formally
ratified by the people until the fourth of March, the anniversary of the raising of the Lone Star Flag.

On January ninth, between six and seven in the morning,
the *Star of the West*, a merchant steamer containing 250 men
and supplies but without artillery, attempted to reinforce Fort
Sumter, though but the day before Buchanan had declared
that none would be sent. But the "gallant lads in grey" under
the direction of Major [P. F.] Stevens gave her so warm a reception, in which Fort Moultrie joined, that she was compelled to leave in search of more hospitable quarters, two of
the balls having taken effect. It was thought that she was disabled and would try to land the troops on the end of Morris
Island and send back of it through a little creek to reinforce
the Fort. The Palmetto Guard, Irish Volunteers, and a detachment of German Artillery were immediately ordered
down to Morris Island to repulse them and guard the creek.
As they were about to start, the Governor received a despatch
from Anderson saying no vessel should go in or out, in other
words blockading the Port, as the guns of Fort Sumter command the entire harbor. What a day of distress that was, for,
Willie, Cousin Willie and Rutledge and numerous friends

3 Founded in 1842, this Charleston military college was then officially
   called South Carolina Military Academy, but was usually referred to as
   the Citadel, its official name today.

were in that steamer and we dreaded lest Anderson should carry his threat into execution. But the order for the troops was countermanded. Then it was decided they should go round by the Stono River. They started at dark, when the tide was high, but they did not get there till Friday. Cousin Willie returned that afternoon, as all danger of collision seemed to have passed away, the *Star* having disappeared.

On Saturday the 12th, much anxiety was occasioned by the appearance of the war steamer *Brooklyn*, but, whatever was her intention, she sailed quietly away after inquiring where the *Star* was from a sailing vessel. The Palmetto Guard remained at the Light House five weeks; for the first few days "roughing it in true partisan style," sleeping on rushes with twenty to thirty crowded into one room, cooking their own food, eating it with "natural" knives and forks, washing their faces in a *duck trough*, etc., but they were soon supplied with necessaries for the "outer man," and most bountifully with every kind of comfort for the "inner man," both eatables and drinkables, by their friends in town and in the country. They all came back as fat and hearty as possible, all much improved in health and personal appearance, having enjoyed the "holiday" of camp life very much, notwithstanding the fatigue and exposure to the weather to which they had been exposed. Most of the time they were down the weather was dreadful: rainy, foggy, windy and generally disagreeable. They came back Tuesday, Feb. 12th [1861]. During all the time they were away, we were constantly expecting Fort Sumter to be attacked.

On the evening of the ninth of January, Anderson had sent a second despatch to Gov. Pickens, saying he would refer all to the Federal Government, thus taking off the Blockade, and requesting permission for Lieut. [T.] Talbot to pass through with despatches. On Monday Jan. 14th [1861], Lieut. [Norman J.] Hall, with despatches from Major Anderson, went on with Col. Isaac Hayne, who went to make a formal demand for the surrender of Fort Sumter. His letter, however, was not immediately presented to Buchanan at the earnest solicitations of many of the late members of Congress of the other seceding States. When he did present it, he received a most insulting as well as *false* reply, for Buchanan, ever since the Revolution commenced, has shown himself to be a pitiful *lying* old driveller, whom we pity as much as we despise, for until then he had always been considered an honorable, truthful gentleman. But now, yielding implicit obedience to the orders of Gen. [Winfield] Scott, whose vanity has impelled him to try the role of a Military Despot, false to his State, false to the South and false to everything, Buchanan has sunk so low that his name and Gen. Scott's have become the synonyms of all that is base, treacherous and false. The glories of the once renouned [*sic*] Stars and Stripes have indeed departed when such men yield the power of a great government.

In the meantime favored by Hayne's delay, the most active preparations were being made to bombard the Gibraltar of S.C. Strong batteries were thrown up on Morris Island, at Cummings Point, Sullivan's Island, and Fort Johnson mounted with Columbiads and other heavy cannon;[4] a floating battery is nearly finished, and all the foundaries [*sic*] were busy casting shot and shell, while the ladies worked for the soldiers and made cartridge bags.

Each day rumor appointed the day of attack, but still the result of Hayne's mission was waited for. Before he arrived here, the Southern Congress met in Montgomery [Alabama] Feb. 4th, [1861] Commissioners from the six seceding States forming it and Texas has since been added. A provisional Government was formed. Hon. Jeff. Davis [was] chosen President of the Southern Confederacy and Alexander H. Stephens of Geo[rgia], Vice President. Thus the taking of Fort Sumter has become a national matter, and a minister will be sent to treat with the Congress of the Northern States. Fort Pickens, in Pensacola [Florida] harbor and even more impregnable than Fort Sumter, garrisoned by eighty men under Lieut. [Adam J.] Slemmer, U.S.A., was during this time invested by an army of over two thousand men from the surrounding States, and we every day expected to hear of its attack. But each party dreaded to be the one to strike the first blow in civil war and, of course, that too has become a national affair. In fact, so many startling occurrences are compressed into so small a space of time that it is difficult to give an account of all, partic-

4   A large cannon first used in the war of 1812, by 1860 the Columbiad was the standard U.S. seacoast cannon. The largest one, a fifteen-inch model, weighed 49,100 pounds and fired a 320-pound shell over 5,700 yards.

ularly as I have not all the newspapers to refer to. I have tried to recall the most important events of the last two months, fraught with the happiness, the prosperity, nay, the very existence, of our future. A Peace Convention of the Border States has been meeting in Virginia, and have done nothing as was expected. The Virginia State Convention met [on the] 13th, but whether she will yet redeem the now tarnished fame of the Old Dominion, or whether, seduced by the insiduous flatteries of the Black Republicans, she will still cling to the sinking fragments of the Federal Government, yet remains to be seen.

February 14   On Monday, expecting the Palmetto Guard from Morris Island, we girls went out to see them. They did not come up till Tuesday, but, while I was running up the marble steps at Dora's [Furman] in the rain, my foot slipped and I fell, bruising it so much that I could not walk on it. I remained at Dora's till Tuesday evening when I came home to see the boys, but have to sit in my chamber with my foot on a cushion until the evening when I hop down with assistance. . . .

February 16   Kate Crawford came to stay with us today. I held quite a levee
Saturday   during the morning in my chamber where I am still kept by my foot. Old Dr. [James] Gibbes of Columbia came to see us this afternoon, and among other facts in his interesting conversation, told us that Gen. Scott had left the army when a young lieutenant because someone else had been promoted above him. He went to Columbia where he either studied law with grandfather [Henry William] DeSaussure, or practiced it. Gen. Wade Hampton, perceiving he had great military talents, persuaded him to return to the army and procured him a captaincy. Subsequently he owed his Lieut-Generalship to the vote of Judge [Andrew Pickens] Butler, and he himself told Dr. Gibbes, who has been intimate with him for the last fifteen years, "That he should never forget So. Ca. Gen. H[ampton] had restored him to the army, and Judge B[utler] had placed him above his enemies." But So. Ca. and Virginia, his native State, as well as the whole South, owes his hatred and treachery to their refusal to vote for him as President years ago. Virginia passed a resolution a short time ago to buy the spot where he was born and so manage it that *no other child*

should ever be born thereon. It ought to be ploughed and sowed with salt that not even a blade of grass might flourish there.[5]

Today we made an excursion to visit the Parsonage [St. Andrew's] and see the beautiful avenue of oaks planted by old Parson [Thomas] Mills, who, when about ninety, married Kate's aunt, who was in her teens. The girls went on horseback, and Mr. [William Izard] B[ull] drove Becca [Bull] and myself in the buggy.[6] From there we went to Skieveling, the family seat of the Izard's, Mr. B[ull]'s ancestors. It is now owned by Mr. H. A. Middleton but quite neglected and uncultivated. The house was burnt down a great many years ago, and the only remains of its former glories are a dismantled porter's lodge and the most magnificent avenue of oaks I have ever seen, wide enough for several carriages abreast and full a quarter of a mile long, with the branches inter-twined in a grand arch above with garlands of gray moss drooping from every bough. It seemed to me a realization of the cathedral avenue of [Thomas] DeQuincey's dream of a mid night ride on an English Mail Coach. We visited "Magnolia" also, but though the river view and the lake looked as romantic and beautiful as ever, the japonicas for which it is so famed were so blighted and discolored by the frequent rains that there was scarcely a perfect one to be found among the hundreds in bloom.

February 21

5 Scott was suspended for one year in January, 1810, when a court-martial found him guilty of conduct unbecoming an officer. In 1813 he became a member of Wade Hampton's staff in New Orleans. Charles W. Elliott, *Winfield Scott* . . . (New York: Macmillan, 1937) discusses the court-martial episode on pages 30–36, but does not mention the Virginia resolution alluded to by Miss Holmes. See her further comments on Scott in the May 30, 1861 entry.

6 William Izard Bull (1813–94) was a grandnephew of Stephen Bull, the deputy to Lord Ashley. He was one of the Carolinas' first settlers and in 1671 established the family plantation, Ashley Hall. William Izard Bull was the owner of Ashley Hall during the Civil War and was one of General P. G. T. Beauregard's special aides. Earlier he had been a colonel in the state militia and a member of the state legislature from 1835 to 1865. In 1865 he was a delegate to the South Carolina constitutional convention. His living children during the Civil War (all friends of Emma Holmes and mentioned in the diary) were William Izard Bull (Willie), Rosetta Izard Bull (Rosa), Sallie Davie Bull (who died in 1864), DeSaussure Bull (Dessie), and Rebecca Theodosia Bull (Becca). The Bull family genealogy is discussed in "The Bull Family of South Carolina," *South Carolina Historical and Genealogical Magazine*, I (January, 1900), 76–90.

February 22 We spent this morning fishing and rowing on the lake. The weather was delicious, as mild and balmy as a May morning. The trees are all budding and the roses beginning to bloom. Ashley Hall seemed to me more enchanting than ever, and we left it with regret, though we came down particularly to hear Jimpsey Thurston speak before the Calliopean Society.[7] Rosa came down to stay with us, and Willie brought Willie Elliott of the P[almetto] G[uard] to join our party. Rutledge and Harry B[urnet] went with us also, the latter driving me in the buggy as I am still lame. We arrived just as Mr. T[hurston] was ending his speech and too late to hear a word, but Mr. [S. C.] Boylston gave a very good well delivered speech on Churchill, Duke of Marlborough. Prof. [J. P.] Thomas gave a lecture on the past and present of S. Ca., but I was much disappointed in it. While we were in the country this morning, we were quite startled by the booming of cannon but soon concluded it was in honor of Washington's birthday.

February 25
Monday This morning we invited a large party to join us and visit Fort Moultrie tomorrow or at least walk outside and see the fortifications, as Mr. [Alfred] Chisolm had told us we could go down. But in the evening, much to my vexation and disappointment, Rutledge said he had not even tried to get us permission from [S.C. Secretary of War] Gen. [D. F.] Jamieson, so the party was completely broken up. After sunset R[utledge] and W[illie] got Mr. Bull's boat and took us rowing. Mr. P[eyre] G[aillard] and cousin Margaret [Barnwell] came just as we were going and were invited to join us. The boys went to company meeting tonight to receive the resignation of Capt. [C. F.] Middleton, and they nearly had a split in the [Palmetto Guard] company. But it was finally adjusted, though they have not invited another captain or rather elected one.

February 26
Tuesday Tuesday evening Willie invited company here and we expected about twenty persons, but only cousins Margaret and Lizzie Barnwell, Mary Davie, and Lizzie Burnet came and of the dozen or fifteen gentlemen invited, only Reeves Shoolbred, Ed. Macbeth and T.[om] Barnwell. But we had *one* too

---

7 The Calliopean and Polytechnic societies were the two literary societies of the Citadel. They held debates and oratorical contests and served as an emotional release for cadets.

many in the person of a Mr. Stephen Smith, a son of Aaron Smith, who defaulted in one of the banks a year or two ago. He walked in uninvited with Edward M[acbeth] and told a different tale to each lady to account for his presence. I soon perceived he had taken a drop too much, not enough to make him foolish but just enough to add to his native impudence and simply to make him the most cooly [*sic*] impudent man I have ever seen. He walked in and out of the room as freely as Willie would. [He] did not wait for particular introductions but talked to every lady and persisted in his attempts at conversation, notwithstanding the freezing cutting reception he met with both from Kate [Crawford] and myself. He is quarter master in the Palmetto Guard and boards at the same place as Mr. Crawford. They liked him very well in his place, but he persisted in calling them all by their Christian name and declaring his intimacy with each and all. He told Kate he had come to see her, well knowing her brother was sick, for Mr. C[rawford] had already refused to bring him here. It was altogether quite a scene, though we were all indignant at his impertinent intrusion and Willie especially so. He still afforded us great amusement, particularly as I thought him the author of two *poetical love letters*, the most ridiculous nonsense possible, which Kate had received in the morning. Both were signed in Latin, one on a half-sheet of blue paper with four words which we could not translate. The other desperate effusion of despairing genius was on pink note paper and signed "*Amo te.*" Both were in the same handwriting and postmarked Charleston. He did not, however, betray any consciousness, though we criticized and laughed at them before him, and [he] even did it himself. However, all things of whatever nature must come to an end, and so did his unwelcome presence, but not until the other gentlemen were leaving.

Judah Benjamin of La. has been appointed Attorney General of the S.C.A. and Henry F. Ellet, Postmaster General, and a bill has been passed raising the postage to five cents, drop letters to two and to twenty for letters over five hundred miles.[8]

Rosa came to go to the Theatre tonight with a large party we had made to see the *Lady of Lyons* performed by amateurs.

8 J. H. Reagan was the Confederacy's only postmaster general.

The proceeds [are] to go to the State. Rumor names Mrs. Henry King, Maria Finley, Chapman, a King St. clerk, and Marchant the Stage Manager as among the actors. Besides the play there is to be a concert and speech. The Governor and suite are to be there and all officers are requested to wear their uniforms, so even if the acting is poor, we will no doubt have a brilliant scene and plenty of amusement. It is, however, postponed till next Monday, so to console us for our disappointment, Mr. C[rawford] & Willie took us to row. We went a little before nine. The night was as calm and warm as an evening in June, and the brilliant lights from Chisolm's Mill, the Battery, and various other streets and houses, reflected in the water, had a beautiful effect. When opposite the Battery, we saw the moon rise as it were directly out of the water and almost over Fort Sumter, which lay so lonely and peaceful in the distance that, in the magic influence of the scene, all the agitations of the last few months and the frowning future seemed naught but a fearful dream. God grant that the terrors of civil war may be averted. I would not fear so much were our troops to meet the fanatics of the North face to face, for we have truth, justice and religion on our side & our homes to battle for, but Fort Sumter is almost impregnable and to take it thousands of the best and bravest of Carolina's sons must be sacrificed. For if the attack is once commenced, it will never cease until it is ours.

Kate and I rowed for a considerable distance, while Carrie and Rosa steered. Then we all reclined in the laziest and easiest positions and let the boat float with the tide. It was delicious idle dreamy repose just suiting the hour and the romantic beauty of the scene.

February 28   The last day of the month. . . . In the afternoon we went to the Citadel to see a review of the 17th Regiment, to which the Palmetto Guard belongs.[9] They turned out very strong, 110

9 The Palmetto Guard was an infantry company made up of men from the Charleston area. It became Company I of the 2nd Regiment, South Carolina Infantry. Along with the 3rd, 8th, 15th and 20th regiments and the 3rd South Carolina Battalion, the 2nd Regiment made up the 1st Brigade (J. B. Kershaw's) of the First Division of the First Corps of the Army of Northern Virginia. The Palmetto Guard saw action at Morris Island during the Fort Sumter crisis before moving to Virginia.

men. It was a gallant sight. Ten or eleven companies in their plain undress uniforms, their bayonets glancing in the bright sunshine, the bands of music, Gen. [James] Simons and his staff in their brilliant uniforms and the Rutledge Mounted Riflemen as their escort with throngs of spectators in all directions. We afterwards drove round the Battery, when the troops had preceded us, and it was thronged with equipages and pedestrians, as on a "music evening" in summer.[10]

Old Abe Lincoln was inaugurated today amidst bayonets bristling from the housetops as well as streets. His speech was just what was expected from him, stupid, ambiguous, vulgar and insolent, and is everywhere considered as a virtual declaration of war.

March 4

This evening there was a grand amateur performance at the Theatre. The proceeds [are] to be devoted to arming and equiping the Sumter Guard. As common report said that Mrs. Henry King and her set were to be the "ladies and gentlemen" who were to act, every seat was taken on Saturday, & curiosity and expectation ran high.

Hattie [White] and Rosa came to go with us, but about dark it commenced to pour rain and, though we dressed, we almost gave up any idea of going. However, the gentlemen came . . . and we went in spite of the rain. . . . Though our seats were taken Saturday, they were not *secured*, for others had encroached, and every inch of standing place was so jammed that our gentlemen had to stand most of the time. "The world and its brother" were there and our glasses were as busy in seeking our acquaintances as looking on the stage. Most of the gentlemen wore their uniforms, and though *very few* ladies wore evening dresses, it was a gay scene. The *Lady of Lyons* was acted, or rather "murdered," and, though we several times imagined we recognized either Mrs. Gamage as Mad. Melnolte and Col. [John] Cunningham, Mr. John Edwards & Mr. John Irving among the actors, we soon found we were mis-

10 The Battery is that area in Charleston directly fronting on the harbor. It gives an excellent view of the entire harbor area and during the nineteenth century was a popular place for walking. Many fine antebellum homes, including several mentioned in the diary, line the landward side of the Battery.

taken. Chapman was a disgusting caricature of Mad. Des-chappelles, in a very low neck and short sleeves, stockinets, and hoops, in fact was a hideous nondescript, but of course elicited roars of laughter from the men. Pauline, whose name we have not yet discovered, nor Mad. M's, was an automaton: wooden in *figure*, *speech*, and *action*. One *tone*, *look*, *gesture* and *dress* serving all occasions, excessively ungraceful, rather plain & walking like "Dot and go one." Mr. Morgan was Beauseant, *barely* tolerable. Covert, very good as Clavis, making it a comic character. . . . The only actor worth looking at was Dr. Couturier, as Gen. Damas, but the whole was the greatest farce I've ever seen.

Then we were treated to an address by Paul Hayne, read by Marchant, of which I only heard the concluding remarks and do not think I missed much. A solo on the violin by Mr. Rothschild of the Abbeville Volunteers. Two songs by Reeves [Shoolbred] and two by a little girl and boy. But the only really good thing was two little girls, one acting sometimes as an old woman or a boy and singing & acting comic songs. Then dressed as Italian peasants, they danced a fancy polka very prettily and gracefully, and the grand performance ended with one of them singing the Marsellaise [*sic*], while she waved the banner of the Sumter Guard. We certainly got our money's worth of laughter, if we were taken in otherwise.

. . . Quite a number of rafts with their pine knot fires were lying off Chisolm's Causeway, the gas light also adding to the picturesque beauty of the scene, and we could imagine we could see the camp-fires of an army, as he [Cousin Willie] pointed out where the different officers, guards, etc. would be.

March 7   Last night after five ballots and many discussions & meetings, the Palmetto Guard elected Mr. George Cuthbert as captain and thereupon Brewster, the first lieutenant, resigned. . . .

March 8   We called for Rutledge & went with Kate Crawford to the de-
Friday   pot and, as we had plenty of time, we all weighed. Kate and Carrie both weighed 143½, R.[utledge] 142, W.[illie] 16 [*sic*], and I 126 lbs. We have been so lively while Kate was here that the house seems unusually quiet without her. We felt as if we had lost something when she went.

... The flag which has been adopted by the Confederate States has a red field with a white stripe, dividing it equally, the white and red being the same width. The blue union on the left extending to the lower red stripe and containing a circle of seven stars, thus:

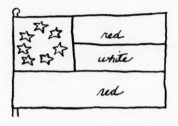

I spent almost all day reading over old letters & selecting those to burn and those to be kept, as I had some hundreds of them, and threw away many uninteresting ones. I had about half a bushel to burn. What pleasant memories of by-gone days did they not record. Little family histories and scenes long forgotten, friends now dead, married or far separated with whom I had forgotten that I ever corresponded. Notes or two or three letters from others with whom I had occasionally or accidentally corresponded. Here and there a stray lock of hair whose owner I scarce remembered. The invitation to my *first picnic* given by the [Citadel] Cadets at Mr. Robt. Macbeth's farm, and my *first ball* also given by them. Mementoes of hours of the most unalloyed pleasure to be remembered and cherished as feelings which will never return.

March 9
Saturday

What treasures old letters are and my old journals too, uninteresting and foolish to any one else.[11] To me they recall scene after scene as vividly as if unrolled by a panorama, nay, the very tones and looks of the other actors in them are brought to mind. Though my too vivid imagination has often proved a serious evil to me, it has also been a source of great happiness, enabling me to enjoy the society of my friends in hours of darkness and pain, almost as much as I do their bodily presence.

11 No trace of these journals has been found.

Mr. P.[eyre] Gaillard came to see us, and told us many interesting anecdotes about his great-grandmother, Mrs. Daniel
Hall of Revolutionary memory, as staunch a *Rebel* as ever
lived, and whose keen wits and sharp tongue made her noted
and feared among the British Officers. She lived to the venerable age of eighty-nine & once told Bishop [Nathaniel] Bowen
she intended to live to a hundred. Mr. G.[aillard] said he used
to sit by her side when he was a little boy while in her graphic
language she described many of the scenes of her youthful
days, and [he] has often wished since that he had recorded
them at the time. Among others at a dinner given while the
British were in possession of Charleston and to which she persisted in going though her husband told her that no American
officer would be there and that she would hear many unpleasant things, a toast was given by a young lady "To the
blood that flowed at Guilford Court [House]." Mrs. H[all] immediately rose and responded: "Thank God the blood of the
British *washed away* that of the Americans." Then she added
in her description, "But I tell you my child, I had to leave
then." She used to convey letters to the American Army
sewed up about her person and said the weather was so warm,
she often had to *dry* them before presenting them to the General. On one occasion when conveying a boat load of supplies
to the army on John's Island, where her plantation was, she
rowed directly past the British gun boats passing herself off as
a dying woman about to visit her mother. She had some very
peculiar habits and pets, among others was a black snake with
the fangs extracted which she constantly wore around her
neck, and on one occasion wore it to the theatre, causing the
lady in the next box to faint from the fright, and another time
so scared a British Officer by taking it off and showing it to
him. Than [*sic*] he took to his heels and jumped over the
balustrade of the portico. Mr. G[aillard] told us he had joined
Capt. G. King's company. The Marion Artillery [are] to go to
Morris Island on Wednesday and the Palmetto Guard are to
go on Tuesday to take charge of the Dahlgreen [*sic*] gun battery on Cumming's Pt.[12]

12   John A. Dahlgren, a Union admiral, was the inventor of this "soda-
water bottle" type gun: it was thicker at the breech and then tapered
toward the muzzle.

How my heart sinks with apprehension for the future, particularly after the last happy month when our boys have been with us.

Our Commissioners, Messrs. [Martin J.] Crawford, [John] Forsyth and [A. B.] Roman, are in Washington but have not presented their credentials. *March 11 Monday*

North Carolina has set the seal of Infamy upon her name by a majority of over 1000 refusing to call a Convention and going strongly for the Union. Monday evening we attended a charming sociable little party given to Allie Gaillard, who has just returned from Paris. . . . Between thirty and forty persons were there. Edward Brailsford was introduced and, as we had heard of each other before from his brother and the Moores, we did not meet as strangers. He is very good looking, pleasant and with an admirable opinion of himself. I did not intend to dance, but he persuaded me to do so, & the delicious music from Messrs. [George and John] Read, [Willie] Walker & [William W.] White was irresistible. They afterwards played an exquisite duet from Travatore & another from Norma. Then Nanna [DeSaussure] sang the Marsellaise [*sic*], several of the gentlemen & ladies joining in the chorus. It was splendid. Altogether I enjoyed the evening very much, though I have no doubt I have made my foot worse. It seems as if it will never get well, and the weather is so beautiful and so inviting for a walk that it almost gives me the "blues" to have to stay in the house.

The Palmetto Guard went down today to Morris I[sland] to take charge of Steven's Battery at Cumming's Pt. They had an election before they went, by which all the lieutenants rose, so Rutledge is now first lieutenant, and Mr. T. S. Brownfield second. Willie is very much disappointed indeed that he cannot go down, but, as he is the only one left in the office, he has to stay. Cousin Willie & *Rush* Gaillard have gone, and Peyre [Gaillard] goes tomorrow with the Marion Artillery. Rumors and telegrams are rife to the effect that the Federal troops will be withdrawn in two or three days, as they find it impossible to reinforce it [Fort Sumter], unless by an immense army on land as well as sea. And Anderson's supplies are *March 12 Tuesday* nearly out, his larder almost empty as the Federal Treasury. The news, however, is too good to be true, and Beauregard is adding to and completing our preparations for the worst.[13] . . .

March 13   Seward has refused to see our Commissioners, after delaying them several days on account of his "indisposition," and now it is "for reasons of public interest." . . .

March 14   The prospect of war certainly does not tend to depress love-affairs, for during the last three or four days I've heard of numerous engagements. . . . Mr. Peter Gourdin and Constantia Moultrie, after very *mature* deliberation, he being fifty and she nearly thirty, have at last made their minds to go *down* the hill of life together. . . .

March 16   . . . This evening Mary Brownfield came to see me and tell me
Saturday   of her arrangements and preparations for getting a flag for the P[almetto] G[uard]. She has fifty dollars already given her and but twenty more is needed. That, many of our friends have already promised to make up. The design is very simple, a Palmetto worked with chenille in natural colors, with the latin motto of the company in a scroll, in gold letters above, on one side. On the other [side] a wreath of oak & laurel leaves in gold bullion, with the name and date of formation. . . . If I am ever able to get there, I shall certainly do a part, as well as Carrie. But my foot swelled so much this evening that I could not walk across the floor.

March 17   Sent for the Dr. today. He came while the rest were at church and I never saw him so grave in my life. He first told me he could not attend me unless I promised to obey his orders exactly, for, if the case should become serious, he would be

13 P. G. T. Beauregard was Emma Holmes's favorite general, and he is often mentioned in the diary. A native of Louisiana, Beauregard was an 1838 graduate of the United States Military Academy and was superintendent there January 23–28, 1861. He was relieved when he said he would leave his post if his state seceded. During the Civil War, he commanded the attack on Fort Sumter and played leading roles at Bull Run and Shiloh. In June of 1862 he took sick leave much to Jefferson Davis' displeasure. When he returned to active duty, he was placed in command of defenses of South Carolina and Georgia and was second in command to Joseph E. Johnston during the campaign against William T. Sherman in the Carolinas.

blamed. So I promised. Then he looked at my foot & told me I would have to lose it. When I said I hoped it was not quite so serious as that, he answered "either that or have a serious operation performed. If you do not keep perfectly quiet, for though the foot does not pain you now, constant use will injure the bone and produce disease."

It was very hard at first to make up my mind to weeks of confinement, with my foot in an upright position and neither allowed to take a step or put it to the floor. After having been so much confined for five weeks already, then to have such a dreadful alternative, a cripple for life. I took a good long cry, then resigned myself to my fate as cheerfully as I could, tantalized too by hearing Peyre [Gaillard] and Johnnie C[rawford] laughing very merrily down in the drawing room.

The morning's [Charleston *Daily*] *Courier* announces that our Commissioners entertain strong hopes of success, and that Uncle Edward [Holmes], who is now in Washington, had written to Gen. Scott asking if Fort Sumter really was to be given up, and was answered in the affirmative.[14] *March 18 Monday*

The paper also had the funeral invitation of Mr. [James C.] Jones, of the firm of Russel & Jones. His death seems to be involved in mystery. The night before he walked until a late hour on the Battery with Rush Gaillard and finally parted with him in a cigar store. The next morning his body was found in Bennett's Mill Pond and his watch & boots on a wharf near.

A dull rainy day and cold as a January day.

To our astonishment when we woke this morning, we found it snowing hard, but it stopped between seven and eight. It was *March 19 Tuesday*

14 Isaac Edward Holmes (1796–1867) was an 1815 graduate of Yale University, a friend of John C. Calhoun, and a founder of the South Carolina Association, an antiabolitionist group. He represented South Carolina in the House of Representatives from 1838 to 1850. In 1851 he moved to California for financial reasons. When secession came, he went to Washington and conferred with Seward, among others, in the hope of maintaining peace. When he failed, he moved to Charleston and became a member of that city's council. After the war was over, he was a member of a South Carolina delegation that went to Washington to negotiate with Andrew Johnson's administration concerning state matters. See February 26, 1862, entry for Emma Holmes's comments on her uncle.

about two inches thick on the shed and everything looked beautifully [*sic*], but the sun soon shone forth very brightly and dissipated the picture. We enjoyed it while it lasted and, though we did not make snowballs, we made milk sherbert or punch.

The Dr. came to see me again, said the foot was better and looked quite encouraging. He says, if I had used it two days longer, I would almost certainly have lost part of it. What a narrow escape I have had from a life of misery, but I cannot realize how near I have been to being a cripple for life.

Uncle James [Holmes] sent me a nice therapeutic chair today, which has made me very comfortable.[15] I can change my position whenever I am tired. It is very cold, but I have not found it uncomfortably so, except for my hands and feet, in my little "sanctum."

My time passes very quickly and busily, sewing, writing, reading and attending to Lila's lessons, for she has now resumed her regular reading of history, studying French and arithmetic.

March 20   The papers announce that a very strong Secession meeting has been held at Charlotte N.C. and the people are as excited and enthusiastic as we ever were. Many of the strong Union men have become as earnest for secession, & they say that the people were deceived & cheated into voting against it. The Virginians are also rousing and in Richmond all are for secession. It certainly is time, when the Black Republicans are talking of making Norfolk [Virginia] the "point d'appui"[16] of seacoast operations against the Confederate States, and are sending troops, ordnance and ammunition, with provisions for a year, to all the Southern forts in their possession, or rather [in] these two States.

A letter has been received from Uncle Edward, saying he has seen Scott, who assured him there would be no collision between the two forces but never even mentioned Fort Sum-

15 James Holmes (1797–1882) was the brother of Isaac Edward Holmes, the son of John Bee and Elizabeth Edwards Holmes. He was first married to Eliza Ford DeSaussure and, when she died, married Charlotte Motte. James Holmes inherited the Holmes family home located at 19 East Battery, Charleston, and seemed to be the family head during the years described in this diary.

16 A base from which a military operation can be carried on.

ter. For several days each one successively has been named as "Evacuation Day," & today a telegraph was received appointing tomorrow, but scarcely any one credits it. Beauregard says he will not allow Anderson to withdraw. He must *surrender*, for the *necessity* which compels the Government to give it up is caused by our numerous fine forts & batteries on Sullivan's, Morris, and Coles Island, as well as Ft. Johnson. . . .

Uncle Edward arrived today, and a Dr. [Gustavus V.] Fox, *March 21*
sent to Anderson. He says his mission was simply to learn the exact condition of Fort Sumter. He was accompanied there by Capt. Harsteine [Henry J. Hartstene], S.C.N. but only staid half an hour and returned directly to Washington.

This afternoon Beauregard reviewed the Cadets on the Cita- *March 22*
del Green, and thousands of spectators crowded every available spot principally to see our gallant General. Mother and Cousin Beck [Holmes] went. A most remarkable event, but the former paid dearly for her first visit there as she fell and bruised both knees severely, &, when she came home, [she] had to go to bed she was suffering so much.

Mother did not sleep at all last night, she was in such intense *March 23*
pain. One knee is very much swollen and bruised. We certainly are a lame family now, but the Dr. told me today that my foot was a great deal better, much more so than even he expected.

I spent most of today reading *Misrepresentation* by Anna Drury, an admirably written picture of real life, but, oh, there is no need for me to turn to the pages of a novel to read descriptions of the misery & keenest anguish of mental suffering. Such *real misery*, so bravely borne, was brought before my eyes today that my heart was wrung knowing my utter powerlessness to help her. The world little dreams of the trials she has already undergone, nor the bitter pills of mortification she daily has to undergo. Misrepresentation has done its work against her, & that too from sources which render her still more helpless. May God in His mercy raise up friends who have the power as well as will to help her in her great need, for we can do nothing.

For several days I have had a constant flow of visitors, and this evening Mary Davie came and gave us a very amusing but interesting account of what the detachment of R.[utledge] M.[ounted] R.[ifles], who had been sent to Battery Island, had gone through. It is a little island of about five acres at the mouth of the Stono just ploughed and ready for planting cotton. In anticipation of another attempt to reinforce Fort Sumter, this detachment was very hastily sent off to keep a lookout & guard the mouth of the river. Being sent so hastily they had no time for preparations, even for food, merely carrying a few loaves or sandwiches, and a chicken or two, which served for supper & breakfast next morning. Then they sent to beg or buy potatoes & turnips, as they were too far from the city to be supplied immediately. There was no shelter for either man or horse, so they slept in "cotton beds" and, as it was cold, rainy & snowy weather, they woke up to find icicles hanging to their hair & beards, as well as the horses' manes and tails. Guards were out every night & they often had quite exciting times when boats were seen approaching. Plantation boats were constantly passing, and once quite a large boat was seen coming. It was hailed & ordered to stop, but, not doing so, a warning shot was fired; that had no effect, and a volley followed, fortunately hurting none of them, for they were a party of drunken negroes from a plantation, who did not understand the summons. But the scene after the firing was supremely ridiculous, all scared to death and each striving to get undermost in the boat. James Fraser, who was one of the troop, described it to Mary. In a few days, food was sent them &, in a week, tents, etc., while a hundred Irishmen went to build a battery there. James [Holmes] was ordered to "Camp Simons" in St. Andrew's to help drill the company, though he begged to stay at the Battery, as in spite of all the hardships, he enjoyed the exciting life. At Camp Simons, each one grooms his own horse. It is rather hard to fancy our elegant do-nothing dandies, such as Joe Heyward, Joe Manigault, the Rhetts, etc., doing such things as contrary to their usual habits, but it shows the spirit which animates all hearts.

March 25   Uncle E[dward] came to see me today. He looks quite well and
Monday   fat and his likeness to father is striking. Texas has deposed Gen. [Sam] Houston from the gubernatorial chair, and [also

deposed] the Secretary of State [E. W. Cave], because they refused to take the oath of office under the Convention.

Another messenger to Major Anderson, Col [Ward H.] Lamon, visited the Fort today, staid an hour and returned immediately to Washington.

The Dr. said today that my foot had improved so much he hoped to let me out at the end of the week. Johnnie bruised his knee, and it festered so the Dr. placed him on the "invalid corps" who have to keep their chambers & *chairs*. I have had him to amuse and keep quiet while enduring headache and toothache, which I have had for a week or more, and it sometimes requires an extra amount of philosophy to bear all. *April 1 Monday*

Today the Permanent Constitution of the Confederate States was ratified by the Convention of South Carolina, though only after many serious discussions, by a vote of 150 against 20. They are almost unanimous in objecting to two provisions, viz, the admission of anti-slave States by even a two-thirds of the House of Congress, and the continuance of a partial instead of a full representation of slaves in the Congressional apportionment. Many also object to the insertion of the prohibition of the Slave Trade into the Constitution instead of leaving it to legislative enactment as formerly. On the whole, however, it is regarded as an admirable Constitution and one well calculated to make us a prosperous and happy people. *April 3 Wednesday*

Much excitement was caused today by the attempt of a schooner without colors to pass the batteries. But she received as warm a welcome as did the *Star of the West* when she immediately hoisted the U.S. flag and turned back. But, [she] got among the breakers. Maj. Anderson sent to inquire why she was fired upon and to say that, if she had received any injury, he would feel obliged to open his batteries upon us. He also asked permission to send to the schooner and make inquiries, which was granted. Nothing further was heard from him, and, when one of our Guard boats went down to examine the matter, she had disappeared.

Excitement increased today when it was known that the companies on duty were to fill up the reserves and those on fur- *April 4 Thursday* lough [were] being ordered to join their corps immediately. Every lady was anxious and speculating upon the next probable move. It became still more general upon two officers from Fort Sumter, Lieuts. [T.] Talbot & [G. W.] Snyder, arrived with a flag of truce and were received by the Gov. [Francis W. Pickens] and Gen. Beauregard. Talbot, having been appointed by *his* government Ass.[istant] Adj.[utant] General for the District of Oregon with orders to go there immediately, asked permission to leave the city to report himself at Washington. Of course, it was granted, and he was escorted to the cars by an Aid. Snyder meantime informed Pickens that the schooner was from Boston, laden with ice and bound for Savannah, but had put in here on account of stress of weather, and told him also that one shot had passed through the sail.

April 5 Last night the graduating class of [Citadel] Cadets received their diplomas from the Calliopean and Polytechnic Societies. The speeches, etc., took place at the Hibernian Hall. . . . Tonight the Cadet's Ball takes place. . . . All are anticipating much pleasure, though it has been somewhat damped [*sic*] by the warlike symptoms, which will prevent a great many of the expected beaux from coming up from the islands to attend. . . . With very many of the girls it is their *first ball*, and what gay visions do those magic words conjure up. I should like very much to go, if not as a participator [then] as a spectator, but my unlucky foot still keeps me imprisoned, though the Dr. made me *walk once round the bed* today and back again and says the same trial must be made tomorrow. Though the foot did not exactly hurt, it felt very stiff and uncomfortable. . . .

This evening I was made very nervous and anxious by a letter from cousin Willie to his sisters saying he heard that the surrender of Fort Sumter was to be demanded today and, if it was not given up, "shot and shells" would be used. I thought it must be certain coming from him, stationed as he is at the most important battery, but Sue B[rownfield] came to see me and relieved my anxiety by saying the same report had been prevalent for *two* days, and other circumstances showed it to be merely rumor. She cheered me with an amusing description of their trip in the steamer a few days ago to visit the fortifications on Morris Island, a gale blowing a tremendous swell in the sea, & Mary & Fannie [Brownfield] dreadfully sea-sick.

Carrie was the personification of Spring last night in a beautiful sea green tarletan with white japonicas in her hair. Her dress was so simple, yet so elegantly neat, &, withal, so cool & fresh looking, besides being the only one at the ball of that color, that she attracted much attention. Gov. Pickens, Gen Beauregard, & ex-Gov. [John Hugh] Means, all inquired particularly who she was, & the latter paid her a high compliment. The ball was a brilliant success. There was no want of either beaux or belles and everybody looked well and seemed to enjoy themselves. Carrie enjoyed herself as much as she expected, a very rare thing, for our pleasures seldom equal our anticipations, at least mine scarcely ever do. *April 6*

Our visions of peace were rudely destroyed today by the return of [Lt. T.] Talbot from Washington with despatches to Anderson, which, however, he was not allowed to present but compelled to give up to the Governor. A Mr. [Robert S.] Chew, private secretary to Chase,[17] arrived with him to inform [Governor] Pickens that supplies would be sent to Anderson *peaceably* if possible, but no reinforcements. A fleet, however, would accompany the store ships to enforce their entrance. So at last, war is declared. But with the same treacherous contemptible policy, they seek to throw the onus of opening civil war on us. The sending of [Gustavus V.] Fox & [Ward H.] Lamon and the constant talk of evacuating the fort were only attempts to blind and beguile us, while the elections for Governor of the different Northern States were going on, and they were preparing their naval force. But they did not deceive our government, how ever much they may have done many of the people, and it only served to increase their force and activity. Talbot & Chew returned to Washington by tonight's train, and a Council of War was held this evening and all arrangements made for the expected battle. *April 8*
Monday

17 Chew was actually a clerk in the State Department.

April 9
Tuesday

A little before midnight seven vessels were reported off the bar. The bells of St. Michael's rang, & seven cannon were fired at the Citadel as the concerted signals for the gathering and departure of the 17th Regiment, Phoenix Rifles, Charleston Horse Guard & various other companies to different stations. All night the tramp of armed men were heard marching to the boats and the streets were thronged and bustling with the preparation for war, through all the pouring rain, which had lasted all day. All this morning I felt restless and anxious, listening to every sound with a beating heart, fearing to hear the announcement of the beginning of *civil war*. What fearful meaning is concentrated in those two little words. All was quiet, however, and cousin Beck [Holmes] came in and told us she had heard from Capt. [Cleland K.] Huger that the vessels had not yet arrived, though hourly expected. It was only rumor when the papers went to press.

All the up-country companies have been ordered down and every train brings fresh ones. . . .

April 10
Wednesday

The Citadel Commencement was to have taken place today, but, in consequence of Maj. [P. F.] Stevens & most of the officers and other public men being on duty or too busy, the public ceremony & speeches were dispensed with, much to the disappointment of the girls generally. About twenty graduated. . . .

Everything quiet today, the telegrams only confirming what we had already heard. . . . The Legislature of Virginia has passed a law acknowledging the independence and sovereignty of the seceded states. The venerable Edmund Ruffin has been elected as a member of the Palmetto Guard and is on active duty.[18] Hon. Louis T. Wigfall, a worthy son of our glorious State, but for many years a resident of Texas & who so lately brilliantly defended the rights of the South in "The *last* Congress of the original United States," has been appointed Gen. Beauregard's especial aid & is on active service.

18 Edmund Ruffin (1794–1865) was rabidly proslavery and a leading agriculturist. Though already in his sixties he took part in the Fort Sumter and Bull Run battles. He killed himself in 1865 in despair over the war's outcome. Two volumes of his massive diary have already been published. See William Kauffman Scarborough (ed.), *The Diary of Edmund Ruffin* (Baton Rouge: Louisiana State University Press, 1972–).

Four six and twelve pounders have been placed on the "Battery" with a corps of Cadets in charge. . . .

[This] is a day never to be forgotten in the annals of Charleston. A despatch was received from Jeff Davis with orders to demand the surrender of the Fort immediately at 2 P.M. Two aid-de-camps [*sic*] went to Anderson with the summons, giving him until six to decide. The whole afternoon & night the Battery was thronged with spectators of every age and sex, anxiously watching and awaiting with the momentary expectation of hearing the war of cannon opening on the fort or on the fleet which was reported off the bar. Every body was restless and all who could go were out. . . .

. . . The first time Anderson said, if the fort was not battered, he would have to surrender in three days for want of food. Beauregard went the second time last night at ten to urge the surrender, but Anderson refused. All last night the troops were under arms, and, at half past four this morning, the heavy booming of cannons woke the city from its slumbers. The battery was soon thronged with anxious hearts, and all day long they have continued, a dense quiet orderly mass, but not a sign of fear or anguish is seen. Every body seems relieved that what has been so long dreaded has come at last and so confident of victory that they seem not to think of the danger of their friends. Every body seems calm & grave. I am writing about half past four in the afternoon, just about twelve hours since the first shot was fired. And, during the whole time, shot & shell have been steadily pouring into Ft. Sumter from Fort Stevens where our "Palmetto boys" have won the highest praise from Beauregard, from Ft. Moultrie, & [from] the floating battery placed at the cove. These are the principal batteries & just before dinner we received despatches saying *no one* has been hurt on either Morris or Sullivan's Islands, and, though the floating battery & Fort Stevens have both been hit several times, *no damage* has been done, while two or three breaches have been made in Ft. Sumter. For more than two hours our batteries opened on Anderson before he returned a single shot, as if husbanding his resources. At times his firing has been very rapid, then slow &

irregular and at times altogether upon Ft. Moultrie. Though every shot is distinctly heard & shakes our house, I feel calm and composed. This morning I was so very restless because I was not able to go out, though the Dr. let me go down stairs, that I felt almost sick, but some one came constantly to tell us the news, & we were comforted by hearing "all well" at Fort Stevens. . . . At one time it was reported between twenty & thirty regulars had been killed at Fort Moultrie by the bursting of one of their own shells, but a subsequent despatch showed it to be false.

There are some few ladies who have been made perfectly miserable and nearly frantic by their fears of the safety of their loved ones, but the great body of citizens [seems] to be so impressed with the justice of our cause that they place entire confidence in the God of Battles. Every day brings hundreds of men from up country, & the city is besides filled with their anxious wives and sisters and mothers, who have followed them.

April 13 All yesterday evening and during the night our batteries con-
Saturday tinued to fire at regular intervals. About six in the afternoon the rain commenced and poured for some hours. The wind rose & it became quite stormy. But this morning rose clear & brilliantly beautiful. Yesterday was so misty it was difficult to see what was going on at the forts. The wind was from the west today, which prevented us from hearing any firing, and we were becoming anxious to know the meaning of the stillness when Uncle James sent to tell us Fort Sumter was on fire. I could not wait for the Dr.'s permission but drove hurriedly to cousin Sallie's [DeSaussure] where I had a splendid view of the harbor with the naked eye. We could distinctly see the flames amidst the smoke. All the barracks were on fire. Beyond lay the fleet of four or five vessels off the bar, their masts easily counted. They did not make the slightest effort to go to Anderson's relief. We could only tell when a gun was fired by the smoke or a white cloud as "big as a man's hand" floating for a few moments along the blue sky marked where a shell had burst. Occasionally when the fire reached the temporary magazines, or a shell struck them, an explosion followed which was felt in the city. The scene at Fort Sumter

must have been awful beyond description. They had soon been compelled to leave their barbette guns, from their exposed situations, many being disabled by our balls.[19] Anderson fired his guns until he was compelled to retreat into the casemates from the fury of the fire on three sides at one time. The men said afterwards the only way they could breathe was by lying flat on their faces in the casemates, for the smoke was stifling. Both on Friday and Saturday Anderson put his flag at half mast as a signal of distress, the barracks being on fire three times on Friday. "His friends" took no notice of it & [the distress signal] was not understood by our men though all sympathized deeply with him and shouted applause every time he fired.

In the meantime the scene to the spectators in the city was intensely exciting. The Battery and every house, housetop and spire, was [*sic*] crowded. On White Point Garden were encamped about fifty cadets, having in charge, five, six and twelve pounders placed on the extreme of the eastern promenade. It was thought the vessels might attempt to come in and bombard the city, and workmen were busy all day in mounting four twenty-fours directly in front of cousin T[a]'s [DeSaussure]. With the telescope I saw the shots as they struck the fort and [saw] the masonry crumbling. . . . We [also] saw the men moving about on the sand hills [on Morris Island]. All [there] were anxious to see, and most had opera glasses which they coolly used till they heard a report from Sumter when they dodged behind the sand hills. On Friday, when a shot struck the iron-battery, battering in one of the trapdoors, [Capt. George] Cuthbert walked coolly amidst the thickest of the fire on the outside, to examine it, and, during the whole battle, the Palmetto Guard, 135 strong, behaved with the greatest coolness, skill and gallantry. They had in charge Steven's Battery (Cuthbert), a mortar battery (Rutledge), and Point Battery (T. S. Brownfield commanding), where were two 42's & the rifled cannon just sent on by Charles K. Prioleau from England, a most destructive weap-

---

19 A barbette is a platform from which a cannon or gun can fire over a wall thus needing no opening or embrasure in that wall. A barbette gun, therefore, is simply a gun or cannon of whatever kind on a platform.

on, whose every shot told with dreadful effect.[20] During the morning a demand for cartridge bags for the Dahlgreen [*sic*] guns was made. The elder ladies cut and about twenty girls immediately went to work, all seated on the floor, while we set one to watch and report. Soon the welcome cry was heard, "the flag is down." But scarcely had the shout died away when it was reported to be up again, but only visible with the glass, the staff being shot off. It was hastily fastened just above the parapet, and very soon after, at one o'clock, the stars & stripes were struck, & the white flag floated alone. We could scarcely believe it at first, but the total cessation of hostilities soon proved it true. After the staff was shot off, Mr. [Louis T.] Wigfall, who was on Morris I. not being able to see the flag when it was replaced, determined to demand the surrender in Beauregard's name. He sprang into a boat and, rowed by three negroes, asked H. Gourdin Young of the P.[almetto] G.[uard] to accompany him & went to the fort while shot and shell were falling all around from the batteries on Sullivan's I. He crept into a port hole, asked to see Anderson, and demanded surrender. He was asked why the batteries continued firing as the white flag was up beside the U.S. flag. Wigfall answered that, as long as the latter floated, the firing would continue. It was immediately hauled down. In the meantime, a steamer had started from the city with several other aids, but they found Wigfall had anticipated them. The terms granted are worthy of South Carolina to a brave antagonist. Maj. Anderson & his garrison are to be allowed to march out with military honors, saluting their flag before taking it down. All facilities will be afforded for his removal, together with company arms & property and all private property, & he is allowed to determine the precise time of yielding up the fort and may go by sea or land, as he chooses. He requested that he might be sent on in the *Isabel* to New York.

What a change was wrought in a few moments in the appearance of the harbor. Steamers with fire engines were immediately despatched to the fort. The garrison gathered on the wharf to breathe the fresh air, & numbers of little sailing

---

20 Charles K. Prioleau was an agent of the Liverpool branch of Fraser-Trenholm and Company, leading blockade runners.

boats were seen to dart like sea-gulls in every direction conveying gentlemen to the islands to see their friends.

During the afternoon a small boat came with a white flag from the fleet bearing an officer who wished to make arrangements with Anderson about his removal.

As soon as the surrender was announced, the bells commenced to ring and in the afternoon salutes of the "magic seven"[21] were fired from the *Cutter Lady Davis School* ship and "Cadet's Battery" in honor of the one of the most brilliant & bloodless victories in the records of the world. After thirty three hours consecutive cannonading, not one man hurt on either side, no damage of any consequence done to any of our fortifications, though the officers' quarters at Fort Moultrie & many of the houses on Sullivan's I. were riddled & though the outer walls of Fort Sumter were much battered & many of the guns disabled besides the quarters burnt, still as a military post it is uninjured.

I have tried to give an outline of this ever memorable day but find it difficult to do justice to the subject and to the gallant men who achieved the independence of our beloved State. Another difficulty is, among the thousand different rumors each day circulated, always to find out which is the true tale even about things occurring before our own eyes.

Major Anderson appointed 12 o'clock today to give up the fort. The Governor, his wife and suite, Gen. Beauregard and suite, and many other military men . . . were down on board a steamer whence they witnessed the ceremony of raising the Confederate & Palmetto flags, which was done at the same time, the former by two of Gen. B's aids, the latter by two of the Governor's. Anderson and his men embarked on board the *Isabel*. . . . But as the tide prevented them from leaving immediately, they were obliged to be witnesses of the universal rejoicing. In Anderson's saluting the flag, an explosion from carelessness occurred killing one man & wounding four others. Two were, however, carried on the *Isabel* and [the] two mortally wounded were brought up to Dr. [G. G.] Chisolm's hospital where one has since died. Howe [Daniel

April 14
Sunday

21 The seven states then in the Confederacy.

Hough], the private who was killed, was buried in Fort Sumter with military honors, the service being read by Parson [W. B.] Yates & the funeral attended by a part of the P[almetto] G[uard]. The command of the fort was given to Maj. [R. S.] Ripley who commanded the regulars on Fort Moultrie during the battle,[22] and, when cousin Wilmot DeS.[aussure] summoned the officers on Morris I. to draw lots for the volunteer company from there which should have the honor of occupying the fort, together with a company of regulars, [Capt. George] Cuthbert withdrew his claim. The others loudly cheered him then did the same. Thereupon cousin W.[ilmot] took it upon himself to appoint the Palmetto Guard which seemed to give general satisfaction.

Sunday afternoon I went on the Battery which was more crowded than ever. The cadets had a dress parade at sunset and the harbor was gay with steamers with flags flying from every point. It did not seem at all like Sunday. Off the bar were [*sic*] still lying the Black Republican fleet, which has won the scorn and contempt of every Carolinian, especially after its grand braggadocio.

Mr. [Edmund] Ruffin fired the first gun from Steven's Battery, & among the soldiers was a little boy of twelve or thirteen named Peter Lalaine who had gone down to see his brother, a P.[almetto] G.[uard], and he had the honor of firing seventeen times.

April 15
Monday

Abe Lincoln has issued a most absurd proclamation ordering the *"rebels"* to lay down their arms and disperse quietly to their homes within twenty days. The old dotard is getting thoroughly scared. [He] has called for 75,000 volunteers & declared Washington under martial law, concentrating large bodies of troops there and has a guard round the White House every night.

22 Roswell Sabine Ripley (1823–87) was an 1843 graduate of the United States Military Academy. He fought well in the Mexican War and was the author of the two-volume *The War with Mexico* (1849). He resigned from the Army in 1853 but remained in the militia. When war came, he commanded and reconditioned Forts Moultrie and Sumter and, in August, 1861, was made brigadier general and placed in command of South Carolina, a post he held until he was replaced by John C. Pemberton in 1862. He served in various areas and commands throughout the war but was always in difficulty with his superiors and subordinates.

Hurrah for old Rip-van-Winkle. North Carolina has woke at last. Gov. [John W.] Ellis has ordered the forts to be taken and sent to beg us to spare him some cannon, but Virginia is wavering still. The heart of the *people* is with us, and they are eager for secession, but [John Minor] Botts & the Convention have knelt in submission to the "golden calf" set up for worship by the Black Republicans.[23]

Yesterday afternoon we were quite disturbed by the booming of cannon seaward but found afterwards it was a salute fired by the fleet of Major Anderson on going with his troops from the *Isabel* to the *Baltic*. Why he changed we do not know, unless he thought it would displease his government for him to go on in one of our vessels. He says he has twice sent in his resignation, once before Lincoln was inaugurated and since again, but his letters were unnoticed. [He says] that he intends to resign immediately & retire into private life, for the last three months of public service will last him for life.

April 16
Tuesday

North Carolina has refused Lincoln's call for troops, taken Fort Macon & is arming the State, but not yet seceded. Kentucky has also refused and says she will support the South in case of war, denouncing Lincoln's policy in violent terms. The P.[almetto] G.[uard] returned to Morris Island today.

Jane [Chisolm] and Emily [Ford] went with Carrie and myself today to dine with Rosa. We arrived there [Ashley Hall] about twelve.[24] Found . . . a very agreeable little party. The weather was delightful, cold enough for cloaks driving up, but the sunshine was so warm we dispensed with them while walking & fishing in the lake under the trees overhanging it. I enjoyed

April 18
Thursday

---

23 John Minor Botts (1802–69) was a member of the U.S. House of Representatives 1839–43, 1847–49. He opposed Democrats on everything but antiabolitionist stands and believed that secession was caused by a Democratic conspiracy. He was defeated in his delegate race for the 1861 Virginia Secession Convention and created a controversy when he said Abraham Lincoln had offered to stop the fleet from resupplying Fort Sumter in exchange for the adjournment of the Virginia convention. This was never proved. In March, 1862, he was arrested under the provisions of martial law then in effect.

24 Ancestral home of the Bull family, Ashley Hall originated in a 400-acre grant to Stephen Bull in the 1670s. It was located across the Ashley River from Charleston just south of Wappoolaw Creek. At this time it was owned by William Izard Bull. See also note 6, of this chapter.

the country, the beautiful scenery, the flowers, & the peace which pervaded all, doubly from my long confinement and the excitement of the last week or two. It is the first time I have walked out in six weeks. We rose from [the] dinner table just after sunset & all strolled into the garden in different groups, finally leaving Rosa and W[illie Guerard] to enjoy a têta-a-tête on the Indian Mound, the result of which was a source of speculation & amusement to the rest of us. He certainly is as much in love as poor H[enry] B[urnet] was (and I think still is, though hopelessly) but he has more tact in managing affairs. W[illie] H[eyward] is another rival, but we can not decide which has most chances of success. We hope *not* the former. . . .

April 19 Friday I believe Virginia is out at last. The [Charleston *Daily*] *Courier* has several despatches to Gov. Pickens from Richmond announcing it. She has certainly taken possession of Harper's Ferry & the Armory, Custom House at Richmond & Norfolk, the Revenue Cutter, the arms stored at Norfolk & sunk vessels in the harbor to prevent the Federal men of war from leaving. It has produced great rejoicing at the South & equal dismay at the North. Tennessee has refused Lincoln's call & offers fifty thousand volunteers. Missouri has also refused to fight her southern sisters. Arkansas is also with us in feeling as well as Eastern Arizona. The tide of Secession is rolling rapidly over the continent; every day brings news of its ceaseless course. Maryland has refused to call out the military, except for the protection of the State and Washington, and only in case of absolute necessity.

The accounts from N.Y. and Philadelphia show that *"mobocracy"* reigns supreme & that a "Reign of Terror" is about to be inaugurated.

April 20 Saturday Yesterday a terrible conflict occurred at Baltimore between the citizens & a regiment of Mass.[achusetts] soldiers & a part of the N.Y. Seventh R.[egiment] who were on their way to Washington. Thousands of the citizens gathered to oppose their passage through the city, attacked them with paving stones, & were fired on in return. Several were killed and wounded on both sides, but, by the efforts of the police, the troops were enabled to reach the station & proceed to Washington. The mob has torn up the railroad track & the President of the Baltimore and Ohio R.R. has issued orders that no troops shall be conveyed either to or from Washington. The whole country is in an intense state of excitement, & Maryland and Virginia are preparing for resistance at all points, &, in fact throughout the north and northwest, and indeed the whole country is arming & preparing for either one or the other side of the contest. It is almost impossible even to make a memoranda of the daily news, so voluminous is it from all points.

It is expected that in a week Kentucky, Tennessee, Missouri, Arkansas, North Carolina & Maryland will follow Virginia's example. Abhorrence of Lincoln's proclamation is strong in the west, and the people are all rising in defence of Southern Rights.

April 22
Monday

Several companies of [Maxcy] Gregg's Regiment left this morning for Virginia. The Richardson Guard go tomorrow, the Camden company has volunteered & the Palmetto Guard will go as soon as Beauregard relieves them from duty on Morris Island. Rosa [Bull] and Sallie W.[allace] came down today to write & send some hundreds of invitations to a fête Mr. Bull is to give on Wednesday. It is given with the intention of renewing his suit to Fannie [Garden] & is really given to her. He says he will never give up until either she marries him or some one else. He has invited "everybody" from the governor & Beauregard, with their suites, to some of Sallie's companions. Half the upcountry is in the city & all are invited. It will be a tremendous crowd, but the comfort is that the lawn & garden are large enough for them & a band of music is engaged. They will dance & dine on the lawn. . . .

Carrie & myself went to Ashley Hall this morning with Emily & Eliza North. We arrived a little after twelve & found quite a number of persons there & until late in the afternoon there were constant arrivals. I suppose there must have been over 150 persons present, most of them strangers to the city & whom neither Rosa nor we knew. [Ex-] Gov. & Mrs. [J. L.] Manning & the Misses Preston were there, all very tall, fine &

April 24
Wednesday

striking looking, but I was as much disappointed in the beauty of the latter, as I was in that of Mrs. [Francis W.]Pickens & Jane Bidon, all of whom I had heard so much of. The collection of ladies on the whole was very pretty. . . . Most of the ladies wore "jockeys" and many of them "Renfrew hats" some being of black velvet with white plumes, others white with black plumes.[25] The effect was very stylish & distingué, though I do not admire them for grown ladies, as they are too conspicuous. However, they afforded variety to the scene which was really very pretty. The band played delightfully, but the guests seemed more inclined to walk about & see Gen. Beauregard and the other "celebrities" than dance. The Gen. is rather above the middle size, very compactly made, &, though not of "commanding presence," he looks "every inch a soldier & a gentleman," not handsome, but his face attracts your looks again & again, & each time you are more impressed with the decision & character of his keen dark eyes. I was not near enough to see the color of them, but they seemed to me a brilliant hazel, my favorite color. . . .

With many acquaintances & sources of pleasure, I did not enjoy the day. I have had "the blues" dreadfully the last few days & the crowd & the gay music only aggravated, instead of curing, it. I believe if I could have danced, the exercise & rapid motion would have exhilarated me & driven them away. But as it was, though provoked at my own foolishness, I could not help it & everytime I looked at Rutledge, Hugh [Garden] & Willie [Heyward] & some of my other friends, the thought of how soon we would have to part with them almost overpowered me. After dinner, which was a scramble in true picnic style notwithstanding the ambitious name of "dejeuner," I found myself walking in the garden with Lizzie Burnet, separated from our companions. She had a severe headache & was feeling very sad at Harry's determination to join the P.[almetto] G.[uard] and go to Va. So we seated ourselves on a swinging grape vine in a remote corner to enjoy the quiet & fresh air for a time, & I took a little cry. The idea of crying at

25 *Webster's Third New International Dictionary* (unabridged) defines this type of hat as "of the kind or style prevalent in the county of Renfrew Scotland."

a fête!!! but oh what a comfort it is to be able to relieve my depression by tears. I always feel gayer & brighter after it, a paradox, but true. Then what added to my aggravation was being obliged to come down just as the full moon was rising, because the coachman was sick, when we expected to stay at least an hour longer, & as the crowd had left, it was just the time to see our friends. . . .

[J. B.] Kershaw's Regiment, of which cousin James B.[land- *April 25*
ing] is Lieut. Col. & in which are Hugh [Garden] and Allie, came up last night & are to leave immediately for Va. It is hard for us to make up our minds to the idea of "our boys" going so far, especially when Virginia has been such a laggard. For if she had proved true to the South two months ago, war might have been avoided. But the only comfort is, that as war must come, it will be carried on on her soil, not ours, and that is the reason our men are rallying to her call. It will be a Border War, for the Baltimorians [*sic*] particularly & the whole state in general are determined to resist to the last any attempts to reinforce Washington through Maryland. A despatch from [Virginia] Gov. [John] Letcher to the Mayor of Petersburg on the 22nd appeared this morning to the effect that he had received reliable information that an engagement had taken place on Annapolis Heights between the Baltimore Military & the N.Y. Seventh Regiment, in which the latter had been literally cut to pieces. It is the "crack" regiment of the state & was composed of the very flower & pride of New York City & has hitherto been deemed invincible. The same rush to arms has taken place on the Border as occurred with us, with the very great difference that everything with us was conducted in a quiet orderly lawful manner, notwithstanding the intense excitement. While mobs are rife in Baltimore, constantly breaking open the armories or hardware stores to obtain arms, all the telegraph wires leading north from that city have been cut & the wires south [have] been taken possession of by the city authorities. The centrifugal steam gun of Mr. [Charles] Dickinson, lately purchased by the city, which is worked something like a steam fire engine & is said to throw three hundred balls per minute, will be placed at the head of the street through which the invaders will attempt to march &

thus sweep the ranks.[26] A great many prisoners were taken by the Baltimoreans in their first skirmish, being half naked, half starved, & unarmed men, which had been deceived into consenting to go to Washington by the false representations of their officers in regard to the political feeling of Maryland & the reception they would meet with there. Most of them foreigners unable to speak English & suffering for the necessities of life, [they] were induced to enlist upon the promise of large wages. Arrangements were made by the city to have them conveyed to Philadelphia, &, when they left, many were completely [overwhelmed] by the kind treatment they had received and vowed never to lift their hands against the south [again].

Arlington Heights overlooking the western part of Washington has been seized by the Virginians & they are busily fortifying it. A Norfolk paper gives a list of the principal property destroyed at Gosport Navy Yard: six war vessels, including the celebrated *Pennsylvania*. The *Germantown* . . . & the *Merrimac*, a magnificent steamer just built, were burnt to the water's edge. Several others [were] scuttled & the Marine barracks & Commodore's quarters with other large buildings & their contents were burnt, but fortunately the attempt to blow up the dry dock, machine shops, & foundry were unsuccessful. But millions of valuable property were destroyed. Retribution will come, however, for such wanton destruction.

Thursday evening Carrie & Hattie [White], who had been driving out with Isaac [White] came for me about dark to spend the night with the girls & hear Mr. [Willie] Walker & Edwin [White] play. Mrs. [Anna Gaillard] W[hite] and Nanna [Hughes] are in the country, so our party consisted of us four girls, those gentlemen, Mr. [William] Ramsey & Mr. Hughes. It was a bright moonlight night & about half past ten we heard the band of music preceding the companies of Kershaw's Regiment, who were about to start for Virginia, & [we] walked out to see them pass. There were only two companies, some more having gone on Friday night, but they had just

26   This attempt to utilize steam power to hurtle balls at attacking troops never proved workable. This particular gun was captured by Ben Butler's troops near Baltimore. See Robert V. Bruce, *Lincoln and the Tools of War* (Indianapolis: Bobbs-Merrill, 1956), 138–39, in the chapter entitled "Patent Nonsense."

received the flag worked by Fan [Garden] & the other Sumter girls for the Regiment. They gathered at the Charleston Hotel just before going to the R.R. & aunt Lizzie Garden presented the flag to [Ex-] Gov. [J. L.] Manning. He in turn presented it to Col. [J. B.] Kershaw with a speech to which the latter responded.[27] Then addressing Hugh [Garden], who is third Sergeant of the Sumter Volunteers (Allie is fifth corporal) & is elected standard bearer, he confided it to his charge. But unfortunately as he handed it to him, the flag staff, which was too slender & not of the right material to bear such a weight, snapped. It was too late to repair the injury, so they carried it with them. How bravely they marched by, their bayonets glittering in the moonlight, though the shadows obscured their faces so that we could not distinguish them. Many were very small seemingly young boys of seventeen or eighteen. We turned away with mingled feelings of pride & sadness, the echo of the music fading in the distance, adding to the melancholy thoughts inspired by the sight.

Friday I remained with the girls to help finish the Confederate flag for the *Pride*, commenced before the battle of Fort Sumter. The circle of the "magic seven" had already been prepared & none of us would add the eighth star for Va. She has the responsibility of this war upon her shoulders, for if she had done her duty at first this would most probably have been avoided. She has just passed an ordinance adopting the Provisional Constitution, &, as the Legislature of Maryland & N.C. meet in a few days, they will follow her example & be really, as they are now virtually, out of the hated Union. The fifteen Southern States will soon be united in a glorious whole, for Delaware is in the hands of the Secessionists, and even in old Abe's own State, Illinois, at Cairo, the feeling is strongly in our favor. In Washington things are growing more desperate every day. Abe has not only a guard of two hundred volunteers around the White House, but has even about eighty "Border Ruffians, horse thieves & murderers" under Jim Lane, all of Kansas Notoriety, *in* the mansion itself,

27 Joseph Brenard Kershaw (1822–94) was the leader of what came to be known as "Kershaw's Brigade"—1st Brigade, 1st Division, First Corps of the Army of Northern Virginia. Kershaw was a native of Camden, South Carolina, and a leading figure in Kershaw County before and after the war. From 1877 to 1893 he was a circuit judge.

as a guard on those without.[28] Southerners, or those with Southern feelings, are in danger for their lives. Annapolis [Maryland] is in the hands of the Federal troops which are constantly passing on to fortify Washington. The greatest alarm is felt at the latter place, & families [are] leaving daily, while in Baltimore everything is settling into a quiet but determined resistance. Order [is] being once [more] restored as the military are being organized & prepared.

The resignations of [Matthew Fontaine] Maury & Col. Robert [E.] Lee will be most sensibly felt by the Northerners, for the former is the most generally known & respected American name in Europe (& [Duncan] Ingraham next) for his discoveries in science & of Lee, Scott said "that it was better for every officer in the army to die, himself included, than Robert Lee," on account of his military genius, particularly in engineering.[29]

Chief Justice [Roger B.] Taney & Judges [James M.] Wayne & [John A.] Campbell of the Supreme Bench are believed to have resigned. Col. Wynder [John H. Winder], who was for years in command of Fort Moultrie, *Maj.* [Samuel S.] *Anderson lately* in command at Fayetteville, N.C., a Virginian as is Maj. Robert A.[nderson] & Col. [Charles] May of Palo Alto celebrity, have all resigned.[30] Every day the list of southern resignations from the Army & Navy, as well as every official position, grows longer.

28 James Henry Lane (1814–66) was lieutenant governor of Indiana from 1849 to 1853 and a member of the U.S. House of Representatives, 1853–55. In the latter year he migrated to Kansas, became president of the Topeka convention, toured the Northeast seeking support for his cause, and, beginning in 1856, led armed assaults on proslavery strongholds. In 1861 he was elected senator from Kansas. When he arrived in Washington in April, 1861, he organized a "Frontier Guard" which bivouacked in the East Room of the White House for a few days. He shot himself in 1866 because of criticism of his support for Andrew Johnson's veto of the civil rights bill.

29 Matthew Fontaine Maury (1806–73) was superintendent of the United States Naval Observatory and Hydrographical Office. He is most famous for devising wind and ocean current charts which cut days off the Atlantic crossing. After secession, he became a commander in the Confederate Navy and spent most of the war in England procuring ships. Duncan Ingraham (1802–91) was chief of the Bureau of Ordnance (1856–60). He joined the Confederate Navy in March, 1861, and commanded naval forces on the South Carolina coast.

30 Palo Alto was the first battle of the Mexican War in which May, then a captain, distinguished himself.

It is a singular coincidence that the first blood shed in the defence [*sic*] of Southern Rights & Independence should have taken place April 19th, the 86th anniversary of the Battle of Lexington. The papers announce that on the 12th a Mrs. Peggy Fite of Wilson Co.[unty] Tenn completed her 100th year. She was 15 when the Declaration of Independence was adopted & has thus witnessed the rise, progress & dissolution of the Union, the most glorious fabric ever raised by mortal hands, now destroyed by the demonic fury & hatred of the Black Republicans.

The accounts of the northern papers of the "evacuation of Fort Sumter by Anderson on his own terms begged by Beauregard" make us wrathy. As Hattie [White] says, it is "throwing pearls before swine" to have treated them as they have been, for they are incapable of acting with such magnamity themselves, therefore cannot appreciate it. But a Nemesis will arise, to make their iniquities recoil upon themselves. . . .

. . . The telegrams are so contradictory now, we scarcely know what is actually taking [place] in Maryland & Va. But every paper gives accounts of outrages against Southerners or those who sympathize with us in Washington & at the North. . . .   *April 29*
Monday

The Palmetto Guard returned from Morris I. this afternoon.   *April 30*
A collation was prepared for them at the Military Hall & a gold medal, costing two hundred dollars commemorative of the Battle of Ft. Sumter, is to be presented to them tomorrow, both being given by "the mothers, wives, sisters & sweethearts" of the corps. The originators of it seem to have [been] the Birds & Bissells & that set in society. None of "our set" would have anything to do with it, as we did not like the idea & thought, instead of wasting the money on a useless medal, it had better have been given to the men to provide uniforms & knapsacks etc., which they need. We will present them with our flag, which is nearly finished, & really beautiful. The wreath on one side is of oak & laurel leaves, in chenille. The acorns [are] in gold & the name and date in bullion. On the other side is the Palmetto in chenille. The cresent latin motto above the tree & the date of the Battle of Fort Sumter beneath it, all being in gold. . . .

This evening at dark Carrie & myself in coming from cous-

in Willie's met Rutledge & Willie Heyward at the Corner & I
felt almost shocked when they asked if the report of Rosa's
engagement to Willie Guerard was true. I had not heard it
and, though I knew he was very much in love with her, we did
not think the "crisis" was so near nor that she was so much
interested in him. In fact, almost all of her friends are disappointed in her choice. We had hoped against it. For he is by
no means a favorite, from his arrogant supercilious manners,
though he can make himself agreeable when he chooses to.
We have not heard it from herself, yet something she said
yesterday makes me fear it is true. But through apparently
direct sources, W.[illie] H.[eyward] heard it in the street, &, as
a "fellow feeling" sometimes makes us "wondrous cruel" as
well as kind, he "enjoyed the pleasure" of telling H.[arry]
B.[urnet]. I am sorry for both, & would infinitely rather have
wished it to have been W.[illie] H.[eyward]. He came home
with us to get sympathy & we sat on the steps discussing it
fully. It really made us feel sad, & it will certainly make a
change in our hitherto pleasant set. Engaged & young married couples are always too much engrossed in themselves to
be as agreeable as before. In truth, we all feel disappointed,
but I like W.[illie] all the better for the way he took it. I know
it is true.

May 1
Wednesday   Every day brings fresh accounts of the demoniac fury & hatred of the Northerners towards the Southerners & South
Carolinians especially. The fury with which the "Sans Cu-
lottes" of the French Revolution sought the Aristocrats never
equalled theirs. Capt. Berry, Mr. W. C. Inglis & several other
well known Carolinians have had to fly for their lives or take
refuge under the British flag which scarcely afforded them
protection. Men even suspected of sympathy with the South
are murdered in cold blood. . . .

   To increase the hatred of the Yankees & the scorn & contempt of the Southerners, Maj. [Robert] Anderson, of whom
we all thought so highly for his bravery, has proved himself a
double faced liar & hypocrite hero. He pretended to appreciate the hospitable & magnanimous treatment he had received
as well as the kind feelings expressed towards him. All here
sympathized with him as a highminded [person] in a painful
position in which duty overpowered personal feelings, but, as

soon as he reached the North, how changed was his tone. He boasted of his prowess in retaining the fort till it utterly [was] untenable, declared he *evacuated* on his own terms, & abused us for our barbarity in firing on him while the fort was on fire. Imitating Abe Lincoln's passage from Springfield . . . [he showed] himself to the mobs, through which he had fought & elbowed his way, being fêted, dined & presented with swords & $500 gold boxes. As "the [Charleston] Mercury" says, he has shown himself in his true colors "with *God* forever on his lips, & *self* ever in his heart." When So. Ca. next meets the renegrade [*sic*], she will know how to treat him.

This morning for the first time I went out shopping with mother, aunt D.[Sarah Boone DeSaussure] having lent us her carriage. It was quite a relief to get out. . . . This evening I walked round to see the Brownfields & the flag. Mary [Brownfield] wrote to Gen. B.[eauregard] today in french asking him to present it. His answer was highly complimentary to the company, but he said he had to go out of town on public business. But we doubt if he would have done it if here; I believe it is not exactly etiquette. So they asked Cousin Wilmot Des.[aussure] under whose command they acted as Artillerists & who is very much beloved by them. He accepted it as a high complement [*sic*], saying he would do it not only with pleasure, but with pride. I think it will take place next Monday. . . .

May 2

Worked a little on the flag today, completing a letter in spangles and bullion. All is done now, but the stem of the tree. Mr. [Sam] Richardson dined with us & at night a large party . . . went to the Institute Hall to see the medal presented to the P[almetto] G[uard]. The Governor & several of his aids, Gen. Beauregard, Mr. C. H. Stevens, Capt. [J. P.] Thomas and several other gentlemen were on the stage besides the officers [of the Guard].[31] Maj. Ellison Capers presented & Capt. [George] Cuthbert received it, giving it into Serg. [J.] Bennet Bissell's keeping. It is attached to a black velvet collar, embroidered in gold with a palmetto & crescent. It is very handsome, but still I do not like the idea. The company were nearly 200 in number, in their war-worn uniforms, many of them

---

31 C. H. Stevens made the floating battery and then operated it during the attack on Fort Sumter.

with bouquets or roses in their guns, & little Peter Lalaine was there with his flag as marker. What gave me most pleasure was seeing Mr. Maurice [A.] Moore. He was among the aids, but I did not recognize him at first, thinking him to be in Virginia. As soon as the ceremony was over, he came to me & we had a long talk. . . . Mr. M[oore] said he did not think it was likely we would have fighting for three months, for neither side [was] even prepared, but that, when it commenced, it would be one of the bloodiest wars on record. The South Carolinians are almost idolized by N.C. & Va. & the more intensely hated & feared by Old Abe & his hordes of abolition demons. He combated [*sic*] my opinions of Maj. [Robert] Anderson & said he still had faith in him, though appearances certainly were against him. But, as the reports of his saying & doings come through Northern papers, it is hard to know what to believe. In fact, we must [wait] for the future to show what he is. . . .

Every day the papers announce seizures by Lincoln of all kinds of goods shipped South from the west or north, as well as vessels & reprisals on our part. He has issued a paper blockade of every Southern port, proclaimed martial law in Maryland, dividing it into five districts. Gov. [Thomas H.] Hicks of that State is his tool & does everything in his power to prevent it from seceding.

Our Congress met a few days ago & this morning the President's admirable message appeared. What a contrast is our government to that of the "Kangaroos" at Washington. Alas, how have the mighty fallen. The name[s] of Edward Ever[e]tt, Caleb Cushing, & many others whom we delighted to honor as friends to the South must henceforth be placed in the list of our enemies, eager to shed our blood.[32]. . . The effect of war is already shown here by the small quantities of goods imported from the North & the increased prices in consequence of the tariff, so that we can not get what we would

32 Edward Everett (1794–1865) was a politician, diplomat, clergyman, educator, and one of the most famous of American orators. He made the "other" speech at Gettysburg in 1863. Caleb Cushing (1800–1879) was a politician and diplomat most famous for his work as commissioner to China in the 1840s. He was, along with Jefferson Davis, one of the two strong men in the Franklin Pierce cabinet. He blamed the abolitionists for the Civil War, was willing to let the South secede peacefully, but later became an advisor to Abraham Lincoln.

choose. Marketing is also very high, that is the meats, for the vegetables which are usually sent to the North at this season, being kept back, are abundant. While, in turn, we cannot get their Goshen butter, upon which we depend generally, the little in the city being sold at 75¢ per lb. & fresh butter has also risen to 50¢ in consequence of the high price of hay.[33] So every body has determined to give it up as a luxury we cannot afford & are willing to do without. It has become quite a subject of amusement to us. . . .

Monday morning we all went to the Brownfields to see the *May 6* flag, which is really beautiful, & in the afternoon it was presented at the Institute Hall by cousin Wilmot [DeSaussure]. Coz [*sic*] Lizzie B.[arnwell] & the Whites dined with us & all of our friends, who were particularly interested, sat together near the right of the stage in full view of the [Palmetto Guard] company, who with their escort, the Cadets, occupied the centre of the hall. A very large & beautiful garland of natural flowers was sent to Capt. [George] Cuthbert for the P[almetto] G[uard] and was raised on the flag. Capt. C.[uthbert] received the flag with a good and well delivered speech, then gave it in charge of Sergeant [Ben] Webb, who sent the garland to Mary & Sue [Brownfield]. In cousin W[ilmot]'s speech he alluded to the girls as Gen. [Thomas] Sumter's grand daughters, & the next morning the [Charleston *Daily*] *Courier* had their names in full, much to their mortification & vexation.[34] The younger B[arnwell]s & some of their friends had carried bouquets which they threw among the ranks & they were eagerly caught. Then they gave three cheers for "The Daughters of Carolina" & their escort. . . .

Every body was out this evening except Lila & I, Carrie spend- *May 7* ing the night with Hattie, so we amused ourselves counting up the persons to whom at different times it had been reported I had [been] engaged, eight in number, a considerable list, particularly as none of them ever addressed me.

---

33 There is no reference to such a butter in J. G. Davis, *Dictionary of Dairying* (2nd ed.; New York: Interscience Publishers, 1955).
34 Thomas Sumter (1734–1832), because of his Carolina area militia leadership in the American Revolution, was known as the Gamecock of the Revolution. Fort Sumter was named after him.

May 8
Wednesday

Just after going to bed last night, we had a serenade from the P[almetto] G[uard] in honor of the flag. About 40 or more of them were in the street. They gave us "Home Again" first & ended with "Then You'll Remember Me." It was very sweet on the wind instruments. They also serenaded the Brownfields & Belle Cohen.

Our Congress has declared war on the U.S. & issued letters of marque & reprisal. . . .

May 9
Thursday

Mr. White lent us a horse today, & Lila & myself spent almost the whole morning at the dentist's, I having five teeth plugged and she one taken out. Afterwards I went to buy some articles for Rutledge to use in his camp life. It was a melancholy pleasure to think of doing these last little services for him. . . . Carrie & myself went to the Depot, accompanied by Dora, Charlotte & Cornelia Davis, with Sam Furman on the box. Quite a number of ladies were there and a dense crowd without. Being dark we could just distinguish the dark line of soldiers as they marched by, escorted by the Cadets & Carolina L[ight] I[nfantry] & a band of music. They expected to disband and be able to seek their friends & say farewell, but were marched directly down, far beyond the depot, where three cars were waiting for them. The only one we saw was Rutledge for a few minutes & Eddie Gaillard who were separated from their company. We followed the crowd to the depot yard, where a dense mass was collected. We could see nothing but the occasional gleam of bayonet by a dim lantern here & there, & the banner as it was carried in, while Maj. [P. F.] Stevens, who was on horseback, gave a short speech, followed by farewell & cheers, and they were gone. The pride of our hearts carried away & probably but few of that gallant band will ever return. But we must keep brave hearts. This is but the beginning; the end no man can see.

I only know personally about sixteen of those who have gone, as a great many were new members joined for the purpose, 115 in number, while over 130 remain to serve our own State. . . .

Mrs. John Astor, who is cousin Tom Gibbes daughter, has lately presented a flag with her own hands to the [First] New York Zouaves, formerly firemen of the lowest, vilest class, &

commanded by Col. Ellsworthy [Elmer E. Ellsworth].[35] They have all taken the most fearful oaths in regard to the extermination of all Southerners & are the terror of the citizens of Washington, who are flying daily. The Shoolbreds [James and Reeves] have taken a solemn oath to each other that, if they come in contact with that company, they will take that flag & bring it to So. Ca. or die in the attempt. . . .

. . . Thomas Francis Meagher, having joined a N.Y. Regiment to aid in coercing us, the Meagher Guards, named in his honor, have changed to the Emerald L.[ight] I.[nfantry] & his name has been stricken from the roll of the Hibernian Society. While Dr. [Francis] Lieber, whose name was once held [in] such high respect in this State, has proved himself a renegade & calls us traitors & rebels. His son, Mr. Oscar Lieber, the State Geologist, has been in the ranks of Capt. [A. J.] Green's company on Morris I. as [a] private.[36]

. . . Old Abe has at last fulfilled his threats of blockading us by sending the *Niagara* here. His *whole fleet* does not consist of more than 24 vessels, though most of them are very fine ones. The *Niagara* is a splendid steam propeller, so contrived that she can withdraw the wheel from the water & thus use either steam or her sails at pleasure, and is probably the fastest ship in the U.S. navy. It carries 12 guns, is manned by 600 men, and fully supplied with provisions, implements & munitions of war.

She has already warned off two or three vessels, some English, others American, but the captain of the English brig "A and   *May 12*

35 Mrs. John Astor was the wife of John Jacob Astor, the heir to the fur trading company and real estate fortune; she was a leading New York society figure.

36 Thomas Francis Meagher (1823–67) was born in Ireland and escaped to the United States in 1852 to avoid arrest for his activities as a member of Young Ireland. He became the leader of the Irish community in New York City and during the Civil War commanded the Ireland Brigade. Francis Lieber (1800–72) held the Chair of History and Political Economy at South Carolina College beginning in 1835. In 1857 he moved to Columbia College, New York, where in 1865 he joined the law faculty. He was the author of several important tracts and, during the war, was frequently consulted by the federal government. His *A Code for the Government of Armies* (1863) was issued in revised form by the War Department. His son Oscar fought for the Confederacy, while two other sons wore the Union uniform.

A" [*sic*] cheated her finely by running into shoal water, from which it was easily extricated by one of our tugs and brought safely to port.

May 13　This morning's paper contains letters from Jeff Davis & Judge [John A.] Campbell, late of the Supreme Court, U.S., showing that the latter had tried to act the part of mediator, when our Commissioners went just after Lincoln's inauguration to adjust our claims. He, it was, who persuaded them to delay from day to day. Their official recognition . . . appeared so unaccountable to us, but Seward, like all the other members of Lincoln's cabinet, lied to him [Campbell] in everything, making promises and assertions which he broke as soon as his back was turned. Thus Judge C.[ampbell] unintentionally deceived us in regard to Fort Sumter, etc.

　. . . The sentiments of the English press are decidedly in favor of the South and warns the North of their failure, when following the exact footsteps of the British during the Revolution. Queen Victoria has sunk into a settled melancholy since her mother's death, & it is feared will not recover her mind. She has been threatened with its loss many times before. . . .

May 14　. . . It is worthy of remark how many of the descendants of Virginia's revolutionary heroes are now holding high positions in the C.S.A. The son of Light-Horse Harry Lee commands the forces there. John A. Washington, from whom Mt. Vernon was purchased, is his chief aid & the only living representative of Gen. Washington. Jefferson's great grandson commands a Battery at Richmond. A grandson of Patrick Henry is a captain in the Virginia forces. Madison left no descendant. Those of Chief Justice Marshall are in the ranks & in command also. . . .

　There is no longer the smallest doubt remaining in regard to the dastardly conduct of Maj. [Robert] Anderson. He is both a liar and traitor to his country.

May 18
Saturday　Since last Tuesday the *Niagara* has not been seen anywheres [*sic*] along our coast. The *Huntsville* which appeared then is supposed to have brought her orders & both have disappeared. So, the much talked of blockade is at an end, not having done us any harm, but plenty to Old Abe, who will have

to answer to the English government for interruption to her trades, by sending away their merchant vessels, thereby causing them to lose their valuable freight of King Cotton. Hattie [White] dined with us today. Carrie & herself went to walk in the evening and Willie Glover came home with them to tea. They left early &, after a pleasant evening, "the skeleton in our house" showed itself in all its hideous deformity—and all was suddenly changed. The tale of "the skeleton in every house" is constantly in my thoughts—the truth of it is daily brought to mind. There is scarcely a family I know, in which though outwardly all appears to be "well within," there is not some secret trouble which the world wots [*sic*] not of. But I do not like to trust a journal with my thoughts upon any subject.[37]

Went to church for the first time in over three months. . . .   *May 19*

Mr. Holland, bearer of despatches from our European Commissioners, was seized at New York by Lincoln's emissaries, who were on the lookout for him. As soon as he landed, his despatches were opened & read—then he was dismissed. The latest news is that great dissatisfaction prevails among the troops in Washington, as they are neither paid nor their families at home supported as was promised, that small pox is prevalent there & at Fortress Monroe, & that the administration begin[s] to fear they will not be able to support the war. Ross Winans, the Millionaire of Baltimore who offered $7,000,000 to the Confederacy, was arrested on a charge of selling the Baltimore steam gun to the Virginians, sent to Fort McHenry & put in the guard room.[38] [He] has since been released on his parole. Such are samples of Lincoln's administration—besides insults to women in churches as well as in their homes, merely for being Southern born. But when Union flags float from the steeples, & the churches themselves are draped in every direction, even the pulpit, reading and desk & communion table, with the same emblems, &,   *May 20*
Monday

---

37 This is a reference to her sister Frances DeSaussure Holmes (Fanny). See the August 21, 1863, entry of this diary.
38 Ross Winans (1796–1877) was an inventor, mechanic, and Confederate sympathizer. He was a member of the Maryland legislature during the Civil War and was twice arrested.

when at the report that Fort Moultrie was in ashes read from the pulpit, the congregation cheered & shouted for joy embracing each other frantically then joining in singing Yankee Doodle or some other such popular tune, it shows such desecration & degradation that we are surprised at nothing now—not even at the unmitigated lies, constantly reiterated, of the hundreds killed among the "rebels" at the Battle of Fort Sumter, and even of Beauregard being positively killed. However, his "ghost" will have considerable effect, I have no doubt, on the "Kangaroo.". . .

May 22   England has recognized our right to commission privateers, a preliminary to a formal recognition of the Southern Confederacy. . . .

. . . The Tariff Bill has just passed &, I believe, in general gives satisfaction. It is a great improvement on that of '57; many articles are on the free list, but the great staples, cotton, woolen, silks, etc., are at 15 per cent. It is in such striking contrast to [the] Morrill Tariff that it will certainly hasten the recognition of the Southern Confederacy by France & England, especially as the latter has only twenty-three weeks supply of cotton.[39] . . .

A flag was presented tonight to the Marion Artillery & we made up a party to go. . . . We arrived at the hall at a quarter to nine &, as the presentation was to take place at 8½, thought, though it was a little late, we would be in time; [we] walked boldly up the middle aisle, secured a good seat high up, and arrived just in time to see the farewell wave of the flag & the companies march out. However, we had the pleasure of meeting several friends . . . as it was early some one proposed to go to the Hibernian Hall and hear the speeches delivered before the Palmetto Lyceum. Of course the arrival of such a large party created a stir; Mr. Edwin Heriot was reading a sleepy speech of which we could not hear a word, so were quite relieved when it came to an end & was followed by a little music which was thought the finale—but alas for our delusion, it was only a prelude to a still more "sleepy reading" by

39 The Morrill Tariff was passed on February 20, 1861, during the last days of the Buchanan administration when southern members had already withdrawn. It raised rates over the 1857 tariff, but its purpose was more for revenue than for protection.

Dr. Hume Simons on Floriculture—every ten minutes we heard a disjointed fragment &, after enduring it for a half hour, a general stampede was proposed—two or three couples first went singly then the rest followed, except cousins L[izzie Barnwell] & B[eck Holmes]. Of course the leaving of the party made more noise than their arrival & to our mortification the doors were closed after us. We all went to Rosa's where we merrily discussed our "disgraceful conduct" & spent the evening very pleasantly. The "chaperones" arrived near eleven, having left in despair before the ending of the speech, so we were comforted & did not break up till twelve.

Thursday afternoon cousin Louis [DeSaussure] gave Mary [Boykin] and Meta [Deas] a sailing party on the *Nora.* There were 29 persons in all. . . . We had a permit to visit Fort Sumter, but the wind was easterly & so high that we could not attempt to land there. So [we] contented ourselves with sailing in the harbor, running sometimes close enough to the Battery to speak to our friends, then sailing up the Ashley, round the "floating battery" of which I had a good view for the first time; it is nothing but a bare rough flat with a sloping shed covered with sheets of iron on one side under which are the four guns. On the other [side there is] a raised platform on which is [*sic*] placed the sand bags as a balance. We saw distinctly where one ball had gone through the roof & several others lodged near the portholes. We did not come in till eight, long after the full moon had risen brilliantly and, though Rosa & Eliza [Coffin] had been a little sick, the evening & party were both so pleasant that we all enjoyed it. The tide was again extremely high this evening covering our street almost entirely and all round the "Corner," but it subsided later & Carrie & myself went there. Cousin W[illie] had just heard from R[utledge]. The P[almetto] G[uard] was still at Richmond where they have been petted & feasted by the ladies & in return gave them a handsome collation of strawberries, ice cream & champagne. We girls really begin to feel quite jealous & fear they will lose their hearts there. R[utledge] sent to ask Carrie & myself to write to him. On the 24th, the So. Ca. troops were to go to Manassas Gap about 27 miles from Alexandria the junction of the R.R. from Harper's Ferry, that City, Richmond, & Acquia [Aquia] Creek.

May 23

May 24   Sallie Bull gave a party this evening, a mixture of all ages,
Friday   most of the girls being much older than herself; the beaux
were principally cadets of 17 & 18 with a sprinkling of mid-
shipmen, civilians & mere boys. She performed her duties as
hostess better than I expected, but there is still great room for
improvement. As many of the girls & gentlemen were our
companions, we found it pleasant, but I principally occupied
myself in introducing those who were strangers & trying to
help entertain them. . . .

May
25
∾
August
5, 1861

War Begins

Virginia is invaded! Yesterday about 5000 Federal   *May 25*
Troops took possession of Alexandria, the few hundred Confederate soldiers who were there retiring to
Manassas Junction. Col. [Elmer E.] Ellsworth, commanding
the [First] N.Y. Firemen Zouaves, attempted to pull down the
Secession Flag from the Marshall House which could be seen
from The White House, when [James] Jackson, the proprie-
tor, a Virginian & staunch secessionist, instantly shot him dead
and was himself instantly cut to pieces. But, he has fallen in a
glorious cause. His is the first blood shed in the defence [*sic*]
of our proud "Stars and Bars." Hampton [Virginia] has also
been seized. Well, they have struck the first blow as we wished
by invading our soil, and the consequences be upon their own
heads. The Northern mail has been stopped & wires cut beyond Richmond, but, as our own P.[ost O.[ffice] Department
goes into operation on June 1st, it will not incommode us.
Congress has adjourned & the Provisional Seat of Government is to be moved to Richmond where it meets again July
20th.

Such contradictory rumors are each day heard in regards to   *May 28*
the movements of the Lincolnites that we do not know what   *Tuesday*
will be the point of attack. Some say the [Manassas] Junction
where between 4 & 5000 of our men are strongly posted;

others [say] Harper's Ferry which is now considered impregnable. The [government] machinery all having been carried to Richmond & put into operations . . . most of the Virginians think their capital [is] in danger. However Jeff Davis has just passed very quietly through Charleston & reached Richmond which already gives the people immense confidence.

May 30   Yesterday & this morning's papers contain extracts taken from personal reminiscences as well as the War Department against [Winfield] Scott, [William S.] Harney & [Benjamin F.] Butler—proving Scott to have been *suspended for a year* from the army for having taken for his own use, i.e. stolen, the pay for his men. But, through the interest of a friend high in office, [he] was afterwards transferred and promoted in the Artillery. Numerous other charges are proved against him, for one, bringing "his religion" as a shield to protect his cowardice when challenged to a duel. When a man is sincerely religious I think he is right to give that as an excuse, not that I favor duelling at all, but when a man's actions do not stand up to his words, he must necessarily be suspected of hypocrisy. As to Harney, he was proved & tried for having whipped a negro woman to death with his own hands but escaped punishment through law chicanery. . . . Both Butler & himself have been guilty of brutality, cowardice & every other misdemeanor which could render them hated & despised by every respectable person, Southerners especially, and such are the men to fight against us.

The Federal troops are committing dreadful excesses & outrages of the grossest description upon the defenceless [*sic*] citizens of Alexandria [Virginia]. On Tuesday the *Minnesota* arrived here in company with three other vessels to renew the blockade here & at Savannah. Gen. Beauregard & suite left yesterday for Va. I am so glad he will command our troops for all have such confidence in him.

Today Eliza Rose & Mr. Trapman were married and left immediately for Europe by the "back track" of Cincinnati, the [Great] Lakes & Boston. He goes as bearer of despatches from the British Consuls. . . .

We had a delightful sail this afternoon on the *Pride*, Willie and Willie H[eyward] getting up the party and furnishing refreshments. . . . Champagne and a *huge* sponge cake was carried. The latter especially afforded us plenty of fun. The *Nora* passed us quite close and we tossed a bottle to them; in return they saluted us three times with their flag & of course we returned it. We had several good voices on board, and they added very much to our pleasure.

Saturday afternoon I spent with Miss Bates, discussing the state of affairs, etc. She & Miss A[gnes Bates] are such strong Southerners & Secessionists in feeling, having lived twenty years at the South & most of that time here, that I told her I claimed them as South Carolinians, especially as they had refused the earnest entreaties of their brothers & friends to go and live at the North. Their brothers sympathize with the South and think that the North broke the Constitution thereby justifying secession, but wished them to go on and live with them, as they could not bear the idea of separation during a civil war especially when the fiercest wrath & bitterest indignation are directed towards Charleston, by "our dearly beloved brethern of the North." They say "the rebellion commenced where Charleston *is*, and shall *end* where Charleston *was*." Such is the tenor of all the letters they receive from those who style themselves their *friends*—not *relatives* however. As Miss B[ates] said, "you would suppose *I* had taken Fort Sumter and commenced the war to hear their outpourings of wrath.". . .

June 1

. . . How attached I have become to this record of the passing hours, personally interesting to few, if any, besides myself, and yet how valuable it will be in after years as a record of the events which mark the formation and growth of our glorious Southern Confederacy.

June 3

Rosa invited a large party of friends to dine with her today at Ashley Hall in compliment to Mary [Boykin], but so many were afraid of country-fever, that it only consisted of . . . [a few persons]. The weather was delightful, a refreshing breeze all the time blowing from the river, but the guests were quiet & needed a master-spirit to bring forth or rather keep in a flame the occasional sparks of liveliness which were emitted. We dined on the lawn in picnic style, with a thunder storm threatening all the time, but only received a sprinkling on our

June 4
Tuesday

ride down not sufficient to lay the dust. On the whole, though, there was nothing to mar the day; there was also nothing to render it worthy of being noted as one of "the charming parties at Ashley Hall." Mr. B[ull] has evidently heard the news of Fan's [Garden] engagement but performed his duties as host quietly & pleasantly, though once or twice he distinctly alluded to it. He was quite attentive & polite to me. I wonder if he wishes he had taken my advice. He is going to send Sallie to Miss Bates' school tomorrow—he begins to realize how spoilt [*sic*] she has been.

June 5   . . . Beauregard has taken command at Manassas Junction to
Wednesday   my great delight, for all our men have the utmost confidence in him. A fearful retribution will have to be suffered by the U.S. troops in Alexandria & Hampton [Virginia] as well as on the Maryland R.R. for the awful outrages perpetrated on the persons of men, women & even children. The heart grows sick in hearing of their vile deeds.

The Ladies of New Orleans, who have lately had a Military Fair, have presented Gen. Beauregard with a very elegant sword. This morning's paper contains a splendid speech of Judge Beverly Tucker's delivered in The Nashville Convention Dec. 12, 1850 prophetic of the course the South has pursued—only he did not believe the North would ever attempt to make war upon us, as it is so much against their own interests, but he could not foresee the blind, demoniac fury which has seized them.[1]

June 6   We attended quite a large party this evening given by Gen &
Mrs. [Abbott H.] Brisbane to Ella [Ingraham] Whiting.[2] It was quite a sociable, pleasant affair in consequent of the mingling

1 Nathaniel Beverly Tucker (1784–1851) was professor of law at the College of William and Mary, Virginia, and a well-known author. All his works support an extreme states' rights position. His most famous work was *The Partisan Leader*, written in anger over the Nullification Proclamation and Force Bill in the 1830s. It was published in 1836 but bore the fictitious date of 1856. It is prophetic of the events leading to the Civil War as Miss Holmes notes in her September 23, 1862, entry.

2 Abbott H. Brisbane graduated from the United States Military Academy in 1825. He resigned from the Regular Army in 1828 but was colonel of the South Carolina Volunteers during the Seminole War (1835–36). In 1836 he was made brigadier general of the South Carolina militia. He was involved in numerous engineering projects and in 1847 became

of all ages . . . crowds of married ladies down to young ladies
"out in society," the girls of thirteen or fourteen of the family
. . . besides plenty of strangers. It was not a regular dancing
party, the entertainments being varied by delightful singing
from Hattie White & Susan North. The house is a very curious old time one, only two stories or rather a basement & one
story, with low ceilings & small rooms running far back,
though last summer the Gen. improved it very much by adding a fine large drawing room running across the whole front.
It was altogether a handsome affair, a very fine supper, & the
numerous rooms ornamented with beautiful bouquets and
baskets of flowers, which are quite scarce now. . . .

. . . I learned to my astonishment that, though Mr. [William
J.] Grayson is the author of "The Hireling & Slave," [he] is a
rank Unionist and Submissionist. I felt mortified to think that
Charleston should be obliged to place on that list some of her
most respected sons. As to Mr. George Bryan, "the correspondent of Henry Clay," he is not worth mentioning as he
only follows like a cur in the steps of his master, Mr. James L.
Petigru.[3] He, one of our first lawyers and the pride of the So.
Ca. bar, is a Unionist, but he is quiet and does not meddle in
politics, &, though he has "fallen from his high estate," we
pity but cannot despise him. If any man ever was to be pitied,
he is—a brilliant mind, with not a solitary thing to solace or
dignify his old age. His domestic affairs have been most unhappy—two of his children, if not Mrs. [Elizabeth C.] Carson
also, have disgraced his name and Mrs. P.[etigru], if not quite
as bad, is most notorious. A home and family circle, he has
none for as he himself told Uncle Wm. [DeSaussure], his
home is his office in St. Michael's Alley, where he often sleeps
and "burries his troubles" digging at his flowers in the beautiful [garden?] attached to it and hidden out of sight of the
world. He is almost, if not quite, an infidel, or at least an
atheist, yet used to attend St. Michael's church until this winter when the prayer for Congress was first changed into "for

---

a faculty member of the Citadel where he served until 1852, at which
time he took up farming. He died on Sept. 28, 1861, at the age of fifty-
six.

3 James L. Petigru (1789–1863) was a leading Unionist during the 1830s
nullification controversy in South Carolina. This position kept him in the
minority throughout his life in Charleston.

the people of So. Ca. in Legislature assembled" then that for the President of the U.S. omitted. He walked out of church followed by his servile imitator, Mr. B.[ryan], and I do not think he has attended since. And, now to crown all, the Union is dissolved and the glory of the Stars and Stripes forever departed—disgraced not by having been hauled down in submission to the emblem of our glorious free new-born confederacy, but the vile deeds of the still viler hirelings and cutthroats of the despotic tryant, Abe Lincoln, who in the three months which have passed since his inauguration, has broken every article of the Constitution which he swore to abide by & defend. And yet his slaves and parasites bend as meekly before each fresh usurpation of power as if he was the Grand Sultan himself. But his Janissaries may yet turn and recompense him with the dog's death he deserves. A strong undercurrent in favor of a peace policy seems to be working at the North already—more than twenty hitherto raving newspapers have suddenly made the discovery that the war is illegal, the Union dead, & never to be revived—while New York is paralyzed, trade totally destroyed & grass literally growing in the streets, while the cost of subduing and conquering 17 States & twenty millions of people, while their own millions are starving for want of our cotton, is beginning to be counted; many moderate people at the North think that if a battle was only staved off till July 4th, when the U.S. Congress meets, it would recognize our Confederacy & thus avert a civil war. Another skirmish took place this week in the N.W. of Va. between some hundreds of the State Militia and 3000 Lincolnites, in which the latter were repulsed with considerable loss.

June 8   Saturday evening Eliza and Edward were to have attended a small party at Sara White's, but a tremendous thunderstorm frustrated all their hopes. I never imagined the city would be so gay when war is impending & so many of our friends are away among the combatants, but it seems to be a reaction after the long depression of the winter and absence of our friends on duty on the islands. During the last month a great many parties have been given, almost all however small, but often two or three on the same night.

... Last week Stephen A. Douglas the author of the doctrine   *June 10*
of Squatter Sovereignty died—of disappointed ambition.

I have forgotten to note a change in "my domestic arrange-   *June 12*
ments" which occurred a few days ago and which promises
well. Mother has promoted Margaret to the honor of being
our maid &, though her appearance is not very prepossing
[*sic*], I find her not only willing but much more capable than I
expected and really very "handy" in her new vocation. I have
undertaken to train her.

Today being appointed by the President as the day of "fast-   *June 13*
ing, Humiliation and Prayer," all the churches in the city were
open for service and the congregations quite large. The service was remarkably solemn & Mr. [W. B. W.] Howe gave us
a most admirable sermon from I Kings 19:33–34 [should be
12:23–24] showing an exact parallel between the separation
of the Israelites from the Jewish Nation under Rehoboam's
oppressive rule and our secession and said that this very case
has often been quoted in the U. S. Senate; the parallel runs
through to the final act, which is here changed, as their's was a
peaceful separation while a civil war has inaugurated our independence.[4]
   My foot has been hurting me lately, and I paid the Dr. a
visit today; he says it is only weakness, gave me a stimulating
lotion and leave to walk where & as far as I please. ...

The papers confirm the account of the [June 10th] battle of   *June 14*
Great Bethel [Virginia]. There was a skirmish two days before
at Little Bethel, a few miles off. ...

Henry W.[inter] Davis of Maryland, the Republican candidate   *June 15*
for U.S. Congress, has been beaten in Baltimore by the Secession candidate; the secession feeling there is stronger than
ever & thousands of arms are concealed by their owners,

4 William Bell White Howe (1823–94) was a native of New Hampshire,
   who moved to South Carolina because of his health. He was ordained in
   the Episcopal Church in 1849 and served in St. John's Parish, Berkeley,
   South Carolina, for the next twelve years. During the Civil War, he was
   rector of St. Philip's Church, Charleston. In 1871 he was consecrated
   bishop of the diocese of South Carolina.

ready to be used as soon as we make a demonstration in their favor. The Gov. of Missouri [Claiborne F. Jackson] has issued a proclamation, calling for 50,000 militia to aid in "expelling the invaders" who have trampled upon their privileges and murdered men, women and children. He has tried to preserve neutrality but found it impossible. Yesterday the Virginia State Convention signed the Ordinance of Secession, which has waited till now for the votes of the people, passing by over 90,000 majority.[5] Received a long letter from Rutledge. The Wilderness is now named Camp Beauregard. The men are all as enthusiastic as ever & busied in entrenching themselves for the enemy, *should it ever come.* That they seem to doubt and are anxious for orders to march against them. They are all getting most accomplished in the art of cooking, washing and mending their clothes; he says Willie Elliott, however, has borne away the palm for the first, and he had just eaten a cake which he had made and baked, "which would do credit to any young lady.". . .

June 20 . . . Several letters written by W. H. ["Bull Run"] Russell, the correspondent of the London *Times*, from Savannah, Mobile & Montgomery, have lately appeared in the [Charleston] *Mercury* and excited universal indignation by their misrepresentations & actual falsehood. The one written from this city just after the Battle of Fort Sumter was disparaging enough, speaking of the "civilians and militia men," their preparations and deeds, in the most slight manner. In these [letters] he says that the "universal voice of the South Carolinians is a wish to be governed by a branch of the royal house of England and a love for English law and institutions." Several pieces have appeared in the papers, correcting many of his statements, and this morning a letter from [S.C. Attorney General] Mr. Isaac Hayne was published, giving an indignant denial in the name of the South Carolinians to such a statement. From what we hear, and [this is] an allusion of Mr. Hayne's, Russell must have fallen into the hands of Mr. Wm. Trapier, one of the most eccentric geniuses I've ever met with, & been completely quizzed by him. I know Mr. Trapier

5 On May 22, 1861, the people of Virginia voted 96,750 to 32,134 for the secession ordinance.

abuses Washington most unmercifully, but whether in earnest or not it is hard to say; at any rate, he is an intense Southerner & hater of the Yankees but has completely fooled Russell who has lost immeasurably in our opinion by having shown himself to be a man of so much less penetration than we gave him credit for. It is aggravation to think that the Europeans are to gain a knowledge of us and our affairs through such channels as the Northerners & Russell, for the latter is implicitly believed, & was sent out here expressly to obtain a true account of the state of affairs. His Montgomery letter is more truthful and creditable to us than almost any other.

Carrie went to ride yesterday evening with Isaac White and, *June 22* as I was going to Sallie's [Bull] met her getting out. The parting was significant &, in connection with slight indications during the last few days, made me suspect they were engaged. She did not go to Sallie's and was asleep when I came home, but this morning confessed my suspicions were correct. He had addressed her Wednesday evening, when bringing her home from taking tea with Hattie [White], but she did not give him an answer til yesterday evening. I have so long expected this that it did not in the least surprise me; he has been fond of her since she was a child, and I think his passion for Susan Clark was only a passing furor; his qualities are not showy, but solid, and he makes such a good son and brother that I am sure he will make a devoted husband. In the last two months Rosa, Fan [Garden], & Carrie have become engaged all apparently sudden[ly] and quite surprising to "the world." I wonder whose turn will come next, not mine I'm sure, for I do not think there is anyone who cares particularly for me & I have not seen anyone whom I like as much as my cousins, and I would not marry any of them. I think I was always meant either to be an old maid (I hope not a disagreeable one) or to die young. As I have never found life very happy, the latter would be preferable. I often amuse myself and my friends with descriptions of my old maid's establishment. This evening he [Isaac White] came to see mother, but Carrie went out walking with a party Jane Chisolm made up; of course, after this, he will be a regular visitor & I will have the pleasure of feeling myself "de trop" upon all occasions.

June 25 . . . Mr. [Dan] Vincent took us to Fort Sumter & what a dif-
Tuesday ferent aspect it presented to that of our last summer's visit.[6]
On the side facing Sullivan's and Morris Islands, large pieces
of masonry had been knocked away and they were much battered, though many places have already been repaired; workmen are busy in rebuilding the officers' quarters, which look
half ruined, while the men's quarters have already been built;
the damages to the outside of the walls are also being repaired; over the gateway a motto in Italian has been placed,
by whom I cannot imagine, for I think it singularly inappro-
priate, "He who enters here, leaves all hope behind." Last
summer the first & second tiers of arches were simply a succession of arches, with the places of the gun carriages marked
on the ground by a few bricks and no flooring to the second
row, nor was there a single gun on the rampart. Now, the first
tier of casemates is solidly finished off, and, as we stood about
the centre of the north side, we looked down the row of
arches & saw each one filled with a heavy gun; the second
tier is finished off into rooms each arch forming a good sized
one, and, as we walked along in front, we saw them fitted up
as mess rooms & sleeping rooms; on the ramparts were guns
of the heaviest calibre, 10 inch columbiads, 64 pounders &
mortars—we saw the only one which was "en barbette" at the
time of the battle & which [Captain Abner] Doubleday in his
haste to fire, while shot & shell were falling around him, completely threw off of its carriage.[7] It stood ready loaded. A 64
pounder was placed at a tremendous angle to give Lincoln's
blockaders a "salute" if they came near enough. We could
plainly distinguish the masts of one [ship] laying off the bar.
Grape shot, canister, shot & shell were piled in all directions.
The two first kinds I saw for the first time, while on the
ground were hundreds of those that had been fired *into* the
fort. Col. [R. S.] Ripley is commandant & Alfred Rhett captain
of one company. Wm. Prioleau is surgeon. Those were the
only officers we saw. Ripley is rather above the medium size
but very stout & quite a jolly looking soldier in his loose white

6 Vincent became a blockade runner. While commanding the *Emilie*, he
was captured in August, 1862.
7 Abner Doubleday (1819–93) later became a Union general, but he is
most famous as the inventor of baseball.

linen suit. The breeze was very light & we had a very quiet sail back. . . .

. . . Uncle Edward came to see us today & staid to dinner. He has lived here so little, he is almost like a stranger; he is a very agreeable companion; his conversation is highly cultivated, and he has lived so much in Washington and in public life that I really enjoy talking to him. He noticed particularly today the remarkable fact that Leonidas Polk the Episcopal Bishop of Louisiana has been made Major General of the Provisional Army of the Confederate States. He was a graduate of West Point and in the army for two years; he now commands the lower division of the Mississippi Valley. Uncle E.[dward] says such a thing has not occurred since the Crusades. *June 28 Friday*

Jeff Davis, a privateer carrying five guns and commanded by [Louis M.] Coxetter, left the harbor today and run [*sic*] the blockade.[8]. . . *June 29 Saturday*

We went to sail this evening on the *Nora* with cousin Sue Screven and a party of over forty persons, most of them married people and several children. . . . The party at first did not promise much pleasure, but we all enjoyed the excitement & fun of the scene. The wind was very high and every wave capped with foam, which shivered into clouds of spray, drenching everyone—gentlemen lost their hats and the ladies their veils. Soon everyone got rid of their hats, for it was as much as we could do to keep our seats & hold on without holding the hats too. No lady was sick, but everyone was so bedraggled & their hair so disheveled that each one was a source of amusement to her neighbor. Soon after we got home, Rosa ran over to show us a comet which appeared without any warning in the northeast, quite startling her. It was quite large with a very long tail. She said the Dutchmen were discussing whether it was not a bomb shell. We went over after tea to see Lizzie Burnet &, on our return about ten, found cousin Willie seated in the portico with Sue and Lila; *July 1 Monday*

8 Louis M. Coxetter (1818–73) was probably the leading Confederate privateer and blockade runner.

we took our seats on the steps & talked there till long after twelve, just as we used to do in by-gone days, he teazing [*sic*] Carrie, repeating poetry and amusing us with inquiries after the lover I should wish to have. As my standard is very high, "the men with the requirements" furnished an endless subject of amusement. How many evenings last summer did we spend on the same place with Rutledge and himself, the hours gaily passing with their merry jests.

July 4
Thursday

How very different today has been from the last anniversary and how little did we dream then that one short year would see such a great revolution and as yet almost a bloodless one. Last year it was the most intensely hot day I have ever felt. Many soldiers who paraded died from sun stroke. I felt completely "wilted" and was only revived by cousin Willie & Rutledge taking us to sail after sunset in Mr. Bull's boat. Today, there has been no parade, but the ringing of the bells and the guns from the forts honor the day. Rutledge & so many of our friends and relatives are in Virginia, either fighting now or daily expecting a battle. Beauregard with "The Army of the Potomac"[9] is encamped at Fairfax and it is thought a few days will decide whether the war will go on and whether the Lincolnites will have to give up for want of the "bone and sinews of war." The Northern Congress meets today and their action will decide much. . . .

July 5
Friday

Capt. Richard Thomas Zarvona of the Maryland Zouaves, together with Capt. [George N.] Hollins late commander of the *Susquehanna* & several others, have lately succeeded in immortalizing their names by a brilliant [June 28th–29th] expedition, in which, though they did not succeed in the most important part of the plan, the intended capture of the *Pawnee*, still succeeded in gaining prizes of great value: the *St. Nicholas*, a fine steamer running between Baltimore & Washington & three brigs laden with ice, coffee and sugar, the cargoes being worth two or three hundred thousand dollars. Cap. Z.[arvona] first went to Philadelphia where, under guise of a Federal agent, he procured a supply of arms which he put in two trunks and took passage from Baltimore disguised

9 Also known as Department of Alexandria and Potomac Department.

as a French lady. Quite a number of friends went at the same time, each going independent of the others, as a stranger. Further down the river, Capt. Hollins & several others went on board, when the two captains immediately recognized each other as old Parisian acquaintances delighted to meet again; both being conversant with French they made all their arrangements. During the evening each man was quietly supplied with revolvers & at one o'clock at night when they had reached a certain bend in the river, Capt. Z.[arvona] quietly informed the captain of the vessel that it had changed owners, for his companions had distributed themselves over the boat, taking possession of the engine room, etc. the precaution having been taken to carry a competent engineer with them. The whole affair was conducted so noiselessly that the passengers did not know until next morning at breakfast that the vessel had changed hands. The aim of the expedition was the capture of the *Pawnee*, which was to have been effected by taking on board a regiment of Tennesseans & with the Federal flag flying, to board, but when they arrived at the encampment only part of the regiment was there, and those the Col. refused to let go. Disappointed in that, Capt. Z.[arvona] turned privateer & carried his prizes safely under the Confederate guns.

Dora went with me just after breakfast today to Dr. J. B. *July 6* Patrick's to have my tooth plugged. I like him so much that I do not mind going and always enjoy talking to him. He is so gentle, manly & pleasant. He talks to one while he is operating, and we always discuss the war news, etc. for he is an ardent Carolinian. If he had staid one day later in Va. on his recent visit, he would have been present at the Battle of Bethel & he regretted not being there very much. Today's paper gives an account of the celebration of June 28th by the P[almetto] G[uard]. Charlie Prentiss was the orator. Rutledge won a brace of pistols, Hopson Pinckney the silver cup & Dr. [J. J.] Goodwyn some other prize for shooting; then they had a grand dinner. I went home with Dora and staid all day with her, amusing ourselves *singing* & reading Tennyson. . . .

Aunt C[arrie] B[landing] dined with us & gave an account of *July 16* the illness of cousin Nora's [Barnwell] infant, occasioned by *Tuesday* the most diabolical wickedness of the nurse, an old negro woman owned by cousin N.[ora] who has minded all her children & one whom they have always considered a good and faithful servant; what was the cause of the act, we cannot imagine. The baby was born soon after the Battle of Fort Sumter and while cousin James [Barnwell] was away on duty; during the first fortnight, the nurse scarcely held it, the ladies of the village almost taking her place. It was a fine healthy child till it was three weeks old, when it went off suddenly into convulsions, without any apparent cause, & has been desperately ill ever since and suffering agony almost constantly in convulsions, then again, lying for hours as if dead, then waking with agonizing screams. The physician said he could do nothing. He had never seen or heard of such a case; everybody thought it was similar to that of Uncle John's [DeSaussure] Carrie & hoped that it would die, as was daily expected. Seven weeks of nursing and anxiety passed when it was discovered that the child had been made to swallow *eleven large pins*, some of which were working their way out of the child's body at the side, while nature relieved it of the others. During this time the nurse was the only servant who had anything to do with the baby. . . . Suspicion was aroused. Cousin James sent his whole family to Mr. McFadden's and all his servants to jail to await their trials, except his house-servant, whom he left in charge of his house, & two guards placed there also. Cousin James himself is obliged to leave for Virginia tomorrow with his Regiment, but Mr. McF.[adden], Dr. Haynesworth and the other gentlemen of the neighborhood have taken the case in hand and are determined to find out everything &, if the child dies, the woman will be hung, as she probably will be anyway. . . .

July 17
Wednesday
For two or three days past we have had most confused & contradictory accounts of skirmishes in western Va. at Rich Mountain & Laurel Hill.

July 18
Thursday
I spent [the day] with cousin Lizzie B[arnwell]. The more I see of her the more I love and admire her. What a strange and varied life has hers been. The belle of Providence [Rhode Island] brought up in elegance & luxury, with most extrav-

agant habits—a hasty marriage at nineteen, brought on abruptly by a sort of persecution from her brother, a continued struggle with small means, an increasing family, with the addition of T[om]'s brothers as well as her own and his children, from all of whom she experienced the greatest ingratitude & meanness. T[om] too is so strange on some subjects that he only adds to her difficulties instead of smoothing them away. And yet with all her troubles, which would have long ago broken down a weak woman and made her peevish & fretful if not worse, she is so amiable & bears all so bravely that I cannot help loving her more and more.

News arrived today of the battle at Manassas Junction, which lasted four hours & a half in which the Federalists were severely beaten with great loss, while ours was very slight.[10] *July 19 Friday*

This afternoon we attended a meeting of ladies held at Miss Hesse Drayton's to form a society to furnish clothing for the Volunteers. The members [are] to subscribe 50¢ a quarter & the gentlemen to give donations either of money or cloth. The ladies [are] to make it preparatory to their winter campaign; about thirty ladies were present, cousin Beck [Holmes] and Miss [Hester T.] D[rayton] being the heads; it was proposed to have a public meeting and invite the ladies of the city to join as all are equally interested. Carrie and myself afterwards went walking on the Battery, met Hattie [White], who returned home with us; Isaac [White] came in after tea & proposed a frolic to the ice-cream garden so Willie and himself escorted the girls, calling for Rosa, & Alester & I went in the buggy. The moonlight was very bright & I drove almost all the time, taking a turn on the Battery also, and quite enjoying the ride.

Congress meets at Richmond today. *July 20*

The telegraph this morning announces a great and glorious victory gained yesterday at Bull's Run [*sic*] after ten hours *July 22*

---

10 This was called "The Affair at Blackburn's Ford" by the Union side and "The First Battle of Bull Run" by the Confederates. There were eighty-three Union and sixty-eight Confederate casualties.

hard fighting. The enemy were completely routed, with tremendous slaughter; the loss on either side is of course not yet known, but ours is light compared to theirs. They have besides lost the whole of the celebrated Sherman Battery, two or three others, and a quantity of ammunition, baggage, etc. Their whole force amounted to about 80,000 while ours was only 35,000; only our left wing, however, commanded by Genl. [Joseph E.] Johnson [Johnston], 15,000 in number against 35,000 of the enemy, were mostly engaged.[11] The centre commanded by the President [Jefferson Davis], who arrived on the field about noon, & the right wing, led by Beauregard, were only partially engaged. The Georgia Regiment commanded by Col. Francis S. Bartow seems to have suffered very severely, the Ogelthorpe Light I.[nfantry] from Savannah especially. Col. Bartow was killed as was also Gen. Barnard Bee and Col. B. F. Johnson of the Hampton Legion. The latter arrived only three hours before the battle and seem to have taken a conspicuous part in it. In Gen. Bee the Confederate Army has lost an officer whose place cannot readily be supplied.[12] He stood so high in his profession that, immediately after his arrival quite late from the distant western frontiers, a captain, he was raised to the rank of Brigadier General; he was one of Carolina's noblest sons, and, though we glory in the victory won by the prowess of our gallant men, tears for the honored dead mingle with our rejoicings. Col. Bartow was one of the most talented and prominent men in Savannah and very much beloved; he left Congress to go to Va. with the O.[gelthorpe] L.[ight] I.[nfantry] as their captain, but was made Col. & was acting Brigadier Gen. during the battle. Col. Johnson's loss will also be much felt; he leaves a wife & eight children. A great many Charlestonians are wounded but only three of Kershaw's R.[egiment] which must have been in the right wing. . . . Rumors are, of course, flying in every direction, none of which are to be relied on,

11 Union forces numbered 28,452 and suffered 2,645 casualties, while Confederate forces numbered 32,232 and suffered 1,981 casualties.
12 Barnard Bee (1824–61) graduated from the United States Military Academy in 1845. On July 21, 1861, during the Battle of Bull Run, he gave General Jackson his famous nickname when he exclaimed: "Look at Jackson's Brigade; it stands like a stone wall! Rally behind the Virginians." He died the next day.

but Willie Heyward went on tonight to see after some of his
friends, whom he hears are wounded.

The telegraph today only confirms what we heard yesterday *July 23*
without additional information, as the wires from Manassas to
Richmond were down for some hours. Several gentlemen
went on last night with servants & nurses to attend our
wounded, and societies for their relief are being organized in
the city. The *northern* account of the battle & the dreadful
panic which seized their troops, followed by complete de-
moralization, is most graphic. They admit that the carnage
was fearful. The "brag" regiment of N.Y., the 69th, was cut to
pieces; the *infamous* Fire Zouaves went into battle 1100 strong
and came out 206. The New Orleans Zouaves were let loose
on them & most amply were the murder of [James] Jackson &
the outrages on women avenged on these fiends; 60 pieces of
artillery were taken including Sherman's which was celebrated as Ringgold's during the Mexican War. [Others taken
were] Carlisle's, Griffin's, the West Point Batteries, & the 8
siege 32-pounder rifle cannon, with which [Winfield] Scott
was marching upon Richmond. The Federal Army left Washington commanded by Scott in all the pomp & pageantry of
the panoply of war—all so grand and impressive in their own
eyes that they did not dream that we would strike a blow but
would lay down our arms in terror. They carried 550 pair of
handcuffs & invited immense numbers of ladies to follow and
see Beauregard and Lee put into irons, expecting to march
directly on to Richmond. The contrast of the picture may be
imagined—gloom and terror reign in Washington, and they
are multiplying fortifications and reinforcing the city.
    Today, by Col. [Richard] Anderson's order, a salute was
fired of twenty-one guns, from Forts Moultrie & Sumter, at
12 o'clock, in honor of the victory, & tomorrow their flags
will be placed at half-mast and guns fired hourly from 6:00
A.M. till sunset in honor of the illustrious dead. Preparations
are being made to receive the bodies in state; the City Hall is
draped in mourning as when [John C.] Calhoun lay in state, &
now his statue gleams intensely white through the funeral
hangings surrounding the three biers. I have not yet visited
the hall but those who have say the impression is awfully

solemn. It seems really the "Chamber of the Dead." The bodies were expected today, but a delay occurred & they may not come till Friday. This afternoon the Ladies Charleston Volunteer Aid Society held a meeting at the S.C. Hall, 192 ladies were there and nearly $1000 collected from subscriptions and donations. Miss Hesse [T.] Drayton was appointed Superintendent, & Hesse [D. Drayton], Assistant, Emily Rutledge, Secy. & Treasurer, & 12 Managers to cut out the work and distribute it. We are to have monthly as well as quarterly meetings. The ladies all seemed to enjoy seeing their friends as well as the purpose for which they came. Mrs. Geo. Robertson & Mrs. Amy Snowden have got up another [society] called Soldiers' Relief Assn. not only for sending clothes, but comforts & necessaries for the sick and wounded, while the ladies interested in the Y.M.C.A. have got up another [group] & already sent on supplies for the hospitals. All are most liberally supported. . . .

July 25   Aunt [Carrie] Blanding and Aunt Mary [Holmes] dined with us today and I read out to them the splendid speech of *Clement L. Vallandigham of Ohio*, Representative of Lincoln's Congress, delivered in Congress last week against the usurpations of Lincoln[13]—it is clear, concise and comprehensive. He brings up passage after passage of the Constitution and shows how total and complete have been the tyranny and usurpations of the American President, when an English monarch whose line of ancestors extended hundreds of years back lost his head for usurpations which were trifles compared to Lincoln's. His scorn & sarcasm is intense & scorching against Old Abe himself as well as his satellites and the whole exposes the foundation and cause of the war. The peace policy was killing the Black Republican party & they, by threats to Abraham if he did not declare war & [by] promises of immense supplies of money, forced the old dotard to plunge the country in all its horrors. But he shows too how all is recoiling upon themselves. All honor is due to one of the few honest men left at

---

13 Clement L. Vallandigham (1820–71) was considered the leader of the so-called copperheads. In May, 1863, he was arrested, put on trial, and banished to the Confederacy. He made it to Canada and even ran for the office of Ohio governor that same year. In 1866 he was a member of the National Union Convention. He accidentally shot himself in 1871.

the North, who not only "dares to have his own opinions" but to stand up boldly and proclaim the truth in spite of the seventy thousand hirelings which surround the Capitol. . . .

Gen. [George B.] McClellan has superseded McDowell, U.S. who was defeated at Bull Run on the 21st. He [McDowell] had telegraphed to Washington announcing a signal victory & by the time the news arrived his troops were routed and flying for their lives.

Mr. [Robert] Bunch of the English Consul says he considers this one of the most remarkable victories ever gained. Not only were the Lincolnites double our number, but all their batteries were manned by *regulars*, well trained and experienced as well as commanded by experienced officers. Those batteries were almost all taken by *infantry* at the point of the bayonet, a thing which has never been done before—cavalry always being sent to charge them.

The new French Consul, Baron St. André, has lately arrived here. He was instructed to *avoid* Washington & to present his credentials to the Mayor, so at least we hear, and [it] seems probable it is but the preparatory step to recognizing us.

Carrie & myself went up today to Mrs. [Anna Gaillard] White's to bid Mary Jane and herself goodbye as they expect to leave at midday for Summersville on their way to Winnsboro. We found a number of the Dragoons collected there, waiting the arrival of the bodies; the train was expected at eight & again at ten, but a telegram announced that a delay had occurred & it would not arrive till one. Mr. [John] White invited some of the dragoons to wait there instead of returning home. A funereal [*sic*] car had been sent to Florence to meet the bodies & another draped in mourning bore the committee appointed to meet it. Business was generally suspended, all the flags were at half-mast & the Liberty pole had crape upon it; everybody was out to see the procession. The Dragoons in their summer uniform of pure white, the German Hussars, & Charleston Mounted Guard met the bodies at the depot and escorted them to the City Hall, four from each company being detailed as especial body guard & the City Guard marching in single file on either side of the hearses; the bodies lay in state for three hours; at four the procession

*July 26
Friday*

moved again, the Dragoons first, Col. [Richard] Anderson commanding & leading the way, with nearly a thousand regulars trailing arms. The W.[ashington] L.[ight] I.[nfantry] was the only volunteer company carrying arms in respect to [Lt.] Col. [B. F.] Johnson, but every infantry company in the city turned out; the pall bearers were all high officers in brilliant uniforms, some on foot others on horseback immediately around the hearses; the flags were furled, at least some were, & draped in crape. There was but little music. The R.[utledge] M.[ounted] R.[ifles] ending the procession on foot leading their horses, a body of Artillery on their way to Va. commanded by Willie Preston were also in the procession. Col. [Gen. Francis S.] Bartow's body had been escorted to the Savannah R.R. by the Mounted Guard.

Carrie & myself dined at Mrs. W[hite]'s; then all went to St. Paul's [Episcopal Church] where the services were performed by cousin Christopher [Gasden] except Mrs. W[hite] and myself—our carriage came for me, and she and I rode out to see the procession. We got a position at the head of Calhoun [St.], and saw it as it turned into Coming [St.] Many of the companies could not get as far as the corner. After the services were over, the bodies were brought out and three volleys fired over them. They were then carried to Magnolia Cemetery, where Col. Johnson was buried & Gen. Bee's remains placed until tomorrow, when they would be carried to Pendleton where all his family are buried. Gen. Bee was mortally wounded in the stomach by grape or chain shot and did not die till eleven o'clock on Monday and, though he suffered fearfully he never uttered a murmur. Col. J.[ohnson] and Col. B[artow] were both instantly killed, the former dreadfully mangled in the face. Thus it was impossible to allow the family a last look ere they were consigned to the tomb, &, oh, how harrowing to their feelings to think those loved forms so near and yet unable to obtain one last agonizing look.

July 27
Saturday

. . . [After Bull Run] 1500 of the Virginia Cavalry pursued the enemy beyond Fairfax till two o'clock in the morning. At that place, they found Gen. [Winfield] Scott's carriage & six horses, with his sword and epaulettes, his table set with silver, champagne, wines and all sorts of delicacies, to celebrate their *intended* victory. But the arrival of the panic stricken troops, flying from close pursuit, had compelled "old fuss and Feathers" to follow their humiliating example. . . .

Congress having appointed a general thanksgiving to be celebrated today in honor of the victory, which will have such important consequences, the services were very solemn, Mr. Howe performing the whole & preaching a most admirable sermon upon the victory & its moral consequences from the text "The Lord has done great things for us, for which we rejoice." He paid a beautiful tribute to the dead who had not only dared to do but to die for their country, their own convictions, "the happiness of little children and the security of women." *July 28 Sunday*

Congress has appropriated $15,000 for the relief of the sick and wounded and appointed a committee of one member from each state to see that they are properly attended to.

Mrs. Elizabeth Barrett Browning died lately at Florence. I have always admired her and her writings so much that I regret her death very much. . . .

A letter was received from Rutledge today written from Stone Bridge on the 22nd. It was merely a few lines in pencil, telling us that the battle had taken place and that Kershaw's & Cash['s] regiment had the honor of turning the tide of battle to victory. President Davis said they had done so. It was a mistake that he commanded the centre; he did not arrive till the enemy were in full retreat. To Beauregard belongs the honor of planning the battle & commanding the army—he has just been made a Confederate General. Col. Richard Anderson has been raised to the rank of Brigadier General. *July 29 Monday*

Bowen Barnwell says the road to Centreville was strewed not only with arms, knapsacks & soldiers' clothing, but delicacies of all sorts and ladies bonnets and shawls. For, a great many of the Lincolnite Congressmen with their wives and friends had gone to witness the "great race" between Federals and Confederates. One of the prisoners said they were told by their officers that we would not fight or at least it would be a mere brush, for our men were so few compared to theirs & they did not believe they would face the regulars, Scott's chosen 10,000, but would yield or run and their army would march immediately on Richmond. The papers which were taken prove the man's assertion true. A bill of fare among other things was found of a dinner McDowell intended to give *yesterday* in Richmond. [Alfred] Ely [of New York], a member of Congress, was taken prisoner also Col. [Michael] Corcoran of the N.Y. 69th, the latter was captured by a mere boy. The P[almetto] G[uard] have captured a flag & two drums. Every Southerner was a hero on that battlefield; every day we learn some new deed of valor, but the taking of Sherman's battery at the point of the bayonet is the most wonderful. Beauregard said it was the greatest the world had ever seen.

Our troops suffered awfully for want of water. Exhausted from want of food, the heat, & hard fighting, their thirst was intense and caused severe suffering.

July 30 ... Mrs. Leo Walker has received letters from an intimate friend in St. Louis giving an awful account of the state of things there. Men walk into their houses and take anything they wish, nor dare they say a word, for a pistol is put to their head, or they are arrested. Little children have been so severely beaten for harraing [*sic*] for Jeff Davis that physicians have had to attend them. She says they do not dare attempt to collect their rents and "we live as we can; God knows that is hard enough—if we had arms we would rise and throw off this yoke of slavery and despotism, but, as it is, we are powerless."

July 31 Went with Sue Brownfield this morning to Miss [Hester T.] Drayton's to help cut out work for the society. It was first intended only to be for the soldiers from the city, but has gradually become a State Society. Very liberal donations have been given both in money and goods and the gentlemen will take an active share in it. The Hospital Society as it is now called gotten up by Mrs. Geo. Robertson is also very active and doing a great deal for the sick and wounded.

All the ministers & physicians & schoolmasters, who are usually exempt from military duty, have been ordered to form and drill as a Reserve Guard—every man from sixteen to sixty is ordered out & *obliged* to drill. It has afforded us a great deal of amusement that the ministers have to drill. I would like to see them practicing the "double-quick step."

Cousin Christopher [Gadsden] has joined the P[almetto] G[uard].[14] He was their chaplain &, when he entered the room at one of their meetings, he was received with such a shout of welcome that he was quite abashed—said he would rather have preached a sermon than face as many young men. After a while, they asked him to offer up a prayer of thanksgiving for the preservation of their comrades on the battlefield and their continued well-fare [*sic*]. After that, he felt "quite at home" amongst them.

We have heard nothing further from R[utledge] or Mr. T. S[umter] B[rownfield] since their notes dated Stone Bridge 22nd, but Mr. Stephen Elliott received a very interesting letter from Willie [Elliott] who is 1st Lieut. Brooks Guard, Kershaw's R.[egiment], giving a sketch of the battle. I feel very proud to think they had such a prominent position and should have had the universally acknowledged honor of turning the battle in connection with Cash's R.[egiment] and Kemper's four-gun battery from a defeat into a glorious victory. For when they rushed to the charge, they met wounded men going to the rear who told them we were beaten & everything which met their sight seemed to confirm it, but undisheartened they rushed onward to victory, to [J. B.] Kershaw's battle cry "Boys remember [Benjamin F.] Butler, [Fort] Sumter and your homes."[15]

It is very difficult to obtain accurate information about either the whereabouts of our friends or those who are wounded, as Beauregard will not allow any but those who are going to join the army to go on to Manassas and the Carolina Regiments are continually on the move. . . .

Spent the morning learning to work the machine & made *August 1* nearly a whole flannel shirt. Both being my particular dislike,

---

14 Christopher Gadsden was ordained an Episcopal priest in 1847. He served as assistant rector of St. Stephen's Church, St. Stephen's, South Carolina, and St. Philip's Church, Charleston. From 1857 to 1871, he was rector of St. Luke's Church, Charleston. During the Civil War, in addition to chaplain duty, he was coeditor of the diocesan periodical, the *Southern Episcopalian*. After the war, he was one of the members of the Board of Missioners to Colored People and Freedmen.

15 On May 13, 1861, Butler took Baltimore. His government of that city and Annapolis proved irritating to area residents.

it needed all my patriotism to bring me to "the sticking point." I've always declared I would not learn to make men's clothes, shirts especially, so everybody laughs at me now.

The paper says Beauregard has lately hung three traitors at Manassas; a civil engineer, a *minister* & a farmer—all having given important information to the enemy. The S.C. Regiments have gone to Vienna, 6 miles from Washington. Whatever is Beauregard's plan, he keeps his own counsel and we can only guess at his future movements.

Among other articles captured have been several wagons loaded with handcuffs—30,000 pairs, to deck their intended victims. I suppose the Lincolnites expected to have a triumphal entry to Washington in the old Roman style.

August 2   Cadwallader [George Cadwalader] and [Robert] Patterson have been dismissed from their army with honorable discharges & McClellan made Commander-in-Chief, thus superseding even Scott.[16] Though all the Northern papers at first announced a great victory *over* us, they have been finally obliged to confess to a most humiliating and disastrous defeat. In fact, some acknowledge the truth that it was a complete rout, but they cannot desist from the most outrageous lies against us to try and support their already tottering nation. Their papers are filled with accounts of our savage barbarity to the wounded & prisoners in hope of inciting their men on to revenge, but they do not tell that they never sent to bury their dead nor to see after their wounded for two or three days. Beauregard sent a dozen of their surgeons whom we had taken prisoners to attend to their comrades, but, instead of doing so, they took the nearest road to the Capital. Their wounded were as carefully tended as our own, but from the numbers of our own, the constant movement of our troops, and the confusion attendant on such an extended battlefield, many were not found for days, and they had crawled into the woods to conceal themselves and there died. Our men finally commenced to bury them, but the task be-

16 Cadwalader was mustered out of Pennsylvania state troops on July 19, 1861, but was made major general of U.S. volunteer troops in April, 1862. He resigned from the army on July 5, 1865. Patterson was mustered out July 27, 1861, under criticism for his alleged lack of aggressiveness at Bull Run. McClellan did not become commander in chief until November, 1861.

came too repulsive. Several days after the battle, a whole Indiana regiment of 700 men, who had been wandering in the woods till nearly starved, were taken prisoners, & every day more are found and brought in.

The Lincolnites do not tell [about] their mean cowardly subterfuges to deceive our men: by fighting under a Confederate flag, obtaining & using the same badges as our men & even the peculiar sort of masonic sign used to distinguish each other, their uniforms being similar & these base deceptions used, in more than one instance. Our gallant troops approached them as friends, nor did they discover their mistake until a deadly fire was opened upon them. It also caused a heart-rending mistake to occur when Jenkins 5th S.[outh] C.[arolina] R.[egiment] came round a hill, the Mississippians mistook them for the enemy & for a few minutes an awful fire met them, till the officers rushed in between and stopped them. Traitors are abundant in our camp, for many of the surrounding farmers are Unionists. The engineer, lately hung, confessed he had been bribed by the enemy to prevent a junction of our forces, & it is more than suspected that [Virginia] Gov. [John] Letcher is as arch a traitor also.

The farmer had been supplying the Hampton Legion with some milk; went over to the enemy & gave such a full account of their dress, etc. that they were immediately recognized & it is supposed that was the reason they suffered so much. . . .

Two young men, members of the W.[ashington] L.[ight] I.[nfantry], Horsey & Walker, have been lately shot for insubordination. The former wrote and published a very mutinous and very improper letter in regard to the alleged treatment of the officers of the [Hampton] Legion. Col. [Wade] Hampton ordered him arrested & he drew a pistol on him. The company then rose in his favor & Col. H[ampton] ordered out four armed companies of infantry to arrest the whole of them. We have not heard all of the particulars, only the fact is known, it being kept quiet for their families' sake. The fathers are both respectable citizens here. Horsey's character does not seem to have been very good, and he nearly murdered a man here before he left. . . .

W[illie] Heyward who reached Wilson [N.C.] three hours   *August 3*
after Capt [Charlie] A[xson] was killed and heard the facts

from several of the company [Richardson's Guards], gives the following account which is now believed to be the true one. Capt. A.[xson] was carrying some melons for friends in Richmond, several of which [Arthur] Davis ate & crushed others. A.[xson] spoke to him about it and he apologized, saying he did not know they were his. It was accepted, & at the next stopping place, he said to Axson—Capt. I owe you something, let's go & take a drink. It was agreed to & they shook hands in a friendly manner. They afterwards got scuffling playfully & Axson grasped Davis by the throat. After that he went out, took another drink & armed with bowie knife & revolver, walked up to Axson in the car & saying "no man shall insult me with impunity," shot him dead. It was the most deliberate cold-blooded murder. Axson's men took almost as lawless a mode of revenging themselves. They took him from his guard & shot him, but his wounds have not proved mortal, as were at first supposed, and it is thought he will recover. He seems to have been a man of the lowest class & very little character.

August 5   Finished my first pair of "drawers" today. I could not help
Monday   laughing at the idea of my being able to teach Lila how to put them together. I do not find the machine as hard to manage as I expected and can sew on it pretty well. A day or two ago, Rosa told me one of her maids asked her if I was not engaged to W.[illie] Heyward. I think it one of the best jokes I've heard for a long time, especially the idea of her telling me. I should like to see his face, when he hears of it—it would be a rich treat and a study for Hogarth.

What curious discoveries are sometimes made from a look or accidental word. Tonight Rosa & Lizzie [Barnwell] came over to see Carrie, who came today from the island, & some trifle made us tell them how grandmother used to do when she was engaged—things that we considered very improper & decidedly "fast" and which would horrify her, if *we* were to do the same, but which she now tells as a good joke. One thing & another stirred up old memories &, after we went upstairs, Sue, Lila & myself gathered in mother's chambers still pursuing the theme. . . . How curiously we have learnt some facts about the other members of the set; almost all are either engaged or in love—Rosa & W[illie] G[uerard]—Carrie & Isaac,

Janie [Chisolm] & Jamie [McCaa]—Alfred [Chisolm] by his own confession in love with Mary B[oykin]. Many believe that Emily [Ford] is engaged to Mr. E.[dward] Thurston, for though she always received a great deal of attention, she has no particular beau. . . . It is very pleasant and interesting to me to stand a spectator with, but not of them, for I'm too old to *belong* to "their set" and watch the undercurrent of life gliding swiftly past. I have never belonged to any particular set mingling as often with those younger as older and really enjoying their society most.

We did not leave mother's room till long after twelve, discussing many by-gone days. . . . After Isaac had left & Carrie came up to bed after one o'clock, she and I talked . . . & from that I got recalling some of my past flirtations, silly girlish memories, but pleasant now to look back upon, though *then* the roses had their thorns. What a bundle of contradictions I am—I wonder if anyone ever *really* loved me. The pretense of some I soon found out. But such recollections are better where they are—even my journal is not to be trusted, but oh, that I had "the gift of the gray goose quill" to weave them into a whole for my own amusement, or that of my friends. It is time for me to lay aside all romance & come down to the practical, illustrated by red flannel shirts & homespun drawers for soldiers. . . .

August
6
&
December
31, 1861

War Rumors and the Charleston Fire

August 6
Tuesday

His [Rutledge's] letter of Aug. 1st from Vienna [Virginia] says he has received a very high compliment not only to himself but to the company by being appointed by Gen. [M. L.] Bonham, Act. Ass. Adj. Gen. the highest appointment on his staff.[1] He says if it had been left to his choice, he would have refused the honor, because he did not like to leave his company, but it was not, so all he had to do was to accept it gracefully & now he likes it very well. He is quartered with the Gen. at a farm house, with the appurtenances of civilized life, & said the night before he had tried for the first time since the eighth of May to sleep in a bed, but found himself so unaccustomed to the luxury that he could not sleep. He said he had just bought a fine horse, as the Gen. wished him to be mounted immediately, so the appointment seems to be a permanent one. He likes Bonham very well.

Edward wrote yesterday that Johnnie C.[rawford] had written home on some of [Congressman Alfred] Ely's paper, stamped with his initials, which they had taken.

1 Milledge Luke Bonham (1813–90) was commander in chief of South Carolina troops in the Charleston area but waived rank and served under Beauregard during the Fort Sumter crisis. He led a brigade in Virginia, but resigned the army in January, 1862, and became a member of the Confederate Congress. He was governor of South Carolina from December, 1862, to December, 1864, then returned to the military and served under Joseph E. Johnston.

Dined & spent the evening with cousin Lizzie Barnwell. This afternoon the German Band voluntarily gave a concert on the Battery for the benefit of the Hospital & Volunteer Aid Societies. Little boys and gentlemen were stationed at different crossings to receive the contributions of the promenaders & riders. $247 was collected.

August 7
Wednesday

Willie has just been elected first lieutenant of the Emerald L.[ight] I.[nfantry] & Willie H.[eyward] Captain, but the election of one of the other officers occasioned a "split" and these boys with twenty-five of the privates have formed themselves into the Sarsfield L[ight] I[nfantry] so named in honor of a great Irish general & patriot.

Rosa, Carrie & myself went visiting. . . . I went to see Lane Deveaux . . . & she told me one of the Boykin Rangers had written home a most ludicrous account of Harry Burnet's turning "laundress" for the company and washing their shirts in a pool of dirty water with *"seven pence worth of soap"* which was all they had, no one but himself having bought any. So we determined to send them some, as a box is about to be sent to Rutledge. . . .

August 8
Thursday
afternoon

. . . It is reported from a private despatch that Beauregard has possession of Arlington Heights and is storming Washington.

August 9
Friday

Cousin John [Holmes] spent [the evening] with us. His wife and children went on to the North with Mr. Welsman a fortnight ago & are now in Philadelphia. I am sorry for him; with all his faults he has a very affectionate heart and, had he a different wife, might be a better man, for he is easily guided by an affectionate hand.

August 11
Sunday
evening

Harriet Post was married to Mr. H. L. Pinckney last week. Her brother's sister-in-law, Miss Stuart, a Virginia lady, residing in the western part was sometime ago kissed in the street by a Lincoln soldier. She drew a pistol and shot him, but I do not know whether she killed him. However, she was arrested and has disappeared—her family know nothing about her. Thus the Northerners war against women. The most horrible outrages upon married women have been committed by the

Ellswith [Ellsworth] Zouaves, yesterday's paper gave a sickening account.[2]. . .

August 14
Wednesday

Prince Napoleon and his wife and suite came on a short time ago to America incog[nito], but [he] has been feasted, wined & dined with Lincoln and his cabinet. His visit, at this crisis, though ostensibly merely a pleasure trip & traveling privately, is considered to be another step towards our recognition, as it is believed the Emperor has sent him on to ascertain the truth & our strength & ability to maintain our government. Last week he visited Mt. Vernon & Manassas also. [Joseph E.] Johnston & Beauregard rode with him over the battle-ground & invited him to visit Richmond which, however, he declined. The French Minister, Mr. [Henri] Mercier, does not seem at all deceived by the furious rhodomoutade [*sic*] of the north, and is decidedly in favor. . . .

Missouri has declared herself "a free, independent and sovereign State, the act of war having broken the ties which bound her to the United States" through a proclamation of Gov. [Claiborne F.] Jackson & [the Confederate] Congress has voted $1,000,000 to support her and authorized the President to call for 400,000 more volunteers.

John Lathrop Motley, who wrote & published only four or five years ago an admirable and most intensely interesting history of the Netherlands, has just been made Lincoln's second Minister to Austria, the first having been rejected by that power. Motley is a Northerner but having depicted in such glowing, earnest, life-like colors the struggle of the Netherlanders for liberty against the oppression of the House of Austria, it seems incomprehensible that he should consider us as *rebels* and take a strong part against us. I admired him not only for the fine execution of his work, which will undoubtedly take its stand as a classic, but for his heart whole enthusiasm in their struggles for that most glorious of all blessings—liberty—but he is an example for party spirit and inconsistency too common to the age.

August 17
Saturday

The telegraphic News this morning confirms the account of a brilliant victory gained at Springfield, Mo. [Wilson's Creek, April 12, 1861] by Gen. McCullough [Brigadier General Ben

2 The Charleston *Courier*, August 10, 1861, clipped a Richmond *Exam-*

McCulloch], over [Nathaniel] Lyons in which the latter was killed & his forces completely routed.[3]. . .

Gen. [J. Bankhead] Magruder burnt Hampton [Virginia] a short time ago, as he found the Lincolnites intended making it their winter headquarters to enable them to dispose of the 900 negroes which [Benjamin F.] Butler stole and has shut up in Fortress Monroe. Several of the inhabitants set fire to their dwellings with their own hands. Everything had been so defiled and ruined that it never could have been "home" again to any Southerner. The village church, the oldest on the continent, unfortunately caught [fire] and was consumed, also.

Hon. Charles [J.] Faulkner, a Virginian, whom Lincoln sent some months ago as his Minister to France, has just returned & been arrested immediately on a charge of treason.[4] I wonder what will be the next step of the despot to whom the Northerners now bow in submission—they are worthy of their fate.

It has been raining steadily for four days, warning us of the approach of Autumn and the loss of our delicious Summer nights. . . .

. . . There is a great deal of that fever not only in the city but all over the country and among our troops in Va. Harry Burnet is much better but Mr. [T. Sumter] Brownfield has had fever and, though he says he is better, he has gone to the hospital and of course the family are very anxious & uneasy. A letter from Rutledge was received today. He said they had moved to Fairfax as Vienna [Virginia] is unhealthy. [He] was well and wrote cheerfully.

August 19
Monday

This companion of months must yield in turn to another but I have a particular affection for this commenced in my lameness and the source of much pleasure to me.[5]

---

iner story telling of two N.Y. Fire Zouaves' alleged rape of a pregnant mother in front of her children.

3 Ben McCulloch (1811–62) fought in the Texas War for Independence and the Mexican War, gaining much popularity in both. In February, 1861, he was commander of the Texas troops who received the surrender of General Twiggs. He was made a brigadier general of Confederate forces in Arkansas. In 1862, while serving under Earl Van Dorn, he was killed at Elk Horn Tavern.

4 Faulkner was appointed by President Buchanan in 1859.

5 This ends the first volume of the diary manuscript.

August 20   . . . It seems to me as if trouble is everywhere. . . . In Va., disease is rife. Measles, mumps and typhoid fever have placed over twenty thousand of our men in the hospitals. The accounts are terrible, for much of the sickness is produced by scarcity of food and what they have is ill cooked.

The Palmetto Guard number 140, & 100 are said to be on the sick list, including Capt. [George] Cuthbert & Mr. [T. Sumter] Brownfield. In [Thomas G.] Bacon's [Seventh S.C. Infantry] regiment, out of 1000, only 200 answered the roll call. Medicine and nourishment they were unprovided with, and the Commissariat was in a dreadful state. The Commissary General, Dr. [Lucius B.] Northrop, is universally blamed as the cause, he being too parsimonious. Want of food prevented Beauregard from advancing with his army to attack Washington immediately after the battle of the 21st, has since prevented him, and is reducing the strength of our army fearfully. I scarcely eat a meal without thinking of our men, perhaps then suffering for want of one, or what they have [is] so scant and ill-cooked as to make them sick. Congress has just passed a bill for providing more surgeons & Mr. [William Porcher] Miles has offered one [*i.e.*, a bill] providing cooks for the different companies. They certainly are more needed than the doctors even. For, the rations are mostly bacon and *wheat* flour and, as very few of our men know how to cook particularly the latter article, the raw or half-cooked dough speedily produces diarrhea, which generally ends in an attack of typhoid fever.

August 22   I see by Mr. [Robert W.] Barnwell's weekly report from the Charlottesville Hospital that he has sent off quantities of all kind of things needed for the sick—bed linen, underclothes, medicine and nourishment to the various Carolina regiments.[6]. . . We are busy as possible, all the time making up underclothes, which is either sent on to Va. or given to those companies about to start. It is a never-ceasing labor of love & patriotism, and the whole country from one end to the other is engaged in the noble work. . . .

What will be the next act of Lincoln's despotism no one can guess. He has gone further than any of the Stuarts ever suc-

6   A deacon of the Protestant Episcopal Church, Barnwell was professor and chaplain of what is today the University of South Carolina.

ceeded in going. His last acts of tyranny have been seizing Mr. Robert Mure of Charleston, who is, I believe, a Scotchman, as he was about to leave for Europe as bearer of dispatches; Mr. Serrill of New Orleans was arrested as he came off the vessel which brought him from Europe where he has been on a visit. 40,000 pounds of English currency and imported papers for the Confederacy are said to have been found on him.

Missouri has just been admitted into the Confederacy by an act of Congress, and a war-tax [has been] passed, a direct taxation of 50 cts on every hundred dollars, on gold and silver plate, watches, pianos, [and] pleasure carriages.

The last steamers for [*sic*] Europe bring current reports that Napoleon, on receipt of the news of the [Bull Run] battles of the 18th and 21st, had determined to recognize us and that [British Prime Minister] Lord Palmerston had declared that, if a single vessel succeeded in running the blockade, it was inefficient. . . .

. . . It has been raining almost all this week making the weather very changeable and disagreeable. Monday night was the only one on which we had brilliant moonlight, though we went to row with Rosa Wednesday night.

August 23

Sue, Lila and myself have made a dozen pair of drawers this week. The weather cleared this afternoon, and the sunset was brilliant. Another concert was given by the Brass Band for the Aid Societies on the Battery, but the proceeds were comparatively small, as few persons were walking. . . .

August 24
Saturday

. . . This afternoon the first monthly meeting of the Ladies Society for Clothing the troops in active service was held,[7] and the reports read—2301 flannel shirts and drawers have been completed, two or three companies going on have been supplied, and the rest sent to the quarter-master. All the subscriptions and donations received have been expended, but the quarter-master is to pay Miss [Hester T.] Drayton's bills and, in turn, the Confederate States [will] pay the State. Thus, in reality, the troops are clothed by the Government, and our society, as it were, has only made an advance for it. Thus, each

August 26
Monday

7 Ladies Clothing Association for Troops in Active Service. See also the June 24, 1861, entry.

[is] sustaining the credit of the other, and the ladies [are] only contributing their work, though we will continue to pay our subscriptions and thus keep the society always going. . . .

August 27   Isaac came this afternoon to teach us how to shoot pistols. . . . We shot a good many times, but as we were in the piazza and too far from our mark, we did not prove very apt scholars. . . .

August 28
Wednesday   . . . The Lincoln despotism is progressing rapidly. Fort *Lafayette* in New York harbor has become the Bastille, into which are thrown without the slightest warning or given cause, not only men of the highest standing and respectability, but *ladies* moving in the most fashionable circles. Mrs. [Rose O'Neal] Greenhow, whom mother met many years ago at the [Virginia] Springs, the widow of the former Librarian and Translator of the State Department and a great politician, has been arrested.[8] Mrs. P. Phillips, whose husband is a well known Counsellor before the U.S. Supreme Court, both formerly from this city but lately of Alabama, was also arrested because she had *intended* to illuminate her house in honor of our victory at Manassas but was dissuaded by her friends. The trunks of Mrs. [William M.] Gwin, wife of the Senator from California, were searched while she was absent, and drawings of the fortifications of Washington [were] found. Orders were immediately issued for her arrest. Four naval officers lately arrived, who resigned their commissions, had their names stricken from the roll and themselves consigned to dungeons. A Miss Cunningham of this city, whose father is a carpenter, has just arrived from N.Y. When there, she went to see Johnnie Harleston. She said she heard the clank of his chains before she saw him, and their marks were visible. She asked him

8   Rose O'Neal Greenhow (?–1864) was a Washington society leader who became a spy for the Confederacy. She informed Beauregard of McDowell's plans for Bull Run through the use of a cipher. She was arrested and her house then became a prison for women—Fort Greenhow. After a number of security breeches, she was sent to Old Capitol Prison in January, 1862. She and her daughter Rose stayed there until the spring when she was released and went south to be hailed as a heroine. She later ran the blockade and met Napoleon III and Queen Victoria. She wrote a book, *My Imprisonment.* After she had returned to the Confederacy, she lost her life in a sea accident in September, 1864, and was buried with the honors of war.

if he wished to write to his family. He said yes & the keeper procured materials. He gave her the letter which she sewed inside her dress between the wadding, which was the only way she saved it. For, she was thoroughly searched at the different stopping places by women who even shook her garments, but fortunately this did not rattle. She went to see his mother and delivered the letter. . . .

Gen. A.[lbert] Sidney Johnson [Johnston], who is to be our Commander-in-chief, has arrived at Mesilla in Arizona, taken possession of our troops there, & prepared to give battle to the U.S. forces there. He is a man of great military genius, considered second to [Winfield] Scott formerly, and capable of moving and managing immense bodies of troops. He is a man of about sixty and gained his reputation in the expedition against Utah, when the Mormons revolted. He started from California, where he has been living, sometime ago, to come to the South, but was detained on the way by a lingering illness. He is accompanied by a large bodyguard and about fifty staff officers. Gen. Braxton Bragg of "a little more grape" celebrity[9] has been ordered to Va., and Gen. Richard Anderson [has] been ordered from here to supply his place at Pensacola. . . .

A telegraph from Wilmington [North Carolina] today announces that the fleet of ten or fifteen war vessels lately gathered off Fort Monroe had sailed South and were heading for Cape Hatteras. Thereupon the Moultrie Guards and a corps of Artillery were immediately ordered down to Morris Island "to make assurance doubly sure" and prevent any barges from landing. . . .

August 29

The Northern fleet, carrying 100 guns & 4000 men, commanded by Gen. B.[enjamin] F. Butler, on Tuesday attacked Fort Hatteras [North Carolina], a mud fort, with several guns & garrisoned by 853 men. The firing was returned with spirit and renewed the next day. When the ammunition gave out, &, after a very brave resistance, our men were compelled to

August 31

9 According to an often repeated apochryphal story, during the Battle of Buena Vista in the Mexican War, General Zachary Taylor rode up to Bragg's battery and said: "A little more grape, Captain Bragg."

surrender [on August 29th]. About twenty made their escape, and about eighty were killed & wounded.[10] The same day two other small forts two miles off were taken. It is a dreadful loss to us, for the enemy have thus acquired a strong foothold and, backed by their fleet, will be enabled to harrass and pillage the country. Great blame is attached to those in authority for the want of ammunition which caused the loss of the place. . . .

John Harleston has written on to his mother to ask her to pray for his death. He says his health is failing very much, & he is very much swollen. He thinks he will be kept in confinement about two months longer, and then "*let loose to the mob.*". . .

September 2   All the families living in the neighborhood of Hatteras & Beaufort, N.C., are flying into the interior, as they are expecting the latter to be shelled. . . . On Saturday evening Caliste & Fannie [Brownfield] had been here & I got them to sing "the Evening Song to the Virgin" by Mrs. [Felicia D.] Hemans & an exquisite French chanson, "Elan d'Amour." This evening I persuaded them to try them again with the piano and several other voices joining in. They are not accustomed to singing except occasionally for their own amusement & never practice, but I was particularly charmed with these pieces. Then Caliste & I tried a redowa,[11] and, as my foot stood it very well, I conclude it is almost well—nearly seven months since my sprain.

September 3   The free colored men of this city have had a meeting, collected $450 for the Soldiers Relief Society, passed resolutions very creditable to them indeed, and presented the money.

September 5   Our shooting club met again this afternoon, but Hattie [White] was the only one of the girls who came. We shot [at] a distance of about twenty feet at a card. Hattie, Willie, Isaac &

10   The Butler expedition consisted of seven naval vessels, 143 guns, 880 men, and a landing party of 319. Thirty-five Confederate cannon and 670 Confederate men were captured.
11   A popular Bohemian ballroom dance of the nineteenth century— either a dance in 3/4 time resembling a waltz or a dance in 2/4 time resembling a polka.

myself were the only ones who hit it, but most of our shots were within a foot of it—*tolerably* good, for such unpracticed shots.

September 6

I walked round to Uncle James' this morning with Lila, who went to take her music lesson, and spent the morning there looking over the bookcases and reading. I brought back quite a miscellaneous collection, commencing with *Noctes Ambrosiance, Life of Petrarch* & Alex Smith's *Poems*, & ending with Florence Nightingale's *Notes on Nursing* & Sam Slick's [Thomas C. Haliburton] *Wise Saws & Modern Instances*. I had heard a great deal of the latter and fancied it to be coarse in its humor, but was most agreeably disappointed and delighted with its life-like pictures of New England life, its rare humor, delicate and yet so true and natural, that everybody enjoyed it thoroughly. It is like the joyous laughter of a merry hearted child. Judge Haliburton shows extensive acquaintance with men and manners, and that human nature in all degrees from the President of the (former) United States, and the Peers of England, to the "down-Easter" farmer, and negro has been the subject of close observation and study and animal nature as well as mother Earth has also shared his regards.

The wisest and most common-sense maxims about life in all its aspects and variety are scattered broadcast through his more comic stories and often clothed in beautiful language. It is a book that can be read & re-read & always with pleasure.

September 8

. . . Since the first of August I don't think three days have passed without pouring rains during some part of the day. The mornings will be bright and almost cloudless and the sun very hot, when a sudden deluge startles everyone. Then the weather clears brightly till next day. Just as we came out of church this morning it commenced. . . .

September 9

Carrie, Emily [Ford] and myself walked this afternoon on the Battery and Hannah Harleston joined us. She says her brother has never been chained except being handcuffed when carried to court. The last letter they received from him was through Miss Cunningham, all written communication now being stopped, but a Catholic priest, who came on a few days ago, had been to the Toombs. The health of the prisoners was so much impaired that the physicians had ordered a change, and Johnnie H[arleston], Mr. [Charles S.] Passalaigue & Capt. [Thomas H.] Baker had been removed from their dungeons & put together in a large room, in which they could take exercise &, though the windows were high up, they could look out. J[ohn] H[arleston]'s health had been much improved by it. The priest took letters from them but was searched so often that he feared they might be found & be detrimental either to them or their friends here, so he destroyed them. Hannah is as cheerful as possible & anticipates no danger for her brother.

September 10
Tuesday

The Fiftieth Anniversary of the "great tornado" when grandmother was so miraculously saved from death & Uncle Henry [Gibbes] born on mother's third birthday.[12]. . .

Uncle Edward dined with us today &, in talking of Beauregard's movements on the Potomac, he said he thought all these slow cautious forward moves, building batteries, taking high hills, etc. with constant little skirmishes, was meant by Gen. B.[eauregard] to keep the enemys [*sic*] constantly in alarm expecting an attack on Washington, while he [was] waiting for affairs in Missouri, where Gen. [Albert] Sid[ney] Johnson [Johnston] has been sent, to get a little more settled. [Then] he will suddenly cross the Potomac (generally low during this month, but lately very high indeed) with a large army, while the batteries still keep the enemy in check. [He will] rouse the Marylanders, free the Baltimorians [*sic*] from the dreadful despotism under which they are suffering and push on to Philadelphia. That seems to be the opinion of many, & we have only to await events & see if they are true prophets.

The Washington correspondent of a Baltimore paper writes a dreadful account of the way in which the ladies are arrested & treated without any charge being proved on them. Soldiers suddenly entered the house, arrested them & treated them in the most insulting manner, not only searching them & rifling their pockets, but [searching] every box, desk, bureau & in fact everyting, even to their *soiled clothes.* Every

12 Emma Holmes's account of this incident is located in the Wilmot Stuart Holmes Collection, Southern Historical Collection, University of North Carolina.

note received passes through their [the government's] hands; the family [is] under espionage all the time, & every possible indignity [is] offered. In Baltimore the ladies are forbidden to appear in the colors of the Confederate flag, men wearing red & white neckcloths are ordered to take them off or be carried to the guard-house, & a man who put a pair of *knit baby shoes*, red & white, in his store window was ordered to remove them. When a government has to resort to such base, low, little expedients to prop its authority, it truly exposes its utter decay to the scorn of the world. Anyone reading the account would believe they were in Italy, during the days of its revolution, when Austrian fear & despotism, as well as priestly despotism, ruled all with a rod of iron.

... Spain has practically, though not formally, acknowledged our Confederacy by a proclamation of the Captain General of Cuba permitting all our vessels "both to enter into its ports, & clear from them," in spite of the opposition of the American Consul, & further he informs all foreign consuls that no interference will be allowed.

September 13
Friday

The first steamer of the line to run between here & Liverpool started on the fifteenth of August. It is owned by Geo. Trenholm & Co.[13] £70,000 was paid for her and the cargo is worth $300,000. The letter informing them of it added that "in consideration of the number of privateers swarming the seas, it had been deemed prudent to put two rifled cannon on board." Of course, we are looking eagerly for news of her arrival in some Southern port near; she sails under British colors and papers.

A hundred and fifty Yankee prisoners arrived last night to be confined in Castle Pinckney. Twenty-five are officers, including Col. [Michael] Corcoran of the N.Y. 69th & Col. [1st Lt. A. T.] Wilcox of [the Seventh] Ohio [Volunteers]. The rest are N.Y. Zouaves. The whole Rifle Regiment & Dragoons were ordered out to receive them, as it was feared the Irish & rabble might attempt to mob them on Corcoran's account. They were under arms from four o'clock Thursday afternoon

13 George A. Trenholm (1807–76) was a Confederate secretary of the treasury, from July 18, 1864, to April 7, 1865. Through his company he was a leading figure in Confederate negotiations with Europe for ships and goods during the war. His ships were leading blockade runners.

till seven, then from eleven till seven Friday morning, awaiting their arrival, an accident having detained them. They arrived early in the morning, & were marched quietly to the jail to remain for a few days, under a guard, till Castle Pinckney is prepared. Richmond is overflowing with them & several have lately escaped, though most were retaken. It was concluded to disperse [prisoners] farther South: at New Orleans, here, & other places.

September 15 I was still so completely worn out & fatigued this morning by my walk to Hattie's [White] on Friday that I could not go to church, as our horse is lame again. Read two most admirable sermons by Bishop [Stephen] Elliott [Jr. of Georgia] delivered June 13th and July 28th and published in the *Southern Episcopalian.*[14] They were a sort of condensed abstract of the causes and events of our most remarkable revolution, showing how visibly the Hand of God was with us throughout all our struggles for freedom. I only wish they could be published in Europe and read by all the civilized world. . . . Oh, the miseries of bad pens are almost as inexpressible as "the unwritten poetry of the soul." I almost despair of ever writing nicely again & pens are so scarce that we will soon have to come down to the "grey goose quill" of olden times.

September 16 The *Bermuda*, [George] Trenholm's steamship from Liver-
Monday pool, which we have been so anxiously expecting, arrived on Saturday at Savannah. It ran down here early in the morning but finding the squadron on the alert, it very quietly saluted it & passed by as a British man-of-war, its two 84 pound rifled cannon thus doing good service. Besides those, it brings 50,000 Enfield rifles, 1500 pair of blankets, woolen goods, etc. 80,000 pr. shoes, 24 rifled cannon, mostly 42's & 32 pounders.[15]

My list of accomplishments is constantly increasing. I can

14 The periodical of the Episcopal Church of South Carolina, it was in existence from April, 1854, to August, 1863, and was printed in Charleston.
15 The cargo consisted of 18 rifled cannon, a 32-pounder; a 42-pounder; two 168-pounders; 6,500 Enfield rifles, 200,000–300,000 cartridges; 60,000 pairs of shoes, 20,000 blankets; 180 barrels of gun powder, and medical stores.

not only make flannel shirts & drawers, the latter being my principal occupation, a pair every morning, but I can load & clean pistols as well as clean [*sic*] them & knit stockings. [The latter] also indeed has become so fashionable that the girls carry their knitting when they go to take tea out just like our great grandmothers. . . .

Last night Isaac gave us the long promised serenade. The moonlight was brilliant, and just at twelve we were woke by the arrival of a Jersey waggon [*sic*], carrying a piano & the performers, Isaac driving Prince & Jerry in the tandem & Mr. Hughes & Mr. W.[illie] W. W.[hite] as outriders. Willie Walker played the piano, Edwin [White] the "fairy-flute" & Messrs. George & John Read on the violin. The two first pieces were delicious waltzes, to which I have often danced, & one particularly has been haunting me ever since. Willie & Willie H.[eyward] then went out and invited them in to take a "snack," & we feared all was over but waited with intense anxiety. Soon we were rewarded by a most exquisite gem from Travatore, a duet, in which the violins and flute strove to see which could *talk* the sweetest. I never heard any music but theirs which made you feel as if you heard the different speakers. Then followed "Let me kiss him for his mother," W. Walker as solo & Willie H.[eyward] joining his fine voice with the others in the chorus. Willie W.[alker] sang another song, very familiar as one of his favorites, but the name I do not know. Then the "sweet music as of a dream" ended in the gay strains of the Storm Galop and all passed away as silently as they had come, to waft their delicious "fairy like music" to other favored mortals. . . . It is really an exquisite pleasure to hear such music, and it is heightened by the scene & the time, all blending into a perfect whole. They gave sixteen serenades, beginning at Hattie's at half past ten & not getting home till five o'clock.

September 18

Last night I went over to the Burnets & was so indignant at their abuse of President Davis from the eldest to the youngest, all joining open mouthed in the cry against him & everything he said & did, that I could scarcely hold my peace & wanted to leave. The whole Rhett connection & clique are indignant that

September 20
Friday

old Mr. [Robert] Barnwell Rhett was not made President & in consequence the [Charleston] *Mercury* daily teems with articles against Davis & the government & how badly & wrong everything is conducted, etc. until everybody is thoroughly disgusted with them.[16]

September 27   ... Quite a storm of wind and rain commenced last night &
Friday   has increased this morning, blowing down fencing & blinds, & [the] rain [is] beating in in every direction. It is several years since we have had such a storm, and our troops on the coast must feel it severely. A sub-marine telegraph has been lately successfully laid between Forts Moultrie & Sumter & an air line one to Battery Island. ...

September 30   Today we heard of Gen. [Abbott H.] Brisbane's death, which took place at Summerville where he had gone for a change. His health has been very delicate for years, but this summer he insisted on doing something in the military line. He was made Inspector General, but the duties were too severe for such a nervous excitable frame, & he twice fainted on the Citadel Green before he would give it up. Though he has long retired from public life & will therefore not [be] much missed there, he will be deeply mourned by all his family and connections, for he was very much beloved, a very warm hearted kind man & a most agreeable & genial companion to young people, of whom he was very fond, as well as elder ones. I shall always remember him with pleasure, & [remember] the delightful party at his house last spring, which was the beginning of a series he intended to give, to draw young people always round him. He was a graduate of West Point and in the same class as Gen. Robert (Lincoln) Anderson, Prof. [Alexander D.] Bache, & many others well known in public life.[17]

16 Robert Barnwell Rhett (1800–76) was a leading "fire eater," member of the South Carolina legislature (1826), state attorney general (1832), and member of Congress (1837–39). His son was the editor of the Charleston *Mercury*, a consistently anti-Jefferson Davis newspaper.
17 Alexander D. Bache (1806–67), a great-grandson of Benjamin Franklin, was a leading American physicist. He was superintendent of the United States Coastal Survey from 1843 until his death in 1867. He was the first president of the National Academy of Science.

. . . Mr. [P.] Fayssoux Stevens has resigned the Superinten- *October 1*
dancy of the Citadel, to the universal regret of all. Even his
family were strongly opposed to it. He is to be ordained & has
accepted a church at Pinopolis, quite too limited a sphere for
a man of his talents, for he is looked upon as one who will
prove a "shining light" in the church. This is the second or
third time appointed for his ordination, but he was so strongly urged to delay it, as his state needed his services & he was
somewhat bound to her having been a beneficiary, that he was
compelled to do so. He intended resigning last January, but
then again the necessities of the state made him delay & now,
though he is needed as much as ever being one of the best
military men in the state & no one being as well qualified as
himself to be at head of the Citadel, a doubly important institution at present, he thinks it his duty to devote his talents
and energy to the service of God. Capt. J. B. White of the
Arsenal is to fill his place.

The *Nashville* has been preparing for sometime past to take *October 2*
our Ministers, Messrs. [James M.] Mason & [John] Slidell to
Europe. The latter intends carrying his family also. He is to
go to France & Mr. Mason to England. Mr. [E. J.] Macfarland
[*sic*] is Secretary of Legation to the latter. The *Nashville* is a
very fast sailer & has been armed with several small rifled
guns for she could not carry a heavy one. She intended running the blockade, when as it often happens, there is only one
or two vessels off the bar, & our "infant navy" was to go down
& keep them busy while she got safely away. The presence of
the gentlemen here has been kept very quiet & indeed [so has]
everything in regard to the aim or destination of the vessels,
while the papers reported that they intended going by way of
Tampico. However, day after day there has been some delay.
Week before last we expected it to go, but the fleet was suddenly increased & it is believed that some traitor has signaled
it. This evening . . . out of the eleven ladies gathered, eight
were knitting stockings, & grandmother showed us a pair of
slippers sent her from London just after she was married,
when it was the fashion for the ladies to make their own for
drawing room wear; it was of yellow marseilles, now brown
with age, embroidered & bound with brown, made all in one

piece, very simple & easy, with a leather sole inside. I intend making some & putting a cork sole inside. They are really quite pretty & becoming to the foot as well as quite a discovery when shoes are so scarce & high. . . .

October 9
Wednesday

A clear, bright & very cool autumn day. I went up to Ashley Hall with Claude [Turnbull Walker] & Rosa & Becca [Bull]. Willie G.[uerard] driving; Mr. Bull arrived soon after we did with a violent ague on him & was quite sick all day. It was the first time I had ever seen any one with an ague, & I did not know [what] to make of it at first. He could scarcely speak when he came in. Dr. [John] Drayton spent the day there also, but, as he is "a sour old maid of forty-five," he is not much addition to the party. The day was delightful & we spent most of it in the garden, practicing with a revolver, sitting under the trees or gathering flowers. . . .

October 14
Monday

. . . Willie heard this evening that Edmund Gibbes' property here had been sequestrated [*sic*]. Allan Gibbes came in to pay a visit and confirmed it. All summer Edmund has not only refused to do military duty or pay his fine, but wrote an insulting answer to the summons. He has never contributed a cent of his immense wealth in any way towards the service of his State. The only thing he did was to offer his services free at Richmond to attend the sick & wounded, or at least he gave out that he was going on for that purpose, but no one believed him sincere, & he has now gone on to the North to try & save some fifteen or twenty thousand dollars worth of property he owns there. Allan says, as far as he understands it, to get his passport he has to swear himself "an alien enemy to the Southern Confederacy," &, on his own words, his property [that] amounted to between four & five hundred thousand dollars has been sequestrated [*sic*]. The miser in attempting to over-reach others had over-reached himself & destroyed the god he worshipped. He is a man no one will pity or regret, save cousin Juliet [Gibbes], who is attached to him despite his faults & neglect of her. He is a man of highly gifted mind &, with all the advantages of European education & travelling over half the world, can make himself a most fascinating companion when he chooses. But, he is an infidel & a notoriously immoral man, not only glorying but boasting of his wicked-

ness & the meanest of the mean in everything. His only redeeming quality was his love for his mother &, since her
death, all is concentrated upon his own vile self.

It poured rain all Thursday & rained steadily all today, but
the weather is so warm we are wearing summer dresses and
sleeping with open windows.

October 19
Saturday

Raining steadily all day, but Willie went out & brought the
news of Capt. Dan Vincent's safe arrival in town from one of
the West India Islands. Yesterday he lay off the bar, & raised a
signal of distress. A carpenter was sent from the fleet to repair
some damage to his vessel, taking him either for a Yankee or
Englishman, &, after getting the news & repairs, he slipped
his vessel last night into Bull's Bay. This is the second time he
has outwitted the Yankee fleet in the same way. The latest
item, which it is believed he brought, is that the Yankees intend attacking our coast very soon in three places. I have no
doubt they think we are awfully scared, but our men are
ready for them & eager for the fray. In case of alarm the bells
are to toll fifteen times, five times in succession, & all the surrounding districts will fly to arms. I read Gen. [W. G.] De-
Saussure's orders two nights ago, where all the companies as
far as Upper St. John's were to take their positions in readiness to move at a moment's warning.

October 20
Sunday

Dull, disagreeable, gloomy weather for the last two days, but
this evening it brightened a little, & I went to see Mary
B.[rownfield] & spent the evening there, with her brother
Robert to escort me home; something quite unusual, as gentlemen are so scarce now.

October 22
Tuesday

Gen. [Nathan G.] Evans has won a brilliant victory at Lees-
burg [Ball's Bluff, Virginia], nearly equalling, if not surpassing, that of Manassas in the complete rout of the enemy.[18]. . .

October 23
Wednesday

Went with M.[ary] Davie to the quarterly meeting of our society [Ladies Clothing Association . . .], paid our subscriptions,

October 24
Thursday

18 After this battle a controversy developed over General Charles P.
Stone's conduct leading to the establishment of the Congressional Committee on the Conduct of the War.

but did not wait for the minutes, as we preferred a walk on the Battery. Wore my new gored dress for the first time, & am by no means well-pleased with it. However, it takes a long time for me to like any new dress. . . .

October 25   Miss [Hester T.] Drayton has responded to an appeal for clothing from the Maryland Volunteers under Col. Gillam [William Gilham] by sending 100 shirts & 100 pair of drawers, & other contributions have been sent also. They are mostly young men of the best families, who are, of course, entirely cut off from supplies from their friends.

October 27   . . . All the Episcopal Bishops of the Confederate States have just been in Convention at Columbia for the purpose of framing a new Constitution; one of the Bishops from N.C. proposed to change the name of our church from Protestant Episcopal to Reformed Catholic, but it was almost universally ruled down. Major P. F. Stevens was ordained by them, & has gone to take the church at Pinopolis.

October 30   . . . Yesterday evening I spent with Miss Bates, & she read me the lecture on the German composers of music which she is going to deliver next week at two concerts given at her house by the Misses Sloman, at which they will play some of Handel's finest music as illustrations. I was very much interested indeed not only in the lecture itself, which is beautifully written, but in the prospect of hearing such grand music on the harp & Alexandrian organ, which can imitate a full band of music. Only a hundred tickets are to be given out for each concert, at fifty cents each, & the proceeds [are] to be given to the soldiers. The Misses Sloman & Misses Bates have for some months past been accustomed to read together plays or pastorals [such] as the *Mid-Summer's Night Dream* or *Comus*, the former playing as accompaniments either Handel's, Mendelssohn's, or Beethoven's exquisit [*sic*] music.

November 8   . . . The bad news from Hilton Head & Bay Point received
Friday   this evening has thrown a gloom over everything. After four hours hard fighting between the fleet & both batteries, the latter being surrounded on three sides with about 160 guns bearing on them & almost every gun dismantled & between

thirty & forty killed & wounded, our men were obliged to abandon both batteries. . . .

We found a room full of persons at Miss Bates' but not the crowd that was there on Wednesday. Miss A.[gnes] said at one time they did not think any one would come for everything was in such a troubled anxious state. Miss B[ates's] lecture was very interesting indeed, & the music [was] very fine. I was especially pleased with Handel's *Coronation Anthem* on the Harp & piano, Von Weber's *Mermaid's Song from Oberon* on the harp, a duet from Mozart's *Don Giovanni* on the harp & Alexandre organ, & the *Beauregard March* on the same instruments—the latter was arranged by Miss Betsey Sloman. It commenced with the "Prayer before the Battle" from Mozart, which is exquisitely beautiful, then comes the bugle call followed by the trumpet, & the March. The entertainment ended with Capt. E. O. Murden's "Battle of Ft. Sumter" set to music & sung by Miss Sloman. The room was decorated with a peculiarly Southern drapery of long grey moss, "the old man of the forest," & in the entries the chandeliers were hung with garlands of moss, rice, cotton . . . & wild oats mingled. I walked home with Henry Walker and he made himself more agreeable than I thought he could have done.

Today James Holmes came to tell us good-bye, as all the cadets are ordered out on duty tomorrow, the arsenal-cadets also, only leaving a few to guard either institution. While he was here, Willie came home to get ready, being ordered out immediately, & left at two for the race course where the whole of DeSaussure's Brigade of over 3000 men are to assemble, prepartory [*sic*] to leaving. Almost every young man that was left here belongs to it, so we will only have the Reserve left. . . . North Carolina has already sent us [Col. T. L.] Clingman's [Twenty Fifth N.C. Volunteer] regiment, including 850 Indians, & Georgia has also sent over a thousand, with thousands more ready to pour down on our invaders, especially if our generals will consent to fight under the "black flag"—no quarter given or taken. *November 9 Saturday*

. . . At midday the brigade was ordered out and James [Barnwell] determined to take his family directly to the farm, with all their furniture & household goods, before a panic should *November 10 Sunday*

seize the people here & he be prevented from carrying anything. As it is, numbers of persons are moving into the interior or making preparations to move by packing up & sending off their silver & other valuables. James could not get his
furniture packed, as almost all the workmen are on duty, so
he has got a box car into which he will himself see that all is
carefully packed & not opened until it stops within a mile of
the farm. . . . We expected Edward down today with the Cadets from the Arsenal, but instead received a letter saying the
Dr. had selected him, because he *looked delicate*, to remain as
one of the guards. He is dreadfully mortified & indignant &
at first wanted a discharge or to desert and join some other
company, but second thoughts have sobered him a little,
though not deprived the trial of its sting. I wrote him a long
consoling letter this afternoon. . . .

November 11   . . . Today Aunt Mathewes [Holmes], who is 85 years old &
Monday   has not been to town for fourteen years, always declaring that
the move would kill her though she is a remarkably active old
lady & does not use spectacles either to read or sew, came
down with cousins Eliza & Mary [Bacot], all running from the
Yankees & dreadfully scared. . . .

November 14   The weather for the past week has been like the most deli-
Thursday   cious spring days. The sky of the deepest azure with here &
there a fleecy cloud floating lazily along the horizon, & the air
is as balmy as if direct from Paradise. I sit in my chamber
busily sewing on homespun drawers, with both windows
open, & occasionally glancing up the Cut, which is [a] scene of
great interest now—the floating battery lying on one side, a
guard boat with several heavy guns on the other, & steamers,
schooners, sloops & numerous smaller craft continually plying its placid waters. The only fault to be found with the
weather is that it is too warm for the season, at least we find
it so when walking & wearing winter dresses. . . .

November 15   Day of Fasting, Humiliation & Prayer appointed by the President. Mr. [William] Dehon gave us a very solemn sermon on
the sins for which God is now punishing us: pride & boasting,
profanity & Sabbath breaking. . . .

This afternoon Lizzie Burnet, Sue, Lila, Alester & myself *November 16*
went up to the race course. Putting the Burnett horses to our
carriage as theirs is broken, we arrived before the rifle regiment paraded & paid a visit to Willie's tent. It was my first
view of an encampment, and camp life & everything was interesting to me. During the parade Walter C[oachman] &
Sam R[ichardson] joined us, & we all returned to the tent
where we sat till long after the moon had risen &, as we passed
through the long crowded rows of tents, we caught many a
glimpse of the scenes within; while without, groups stood
around the camp fires where we saw numbers of servants &
coffee pots. . . .

Rev. Richard Trapier preached for us both morning and *November 17*
afternoon, Mr. Howe & Cousin Christopher [Gadsden] both *Sunday*
being away, the latter having gone to preach to his company, the Palmetto Guard, Mr. [P.] Fayssaux Stevens supplied
his place & Mr. [William] Dehon some other pulpit. Mr.
T[rapier]'s sermons were both vigorous and excellent, especially the first, which was explanatory of the denunciatory
passages contained in the Psalms. He spoke of the recent invasion of our coast and of our wishes for the destruction of
our enemies in strong terms. His feelings of antagonism to
the north are very strong and especially since he and all his
parishoners have been compelled to fly from their homes on
John's Island. . . .

A thunder bolt has fallen upon us in the news of the seizure *November 20*
of Messrs. [James M.] Mason, & [John] Slidell, [E. J.] Mac-
Farland & [George] Eustis. The English mail steamer [*Trent*],
on which they had sailed from Havana & in which they considered themselves as secure as if on English ground . . . [was]
boarded by an officer & 35 men from the U.S. War Vessel
San Jacinto. [This vessel is] commanded by Capt. [Charles]
Wilkes who by the way is a brother-in-law of our old Mr.
Wilkes. . . . The gentlemen [were] forcibly seized notwithstanding the protest of the British Captain. Mrs. Slidell and
her daughter were allowed to continue the voyage unmolested &, as far as we can learn, so were the despatches. The
prisoners were taken to Fortress Monroe whence a flag of

truce conveyed the news to Gen. [Benjamin] Huger.[19] Then they were taken to the Bastille. The shock has been dreadful and at first I was very much troubled. Opinions varied so much upon the laws in regard to such an outrage to a neutral flag and to the course England would pursue that I felt really low spirited. But hope soon brightened all. For most of the gentlemen think it will do us more good than harm and that Mason and Slidell in prison will plead our case more powerfully than if at Tuilleries & the Court of St. James. [This is] especially [so] since the shipwreck of the French corvette, the *Frony*, off Hatteras when the signals of distress were so inhumanly disregarded by a number of Federal vessels passing by.... Our small navy, by hard work, ... [succeeded] not only [in] rescuing the whole crew but their whole baggage & every courtesy and kindness [was] extended to the sufferers. ... The captain expressed his gratitude, adding that it should be especially made known to the emperor....

November 22 Cousins John [Holmes], Liz [Barnwell] & Mary [Holmes] were here this evening. He gave us some interesting accounts of his camp life, of picket duty, and the various signals used, & sketched the new battle flag just prepared for our Army of the Potomac [Army of Northern Virginia]. One [is] for each regiment, which cannot be readily imitated by the enemy, as they did the Confederate flag at Manassas, at one time causing a Miss. regiment to fire into [Micah] Jenkins' So. Ca. reg. through a fearful mistake. The flags were prepared in Richmond, and Sam Ferguson, Beauregard's especial aid, carried

them to each general and but few had seen them. The field is a delicate pink silk, with a yellow border an inch deep. The cross [is] of blue and the stars [are] white. He says the whole really has a beautiful effect....

19 Confederate commander of the Department of Norfolk.

... Jane and Anna Gadsden came to see me today, then Claude [Turnbull Walker]. The war really has wrought wonders in the latter. Until this year she lived wholly among books, & her ideas always seemed confused when she came in contact with the practical every day world. Now she has devoted herself most enthusiastically to working & knitting for the soldiers & her Italian & French has given way to drawers, shirts, & socks. She is always bright & cheerful notwithstanding the change which has for the present clouded their fortunes. The whole family have always been accustomed to have money as freely as possible, & now, not being able to sell their cotton in Miss., Mr. T[urnbull] cannot send them on any money. Now Mr. [George] Walker gets a dollar from his property in St. Louis. He has always [been] a gentlemen of elegant leisure brought up in the lap of luxury; but Mrs. T.[urnbull] told him a few days ago that, as for eleven years since his marriage, he & his family have always lived freely and without expense with her, she would now have to turn the housekeeping over to him & he would have to maintain them with his salary as Asst. Adj. General of $2000 a year. Rosa says that this summer their breakfast has generally been merely hominy & coffee & sometimes not even the latter. If the Yankees think to conquer such a people they are mistaken. . . .

I was so fatigued from walking yesterday, that I could not attend the lecture delivered by Rev. R. W. Barnwell before the Ladies C.[lothing] A.[ssociation], much to my regret. But all the rest went & gave me a full account of his most eloquent appeal in behalf of the soldiers, to the ladies—not for anymore contributions—for the hospitals were amply provided at present. 150 bales & boxes [have] not yet . . . been opened & a rough calculation of the value of the contributions sent from S.[outh] C.[arolina] amounted to $45,000. But, what was needed was the presence of the ladies themselves, not so much as nurses, as to superintend the different departments, to read to them & in fact to supply all the charms of home to soothe the sick beds of our noble soldiers. He wanted about twelve or fifteen to go on, if only for a month or six weeks, for the ladies there were exhausted & [so were] all the Virginia ladies within twenty miles of the hospital. . . . Any over eighteen could be of service. He said the Va. ladies had done

November 23
Saturday

December 2

& given everything they could & that, when the war was over, they would not have more in their houses, of house linen etc., than they could barely get on with. His tribute to the women of our state & especially to those of our city was as noble as it was just. "WITHOUT YOU, THIS WAR COULD NOT HAVE BEEN CARRIED ON, FOR THE GOVERNMENT WAS NOT PREPARED TO MEET ALL THAT WAS THROWN UPON IT."

December 3 . . . Cousin W.[illie] told us Mr. [John] Gourdin had read him a letter from Henry Young, who, as one of Gen. [Thomas F.] Drayton's aids, had gone [to Port Royal] with the relatives of Dr. E. L. Buist to search for his body under a flag of truce. They had been very courteously received & treated. The officers told them that the body had been buried with military honors & the funeral attended by all their surgeons, a coffin having been improvised from a gun box, but requested them to wait until they could have a better one made in which to remove the body. . . . They remained nearly ten hours altogether. All Dr. B[uist]'s valuables: watch, papers, etc., & even some of his hair had been put into his trunk to be sent to his relatives. A head board had also been placed at his grave, with his name, etc.—nothing offensive by word or look was offered them among the officers except one & he was treated with silent disregard by the others, who spoke loudly in praise of the bravery of our men & said they only wondered they had been able to remain there so long & said our firing was a little wild. But when our gentlemen passed the men's quarters, the scene of debauch there with the negro women was so dreadful and so revolting that the officers were actually ashamed & had to apologize & said that after a victory they were quite unable to control their men.

December 4
Wednesday . . . Today was spent in a visiting tour, starting at half past ten. . . . I went to Miss [Hester T.] Drayton's to get the clothes for the crew of the *Lady Davis*. [I] only saw Hesse [D. Drayton] & received a polite refusal that what little was in the house was promised away, but objecting also because they were in the navy. I was provoked because I thought they had as much claim upon the society as the soldiers, but, as she was so very polite, but decided, I could say nothing. . . . I went to Mrs.

Snowden's, or Miss Amy as we still call her. She received me very pleasantly, and I arrived just in time for dessert, after which I told my errand, received a favorable answer and directions how the application should be made—through the officers. Then she told me how Miss [Hester T.] Drayton had insulted Emma Rhett in the most unjustifiable manner in regard to her uncle, Reverend Mr. [Albert] Walker, in consequence of which all the R[hett]s have withdrawn from the Society. I had heard the fact some time ago, but not the particulars. As I knew Miss D[rayton] of old, I was not surprised at that as much [as] I was at another of her tricks . . . [which] was downright bribery and corruption. Capt. C. Gaillard applied to her for clothes for his company. She wrote back to say that she was then largely employed in working for Kemmer's Company, but to send back in a fortnight & she would see what she could do for him. Next day, he received a note saying she had kept 200 pieces for a company to which her nephew belonged. But, as he had now left it & she had *no further interest* in it, she would give them to him, provided he would *give her nephew an office* in his company, which was declined & the clothes got from the Relief Society & Ladies C[lothing] Ass.[ociation]. These latter always give by a vote of the managers or committee, but Miss D[rayton] never consults anyone but herself & announces the result at the monthly meetings. In consequence, numbers of ladies have left & joined the others as much more satisfactory to work for & unfortunately on Tuesday I sent for a dozen shirts. But, when those are done, I shall also drop off. I have worked steadily since the formation of the society, &, though I may not have accomplished a great number, I know what I did was always *well* done. . . .

Today was cold, but as beautiful, bright and clear a day as could be desired to gladden the heart & so calm that scarcely a ripple disturbed the blue waters of the Ashley. Rosa took Mrs. Leo Walker and myself up to Ashley Hall where we spent a delightful day most of the time out of doors without our shawls, luxuriating in the sunshine & flowers, the pure country air &, above all, the peace which reigned over all things. But the signs of war were on the road, where "infantry intrenchments" had been thrown up in front of a long sweep

December 5
Thursday

of woods, as well as a flat platform for cannon to rake down the road; &, as we neared the bridge, soldiers & baggage wagons, "a solitary horseman" or squad of mounted guards, were met at almost every step.

December 6   Mrs. [Leo] Walker & myself had a long talk yesterday about
Friday   Gen. [Thomas F.] Drayton's conduct at Port Royal; Mr. W[alker] being [R. S.] Ripley's Adjutant, of course, was excellent authority.[20] Ripley said he would himself have commanded but, as Gen. D[rayton] had planned the battles, he did not like to hurt his feelings by doing so. And Drayton assured him so solemnly that he would never leave the fort, unless as a corpse and every man killed, that tears started to Ripley's eyes & he said: I will go immediately for reinforcements, every one of his aids having already been sent off. He had scarcely arrived at Hardeesville, when courier after courier galloped panting in, almost fainting from exhaustion, to say that our men had retreated. At first it was not believed, but when successive ones arrived with the same astounding news, he asked, "of course in order," but was horrified by the answer, "No, in great disorder." Gen. Drayton has fully proved his utter incompetency for his high position, but I sincerely pity him. To have been raised from an honorable position as a citizen respected by all to a distinguished military one from which he has gained nothing but contempt. However, I think the battle of Port Royal has been of great service to us, by arousing everyone from their dangerous security to the utmost vigilance & activity. The Beaufort planters will no doubt suffer greatly, but they deserve it in a great measure, for they would not remove their negroes and valuables in time, as they were long ago warned to do; as to the Yankees, the little cotton & provisions they have obtained won't pay half the expense of the expedition, and I have not the slightest doubt their dreadful treatment of the negroes, at least the men, will assuredly strengthen our "peculiar institution" by

20 Thomas F. Drayton (1808–91), son of William Drayton, the last president of the Bank of the United States, was a graduate of the United States Military Academy and a classmate of Jefferson Davis. During the Civil War, he was commander of the military district around Port Royal, South Carolina. In July, 1862, his brigade moved to Virginia, but it was soon demobilized because of his incapacity as a commander. After the war he was in the railroad and insurance businesses.

teaching them who are their true friends. A gentleman told cousin Alex [DeSaussure] that he had *himself seen* a negro man, who escaped from them to his master, *handcuffed* & perfectly naked. He told him that during the day they were made to pick cotton with soldiers standing over them with bayonets, with which they were pricked if they did not work fast enough to please their "white brothers," & at night they were handcuffed & their clothes were taken from them to prevent their escape. . . .

The past week will never be erased from the memory of Charlestonians. The terror! the misery, & desolation which has swept like a hurricane over our once fair city will never be forgotten as long as it stands. On Monday, Willie came up on business & was to have returned on Wednesday but was twice prevented by accidents. Those three days were as warm and balmy as if it were June, with scarce a breath of air to ripple the calm waters of the Ashley. All was fair and smiling till a quarter before nine at night when the mournful sound of the alarm bell fell on our ears, followed by the cries of fire. At first we thought it was at Rosa's so near was the cry, but soon found it was high up town and raging fiercely. Till then, the wind was still, but, as the fire rose, so did the wind, showering sparks & flakes around or bearing them far aloft in the air where the floated like falling stars. Edward went to see where it was, returned to change his clothes, and at eleven went out again. Even then the sparks were falling so near us that Willie would not let Dudley go, as he might be needed at home. Then Willie himself went to see after the fire, before deciding whether he would go, as he might be needed at home. Then Willie himself went to see after the fire, before deciding whether he would go, all his baggage being on the steamer. Willie Guerard had just come to town & was with Rosa, who came over to us while he went also.

Hour after hour of anxiety passed, while flames raged more fiercely and the heavens illuminated as if it were an Aurora Borealis—it was terrifically beautiful. The tide was rising & every wave crested with foam, while beyond the rosy clouds floating overhead was the intense blue of the sky & Sirius sparkling like a brilliant diamond. As time passed, the sparks were so thick that we had water thrown on the shed &

December 16

servants watching it. About one, W. Guerard returned & reported the Institute Hall & Circular [Congregational] Church as burning & cousin Henry [DeSaussure]'s in danger. A light rain was then falling & we earnestly prayed for more, but it only lasted a short time & Rosa went home. We heard the roaring & crackling of the flames, the crashing of the roofs falling in, & occassionally [*sic*] the report of an explosion as a house was blown up to try and stop the ravages of the fire. But God had decreed that we should be purified through fire as well as blood, & still the flames swept on with inconceivable rapidity & fierceness, not withstanding the almost super-human efforts of the firemen.

At two o'clock, Willie returned and told mother it was time to pack and move. We had already commenced to put up our jewelry, silver & money &, by three [A.M.], we had packed all our clothing and started for uncle James [Holmes], each laden with what they could carry & leaving the servants to see after their own things. The scenes all along the streets were indescribably sad. The pavements [were] loaded with the furniture, clothing, & bedding of refugees who cowered beside them in despair, while others were hurrying with articles for safety to the side from whence we came. When we reached the Battery, the wind was so high we could scarcely breast it. The heavens [were] black as midnight while the waves were white with foam and all [was] illuminated by the intense lurid lights. The boys all returned & soon came cousins Liz. & Mary [Bacot], their aunts having gone with the children up town to Mr. [John] Harleston. Mrs. Paul Gervais with her four children & cousin Mary Bacot had also gone to Uncle James. . . .

Throughout that awful night, we watched the weary hours at the windows and still the flames leaped madly on with demoniac [*sic*] fury, & now the spire of our beautiful Cathedral [St. John and St. Finbar] is wrapped in flames. There it towered above everything the grandest sight I've ever beheld; arch after arch fell in & still the cross glittered & burned high over all. Then the roof caught & we saw that too fall in. At five [A.M.]. the city was wrapped in a living wall of fire from the Cooper to the Ashley without a single gap to break its dread uniformity. It seemed as if the day would never dawn. Oh, it was the longest weariest night I ever spent. No one felt fatigue or thought of sleep, and, when the sun rose, the fire was still raging so fiercely that its glare almost overpowered that of the sun.

The fire, evidently the work of an incendiary, broke out in a shed next to [H. P.] Russell's extensive machine shop & soon spread to Cameron's foundry, where an immense amount of Confederate work was destroyed, in rifled cannon, shot & shell. It swept all the upper part of Hasell & many small streets near, down East Bay where Miss Harriet Pinckney's splendid mansion, once the palace of the Royal Governors & for long successive years the residence of her forefathers, was destroyed. Just one year ago, I went with mother to see her on the 17th, her 85th birthday and my 22nd, but principally to see the interior of the house, which was hung with tapestry, in antique style. Fortunately almost everything was saved through the strenuous exertions of Captain [John] Rutledge and the crew of the *Lady Davis*. All the small streets between that & the Charleston Hotel were destroyed. Fortunately that & Hayne Street were saved, but the fire leapt across to the south side of Market Street which was swept away in a few moments; consisting of small wooden tenements—down Meeting on both sides to Queen—destroying the Theatre, Apprentices Library, Art Gallery, & Savings Institution, Drs. [B. A.] Rodrigues, [Edward] North & [Henry] DeSaussure, Southern Express Office, Circular Church, and, more regretted than all, the Institute Hall, one of the largest in the South [and] the scene for many years of almost every public event. There were held all our fairs, concerts, presentation of flags, The Democratic or National Convention of 1860, and, above all, there was signed our Ordinance of Secession, the instrument which broke the fetters with which the North is seeking to bind us down to everlasting slavery and disgrace. That loss can never be replaced, those hallowed associations will linger around the ruined walls. The Circular [Congregational] Church is where all my ancestors worshipped and are buried for 175 years [sic]. That pulpit has been filled upon the same spot though not in the same church. This was built in 1806, and a few years ago thoroughly done up & refurnished, making it the largest and one of the handsomest churches in the city. Uncle James saved the Bible & Hymn Book. The fine collection of our art gallery was entirely destroyed, but the Savings institution fortunately saved most of its papers.

Cousin Henry Des.[aussure] by the exertions of his friends, saved almost everything except his heavy furniture, but Dr. [Edward] North lost immensely. The square on which the Mills House is built was saved, but the whole other side of Queen was burnt down to the Roper Hospital, fourteen houses being blown up to save the latter & the Medical College, Marine Hospital, Jail, Workhouse, & other public houses which otherwise must inevitably have been destroyed. For the wind circled in eddies, driving the flames in every direction & carrying showers of flakes to an immense distance. Horlbeck's Alley is burnt and the greater part of Kings' St. on both sides below Enslow's as far as the Quaker Church on the east side, & nearly to the corner of Broad on the west side. In Broad, where were some of the finest private residences in the city, were burnt on one side. The Cathedral, which was filled to overflowing with the silver, clothing, furniture and valuables of scores of people, believing it to be fireproof, [was lost]. Bishop [Patrick N.] Lynch's splendid library was also lost there. The residence of the Sisters of Charity was partially burnt. Mr. Coffin's, Mr. Isaac Porcher's, Mr. James Heyward's, Mr. Alfred Huger's, the latter [house] quite an antique & for very many years occupied by the same family, Miss Bowman's, Mr. John Laurens', Mr. G. Manigault's. Mrs. Ben Rutledge's & another fine brick house, Dr. Wraggs', & just back of his, Rev. Mr. Campbell's. On the south side of Broad, Miss Marshall's, an old crazy wreck a century old [and] a nuisance to the city, was destroyed. The fine residences of Mr. Belin & Mr. Smith were spared but all below burnt, including Mr. Petigru's & Mr. James Legare's. The whole of Friend St., from Queen, was burnt, including the very large new Public School, nearly to Tradd. The whole of Lagin St., including St. Peter's Church, was burnt, except Mr. Tom Frost's & Judge [Edward] Frost's —down Tradd it swept destroying everything on the north side—on the south, sparing Mr. Winthrop's old wooden timber house & destroying the old Rutledge house from which poor old Miss Pinckney had to be moved a second time. Skipped Mr. Sol. Legare's next door, but swept everything below it but the lower part of·Limehouse St. on both sides below the fine brick houses of Messrs. Shingle's and Addison on either side. Col. Edward White's fine new house was destroyed. The whole of Council St. is gone. Mr. Lucces' & Mr.

Bull's [were lost], but Mrs. Alston's spared. The whole of New St. commencing with Mr. Cordes Harleston on one side, Mr. Gibbon, Mr. James Wilson, Miss Torre, Dr. Sam Wilson's occupied by Mr. Stevenson, Mr. [Aaron S.] Willington, Mr. A. H. Brown, Mr. Otis Philips, Mr. Geo. Reid, Mr. Paul & his daughter & Mr. James Elliott, on the other side from Mr. O. Middleton's, Mr. Kerrison's, Mr. Gibbons, Misses Muir, Mr. Richard Bacot, Mr. Gibbons' daughter & Mr. [Alexander] Flinn, all are gone. But Mr. Charles Edwards' [is] left standing at the corner, while everything on every side was burnt. The whole of Savage Street is gone and all above & below the Huguenins' on Broad St.

Our brothers & cousins, after working at Dr. [Henry] Des'[aussure] & other friends, went to our houses and, with our servants who worked most zealously, tried to save what they could. But the flames were so fierce and rapid that they were soon cut off from communication with the rest of the city &, as the water was on the other side from our house, they were only able to save *all* our clothing which was packed & all our beddings. . . . They opened mother's work press & linen press and swept everything into blankets, which were safely brought round—our sewing machine & the antique mahogany round table, about a century old, our clock, & a nest of card tables, most of the books from our chamber & all the china ornaments, most of the books from the bookcase & many from the étagèrs. The knives & forks & some of the dinner set that was in use, everybody's desk except Willie's, which he valued very much as it was father's, & many other minor things, each with its own peculiar value, but no other furniture. Some pieces were taken out but burnt in the street. Our carriage was also saved & the mirror from the drawing room. As the Burnets had already sent away most of their things to Camden, they saved a great deal. Cousin Willie saved almost all their clothing and the furniture from his chamber & the drawing room, carpets also. [He also saved] their machine, silver and a good deal of fine old china & cut glass of great value—not only for their beauty but because the china had been brought on by Mr. Charles Deas & the glass belonged to their great grandfather, old Mr. Humphrey Lomers—a few mattresses & some bed linen. At Rosa's almost everything was saved, as her house did not burn till much later than ours, & numbers of gentlemen went to help, after their own or relatives' houses were gone. All their clothing, even to ball dresses, elegant drawing furniture, curtains, three immense mirrors, piano, sideboard & even Rosa's sweetmeats were saved. Most of the silver had been sent off to Columbia by Express that very day. From St. Andrew's Hall, many of the portraits were saved, and the walls now stand in their strength, swept bare within. The Cathedral & Circular Church are beautiful, though melancholy, ruins. But the shock has been so great in extent, so sudden & so awful, that private feeling seemed merged into public feeling, and each one seems to forget their own losses to regret that of their friends.

On Friday, I walked out to inquire after cousin Mary Des.[aussure], found her bright & cheerful & thinking of our loss, while we had feared so much for her in her situation, everyday looking for an addition to her family circle, as is Mrs. James Elliott. . . . Mrs. Dan Vincent's infant was but three days old & her husband away, [so] she was carried off to Mr. Hugh Vincent's when the house was burning, but has not felt any ill effects. Afterward I met Mr. Louis Robertson & we walked down what was once Broad & New Sts., but, oh, so changed that I could not realize where I was. All seemed a frightful dream, though I stood among a forest of chimneys. I went home to dine with him &, though his family had been obliged to move, they were at home again and everything was so handsome and so comfortable that it was impossible [to] feel that their house looked upon the ruins of ours, a few hundred yards off. Mr. R[obertson]'s niece, Pamila Joyner, is staying with them & after dinner we went out walking amidst the scene of desolation and smouldering ruins. For the week before the fire I had been so unwell and so prostrated as well as in so much pain, from having taken too much exercise previously, that I was scarcely able to walk across the floor, and the doctor had made me begin to take a tonic again. But that memorable night, I was on my feet almost from nine o'clock until Thursday night. For, during the days, throngs of friends came with offers of houses or rooms in their houses, clothing or anything else they could offer, with their heartfelt sympathy and condolence. Girls who are merely friends as well as relatives came & ever since we have had numbers of kind offers from all the Gadsdens, DeSaussures, Gibbes, Mrs. Leo Walker, Miss Bates, Mr. Frederick Porcher [and] Jimmie Davis who offered his whole house. The Gatewoods offered clothing, & Mrs. Kirkpatrick offered two chambers & some dresses. Our troubles have indeed shown who were friends, and "The milk of human kindness" seems to overflow for the suffering Charlestonians from every part of the Confederacy, as well as our own state.

By Friday $30,000 were subscribed in the city for the sufferers, & numbers of societies & committees formed to feed, shelter, & clothe the poor & destitute, as well as hundreds of the better class who had lost everything. President Davis proposed, & Congress voted, $250,000 to South Carolina in part payment of the national debt to her. Savannah has voted $10,000—Augusta sent nearly $7,000 already, & intends to make $15,000—Georgia voted $100,000—Columbia $30,000 & numbers of the most munificient [*sic*] donations from $1,000 down, from private individuals all over the state. How sweet in adversity to feel that the bond of sisterhood is drawn even closer between states of our glorious Confederacy by our sorrow. I look beyond to brighter times & firmly believe that God has permitted this to unite us still more closely than before & to prepare and purify us through suffering for the great position he means us to occupy.

On Sunday Mr. Howe gave us a most beautiful & appropriate sermon. The text [was] the most appropriate that could have been chosen: Job's reply to his wife, "We have received good from the Lord & shall we not receive evil also." Many of the congregation had lost their homes & almost everything. . . . It was only by great exertion that the church itself was saved. There were but few dry eyes when he finished & the hymn "How firm a foundation, ye saints of the Lord!" seemed to soothe and strengthen all in their trials. . . .

December 17

My birthday was spent very quietly writing & seeing friends & after tea . . . [several of us] walked among the ruins principally to see the Circular [Congregational] Church & the Cathedral [of St. John and St. Finbar]. The walls of the former are perfect & part of the steeple [is] still standing, and, with the moonlight streaming through the windows & the monuments gleaming beyond, the effect was beautiful & reminded us of the Coliseum. While the front view, with the row of Ionic columns standing as if to guard the sanctuary, brought the ruins of the old Grecian temples vividly before us, as did the broken arches of the Institute Hall. The Cathedral is also very beautiful, the walls all standing and the spires all along the side reminded me of the statues on the Vatican while the general offices was that of some old Gothic minister [*sic*]—indeed everything is so transformed by the work of a single night that it seems as if we were carried centuries back and stood among the ruins of some ancient city. How desolate seemed the few solitary houses still standing. . . . Nothing but ruins on every side; it is more dreary than living by a cemetery. We walked where once our beloved home had stood, and, as we listened to the passing sound of the oarsmen & their songs & the chimes of old St. Michael's bells, they seemed to ring clearer through the silence which reigned above. The moonlight was brilliant, but the atmosphere very hazy. Thus our view was not as beautiful as expected. . . .

Isaac White has been in town and is about to return to make some arrangements about his family and ours moving together—he has just been made one of [R. S.] Ripley's aids. Half a dozen plans have already been proposed & rejected, first Orangeburg, then the two families to go to Mrs. David Gaillard's plantation, 12 miles from Winnsboro, then Pineville & lastly for us to spend the winter at cousin Alek's [De-Saussure] house in Charlotte St. which being so near the Whites and Gadsdens would be very pleasant. . . .

December 19   I have spent the last two days writing letters to friends anxiously inquiring of our welfare. . . . Mrs. Kirkpatrick, whom Sue & sister F[rances] have visited for two or three years, has been very kind indeed. She at first sent to offer two chambers & some dresses, but, as we did not need those, yesterday she sent Sue a very kind note asking her to accept "a pair of vases & a few odds & ends" which proved to be two or three of each article of house linen, two cups & saucers, a decanter & pair of preserve dishes. The delicacy of the gift was as great as the sympathy it expressed. The news from England is glorious—

the excitement in Liverpool was intense on learning [of] the
seizure of Messrs. Mason & Slidell, and a public meeting [was]
held denouncing the [*Trent*] outrage. The Queen has sent a
special messenger to Lord Lyons demanding the immediate
release of those gentlemen & their secretaries and a safe passage to England for them, as well as the most ample apologies
for the insult.[21] The Yankees cannot get off from the dilemma. As they were so sure that England would take no notice
of it. . . . They gave public addresses & dinners to both Capt.
[Charles] Wilkes & Lieut. [Donald M.] Fairfax, thus sanction-
ing the act after, if not before, which we feared would be their
excuse. Their wonderfully courageous & patriotic officers
have not only openly boasted of their act, but have published
all their orders etc. in the papers. The Queen also ordered
Lord Lyons, in case his demand was refused, to demand his
passports immediately. All the northern papers are exceedingly indignant and declare the "British Bluster" must be put
down & that our ministers shall not be given up. Hon. C. J.
Faulkner, ex-ambassador from the U.S. to Spain or France
who was seized as a Secessionist as soon as he landed, & carried to the Bastille, has just returned to Va. released in exchange for [Congressman Alfred] Ely. He says the Yankees
are for "war to the knife," & I have no doubt they will have it
to their hearts content, for England has already sent a large
number of troops to Canada as well as a quantity of Arm-
strong guns and Enfield rifles. . . . The London *Times* predicts
that the next movement will be the Southern ports opened &
the northern ports blockaded and the Confederacy recognized by England and France. With our ports opened, we will
soon have a navy & will soon sweep the Yankees from our
shores. If we had had a navy, they never would have polluted
our soil.

The first anniversary of our Secession and Independence.   *December 20*
Though the season is one of public, as well as private, distress and this glorious day cannot be celebrated as we would
wish, still it will be gratefully remembered and rejoiced in.
   All the northern banks have suspended specie payment &

21 Lord Lyons was the British minister to the United States.

Mr. [Charles Francis] Adams, U.S. Minister to England, has demanded his passport after the Queen's proclamation—better and better.

December 21   I was on the bed all day yesterday, feeling very badly, & had quite given up all notion of being able to go to the oration at the Citadel when Mrs. John Ashe Alston stopped to see me for a few minutes and offered to send me her carriage, which of course I accepted. . . . Cadet [William B.] McKee read a long paper giving the causes for Secession extending almost as far back as revolutionary times & ending with the Ordinance of Secession of South Carolina. He was not a good reader, and we were disappointed, but our expectations were more than fulfilled by the fine oration of Cadet [Dan] Campbell. It was exceedingly interesting and well written, giving a retrospect of the past year from the time when the Palmetto State stood alone in its glory, defiant of the world, till now, when, at the close of this most eventful period, it forms with its Sister States a circle of thirteen brilliant stars. [Thirteen was] the original number which formed the Union & now the Confederacy with a Permanent Government, a president & a vice-president beloved by all or at least by almost all (for the minority have made themselves contemptible from their spitefulness)—an immense army & its resources greater than at the commencement of the struggle, its internal resources & advantages improved & its people more united than ever, we have indeed cause to be grateful and to look forward with bright hope to our future career. Mr. Campbell's delivery and manner was so graceful that it added a great charm and everybody was delighted. We wanted to send and congratulate his father, whom we saw. The room was very prettily decked with evergreen & flags and was crowded. A band of music added to our pleasure and, as we kept time by our steps to a gay polka as we passed through the wide corridor, everyone seemed as happy as if peace was at our doors instead of grim war. At least all went home cheered, particularly as the Yankees have, to use an expressive old saying, "bitten their nose to spite their face," by sinking seven large vessels in our channel. Thus . . . [they have prevented] their own ingress by what the old sea captains think will be very beneficial

to our harbor. I returned to cousin Martha's [DeSaussure] to
share Sue's room.

December 22

For the first time I have seen all cousin M's [Martha DeSaus-
sure] family and they are eight of the most interesting children I have ever seen. . . . Both cousin Wilmot & cousin
M[artha] are so talented; she especially is at once one of the
most intellectual, sprightliest, & practical women I have ever
met. . . .

December 29

. . . The past week has been spent very quietly, but pleasantly,
the three first days were passed in the enjoyment of cousin
Wilmot's [DeSaussure] library, looking over the books & selecting those I wished to read in the afternoons. Susie [De-
Saussure] & I went on the Battery, & the evenings were
shared between cousin Sallie's [DeSaussure], Uncle James &
Uncles [Henry Alexander DeSaussure]. Christmas day the
weather was very beautiful, as it has been for some time, clear
& brilliant & the sunshine so warm & pleasant that it wooed us
to walk. . . . Sue & myself went to see Mrs. Edward White,
who is staying with Mrs. [Abbott H.] Brisbane. She bears her
great loss very well for her loss was greater than ours. Her
house was only built about three years ago, was very handsome, as well as built expressly for her comfort & convenience. She lost all her handsome furniture except two or
three marble tables etc., piano, sewing machine, 12 carpets &
as many mattresses, and about $4,000 worth of books, besides
hundreds of other valuable things. . . . Friday morning I got
up tolerably early to take a survey of our home for the winter
& was most agreeably surprised. There are three rooms on
each floor & large entries running through the house. Our
chamber, in which Sue, Lila, Carrie & myself sleep, is large &
looks on the street, from which, however, it is separated by a
front yard & some large trees. Our room opens into mother's
which is bright and sunny, with a piazza attached. The boys'
room, opposite ours, also has a piazza & below is a drawing
room, closed however. We use the parlor & dining room,
which connects by folding doors. Closets & other conveniences are lavished on every side though we have not many
in use. But the house is cold as it was built for a summer

house. The yard & garden back are large & quite cheerful looking. . . .

"Busy all day getting to rights." Unpacking some trunks, to repack others & arranging & putting away all the books, for another box of them was found at Mr. Edmondson's high up town. . . .

December 31   Rosa brought us the joyful news this morning that our darling Rutledge had come on a thirty days' furlough, & this afternoon Lila & I went to see him. I could scarcely realize our happiness in having him once more with us. He has grown much stouter & is remarkably handsome. He says Charlie Furman has grown almost as stout as himself &, when he left, he was a pale delicate youth, apparently not more than seventeen. I am delighted for I hoped the change would benefit him. We don't have time to feel lonely up here for our friends & neighbors are calling all day and after tea too. Rutledge is our best New Year's gift & his arrival has made everything look bright.

January
1

May
7, 1862

Life in Wartime Charleston

The New Year opened very brightly and as warm and pleasant as a spring day. The Pinckney lecture on the goodness of God was delivered at St. Philips by Mr. Howe and all the other Episcopal congregations invited to attend. The Whites & Gaillards went with us and after service we went to the Guard House to see the Fire and Alarm Telegraph. Mr. Westervelt has in charge the telegraph to Coles' Island in the same room &, while we were there, [he] sent several messages to his brother, who is the other operator. None of us had ever seen the machinery or its operation before, and it really seemed like magic. . . .

Our reading club met for the first time at Hattie's [White] today & commenced [Henry] Reed's lectures on English History, as illustrated by Shakespeare's Plays. This is the third time I've read it but it is always interesting. . . . To-night Harriet & cousin Mary [Holmes] came over, and then cousin W[illie] & Rutledge. The boys stayed till nearly eleven, and it seemed almost like our old home to have them once more with us. Cousin W[illie] was very merry but R[utledge] subdued; he spoke very highly of Charlie F[urman] and said he thought Fan [Garden] had done well—camp life is a fiery trial for any man and, if he has a single mean trait, he cannot help showing it. Rutledge said the Palmetto Guard had refused to volunteer for the war & he intends to raise a company himself.

January 4 . . . The news of the surrender of Mason & Slidell is confirmed. Surrendered after all the Yankee bluster by Seward. Through necessity, as he knows; The U.S. could not support a double war. We expected just what had occurred, but it has done us a great deal—England's demands are said to have extended further, in regard to the Stone Blockade.[1]. . .

January 9 . . . Our club read this morning in Mrs. [Anna Gaillard] White's room. . . . I had quite a curious adventure on my way home. When I left, I found it quite late, but the brilliant moonlight had deceived me into thinking it much earlier. I walked quietly along, &, as I crossed from the Citadel to Flinn's [Second Presbyterian] Church Square, I observed a gentleman behind me. Just after I reached the pavement I heard him say "Good evening Ma'am." I turned and said "Good evening sir," first thinking it was Isaac W[hite], he having a large white dragoons' overcoat like Mr. W[hite]'s. As he did not speak again, I concluded it was either some acquaintance whom I did not recognize, or he had mistaken me for someone else, & I said "You must excuse me sir, but I really do not recognize you," giving him thereby a hint to announce himself. He looked like a gentleman, & his dark blue uniform was that of an officer, though his great coat concealed his stripes & shoulder straps. He answered in the most respectful manner, "I hope I don't offend." I immediately guessed he was an up country man, for I had heard of their joining the ladies frequently on Sullivan's Island saying they had left all their friends at home & *did want so much* to get acquainted with the Charleston Ladies. I answered, "Oh, no, but I thought I recognized your voice, as an acquaintance," then I added to draw him out, "I am not at all surprised you think it late for ladies to be out, it is much later than I intended." He replied that he did not think it very late. I said it was later, however, than the ladies here were accustomed to walk. As he

1 The Union navy unsuccessfully tried to blockade several southern ports by sinking old vessels loaded with stone in main navigational channels.

still remained quiet, (I forgot to say that just before, he asked
if I was going home, I said, yes, & he asked if I would permit
him to escort me. His manner throughout being most respectful, I told him yes.) I asked him if he was one of our brave
defenders come to fight the Yankees. He replied in the affirmative, & I said I hoped he would soon have an opportunity of meeting them. "Yes Ma'am," then a pause and I recommenced: "Are you from the up country?" "Yes Ma'am." I
wanted him to announce himself so I went on: "I have a great
many friends there." "What part Ma'am?" "Spartanburg &
Glenn Springs & about there." "Yes Ma'am." I ventured
again: "My mother was from the up country & I always feel
great interest in it." "What may be your name Ma'am?" "Miss
Holmes," "Do you live in this street?" "Yes, only a few doors
further." Another pause & I started on the beautiful weather
& moonlight & he answered that it was very pleasant especially for walking at night. So I asked if he had been on the Battery. He said no. I answered: you don't know where our
Battery is, why it is our pride & where the ladies walk a great
deal in summer, especially on moonlight nights. By this time,
we had crossed over to our side of the street, & he asked if I
would not extend my walk a little tonight. Love of fun and adventure would fain have lead [*sic*] me to say, yes, but propriety
said, no, & I answered just as I would have done to an acquaintance: "Not this evening, I have been out all the afternoon, & I think I ought to go in now." Another pause, and I
added, "but in turn you ought to let me know the name of my
escort." "Mr. Jones, Ma'am." He stopped, evidently thinking I
had arrived home though I was three or four doors from it,
said good evening in the politest manner, which I returned as
politely, & each went their way. I have amused the family very
much by my account, &, of course, we are all curious to find
out who he is. . . .

I find a long hiatus, which I must endeavor to fill from recol-   *January 20*
lection, but so little of importance has happened that it is
scarcely worth recording. . . .

The weather changed and it became gloomy, rainy, raw &   *January 21*
generally disagreeable, continuing so the rest of the week.   *Tuesday*
However, the club met that day, though Thursday was too

rainy. Friday evening the Quarterly Orations of the Cadet Societies were to have taken place & a large party [to have] gone with me. But just as we were dressing, Edward sent to tell us it was put off on account of the weather . . . so we got up a dancer & quadrille & found we had almost forgotten all the figures it was so long since we had danced. Willie was offered the Adjutancy of his regiment, but declined as he had helped to get up his company. They expect soon to be relieved & reorganized. He told us an amusing incident of their camp life. A few days ago, the Commissary informed the Colonel that no more coffee would be served at rations, the small quantity on hand being kept for the hospitals. The Colonel informed the men at dress parade & that night after supper they had a grand torchlight procession. The men [were] all . . . disguised with blankets & great coats & carrying a transparency, bearing on one side a dilapidated coffee pot on two broken down legs with an arrow through it and, above, the motto, "No more *grounds* for complaint." On the other [side was] a broken coffee mill & above "The last grind." Behind was borne a worn out coffee pot which was buried with appropriate ceremonies and a German funeral sermon and song. . . .

January 27   Another week since I have opened my journal. . . . Saturday morning [January 25, 1862] the sun rose brilliantly on a cloudless sky, and the sunshine was so warm & delightful that it moved us to forsake the cold dull house to enjoy its beauty. We spent part of the morning reading aloud the poems of W. Maxwell Martin of Columbia, who died a year ago.[2] Some of them are exquisite gems & breathe the very spirits of a true poet, especially his "Sunsets' prayer." Then being personally acquainted with him & many of the persons

2 William Maxwell Martin (1837–61) briefly attended South Carolina College but graduated from Wofford College in 1857. He was elected principal of the Palmetto School in Columbia but remained there only one year. He then taught in several other places and was preparing to enter law school when secession came. He joined the Columbia artillery and went with them to Fort Moultrie in Charleston harbor. He caught a chill there and died from typhoid fever on February 21, 1861. Martin wrote poetry and prose, and upon his death friends published some of them: William M. Martin, *Lyrics and Sketches* (Nashville, Tenn.: Methodist Publishing House, 1861).

& things to which he referred, we enjoyed them the more. [We] also [read] two exquisite little poems written by Professor [James L.] Reynolds, upon his death. Mr. Martin was a most genial companion, as well as true poet. Humor flowed with every word but, unfortunately like too many geniuses, he yielded to the temptor, drink, & was quite dissipated. This pretty little volume, which by-the-by was entirely of Southern manufacture being printed and very neatly bound in Nashville, Tenn., contains, besides his poems & prose, sketches, almost all of which had just appeared in the newspapers, a few poems, remarks and notices of him by different friends, & extracts from many of his very interesting letters down to the time he was taken sick on Sullivan's Island. At the call for volunteers for the defence of our city a year ago, he had joined an artillery corps, was soon promoted for soldierly conduct, & shared in the attack on the *Star of the West.* When the *Brooklyn* was expected in, his corps was very much exposed one dreadful night, & he took cold, was in the Hospital for a time, went home & the disease turned typhoid, & he died in February, in his twenty fourth year.

On Sunday [January 26, 1862], there was no service at St. Philip's as, during the stormy weather a few days before, a piece of the steeple had been blown down, injuring a passer-by, and it was thought best not to have service till it was repaired.

Beauregard has been sent to Kentucky to replace [Felix K.] Zollicoffer & Gen. Gustavus Smith is to take his place. There seemed to be no prospect of a battle on the Potomac & the name of Beauregard is a tower of strength. . . .

January 31
Friday

Rosa & Carrie returned to the country while Hattie [White], Edward, James [Holmes] & myself went down to Chisolm's Mill at three o'clock to join a sailing party on the *Howell Cobb,* [with] Capt. Frank Bonneau. . . . We took a hasty dinner & hurried down as fast as the buggy could go, fearing we should be too late & [then] had to wait more than a half hour. . . . When we did start, the tide was very low, no wind & the weather very cloudy. In fact, it was sprinkling rain occasionally. We were to have gone to Fort Sumter but never got fur-

February 1
Saturday

ther than the guard boat off James Island. The wind sprang up & blew keenly. We all found it cold, damp, & rather disagreeable, but on our return [we were] stuck in the mud for about an hour &, as it began to rain quite hard, the whole party of ten ladies . . . and fourteen cadets had to crowd in the captain's little cabin, which of course was so close that it was very unpleasant. . . . I was in a very quiet dull humor, &, as very few of the cadets knew the girls who were all of an older set, the feeling seemed contagious, though some seemed to enjoy themselves very much when we were in the cabin. Hattie was pleasantly situated among agreeable & intelligent companions, while I was confined to a corner from which there was no escape, & uninteresting people. Mrs. [William] Ford afforded us some amusement by her silly affectation of girlishness, sentimentality and flirting, for which she was well laughed at.

February 2
Sunday

. . . Old Mr. [Aaron S.] Willington, the senior editor of the [Charleston *Daily*] *Courier* & probably the eldest editor with one exception in both the U.S. and Confederacy, died this morning of apoplexy. He was 81 & by birth a Massachusetts man but a devoted southerner in feeling.

February 3

Edward received an appointment today as drill master to Col. [James M.] Gadberry's [Eighteenth S.C.] regiment, his pay being either $63—or $50 & rations. The regiment is stationed over in St. Andrews and he leaves for it tomorrow. . . .

February 4
Tuesday

[This] afternoon our club met at Mrs. [Anna Gaillard] White's & the girls & myself finished Macauley's *Essay on Warren Hastings.* Though I have read it many times before, his life & the remarkable scenes & events of Indian life, are so romantic & intensely interesting and so graphically portrayed, that each time it is perused with new enjoyment. Truth is, indeed, stranger than fiction.

February 7
Friday

Willie & myself attended the dress parade at the Citadel this evening. The band of music had attracted a crowd & we met many friends. . . . Harry Burnet came in after tea this evening as great a croaker as ever & more pompous & conceited than ever. I used to like him and to take up stoutly for him, but he is too much changed. We spent the evening playing whist which I have not done so long that I felt as if I was almost doing wrong instead of knitting. Fort Henry on the Tennessee river has been captured by the Yankees after two hours fighting. . . .

The telegraphic news this morning is most distressing. On Friday, part of the [Ambrose] Burnside fleet attacked Roanoke Island and were repulsed. . . . The fight was renewed the next morning. . . . Elizabeth City [N.C.] is said to have been shelled & burned, and the enemy pushed on to Edenton [N.C.]. On the Tennessee river, they have occupied Florence [Alabama], thus cutting off our communication with Memphis both by railroad & telegraph, & they have gone further down the river. Both blows are severe & have depressed me more than anything else has done. The clouds are indeed dark and threatening, but I am still hopeful and trust they are but the precursors of a brilliant dawn. . . .

February 11
Tuesday

Carrie, Harriet and Maggie H.[olmes] and myself attended the dress parade at the Citadel this afternoon. The band was there & attracted a crowd. Our party, with several additions & some of the cadets, went to the society halls and, in coming down the long corridor, I started to polka with Harry Des[aussure], but my stiff boot must have strained the lame foot which I thought quite well, & I found on coming home that it was swollen and hurt me when I walked. Visions of dissecting instruments and doctors floated through my mind, but I hope a few days rest will cure it.

February 14
Friday

. . . The war seems rather incentive to love than a check. Harriet Ingraham is to be married on Thursday to Lieut. Hall, of the Navy, at St. Philip's church, & is to have twelve bridesmaids who are to wear white dresses and blue scarfs, the ends being of Confederate colors; and the groomsmen, all naval officers, to wear Confederate uniform[s]. . . .

February 17
Monday

Tuesday morning it was reported through the papers that Fort Donelson had fallen & with it 13,000 men captured in-

February 20
Thursday

cluding Gens. Johnson [Albert Sidney Johnston], [Gideon J.] Pillow, [John B.] Floyd and [Simon B.] Buckner & that Nashville had also surrendered to the enemy.[3] The gloom, dismay, & consternation spread by such dreadful tidings were overwhelming. Doubts were circulated of its authenticity, for the magnitude of the reverse was too great & awful to be believed. Beauregard, too, has been reported ill at Nashville & the idea that he should be captured, and that Johnston, in whom such unbounded confidence had been placed, had surrendered without striking a blow, as well as such an army, was enough to make the stoutest heart sink. But yesterday glad tidings were received that *Nashville had not surrendered* but that Johnston was determined to make a desperate resistance, in which he was seconded by all the citizens. Fort Donelson has fallen, after a hard fought battle; it was surrounded by the enemy. Our loss is not ascertained, nor is it believed that any of our men are captured except a few stragglers, perhaps those who have been cut off. . . . All our generals are safe, but it is said that 10,000 of our men are surrounded by the enemy, but bravely cutting their way through. There is still great uncertainty about the reports. It is now believed that the first news was expressly & malignantly manufactured for some purpose, either by a man in the telegraphic office, who has been arrested, or by speculators in Tennessee.

The surrender of Roanoke Island [N.C.] seems a most unaccountable thing. The first news being [*sic*] of such slaughter on both sides until our troops were surrounded by such a superior force, & now it seems we only lost 10 killed in all . . . and 30 wounded.[4]. . . The account of Gen. [Henry A.] Wise [Confederate commanding general], on seeing his son's body, is most affecting. The old man bent down & kissed the lifeless face, still retaining the dauntless countenance with which he met his glorious death, and exclaimed, "My son, my son, you died for me." The body lay in state for two days and was visited by hundreds with tearful eyes. He was a noble young man and very much beloved.

3 Only Buckner was captured; Pillow and Floyd both gave up their commands and escaped with some of their troops before the Federal victory was complete. Official Confederate records list 14,623 missing.
4 Actually 149 were killed, wounded, or missing, and 2,500 were taken prisoner.

Today was observed as a day of Humiliation and prayer throughout the city by the mayor's order on account of the gloomy state of affairs and next Friday, the same has been commanded throughout the Confederacy by President Davis. I went to St. Philip's and was disappointed in not hearing Mr. Howe, but heard an excellent sermon from Mr. [Lucien C.] Lance. . . .

February 20
Friday
[should
be 21]

The inauguration of President Davis will take place, the birthday of Gen. Washington having been selected from which to date the event of the inauguration of the first president of the Southern Confederacy. But already a storm of invective has burst over him, & the faith of many in him entirely gone. His defensive policy, suppression of Beauregard's real report of the battle of Manassas, and the displacing or rather promoting [of] two of his relatives over Gens. William H. T. Walker and [M. L.] Bonham in consequences of which they resigned, have gone very much against him. But I will not yield my faith in him until I see further proofs brought against him.

February 22
Saturday

  We went to Harriet Ingraham's wedding tonight but were disappointed in the pretty sight we expected, for the bridesmaids only wore shoulder knots of red, white & blue, instead of scarfs & as several of the groomsmen were unable to come, several of her cousins waited in citizen's dress, though neither of her sisters had groomsmen but walked together. Lieut. Hall is quite small & youthful looking. After the ceremony, Eliza stepped up, threw back her veil & kissed her, then her mother did the same.

I went to St. Luke's [Episcopal Church], which is really a beautiful little church, though I should not call it little, for it is larger than it appears at the first view. The roof is of light Gothic arches, springing from a cluster of small pillars & intermingling at each point. Where the arches intersect, they are ornamented with bosses of rich Gothic tracery. The church itself is in the form of a Greek cross. The galleries are small & low. The balustrade is of carved open work & lined with crimson. The effect of the whole is beautiful. The windows are only of ground glass colored on the inside, as the stained glass cannot now be procured from Europe. Nor have

February 23
Sunday
morning

they any organ or pulpit, as they are still using the Alexandre organ used in the Tabernacle.[5]. . . Cousin Christopher [Gadsden] likes the reading desk as a pulpit also. It is made of Carolina wood & entirely of native manufacture. . . .

February 24
Monday

As prayer meetings are to be held every day this week at the different churches, our club is to meet in the afternoon instead. . . . We have commenced *Paradise Lost.* . . . After the reading, Janie [White] & I took a walk round the Citadel square & arranged for our taking regular walks together in the morning.

February 25
Tuesday

Janie and I took a delightful walk this morning, starting at seven, visiting the artesian well, which brought back many pleasant memories of Mr. [T. Sumter] Brownfield & Rutledge & other friends. We extended our walk to the Battery but did not go on it, as a great change has taken place in the weather & the wind was blowing keen and cold. Nashville has been surrendered to the enemy who say they will not molest anything. . . .

Mr. [Henry S.] Foote of Tennessee has made a motion in Congress for making the war aggressive and strongly animadverted against [Secretary of the Navy, S. R.] Mallory & [Secretary of War, Judah P.] Benjamin.

A general exchange of prisoners is about to take place. [Michael] Corcoran and all the prisoners from Columbia [are] being sent off, & Johnnie Harleston & his companions, as well as those recently taken to Roanoake, [are] being sent in exchange.

This afternoon after our reading club, we nine girls . . . went to walk, but commenced & ended it by a race, down the broad gravel walk of Flinn's [Second Presbyterian] Church Square, which we all enjoyed very much. It is so quiet & secluded there among the beautiful mock oranges. We felt almost as free as if in the country. Our walk was only around the Citadel Square, but I told the girls I felt quite reconciled to living up town, if we could enjoy such freedom and frolics.

5 Also called the American organ, this instrument is similar to a harmonium; the reeds are made to sound by compressed air drawn in rather than forced out.

Mother has hired Mrs. Toomer's house in Chapel St. just back of Harriet's [Holmes] so we will still be near; it is a fine house, with many modern conveniences, a large garden, & figs & grapes ad libitum. . . .

. . . This afternoon mother told us a great deal of family history, of Uncle [Charles] Rutledge's [Holmes] death, [and about] Uncles Wm. and John [DeSaussure] and Uncle Edward [Holmes]. I feel the sincerest sympathy for Uncle E[dward]. He is comparatively desolate & isolated even in the midst of his brothers and sisters. Such a devoted husband as he was and such a lover of children, he has neither wife nor child—no one belonging as it were solely for him, to cling to in declining age, his intellectual resources much curtailed by his deafness & weakness of his eyes one of which was destroyed in infancy by smallpox, with which he was inoculated. And now he, who once revelled in wealth & whose hand was ever opened to the friendless & needy, is reduced almost to poverty. Twice, great speculations first brought him wealth, then as suddenly was the golden chalice dashed from his lips. Last year he came on to see us, leaving the beautiful little farm, the cultivation of which he so much enjoyed, near San Francisco, and a good deal of other property, his right to which he had but lately succeeded in settling. After several years of law-suits, he has never been able to return, nor to receive letters for a very long time, and it is most probable that all will be confiscated as the property of a rebel. He has only two or three negroes here, upon whose wages he is dependent. In the meantime he devotes himself entirely to reading, until he says, Uncle James scolds him and makes him take exercise, being fearful such close application will injure his eyes as well as his health.

February 26
Wednesday

Our club met at Harriet's [Holmes] and we took our usual walk afterward. . . . I have taken up my Italian again and find it very easy from its similarity to French & Latin. . . .

February 27
Thursday
evening

[Today] was observed as a day of Humiliation & prayer in all the churches. Mr. Howe gave us an admirable political sermon very warlike in its tone. . . . We went to see Sue, Jane &

February 28
Friday

Minnie Robertson. . . . They heard through a number of different gentlemen that all the clothes which the ladies have subscribed for & made, working so hard as we have done, and which were sent to the soldiers as voluntary contributions, have been *sold* to them by their quartermasters. It is a detestable meanness & ought to be investigated. Mrs. [Abbott H.] Brisbane is going to take all her negroes to Georgia. She wrote mother a very affectionate farewell and a most complimentary wish to have me go with her to cheer and amuse her loneliness. She is such a highly intellectual & most uncommonly cultivated lady that I consider it a great compliment. . . .

March 3   . . . I have just finished [Matthew L.] Davis' *Memoirs of Aaron Burr*, in which I was exceedingly interested, particularly by the letters between his daughter, Theodosia Allston, and himself. He certainly seems to have been a devoted father & husband, notwithstanding his flagrant want of principle and immorality. The latter is merely noticed as a dreadful blot on his character, which could not be denied, but which it was best to pass over in silence. Miss Agnes [Bates] had read it and told me of the frequent references to Natalie DeLage, Mrs. Sumter, who was very intimate with his [Burr's] daughter & who went to live with him as his adopted daughter until she returned to France to her mother. The references are exceedingly interesting to me having known her most romantic history & [being] intimate with her descendants. The letters from Gov. [Joseph] Allston to his wife are most affectionate, & Mrs. Sumter always denied (so Miss Maria Furman told me) the reports of his indifference to her and the idea, which has been generally received, that the voyage which proved so fatal to her had been undertaken at his instigation, with a secret understanding with the captain. For his private character & those of his two brothers are held in utter contempt and abhorence by their contemporaries. I have often heard Grandmother say she knew them all, and they were all considered bad enough to be capable of anything. However, Mrs. S[umter] insisted that he did all he could to dissuade her from going, but no obstacle hindered her where her father was concerned.[6] . . .

6   Theodosia Allston (1783–1813) was the daughter of Aaron Burr and the wife of South Carolinian Joseph Allston. Though there were accusa-

. . . Mr. Bull came for Rosa; he came in & began talking to Uncle E[dward]. Now comes the richest scene I've enjoyed for a long time. He said he wanted a good wife, but could not find any of these young ladies foolish enough to take him. "You mean wise," said Uncle E[dward]. "No," said he, "I mean foolish, but I expect I'll soon find one." Just for a little banter, I told him he seemed quite confident. He answered, "Take care Miss Emma, I might come to you." "Well suppose you did?" "What would your answer be?" said he, "No, of course." After that, he seemed to forget everybody & everything but me. He was sitting near me & kept up the conversation, in a low tone on my part. It was merely a laughing repetition of the same answer. Uncle E.[dward] & the others, finding themselves detrop, dropped out. Rosa had gone to the carriage, having repeatedly told him she was ready, & urged him to go. Carrie & Sue were getting ready to go to our club & I wanted to do the same, but I could not get away, for he insisted he was serious in his offer, & implored me to accept him, offering every inducement he could think of to persuade. I told him I was serious too, in my refusal, but he would hear nothing. He knew I could make him so happy, I told him I knew both of us too well & knew we could never make each other happy, for we did not suit each other. I tried to end the scene by telling him all the girls were waiting on me. For, he had been interrupted by two or three messages and rising to go & leave him, as he would not go, I offered to shake hands with him as usual. But that only made the matter worse, for my hand was seized as if by a vice & covered with kisses, while I struggled in vain to get it away and almost ready to scream with laughter. For it was really December and May, & I remembered cousin Martha's [DeSaussure] prophecy about he and I, the truth of which was then being proved. At last I freed my hand & was about to go, while he persisted in asking whether I really refused him, when Sue came in for

tions of a political bargain, Theodosia seemed attached to her husband. She was with her father during his famous trial and later tried to smooth the way for his return from exile. On her way to visit Burr in December, 1812 (without her husband who had been prevented from accompanying her because of business), her ship was lost at sea. Stories later circulated that pirates had captured the ship, and one account even had her walking the plank. Her story was a subject for romantic and exciting conjecture for many years after her demise.

the books & stopped for an instant to speak to him. I thought it a good opportunity to make my escape but he again caught my hand & detained me, insisting if I did not accept him he would commit suicide, etc., for he was desperate. But I told him no, he would not, I knew him of old. But why won't you marry me, he persisted, "Because I don't love you." "But I thought you did once." "Mr. Bull, we were once very good friends"—"well why cannot you marry me?" "Because I say no and no means no." As all the time I was trying to free my hand from the vice in which it was nearly crushed, he released it after covering it with kisses & saying: "Well farewell, and if forever, still forever, fare thee well." I ran out of one door shaking with laughter while he went to the carriage, where poor Rosa had been waiting most impatiently for him, and I have no doubt quite provoked with me, though it was not my fault. But I should certainly have been so in her place. Thus ended my first offer, not a very complimentary one I must confess, for I was not the *"Seventeenth Selection of Same from Grace Church"*; it is almost as bad. Besides he is not only getting bald & gray but has lost two front teeth. Moreover, I could readily perceive that he had been drinking wine & was quite excited. . . .

March 6
Thursday
. . . Mid day Rosa sent the carriage for me to come up and stay with her [at Ashley Hall] while her father has gone to remove Mr. Erestis' negroes from Timothy to some place of safety on the Santee. The country is enchanting. The golden bells of the jessamine drape every tree & shrub while the air is perfumed with the starry white blossoms of the machella berry. The clusters of tiny stars forming [*sic*] fit carpet for a fairy dance, while interspersed are the deep purple and white wild violets.

March 7
Friday
We woke this morning to find the ground covered with a light fall of snow, much to our surprise, & very cold and windy. However, it cleared off about midday brightly and Rosa and myself went to dine with Mrs. [John] Parker. . . . We spent a quiet but very pleasant day. The house is a very nice one and seems fitted with every convenience and comfort. The drawing room especially took my fancy. On either side of the large

fire place was a Gothic alcove fitted up as a bookcase. On a large étagèr in one corner was collected relics of her travels in Europe & Egypt for her husband's health, from the U.S. flag which floated over their boat on the Nile and a mummy's hand, an ostrich egg, etc., to engravings and other objects of virtue. The room is hung with exquisite engravings or photographs of the most celebrated pictures and statues. The lamp, vases & other ornaments of bronze were all of antique style and everything, even the water pitcher, showed a classic taste & love of the beautiful. It is my ideal of a country home. . . .

President Lincoln has just lost one son, Willie, & in imitation of royal custom, the body has been embalmed and the festivities prepared to celebrate February 22nd put off for the capture of Savannah or Charleston. Another son is also desperately ill.

Rosa and myself took a delightful ride today on horse back of several miles, accompanied by a servant, the first time I've ridden since August 1860. After dinner, as we were walking in the garden, the "inevitable Dr. [James] Morrow" rode up, joined us & spent the evening. I had heard so much of him that I was really curious to meet him. I have read of such characters, but never met one in real life. He is a South Carolinian by birth but a traveller all over the world, except Europe. He says he has not a relative living but knows everybody, & everybody has heard of the ubiquitous Dr. Morrow. He is seen everywhere in the most unexpected places. It is said that when Perry's Expedition to Japan was about to start, someone remarked, "Well, at any rate, we are now going to a place where we won't meet Dr. Morrow." But to his astonishment, in a little while that remarkable individual came on board and joined the expedition. Everybody knows Dr. Morrow, yet nobody knows his history or anything about him. He is a very fine looking man, over six feet and proportionably large, with a red face & full long black beard. His manners are very pleasant & sociable; he is intelligent and cultivated and converses most agreeably.[7] Our conversation was most

March 8
Saturday

7 James Morrow (1820–65) was born in Willington, South Carolina. He attended the Literary University of Franklin College (today University of Georgia) and received his M.D. degree in 1846 from the University of

varied in subjects, & I once caught him completely. He was relating his accidental meeting a number of years ago with a most fascinating young lady of seventeen or eighteen, a budding poet & author, who has since written a number of prose tales. They met on the cars & continued their journey on the steamer a short distance. Short as it was, it was time enough for a most lengthy flirtation. They did not meet again for years, for he went to the East Indies, while she met and married the editor, a middle aged man, in whose paper her poems & prose tales [had appeared]. He died four months after. After several years she visited Charleston where she met Dr. Morrow and he accompanied her on a visit to the Orphan House. She afterwards wrote a story founded on fact, in which she introduced him as one of the characters, and has also sketched him in several others, etc. The more he told, the more convinced I was that I knew the lady's name &, when he finished, I very quietly remarked that her sister had been spending some time here & had recently left. He looked at me in utter astonishment. Then followed an explanation and confession. She was Mary Bradley, Kate Rodgers half sister, who just married Joseph C. Neal, then Mr. Haven. Her "nomme de plume" is cousin Alice & the story is "Patient Waiting No Loss." I have always enjoyed her tales and long ago Miss Agnes [Bates] told me her story. He asked me to go to ride with him on Monday to Rev. Mr. [J. Grimke] Drayton's plantation, Magnolia.[8]

Pennsylvania. He practiced medicine in Charleston and pursued graduate studies in the South Carolina Medical College. He was appointed "agriculturist," that is collector of seeds and plants in the Perry expedition to Japan. After the expedition he and Perry had a severe disagreement, which also involved Asa Gray, over the disposition of the plants and Morrow's journal. He then returned to Charleston to practice medicine. When the Civil War broke out, he was made acting assistant surgeon on Morris Island and later was on James Island. He received his discharge from service in June, 1865, at which time he returned to his home in Willington. He was married on November 18, 1865, but died less than a month later. Accounts concerning Morrow's role in the Perry expedition may be found in William B. Cole (ed.), *A Scientist with Perry in Japan: The Journal of Dr. James Morrow* (Chapel Hill: University of North Carolina Press, 1947); A. Hunter Dupree, "Science Versus the Military, Dr. James Morrow and the Perry Expedition," *Pacific Historical Review*, XXII (February, 1953) 29–37; and Samuel Eliot Morison, *"Old Bruin" Commodore Matthew C. Perry, 1794–1858* . . . (Boston: Little Brown, 1967).

8 The Reverend John Grimke Drayton is most important for his work among blacks in the area of St. Andrew's Parish, where he was rector

... For the first time I attended service in the beautiful parish church [St. Andrew's], built in 1706. About four years ago, the wood work was so thoroughly decayed that the whole of the inside was pulled down only the walls left standing, & the whole entirely renovated. It is built in the form of a cross, the alter forming the head, with a pew on either side, one of which is Mr. Bull's. ... Above, he has erected two beautiful and chaste tablets to his ancestors, the Izards & Bulls. He was the principal person who directed & paid for the renovation & says he designed the inside of the church. The pulpit and reading desk are at one angle near the altar, the doors being at the three arms. Mr. [J. Grimke] Drayton preached to a tolerably large congregation, composed of mostly soldiers. Of course Dr. M[orrow] came to our carriage for a talk and rode beside it. About dark Willie Guerard arrived unexpectedly and I found myself detrop.

March 9
Sunday

W[illie] G[uerard] left soon after breakfast and, just as we were ready to go to ride with Dr. Morrow, Cousin Lenora Wilson drove up to pay a visit and of course took a walk round the garden. However, as soon as she left, we mounted & had a charming ride, walked all over Magnolia garden, where all was silent and deserted, Mr. Drayton having just gone away & his family being in the up country. Thousands of japonicas of every variety were wasting their beauty on the deserted scene, for though the snow had injured & blighted them very much, still we found a quantity of fresh and blooming ones. On coming home we found Willie Bull just arrived and Mr. B[ull] expected, so the Dr. did not stay to dinner. Today's paper brought glorious news. The *Merrimac*, burned to the waters' edge by the Yankees, has been converted into a steel battering ram, re-christened the *Virginia*, & carries eight 10 inch columbiads & two rifled guns, one at each end. On Saturday, it attacked the *Cumberland* & *Congress*, blockading the James River, sunk the former, & the latter was run ashore to prevent from sinking. The *Virginia* with two gunboats then attacked the fort at Newport News. The battle was terrific.

March 10
Monday

from 1851 until the church's destruction during the Civil War. (William Izard Bull was St. Andrew's church warden from 1833 to 1865 and directed the church's refurbishment.) Mr. Drayton's plantation, Magnolia, located near St. Andrew's, was well known for the beauty of its grounds.

The *Minnesota & Colorado* came to its assistance and were also attacked. The former was run ashore, but still fought bravely though it had been on fire at night. The confederates [set] the *Congress* on fire, after taking off a number of prisoners, that they might see to continue the attack on the *Minnesota* which was completely riddled, & part of her stern works shot away. A large tug, which was coming to get her off, was shot into & immediately blew up. Sunday morning [the *Monitor*] the famous Yankee iron clad Ericson [John Ericsson] battery appeared, and attacked the *Virginia*. The battle lasted some hours and finally the latter ran into it, damaging it considerably. Thus three of their finest vessels have been destroyed by a single one, and it [is] thought the entire force of 10 or 12,000 men at Newport News will be captured, as they are now cut off from assistance. Com. [Franklin] Buchanan commanded the *Virginia* & was slightly wounded as were two or three others, and three or four men killed on the *Patrick Henry*. . . .

March 11
Tuesday

It rained all day & I spent the morning partly in calling Mr. B[ull] to account for the speeches he made of me, two winters ago, and gave him some very plain talking, which settled everything between us & placed our acquaintance on a pleasanter footing than it has been for a long time. The rest of the day passed in writing in this, embroidering and reading.

March 12
Wednesday

I shall not easily forget such a frolic and [such] flirtation I have not enjoyed for a long time. . . . Edwin [White] rode with Rosa & the Dr. [Morrow] with me, while Mr. B[ull] followed on horse back and Dr. [John] D[rayton] in his sulky. At the [Ashley Dragoons'] camp we found Dick Macbeth, Sam Wilson and Willie Vincent, all of whom I knew, & Mr. Maclaine [William McLean] a young Irishman, a protege of Dr. Morrow's whose aunt brought him up.[9] I was not introduced till after we left, but the Dr. gave me a slight sketch of his life. He has a great genius for mathematics and mechanism, but, like most natural & uncultivated geniuses, [he is] erratic & constantly

9 The Ashley Dragoons were Company H of the 3rd South Carolina Cavalry Regiment. This regiment, which never served as a unit, was primarily involved in coastal defense in South Carolina, although it also engaged Sherman and surrendered at Greensboro, North Carolina.

running off to sea. But [he is] a man of good principles & character. He is young & red headed, with a pleasant mischevous face lighted up with real Irish humor. But he interrupts the thread of my story. We dismounted and sat around the camp fire till it commenced to rain and we adjourned to Edwin's tent, a wall tent, floored & carpeted with sail cloth & in very nice order for our express benefit. We waited for lunch, as I wanted to taste their famous camp pudding, of bread soaked in molasses & fried bacon. When it was ready, we went to the mess tent a few steps off, & I took lunch in true soldier style; a pine table with tin plates and a *calabash* from which to take a "slight *refreshment.*" The bill of fare was beefsteak & bread & pudding. The latter with a little whiskey or "kitchen wasser" poured over it, the gentlemen declared, tasted like mince pie, but a few mouthfuls soon satisfied me. When we started [back] as it looked as it was going to rain again, Dr. Morrow carried his india rubber cloak for my benefit. Mr. Bull introduced Mr. Maclaine [McLean], but I had nothing to say to him till much later, for, just after, we made a turn into another road, & he went to tell Rosa and Edwin where to meet us, as they were far ahead.

Early in the morning I had expressed a wish to visit Peaceful Retreat, my great grandfather [Robert] Gibbes' plantation on John's Island, now owned by Mrs. Tom Roper, and where uncle [Alexander] Garden & so many of the old members of the family are buried. It was also the scene of Aunt Mary Ann Garden's heroic conduct, when a girl of thirteen, in rescuing her little cousin John Fenwick (afterwards a Colonel in the war of 1812) when the house was in possession of the British. Mr. Bull said he would take us the next day, & we went over to Mrs. Wilkes' to see and arrange with her overseer to take us across the river. The by roads through the woods were nothing but a succession of logs, but we were determined nothing should stop us. When it commenced to rain, Dr. Morrow put the cloak around me & it not only kept me dry but warm for a little while. We took shelter under a shed, but soon pushed on to the redoubts, through logs, cotton fields, newly cleared ground & altogether the roughest road I ever travelled. But I enjoyed it all the more. I found Dr. Morrow had not only been on Morris Island all last winter & knew Cousin Willie & Rutledge, but that Mr. Maclaine [McLean] had been a P.[almetto] G.[uard] and was at the battle of Fort Sumter, had gone to Virginia as Commissary of the company, then became [M. L.] Bonham's orderly, and knew Rutledge and my other friends very well. That was enough for me, and we had a long and interesting conversation in regard to the company and its affairs. He had returned home last October. We did not see the overseer &, after taking shelter under a shed for a few minutes, we pursued our ride passing again through the camp and Mr. [Simon] Magwood's plantation. I never saw such tumble down hovels in my life as on this place, but his garden and walk around the house are very pretty & carefully cultivated and trimmed. Dr. Morrow had dropped his stirrup; so I got far ahead with Mr. Maclaine [McLean], and as we rode up Mr. Bull's avenue, we had a regular John Gilpin race, and I know I "cut a curious figure."[10] The cloak flying & flapping, my hair streaming down and my hat coming off and I so convulsed with laughter that I could hardly keep my seat.

As we dismounted, the children met us, just from town with the news that Gens. McCullough [Ben McCulloch] and Mackintosh [James McIntosh] has been killed in a great battle [Pea Ridge] in Arkansas [March 7–8, 1862] & [Sterling] Price severely wounded. The shock was dreadful, for, but a few moments before, Dr. M[orrow] & myself had been speaking of McCulloch whom he knew very well & Des. Garden who is his Adjutant General. Dr. M.[orrow] had been teasing me about him &, in answer to some remark of his, I had said that "we could have friends without their *degenerating* into lovers." . . . He had been teasing me about it every since. I could scarcely think of anything else but Des. & I felt so anxious about him that it made me quite dull &, but a few minutes before, I had been in the highest spirits.

We dined at dark. . . . I spent part of the evening talking to Dr. M.[orrow] & the rest in playing cards, in which all joined except himself and afterwards told us why. When he was a boy someone gave him a pack of cards, & he became so in-

10 John Gilpin was a Londoner whose adventures are related in William Cowper's humorous poem, "The Diverting History of John Gilpin, showing how he went further than he intended and came home safe again." The poem tells of Gilpin's misadventures because of his poor horsemanship.

fatuated with learning to play that for a week he did not study
a lesson, but spent the time in the woods with some boys playing various games. But his school master gave him a whipping
for every lesson he did not know at the end of that time, [so]
he concluded he had had enough, threw the cards into the
fire & resolved never to play again. The gentlemen left about
ten, all hoping for fair weather, for our proposed frolic.

The morning paper brought a full & most graphic account
of the glorious victory of the *Virginia* commanded by Capt.
[Franklin] Buchanan. . . . Pres. Davis has suspended Generals
[John B.] Floyd and [Gideon J.] Pillow from their command
until they give more satisfactory accounts of the battle of Fort
Donelson, as in neither of their reports do they state that they
asked for reinforcements, & Johnson [Albert Sidney John-
ston] was only 40 miles off & with railroad connection. He
further says it is not shown that their position could not be
evacuated, nor the whole army saved, as well as part, nor by
what authority two senior generals abandoned their responsibility by transferring the command to a junior officer. Our
troops have also fallen back from Manassas not from necessity
but as a most brilliant strategic movement & every preparation being made for the opening of the spring campaign very
soon.

March 13
Thursday

We woke to find a heavy fog wrapping everything in its misty
mantle. . . . However, between one and two, Dr. M[orrow]
rode up, bringing the paper, & we went to ride, which I
hoped would be very pleasant, [but it] was as dull as possible.
Neither seemed talkative. The roads were dreadfully boggy &
uninteresting. We had to walk single file most of the time. We
rode to the camp & invited the gentlemen to come to an oyster supper & asked Edwin [White] to bring his flute. Dr. Morrow dined with us. . . . They got [to] playing cards &, as it was
quite warm, Dr. M[orrow] and myself walked in the piazza till
supper time. . . . [Then] Edwin enchanted us with the exquisite melody of his flute. He must have played an hour or more,
all my favorite tunes, & we were all surprised when, on looking at their watches, they found it was nearly twelve, so pleasantly had the evening sped away. The Dr. told us (some only
to me) various incidents of his life, one of which was his most
remarkable likeness to a young man not at all related to him,

but with whom he became intimate—the likeness was so extraordinary that Mr. Johnston's sister could not tell them apart and often his sweetheart also. Then he told me of a young lady with whom Gen. McCulloch & himself were in love & whom he would have addressed but for her dreadful health. And at dinner he told us of another disappointment. He was prevented from addressing a young lady before he went on a voyage for want of an opportunity, it only being a few days before he left. He returned two years after & one of the first persons he met was her uncle of whom he immediately made inquiries and was told "she was married last Thursday." I suppose these are the reasons why he has not married. Rosa & I ended the evening after "the concert of sweet sounds" by a ridiculous dog chase trying to get the children's pet dog out of the house, before shutting it up. Our endeavors were in vain for some time & the scene almost absurd.

March 14
Friday

Rosa & I came down this bright beautiful morning, I feeling very loath to leave when I enjoyed it so intensely after my long weary lameness. . . . However, I hope to return later. . . . I was very much amused to hear the first thing on coming home that it was reported everywhere over town that I was engaged to Mr. Bull. On the other hand, the club had already heard of my wearing Dr. M[orrow]'s cloak. . . .

One of [George A.] Trenholm's iron steamers, the *Economy*, ran the blockade here early Thursday morning, during the dense fog, bringing a large quantity of arms and government stores, besides other things, but of course, as yet, rumors of the amount are various.

March 22
Saturday

The concert given on Thursday night by Susan North, Emma Taber, Willie Walker, Pauline Walker, Rheeta & Henrietta Simons and other amateurs for the gunboat fund was so crowded that it was repeated last night &, on both occasions, numbers were obliged to return home because they were unable to get in. Those who heard it say the music was delightful & the singing exquisite. After one of Susan North's songs, the Baroness St. Andre, the French Consul's wife, let fly a white pigeon decked with Confederate colors, considered a great compliment. The idea of the concert was started by the girls of the Normal School & a number of them assisted in the chorus. Emma Taber sang the *Marsellaise* & *My Maryland.* I believe it is to be repeated next week. Willie & Edward dined with us today. Willie has got with a very nice mess, consisting of Tom and Willie [Heyward] and [Benjie] Guerard and Jamie H[olmes], Willie Guerard, Mr. Boliver Furman, Edward Gadsden, & several others. They are nicely fixed. They have a wagon and horses, their private property, with all kind of kitchen utensils and Tom's servant is an excellent cook. . . . Carrie asked Mr. [Isaac] White tonight and informed me that Dr. Morrow's name is James.

This afternoon we rambled through the Circular [Congregational] Churchyard & saw there some very old and curious tombstones, but it was really sad to see the destruction by the fire, many utterly crushed and burnt to powder.

March 23
Sunday

Last Monday [March 24] I returned with Rosa to Ashley Hall quite unexpectedly. Carrie & I had been to Miss Bates' lecture and on our return found Rosa who wished one of us to stay with her. . . . Tuesday [March 25, 1862] Dr. M[orrow] came in for a few minutes, but soon left with Mr. Bull & other gentlemen who were going to try and find the camp of forty of Mr. Evans Edings' negroes, men, women, & children, who went off two or three days ago, carrying all their baggage & two of Mr. Bull's house boys also. In the afternoon we went to [the] Ashley Dragoons' camp to see Willie, taking Alester as our escort and a servant also. Allie was on a half broken colt, which was continually darting into the bushes and trying to throw his rider off, while my poney [*sic*] not only was very obstinate in always taking the wrong way and not obeying the rein, but would suddenly stop and commence to trot whenever we met anybody. So we were kept laughing at one another all the time. . . .

March 29
Saturday

. . . I felt grievously disappointed by receiving a note from Willie saying they could not come for us, as an election was to take place for corporals, & they were running Benjie G[uerard]. So we took a solitary ride after dinner, with Hattie [White] on the same unbroken pony and a servant. . . . The only thing we had to break the quiet of the evening was Hattie's horse, throwing him [the servant]. He flew into the air, took a somersault and rolled over on his back in a pool of water till his head went under. The scene was so comical we laughed till we cried, and the woods rung [*sic*] with our merriment. . . .

March 30 Sunday   We went to church this morning & waited an hour, but no minister appeared, though the congregation of soldiers was quite large. Sallie Parker was the only female besides ourselves. We finally concluded we might as well return though we at first proposed Dr. M[orrow] being a communicant as lay reader and Edwin White & Willie H.[eyward] as the choir. . . .

March 31 Monday morning   We were surprised by the arrival before breakfast of cousin Wilmot Des[aussure] and Gov. [Francis W.] Pickens, who had come for Mr. B[ull] to take them over the different lines of fortification. They went soon after breakfast & returned about one to lunch. The day was so warm, Mary [Davie] and I did not take our usual walk, but after dinner, we rode to see the Ashley Dragoons drill. Mr. B[ull] and Mary [rode] in the buggy & I on Willie's Cavalry horse, a large and very fine animal, which was so excited and restless that I had to keep it walking up & down all the time. After the parade, Willie Colcock & Willie joined us & we took a short canter, then went to their camp. Supper was not ready, but Tom H.[eyward] took me to visit the kitchen & see the loaf of bread in the oven. We went to their tent and took a "slight refreshment" of "peach and honey" & biscuits. We came home dreadfully sleepy, but looked for them to come and play cards. We waited till ten then went to our chambers &, as we were about to put out the candle, we heard the first notes of a serenade which they had promised us. True the instruments were decidedly rustic, being the banjo, violin, tamborine, triangle & "bones," but we only enjoyed it the more. It was varied by vocal melody and, [after] they [had] sung five or six songs, to reward them, we flung bouquets of orange blossoms, with an old candlestick & broken knife, as make weights, amusing ourselves with their efforts to find them in the dark. Mr. Bull was so fast asleep in the drawing room that we could not wake him up to ask the gentlemen in.

After teasing us for a long time this morning in the most provoking manner, till we did not know whether we were going or not, Mr. Bull drove us up in the carriage to Camp Wallace, about twelve miles off. The day was delightful . . . we spent the morning under a grove of pine trees near the tents . . . we walked to visit the fortifications or rather where they were commencing to rise on either side of the railroad track. Instead of camp fare, as we expected, the gentlemen had provided us with fruit cake & champagne for lunch. The dinner was laid in a tent & was very nice, but camp life was shown by the deficiency of china . . . its place being supplied by tin ware. It only added to our pleasure & sociability. After dinner, Edwin [White] gave us some delightful music on the flute. . . .

April 1
Tuesday

. . . Mr. Bull drove us again this morning in the carriage to Capt. [Willie] Preston's camp, where we arrived punctually at eleven. . . . Sometime after our arrival, Mr. Edward Peronneau & the four girls came, then Lieut. O'Brien, who had been engaged on a court-martial. He is a gentleman from Texas apparently about twenty three or four & quite good looking. He is as merry & full of humor as Rutledge & reminded me of him in his funny ways. He has one peculiar habit, which was irresistibly comic. In the midst of gaiety he would suddenly pass his hand, (by the way, it was quite small, white & pretty) down before his face, & it would become as grave & stern as if about to pronounce sentence of death. Notwithstanding our merry peals of laughter, his muscles remained as rigid as possible, & he talked in the most solemn manner. Then suddenly, he would make an upward pass & the change was as instantaneous as a burst of sunshine after a thunder storm. He has a large mouth but very fine white teeth and altogether is a most agreeable companion. . . .

April 2
Wednesday

Col. [Thomas] Wagner & Mr. Leo Walker came up about twelve to inspect the battery, & we went into an old field to witness their evolutions which were very pretty & quite exciting. The firing, however, was not equal to their drill, for but one shot struck the target. After, we returned to the house. . . . We went to dinner about two [o'clock] in a large tent in the garden. The dinner was in regular city style, boned turkey, ham, lobster, salad, etc. but it was also laid in camp fashion all the dessert being on at the same time. We had brandied greengages, fresh preserved peaches, jelly & pound cake and afterwards ice cream and of course champagne and wines. It was all very fine, but I did not enjoy the day as I did Tuesday for almost all the gentlemen were strangers to me and I was disappointed in not seeing the familiar faces from Camp Wallace. . . .

. . . After dinner we adjourned to the greensward in front of the tent while the gentlemen smoked to keep off the sand flies, which were very troublesome. . . .

April 3 Ashley Hall Monday [should be Thursday]—This is really a curious book for me to use as a journal[11] but as the Sarsfield L.[ight] I.[nfantry] are entirely broken up, & this useless, I begged Willie Heyward for it. This morning Rosa, Mary [Davie] & myself drove to town through a thunder storm to attend the speeches to be delivered tonight before the Cadet Literary Societies. . . . Col. [A. P.] Aldrich gave a plain, short speech saying his camp duties had prevented him from making any preparation—it was of course on the times. Mason Smith's speech in delivering the diplomas to the Calliopean Society was as pompous and grandiloquent as we expected, but minus an original idea, & their orator, [J. H.] Moses, was tedious & sentimental. [J. S.] Dutart delivered the diplomas to the Polytechnics, & Dan Campbell delivered the valedictory. It was very pretty, his quotations apt & choice and his delivery altogether very graceful. The others had one or two bouquets—he had a shower.

April 5 We returned to Ashley Hall yesterday to dinner & found Wil-
Saturday lie and Benjie Guerard here. They staid till dark & bid us goodbye as they were to leave this morning for Hardeeville. Benjie has quite won my heart with his gaiety & sociability & withal is so boyish that he seems to me just like one of my cousins. . . . When he went, I promised to write to him & Rosa & I both let him kiss us. Just about nine, as I was trying to rouse up from a sleepy fit, I was startled by hearing the first notes of a serenade, just in front of the house. Rosa expected them, but it was a most agreeable surprise to me and so quiet-

11 This is the first entry in the third volume of the diary manuscript.

ly did they come that we did not hear them till close to the house. After one or two tunes we invited them in, Benjie having previously climbed through the window. . . . Mr. [Prioleau] Chisolm played very well on the banjo, which was an excellent one & almost as good as a guitar. John C[olcock] played remarkably well on the violin & Benjie & Willie joined in with the triangle & tambourine. The music was really very sweet, & the evening passed most agreeably in singing, playing, talking & supping. They did not leave till half past one, all feeling very loath to say goodbye. For, we did not know when we should ever meet again and certainly the *whole* party *never* will together. . . . Though we had never seen three of them before, we felt an interest in each other before we parted. Rosa & I got all to write their autographs in our albums on the same page, we girls doing the same as a memento of our delightful evening. After they mounted, they drew up in line & we joined with them in singing "My old Cabin Home." Benjie went off with his hat gaily decorated, for Rosa gave him a palmetto tree & I a beautiful crimson japonica and bud, besides a spray of orange flowers to be worn in remembrance of us. It really made us sad to have them all go and we already miss them very much. This morning Mr. [Tom] Fuller came to breakfast, expecting Mr. Bull to go to hunt, but cousin Wilmot [G. DeSaussure] brought the Governor [Francis W. Pickens] up again for Mr. Bull to take them over James Island. They all returned to dinner & the Governor amused himself by teasing Rosa & myself, putting me on the list of engaged young ladies. He made himself very pleasant, however, & when he left, took leave of Rosa according to the Russian custom of kissing the hand of the hostess. Mr. Fuller did not leave till dark.

We went to church and heard Mr. [J. Grimke] Drayton. The congregation was very small, and it really looked deserted without the soldiers which generally filled it. We missed the familiar faces of the Ashley Dragoons very much. . . .   *April 6*
Sunday

We were up early, preparing for the party Mr. Bull had invited to go on a boating excursion to Mr. William Middleton's place. Quite a large party, at least twenty odd were expected, but   *April 7*
Monday
morning

only . . . [a few came]. It was quite a disappointment. . . . We all went in a large plantation boat, rowed by four negroes, while the boys sailed in the smaller boat. . . .

We found it was too far to go to Mr. Middleton's, as we had waited till late hoping some one else might come, so we landed at the Rev. Mr. [J. Grimke] Drayton's [called "Magnolia"] & walked over his extensive garden with him. The azalias, of which he has over ninety varieties from the purest white & white pencilled with rose color, to every shade of pink, scarlet or crimson & even magenta, were in full bloom, & I never saw anything more beautiful. The clusters of blossoms were so thick you could scarcely see a leaf between. Mr. Drayton gave us some exquisite japonicas to bring with us. . . .

April 8
Tuesday

The telegraph has brought us tidings of another victory gained at Shiloh about eighteen miles from Corinth in Miss. on the Memphis & Charleston RR. It was fought on the sixth & lasted through ten hours of the deadliest strife. But thank God our holy cause was victorious, though purchased by the severe loss of Gen. A.[lbert] Sidney Johnson [Johnston] & numbers of other brave Southern hearts. But the enemies' loss is tremendous. . . . Beauregard is now commanding, and the fight going on; he says it is a second Manassas. . . .

April 13
Sunday

. . . The first anniversary of the surrender of Fort Sumter. We scarcely feel like celebrating it, when [Fort] Pulaski [Georgia] has just fallen.[12] . . .

April 15
Tuesday

We expected to visit Mr. William Middleton's beautiful country seat today, about ten or eleven miles from here, but, as is our common lot, we were disappointed by the steady rain. Willie Guerard has just arrived & says that [Fort] Pulaski has really fallen which many doubted. But nothing further is known as none of the garrison have escaped as was reported. We only know that the detested flag of U.S. now waves over it & that yesterday, when he left, twenty vessels were in sight of Savannah which he says they do not expect to be able to defend and of course a great many families are leaving. . . .

12 Fort Pulaski guarded the ocean approaches to Savannah.

This morning we took the trip to James Island which we had so long anticipated. Mr. Bull driving Mary [Davie], Rosa, & myself in the carriage with all the blinds rolled up and Edward and Sallie [Bull] in the buggy. We crossed Wappoo Cut on the Pontoon bridge at [Frank] Simon's farm, passing through [Col. James M.] Gadberry's camp & near part of [Major Edward] White's battalion. Near Elliott's Cut on the Stono, [where] Isaac White is superintending the erection of a very fine battery, we stopped to see him & Maj. Allen Green whose headquarters were on the same farm. . . . We rode almost from one end of the island to the other, most of the time through fine roads and beautiful forests or green hedges on either side—passed a very pretty Episcopal church [St. James], where, it being Good Friday, Mr. [Stiles] Mellichamp was holding service to a congregation of three ladies, scarcely any being left on the island. Soldiers & camps dotted the landscape while a strong line of breastworks meandered like a river from near Wappoo quite across the island & redoubts & other breastworks were still in progress. We went to Fort Johnson where Col. [T. G.] Lamar, Mac DeSaussure's uncle, is stationed; he invited us in & there we met Gen. States R.[ights] Gist in all the "double agony," as Willie Heyward says, of his handsome and becoming new uniform.[13] They urged us to stay to dinner, but as we carried lunch we declined, though dinner was on table. . . . [We] proceeded on our way to Lazaretto point on the beach opposite Fort Sumter, whence we had a beautiful view of the harbor and surrounding islands, as well as seeing for the first time the new fort being built in the harbor very near the city. We partly retraced our steps, then went across the island near Secessionville, another summer residence where [L. M.] Hatch's regiment is now quartered, and after a long drive, arrived at the Presbyterian church, where we stopped to dine under the trees. We could not find water anywhere near & were forced to quench our thirst with claret and cordial. We spent nearly an hour to rest the horses, amusing ourselves with rambling in the church yard, which was neatly railed & contained a number of marble tablets and monuments—one as old as

13 Adjutant general of the South Carolina state troops, Gist was killed on November 30, 1864, while leading his brigade at the Battle of Franklin.

1766. Our ride home was very pleasant. As the sun was sinking, the fresh sea breeze, which we had enjoyed all day, prevented us from feeling its warmth and when we arrived at the pontoon bridge, we had quite a merry scene. A sloop had just passed through, and, as it was dead low tide, it was some time before the bridge could be got into place and, when it was, the descent & ascent was quite precipitous. Mr. William Wilson & Stoney, Mr. Alex Mazyck & Eddie Wilson & a P.[almetto] G.[uard] in another buggy, Lieut. [Ben] Webb of the P.[almetto] G.[uard] & an old gentleman with his son in a third buggy, all came across; and it was amusing to see the faces as the sentinel cried Halt. Mr. Wilson presented his pass, but Mr. Mazyck had none, so [he] gave his name and residence & said he was going wherever the other gentleman, pointed to Mr. W.[ilson] was going—which was to see Willie Ramsey. They let him pass, & he remarked to us that it seemed hard to prove himself an honest man. The other old gentleman was also without a pass, but his explanation seemed to satisfy the corporal and he was permitted to pass, everybody laughing at each other. We certainly never, in our wildest dreams, two years ago, ever thought we should be challenged by a sentinel, two or three times a day, on our quiet roads. We met Mr. [Tom] Fuller and his daughter Celestine on their return from having been to pay us a visit & leave a bouquet of "Cloth of Gold" roses for *Mary* [Davie]—the latter affording us a great source of amusement. We arrived home at dark, after a ride of nearly 40 miles.

April 19
Saturday

The day was as quiet as possible—but *Easter Sunday* arrived and with it Mr. Fuller with another bunch of superb roses for Mary. Though she had before declined going to church on account of a headache, he persuaded her to let him drive her to church in his buggy and, though he pretended to be dreadfully shocked at our going on a frolic on Good Friday, yet he was a member of the church & not only did not stay to communion but took to ride afterwards—all of course contributing much to our fun. Major Edw.[ard] White & Lieut. Willie Earle, now his adjutant, were at church and Mr. Bull invited them to dinner. Cousin Louis [DeSaussure] also came in for a short visit and altogether we had a charming day. . . . He [Earle] is a fine looking man, six feet in height & quite good looking. He is intelligent and cultivated & quite an agreeable addition to our circle of beaux—particularly when we are so deficient in those articles as at present. We invited Jamie Furman & himself to join our party to visit Mr. [William] Middleton's place tomorrow & also promised to visit their camp at Simon's Landing on Wednesday, when they would have a review & I should have the pleasure of firing a 32 pounder.

There seems a fatality against our intended frolic, for it rains every time we intend to go. However, we will hope for tomorrow. . . . I received two letters by the return of the carriage . . . also a paper containing an account of the late daring & deeply laid scheme of the Yankees to burn all the bridges on the railroad running through Georgia & Tennessee and which passes just behind Lizzie's [Barnwell] home and thereby to cut off all communication with our Western army. The consequences would have been fearful. The plan was perfect and the way in which it was defeated as daring as itself. Altogether it was one of the most exciting incidents of the war— besides being the only thing of the kind on record: a race for life or death (not merely of a few individuals, but we may almost say of a great nation) on two fiery iron steeds. But the account is so interesting and so long that I must insert it in this.[14]

April 21
Monday

Mrs. Fred Fraser has another daughter & Congress has increased the postage on any letter to ten cents—two important items—the latter particularly & one which I will feel considerably as it will restrict my correspondence in these hard times. A Ladies Fair for the gunboat is to be given the first week in May and all the silver, jewelry, etc. sent for it will be disposed of. Some persons, I don't know who, are getting up Tableaux in aid of it also.

A clear bright day, but the wind cold and keen, and winter clothes quite comfortable. Only Mr. [Willie] Earle came this morning to go with us to Mr. [William] Middleton's. Rosa and

April 22
Tuesday

14 No newspaper account was discovered with the diary. This escapade is the famous Great Locomotive Chase in Georgia, April 12, 1862, between the "General" captured by Union volunteers and the pursuing "Texas," under Confederate control. The "General" ran out of fuel, and the Union raiders were captured and several executed.

himself rode on horseback, Sallie [Bull] taking her place when coming home. The rest of us [were] in the carriage. The ride was so pleasant that the ten or eleven miles there did not seem more than five. We found Mr. & Mrs. M[iddleton] at home, having come up only to spend a day or two; we looked first at the pictures, with which the walls of the house are literally covered—some of them are exquisite and very rare. He has the only Claude L.[e] Lorrain in America, and it has been 120 years in the family, brought direct from Italy by one of his ancestors—the scene I think is part of the bay of Naples, with the vessels of various nations at anchor and the sky all aglow with a distant conflagration. There were two others, which I admired particularly from the wonderful art with which the lights and shadows was effected, but I do not know either their names or that of the painter, for Mr. M.[iddleton] spoke so peculiarly & indistinctly that I could not catch any name accurately, though I asked him once or twice. One has two or three old monks in the foreground under a thick grape arbor with the rich clusters hanging around and in the background the convent lighted up by the setting sun—the other [shows] two nuns walking in the street—the night is dark, but their faces are brought into strong relief by a lamp fixed high up in the wall at some shrine before which they are passing and telling their beads, while in the distance, Vesuvius glares luridly. He also has a most exquisite full length miniature on ivory of Mad. Racamier taken by her permission for his uncle who was quite intimate with her. I can only remember the few which we particularly noticed, for our stay was short & the rooms were lined with him. But what attracted me most was a marble statue, a copy of a Nymph by some German artist at Berlin & by the Germans said to be worth its weight in silver. It is a young girl, apparently just from the bath, the drapery loosely thrown around her as she is seated tying on her sandal and revealing most of the upper portion of her body and the left leg, the right being thrown across to tie the sandal—that leg is perfect and the most beautiful I have ever seen. How I wish for Dora [Furman] to enjoy it with me. In his study, he showed a most magnificent bust of Washington—an original taken by an artist who came on from Paris to do so. But again, I lost the name, much to my regret. The head is massive, and the face grandly beautiful, the eyes the most expressive I ever

saw in marble except [William Randolph] Barbée's Coquette
and the mouth very beautiful. But I did not recognize it as
Washington's till I was told. In the study he also showed us a
water colored sketch of a drawing room scene in St. Petersburg when his father [John Izard Middleton] was Minister to
Russia; two of his sisters being present among a numerous
circle of Russian nobility. The grounds are beautifully laid
out in the English style, with a great deal of shrubbery and
long walks of green sward between. It is on a high bluff and
terraced down to a rice field with the blue waters of our
beautiful Ashley winding beneath us and along as far as the
eye could reach along its meanderings—the view was beautiful. The pride of Mr. M[iddleton]'s garden, the camelias,
were almost out of bloom but his trees were very large, from
twenty to twenty five feet high and the trunk as large as a
man's leg. They were some of, I believe Mr. Bull said, the first
brought to this part of the country. He had a variety of beautiful roses growing on a large round frame of trellis work, like
an arbor, which was very pretty. Mr. Earle walked with me
during the greater part of our visit and I am more than ever
pleased with him. . . . Mr. E.[arle] was very much struck with
a comparison I made between the "shrub" and a person
whose beauty lies not upon the surface but only perceived
upon close intimacy, when the "inner heart" is revealed. He
declared if he was a poet he would immediately seize on it as
the subject of a poem. We stopped to lunch and arrived home
about four. After dinner, cards were proposed & we played
whist the whole evening until he left at eleven—the luck as
usual always being with Rosa & affording us a great deal of
amusement. . . .

Another memorable day of pleasure. All of us . . . went to see
the review of [John] Waties company in White's Battalion,
[Palmetto Battalion Light Artillery] at Simon's Landing. As
we passed the Major's [Edward B. White] headquarters, Pre-
vost's farm, he rode out with his staff & several other officers.
. . . We first had a review of two companies of infantry, lately
mustered in, and quite an awkward squad—then the evolutions of Waties battery of four six pounders, two brass and
two iron, then we were invited to headquarters of Lieut. Wad-
dell, 1st Lieut. of Waties' company, the latter being absent on

April 23
Wednesday

a court martial. There we took "slight refreshment" and were introduced to a number of officers. . . . I did not expect to see so many gentlemen, for I did not know the battalion was so large. It now contains six companies and is the largest battalion of Light Artillery in the Confederacy and will soon be a regiment. As many of the guns were lost when Cameron's [Foundry] was burnt, they only have about eighteen guns now, when they ought to have thirty. We next adjourned to witness the firing at the target placed in the marsh 500 yards off. The shooting was certainly much better than that of [Capt. Willie] Preston's battery, but there was still great room for improvement. Sallie carried a large bouquet to be given for the best shot and the sergeant who won it looked "as pleased as a basket of chips—Dr. M.[orrow]." . . . After Waties' battery had ceased shooting, our party with a long train of officers, went over to James island to a battery on a bluff, mounting a 32 pounder, and commanded by Capt. [James F.] Culpepper of White's battalion. The view of the windings of the river, through long strips of marsh & heavily wooded points of land jutting out on either side, with batteries & white tents gleaming between the trees, was lovely, & Dr. [Octavius] White has promised me a sketch of it. Mr. Earle had promised that I should fire the 32 pounder and asked the Major [Edward White] to take us there. . . . Accordingly I fired the first shot, much to the amusement and interest of the surrounding groups of soldiers. The other girls followed my example & both solid shot and shell were fired—all were very fine indeed, ranging from 700 and 800 yards to over a mile. It really did Capt. C.[ulpepper] credit—we were very much amused by his taking Mary [Davie] and myself for Mr. Bull's daughters when giving us an urgent invitation to visit his battery again. . . . Mr. [Frederick C.] Schultze invited us to come and visit his camp & eat camp pudding as soon as they got settled, he being in Capt. Smith's company just mustered in. We told [him] the difficulty was want of an equipage as we were about to return to the city so he asked us, if he brought a wagon and four, if we would ride in it. I told him of course, but, as that unfortunately cannot be done in the city, I am going to ask him to give us the ride up here. On our way home, between three & four, I suppose, the Major invited us to headquarters where we found a very nice collation of cake and wine. There we arranged the party to visit Battery & Coles islands on Friday, & the Major appointed "an especial aide de camp" to each of us. . . .

. . . Rosa returned with the girls just after dinner, bringing quite a budget of news—first mother has just moved into our new house in Chapel St. and sold Beck who run away a short time ago for a week or more then returned as quietly as she left. It is very provoking that she should give us so much trouble after [our] having taken such pains to train her for a seamstress and maid & when she had learnt to embroider so nicely too. But she was such a bad girl that I think mother has done wisely to get rid of her. . . .

April 24
Thursday

We started home about eleven for our trip to Cole's island— as we passed Major White's headquarters, Mr. Earle joined Rosa, Mr. [George] Parker rode with Sallie [Bull] & Jamie F.[urman] took the extra seat in the carriage, giving his horse to one of the boys. Mary [Davie] to our very great disappointment as well as her own, had such a severe sick headache that she could not go with us & Wilding [DeSaussure] and myself rode in the carriage with Mr. Bull. I had expected to have ridden on horseback, but there were only two lady saddles & Sallie said she would not go unless on horseback nor would she consent that, as the ride would be about 45 miles, that we should exchange, she riding there & I on the way home. By persistence & selfishness equal to her own, I could have ridden all the way, but I would not make myself so disagreeable & gave up to her, though I was grievously disappointed. Our party was much smaller than we had expected, as the Major had to go to town & Lieut. Schultze got sick out of sympathy with Mary. We carried him a bouquet from her to console him for her absence & finding him sick despatched it by one of the boys with a message. Rosa & I each carried a bouquet for Walter C.[oachman] whom we thought was on Battery island, but when we arrived near the end of James island & the equestrians were far ahead, we saw a company encamped and on inquiry found it to be the Palmetto Guard. I immediately sent for him & gave the bouquets; of course he was delighted to see us and invited us to dine, which however we declined, promising to stop again on our return. When we

April 25
Friday

reached Battery island, I did not know we were on it, for it was connected by a causeway and surrounded by a sea of marsh, not water, though the broad and beautiful Stono flowed directly in front [with] Legareville being directly opposite, on John's island. Battery island contains about four acres and has several cannon on it—with wooden barracks for the troops. The P[almetto] G[uard] is to go down there shortly, and they will be very much crowded, for they will not have room to pitch their tents. Between James & Cole's islands, there are a succession of small ones, quite narrow, surrounded by wide extent of marsh on either side & connected by bridges or causeways, with here and there a creek running up. Sentinels were posted at the bridges and, at one, a howitzer to rake it & the Wellington Rangers were going the same way as ourselves. On Cole's island, we found Col. Clem Stevens stationed & several companies of regulars. . . . Col. Stevens first took us to visit a small fort built during the war of 1812 of tabby work or a kind of concrete of oyster shells, mounting two rifled 48 pounders. The grass was growing on the outside up to the rampart and on one side a palmetto tree flourished and waved its green banners in the bracing sea breeze. A beautiful bay lay before us with Folly island a long strip of wooded land quite near us on the left. Goat & some other small islets [were] to the right, and far in front of us stretched Bird Key a long low sand bank scarcely distinguishable from the breakers beyond. None of the blockading squadron were in sight, as they generally are. We visited two or three of the batteries, and some shot and shell were fired in honor of us. At one battery there was a 10 inch columbiad, two 42's and a 32 pounder—at another 32 & 24's. We were not invited to shoot them off as we wished, for I was especially ambitious of firing the 10 inch. Col. S.[tevens] also showed me the furnace for heating hot shot & showed us where were the bomb proof magazines and hospital. We retraced our steps to James I. and stopped about a mile or so from the "P. G." in a pretty grove and, when we started, Jamie drove me in the buggy, making George [Parker] & the servant go in the carriage. I enjoyed that part of the ride most of all, for not only was the sun declining behind the trees and the air delightful, but Jamie talked more freely when we were alone. For he is reserved and generally very quiet in company. He told me

Mr. Earle has been engaged for a long time to a very pretty girl, Miss Price of Virginia, & wears her likeness in a seal ring he has on. I must get him to show it to me. I begged Jamie to make friends with him, but do not yet know whether my wishes have had any influence. While we were at the fortifications & at dinner, Mr. E[arle] was with me, but the rest of the time with Rosa. He has found out her engagement, but she is not yet certain of his, though she suspects it. We stopped to see Walter [Coachman] & Bentham Simons & gave them a bundle of cake and kisses. We arrived home between seven & eight, after a charming day; the gentlemen staid to supper & [to] play cards and, as Mr. [Parker] had gone without express leave from the Major [White], I wrote a note to the latter begging him to excuse Mr. P[arker] and we girls signed our names, giving it to Mr. Earle to carry. He told us he meant to show it to the Major then to keep it.

The day was as quiet and as dull as possible &, after supper, when we were in the midst of a game of whist, Mr. Earle, Mr. [Tom] White and Mr. [Augustus or W. R.] Fludd were announced. After some pleasant conversation, "Old Maid" was proposed & played, affording us much amusement and opportunity of teasing Mr. Fludd, who denied his engagement to Miss Richardson and tried in vain to find out where I had learnt it, or knew anything of him. None of us dreamed that Mr. White was a married man—he is so small & delicately made that he does not look over twenty, at least by candle light. At last I asked Mr. Earle who he was and when he told me he was the Major's half brother, I told him he was mistaken; he had none so young. He insisted he was right and not only that, but that he was the one married to Miss Edings. That was too much for my credibility, for I thought Mr. Earle intended to play off a joke, and I would not believe him until after repeated assurances on his honor that it was Mr. Tom White who married first Ella, then Posy Edings & I knew had three children. Still I doubted against positive testimony for I never saw such a change. Most men grow large from their rough camp life, but he has grown smaller and looks as different as possible from what he did two or three years ago. The gentlemen rose to go quarter of twelve but their horses were not ready & they stood laughing and chatting for more

April 26
Saturday

than a half hour till at last Mr. Earle in despair of getting them to go said "Mr. White it is time for you [to] go, for Mrs. White will want you in town tomorrow." He jumped as if he had been shot and run [*sic*] for his horse, leaving us screaming with laughter. We promised them to take a wagon ride on Thursday & dine in camp with them on Wednesday—we are to go again to Cole's island for Mary's [Davie] benefit.

April 27
Sunday

We went to church & heard the most solemn, home, heart-searching sermon, extempore from Mr. [J. Grimke] D.[rayton] on the motives which carried us to church. It struck right and left because we certainly had not the deep sense of the solemnity of the service with which he impressed us and I had nearly laughed out when during the service Mr. Bull looked at me and signaled that some one was coming. I thought he meant some of the gentlemen who had been to see us on Saturday night, for I had promised Mr. Fludd if he came, to tell him my informant. As they did not appear, I concluded it was Dr. M.[orrow] who had taken a seat low down, where I could not see him. But what was my astonishment and amusement to see Mr. [Tom] Fuller walk in accompanied by Lou Heyward & then to catch his glances at our pew. After church, he presented Mary with some beautiful flowers. . . .

April 29
Tuesday

Dr. [John] Drayton spent the day here—while at dinner we received a note from Major White saying that he and his staff would be quite unable to escort us on Wednesday as the battalion muster was obliged to take place, and, as it would really "break their hearts" to be unable to accompany us, he begged that we would postpone our trip for another day—so we appointed Thursday. . . .

April 30
Wednesday

Rosa went to town & Dr. D.[rayton] spent the day, but he is not much addition to our social circle—when Rosa returned, she brought plenty of bad news. New Orleans has surrendered [April 25] as Gen. [M.] Lovell had withdrawn the troops from the city and it was defenceless [*sic*]. The Mayor's answer to Commodore [David C.] Farragut was most manly, but nothing else could be done. The *Mississippi* which was to have been a second *Virginia* and was nearly completed, was burned to prevent its falling into the enemies' hands. The *Louisiana* proves to have been only an old steamer, or ship iron-clad, and its timbers were not strong enough to stand the tremendous force of the balls fired against her, and she was sunk. . . . Forts Jackson & St. Philip still hold out however.[15] Fort Macon, N.C. has capitulated, but its garrison marched out with all the honor of war, after a brave defence [*sic*]—but it was completely at the mercy of the heavy Parrott guns, which were placed behind a sand bank, 1100 yards distant.[16] The Northern papers give a full account of the bombardment of Fort Pulaski and say that our men fought gallantly but, after eighteen hours of hard fighting, the fort was in such a dilapidated condition that the walls trembled and tottered with every discharge or ball which whistled clear across the terra plane and struck the magazine. If the firing had continued half a day longer, the walls must have fallen and all been buried in it, or all blown up. We had but four men killed and a few others wounded. And the enemy say they only had one killed and two or three slightly wounded. . . .

My dear father's birthday—what pleasant memories cluster round that date. We girls were downstairs by half past six and by half past eight were all ready to start, having put up the lunch, gathered a number of bouquets, eaten breakfast and done various other things. . . . I rode one of the boys' horses, which had never been ridden but once or twice by a lady, and that long ago—is very lazy and full of tricks. I had to make a servant lead it when starting & before we reached Judge [Edward] Frost's, it had tried to throw me two or three times. But finding its attempts unsuccessful, [it] cantered very well by the persuasion of a huge switch. . . . When we reached Headquarters, Mr. Earle joined us, the Major having let him off and he made Rosa and I promise that either one or both were to ride with him all day never mind who else was with us. As this was the day we [had] promised to dine with Lieut. [Tom] White, Mr. [Augustus or W. R.] Fludd, etc., we rode to their camp at Elliott's Cut to say we could not go and invite them to join us. But unfortunately they could not. . . . After convers-

May 1
Thursday

15 They had already fallen on April 28, 1862.
16 A Parrott gun was a rifled muzzle-loading cannon designed by R. P. Parrott and easily identified by the thick band around the muzzle.

ing with them for a little while, we stopped to see Isaac White
and the fort which he is superintending the erection of—he
was unable to join us either. Our ride was very pleasant, Rosa,
Mr. E[arle] and myself keeping behind and out of the dust of
the equipages. Though the sun was very warm when we started, the sea breeze on the island soon cooled the air. But about
half a mile before reaching the shore, my horse gave symptoms of exhaustion & I gave my switch to Mr. E[arle] as I
found my efforts useless. The scene was as ridiculous as on
that memorable day when we took lunch at Camp Magwood
—he switching the horse all the time & going at full speed and
screaming with laughter. We stopped at the store and I rode
with Ann [Frost], Lizzie [Frost] having changed to the carriage previously, & Mr. Bull taking her place while the servant took my horse. We left it at a plantation further on. We
stopped at the Palmetto Guard camp. . . . By that time symptoms of a thunder storm were rapidly approaching but, as we
were so far, we would not turn back. When we reached Cole's
island, it sprinkled a little, but the keen easterly wind was so
furious and the sand storm so blinding that we did not stop,
merely riding round the fortifications. . . .

As we reached Battery island, Jamie [Furman] & Lieut.
White joined us, Jamie of course riding with me, for I have
been unsuccessful in making up the quarrel as I hoped. Long
before we reached our dining place, it commenced to rain
quite hard, & we took shelter in the dilapidated ruin of a
house near our bower. The boarding at the side was all gone
& the floor was covered with fallen plastering, with two or
three old ploughs by way of furniture. Our horses were put
in a room back of that & about a foot lower & they were continually putting their heads into "our" drawing room. The
"P. G.'s" met us there, and I am very much pleased with Mr.
[Ben] Webb. His face is not merely a pleasant one, but as
frank and honest one as ever I have seen, and his character &
manners correspond. We soon became social, as we have
known of each other a long time. Bentham [Simons] went to
camp and brought the fly from two tents, with one of which
they fixed a kink of roof by fastening it to the trees and the
other served as a carpet. The dinner was very merry & I had
Mr. Earle on one side & Jamie on the other. The more I know

of Mr. Earle, the better I like him—he is so thoughtful & considerate towards ladies and so kind & respectful that we call upon him or are willing to receive from him various little attentions and services, which we would not permit from the others, except Jamie. Before he left at night I told him I knew of his engagement and made him promise to show me her likeness.

When we had taken a game of "old maids" after dinner, the rain had ceased and the air was more delicious than before. We started for home, Mr. Earle driving Rosa in the buggy & Sallie taking her horse with Mr. [Tom] White as escort. We had intended passing him off on Ann [Frost] as an unmarried man & expected a great deal of fun, but Mr. Bull, thinking he would not come, told on us; still he was so gay & lively that he added a good deal to the party. He declared he was only seventeen & put himself under my care. He certainly is the most youthful looking man I know and, though the Yankees have deprived him of all his wealth, he seems as light hearted as if he really was only a boy. He is a consummate flirt too, that I read in his eyes in a few moments & he has a plenty of conceit and that article, vulgarly called "brass." On our way home, Jamie spurred my horse, in the most quiet manner possible, & set it running races, and, after it got into the spirit, I could scarcely stop it. We took several races, which considerably added to my enjoyment, Dessie's [Bull] wrath, (for it was his horse) and the astonishment of the people we passed. Jamie [Furman] & Mr. White had to leave us at the Pontoon bridge &, as the rest of the equestriens [*sic*] had gone ahead, I had to ride alone behind the buggy, not at all agreeable when passing through the camps. We stopped at headquarters and invited Mr. [George] Parker to tea, but he did not join us till we reached the gate about a mile from the house. So, most of the way I rode alone far in front of the buggy in the soft evening twilight, with my hat off enjoying the cool spring breeze. When I got home I was so stiff & bruised from my long ride that I could scarcely move, but I had expected that so did not mind it. I am willing to take all the pain for the pleasure I have enjoyed. Poor Mary [Davie] had to retire early with a severe headache, but the rest of us ended our day very agreeably.

May 2 . . . Everybody in town [Charleston] has a face "two miles
Friday long." They report an attack upon the city is expected very
soon & gentlemen are sending away their families. There has
been fighting for two days at Yorktown [Virginia], but no further particulars are allowed to come on. The seat of Government has been virtually changed to Columbia [Virginia] from
Richmond, important papers, etc. having been already
moved.[17]. . .

May 3 . . . Sunday morning before church we were agreeably sur-
Saturday prised by a note from Mr. Earle, saying he and the Major
would dine with us. . . . We all went to church as it was to be
the last day; Mr. [J. Grimke] Drayton gave us a fine sermon
and a most solemn and affecting farewell. It saddened me to
think we might never enter these walls again, and probably it
would be the last time at least for [a] year that I would pass
over those now familiar roads, associated with so many, many
pleasures. Mr. E[arle] met us at the door, having arrived too
late for the service, but in time to ride home with us and the
Major came later. Mrs. Parker came in after church & we all
went walking round the garden. . . . We had a long talk about
the Major who had provoked us both by putting Mr. Parker
under arrest in his tent, because he had not asked his express
permission to go the night he took tea last with us. The Major
is exactly what I expected him to be as a military man: an
irascible, conceited martinet, who makes the greatest fuss in
the world about trifles, thereby sacrificing the respect of his
officers. He is unjust to Mr. P.[arker] and we were right provoked as it was a disappointment to him as well as ourselves
not to see him. On our return from walking, Mr. Earle & I sat
for some time on the steps as we did last night, talking & he
always sits by me at meals; at supper I was much amused
by Mr. Bull's expressive looks & told Mr. E.[arle] that Mr.
B.[ull] thought us, what he would call, "an evident case" &
he proposed we should keep up the joke; but, unfortunately
after they left, Willie G[uerard] told him of Mr. Earle's engagement, and he rapped at my door on his way to bed to say
he had just heard some terrible tidings, which would shock

17 On May 1, 1862, Jefferson Davis gave General Johnston permission to
    withdraw from Norfolk and the peninsula; Richmond was not evacu-
    ated.

me, but would not tell me what it was. I guessed immediately & laughed most merrily at his mistake, especially when I found next morning that Willie G.[uerard] thought I was the only one of the girls who did not know it.

Willie G[uerard,] Wilding [DeSaussure] himself [*sic*] came down [to Charleston] Monday morning. I did not mind coming half so much since I knew headquarters were to be moved that afternoon to James Island, & Rosa was not likely to have any frolics without us. I stopped to see Mary Davie & found her in the midst of packing, as they are going off this week and almost everybody we know is going also. As whether the city is burned or is defended street by street, the women and children, they think, ought to be away. Mother I found in a most unsettled state undecided whether to go or stay, as our new house, which is a most delightful one, cool, comfortable and quite convenient, is hired for a year, at $700, and all the gentlemen think we will have to pay the whole. If so, we cannot afford to hire another in the up country, besides the great difficulty of getting one.

Mary Hume came to see us and say goodbye as she leaves on Sunday; each farewell with our friends causes new sadness, for we do not know that we will ever meet again, at least in this dear old city. . . .

May 7
Wednesday

May
10
&

December
30, 1862

Life in Wartime Camden

May 10
Saturday

Last night I went to the [Ladies Gunboat] fair with the children & had a delightful evening, meeting a number of friends, among others, Dr. [James] Morrow, who seemed very glad to meet me & I spent about an hour or more with him. . . . [I] heard Mr. E[arle] was quite sick, so this morning as soon as I woke, I wrote a note to Mr. [Tom] White, asking to stop and inquire after him. I am so afraid he will contract fever, & he is not strong. The Dr. says the reason he did not come to see us is that he was continually being sent off on business and last night he was told that they wanted him to go to Knoxville. Almost everything at the fair is raffled and today there is to be a grand lottery of all the silver, jewellry [sic], watches, china sets, etc. which have been given. 4000 chances at one dollar each and 200 prizes. Some of the articles are very elegant—an entire pearl set and a diamond ring among others. . . .

May 10
Saturday
afternoon

I attended the grand raffle which was admirably conducted. The pearl set was won by a Miss Broadie, a Baptist, a respectable woman in the lower walks of life [but] one certainly who will never make any use of it except to sell it. I don't know who got the other handsomest prizes.

The news of yesterday and today is so dreadful and so discouraging that I really feel despondent. Norfolk & Portsmouth [Virginia] evacuated [May 9–10], the Navy Yard & *Merrimac* destroyed [May 11]—the last especially is a dreadful blow. The evacuation was intended to have been another brilliant strategical movement like that of Manassas, & the *Merrimac* to have gone down to Craney Island at the same time. But the Captain of a tug in the Confederate service went over with it to the enemy, carrying such information as compelled the hasty evacuation of Norfolk & the destruction of the *Merrimac* to prevent her falling into the enemy's hands, as she could not run up the river. I do not yet understand it, but can only suppose Tatnall [Josiah Tattnall] knew best.[1] Then yesterday morning we were horrified by learning that the negro crew of the *Planter* which, besides being armed with a 32 & 24 pounder, was laden with four heavy guns for Fort Ripley, the new fort on Middle Ground, had carried her over to the fleet; the captain, mate & engineer, all white men, being absent as they ought not to have been, nor was there a guard on board as ought certainly to have been to protect the very valuable guns & ammunition. . . . All [R. S.] Ripley's books with the orders and countersigns for the various posts were onboard, which was another dreadful piece of negligence on the Captain's part. He, [C. J.] Relyea, is an honest man, but has shown himself most culpably careless in this instance. He and his two assistants have been arrested and put into jail, but the irreparable mischief is already done. At daylight, the crew got up steam &, though there was a sentinel on the wharf, put there since Ripley's barge was stolen ten days ago by his negro crew, who carried off a number of others with him, he did not stop it, thinking all right. They ran down to another wharf and took a number of negroes, including their families, on board & went off & this morning we learn that they went up the Stono and carried off the *DeKalb* also. Whether that is laden with the guns from Coles island & the other batteries on the Stono, which are being dismantled, we do not yet know. . . . In passing Fort Sumter, they raised the night signals &

1 Commander of the *Merrimac*, Tattnall requested a court of inquiry to clear him of wrongdoing in destroying the ship. He was censured but later was acquitted by a court-martial also convened at his request.

were allowed to pass as usual. It is not only one of the boldest & most daring things of the war, but one of the most disgraceful, as showing utter negligence on the part of the authorities in having the city so miserably guarded.[2] Martial law did not go into effect till yesterday, & hundreds of soldiers were out guarding but it was too late. The serious thing is that the *Planter* & *DeKalb* neither draw more than four feet water, so can come in at any time & run through Stono and Wappoo and, as almost all those batteries have been dismantled, there is nothing of importance to stop them. Then the *Bermuda* & *Ella Warley* were both captured lately, the former having a British crew and running under British colors and heavily laden with arms and ammunition and running from one English port to another, the latter was also running under English colors. . . . The last telegraph is that several gunboats including the *Monitor* have gone up to Richmond and it is supposed to have fallen by this time. Truly the clouds grow darker and darker & it needs all our faith to keep the silver lining of God's mercy and goodness in view. . . .

Mother received a letter from aunt Lizzie Garden two nights ago, giving us a warm invitation there—we to rent the house & Fan and herself to board with us, their board to counterbalance our rent, so that neither would pay anything. Though I dislike Sumter very much from the prevalence of sand & Jews, my great abhorrances, and we will be crowded, still I do not think we can do better. . . . We have accepted it, as we conclude Mr. Bennet cannot hold us to the rent of this house if we pay the first quarter, though mother has not yet seen him. I have advised mother to send off our winter clothing, machine, table & books in a few days, so that we shall be less encumbered later. . . .

May 16 The report about the *DeKalb* is false, it having only run
Friday aground, and the news from Richmond is cheering—[yesterday] five gunboats including the *Monitor* and *Galena* had attacked the lower batteries & been beaten off [at Battle of Drewry's Bluff].

2 The leader of this daring venture was Robert Smalls, later a member of the United States House of Representatives and one of the key black political leaders in postwar South Carolina.

I spent the day visiting among my friends and, as I passed round the battery to go to see Rosa, found White Point Garden filled with soldiers—[Peyton] Colquitt's Georgia regiment, 1150 strong, being encamped there. The Dixie Rangers are in Mr. [Samuel G.] Barker's vacant lot in Meeting St. and indeed soldiers are encamped all over the city, but martial law keeps them quiet and orderly as every soldier found in the street without a permit and furlough is imprisoned. Uncle Arthur told us today that a few days ago a negro was caught on his way to the fleet with a complete diagram of the city and fortifications and all necessary information attached, signed by Dexter Leland, whom he says has been a writing master here for over forty years, though a Yankee by birth. Leland was arrested and confessed to his hand—he has been put in jail, but I think ought to be hung without judge or jury. We have too much treachery amongst us. . . .

The citizens of Richmond, as well as the President, Governor & Mayor, have determined to resist to the last. All are enthusiastic in their preparations to defend it—but a letter from aunt Lizzie Gibbes says Uncle Ta writes that they talk of giving up Mobile [Alabama] after all the preparations there, & he will have to remove with the Government property—he is Captain of Ordnance & employed in the manufacture of arms.

Another letter from Aunt L.[izzie] Garden has considerably changed our plans. She does expect rent to be paid while she is away and at the rate of $600 a year, which is very high, particularly as her house is very inconvenient & we would be crowded and besides the servant's accommodations are not sufficient & mother would have to hire another house for them at some distance at $12 a month which will not do at all. . . .

A passenger on a Confederate schooner lately captured by the fleet who was sent to Sullivan's island by flag of truce, says he was shown the Charleston papers daily, while with the fleet, and that they are well acquainted with our minutest movements. With such treachery without and within to contend against, we have indeed a hard battle to fight. The Yankee commander moreover says they don't want any more negroes & are willing to give up those they have on a demand from the owner, for they are all disgusted with them. . . .

. . . Mr. [John] Greene & two others had permission to make their escape [at Island No. 10] *if they could.* He had only been married about two months & he thought for a few moments of months spent in a gloomy Northern prison & determined to try his fate. They set out at one at night and reached Reelfoot Lake [Tennessee] in safety, but to their dismay found no boat to cross it and it was eight miles wide. They soon remedied that, however, by tying two logs together and on that frail raft they started. They could have landed that afternoon, but, knowing the Yankee scouts were in the vicinity, determined to wait till night. But about sunset a terrific storm commenced which lasted all that night and the next day. During all that time they tossed about at the mercy of the waves, but a merciful Providence saved them from a watery grave, & they finally reached the shore after suffering from the most intense cold. Though Mr. G[reene] was out with [General John B.] Floyd all last winter in the mountains of western Va., he said his sufferings then were not to be compared with what he had just endured. They obtained horses & a guide by paying a large sum, and, after riding 60 miles over almost untravelled roads, reached a depot from which they soon went to Memphis. . . . The many thrilling incidents and escapes during this war fully equal if they do not surpass the revolutionary tales of our great grandfather's. Lizzie also writes that her friend Carrie Pyncheon, who lives in Huntsville [Alabama], wrote her just before that city was occupied by the Yankees [April 11] that she had spent an evening in company with the now famous Capt. Jack [later General John Hunt] Morgan "our second Marion." She said he was extremely different from what she had imagined. [He was] so mild & gentle in his manners that she would not have taken him for a soldier but for his boots & spurs, so unwarrior-like did he seem. He is one of the most interesting characters of the war, except our beloved Beauregard, and each new feat of daring and valor we hail with delight.

May 20 The enemy's gunboats run [*sic*] up the Stono today, shelling
Tuesday Coles & Battery island; our troops retired as they advanced, according to orders, burning the barracks & falling back to

the fortifications on James Island; the obstructions at Battery I. prevented the Yankees from coming further for the present. . . .

I . . . went walking on the Battery and was joined by Dr. Moore, quite unexpectedly. It was so long since we had met that it was quite a pleasure. He was engaged to tea with Mrs. [George] Parker, so did not walk home with me. I saw Dr. [James] Morrow seated alone looking as grave and forlorn as possible. The children say they think, when he saw me coming by the second time, he made a move to join me when he saw Dr. Moore. I do not understand his behavior exactly, after our intimacy I may say, and he seemed so pleased to meet me at the fair. I like friends to be the same always, & I really like him—he interests me, because he is different from those I generally meet. He has not been to see me and there are a dozen things I want to ask him. It is such a "positive pleasure" to meet any of those with whom I enjoyed our frolics in the country.

. . . A short time ago, the vestry of St. Philip's wrote Mr. Howe a most complimentary letter saying his services had been most acceptable to our congregation and enclosing him $800 with which to send away his family. It was well deserved and very gratifying to us who are so fond of our "old" minister. *May 23 Friday*

Gen. Picayune [Benjamin F.] Butler has published one of the most infamous proclamations ever heard or dreamed of among a civilized people, and, if it does not forever blast the reputation of the United States among European powers, all sense of virtue and decency must be dead. Beauregard had it read at the head of his army and it has everywhere roused the Southerners to a deadlier hatred and made them grasp their weapons with a fiercer determination to sweep such fiends from our beloved country. It runs as follows—"If any of the women of New Orleans shall dare to insult or show contempt for a Federal officer, *by word, gesture, or look,* they *shall be held liable to be considered and treated as women of the town, plying their avocations.*" [Butler did this] because in every town held by our despicable enemies, the Southern women have avoided them and treated them with marked contempt and disdain. . . .

Gen. Butler also took by military force from the person of

the Belgian Consul the key of the vault, in which was deposited $800,000 in cash, placed there by the citizens in payment of a debt to the Belgian Government.... [He] also placed guards around the residences of the French and Spanish Consuls, though he afterwards withdrew them during the day. He is certainly trying to see how far he can possibly outrage every law known among civilized nations.

May 24
Saturday
Yesterday morning was spent shopping in Hayne St. alone, for I have become quite an independent business woman. The prices were enormous as the articles are scarce and the long cloth had to run the blockade from England. I had to give 55¢ for thin indifferent English infinitely inferior to the Northern at 12½ which we are accustomed to wear. For the former is always mean cloth, & we never even bought it for the servants. I was horrified at having to pay $32.45 for a piece of 59 yards. We have to lay in a supply for the autumn as we are going away & don't know when we will be able to get any more. Then I had to get *curtain dimity* for petticoats or night dresses at 28 cts. because it is the best and cheapest cloth to be found. The rest of the morning was spent packing most busily, preparatory to our expected move in a few days to Reidville. . . . In the evening we received a letter from Uncle John [DeSaussure] saying he had hired the house, for which we had applied, for $375. for seven months, from June 1st to December 31st. It is fully and handsomely furnished, has a large vegetable garden and is pleasantly situated among hosts of friends and relatives. . . . It has nine rooms. . . . I don't want to leave the city for myself until obliged to, for I neither fear the Yankees or our own soldiers, but, as mother is anxious to be settled & the boys for her to go, I of course have to go too.

Mr. [T.] Sumter Brownfield, Mr. Hughes & Isaac [White] all spent the evening with us. . . . Mr. B[rownfield] said in the retreat from Yorktown they had to march 75 miles on the railroad track, & in many places the trestle work was 60 feet high. They lived on three ears of parched corn a day to each man, he himself having been quite sick. . . . He says we have as many men as we want and a magnificent army. Johnnie C[rawford] wrote that for eight days they had had no rations served, living only on what they could kill or find on the way, the Yankees pushing them all the way. Mr. B[rownfield]'s visit made me feel rather sad[der] than otherwise, though it was a great pleasure to see such an old and intimate friend, but he is very much graver as we noticed of Rutledge when he first came, and somehow there was a change from the happy old times of which his presence reminded me so forcibly. We recalled the time and place where we first saw each other, though we did not become acquainted for some little time after, and, oh, what changes since then.

Saturday afternoon just after dinner, as uncle James [Holmes] and we girls were standing in the piazza, a soldier stopped and asked for a glass of water. We asked him in, and uncle James talked to him. We found he was Mr. Witherspoon of Clarendon, a cousin of our old friend, Dr. W.[itherspoon] of Sumter. His father was a member of the State Legislature and his grandfather of Congress—the latter, uncle J[ames] had known very well. Mr. W.[itherspoon] is a private in [R. F.]Graham's regiment which has been stationed for six months at Georgetown & passed us a half hour after on their way to the railroad. He said to Richmond, but we have since heard they were only going to Mar's Bluff to guard the railroad. He said he had a wife and five children & his term of enlistment would have been out on Sunday, but for the new law,[3] and he had to pass by his home. From his appearance, in his rough travel stained dusty uniform, with his blankets, knapsack & shoes strapped on his back, I never would have taken him for a gentleman, but soon saw from his conversation even before we learned his name that he was above the common class. He was so grave &, though he said but little of himself, seemed to feel the longer separation from home so deeply that it made [me] right sad. When the regiment passed, we were in the upper piazza, and all turned to look— many officers, as well as men, taking off their hats and saluting us with "Farewell—Goodbye ladies" and one boy called out "goodbye gals." We returned them, waving our hands, &

3 Confederate Conscription Act of April, 1862, called for the draft of every white male between eighteen and thirty-five years of age for three years of service. At first there were no exceptions, but these were later added causing controversy.

answering whatever they said. It was the first time I had ever done such a thing, and, though I did not know any of them and they were all in high spirits, it made me feel more sad. . . .

May 26
Monday &
May 27
Tuesday

Very busy packing and sending off all we could spare, as there is so much freight now that it has to be sent several days beforehand to reach its destination in time. Tuesday afternoon Carrie & I went walking on the Battery. . . . Dr. M[orrow] was there & I am convinced intended joining me as I passed him. He had followed us on the Battery & I saw was watching me as we stopped to speak to some friends but Carrie refused to walk on as usual & turned suddenly back—so he lost the opportunity. . . . I was disappointed & I am sure he was; for we will perhaps never meet again & it would have been pleasant for both parties. . . .

May 28
Wednesday

. . . I went . . . to Rosa's to see her ride off—how it recalled our charming frolics in the country and the friends with whom we had ridden. The Dr. [Morrow] went to see Rosa a few nights ago. It is singular he did not come to see me too, but he passed me on horseback this afternoon, as I was promenading with Christopher Winsmith & stopped to say goodbye as he leaves tomorrow for Richmond. I told him I was going to Camden & asked him if he had been to Nashville, as Rosa insisted. He said no he could not get there, he had been to Knoxville, as I thought. And thus ended our farewell meeting, without a shake of the hand, for as I [was] with a stranger he did not come close up, merely spoke as we were passing. I suppose I will not have the pleasure of seeing either Mr. [Willie] Earle or Jamie [Furman] again either, and all the pleasures of the spring will have passed away like a happy dream. . . .

Stonewall Jackson has achieved another glorious victory near Winchester, or rather succession of them after three days fighting [May 24–26]—each day defeating a portion of [General Nathaniel P.] Bank's army & finally completely routing it "in worse than Bull Run style"—large numbers of prisoners and immense quantities of camp equipage and stores of every kind having fallen into our hands. Mr. James Rose thereupon perpetrated the following verse, which I think admirable:

While Butler plays his silly pranks
And closes all the New Orleans banks,
Our Stonewall Jackson, much more cunning,
Keeps the Northern Banks running.

One week ago I took my last walk on the Battery—the next *June 4*
day I was too wearied after all the packing. Friday morning *Wednesday*
[May 30] Alester came up with the majority of the servants *Camden*
and we started the same evening. . . . Our journey was pleasant for the [railroad] cars were not very full and the night air
cool enough to make a shawl comfortable. . . . We arrived at
Kingsville at three in the morning and remained there till
eight for the Camden train arriving here at eleven. Mr. Elliott
kindly met us with his and uncle J[ohn]'s [DeSaussure] carriages. We met Mrs. Villepigue here waiting to give us the
keys and point out the closets, etc. reserved for her own use.
She is a young widow with three children & sister in law of
Gen. [John B.] Villepigue, now in command of Fort Pillow
[Tennessee].[4]

The house is a remarkably nice one, with five large rooms
on the first floor, two drawing rooms, two chambers & a
dining room back with a pantry attached, & wide passage
through the house—two large upright rooms & wide entry
upstairs, and in the basement a kitchen, storeroom and another which we will make a bathroom. The rooms are fully, &
the drawing rooms handsomely, furnished—with a number
of closets, presses, tables with drawers, and other conveniences and comforts—several nice outbuildings for servants,
two vegetable gardens with a variety growing and a number
of peach and plum trees and one Murillo cherry tree. It is the
first time I ever saw a *cherry on the tree* and could pick it. We
are altogether remarkably fortunate in getting such a pleasant home. As Mrs. [Cordes] Harleston and Mattie are coming
to stay with us, Carrie, Lila & I are going to take one of the
drawing rooms as our chamber, as there is no danger of our
needing a second drawing room to entertain lovers or even
gentlemen visitors—the latter being very scarce here.

Cousin Sarah [Elliott] is just opposite & the Burnets just

4 John B. Villepigue (1830–62) became Bragg's chief of engineers and
artillery. He died from illness at Fort Hudson.

moved back of us; uncle John's [DeSaussure] family including uncle Louis' [DeSaussure] and Aunt Carrie B[landing] and uncle Dan's [DeSaussure] family are about a half mile off, and the Heywards a little further, besides many other neighbors near us. . . . Sunday morning [June 1] we all went to church. . . . Uncle John has procured the Seminary pew for us, rent free, and indeed the citizens here are very kind and liberal to us refugees in every way. Though the walk to church was long, we did not mind it, as the roads are good and quite shady. The Bishop [Thomas F. Davis] preached & Mr. Stuart Hanckel read prayers. The Bishop and Mr. Tom Davis [Thomas F. Davis, Jr.] are both in such very wretched health that they preach but seldom and then always sit, & the bishop generally takes a faint in the vestry room immediately after. It is really a sad and pitiable sight to see father and son—the one blind, and the other reduced to a skeleton and looking death smitten.[5]

We all got rides home from different friends—it was quite hot and in the afternoon we had a hail and rain storm. . . .

Rain all day Tuesday, which I employed in writing six letters, besides sewing. Mother has inaugurated our sojourn here by family prayer, morning and evening, which we have never had before. The news from Virginia during the last few days has been most cheering, though many a home will be saddened by the loss of beloved ones who have fallen in their country's cause. . . .

Our friends of White's Battalion, Lieuts. [Frederick C.] Schultze, [Augustus or W. R.] Fludd and Tom White, had the pleasure of a few shots at the Yankees, from Dill's Bluff, James island, (just before I left town) disabling one gunboat when all retreated. It was the first time they had had an opportunity of testing their mettle, & I wanted so much to see and congratulate them. . . .

---

5 Bishop Thomas F. Davis (1804–71) became rector of Grace Episcopal Church, Camden, in 1847. In 1853 he was consecrated bishop of the diocese of South Carolina. Instead of moving to Charleston as was the usual practice, he remained at Camden. He began a seminary there in 1859, but the building was the victim of arson on March 31, 1865. The Reverend Thomas F. Davis, Jr. (1828–65) was associate rector of Grace Church from 1854 until his death.

The affair of the *Merrimac* is undergoing a court of inquiry in Richmond, for the pilots have published a plain, straight forward letter, totally contradicting Com. Tatnall's [Josiah Tattnall]. A long and very interesting letter has also appeared explaining the cause of the fall of New Orleans. The obstructions which had been the labor of months and were considered so strong that "the bottom of the Mississippi must be torn up before they could be destroyed" were carried away in one night by a tremendous flood in the river, the greatest ever known, and the overwhelming current. They were immediately replaced by vessels moved between the forts and sunk with stones, but again the flood, which had put Fort Jackson waist deep in water, swept away the hopes and confidence of thousands. A third time they attempted to replace them, but the storm of shot and shell from the Yankee gunboats compelled them to desist. The river was considerably higher than the city and the levee had already given way in some places. [Mansfield] Lovell's force there did not consist of 3000 men, and the city was entirely unprotected. For, as fast as he could get guns, he had been ordered to transfer them to Beauregard. Besides, every one thought the obstructions rendered it perfectly safe, but an all Wise Providence saw fit utterly to discomfit all the calculations of man. . . .

June 4
Wednesday
evening

Lila & I walked this morning at half past five with Fanny Hays to see where "the town" is. Nothing new was then on the bulletin [board], but during the morning the Misses Anderson called and told us a telegram had just arrived saying Beauregard had been compelled to fall back 46 miles from Corinth on the Memphis and Charleston RR on account of want of water. The artesian wells . . . [had] proved failures; also that Mrs. [Rose O'Neal] Greenhow had at last been released and sent to Richmond by flag of truce and she reports McClellan as very ill.

June 5
Thursday

Mrs. Villepigue & her sister also called and we have since learned that she is not a widow but her husband deserted her some time ago and went to New Orleans leaving her with six little children & she does [not] look more than thirty. Lizzie Burnet & Meta Deas came to see me this afternoon. I suppose for the next week or two we will have a number of visitors, and they do not mind coming during the heat of the day either.

June 6
Monday
[should
be 9]

A letter from Lizzie Smith a short time ago says she has taken the village school at Liberty Hill, where she is living with Sophie. Her father and brothers were much opposed to it at first but she, like myself, was very desirous of doing something for herself, especially in these times, and they at last consented that she should do so for a few months. It is exactly what I have always wished myself to be, a schoolmistress in a pleasant village among friends. The Parsonage is only next door to the Academy, so she has everything pleasantly arranged. . . .

. . . The James river has risen to an enormous height and is still rising & Richmond is partly flooded. It seems a very singular fact that, when almost every one of our important positions have been attacked this year, the floods have risen to an unprecedented height, enabling the yankee [*sic*] gunboats to come to our very doors, and often destroying our fortifications. Fort Donelson, Island No. 10, New Orleans, Fort Jackson, & Richmond would seem to show that the hand of God was against us, but our trust is in his goodness and mercy that he will not desert us in our great need. . . .

An exceedingly interesting letter from Dr. Josiah C. Nott has also been published written just before the evacuation of Corinth [Mississippi], and giving the many admirable reasons for it.[6] First, the want of water. From the very peculiar nature of the country . . . all the streams etc. seem to dry up and disappear from May to October, during which time the people are dependent on cisterns. But those could not supply our army a week, and both men and horses had been suffering fearfully. 2nd Because the enemy's position and entrenchments were stronger than ours, their guns of greater calibre, so that they could shell us at any moment, & they were in a region where the water was abundant and good, and provisions readily procured—while for fifty miles around ours, the

6   Josiah C. Nott (1804–73) was a leading southern physician and surgeon, most famous for his coauthorship with George R. Glidden of *Types of Mankind* . . . (1854). In this work, they attempted to prove that each of the different races of man stemmed not from a common origin but from a different fixed type. This book had a significant impact on proslavery thought.

country had been perfectly drained. Fort Pillow could be easily taken whenever the enemy seriously took it in hand; if our army was defeated there, it would be totally cut to pieces, & a prisoner had told them that [General Don Carlos] Buell thought he had them in such a position that he could "bag the whole." Again there was nothing left to fight for at Corinth, for the railroad east had been cut off and it [the evacuation] altogether would be the severest blow we could give the enemy. For, they had already twice refused Beauregard's offer of a battle, and, to follow us, they had to pass through a desolate region where they would be surrounded by enemies and be at a great distance from their supplies and gunboats. Beauregard had retired about thirty miles down the Mobile R.R. carrying off everything of value from Corinth—constant skirmishing still ensued.

We do not know whether Fort Pillow is really evacuated or not—one account says it is, another that the Federal bombardment there is more terrific than at Fort Jackson—The storm of shells being at the rate of *fifteen per minute.* . . .

Cousin Wm. DeS'[aussure] regiment had gone to James island where there were between 8 and 9000 men; the two first classes from the Citadel have also gone there. A breastwork of some kind is being erected in Meeting St. near the Circular Church. Edwin White was erecting a battery at Shepherdsboro before we left town & one battery is to be placed on our lot and another at Lawton's opposite, with obstructions between.

Saturday evening the telegraph announced that all the Yankees had left James I. so that we could now continue our work on the obstructions in the Stono.

We heard this evening that the most execrable wretch Picayune Butler [Benjamin F.], had been assassinated in New Orleans and rejoiced exceedingly at his righteous doom, but found it to be a mistake.

I commenced my school yesterday & have found John my greatest trouble, for he has got into an obstinate humor & will not do anything I wish. . . .

June 10
Tuesday

Hattie Shannon called this morning—The Camden ladies take the morning as the time for most fashionable visiting,

June 11
Wednesday

even in very hot weather, much to the dislike of all the Charlestonians and we have determined to carry out our much more agreeable custom of visiting always in the afternoon during the summer. Sue and I myself started this evening & met the girls in the street, so went to Uncle John's [DeSaussure] where we met grandmother, just come from cousin Sallie Boykin's and brought her home to stay with us. She told us of the most scandalous affair between Mr. Bull & Mr. A. H. Brown which occurred a few days ago; Mr. Bull went into Mr. Brown's office quite *drunk* to see him on business—got quarrelsome & very abusive; finally Mr. Brown gave him the lie, upon which he knocked him down & Mr. Brown stabbed him six times in the back & stomach very severely. Uncle James [Holmes] and cousin Louis [DeSaussure] have had to sit up with him—truly Rosa's cup of trouble seems overflowing. . . .

June 13
Friday
Tom [Heyward] brings news that [General John C.] Pemberton has stopped all the batteries being erected in the city and arrested Gen. [William Duncan] S.[mith] because he said another ought to be erected. This is certainly very singular behavior on Pemberton's part and, as he is a Pennsylvanian, engenders suspicion about him.

June 14
This afternoon [I] went to see Hattie Grant & staid to tea. She took me in to see her grandmother, Mrs. [Mary Cox] Chesnut, who is 86, & was one of the young girls who strewed flowers before Washington on his triumphal passage over Trenton bridge.[7] All her faculties are as active as ever, except hearing, which is completely gone, & they use a slate to converse with her. She has not a gray hair and her memory is remarkable. She is gouty and has been confined to her chamber about ten years, until this spring when they moved into town to be near the telegraph & news. She is small & her face quite pleasant & very smooth, showing but few wrinkles. She talks a great deal & most agreeably. She kissed me & invited me to come again. She is very fond of grandmother and aunt [Carrie] Blanding and was pleased to see me for their sake.

7 Mary C. Chesnut was the wife of James Chesnut, Sr. (of Mulberry), mother of Senator later Colonel James Chesnut, Jr., and mother-in-law of Mary Boykin Chesnut, the author of *A Diary from Dixie.*

Her husband is 88 and though he shows his great age more than she does, still bears his years well. Miss Sallie, their daughter is *"fair, fat and forty."*

Skirmishes of almost daily occurrences on James island. Lila is going to be confirmed & Lizzie Burnet also. I at one time thought I would present myself as a candidate but I do not feel sufficiently interested in the subject nor prepared and think the vows are too solemn to be taken lightly.

Mr. Elliott very kindly arranges so that he gives two of us seats in each turn of the carriage, both going to & from church, & other friends are also very kind in bringing us home. We are over a mile from church and the heat of the sun at midday is *intense*. We had a thunder storm in the afternoon, as we were returning, with hail a few miles off. Mr. [Thomas F.] Davis preached both morning & evening Confirmation. His manner is quite energetic and his sermons good and pointed &, though his voice is rather sepulchral and he sometimes drawls his words very much, on the whole I am agreeably disappointed, for I had anything but pleasant anticipations of his ministry. . . .

June 15

. . . Gen. Lee has telegraphed to [Gen. John C.] Pemberton to continue all the fortifications on Charleston and to defend it street by street to the last. It is also currently reported & believed that our idolized Beauregard has come on to inspect everything. I trust it may be true, for his presence alone will inspire that confidence which Pemberton fails to give. The latter ordered out the Cadets to James I. about ten days ago, whereupon Gen. [James] Jones head of the board of visitors writes to the President to know if they cannot be allowed to return to their studies. He said yes and immediately eighty of them left, enraged and mortified at the treatment received a second time. It is really very hard on them—at one time ordered to take to the field as men and soldiers, and the next moment treated as mere boys in a military academy. . . .

June 16
Monday

We learned today from good authority that Gen. [Sterling] Price has been ordered to Charleston, much to the general's joy, for he is next to Beauregard who has himself gone to the Peninsula. Lord Lyons has gone to England, quite a signifi-

June 18
Wednesday

cant fact, & it is generally reported at the North, as well as South, that France has recognized us. But I will wait for official confirmation before belief. The London correspondent of the New York *Times* says the distress in the manufacturing towns, Manchester particularly, is awful; after all the talk about India cotton, they find it cannot supply the place of ours, and that *cotton they must have in less than thirty days*. Many other facts tend to make us believe that our recognition is near at hand but from nothing but the most selfish interest on the part of England & France.

The Northern papers, even the N.Y. *Herald*, seem to recoil in horror from Butler's infamous proclamation, but to add tenfold insult to injury, swear it is a fabrication of Beauregard's. . . . Col. Wade Hampton was made Brig. Gen. at Chickahominy. I fear very much that he is not qualified for that high and responsible position, though he did very well as Col. . . .

June 19　. . . The accounts from the west state that Halleck did not know of the evacuation of Corinth for five days, so admirably was it managed. Then he actually raved with rage that his expected prey had so completely outgeneraled him. His lines were 27 miles in length & he thought he had Beauregard completely in his toils [*sic*]. It is not probable now that he will make any further movements for the present—at any rate, Bragg is there to give him "a little more grape." Gen. Price has fought thirteen battles, without losing one, & it is said that he says that the day on which they evacuated Corinth, when he commanded the rear-guard, "was the proudest of his life." The enemy are in possession of Memphis, after a brilliant & hardfought battle. . . .

. . . The Yankees have got nothing by the possession of Memphis, for all the cotton has been burnt [and] government stores & other valuable public property as well as a great deal of private, removed. . . . In fact, all that they will get is the pleasure of insulting the inhabitants. . . .

June 20　My little school does not progress very smoothly, for neither
Friday　of the boys are studious and give me a great deal of trouble—besides being very much spoiled & telling me "I will and I

won't" very frequently. . . . Today both lost their tempers, &
we had a most disagreeable & painful scene, at least, mother
did, for she had to punish them. But as she does not give me
any authority nor uphold me at the very point I most wish it—
viz—in making them study & recite their lessons over again if
they are missed, as they are daily, without reference to her, &
making them obey me implicitly in the school room—it will
not have any effect and it is a most unsatisfactory way of
teaching. . . .

. . . I am luxuriating in [John G.] Lockhart's *Memoirs of Sir*   *June 21*
Walter Scott and though I have long ago read almost all his
poems and novels, a new interest has been excited by finding
how most of the scenes, incidents & descriptions of scenery,
so vividly portrayed, have been drawn from his own life &
wanderings over his native land & that many of his most
unique characters were copies from life of various friends, or
persons met in his yearly rambles to the Trosachs [Trossachs].
The very time, cause, & scenes in which his immortal works
were composed, add intense interest, and it is altogether the
richest intellectual feast I have enjoyed for a long time. Besides, Mrs. Villepique has sent me the key to her bookcase,
which, though containing a most miscellaneous collection,
contains also many valuable standard works and biographies
and is a perfect treasure to me.

. . . Mr. [Edwin] White says [Sterling] Price is not in the city,   *June 22*
nor has he heard anything of his coming, but everybody has   *Monday*
lost confidence in [John C.] Pemberton and many even sus-   *[should*
pect treachery, though it cannot be proved of course. His   *be 23]*
affair with Gen. [William Duncan] Smith was: he ordered the
latter to build a certain battery, which Gen. S.[mith] said
would occasion great sacrifice of life, & if he still insisted on it,
he wished he would give him a written order. Whereupon
Gen. P.[emberton] said angrily "I believe I will arrest you, I
will arrest you, you may consider yourself under arrest."
Nothing further was said, & he was released before the day
was out.

The Capt. Smith of White's Battalion, who said he was a
U.S. officer and had been in forty battles, which last [point]

Jamie F.[urman] and I very much doubted at the time, has proved to be a man who kept a well known restaurant in the city. . . . How he could have so completely fooled the gentlemen for so long, I cannot imagine. He certainly is a very handsome, fine, military looking man & [has] very good manners, though when I saw him I told Jamie I did not think he had been *born* a *gentleman.* However, Tom Heyward says he was one of the best recruiting officers he has ever met, his manners are very plausible, & he seems to have a tact for persuading men to join. He fired at the gunboats at Dill's Bluff against orders & was arrested & then Mr. [Frederick C.] Schultze caught him in so many falsehoods that he was broken from his command & Mr. Schultze is now commanding. Mr. [Willie] Earle has returned to his company, as he told me he would probably do, disgusted with the Major [Edward White whom as I feared has been tippling a long time, adding to his natural irritability and imperiousness. . . . Dr. Morrow is quartermaster on [R. S.] Ripley's staff on the Chickahominy. . . .

June 26 Alester has proved so very unruly that mother has determined to send him to Mr. [Charles] H. Peck's tender mercies.[8]

We all walked this evening to see the Factory Pond, a most lovely sheet of water as clear and still as a mirror, and on one side the trees drop down from the hill touching the water and reflecting every leaf distinctly, while at our feet the rushing of the water through the floodgate formed a miniature cascade, the sound of which added another charm to the beauty of the little lake. It only needed a dark mass of cloud mountains to transport me to Loch Katrine, or some other which Scott has made immortal. I have been reading many of his poems again and enjoyed them much more now that I understood the personal allusions, etc.

Fighting commenced again today [June 25] on the Chickahominy.[9]

8 From 1859 to 1863 he conducted a semimilitary school in the Male (or Eastern) Academy.
9 This marked the beginning of the Seven Days Battle near Richmond, the culmination of McClellan's unsuccessful Peninsular Campaign.

The sad news of the last two days has brought sorrow and desolation to many homes and particularly among our friends and acquaintances. Gadsden Holmes has fallen on the field of the battle—a glorious death, but most overwhelming to his family who have scarce recovered the shock of Robert's sudden death. I fear his mother will not survive it. He was decidedly the flower of the flock, among the sons, and a most promising youth. His death has made me very sad and that of Mr. George Coffin added to it. His loss is as great to the public as to his family, for he was "the friend of the soldier, the orphan, the widow, the poor & needy—the philanthropist and Christian." He went to Virginia to see Eben [Coffin], was taken with dysentery & so ill that his wife went on to him and he died in Richmond. . . . The war is indeed coming home to the Charlestonians, who have scarce felt its horror before. . . . All the guns in Charleston and its vicinity were fired yesterday in honor of our victories [in Virginia]. Alas, we have scarcely the heart to rejoice, for our land is filled with mourning for the heroes who had shed their life-blood for its liberty. . . .

July 2
Wednesday

The tide of sorrow grows fearfully great—a telegram from Judge [Thomas J.] Withers[10] today announces the death of cousin Henry DeSaussure in Tuesday's battle—he the idolized son, brother, husband, and father of four little boys—it is too terrible. . . .

July 3
Thursday

Judge Withers has written Mary [DeSaussure] that he [Henry] fell Monday night, while gallantly leading his men to the charge. He had just cheered them on, when a bullet struck him in the head and, without a moment's pain, his soul winged its flight to his God. She is as unnaturally calm and has not shed a tear, has been at aunt Eliza's [DeSaussure]— poor girl, I fear the reaction when his body arrives—she has a sad and heavy responsibility left upon her and so young.

July 4

10 Thomas J. Withers (1804–65) was from 1846 to his death one of the common law judges who also sat on the South Carolina Court of Appeals. He was one of the six South Carolina delegates to the convention which organized the Confederacy and was a member of the Confederate Provisional Congress. He resigned his post to return to the bench.

July 5 I have given up John as a scholar, for he is so spoiled and unruly that he never said a good lesson. . . . Instead of finishing at twelve, my whole mornings were spent in hearing missed lessons three or four times over and running down to mother, who neither allowed me even the shadow of authority without which no one can teach properly, nor could she scarcely make him obey her, and not without punishment. . . . As besides I was subject to a continued stream of rudeness and impertinence, I concluded it was wasting my time, which could be much more profitably employed and not doing him any good. He & Alester are both dreadfully spoiled, but mother won't acknowledge that at all. I really am disappointed, for I was anxious to teach them and I know I was very patient and tried to explain and make their lessons as interesting as possible. But neither were inclined for study when the time came, though John especially was so anxious to have me teach him, begging me over and over before we left town to let him study with me. I shall now devote two hours every day to Eliza, who is studying French and reading French on the Study of Words and [Alexander F.] Tytler's Universal History. . . . No letters or papers for anybody tonight, because yesterday was the fourth. . . . Oscar Lieber, late State Geologist, has died of his wounds received in May. He was a noble man and died for his adopted state, while his renegade father, for very many years professor in S.C. College & who always pretended to be an ardent Southerner, and his two brothers, born here and named after some of our most distinguished men, are all fighting against us.

July 7 The paper this evening says the series of terrific battles, which had lasted a week [Seven Days' Campaign], seem to have ended Saturday evening. The enemy are thirty miles from the original battle field, and it is difficult to say exactly where they are, but (I sigh for some good pens) Jackson and Longstreet are pursuing them and will give a good account of them. The sum total seems to be that McClellan's Grand Army is totally routed *and the end is not yet.* . . . The victories have been signal and glorious, but dearly bought by the heavy sacrifice of the chivalry of the South, but there can be no nobler death bed for our loved ones than the battle field where they died for their country's liberty and their God. . . . Dan [DeSaussure] was expected today with cousin Henry's [DeSaussure] body, but instead came a telegraph "that on consultation, it was found impossible to move the body"—leaden coffins cannot now be procured—it is another distressing blow to the family. Mr. [Alfred] Brevard, the second lieutenant who has come home wounded in two or three places, says cousin H.[enry] went into battle as the *senior officer* of the left wing of the regiment, all the others having been previously killed or disabled. . . . Cousin Henry's name has already become a proverb of bravery in the regiment—whenever any man fought particularly bravely, they say *"he fights like Harry DeSaussure."*. . . A British steamer, the third recently, has just arrived in Charleston, laden with salt-petre, sulphur, coffee, etc. & *others expected*. The European powers are talking very strongly of immediate recognition and intervention—not that they care one iota for us, but because their own intensely selfish interest is pushing them to the wall—starving manufactures, revolts and commercial ruin is staring them in the face. The N.Y. *Herald* says two leading Powers have informed the U.S. that the war must cease immediately—which corroborates all our direct European news—from Mr. [John] Slidell. . . . The news from Va. today is not what we had hoped—prisoners say McClellan has been strongly reinforced by [James] Shields, and is now at Berkeley [Harrison's Landing] with between 80 and 100,000 men. Our generals give him the greatest credit for his skillful generalship, which has saved his army from total destruction by plunging it into the thick swamps and forests of that section of the country. . . . Though our men follow closely, it is almost impossible to find them, or, if they do make a stand, it is almost equally impossible for the regiments or even companies to fight to advantage, so lost and bewildered do they get in those dark ravines.

Have finished the *Life of Scott*, which I hope to own some day, as well as all his prose works—skimmed over *Dombey & Son* and *Gil Blas*, for the sake of the stories of which I had heard so much, am disappointed in the former & disgusted with the latter. . . . Oh, in these terrible days of doubt and suspense, we know not what to believe. One day Mrs. Beauregard is said

July 11
Friday

to be dead, the next day it is contradicted. "Personne" writes that Capt. [George] Cuthbert has had his arm amputated— then that is denied.[11] It is very singular that Beauregard's name is never mentioned anywhere, no one seems to know what has become of him, though it is generally reported that his health is so bad that he has retired for its renovation.

July 15
Tuesday

... Oh, I can scarcely write the too terrible news of Mr. [T.] Sumter Brownfield which gave me such a dreadful shock Sunday night. ... Dan [DeSaussure] has just come on and says he inquired for him and learned that a man answering to his description, and with a similar wound, from which it was impossible for him to recover, had died and was buried and that was all they knew of him—oh my God, can it be possible that he, that beloved, idolized brother and son, should have lingered through days of mortal agony, without mother, father, sisters or brother to soothe his dying bed and that he should have died and nothing known of him—a first lieutenant too, of so famous a company as the Palmetto Guard. It is awful to think of it. His death bed has haunted me ever since and the heart breaking misery of his family. I can scarcely write for the scalding tears which fall for him and all his family—had he but died on the battle field, without a moment's pain, like cousin Henry [DeSaussure], it would have been consolation. But to know that he is gone, disappeared and left no sign is misery unutterable. When sought for at the hospital and not found, he was reported missing—oh, that fearfully agonizing word—such depths of woe does it open to the stricken friends. And we were made so happy yesterday afternoon by a letter from brother Henry, announcing the birth of a little daughter "Caroline Pasteur" on the 6th. ...

July 18
Friday

... Wednesday Mamie Boykin paid us a long visit and told us a variety of interesting news from Va., Mr. [James] Chesnut

11 "Personne" was the pen name for Felix G. De Fontaine, who, according to historian J. Cutler Andrews, was one of the two best southern Civil War reporters. He appeared in Charleston in April, 1861, as a reporter for the New York *Herald* and, through his friendship with Beauregard, supplied the *Herald* with a report on Fort Sumter. He worked for the Charleston *Courier* as a reporter until the end of 1863 when he became editor and part owner of the Columbia *Daily South Carolinian*.

[Jr.] having lately come on. Gen. [Benjamin] Huger's command has been taken from him as the failure of the plan of capturing McClellan and his army is laid on his shoulders, his division having failed to take their appointed position, thus allowing the enemy a loophole for escape. It is generally believed that he drinks and that that is the cause that two or three times his troops have failed in the hour of need. Others, again, positively deny that but say that he is quite incompetent to manage so large a body of troops as a division, he having always been at the head of the ordnance department in the U.S. army and well qualified for that, but not for the command of troops in the field. . . . Willie writes that, a few days ago, René Beauregard told Willie Heyward that his father did not have a black hair in his head, both hair and beard being snow white and his face covered with wrinkles—so much has he been changed by ill health (which has compelled him to retire from the army for a time to recruit), by care and anxiety for the public welfare, as well as [by] his own domestic concerns. For his wife is still in New Orleans & been twice reported dead. René was unable to move her before the fall of the city, as was generally believed, as he found her very ill. . . .

Stonewall Jackson & Gen. D. H. Hill are brothers-in-law, their wives being daughters of a Presbyterian clergyman of N.C. & both generals are elders of the church.

Mr. [Edwin] White came up very unexpectedly today on a visit, Pemberton having given him a week furlough. Col. [Tom] Wagner is dead, after having suffered two amputations. Mr. W[hite] told us Walter Coachman had been very ill on James island with typhoid fever, but was better and a short time after the paper arrived with the invitation to his funeral. Poor Walter, he will be long mourned by all his friends, for of none can we say more truly "None knew thee, but to love thee, none named thee, but to praise." His very name was a synonym of all that was joyous and bright and loving—with our set of girls he was always an especial favorite—how Rutledge & Willie will grieve to hear of it. . . . What a sad return will it be to our dear old city when so many of those friends with whom we enjoyed the few bright intervals of pleasure of the last year have passed away.

July 19
Saturday

July 20
Sunday

. . . The idea of the battery on our lot was abandoned, but very heavy ones placed on Wappoo and the "grove of pines" at Lawton's. When Adj. Gen. [Samuel] Cooper came on to Charleston a short time ago, the first thing he ordered was that the second tier of casemates at Fort Sumter, which had hitherto been only fitted up as rooms, should be immediately fitted up for guns and some of the heavy ones captured at Chickahominy are to be sent for it. All the idle negro men in the city were impressed into service immediately, and the work has rapidly progressed. . . .

July 22
Tuesday

Mr. White spent this morning with us reading aloud Shelly & Tennyson. A letter from Rosa tonight gives a variety of news, most of it very bad. . . . Cousin Wilmot's [DeSaussure] daughter, Elouise . . . died . . . very suddenly after two days of . . . slight indisposition. Cousin Martha was alone in Pineville. . . . Mary Davie is really engaged to Major Edward McCrady. . . . I can not admire her choice. . . . I don't think he was half good enough for such a charming girl.

Rosa says also that our friend J. C. [John Colcock?] both drinks and gambles—camp habits I suppose. I sincerely grieve for it for his family's sake as well as his own—the consequences of this war are frightful in every way.

July 23
Wednesday

. . . Wed. evening I went round to see Hattie Grant, met Sallie & Essie Reynolds & Fanny Hays going in also. We spent the evening there &, as it rained, Hattie proposed that, instead of walking home in the wet, though we are just round the next street, I should stay and spend the night, which I did, after writing a note home. Only old Mr. & Mrs. [James] Chesnut [Sr.] & Miss Sallie C.[hesnut] live there, besides herself, and they all treated me so kindly and sociably that I felt quite at ease. I used to stand quite in awe of Hattie when I first knew her. I thought she was much older than myself and had heard so much of her talents and cultivation that if anyone had told me then that I would ever be on such sociable terms with her, I would have thought them daft. We had prayers soon after the others left & went to our chambers. Miss C[hesnut]'s opened from Hattie's and, after we were undressed, we sat and talked for more than an hour. Miss C.[hesnut] took me into her room to show me its arrangements, the house having been built expressly for her by her father and lately finished. Hattie had planned her own large comfortable room and dressing room, which are luxurious, yet tasty in everything....

Cousin Beck [Holmes] writes that many ladies are returning to town. The prices of provisions are enormous. Rice $4. *a bushel—grist $3.*—wheat flour 12½ cts per lb—molasses *$1. a quart*, sugar, common brown, 50 cts per lb—but in Richmond, they are frightful.

Carrie & myself started this morning at seven on a shopping expedition; after our walk of a mile & a half we found very few stores open and those that were had no one to serve us, negroes opening them. We met Dan [DeSaussure] just going to his office where we sat about a half hour, waiting for the stores to open. When they did, we could scarcely get anything we wanted & reached home quarter to ten, having walked about five miles. . . .

I have read lately an interesting *Life of Mrs. Siddon* by the poet [Thomas] Campbell; *The Siege of Florence* a graphic and well written tale of the troubled days of Michael Angelo [*sic*] & Machiavelli; *Tit for Tat, an answer to Dred* by a lady of New Orleans, a frightful picture of the slavery & barbarity practiced on the chimney-sweepers in England, as proved by the reports before the House of Commons in 1854; *Ramsey's History of South Carolina* with which I was delighted; & *Tales of the Irish Peasantry* by Mrs. L. C. Hall. I have given up teaching Eliza, as she took very little interest in her studies & was quite irregular and did not like it when I spoke to her of it.

. . . Mary Louisa [DeSaussure] went on to Richmond with cousin Wm. [DeSaussure] and is at a private boarding house at *$75 a month*, the cheapest there. Carrie & myself again went visiting this evening and staid to tea with Lizzie Burnet, the most pleasant evening I've spent there for a long time, no politics or other unpleasant subject having been broached by either her father or mother—she always avoids them. I have just finished *Incidents of Travel in Central America, Chiapas & Yucatan* by John L. Stephens, which gives an interesting account of the very remarkable ruins at Copán, Juirigua and Palenque. . . . Read also Gen. Waddy Thomson's *Recollections of Mexico*. . . .

July 29
Tuesday

August 2
Saturday

The Confederacy has lost one of its greatest theologians and most brilliant ornaments in Dr. [James H.] Thornwell, who died yesterday in Charlotte, N.C. of Typhoid Pneumonia. . . .

August 4
Monday

Took another four mile walk after breakfast this morning to shop, got some fine nice boy's socks for myself, to which I am going to knit tops while the other girls are doing the whole stockings themselves. . . .

Col. [James] Chesnut [Jr.], who was on the field with the President [May 31] says it [Seven Days' Campaign, Virginia] was the most terrific fighting the world has ever seen. Manassas was child's play to it and it [is] said that those two terrible days in which we lost Henry [DeSaussure] and Mr. Brownfield were just so much useless sacrifice of the best blood of the country, because [John B.] Magruder & [Benjamin] Huger did not bring up their forces in proper time to support them.

August 5
Tuesday

We are commencing our troubles with hired houses, from which we have been so free all our lives. We have been obliged to pay Mrs. Toomer six months rent $350 for six weeks stay in it, and we thought $375 for seven months for this house high and almost extravagant for us—indeed we could not have taken it but that the Harlestons and Mattie [Harleston] boarding with us. But, when mother sent Mrs. V.[illepigue] the monthly rent, $53, she said it was $75, which we could not understand, as Uncle John [DeSaussure] had distinctly written $375 for seven months. The matter was referred to him as the agent for both parties. He was sure he was right, as he had taken a memorandum as soon as he went home. But on examination, to his dismay, he found it was $75 a month, a most enormous rent, at the rate of $900 a year. Of course, it worries him very much. He tried to get her to compromise for $60, but she would not. . . . He wants mother to let him pay half of the extra $22, but mother is not willing, & I do not know how it will be settled. But it is a burning shame: such extortion from refugees & burnt out people. I do not know how we are to get along, and I am more than ever determined to try and get a situation as assistant teacher in Mrs. [Fanny]

McCandless' school, as I have been intending for some time. . . .

This evening's paper contains a letter from the President to Gen. Lee in regard to the way in which Gen. [John] Pope and his officers are to be considered and treated. Immediately after the cartel for a general exchange of prisoners had been signed, Maj. Gen. Pope issued an order to murder any of our peaceful inhabitants who were found engaged in tilling the farms to his rear & Steinwheir [Adolph von Steinwehr], one of his brigadier generals, has seized upon a number of innocent peaceful inhabitants to be kept as hostages in case any of his soldiers are killed by the guerillas [*sic*], whom he calls Bushwhackers. Besides, the U.S. Government have passed an act confiscating all rebel property, wherever found.[12] For these reasons, Gen. Pope & his officers, if captured, are not to be considered as prisoners of war or entitled to treatment as such, but as robbers and murderers. For the present, the privates will be treated as prisoners of war, but, if after this notice to the U.S., their barbarous practices are not put a stop to, we will be compelled to retaliate in full. Such is the tenor of the letter & I am delighted to see our government is at last trying to stop, most probably vainly, the frightful barbarities and enormities committed by the boasted "most civilized nation on the earth," deeds which would disgrace a savage.

An admirable and most just tribute to our ever lamented friend, Mr. [T.] Sumter Brownfield, appeared in today's *Courier* and a few days ago an editorial. The obituary was written by Captain [George] Cuthbert and did not contain a word too much or too little in his praise. Generally such notices are much too highly wrought, and I was glad that this was as simple and as manly as the character of him we mourn.

. . . Rosa writes she is enjoying herself very much, for besides W[illie] G[uerard], she sees a great deal of company, gentle-

August 6
Wednesday

12 The Second Confiscation Act was signed by Lincoln on July 17, 1862. Its terms called for persons convicted of treason to be punished by fine, imprisonment, or death. Those involved in "rebellion or insurrection" were subject to a fine, imprisonment, and loss of slaves. All property of Confederate government officials was declared confiscated immediately; others in the South were given sixty days warning.

men dropping in almost every evening. A French frigate has been at Charleston to take Monsieur St. André & his wife on to the North on a visit. The officers dined at Mr. Bull's with Mr. & Mrs. [Robert] Bunch, who spoke french very well, but neither Willie G[uerard] [n]or Rosa could, though they managed to keep up a kind of conversation with the Frenchmen, who did not speak English or very little, by a jumble of the two eked out by gestures. Mr. Bull understood nothing of French & thought by talking very loud and distinctly, as if they were deaf, they would understand. Rosa guessed at most they said, only she could not answer them. She says it was one of the most amusing scenes possible, & I can readily imagine it. She says none were fine looking men, all small & the Dr., a little fellow in a long blue swallow tail coat, almost killed her laughing. She knew the French were a polite nation, but her imagination had never conceived such bows & apologies. One young past [*sic*] midshipman, only twenty-four, had been all through the Crimean war. Before the vessel left, her father sent the boys in the boat with some melons & vegetables and in return they sent him a small bag of very fine coffee then wrote a note of thanks and called to say goodbye. I should like very much to have been down to enjoy meeting real Frenchmen and gentlemen.

August 11
Monday

The crews of the various privateersmen lately prisoners, have arrived in Charleston. We rejoice in the release of all, particularly of Johnnie H[arleston]. Mr. [Edwin] White writes he looks very badly, for his health has suffered from his long and rigorous confinement. All our men agree that their treatment has been most brutal & particularly where their guard have [been] Pennsylvania Dutchmen. At one fort, the majority of the guard having been sent away to reinforce McClellan, our men were ordered to do police duty and perform other degrading services & on their refusal they were heavily ironed till their release, their watches, money, and other private property taken from them and never returned. The ladies of Baltimore made up a supply of clothing, which was sent to the captain of the *Petrel*. . . . After his men were supplied, he gave the rest to Captain [Augustus A.] Gibson, their jailer, to distribute to the other privateersmen. But he coolly informed them he would give it to his own men or those of the Confederate prisoners who had been seduced into taking the oath of allegiance and, upon Mr. Henry A. Rowan of Charleston remonstrating with him, he put him into irons and close confinement. Our men declare they will never take a P. Dutchman prisoner after this, and they will suffer death before the horrors of a Northern prison again. The gallant Col. [Richard Thomas] Zarvona is heavily ironed and immured in a dungeon from which all light and air is excluded save by an auger hole about an inch in diameter, his dungeon being a casement from which he is never allowed to go out for an instant, he having once made an unsuccessful attempt to escape & his window closed up because he was found communicating with his fellow prisoners. His food is wretched and scanty, & he is neither allowed to receive the delicacies his friends send him nor the use of pen, ink or paper. He, however, contrived to write a few lines to President Davis, telling his situation & conveyed them to some of our men, and it has been published in the paper. He has been ten months a prisoner, and his health has suffered very much from the inhuman treatment. The U.S. Government refuse to give him up, "as he is neither a prisoner of war, nor a political one, but simply a disloyal citizen of Maryland." Such brutal treatment I had just read of in [George W.] Kendall's account of the Texan Santa Fe Expedition in 1841, of which he was one, or rather he accompanied the Texans merely with a view to their protection across the prairies, he being a Northerner on a journey to Mexico for health and pleasure. But the Mexicans chose to ignore his passport & letters & confound him with the Texans many of whom were gentlemen of the best families and education & yet they were all treated *almost exactly* as the Yankees treated our men, as the vilest criminals. But retribution will as surely come as there is a Heaven above us. . . .

This morning I went out to walk a little after five to the Factory Pond. The dewy freshness of the air was delicious— the only cool moments I have enjoyed for some time. . . .

. . . This evening, Mother, Sue, Carrie and I walked to the *August 13* Factory Pond. The water was so beautiful and the breeze so pleasant it made me think of our dear old home and [made me] rather homesick. . . .

August 15   . . . I have just "skimmed over" or, as Lord Bacon says, "tasted," *Stansbury's Survey of the Great Salt Lake* including a sketch of the Mormons, their religion and government. I was as much astonished at the wonder-working effects of the combination of those and how they had truly made the dreary wilderness "to blossom like the rose" in the short space of three years as I was at the account of the Lake, a vast inland Dead Sea, embosomed amidst barren rugged mountains, from which vast wildernesses stretch, often covered with an unbroken sheet of salt, like snow, and more than a half inch thick, capable of bearing the wagon trains. . . . Yet the next day after he crossed, it was dissolved into mud and water by a heavy rain. As the report consisted principally of geological terms and [an] account of the road to be taken over prairies, etc. and I had no map on which to trace the route, I found it generally uninteresting. I have also just read Lieut. A. W. Habersham's (Essie's [Reynolds] uncle I'm sure) *Last Trip to the Pacific, on the U.S. Surveying Expedition.* It is quite interesting. . . . When reading too, of their visit to Japan and Loo Choo, Dr. [James] M[orrow] was brought forcibly to mind.

August 16
Saturday   After April weather yesterday we are today enjoying a delightful autumn day—the sunshine warm and bright, the sky brilliant and the breeze bracing and invigorating, and as it sighs through the trees, their rustling affords a delicious contrast to the late "dead calm" of the "Ancient Mariner". . . . Carrie and I this afternoon called on Mrs. [Fanny] McCandless to inquire whether she needed an assistant in her school, but she said she could not tell—everything was so unsettled, she did not know whether it would be worth while to continue the school, and, if she did, she expected Miss [Lucy] Fisher and Miss [Hattie] Young, who have been with her a year or two, to continue. But should they make any change, she would let me know. We had a long and interesting conversation in regard to each other's views, and we agreed very well. I found her quite a pleasant sociable little lady. . . .

August 17
Sunday
evening   Mrs. Arthur's little daughter who died yesterday of diphtheria was buried this evening—the funeral taking place at the Episcopal church and that service being read instead of

the afternoon service. Then the minister gave an address—a very curious Camden custom. We did not go.

August 19

Mrs. [Henry M.] Hyams of New Orleans, the wife [of] the Lieut. Governor of the State, has rendered her name historic among Southern women, who have nobly avenged the insults of "Butler, the Beast." A few days ago, she was walking in the street and passed a group of Yankee officers, sitting in a doorway. One of them followed and stopped her saying that she had forgotten to bow and asked her if she remembered Butler's order No. 28 in regard to the treatment of Union officers. She attempted to pass him, when the vile wretch threw his arms around her and kissed her; as he released her from the loathsome embrace, she drew a pistol and shot him dead in all the flush of his insolence. Another sprang forward and exclaimed loud enough for all to hear that she must go with him to Butler. He called a cab, but instead of taking her to his "Den," he conveyed her beyond the lines into those of the Confederates and delivered himself to be treated as a prisoner of war or otherwise. He told her that her heroic deed was just, and his admiration made him resolve immediately that she should not be subjected to Butler's revenge. His name has not been published, but I hope will be that due honor may be given to almost the only spark of Christian humanity or the noble spirit of a *man* and *gentleman*, which has been exhibited in that army of fiends. . . .

August 20

Carrie received a letter today from Rosa filled with the saddest news—her grandmother, old Mrs. Robert Turnbull, nearly eighty years of age, has gone quite deranged, even to violence, from nervous excitement brought on by this unholiest of wars. . . . Mr. Bull and Dr. [John] Drayton have gone on a trip to the mountains in the buggy, for three weeks, Mr. B. says, and for his health, but everybody is sure he has gone to see Jane Fraser—"a fool's errand" but I think it will take many more "touches of prunella" to convince him that it is "Love's Labor Lost" for him to seek another wife.

Rosa sent me two photographs, one of poor Walter [Coachman], which does not do him justice at all, but Mr. [T. Sumter] Brownfield's is the *most speaking* one I've ever seen. It was taken just before he went to Virginia last year, I think, when he was looking remarkably well and handsome. It is so natural and the eyes particularly so good that he looks as if about to make some smiling remark. How vividly did it recall the happy past to gaze upon the features of these sad fated friends and how almost impossible to realize that their presence will never more bring a smile to the lip and a bright sparkle to the eye, but rather that their names will ever be cherished and consecrated by the unbidden tear—their monuments are in the hearts of their friends. . . .

August 22 The [Charleston] harbor defences are a complete success. A few days ago, a vessel was towed against the obstructions by three steamers & was unable either to break it, or cross. . . . James Island is considered impregnable. We have 15,000 men between Charleston and Savannah who can be readily and quickly concentrated. Gov. [Francis W.] Pickens, like the goose he is, wrote to the President that our generals had had a sufficient number of negroes all winter and had done nothing, so [John C.] Pemberton went on to see the President and brought on as many guns as we want, among others, 3 15 inch and eleven ten inch, some of those captured in the late battles. Mr. [Edwin] W.[hite] says one battery is in the Pines, another on Plum island and a third on the bend in Wappoo, all within sight and almost opposite "our home." Three vessels have run the blockade during the last fortnight, but prices are getting more exorbitant, even at auction, the Jews outbidding all others and setting up a quantity of little shops. Toothbrushes at *$2 each.*

August 25 . . . We nearly went into hysterics of laughter this evening,
Monday over a "declaration" which Lila has just received from Johnnie Mac. [DeSaussure]. I have seen a variety of love letter, but this surpasses all, even Mr. Bull's "Essays on Gardening." Though he is nineteen, he is dwarfed both in mind & body, but not in conceit,—a most striking contrast to Cousin Henry [DeSaussure], whose loss cannot be supplied by the sons who are left. Lila does not care for boys or their attentions and enjoys the fun as much as we do. I composed the answer for her, the whole affair is "food for mirth" for many a day. . . . Jack [Kershaw] told Alester of a very severe fall our dear Rutledge

had the day before they started. His spur got entangled in his bridle, and, in his effort to disentangle it, he accidently spurred his horse, which reared up and fell back with him, striking the back of his head very severely on the very hard road, while the horse rolled over his legs. The men immediately cut the bridle & released the horse, but Jack who saw it says Rutledge had a regular convulsion or fit; cold water revived him but he could scarcely stand when he got up. He laid down in a house nearby for about two hours, then said he felt well and insisted on going on with the brigade, which was on its march for Hanover, C[ourt] H[ouse] [Virginia]. It makes me feel right anxious about him, for he had just before been sick for several days. A letter from DeS [Garden] dated Saltillo Miss. says he is with [Sterling] Price. . . . He has no confidence in Price as he does not think him anything of a soldier and laughs at me very much for what he calls "my blind admiration of the humbug." Uncle Ta [Gibbes] and himself both have strong faith in [Braxton] Bragg. . . . I have recently finished reading an interesting Life of Com. [Stephen] Decatur & Vincent Nolte's *Fifty Years in Both Hemispheres* one of the most interesting autobiographies I've ever read. It is like "a peep behind the scenes" of most of the great public events of his time, particularly regarding Napoleon. Nolte was a volunteer at the Battle of New Orleans and gives a graphic description & was on the first steamer which Fulton succeeded in carrying from New York to Albany. In fact though his own life did not contain any very remarkable events, save as connected with the times—being a series of failures . . . yet the scenes of which he was a witness form a brilliant panorama. . . .

I suffered so much from toothache last night that this morning I borrowed cousin Sarah's [Elliott] carriage and called for Uncle Louis [DeSaussure] to go with me to Dr. [M. W.] Bissel, who has been practicing for many years in Beaufort. I expected to take chloroform, as I knew the tooth was such a shell that it would break to pieces, but he had none and I had to try it without. It broke as I expected, and he had a good deal of trouble in getting it out, having to make six or seven attempts. He was very kind and gentle and considerate towards my nervousness, though I suffered more from the expecta-

August 29
Friday

tion of pain than the reality. I felt quite ashamed of my nervousness, but Uncle Louis gives me quite the credit of a heroine. . . .

We met several of the family shopping, and everybody had the same cry, "Our money won't pass," it being mostly in Confederate bills at $10, 20 or 50, which have been lately counterfeited to an enormous amount by the despicable Yankee, *authorized by their government*, for the purpose of destroying our currency and bringing ruin and destruction in our nation, as they cannot do it in any other way. Mr. [John] Harleston wrote to say that two of the Columbia banks found that they each had $10,000 in counterfeit of $20, 50 & 100—so everybody is afraid to take them. Our government has taken steps immediately towards calling in those issues and making different ones, but, in the meantime, it occasions a good deal of trouble & distress, particularly as bills of small change are almost as scarce as silver. If no other instance of their depravity were known, this contemptible low trick would proclaim a Yankee anywhere and proves them as "foemen unworthy our steel."

September 1
Monday

. . . Mr. [Thomas] Girardeau's affair is one of the most disgraceful intrigues I've ever heard of. Before he was married, he used to live with Mr. & Mrs. Henry Lucas; he a brother of Maj. J. J. Lucas and she was a Miss Magwood. Her husband has been gone to the wars so long that when she gave birth to an infant lately, suspicion was aroused and fell on Mr. G[irardeau], though a minister of the Gospel & himself a married man with one child & his wife about to give birth to another. He confessed everything & that this has been carried on for *four years*. His wife is indeed to be sincerely pitied, but for Mr. L[ucas] I think death in battle would be a blessing rather than to return to a dishonored home—the mother's awful sin will ever rest on the innocent little children—it is fearful to think of such crime. Mother has at last sent John to school to Mr. [Charles H.] Peck, much to my satisfaction.

September 2
Tuesday

The telegraph announces officially another great victory at Manassas [August 29–30]. . . . I have never before felt such a dread of seeing the list of killed and wounded. All that I heard today contributed to depress me. Mary Boykin came to see us, just from Columbia, and says Beauregard's nephew, Proctor . . . has left the Arsenal, and said James B.[eauregard] had received a letter from his family saying his father was deranged. I felt as if it had happened to a personal friend. But this evening's paper says he has been assigned to the command of Charleston and will soon be there, which completely puzzled us, until some one said that the mistake must have arisen from Proctor's saying that his uncle must be crazy to have written the letter he did to Maj. [J. F.] Thomas about him. Gen. B[eauregard] thought the Arsenal was conducted on the same principle as West Point, where leaving without a regular discharge is desertion and punishable with death. . . . He wrote to Maj. T.[homas] to put Proctor in irons and send him to Fort Sumter, and, if he still proved unmanageable, to shoot him. A Spartan example, to check other insubordination, but powerless in this case. The Arsenal Cadets have been very rebellious, breaking all kind of rules. Some have been expelled and others left and joined the Cadet Rangers. . . . Then [too] Sallie [Bull] & Lilly [DeSaussure] are going on outrageously—encouraging those cadets who jumped out the windows to go to the theatre with them. . . . One night while there the boys received a note saying they were discovered and expelled and had to leave the girls & go to the Arsenal. The latter would have been in a considerable dilemma but for James. Then [too] they [Sallie and Lilly] have taken to *rouging* & Sallie won't submit even to her grandfather's control. I had hoped so much from his firm but gentle authority, and cousin E.[liza DeSaussure] says, since Sallie came, she cannot manage Lilly. It makes me too sad to see such young girls going to ruin, & Sallie has the element of such a fine character, but her father's overindulgence has already caused many a heart ache to her friends.

. . . The story about Beauregard's derangement turns out to be "the three black crows." Proctor [Beauregard] was speaking in French to Mary Preston with whom Mamie B.[oykin] was staying & she misunderstood him. . . . We read a letter from uncle Ta today, written [August 20] from Chattanooga, the night before Bragg's army left. He says they are 55,000

September 4
Thursday

strong, and destined for Tennessee, Kentucky & the enemy's country, and that "they may be annihilated, but *never conquered"*. . . .

. . . Saturday evening Sue & I went to aunt Eliza's [DeSaussure] and staid to tea—while there, Mac and Douglas [De-Saussure] came in rather unexpectedly, he looking so fat and well, and wearing a little beard, that I did not recognize him till he came near. . . . Douglas conversed most of the time with uncle John & Louis about the war and was very eloquent. It was delightful to hear him speak of our army in Va.—the hatless, shoeless, shirtless, ragged men who had achieved such great deeds. He said he had heard nothing of the 20 or 40,000 men said to be sent or about to be, to defend Charleston, and did not believe it, for there are none to go—all the new troops, conscripts, being sent off to Va. as fast as they are prepared.

[Alfred] Rhett's duel with Vanderhorst was on account of an insolently contemptuous speech about Col. [Ransom] Calhoun, his superior officer. . . . The first shots missed—at the second, V.[anderhorst] aimed at Rhett's heart, and the latter fired into the air. He had no personal difference with V[anderhorst] with whose family he is connected by his sister's marriage, but all his insolence and arrogance have been directed against Calhoun, about whom he has made many insulting speeches. This has been going on for two months, but the affair was to have been settled after the war. The first duel, however, brought on the second, which terminated so fatally. Col. Calhoun has known, as well as many others, for some time past, that Rhett has been practicing constantly with a pistol for the express purpose. The Rhetts have been hitherto hated enough, now the name is almost execrated—the public are almost unanimous against him. Duelling is expressly against the rules of war & the penalty very severe, and it is universally hoped that he will be arrested, court-martialed and broken of his commission. We hear that Pemberton has arrested all parties and that it will go very hard with them. . . .

My heart grows sick and sad at the fearful array of killed and wounded which comes slowly in. . . . Old Charleston mourns her gallant dead at each new battle.

Thursday evening I took tea at Dan's [DeSaussure] . . . but both Douglas [DeSaussure] and herself [his wife] were very grave and silent—everything is so changed since the happy days I spent there in '54. . . . It was the first time Douglas and I have met there since and, when I thought of the change in him and the cause and the changes generally, it made me very sad. The innocence and unsophistication of early youth, with its frankness and confidence in the truth and sincerity of all, can never return but must bring sadness at the thought of how "the world," which then seemed "couleur du rose," was gradually revealed in its true colors. Then I stood on the threshold of life, not yet sixteen, a merry unsuspicious child in everything relating to "the world," that gay realization of dreamland. But my awakening has been bitter, as I suppose has been the experience of most girls. Whether I have profited by its lessons, I scarcely know. I have sometimes doubted the faith and sincerity of all.

Last week I was dreadfully homesick "for the old familiar haunts and faces." Here we feel "we are strangers in a strange land," for though we are surrounded by neighbors and acquaintances, they do not seek us sociably to walk or ride in the afternoons or come over to see us after tea. They pay pleasant afternoon or morning visits at very rare intervals, then we are left to our own resources and loneliness. And it is in the afternoons and at night that we particularly miss our home friends. If we go out to walk, we find a disagreeable sandy uneven road and scarcely ever meet an acquaintance to enliven the way. But the girls here go to ride or walk constantly with one another.

Willie came up Saturday morning to spend a few days furlough with us and "capped the climax" when he inquired of mother what her plans were for the winter. . . . She said that, even if we could return to the city, she might remain here, as being more economical—and I have just been living in hopes of our return from this exile in January. . . . I should like much to know why Mr. W.[illington] let a sketch of Col. Ransom Calhoun's life appear in Saturday's paper.[13] . . . I learned

---

13 Aaron S. Willington died on February 2, 1862, as noted in the diary entry for that date. He left no son.

for the first time that he was a graduate of West Point & had since then devoted part of his time to military affairs, before going with Mr. [James M.] Mason to Paris[14] as Secretary of Legation, & that there he had also taken pains to improve himself. He had resigned his position on account of ill health (the climate not agreeing with him) a month before the duel & was on furlough. He had requested to be sent to Virginia, and Willie says was considered such a fine officer that he was soon to be promoted to Brig. Gen.—though unfortunately he did drink, as so many of our officers most unhappily for themselves & country do. It was not a regular habit, and he only frolicked at times. . . . Mr. Howe read his funeral service, and he was buried in St. Philip's Churchyard near, I suppose, to his uncle, the great John C. [Calhoun]. Mr. Howe next day preached a very impressive sermon on the subject. The Rhetts will indeed be execrated and hated. . . . Lee's army, instead of attacking either Washington or Baltimore, though our lines extended within ten or fifteen miles of the latter, has pushed forward into Pennsylvania in the very heart of abolitiondom. They were forbidden on pain of death to take or destroy anything in Maryland. . . . But our men swear that every acre of ground that they visit in Yankee land shall be devastated & left desolate and that all the horrors of war which we have suffered shall be returned ten fold on their own heads. . . .

September 18
Thursday

Day of Thanksgiving for our recent victories appointed by President. Willie left this morning & we were all up & dressed by half past four to bid him good-bye. It was worth getting up so early merely to see the stars in all their magnificence. Mars the evening star was setting in the west, Orion & Sirius in the south and Venus, the morning star, rising in the east—all sparkling with the intensest brilliancy—each a "Kooh-i-nor" [Koh-i-Nûr][15] in the pure expanse of azure while the moon shed its soft radiance over all—then the gradual fading away

14 Mason was stationed in Great Britain not France.
15 Koh-i-Nûr, meaning "mountain of light," is a large diamond originally owned by the Mogul conquerors of India. In 1849 it came into the possession of Queen Victoria of England. India and Pakistan have both recently demanded its return.

of those beautiful angel's eyes before the dawn; and we watched the rise of Venus, till its glory was eclipsed by that of the sun. Oh, how many exquisite pleasures are lost by those who prefer bed and a morning nap to the freshness and beauty of nature. The dew prevented me from going to walk, and I could only wish for the ride on horseback, which we saw the Misses Young taking later, so we contented ourselves by sitting in the piazza and knitting while we watched the sun rise. I knit half the leg of a soldier's stocking, and I could not but reflect on the various changes produced by the war. A year ago we were just learning to knit socks—but we never thought we should so value time as to be knitting before it was light enough for us to see the stitches, instead of going back to bed.

Robert Wilson read the service, very well and impressively—his intonations are very good. It is the first time I have heard him & how it recalled the days of childhood, when I knew him well—he is only a few months older than myself, but looks thirty and is so in manners. The Bishop [Thomas F. Davis] was present, & Mr. [Thomas F.] Davis [Jr.] preached. I was disappointed in the commencement of his sermon in which he merely gave a slight sketch of the position and deeds of our armies two months ago and now, showing it was entirely owing to grace of God, as acknowledged by our generals, that we have been so successful in driving back our foe. But I could not help thinking how much more interesting, to me at least, Mr. Howe would have made the subject, for I think all his thanksgiving and war sermons have been particularly fine. Mr. D[avis]'s unfortunate delivery, to me, detracts much the interest of his sermons. One moment he drawls a word to its utmost extent, as if seeking what word he shall use next, then that is brought out with a jerk, as from the depths. Uncle Louis thinks him remarkably eloquent & a mind probably superior to Dr. [James H.] Thornwell's, but he is just the opposite of my idea of eloquence. . . . Mr. Howe is my favorite minister, and I think him eloquent when "his spirit deep is stirred within him" by such an occasion as this—however, Mr. Davis ended with an admirable address on duelling, strong, earnest and sinking deeply into every one's heart. A collection was taken up at all the churches today for our sick and wounded soldiers in Virginia, by request of. Rev. Robert Barnwell, who has been their "guardian angel"....

September 19
Friday

I spent the morning with cousin Sue [Screven].... She says the city [Charleston] looks deserted—she was the only person in Water St. & only three or four families in Meeting St.— food enormously high—chickens a *dollar and a half apiece*— eggs 10 cents apiece & a ten cent loaf (for five cent ones are now unknown) gave six thin slices—for all that, it is home, and I cant [*sic*] help yearning to go down, if even only on a visit. It will be very dreary for us here this winter, when cousin Sarah's [Elliott] family go to their plantation in Sumter, "Miss Nannie" & Mattie [Harleston] go down, the Chesnuts go to their plantation, the Burnets probably move two miles down into Camden, and the Gatewoods also go farther into town— however, I am going to try and produce sociability by a reading club next month. The girls to whom we have mentioned it seem delighted at the idea....

September 20
Saturday

I have just finished reading *Cinq Mars* par Le Comte Alfred de Vigny—the best French book I've ever read. It is one of the most graphic-historical novels I have ever read by any author. The style is excellent, so natural and vigorous—in decided contrast to French literature generally—for I think both prose & plays are generally written in the most exaggerated, sentimental, theatrical style—everything seems bedecked with tinsel, ornament—but this is "life in earnest" each character is in bold strong relief, and so "individual" that you feel as if you had lived and moved among them, and withal, the truth of history is admirably preserved. It is an intellectual treat and, when I finished it, the tears were in my eyes, and I felt as if I had lost personal friends in Cinq Mars and the "sublime" de Thou. The scenes are all so graphic, particularly those in which Richelieu mingles, that, could I draw, I am sure I could reproduce them vividly, at least if my skill was equal to my fancy. A few days ago, I re-read *Rutledge* and was more delighted with it than at first—though I liked it then—the characters are all admirably drawn and well carried out. "Rutledge" is my ideal of the man I would marry— intellectual, kind-hearted & so tender and loving to the wayward, impulsive heroine, who, singular to say, has no name. I sympathized with her very much, for I think her character *very natural*, and I am sure I should have done the same under similar circumstances. But in Arthur Rutledge there is that indefinable "something" which makes you feel you have met a master spirit, such a one, as *even I* should love to obey—to feel that it would be a pleasure to do his wishes—one whom I could reverence as a superior, yet love devotedly—one, too, who should open "the temple of his inner heart" to me alone, that the cold outer world should never know the depths of tenderness hid therein. How natural are those delicious "library scenes"—I felt their truth. Some one, I forget who, objects to the word *tender* as applied to a man—but I love it, for it conveys a world of meaning—far beyond *loving*. I always think of Miss [Dinah Maria Mulock] Muloch's most beautiful lines "Mine to the core of the heart, my Beauty" and "Douglas, Douglas, *tender* and *true*". . . .

All our club, except Charlotte B[oykin] met here to discuss the arrangement we agreed upon: Tuesday from 12¼ to 2¼ & Saturday from nine to eleven, as the Gatewoods teach their younger sisters. We are all anxious to read the *Partisan Ranger* by Judge Beverly Tucker of Va. written thirty years ago, but prophetic of the leading events of this war, but as we cannot procure it yet, in the meantime we will read I think *Border War* a tale of a similar kind. I do not think this club will be near as pleasant as any of our former ones, but it will serve as a source of interest to the girls of the neighborhood. This evening's paper announces another terrific battle [Antietam] at Sharpsburg, Md. in which the strength of both armies were engaged. It took place on the 17th and is the most dreadful battle of the war. The loss on both sides [was] very great, ours about 5000, the enemy's much greater, but the advantage was decidedly on our side.[16]. . .

September 23
Tuesday
afternoon

This afternoon Carrie, Mrs. H.[arleston], Lila & I went on a journey of discovery down in Camden in search of some spin-

September 24
Wednesday

16 Union losses were 12,410; Confederate losses 13,724. This battle convinced Great Britain not to intervene on the Confederate side and provided the occasion for Lincoln's Emancipation Proclamation.

ners of cotton & silk yarn for gloves; at one house we saw an old woman 94 years old who told me she remembered the first revolution and the declaration of peace as distinctly as if it occurred yesterday. She is quite deaf, but her eyesight very good, & she can card, knit and sew very nicely on fine cross-bar muslin, for she showed me some of her work. We did not get home till quite late. . . .

September 27
Saturday

Our club met and commenced to read *Border War*. Charlotte [Boykin] reads delightfully—her voice is so musical & so expressive in its intonations—her face equally interesting in its constant changes. . . .

September 29

. . . Johnnie C[olcock] came to pay us a morning visit & asked Lila & myself to go to walk with him, which we did in the afternoon to the factory-pond. The clouds were magnificent and we sat watching them till they faded into dark grey masses, when Fanny Hays & sister F[anny] joined us. They returned to tea and as I had sent for Johnnie's violin we had some delightful music from Lila and himself. They did not leave till near eleven, quite a piece of dissipation for Camden. . . .

October 1
Wednesday

I came over to Sumter. . . . Mr. [Albert] Walker escorted me here, & I was warmly welcomed by Fan [Garden], who was just dressed for a ride on horseback & was really a beauty, with her hair cut short & curling off from her brow & a sort of tiara-shaped cap of black velvet and a palmetto interwoven. . . .

Lincoln's [Emancipation] proclamation, which has just appeared, announcing freedom to all slaves after Jan. 1st, 1863 and inciting them to insurrection, has been answered by our Congress with another, proclaiming that after the same date, all officers captured, whether commissioned or non-commissioned, shall be put to "hard labor," either in prison or otherwise; and of the enemy captured on Southern soil shall be considered as inciters, aiders and abettors of servile insurrection, and as such shall be hung—it is certainly full time that the severest retaliatory measures should be taken. It was only a few weeks ago that a plot of insurrection was discovered among the negroes in the upper part of this district—it was very weak and ill-arranged and was confessed by one of them. A number were put into jail and are to be hung this week.

Friday morning we went with Eliza Cooper, Fan's intimate friend, at daylight to the depot to provide the soldiers with refreshments. About a dozen other ladies were there, with most tempting looking waiters, but there were no soldiers & we heard they were forbidden to come this way on account of the fever at Wilmington [N.C.]. So next day no one went & a number of famished soldiers were begging for food. The ladies here have been devoting themselves to this "heaven born charity" for months, and they say they have been more than repaid for their exertions by the unbounded gratitude of the soldiers, who are almost all from other states; our troops always taking the other roads. The soldiers say there is no state in which they are treated so generously as our own beloved South Carolina. . . .

. . . Got letters; mine contained one from Lizzie Greene, one from Rosa and another from Carrie, which gave me "the blues" badly for a time. Mr. White has just been there and urged their marriage, which has been settled for Nov. 12— just a month, and of course she will have so much to do that I must shorten my visit. . . . Then, too she will leave us, and I will miss her dreadfully—our prospects for the winter were dreary enough without this. . . .

October 9
Thursday

Yesterday Caesar, the faithful servant of Lieut. [Sam] Pringle, who arrived a few days ago, came round to see aunt Lizzie [Garden]. He is quite an intelligent man, very respectful and perfectly devoted to Hugh, who he says was always like a brother to his "Mas Sam." I have been quite interested in the account of this young man, the youngest and darling of his family, and his bright, gay disposition made him a general favorite. Hugh speaks of him in the highest and most affectionate terms as a noble christian soldier and patriot. Caesar gave us the particulars of his [Lt. Pringle's] sad death—he was taken to Winchester [Virginia] to the house of Mrs. Lee, sister of Mrs. Rose Greenhow who was staying there and with their daughters nursed and tended him as kindly as if they

October 14
Tuesday

were his mother & sisters. The young ladies would not allow a servant to make his nourishment but cooked all with their own hands. After the amputation, fair hopes were entertained of his recovery by his friends, though he himself would often tell Cesar [*sic*] that he knew he was going to die, but he was prepared and willing. He would laugh and chat gaily with the ladies, enjoying their society very much, but when alone with his favorite servant, who never left him, he would speak of his approaching end. At last, secondary hemorrage [*sic*] took place &, though a physician was immediately sent for, one could not be procured for some time, and, [when] he came, it was too late. Nature could not rally from this fearful exhaustion, and he died the next day in Caesar's arms as quietly as an infant going to sleep; so gently that Caesar could not believe it for a little while.

Five minutes by the watch before he died, he feebly traced a letter to Hugh [Garden] saying that, after Caesar had been home for two months to rest, he was to return to camp to wait on him and the mess of which he is so proud and so thoroughly identified. Caesar has been with them ever since they first went into service on Morris island—and most devoted has he been to their interests. He always speaks of them as "our mess, our battery, our division, etc." as if he was a soldier himself, yet so respectful and so entirely without that pomposity which is so apt to characterize the negroes who have been traveling and to the wars. On his return home and meeting his master's family he fainted, overcome partly by emotion & partly from the fatigue and exhaustion of nursing. A few years ago, one of his brothers was sold to a gentleman out west, and, after one of the late battles, hearing great weeping and lamentation of the field, he went to see what it was & found his brother mourning over the dead body of his young master—would that we had many more Caesars. He gave us quite cheering accounts of the conditions of Hugh's company, at least for shoes and clothing—he says they are well supplied with both, only one man being barefooted & his were lost through carelessness. But he explains why they are so often barefooted. On the march, their feet get so heated that they slit the shoes for air, and these repeated slittings, together with the rocky roads, soon cut the shoes to pieces.

They were also well off for provisions, for, if there was any to be had, Caesar would get it for them, so they write, for he was very modest. In Maryland when the soldiers could not get anything from the Unionists with Confederate money, it was only necessary for "the colors" or "boys of color," as he called them, to put on citizens dress, and they could readily buy. He picked up some U.S. money on the battle field and made it go a great way. The Unionists showed their anger in every way—some of Hugh's company amused themselves by saluting politely the Union ladies & speaking to them. . . . In return they abused them and stamped their feet at them. One young man offered them some apples, which were taken, but only to pelt him with them. Some of them ridiculed & sneered at our soldiers for being barefooted, comparing them with the well clothed Yankees. Mr. Hill, the same fun-loving man, answered very politely that the reason was they had their shoes off when the Yankees commenced to run & run [*sic*] so fast that our men did not have time to stop and put them on while pursuing them. Caesar said "that bunch of them had enough, they went in and shut the door, and I guess they telegraphed to the other side of the street to let us alone, for none of the others troubled us." He also observed "that there was as much difference between those Union people, *who called themselves ladies*, and our Southern ladies, as if they were of another color."

A most delightful autumn day. Mr. [Albert] Walker read prayers remarkably well and Mr. [Thomas F.] Davis [Jr.] gave us an admirable sermon on the "opening of the sixth seal." Mr. Walker preached in the afternoon, for the first time before Mary [Boone, his fiancee] and this congregation, and, though he gave us a beautiful sermon on the text "Peace I give unto you; my peace I leave unto you" and his delivery was graceful, the words flowing smoothly and his intonations remarkably good and impressive, he was so agitated that we were all sorry for him—his quick, hard breathing could be heard by all around him. Everybody was pleased, however—I was very much so. He has a very pleasant face and looks particularly well in his black gown. He preaches alternately at Sumter & Bradford Springs. . . . I told the B[rownfield]s to-

October 19
Sunday
morning

day about Hattie Grant's peculiar behavior latterly, having at first sought me in the most friendly manner then neglected me altogether. They said that was her character, fickle as the wind. I had thought she was a sincere friend, but she may rest in peace now. . . .

October 20
Camden

. . . [We attended] a public meeting to form a Soldier's Aid Society, but found only [six persons] . . . so nothing was done but to appoint a committee to go round for subscriptions & Col. M[oses] of course had to say *something*—his remarks affording us much amusement. We went subscription afterwards, rather unsuccessfully. . . . [The next day] we got up between three & four to dress, then had to wait a long time for daylight sufficient to appear for it to be proper for us to walk to the depot, even with a servant. I was agreeably surprised by meeting James Barnwell on the cars, on his return from Wilmington [N.C.]. . . . On my way to the Camden car, met Dan [DeSaussure] & Major E. McCrady, both coming here, and saw Mary Caldwell on the Charleston cars—how pleasant it was to see a familiar face from our city home. . . . Mr. [John] Harleston, I also met on the cars, coming to take his family to Columbia, as he is not willing for them to go to the low country and has procured rooms. . . . When I got home, I found I was not expected as mother had written me not to hurry home. But I did not receive the letter. I am very glad, however, that I came, for Mary Jane & Hattie [White] are coming up this week to stay with us. Uncle James [Holmes] and cousin Beck [Holmes] are coming to the wedding & perhaps cousin Willie also—we hope for Willie and Edward, but I fear they will not be able to come. All our friends here have been very kind in their offers of assistance on the occasion, knowing that, as burnt out refugees, we are ill provided with many necessary things. . . .

October 21
Tuesday

. . . The celebrated "No. 290" now the *Alabama*, under the gallant [Raphael] Semmes, is again making his name a terror to the Yankees—having already destroyed fourteen merchant ships and whalers of over $1,000,000 by their own account, and they acknowledge that they have no vessel which can compete with her. . . .

... This closes a busy week, employed in mantua-making—remaking old dresses, etc. varied by visitors and afternoon walks. ...

Nanna [Hughes] & I wrote the invitations to the wedding; only to the heads of families on both sides, and a few particularly intimate cousins—besides, Mary W.[alker] and Mary Lang Boykin were invited as the latter's mother has been particularly kind to us as refugees, yet without being at all acquainted. Charlotte B.[oykin] and Lizzie Burnet were also invited. ...

This week was again most busily occupied with making the wedding dress, which was swiss muslin with three flounces, infant waist and thread lace trimming, & altering dresses, Mary J.[ane], Hattie [White] & myself each being engaged in that delightful occupation, besides making a boddice [*sic*] to my brown silk, to wear as my wedding dress.

[The day] was bitter cold. Early in the morning, the frost lay like snow, but the warm sunshine made it pleasant going to church—but last Sunday evening was so warm that we took tea in the moonlight in the piazza. Carrie went to church both morning & evening. Rev. John Elliott read prayers in the afternoon.

On Friday 1st, mother received a letter of twelve pages from brother Henry, dated Tenn. they having just recrossed the mountains. His company was in the battle of Richmond, Ky. [August 29–30, 1862] and received the credit from Maj. Brown, chief of Gen. Kirby Smith's staff, of winning that battle by enabling our forces to outflank the enemy.[17] ... Brother H.[enry] said once, in sighting his gun, it was struck and he felt the splatter of lead in his face, but escaped unhurt—he is still only sergeant, though acting surgeon also. The medical department refused to commission him as a surgeon to the company, as it is too small. During the retreat from Kentucky, he went through some of the experience of our troops in Virginia—suffering from cold & the snow on their weary marches, often both night and day. At one time they did not

17 This was part of Kirby Smith's August–September invasion of Kentucky.

see their wagons for ten days, and a cup of flour, scarcely a pint, was served to each man and lasted seven days; again they had plenty of good beef, but wanted bread, so punched holes in a tin plate and grated corn on it, husk and all, then with a little water made into "journey or johnny cake" and baked it on a stone. He ends by saying they are ordered to Cumberland Gap, where they expect to winter, or rather to bury the majority of the Florida brigade, now reduced to the size of a regiment. Most of the men are those who went to Florida for their health and are unable to stand such a severe climate. . . .

November 11
Tuesday

We arranged the drawing room & bridal chamber, and in the afternoon I went with uncle James [Holmes] to visit his old friends—Col. [James] Chesnut [Sr.]. Forty-three years ago Uncle James came here, a young married man, to practice law; Mrs. [Mary Chesnut] Reynolds was then a beautiful girl of fourteen & they had not met since till now, when she has five daughters and four grandsons. . . .

November 12
Wednesday
morning

. . . None of us here felt as if we were preparing for a wedding, it only seemed like arranging for a little party. Carrie herself was just as usual, only all of us felt rather sad at the absence of "our boys" and the illness of dear aunt Carrie Blanding. She was very ill Tuesday night and still so very sick on the wedding night, that Uncle Louis and Aunt Jane [De-Saussure] returned home soon after the ceremony. Uncle John [DeSaussure], too, had just gone on for cousin Henry's [DeSaussure] body & Douglas [DeSaussure] has just lost his little daughter Constance, so cousin Ta [DeSaussure] did not come. We were all dressed an hour before the appointed time and gathered in Carrie's room. We got so tired waiting that she as well as we thought we should send for our knitting, and some of the girls actually got theirs. Carrie was as quiet and self-possessed as possible, said she did not realize any more than we did that she was going to be married, but Isaac [White] said that during the ceremony she was trembling very much but recovered her equanimity almost immediately and was her usual & natural manner. Our party was much smaller than we expected, there only being thirty persons present besides the bride and groom. . . .

We have had a great deal of fun over Carrie's presents—silver cannot be procured, as the Jews have bought up all in Charleston, Columbia, Camden, Augusta & Winnsboro, as well as most of the jewelry. Furniture and other useful articles are equally hard to procure, so all of Isaac's family and many of ours, gave money, to be laid out as she pleased when going to housekeeping, but cousins Sue [Screven], Fan [Garden], Mary W. Boykin, Lizzie H.[arleston] and Mrs. [Cordes] Harleston each sent a pair of vases—cousin L's were exquisite, of Parian china, Mrs. H's also are remarkably pretty, cousin Sue's pretty, of Parian china. Nancy E.[lliott] and cousin Mary [DeSaussure] each sent a beautiful pair of Bohemian scent bottles. Mrs. Nayler & aunt Carrie B[landing] each a prayer book, the latter's a beautiful copy in blue velvet—cousin Beck [Holmes], a very pretty pair of china candle sticks, aunt C.[harlotte Holmes] a mother of pearl card case, uncle Louis [DeSaussure] a silver pickle knife & fork, Johnnie [DeSaussure] a silver fruit knife, cousin Sallie DeS[aussure] a pair of coffee cups, mother, a pair of gold shawl-pins & belt buckle and Rosa a very handsome work table. Mr. [William] Ramsey gave her a[n] elegant gold bracelet, & Isaac [White], a beautiful cameo brooch. They really made quite a pretty show mingled with the flowers sent by various friends. Her room & the drawing room were really gay with baskets and vases of flowers. Mary Des[aussure] wrote Carrie a pretty little note, sending a bouquet, which was particularly appreciated at this time when her own heart is so filled with sadness. Mrs. [Mary Withers] Kirkland also sent a bouquet, & Carrie has not met her for years. The supper table was very creditable for war times. We had a hot supper, ham & turkey & rice, chicken salad and oysters, apple float, syllabub, charlotte russe & custard. . . . Rosa made the pound cake, & we had tea—real *tea* also,—all of these are luxuries we have not tasted for eighteen months & we enjoyed them the more. Uncle James [Holmes] furnished the wine; madeira, scuppernong & port, all older than the groom himself. When we commenced to prepare for the wedding, I did not think we would be able to get up anything but corn bread. . . .

Charlestonians now feel very confident of being able to defend our beloved city, since the genius of Beauregard has

November 13
Thursday

been at work. New fortifications and redoubts have sprung up all around and in the city, till now it is one of the most strongly fortified in the world and still they are being multiplied. Among other places, forts have been erected on Tucker's green & Half Moon Battery, the latter a revolutionary spot. Between 7 and 8000 negroes are working on the fortification, of which nearly 3000 are under [William] Ramsey, working in St. Andrews, and I am sure from his description we would not be able to recognize the places which became so familiar in our ever memorable excursions last spring. A large drawbridge has been thrown across the Ashley at Bee's ferry and redoubts on either side of the New Bridge and on Mr. [George] Crafts' place. . . .

November 14
Friday

. . . McClellan has been superseded by [Ambrose] Burnside [November 7, 1862], because he would not advance & all Yankeedom is in an uproar about it.[18] . . .

November 22
Saturday

Mrs. James Chesnut,[19] the senator's wife, & Mrs. Kirkland, the far famed beauty, Mary Withers, called to see us today. I was dreadfully disappointed in the latter; I expected to find a vision of loveliness & she may be in ball dress, but not in visiting dress. She is a tall & very fine looking woman, with dark hair & eyes & by no means a beautiful complexion—it was ordinary and I expected an extraordinary one, from all the praises bestowed on it. I could not judge of her gracefulness, but her manners were charming. Perhaps her beauty may grow upon me, but I expected to be dazzled by its exceeding loveliness.

Saturday evening we all went walking, then I went to aunt Eliza's [DeSaussure] to spend the night & sit up with aunt [Carrie] Blanding—it was the first time I ever sat up with anyone, & I felt a good deal of trepidation at first. But a very attentive servant & excellent nurse slept in the room &, as aunt C[arrie] had a very quiet night, we had little to do.

18 Here, obviously to save paper, she begins writing two lines to a single line of her ruled paper.
19 This is Mary B. Chesnut, the author of *A Diary from Dixie.* Unfortunately, the part of the Chesnut diary covering this period is a "memory" not a journal, and there is no mention of Emma Holmes. Judging by the entry above, Emma Holmes was not particularly impressed with Mrs. Chesnut either.

I went round to sit the morning with the B[rownfield]s and found them just going to ride with Hattie [Grant]. She [Mary Brownfield] got out to walk with me, &, as it was a clear, bright cold day, we took a long pleasant walk, during which she gave me a full account of all their troubles & told me minutely the sad tale of the mysterious fate of their poor brother. It is certainly one of the strangest occurrences I have ever heard of. When he [T. Sumter Brownfield] rose, after being struck, the ball entering the temple & coming out over the eye, he turned to Ralph E.[lliott] and said: "That ball made me see a thousand stars." [He] said it was but a slight wound & seemed to think nothing further of it. Soon after, they were ordered to fall back into a wood, which was being cut to pieces by the shot & shell from the Yankee gunboats & where the undergrowth was so thick they had to tear a way with their hands. The regiment . . . [was] entirely dispersed during the darkness and next morning, when he did not join the company, they concluded he had either lost his way like themselves or had found his wound needed dressing and had gone to a hospital. In the meantime, he had sent word to his servant, before he was wounded, which occurred near dark, to go to Richmond, 20 miles distant & not four or five, as we understood, & telegraph to his mother, that Robert [Brownfield] & himself were safe. Robert, soon after he went to Va., was taken into the office of the adjutant general of [Lafayette] *McLaws'* Division and was told to remain in charge of the important papers by which he could be of more service to his country than on the battle field. Thus he heard nothing of his brother's wound till Wednesday evening and it had occurred the day before.

Wednesday morning, about ten o'clock, Dr. Daniels, the surgeon of the *2nd* Regiment, in passing an infirmary or field hospital, saw Mr. [T. Sumter] Brownfield assisting some of the wounded. He called him & inquired if he was not wounded. He said, "Yes, slightly" and, when asked if it hurt him, said "only at times." Dr. Daniels then examined it & said he was shocked to find what a dreadful wound it was. He did not think it mortal then, but very serious. He said he had no instruments with him to probe it & nothing but cold water to dress it & a coarse towel he took out of his knapsack to bind it with. He advised him to go to Richmond as quickly as he could & have himself properly taken care of. He told Mr. William B.[rownfield] that his son was then as conscious as he was, gave a clear, animated & distinct account of the battle & was in excellent spirits. This was 16 hours after he was wounded. About eleven or twelve, Dr. John Darby, who was not an intimate friend, but only a casual acquaintance, found him lying down about three miles further on & recognized him. He was then at times conscious enough to give a minute account of the battle but became confused when questioned about his regiment. Dr. Darby saw that his wound was mortal. The brain was protruding & the action of the intense heat had doubtless aggravated it. At times he was quite delirious. . . . When the Dr. dressed his wound, he pressed an ambulance into service, all those of his own division being engaged, put him into it & asked him where he was going. He was then sitting up and answered, "to a private house in Richmond, where [George] Cuthbert had been nursed and where he knew good care would be taken of him." This was the last ever seen of our dear friend, but the last ever heard of him was from a wounded Mississippian, who told some one, a young South Carolinian officer had died in the same ambulance which he had been [in] & described him so minutely that his friends concluded it must have been him. But when Robert [Brownfield] heard it, he sought most earnestly for the wounded man but could not find him, and it is supposed he had also died. Neither could the ambulance driver ever be found. Robert learned from their servant that his brother was wounded & gone to Richmond. They immediately followed and sought him at the hospitals and private houses where the wounded usually went, but not finding him they went back by different routes to search the wayside hospitals. Meeting Cuthbert, he said he had telegraphed to the *Courier* office to say that among others Sumter was slightly wounded. Robert said he was sorry he had done so, for it would alarm the family & he thought the best thing he could do would be to telegraph home that he knew also that his brother was wounded. He did so, saying "Brother is wounded—not seriously—*I will write.*"

But, poor fellow, almost crazed by the agony of suspense, he vainly sought until the *following Friday week*, when he accidently met Dr. Darby, whom he had also vainly sought. Dr. D.[arby] told him his brother's wound was mortal &, from the nature of it, he thought he could not have lived long and must have been buried by the wayside,—that it was no use for him to seek his grave, he was sure he would not find it. But he did seek, & William even opened graves by the wayside, hoping to recognize his beloved master's body. But a mysterious Providence seems to have decreed that the past shall never be revealed. . . . A long advertisement which Robert lately put in the Richmond papers, minutely describing him & seeking some last information of him, has been unanswered. The morning after the battle Maj. Franklin Gaillard & Dr. [Thomas W.] Salmond of Camden, who was a devoted friend, each sent an ambulance for him, hearing he was wounded. On their way, neither knowing the other was sent, they were met by Gen. [Richard S.] Ewell who inquired where they were going & why they dared to pass wounded men unregarded. The drivers said they were sent for Lieut. [T. Sumter] Brownfield. As it was against orders in Jackson's corps, to which he belonged, to send after friends, he concluded it was the same in Johnston's and commanded them to turn back and take up the wounded lying round. On their refusal to disobey orders, he pulled out his pistols and said he would shoot them if they did not. So they had to obey and thus probably all chances of saving our poor friend were lost.

Mr. Brownfield went into battle without his coat. From a series of peculiar circumstances, he had been wearing the old uniform of the Palmetto Guard—blue coat & brass buttons, so similar to the Yankee uniform. On his visit on sick furlough this last spring, the family begged him to change it for the Confederate grey, like the other officers, which he promised to do, but could not procure the cloth in Charleston & said he would get one in Richmond. But we suppose [he] put it off when there. . . . A few days before the battle of Malvern Hill, where he received his death wound, he was sitting with some officers in Confederate grey—he alone wearing the blue—their flag was standing back of them. Three Georgians passed, and they had become so exasperated during those battles by the loss of so many comrades that they would take no prisoners nor allow others to do so, & thinking Mr. Brownfield from his dress to be one, they fired at him, exclaiming with oaths that no Yankee prisoner should live. The balls just missed him & his friends told him that he must not wear that coat on the field, for he could certainly be shot by mistake. So he led the company in his shirt sleeves—he seldom wore a sash, but carried his sword & pistols in his belt. He had no watch, but wore the medallion with Mattie's [Brownfield] likeness, his ring and studs and sleeve buttons to match. Thus after the battle, he had nothing about him to denote his rank, and unselfish as he ever was, allowed others to be attended to before himself. He had nearly a hundred dollars with him & always wore it about his person, &, as nothing was found in his trunk but his clothes, prayer book & bible, not even a line of writing, Mary [Brownfield] said she sometimes feared he had been robbed after death, & therefore the ambulance driver feared to come forward.

Mr. [T. Sumter] Brownfield had been acting not only Captain but Adjutant, of the regiment at the time of his death, and, besides being thus closely occupied, he was so weakened by camp diarrhea, of which he had been sick for months, that he could scarcely drag himself along. Yet during the year he was in Virginia, he never uttered or wrote one word of complaint of the hardships he endured or of his sickness during those many months. His sufferings and illness were afterwards learned from his companions. Thus has passed away one of those amiable, unselfish, loving men who were made to be the joy of their family and friends—Little Brazilia, after his death, could not bear to hear his name mentioned. She would break abruptly away. One day, Sue [Brownfield], fearing she might forget all his devotion to her, called her & began talking of him—she struggled hurriedly to get away— then afterwards said; "You all think I have no feeling and that I don't love my *precious Bubba*, but I do and I go by myself and cry.". . .

I dined at the Chesnuts on Friday & spent the evening & went there again Saturday morning, till the girls left by the mid-day train. As Mary [Brownfield] said, it seemed like old times for us to have been together, but it only made me feel more forlorn when I came home and missed Mary Jane and Hattie [White] also. . . . Cousin Henry Blanding came up last week to see his mother, and, though at one time he hoped her recovery from this attack, he has now given up all hope— she has consumption, and he does not think she can last much longer. Dear aunt Carrie, the last time I saw her in health and cheerful spirits was when she called to see the Whites, who fell quite in love with her, and she staid to dinner. Mother says she is so dreadfully emaciated & weakened she can scarcely speak at all. I sat up with her a week ago, for the first time in my life, & the next day, Sunday, she was considered a great deal better.

. . . Aunt Mary [E. Holmes] has lately proved the industry and ingenuity of the Southern ladies. While in Athens [Georgia], she made Oliver, her little negro boy about twelve years old, whom she taught to work on the sewing machine and make all kinds of garments on it, as well as to spin—go every day to the depot and pick up the loose cotton lying about and spin it —then ravel and card up scraps of red flannel & other woolen which he also spun. Then she paid a woman ten cents a yard to weave it and made 14 yards of stout warm cloth—enough to clothe him for a year—and at the cost of $1.40 and some trouble and perseverance.

December 1
Monday

. . . Yesterday evening we learned the death of our good pastor, Mr. [William] Dehon. He went down to the city about a fortnight ago and was taken sick immediately after—his already weakened frame was unable to stand the ravages of typhus fever and pneumonia, and he sank to rest on Friday night. He was an eminently pious and good man and will be mourned by his congregation and the church generally. Though he did not interest me in the pulpit, I have always liked him otherwise and felt much interest in him. The Bishop preached this morning but before he commenced, gave a tribute to his memory. Rev. John Elliott preached in the afternoon, from Galatians 4-4 "When the *fulness* [sic] of time was come, God sent forth His Son." One of the most beautiful and interesting sermons, I've ever heard. . . .

December 7
Sunday

. . . It is intensely cold up here, morning and evening, though the sunshine is delightfully warm at midday. This cold spell seems to have extended even to Charleston where the suffering for fuel is great. Oakwood is $20 a cord and very scarce at that—owing to the removal of the negroes, the interruption of water carriage, as well as the scarcity of boats, and the incessant use of the railroads for military purposes. . . .

December 8
Monday

December 10
Wednesday

The weather seemed to have moderated expressly for Mamie's [Boykin] bridal. . . . It was a fine moonlight night, & by no means very cold, but all enjoyed the large cheerful fire & rooms well lighted with wax candles. The guests were not near as numerous as I expected. . . . Mamy [*sic*] looked very sweetly, her veil being fastened on by a tiara of orange buds; her dress was simple but elegant, tulle over silk & her pearl set were a bridal gift from Mr. [Ned] Cantey. I think the ladies gathered there were on the whole a very pretty set & almost every one looked their best. All the Boykins are pretty, but Charlotte, Sallie and Ella [Boykin] are very handsome. Charlotte was decidedly the handsomest young girl present, her dress was peculiar, but very elegant & becoming—gold spotted tulle or organdy, with crimson velvet corsage bouquet and head dress. Mrs. James Chesnut also looked remarkably handsome. I really feasted my eyes on the beauty around me. Col. Blanton Duncan from Kentucky who was there is also quite handsome, a tall fine looking man, with handsome eyes —he has settled in Columbia with his family and is engraving bank notes, etc. Mr. Bull introduced him to me, but I did not have much opportunity of conversing with him, as Mrs. Chesnut engrossed him and Mr. Bull me, the greater part of the evening. Mary had five bridesmaids . . . [and] gentlemen were so scarce & at such a premium, especially *lame* ones, that the girls did not know whether they would be able to find groomsmen until the last moment. All the lame ones had discarded sticks & crutches, but "cousin Ned" [Cantey] had to sit down most of the evening. Everything passed off pleasantly, though at one time I feared it would get still, as there were only one or two dances and a little singing, but as the "feminines" predominated they gathered in knots and got sociable. I enjoyed the evening very much, feeling completely at my ease & wandering like the renowned goose of baby songs "upstairs and downstairs and in the lady's chamber," for every now and then, a group of ladies would gather in the bridal chamber looking at the handsome presents or talking round the fire.

Mr. Bull devoted himself to me much of the evening, talking as usual much nonsense about young ladies, for he is still on the lookout for a wife, then of our last spring frolics. . . . He gave me most urgent invitations to spend Christmas with

Rosa at Ashley Hall. Col. [Blanton] Duncan and several other strangers are to be there, & I know I should have a delightful time, but alas, I had to refuse. Then he told me of Sallie's [Bull] engagement to Edward Trenholm, of which I had heard a rumor. He is the son of Mr. Edward Trenholm, twenty one, and his father is about to give him a plantation—that is all he knows of him & he told him he could not expect him to give his daughter to a man with whom he was quite unacquainted. Besides Sallie was much too young and her education half finished, but he supposed there would be no objections when she was old enough. In the meantime he might visit her & let her become acquainted with him—so that he does not consider it a regular engagement, but he allows them to correspond, for he brought her a letter. At first the idea seemed ridiculous—Sallie, the wild ignorant, uncultivated spoiled child of fifteen, to be engaged. At first we heard he was seventeen, but for a youth of twenty one it seems stranger still, unless he is a man of sense who has discovered the *rough diamond* of her nature & hopes to polish and refine it. If he is such a man as his cousin William Trenholm, as I trust for her sake he may be, one to influence her gently and lovingly, &, if the hearts of both are really interested, it may be the best thing for the poor child, who has been nearly ruined by her father's not merely indulgence, but culpable want of control. . . . I fear she will have some hard trials & struggles before the pure gold of her character can be refined—for she has the elements of a fine woman.

I sat up with aunt Carrie [Blanding]—she is so weak and emaciated that she seldom speaks except to call for what she wants, and seems to suffer much. Her son Henry is unwearied in his devotion to her, is as gentle and thoughtful as a woman, and scarcely ever leaves her except to procure something to alleviate her pain. It is a redeeming point in his otherwise not very estimable character. It is easy to see that he is a disappointed man and has taken to evil ways.

December 13
Saturday
night

[Today] was my twenty fourth birthday—it passed so quietly that I forgot it, till an accidental trifle reminded mother of it. I do not feel older than I did eight years ago.

December 17
Wednesday

December 20
Saturday

The battle of Fredericksburg is over [December 15], but our details have been very meagre, as a squad of Yankee cavalry [on December 17] made a dash on the Wilmington railroad near Goldsboro [Goldsborough, N.C.] a few days ago tearing up the track for three miles, cutting the wires, etc. which caused delay till they can be repaired. . . . Several private telegraphs have been received here, & we know that Rutledge & Jamie Davis & the other Camden men are safe, but Ralph Elliott has been severely wounded in the leg & is expected here today. The Palmetto Guard has thus had every officer killed & wounded & as Capt. [George] Cuthbert is acting major, I do not know who is to command it now. . . . I sometimes think my journal will be nothing but a record of death, for our friends & acquaintances are being swept away like autumn leaves. . . .

. . . Cameron's [Foundry] workshops in Charleston & the Government sheds attached have again been burnt to the ground just one year since the first great loss & whether it is incendiarism or accident cannot yet be determined. Fortunately his tools were saved, but the loss at this time and the delay it will occasion will be great. One of the new gunboats was also nearly burnt on the stocks, in Marsh's adjoining shipyard, but by strenuous efforts was saved.

December 21
Sunday

Aunt Carrie Blanding died last night so calmly & peacefully that those around her could not tell the precise moment when her spirit gently winged its flight to heaven. All had feared a death of suffering by suffocation or strangling while coughing, and it was inexpressible relief—she was conscious almost to the last, taking nourishment constantly. Cousin Henry [Blanding] is to take the body down tomorrow to Charleston, to be buried by her husband in the Circular Churchyard. I cannot realize that the dear gentle aunt Carrie, whom we all loved, has passed away & will never more gladden us with her presence—her heart was so warm & loving and her disposition so even and sunny—she entered into all the affairs and pleasures of young people with so much interest that she won all hearts & she was ever welcomed with joy. Dear aunt Carrie —she was one of the few who ever noticed me in my childhood & I have never forgotten the kindness with which she taught me the rudiments of French, in which she was such a proficient.

I feel so sorry for cousin Henry—he really is alone in the world. His brothers are all scattered, and as he told mother— "I have no home, no wife, no sister, & so on shall have no mother—the only one to whom I could come and talk freely of all my troubles & who was always ready with her tender sympathy."

Carrie gave me William Maxwell Martin's poems. We all went to church, as much to see our friends & pass the time, as anything else—the church was beautifully decorated with garlands & mottoes of evergreens & holly & mistletoe berries, which last I saw for the first time. . . . *December 25* *Christmas*

. . . [Mary Gibbes] writes very happily [of her future marriage] & says she has no fears for her future happiness. But we hear from another souce that Mr. C[ampbell]'s habits are bad & that he is a very good-for-nothing, idle man, which was probably cousin A[rthur]'s [Gibbes] cause of refusal. . . . We hear that Mr. [Edward E.] Bellinger the minister & his cousin warned her of his habits—but I suppose love is *deaf* as well as blind. *December 26* *Friday*

On Saturday mother received a note from Mrs. Villepigue, saying her brother had sold this house & would have to give possession of it Jan. 1st, thus giving us four days notice to quit, when she knew no other house is to be had. Sunday we learned that Mrs. [Hester N.] Cunningham had bought it for her daughter, Mrs. [Elizabeth] Kennedy, the Colonel's [John D.] wife. . . . Yesterday a note came to ask when we would give it up, as Mrs. V. has bought Mrs. K's house & wishes to move in immediately, so Mrs. Kennedy must have this on Thursday as all arrangements have been made—an agreeable prospect truly for us, homeless & without either furniture or carpets in midwinter. Mr. Elliott and the Gatewoods are in similar predicaments—obliged to give up their houses, tho they have furniture & carpets. . . . We are by no means stray examples of the ungenerous treatment which the refugees have received—dozens of others have had the same—and *December 30* *Tuesday* instead of the Upper and Low country being more closely united, I fear the feelings of both, especially the latter, will be more than ever embittered. . . .

Isaac [White] has come up to take Carrie down to stay first with Rosa, then Mrs. P. G. Fitzsimons and themselves will keep house together at Runnymede, Mr. Bull Pringle's place, about five miles above Ashley Hall. Capt. [William] Ramsey will stay with them & probably Eliza Stoney will go down also. I cannot help envying Rosa & Carrie—so pleasantly situated & so near each other—so near the city and in the midst of the fortifications, which they can visit constantly—while I will be up here so lonely without Carrie or any intimate friend or companion & nothing particular to interest me to keep me from the blues and home-sickness. If I only had a class to teach or Eliza would study or read with me, something which would employ me regularly & make me think of something besides the happy past, or idle day dreams, I know I should be happier.

A letter from Rosa mentioning several of those officers with whom we enjoyed our visits to the camps last spring brought all so vividly to mind & made me wish to go down more than ever. She says "the everlasting Dr." [Morrow] is up there again on duty & leaves the newspaper almost every day, as he used to do. He brought us the first news of the *Merrimac–Virginia*—how well I remember the day.

James Holmes,
Emma Holmes's uncle

Dr. Henry M. Holmes, Emma Holmes's
father

Eliza Ford Gibbes Holmes, Emma Holmes's
mother

Caroline Octavia Holmes (Carrie),
Emma Holmes's sister, who married
Isaac White during the Civil War

Rutledge Holmes, Emma Holmes's cousin

Home of James Holmes (19 East Battery, Charleston, South Carolina), which was
torn down around 1920

January
1
∽
June
29, 1863

Camden as the War Worsens

January 1

New Year's day was spent by mother and myself house hunting most unsuccessfully, and our last hope now is the Methodist parsonage, as Mr. Manning Brown has just lost his wife.

January 5
Monday

. . . .Johnnie came today to ask me to teach him French, which I gladly promised. He seems to be taking much more interest in his studies lately, as well as in reading—preferring history & historical tales to anything else & putting up his money to buy books and a desk. I am so glad to encourage him in such good resolutions & mean to devote myself to his cultivation this winter. . . . Gen. [Lafayette] McLaws has just recommended Robt. Brownfield in the highest terms to the Sec. of War for a commission in the "Signal Corps," he having been all this time on the Gen.'s staff, but without rank. He was lately elected lieutenant in the dear old Palmetto Guard, but declined, as he preferred this position. His servant has just come on and says the P. G. have scarcely *ten* of the original members left. Yet it went out with *115* rank and file, afterwards increased to 150. He says too they have lost almost all of the high, gay spirits which they used to have. It makes me too sad to think of the mournful changes wrought by disease and battle in that gallant corps, of which we have always been so proud. At one time, I knew almost every name & certainly half of them personally, or by sight. Now I do not know even the name of any officer besides Capt. [George] Cuthbert & Ralph Elliott & scarcely any of the privates.

[Henry] Timrod, who is one of our most promising young poets, has written a most beautiful Christmas Ode with a fitting tribute to our loved and lost. Oh, that the blessed holy peace which he prophesies for the coming spring may be fulfilled.

January 6   Received a letter from dear Rutledge last night from Fredericksburg which he says resembles Goldsmith's Deserted Village, more than anything else,—that Burnside's army would not let him renew the fight is evident from what the prisoners say &, the morning he wrote, a Yankee picket had called across the river to know if there was a *corporal* in our army that we wished to *exchange for Burnside*.

Vicksburg has been abandoned by the enemy as a nut too hard to crack. President Davis just passed through Columbia, on the way from the West, where he went to visit the armies & see how matters stood.

January 10   Last night I sat up with cousin Beck [Holmes] (who is staying
Saturday   with us) till after one o'clock taking a long confidential talk. Oh, it did me so much good to open my heart freely to one who really understood and could sympathize with me. Dear cousin Beck, I have always loved her, but more than ever now, for she comforted & strengthened me. . . .

January 13   . . . To universal indignation, Alfred Rhett has been placed in
Tuesday   command of Fort Sumter, the Board of Inquiry having decided it was inexpedient to try him now.

Sue & myself today joined the Soldier's society here, of which Miss Sallie Chesnut is president. It meets regularly every Tuesday over [Anthony M. & Robert M.] Kennedy's store, everyone carrying sewing implements & two or three hours are spent there very pleasantly sewing & talking. Almost all the girls I know were there, & I think I will find it very agreeable & inducing to sociability—we all had Beauregard caps to make for the Wateree Rangers. . . .

. . . I am afraid we cannot get the Ancrum's [house], but will have to be "cabined, cribbed, confined" in Mrs. [Hester N.] Cunningham's tiny cottage, which she has offered us. Besides the house being so very small, it is so close to the neighbors that, when sister Fanny gets into one of her half insane fits, every word she utters and all that we have to undergo can be heard distinctly. Oh, how I miss our dear old home. This afternoon reminded me particularly of the hundreds of times I have sat [on] just such an evening, reading at my west window, enjoying the sunset over the Wappoo or the Dardanelles, as uncle Wm. [DeSaussure] always called it, with the fresh sea breeze blowing in my face, as I watched the shadows falling on the blue waves of our beautiful Ashley—the whole landscape is so vividly mirrored in my mind.

January 15
Thursday

Mother had just made arrangements with Mrs. Cunningham to take her little cottage, fully furnished, though there were but three bed rooms & the servants' accommodations equally crowded, at $40. a month till next November—the old lady only giving it up & going in the country to accommodate us—when Leila Ancrum wrote today if their house was not sold by Saturday week, we could have it at $500—so of course all our plans were again unsettled—as of course we would prefer the larger one, especially as grandmother says she will come to live with us if we have a room.

January 16
Friday

. . . Beauregard's staff last week gave a Soirée—they called it —for they did not pretend to have a handsome supper—but otherwise it was a ball. A carload of ladies went down from Columbia—the fashionables there, as well as those who had taken refuge from Charleston. The dresses seem to have been very elegant—velvets, moiree, antiques, & other rich materials were common. The Baroness St. André, the French consul's wife, wore a stomacher of diamonds & had her hair dressed in the style of Louis XVI, with a japonica on top in the middle of her head. Rosa & Sallie [Bull] went. Rosa says it was a ball of strangers, for the city is full of them, foreigners too, &, though she enjoyed it, it was not thoroughly—one partner was a Frenchman, whose English was indescribable— only three square dances all evening, and she staid till near

January 20
Tuesday

three o'clock. There are both an English & French vessel in the harbor & the officers have been dining at Mr. Bull's. The Frenchmen were there last Summer & belong to the *Milan*. A number of persons who lost relatives during the Summer were there. . . . I cannot understand such heartlessness & frivolity—but the storm of war, which has swept away hundreds of our brave soldiers from our homes, seems to have many of those left callous. . . .

January 21
Wednesday

Well, I could fill a page in the style of Mad. [Marie de] Sevigne's letter[1] about the marriage of Madimoisselle Monpensier to the Duc de Lauzeen [*sic*]—to express my astonishment at the news which arrived tonight, and which was like a thunderbolt. Willie writes that he is engaged to Mrs. Ben. Scriven, a widow with *five* children, & begs mother please to send his wardrobe as he will be married soon—not a word more concerning the astounding fact. We have only heard her spoken of as a very pleasant lady, who has been very kind to Willie. In my last letter I joked him a little on the subject, never dreaming there was anything serious in it—and he wrote back contradicting all reports too positively & even rather sharply that I thought nothing further of it & consequently felt perfectly dumbfoundered [*sic*] when I read his letter. Mother burst into tears, frightening us, for we thought something must have happened to Edward, & the letter was passed from one to another without a word. If it was a young lady, we would not have felt it so much—but the idea of marrying a widow, who must be at least five or six years, if not more, older than himself—an idea so repugnant to my feelings— then the five children—such a heavy responsibility for so young a man. She must have some property, for he certainly cannot maintain a family otherwise. He is not generally rash, so I suppose knows what he is about, but we feel as if he is already separated from us entirely. I laughed till I cried over Ann's amazement and disconsolateness—to think of Mass Willie going to be married and not even come home to see us before hand.

I was determined to make the best of it, & I spent the rest of the evening making every one laugh at my merry remarks

1 Probably the most famous of all letter writers in literature, her letters form an invaluable collection of material on the seventeenth century.

—indeed it seems preposterous and absurd in the extreme and I can scarcely believe the evidence of my senses. Of all the strange marriages & matches made by the war, this takes the lead. . . .

Ancrum House—The last two or three days have passed in a whirl of excitement. Monday and Tuesday we were busy packing, preparing to move Wednesday. Tuesday morning, Willie Heyward and Johnnie Colcock, who had just come up, came to see us & tell us all they knew about Willie's choice. They say she is a tall, handsome lady, who has been the life of the village, and speak very highly of her. They think she is about thirty one or two, & her eldest child, a daughter about twelve. Her name was Maria Broughton, so we will certainly have a new name in the family—though not a pretty one. The engagement only took place the night before he wrote, but it is very strange he has not written us again. Tuesday night I got a letter from Carrie, written from Uncle James' saying *cousin Willie*, our darling cousin, whom no one dreamed would marry again, just now is engaged to Mary Hume, who is on a visit to aunt Charlotte [Holmes]. She had just heard too of Willie's engagement, reported by Willie H[eyward] in the city, & said she felt perfectly bewildered between the two astounding pieces of news. I don't know which electrified us most—it was about equal I think. Mary [Hume] is a very warm-hearted, sincere girl, whom I have always liked, & I doubt not will make him an excellent wife. . . . I feel as though I am very glad he is going to marry, for I always hoped he would, he was too loveable not to make some one happy as well as himself, & I am glad it is Mary whom we all know, but still [I] cannot help feeling rather jealous of *anyone*, for his marriage will necessarily make changes in our old associations and we will not see so much of him as we used to. We all look forward to "our boys" getting married, but it is so hard to give them up when the time comes. When Rutledge's turn comes, I expect to cry for a day.

Yesterday morning we woke up to find it snowing, and, though we had ordered wagons, as they did not come, we made ourselves quite easy, not dreaming we would be pushed out of doors [on] such a day, for it was both snowing and raining. But we calculated without our host. First came the

Villepigues to move all their goods and chattels, then Mrs. Cunningham to move her daughter's things in. As we had no wagons, she lent us hers, after they had brought her things, & her carriage. I must say that though we were literally pushed out, it was done very quietly, gently & politely. Of course, moving in such weather was very disagreeable, but, as it was not very cold & the snow melted as it fell, I soon became used to it & ran in and out doors continually. Lila came over and received the loads, putting things in their places, & about four o'clock we had our beds made and "our furniture" consisting of boxes & trunks arranged to advantage. In the sitting room we have the sewing machine, work table, basket stand & several small tables, by way of furniture. . . . At dinner, we borrowed a table from the wash room &, as we only boast of two old chairs, formed a circle on stools around the lit [*sic*] of carpet before the fire. This morning Sue & I got tired standing at breakfast, so we knelt. Though as yet living in marooning style, we will soon be comfortable through the contributions of our friends, and think we have gained greatly by the exchange of houses. This has four rooms in the basement, the two front ones (only bricked but large & with four windows) were carpeted & used as chambers by the Ancrum's. The rear South room is a smaller, but comfortable, dining room with convenient press & fireplace, as have the others. Opposite is a large store room, also a wide entry extending from front to back piazza, all bricked. Upstairs are three rooms on either side [of] a wide entry—on the south the sitting room, mother's & sister Fanny's, all warm and sunny with fireplaces & leading from each other—on the north, the front one will be ours, as [it is] large enough to contain two beds, at need—the middle, which Lila & I now occupy will be grandmother's, but contains the only two closets, which are in the chambers—a great desideratum, without furniture. The boy's [*sic*] have a snug little shed room without fireplace. Then near the house is a large, well built room with fireplace—for a library, but suitable for a chamber. The servants have abundance of room, and the yard, fine vegetable garden, & planting lot are all quite large. This we hire for $500. a year till next January. As it is under mortgage, it will then be sold if possible, but I hope by that time we may be able to return to our dear old city—though home, alas, we have not.

Friends have sent their contributions toward our beginning in *January 31* housekeeping as the Villepigues declined renting furniture, *Saturday* preferring to sell what they did not want but asking enormous prices. We quietly let them alone, glad to be rid of their low breeding & disagreeablenesss, which was shown particularly at the last.

. . . We received letters from Willie & Edward & cousin Lizzie Barnwell. . . . [Willie] wrote that he went on picket the morning after he became engaged & only had time to announce it. . . . As most of the non-commissioned officers were absent, he had to go on picket again during the week, which prevented him from writing earlier. They are to be married Feb. 18th at half past eight and start at ten for Camden by way of Charleston to spend a few days with us. Capt. [G. C.] Heyward told him he had drawn a prize & congratulated him heartily, saying she is a lady of fine mind, highly cultivated & of great moral worth. Willie said he did not mean to give us such a surprise but that he did not dream of such a thing when he last saw us a few weeks ago. The feeling had stolen over him almost unawares. He says "she has a beautiful form and is graceful as a queen." He does not mention the children, but Edward says she has *three*: a girl and two boys—which is correct I wonder? He says he was most warmly received by her friends, & she says, if his friends welcome her as warmly, she will be quite contented & happy. He begged us all to write to her & I did so yesterday. I know my letter was as sociable as if to an old acquaintance but rather a queer one perhaps under the circumstances. But I wrote just the thoughts that came into my mind spontaneously; I could not labor my dull brains Thursday night.

When I had everything packed, I thought I would go down stairs for some of the lunch the children were cutting for me, missed my footing, slipped and turned my right ankle. I can not describe my first feeling—all my former imprisonment and suffering rushed to my mind and made my heart sink for an instant. I soon recovered myself and walked to the sitting room where I announced that I would not be able to travel, but all hoped it would be well enough. However, it hurt me so much when I went to bed that I quietly dismissed all thoughts of my trip for another month, for I would not like to go when Cousin Beck [Holmes] does, just a week before Willie's arrival. The constant pouring of cold water has benefited it very much, but I felt sure, if I had had a "salt fish" & Cousin Willie to administer it, I should have been quite cured by this time. However, greviously disappointed as I have been, I have had much sympathy from all quarters to console me & Cousin Sallie's [Boykin] therapeutic chair to make me comfortable. I am sure every invalid or lame person who has ever used such a chair, ought to shower down blessings on Uncle James' head. I cannot help contrasting the circumstances and surroundings of my first imprisonment within a fortnight of two years ago & the foot not perfectly well yet. Then I had our beautiful Ashley & its ever-varying scenes spread out before me, while the dash of its waves was music to my ears. There in my own snug little room, surrounded by articles endeared by childhood's associations, I held constant levees, the bed as well as the chairs being occupied by a merry circle of girls and "our boys" just up from Morris I. Here, no views, but leaf-less trees with the wind sighing thru them and all those friends widely scattered by the events of the war. Alas, how many have lost their best beloved ones. . . .

February 3
Tuesday

The weather here is as variable as if it were April. Last Thursday it cleared up brilliantly, the sunshine being deliciously warm. Yesterday was as balmy as a spring day; at night we had sleet—the servants say thunder and lightning also—then snow, which lay in patches on the ground this morning—but soon melted by the sunshine. On the Rappahannock, the snow lies six or eight inches deep—and the Yankees in their *fifth* attempt to march "On to Richmond" stuck so deep and fast in the dreadful Virginia clay that they gave up in despair & went back to camp. Jamie Davis writes that the Texan Brigade (Hood's) & Kershaw's drew up in line of battle & fought each other with snow-balls, but alas the gallant Carolinians had to yield to the sturdy Western boys and were fain to try a "Bull run." Of course, no battle can take place in such weather, and Gen. [J. B.] Kershaw & Lieut. [Alfred E.] Doby, his aid, have just arrived. . . .

February 6
Friday

. . . Dr. [John] Bachman has just published a long and interesting letter giving an account of his visit to our western army to inspect the hospitals and learn the wants of the So. Ca. regiments out there.[2] He says the army is well clothed, and he found but one man shoeless, he having lost one foot in battle. But, the surgeon said shoes and clothing were ready for him as soon as he was well enough to leave the hospital. The hospitals were almost all well kept and attended to, but little mortality among the patients, nine tenths of whom were up and sitting around the stoves. Dr. Sam Logan is Surgeon General over those in Atlanta. . . . Dr. B.[achman] held service for our troops. Many of them had heard no religious services for many months. He says the sight was sublime and the most touching he ever witnessed during his long ministerial course. Hundreds of war worn soldiers, far as his eyes could reach and almost beyond his aged voice, were ranged around him, each bringing his own camp stool, and the tears stealing down many a face, as they united in the holy services which recalled their homes and past days of peace and happiness.

There having been a large surplus of the funds subscribed for the sufferers of the Great Fire, Mayor [Charles] Macbeth recently sent $5,000 to Rev. R. W. Barnwell for the use of our hospitals in Va. . . . He writes that he has laid a good deal of it out in purchase of clothing to belong to each hospital that the patient might have sufficient changes and also a wardrobe for the small pox hospital—of course, that needed a large supply, as it [clothing] was constantly burned. He also spent $1,000 in purchase of good French brandy, Madeira & Sherry, for the use of those patients who needed more delicate stimulants than the whiskey furnished by [the] government. Truly he is the soldier's friend & showers of blessing ought to be poured upon him from every part of the Confederacy, for he was foremost in the good work. But So. Ca. owes him a debt of gratitude that nothing can repay. . . .

Lila & Johnnie took advantage of the [railroad] stockholder's free ticket to go down yesterday with cousin Beck [Holmes] to spend a week. It is Johnnie's first trip so far from home without the whole family and of course quite an era in his young life. What untold happiness is enjoyed by youth in its first travels or first ball, etc.—mere trifles not worth noticing to the

February 11
Wednesday

2 John Bachman (1790–1874) was one of the South's leading scientists, the pastor of St. John's Lutheran Church, Charleston, and the founder of a Lutheran seminary, later Newberry College.

old. How vividly such eras are impressed on my mind—so few and far between, that they are like the milestones of my inner life. My first ball—how it recalls poor dear [T.] Sumter Brownfield—a friend who was indeed worthy of the name.

The last two days have been as balmy as June mornings. The warm glad sunshine, the warbling of the blackbirds & the gentle rustling of the leaves as they are stirred by the trees, which seems almost as if borne from the sea, are the first whisperings of spring and always makes me dreamy and melancholy. The dear bright afternoons fading into twilight when the song of the frogs commence make me yearn more than ever for our home and the blue waters of the Ashley. Such evenings I used to spend at my west window watching the changing shadows of the waves. Here, though, I feel as if entirely secluded, shut out from the world, the trees so close around the house form, as it were, a cage barring me in. Mrs. [Elizabeth] Barrett's [Browning] Sea Man's yearning for his boundless ocean home finds a strong echo in my heart. I never thought I should find music in the evening song of the homeliest of animals—a frog—but it seemed to chime in with my sad musings of friends separated or passed away forever and brought vivid memories of the family gatherings at our old homestead, of the many dear old relatives gone forever, but whose names & memory still live in our hearts . . . of "our boys," as we shall always fondly call them, and the many, many changes over all.

February 12
Thursday

. . . Gen. [J. B.] Kershaw came with his wife to see us today for Rutledge's sake, & as usual whenever I would wish to appear to the best advantage to any one I admire or respect, always appear at the worst. I was in the drawing room with my knitting, and they came in rather suddenly. I was so awkward and confused and blushing as if I was a shy school girl—and as to the conversational powers upon which I have been complimented, of course, they flew as usual, when most needed. I could talk or think of nothing but Rutledge & the Palmetto Guard & I have no doubt he was much amused. He said there had been 36 deaths in the company & transfers & other changes have almost entirely changed it. He looked me so full in the face when speaking that I could not scrutinise him as I wished. He is, I think, about the middle height & [has] a small but compact frame, very clear healthy complexion, good features, & a large clear blue eye, which I am sure would flash and burn in excitement. I like his appearance & [his] modest, unassuming manners very much, & I'm sure, though not a distinguished looking man, he must look "born to command" when at the head of his brigade. He is very fond of Rutledge, spoke of him in the highest terms, said everybody who comes in contact with him likes him, & that he is never out of spirits. He thinks Rutledge will be able to get a furlough when he returns, &, if so, I am almost sure cousin Willie will persuade Mary [Hume] to be married then.

I am afraid, as Edward writes, that Willie will not be able to get a furlough to visit us, as all are now stopped & they have been ordered to hold themselves in readiness to march either to Charleston or Savannah, whichever is first attacked. Willie has been away during the past week, removing the negroes of the Guerard estate for the captain. Maria is to have six bridesmaids, but I have to wait for further particulars.

Alester has just donned a coat & has consequently commenced to *trim up*, a decided improvement, & visits out a great deal among the girls. Brother Henry & Edward both write they are growing so fat, having always been among the "lean kind," that they cannot wear their old clothes. I never thought brother H.[enry] would ever complain of that.

February 14
Saturday

Mr. [Robert] Bunch, the English Consul, has just been recalled after a residence of ten years in Charleston, to the mutual regret of both parties. A handsome public dinner with farewell addresses was given him. Mr. H. Panckney Walker has taken his place.

I have lately read *The Partisan Leader* aloud & though much disappointed at its very abrupt breaking off in the midst of a *"crisis"* am very glad I read it. It certainly is remarkable how closely judge Beverly Tucker's prophecies in regard to Secession, Virginia's course, & many minor points have been fulfilled, and how well he understood the baseness and treachery of the Yankee character and the baleful influence of the Federal government as well as its despotism. Three years ago we would not have believed it possible that those with whom we had been so long and so closely connected, whom we considered as brethren, could have been guilty of such lying & vilest treachery, which has marked their course in every step of this unholy war. Each day, new cases of it are shown. . . . Is it possible for any sane man to dream for an instant after such reiterated acts, of *Re-construction*,—rather let every man, woman and child perish in one universal self-immolation and our blessed country become a wide-spread desert than become the slaves of such demons as they have shown themselves. We, the free-born descendants of the Cavaliers, to submit to the descendants of the witch burning Puritans, whose God is the Almighty Dollar. Never! I thank God I am a Southerner and South Carolinian.

February 18
Wednesday

Ash Wednesday—Willie was to be married this morning at church at half past eight. The rain has poured drearily and pitilessly from an early hour all day. I hope they had fairer weather for their bridal.

February 19
Thursday

I busied myself today preparing the bridal chamber, decking it with some of Carrie's wedding presents and the "fairy bells" of the white hyacinth, mingled with geranium leaves & violets. I scarcely expected Willie & Maria, for Beauregard has just issued an order, dated 17th, forbidding any more furloughs to be given, & withdrawing those already given, as he expects an attack in a few days and has requested all non-combatants to leave the city. We certainly expected Lila & Johnnie & perhaps Carrie—but were too sadly disappointed. No one came and not even a letter or paper from Charleston—only a note from Mary Davie, which almost gave me the blues, saying Col. [Edward] McCrady had come home & persuaded her to break her resolution of not being married till the war was over. So at a week's notice, she is to be married next Tuesday & on Thursday go down to Clarendon to his family. The marriage will be strictly private, none of either her or his family, but Mr. [Fred] Fraser's household being there. I think Rosa Bull will probably follow her example in April or May. Oh, how broken up our merry circle will be by so many marriages. It begins to make me feel quite old-maidish. . . .

February 27
Friday

A week ago, Willie & Maria came up with Lila & Johnnie, just when I had given them up entirely, though hoping that Carrie might come. The business which had procured him leave of absence had delayed him a day in the city. At first I was quite disappointed in Maria's looks, having heard from so many persons flattering accounts of her personal appearance. Her face, however, is pleasant and improves upon acquaintance. She has lost the freshness and bloom of youth, and I think looks her age—thirty three. Willie says it is caused by all the trouble she had gone through. She is about two inches shorter than Willie, but at a distance looks quite as tall. Her figure is good, without being at all handsome, as I expected. . . . We could not judge much about her grace, though W.[illie] says black was much more becoming to her. But one day she braided her hair & handsomely dressed she was much improved in appearance. She was very quiet at first & was always so when visitors came, but very soon became sociable with us, & I was forcibly reminded of Chick's [Sidney Pasteur Holmes] introduction into our very large family circle. She seems to be a woman of good sound practical common sense, naturally very gay and lively & fond of fun and frolic, without going beyond the bounds of dignity. We all like her, and I think she will be a pleasant addition to the family, & I am glad Willie is married & will have a happy home of his own. They were married in the midst of a pouring rain, & she only returned to change her dress before going on the cars. . . . Aunt Eliza [DeSaussure] sent her carriage for us to ride, & we took Maria to visit "the lions"—viz. "The Cemetary, Main Street, factory pond & past Miss [Scota] McRae's garden and Mr. [William E.] Johnson's pond"—the longest ride I have taken since I've been here. . . .

Lieut. [Frank] Conover, who was in command of the *Isaac Smith*, is a nephew of old Mrs. [Mary Cox] Chesnut, & Hattie Grant, (who, by the bye, has again become quite sociable & friendly to me) when visiting me a few days ago, told me about him. A letter from him to his wife, found when the boat was captured, in the form of a journal & unfinished, was published in the [Charleston] *Mercury*, those parts relating to family affairs being omitted. Hattie, like most of Mrs. C.[hesnut]'s daughters & granddaughters having been educated in Philadelphia, the home of the Coxes one of whom married a Conover, knew all her cousins well & his brother intimately, though Lieut. Frank C.[onover] she had never met, he having been in the Navy from an early age. Therefore, she was ex-

ceedingly anxious to get hold of those parts of the letter sup-
pressed, as of course, it would tell her of those who had been
her intimate friends. But, she said she could not help feeling
glad he was captured for now the family would experience
some of the anxiety and suspense we had been enduring so
long. But the spirit of his letter was so thoroughly that of a
gentleman—a high toned honorable man, who was merely
obeying the laws of the country and service to which he belonged and to which he had been educated from childhood,
without the faintest shadow of that brutal, malignant devilish
spirit of hatred & destruction so generally evinced by our
foes, that I could not but respect him & sincerely hope he will
never be doomed to suffer the fearful penalty of death on the
gibbet on account of Lincoln's insurrectionary proclamation
& President Davis' counter proclamation. Indeed the first of
January passed away long before I accidentally remembered
either & I trust our government will never have to imbrue
[*sic*] its hands in judicial murder, where the innocent may
suffer for the guilty. The prisoners are closely confined in
Columbia & uncle Wm. DeS[aussure] went to see Lieut.
C.[onover] for Mr. [James] Chesnut [Sr.], found him a very
pleasant, gentlemanly person. Col. [John S.] Preston said his
relatives might send him anything but newspapers and liquor.
Such is one of the many episodes of this war in which relative is arrayed against relative.

March 3   . . . An old and trustworthy negro man, sent two months and
Tuesday   a half ago by Gen. [W. S.] Walker to live among the Yankees
and learn their plans, has just returned & given some valuable
information. He says he was suspected & therefore not allowed to mingle freely even among the negroes who are like-
wise suspected by their white brethren and kept under many
constraints. They would most of them gladly return to their
masters, but fear their reception & equally fear the severe
treatment they would get from the Yankees in case they were
found out or even suspected of an attempt to escape—900 of
them are drilled as a regiment. . . .

March 4   I have just finished [Edward George] Bulwer's [Lytton] last
Wednesday work *A Strange Story* verily, the strangest, wierdest tale I ever
read—yet bearing throughout the seal and impress of Ge-

nius. It is a wondrous mingling of the everyday world—the hard dry common sense which tries all by its standard with vision, shadows, and glimpses of the unreal, supernatural— the magic arts as practiced by Dervishes & Sages in the far off realms of the East—Shadows which make you hold your breath in awe and almost believe in the midst of incredulity of their possibility—deep philosophy which requires solitude and thought to take in and comprehend—subtle reasonings of a kingly intellect to prove that Man has no soul—nothing but intellect, besides the common gift of life, with the lower animals—Margrave being the embodiment of his theory—all rounded into a perfect Whole—of a Grand Idea. The Kingly intellect of a Materialist & skeptic brought at last to bow in Faith & Prayer before an Omnipotent God and acknowledge the existence of Soul and an Hereafter—to become once more as a little child and to feel and receive through Faith, the great mystery of the Christian religion.

I know nothing of Bulwer but his name and the fact that many of his earlier works are very reprehensible, while his later ones are quite free from that stain, but none but a Christian could have written this tale, and I am convinced it embodies the struggles of his own Soul to escape from the shackles of materialism & skepticism. How closely is the far off author drawn to us by such a belief, however unfounded, and what would I not give for some glimpses of his private life— not merely the outward shaping of it, but the inner Man—the springs of action & thought, the incidental circumstances which give a glue to many of his writings—such as afforded by Lockhart's *Life of Scott*—the most delicious of biographies.

... Cousin Willie is to be married on the *twelfth*—it will be quite private, none but brother & sisters, aunts & uncles invited. All "our boys" married without our being present—and I had so surely anticipated being in town when Rutledge should come. It is a bitter disappointment to be obliged to remain here, like a caged bird, vainly beating its wings against its prison bars and pining for freedom & its old companions —while Carrie & Rosa are enjoying themselves & will see so many of the family gathered together. ...

March 7
Saturday

A few days ago, cousin Beck [Holmes] received a long letter from cousin Mary Elizabeth Holmes, brought by the French

Vessel, so strongly Southern in its tone that uncle James published the political part in the *Courier* to show the feelings of a Bostonian, who was brought up & lives there, having only spent a year or two after her marriage in Charleston. . . . She says they have always expressed their sentiments openly & earnestly pray for the success of the South which had the plainest right to secede. She says she is sure some awful tribulation will fall upon the North & especially upon Lincoln for its wickedness and his infamous proclamation—that the army is being disorganized from it, for the men refuse to fight for the negro and all the horrors of servile insurrection, that a great reaction is everywhere taking place, & she hopes much from the retirement in May of two years and nine months men—over 300,000 in number. But as the Yankee Congress have just made Lincoln Supreme Dictator, giving him unlimited power over Purse & Sword, I fear the war will last as long as his administration, unless some fearful retribution overtakes him.[3] She adds "far better that Charleston should fall a voluntary sacrifice to the flames of patriotism & become a heap of ashes, than under the domination of such a fiend as Butler—for it will assuredly rise, Phoenix like, more beautiful than ever.". . .

March 9　. . . The different letters I get, all telling the same story, of
Monday　either visiting about or meeting and enjoying the society of old friends and new acquaintances, makes the dullness & monotony of Camden greater by contrast & of course my disappointment [increases]. I try to bear it patiently and not make myself discontented but there is absolutely nothing up here to interest me. I read & knit all day, but it does not satisfy me. . . .

March 10　. . . I was . . . surprised to learn that Walker Adams, whom we
Tuesday　all thought dead months ago having been considered mortally wounded through the brain at Sharpsburg [Maryland,] I believe, was still living with prospects of recovery—though he had been almost wholly paralyzed. How wonderful and mysterious are the ways of God that such a man, such a drunkard

3 Lincoln was given the authority to suspend *habeas corpus*. Congress also passed a draft law and several finance measures.

that he was, a disgrace to his family & turned out of society, should have lived after such an awful wound not only to be brought home and tenderly nursed but even with a hope of recovery, while poor Mr. [T. Sumter] Brownfield, the idolized son, brother & lover, one so useful to his family and society and so generally beloved, should have had such a fearfully mysterious fate. The insurrection in Poland, which was at first considered a light affair, has proved to be a formidable rebellion which will engage the time and attention of all the great European powers—to our exclusion.[4]

March 12
Thursday

... Mother received a letter last night from Carrie, which she had not read to us, & she only seemed so troubled that it affected me & I feared Carrie might have been more sick than she first wrote. But today she told us the dreadful truth. Margaret had become so excessively negligent & indifferent to her duties & withal so impertinent that Carrie asked Isaac to punish her. He, who is always so kind & thoughtful even towards a servant, would not do so during the day so as not to disgrace her before the other servants but took her after dark to an extreme end of the garden, intending to reprimand her & with a light strap gave her two or three cuts across her shoulders. She tore away from him with one wrench, tore off all her clothing, which must have been previously loosened purposely, and to his astonishment sprang into the creek. He called to her to come out, for she stood waist deep, and [then he] stepped behind a tree. Without answering she *plunged head foremost* & he only saw her head rise. He hastened to the house & sent Marcus to assist her & persuade her to come out, but he could find no traces of her. Mr. Bull had the creek dragged unsuccessfully for the wind was high & the current must have swept the body out. Marcus who had taken great interest in her & talked to her to make her behave better then told Isaac that she had told him a few days ago that if she was ever touched again she would drown or kill herself—yet confessed she had plenty to eat & to wear, had little to do, and was kindly treated, as all the servants bore witness. But none dreamed of such a demoniac temper, for as long as we had

4 This Polish rebellion against Russian rule threatened to develop into a general European war, with England and France cooperating against the Russians.

had her about us, often punishing her necessarily in various ways, it had never been shown to any of us.

It put poor Isaac nearly crazy, for he blamed himself as the cause of her suicide, accusing himself of undue severity. Carrie says she hopes never to spend such another awful night—to see a strong man bowed with fearful anguish, weeping like a little child and accusing himself almost as a murderer—[it] was *too terrible.* The first night they hoped she had crept into the marsh & was ashamed to come up in the day without clothes, was probably waiting for night to come back. . . . Carrie was so worried about her, for the weather was cold and bleak. Her body was not found for two or three days, then Isaac had it examined by physicians and other gentlemen to prove that there was no mark of violence, then staid himself to see her buried. But it was too much for him. Again that terrible anguish swept over his soul—that the public might think him the cause of her death. Poor fellow, to have his peace of mind destroyed by the blind rage of such a creature is too dreadful.

Mother told Nina to break it to Judy; the latter took it more calmly than we feared, exculpated Isaac & only blamed her daughter's temper which all the servants knew, but we did not. Nina says her aunt on Washington plantation did *exactly* the same thing when about to be punished by the negro driver, and she was only saved from being drowned by some boats that were passing by. It occasioned [in] her a serious fit of illness, & when I knew her, [she] always appeared to be as good natured as possible. The servants say that among them she showed her temper as rude, rough & headstrong as possible, & as impudent to all, even her mother. But still nothing like this had ever been shown nor would any have ever dreamed it possible. Ann said, "Why missis, that girl had a wicked heart, & my last charge when she went off was to behave herself, and not have Miss Carrie scold her for her carelessness." But ever since she went down she has given a great deal of trouble. We always thought her a rather dull girl, who was hard to teach anything, but that she would go to a beaten track, though we soon found her very careless & slovenly &, though often sullen when scolded or punished, we never saw an outbreak, therefore, never guessed it. Nor did she show any temper to Isaac; if he [had] dreamed she was angry, he would never have touched her, but she had often taken whippings with utmost indifference, either physically or mentally, then gone back quietly to her work. At the time of the fire, she had worked so well & so voluntarily & eagerly, saving all my books & other things that it raised her in our opinion & we thought she would outgrow her carelessness. No wonder, then, that with *our* knowledge of her disposition, the shock has been so dreadful to Isaac and Carrie—poor fellow, my heart aches for his suffering.

The more I think of it, the more extraordinary the whole thing is—it seems like a nightmare.

... Alester could not go to school today, for want of a pair of shoes, so he borrowed mother's carpet overshoes, while Dudley made him a pair & he took Dudley's place in carrying corn to mill. We had determined on a little frolic & persuaded Charlie to take holiday, (as he is entitled to, by Mr. [Charles H.] Peck's rules, having had no demerits during the past month) and accompany us in a ride to mill. Such a miserable old mule came that at first we declined going but the boys laid an old quilt over the corn sacks & persuaded us to try it. As the mill is on the outskirts & away from gentlemen's residences, we did not care whether we shocked the propriety of the good people of Camden or not. We met the Misses Lang from whom we received a prolonged stare of amazement & several country crackers, but it only added to our enjoyment. The sunshine was so warm & the air so cool & bracing & the Lake of Geneva, as uncle John appropriately calls it, so "deeply, darkly, desperately blue" & lovely in its repose that it carried me back to old times & our merry cart rides of "auld lang syne" when cousin Willie, Rutledge & the other boys & girls used to have such merry frolics together. The miller was highly amused &, while he was grinding, we rode two miles and a half through the pine woods, where I had never been before. It really reminded me of our old country home and the very freedom we felt made me enjoy the unusual excitement more —a break in the monotony.

March 13
Friday

We spent the morning reading aloud *Eric, or Little by Little*, the most natural history of the trials and temptations incident to a boy's school life I have ever read. It is admirably written

March 14
Saturday

and so closely are we drawn to the various characters that tears involuntarily steal down at the death of Russell and the errors and waywardness of Eric as well as his mournful death. We feel as if we had lost dear boy friends.

In the afternoon I took my first walk after six weeks imprisonment, two squares off—while the girls went visiting. At night [we] received a letter from Carrie, saying Isaac was calmer but that he had suffered such agony through three sleepless nights that they no longer spoke of it & she tried to cheer him. . . . Cousin Beck [Holmes] writes that Sallie Bull has broken off her engagement as she says Edward Trenholm is too jealous and does not wish her to dance with anyone but himself. But I am not surprised as she persists in dancing "the round dances" which her father has expressly forbidden. Poor child, I fear her naturally fine character has been totally ruined by want of control & mismanagement.

March 14
Saturday
night

Fanny [Brownfield] slept with me and we talked far into the small hours. I gained a closer insight into her character and disposition than I had ever done before, only raising her the higher in my esteem and love. She has a fine, well cultivated mind and, in many of our tastes and pursuits, she is indeed "a kindred spirit" whom I would thoroughly enjoy having as a companion in my studies. Then she has such a warm, tender, affectionate heart, withal so sensitive at having given or received pain and with such true Christian charity, that she is ever eager to repair even a fancied fault. She is an humble, earnest, devoted Christian, whose Faith has sustained her through all her heavy sorrow. My proud rebellious heart and sinfulness felt rebuked and oh how far above me in goodness and holiness she is. How earnestly I trust that I may become like her, a meek and child-like disciple of Christ.

March 15
Sunday
morning

. . . It has rained for several days, making quite a cold change & causing great solicitude on account of the fruit, for the late warm weather has made the peach & plum trees to blossom fully, while the apple trees are commencing to put forth their leaves first. We have two peach trees of different kinds directly under our north window, & Lila & I watch their daily changes with the greatest interest and anxiety lest a frost should destroy their beauty—present as well as future. . . .

The latest item of news is that the Emperor [Napoleon III] has demanded the dismissal of Seward, for having given [French Minister Henri] Mercier "the lie indirect" in regard to their late ministerial intercourse.[5] The official correspondence has been published & proves Seward to be *the liar direct.* The truth would have done him & his cause no harm, but he is such a habitual liar that the other was easier to him. If true, this is quite important, for Seward is decidedly the *Head* of Lincolndom.

By the Bye, a few days ago, a Kentuckian "one of [John Hunt] Morgan's original squadron" published a short sketch of the early life & origin of Abraham Lincoln—President of the *late United States.* He says he knew both his father & mother & had heard them say Abe was their child. They only lived 30 miles from the writer's Kentucky home. The mother, *Hanna Hanks,* was a woman of the lowest character & situation, with a mingling of *African descent* & was an associate of the negroes. The father, Abraham Inlow, to whom she was unmarried, was a tall, rawboned laborer, of six feet, three inches who always went coatless & barefoot. When Abe was four years old, his mother married a man named Lincoln, & her child took his name, but one day he found Inlow at his house, which caused a fight between them, in which one lost a joint of his thumb, & the other had pieces of his nose bitten out. Abe was consequently treated so badly that his mother sent him to live with a Mrs. McBryde, who gave him the elements of an education. The writer says he spoke to Mrs. McB. a year ago and can swear to as well as prove all these facts. Abe afterwards returned home where he was worked & treated so hardly that he ran away & went first on an Ohio flatboat, then as deck hand on a Mississippi steamer—afterwards commenced to study law in Springfield, Ill. His subsequent career belongs to the public history of the once great powerful and respected United States.

Brother Henry has written me an account of a 12 days trip in the Cumberland Mts. hunting bushwackers, as the Tories there are called, in which they underwent frightful cold exposure & fatigue, and it was nothing but climbing up & down on foot the steepest Mts. & ravines, through pouring rains,

5 Mercier proposed French mediation of the war and Seward refused.

snows, sleet & hail, without blankets & almost without food, the wagons having to be left behind or take circuitous routes; he says they would toil up till drenched with perspiration, then on sitting down to rest, the cold mountain winds chilled them so thoroughly that their limbs became so stiff they could scarcely rise. Over 50 officers & men, worn out, were compelled to turn back, & he says nothing but *will* carried him through for his hip joint ached at every step and the night of the 28th February will long be remembered for its suffering. The people all about there are Tories, thieves & vagabonds, & civilization almost unknown—a people peculiar to themselves; a man told him he knew many others who had not had a home in ten or fifteen years, but rambled through the Mts., the women being as hardy as the men, like Gipsies [*sic*], stealing everywhere. They went from Tennessee to Western No. Ca.

March 27
Friday

Day of Fasting, Humiliation and Prayer appointed by the President.

Uncle Louis says the annular tendon of my ankle is strained, which will best be cured by time & patience; has, however, said that I must not walk out at all & given me a liniment of turpentine, camphor and hartshorn.

March 30
Monday

It has been raining hard for two or three days, with prospects of a continuation, cold and quite disagreeable—however, aunt Sue borrowed cousin Sarah's [Elliott] carriage to go shopping & I took the opportunity for a little exercise and to get what I had long wished for—A Webster's Dictionary, my old school friend. My wishes only soared as high as an abridged, but Dr. [James A.] Young had none but the unabridged at $12.—the original price having been six. But I could not wait till the war was over, though it was far beyond what I had expected to give. But it is a perfect encyclopedia and contains 1500 well executed illustrations. I could not resist so many charms, particularly as I needed something to console me for my repeated disappointments, Rutledge's non-arrival especially, so I determined to treat myself. I brought home my treasure & mother kindly gave me $5 which with the $5 she gave me on my birthday & which I had laid aside for the purchase of books, nearly paid for it. "Old

Webster" is always associated with my happy school days, dear Miss Agnes [Bates] & Dora [Furman], & I chose a binding as near as possible with *that* one, but I have always loved the study of words and their derivations, and am as fond of "reading the dictionary" as any other book.

Still raining hard. Carrie writes that she does not think she will come up just yet, as Rutledge has not been able to do so, but may come the end of this next month or perhaps not till the end of May. . . . She does not wish to leave "her husband" till she is obliged to as she will be with us all summer. I never realize her as a married woman & "my husband" always gives me a slight shock. I have looked so long for Isaac & herself to come up with Rutledge that it is a great disappointment, but I ought to get used to them by this time. . . .

March 31
Tuesday

A letter from Willie says Maria has been a week sick with bilious fever, making him very uneasy. He & Willie Heyward have resigned their offices of sergeant & gone back into the ranks, but he does not say why—& Willie Guerard has just joined the company of their mess. We have to thank Maria for a suggestion of having *gruel* as a good substitute for coffee which mother has just tried; we were always fond of it, and I think it is a capital notion. We really enjoy a hot drink at tea time, after having had nothing but cold water for so long.

April 2
Thursday

The Bath Paper Mills near Augusta have just been destroyed by fire—a dreadful loss, as it furnished excellent printing paper for the newspapers, always supplying the *Courier*, which will suffer severely thereby. Newspapers are such blessings that it affects us nearly [*sic*].

April 3
Friday

. . . Last November [8, 1862] Grant's Grand Army, numbering 100,000[6]. . . (by the bye Mrs. Grant's father & brothers are strong Secessionists & she does all in her power to soften the Yankee yoke) occupied . . . [LaGrange, Tennessee] & its neighborhood &, after remaining a month, set out for Mississippi carrying its train "like a huge anaconda" threatening to crush everything before it & determined not to return "till the rebellion was swept away."

April 4
Saturday

6 In his *Memoirs*, Grant said he moved with a 30,000-man force.

But [Earl] Van Dorn's raids, particularly the one on Holly
Springs [Mississippi], completely destroyed Grant's great
plans in consequence of the utter destruction of all his supplies, and the anaconda came rolling back, its huge folds in
such famished condition, that it swallowed everything. The
Provost Marshall was sent to take all supplies from the inhabitants, except enough for two weeks, promising to return
them afterwards. The Marshal [*sic*] cleared [a] Mrs. A[nder-
son's] house so effectually that she told him she would recom-
mend him for promotion. Her supplies were nearly sufficient
for the year. A gentleman from Illinois interested himself in
her behalf & got her 100 lb. of bacon, same of sugar, and a
barrel of flour, more than they expected, for the Yankees
steal everything they can lay hands on,—not only everything
eatable, even from the negro quarters, besides carrying or
coaxing off the negroes, but everything moveable, even ladies
entire wardrobes, babies & little children's clothes & shoes,
ladies work boxes, guitars, in fact everything including jewelry & money, sending them off to their wives and sisters. Many
ladies with their families of little children were turned out of
their houses, which were either occupied as headquarters or
hospitals, while our wounded soldiers were turned out to give
way to negroes. A very old gentleman of 84, Dr. Millington, a
very learned Englishman, who before leaving his native land
had been invited to be the Queen's Tutor & since then had
been presented with a sword by some Committee in London
about a year ago, went to LaGrange to spend the rest of his
days in peace. The Yankee Gen. [James B.] McPherson made
his house his headquarters, & it was hoped would thereby
afford them some protection, but he allowed his soldiers to
steal everything, even to every suit of clothing except the one
Dr. M.[illington] had on, even the sword which he refused to
have returned at Mrs. M.[illington]'s request. His table was
furnished from her supplies & now Mattie [Trent] says a family who one year ago was worth $200,000 has now to *draw
rations* from the Yankees or *starve*. One of their churches was
turned into a hospital, the pews being made into coffins or
burnt & one evening she saw a horse being fed in one. So far,
none of their servants had gone off & their family of six ladies
& several children kept up brave hearts, the blues & low spir-

its were not allowed and, in fact, she adds we can get used
to anything if we know our brothers are safe. They never get
any southern papers, & her letter was carried to Jackson,
Miss. by a lady who was going to see her son. . . .

Easter Sunday—What pleasant memories are recalled by these *April 5*
dates, though last year they were not coincident. I commenced this book on the 3rd, & on the 5th the Ashley's gave
us their farewell serenade, and it is the last time I saw Benjie
[Guerard]. . . . Easter Sunday dates my acquaintance &
friendship with Mr. [Willie] Earle & much subsequent pleasure. I went to church in the morning, just yearning to hear
the gloriously triumphant chant "Christ the Lord is risen today" which Harriet Hall used to open the service with. Her
clear, flute-like tones, ringing joyously as the bird's, would
haunt me days. But I was sadly disappointed. We had a full
and very powerful but not very sweet choir &, though they
sang the same words as the hymn, it was to a far different
tune, & it actually made me homesick till the tears quivered
on my lashes. Mr. [Thomas F.] Davis [Jr.] gave a short and to
me uninteresting sermon—& more than ever I felt "a stranger in a strange land."

The schools here are much broken up. Mr. [Charles H.]
Peck & Mrs. [Fanny A.] McCandless [are] both ill; Mr. [Leslie]
McCandless [is] much in disrepute for his extreme severity
which made Wade Hampton, Junius Davis, Ben Shannon &
one or two other boys run away a fortnight ago for the army.
Jamie Davis went after them & brought three back, who returned to school, but Wade & Ben have since gone to the
army with their parents' consent. . . .

Saturday night we had white frost & ice, & I fear all hopes
of a full crop of fruit are gone. . . .

Tuesday morning rumors led us to expect an hourly attack & *April 9*
in the afternoon rather unexpectedly Carrie & Rosa came up. *Thursday*
That night, late, we heard the attack had commenced on Fort
Sumter by eight or ten iron clads, but some of the latter had
been disabled, & all had retired. Wednesday paper confirmed
it. . . . Ann Frost broke off . . . her [engagement] to Duff Calhoun a week after,—What a sad feeling it gives to think that

such a great man as John C. Calhoun should have for his eldest grandson a youth without brains or common sense, whose chief boast is that no girl will refuse the name of Calhoun, though oft repeated failures ought to have convinced him by this time. Rosa says the "Ashleys" are in trouble. Almost all the non-com officers resigned or been broken— among others Benjie [Guerard]—for allowing the pickets to leave their posts a little while when he was in command of them. . . .

April 10
Friday

. . . The fleet came up to within 800 yards or at least the [*New*] *Ironsides* did of Fort Sumter,[7] in which several breaches were made, but quickly repaired. It is now considered stronger than ever.

Rosa told me today that the Marquis of Hartington, eldest son of the Earl of Devonshire & Col. Leslie, M. P. dined at Ashley Hall & the former gave her an account of their trip from Baltimore; he & six others, including Poinsett Pringle, wished to come South, but feared if they asked Lincoln's permission it would be refused & then they would be closely watched. So they determined to "run the blockade" of Yankee pickets and spies & started on horseback each with his wardrobe tied up in a "ticking bag" carried behind. After many breathless escapes & much caution, they arrived safely in Richmond, where ashamed of his ticking bag, he procured a small trunk which he lost on his way to Charleston. So he had nothing but the suit he wore, including a gingham shirt.

In January, strangers & many foreigners were almost daily dining or visiting there, & Rosa lived in a continued round of company, till she says, she became quite tired of it and longed for a little quiet and time to read. The Marquis said it was a fact that, when introduced to Lincoln, the President of the U.S. acknowledged the acquaintance by saying "Hartington, Hartington, why that rhymes to Partington.". . .

April 11
Saturday

A quantity of longcloth, calicoes, muslins, stockings, handkerchiefs, shoes, etc. which Mr. Bull sent on to Nassau for, through [blockade runner] Mr. [Theodore D.] Wagner, ar-

7 One of the most powerful warships in existence, the *New Ironsides* had fourteen 11-inch guns.

rived a short time ago, and the girls brought up a great deal. Carrie had sent through him for some of each for herself & us, so we are quite supplied, each with a pretty spring calico & a few other articles as we need them, almost all of very good quality and reasonable prices. Mr. Bull sent cotton, which sold at $1000 a bale, but the list sent out was so large that he will have to send more to get the winter goods. This lot cost, including percentage & duties, nearly $4000.

April 13
Monday

A week before the city [Charleston] was attacked, the Yankees published its capture at the North, of course causing much rejoicing though it was soon found to be false. But they declared they would spend the anniversary of the Battle of Fort Sumter in the city, & everyone hoped & expected the attack would take place either yesterday or today. But, to the astonishment of all, yesterday all the Monitors left the harbor & went southward as well as all the wooden vessels leaving only the [*New*] *Ironsides* as blockader; that & one of the Monitors had to be towed from their moorings. That is all that can be ascertained of the damage done. A number of transports have also carried off all the troops from Stono & it is reported they are also evacuating Folly I. Our men captured one man from there. . . .

April 14
Tuesday

A letter from Maria says Willie & the Captain are again on good terms, & he & Willie Heyward have been restored to their commands, much to the delight of the company.

Hermine Petit has just been married to Mr. Barbot. She is certainly a musical genius—at seven she played delightfully on the piano and at nine at concerts. She played at the last concert [Sigismond] Thalberg gave her a few years ago; he was charmed & said Litz [Franz Liszt], the only rival he had, was the only person beside himself who could teach her, and, if he had known her before his arrangements were completed, he would have invited her to accompany him on his professional tour. I really respect and like Hermine. She had a hard life with her father who was very severe to her. He died of yellow fever in 1856, and she has since maintained herself and her stepmother by keeping school with her and giving music lessons. She is not twenty two yet, has won universal respect, and is invited into the best society. She is a perfect lady in everything but with a great deal of childlike naivete and enthusiasm. Being intimate with the Brownfields, I have known her long and familiarly. . . .

April 15
Wednesday

The [Citadel] Cadets, twelve in number, graduate today. Harry DeSaussure, Mason Smith and Robt. Cooper are the only ones I know. One year ago, at the last graduation, I met and parted with poor Gadsden Holmes and Henry Walker for the last time—Dan Campbell too, the young and graceful orator, who was greeted with such showers of bouquets, all have laid down their lives for their country.

From British officers we learn the capture of the city of Mexico by the French troops. . . .

April 17
Friday

Mrs. Perkins an old friend of aunt Carrie Gilland's came today to see mother & grandmother; Sue & myself happened to be in the room &, though grandmother instantly recognized the face, she could not remember the name to introduce her to us, though she did us to her. So for a time we were completely puzzled but soon guessed from her remarks. . . . Just after Secession, she married her cousin, Mr. Perkins, who took typhoid fever in camp & died eight months after his marriage, leaving her a widow of eighteen. Mrs. P[erkins] I like very much. She is perfectly plain and straightforward in her way of talking; said the reason she had never called to see any of the refugees before was that besides her son-in-law's death, she thought the Charlestonians were so fashionable they would not care to see her. . . . [She] said she always thought Camden the dullest place in the world, which quite amused me, but in which I fully agreed with her—said she believed in being independent and doing as she liked, and, though she knew she was called queer, she did not care. Altogether I was quite pleased with her and really enjoyed her visit.

April 21
Tuesday

Rosa, Aunt Sue & Mary Coffin DeS[aussure] all dined with us today and we had a regular milliner's shop in operation, Rosa & aunt Sue being head workers & Lila & I apprentices: she making a *corn shuck* Garibaldi hat, & I one out of an old dyed cloth talma, ten years old, while aunt Sue was cleaning, whitening and trimming sister Fanny's hat. We certainly strikingly developed "the native resources, talent, and industry of the South."....

Young Mrs. [Callie] Perkins called for Carrie to go to ride this evening, bringing a bouquet of pretty garden flowers and, after a long and delightful ride down a beautiful road lined with wild flowers on either hand, she gave her those they picked which filled the room with their fragrance. The first attention of the kind any of us have received—she told Carrie her mother was quite delighted with us, which she replied was mutual.

April 25
Saturday

Lila's eighteenth birthday—how vividly the scene comes before me of the breakfast table at Willow Grove, when father came in from mother's chamber and put it to the vote what the baby should be named. . . . Without a dissenting voice, she was named after mother. Alas, how many then present have gone down to the silent grave, the young as well as the old. . . . Congress has at last settled upon our National Seal & Flag, so many objections having been raised to the "Stars and Bars" as too nearly resembling the Yankee emblem of cruelty & oppression. The seal bears an equestrian statue of Washington, taken from the one by [Jean A.] Houdon in Richmond, surrounded by the agricultural products of the South; the motto *"Deus Duce Vincimus."* Our flag consists of three equal bars, of blue between white, indicative of faith and purity, while the union occupying two-thirds of the whole, consists of the battle flag, the cross studded with stars, under which so many of our great victories have been won. I think it is beautiful as well as appropriate and elegantly chaste and simple.

April 30

Walked out this evening into Mr. [William E.] Johnson's garden, as uncle Louis said I might try my foot. It is the first time I have ever been over the garden and it is prettier than I thought, at least in its fresh spring garb—though it is on a "finiken" scale to my eye, accustomed to the broad extent of the beautiful ones in St. Andrews, and I do not at all admire his fancy for trimming evergreens to look like lank sentinels all over his grounds varied by others resembling huge glasses of syllabub. Still the old gentleman deserves great credit for his labor & perseverance in laying out his grounds and actually making the soil in which to plant his flowers and evergreens. For the original was nothing but a sandy barren. As soon as he perceived us, he rode up & forthwith launched into his favorite theme—his plans for bringing up from the numerous springs of deliciously cool water, which supply his artificial pond fifty feet below his garden, sufficient quantity not only to fill two circular ponds in the garden, (giving a jet d'eau of twenty feet) but enough to fully supply Messrs. Tom & Willie Ancrum & Mr. Wm. Shannon with abundance of the purest water in every chamber—by means of pipes, for which he was in contact with the Philadelphia engineer, & but for the taking of Fort Sumter five days too early, he lost them. He had [a] written contract with those gentlemen to supply them forever, his grounds being mortgaged to repay the sums they were each to pay him at first on completion of the work & which would have fully indemnified him for all his previous outlay—in case the supply should fail.

The old gentleman's hobby is an excellent and public spirited one, for he likes persons to visit his garden and grounds, & they are certainly the *Battery* for the young people. But like hobbies, it is often ridden too far and too hard and often at his neighbor's expense, for his zeal for improvement carries him frequently to cut and trim trees in their grounds and in the public road & parks much to the general annoyance. But he is a privileged character &, though often grumbled at behind his back for such deeds, everybody lets him have his own way. He is an old friend of uncle James' & came here a poor boy; by industry, steadiness & perseverance, he has made a fortune & is President of one of the banks here.[8]

May 1 . . . I went tonight with Nancy & Lizzie Burnet to see some
Friday tableaux for the benefit of the soldiers got up at the Town Hall by the Misses McDowall. A great deal of taste and immense labor was expended & the dresses & scenery & decorations were rich and handsome. But judgment was much needed in the selection of scenes, which though pretty pictures, did not tell their tale, &, though the audience had pro-

8   William E. Johnson (1797–1871) was founder of the Johnson family in Camden, coming there around 1818. At first he was involved in some type of mercantile business, but in 1845 he was elected president of the Bank of Camden, a position he held until his death.

grammes, they had no light to read them by & scarcely anyone knew what they were. Then they had no footlights & all the light being at the back & the curtains raised & dropped three times so quickly that I could not distinguish the various figures, & to Lizzie & myself who sat aside, they seemed almost farcical. But those in front thought them beautiful and all the children in town were made very happy, for numbers of them acted. Alester wore Willie's black velvet fancy suit, which recalled memories of the happy past. . . . Food of every kind is enormously high there [Charleston], but I would rather live there on the humblest fare than up here in abundance, though that is by no means the case now. I am so homesick & heartsick all the time that many a night I go to bed early just to indulge and relieve myself with a quiet cry, unknown to the others. Dora [Furman] little knows how many bitter moments her silence and neglect have cost me; I sometimes become almost misanthropic. Here everything is so utterly stagnant & monotonous that I have absolutely nothing to interest me. I read & sew & knit, till my brain & arm are weary and I have no one who sympathizes with my tastes or pursuits, who can enter into my feelings, or enjoy what I do—no one to discuss the books I read. Mrs. [Abbott H.] Brisbane writes me I have too many resources to feel my long imprisonment —but all the intellectual treasures of the world did I possess, even one talent cannot fill and satisfy the heart yearning for love and sympathy. Bodily weariness as well as mental often indispose me for exertion of any kind, and the future presents such a blank that everything becomes distasteful to me. If I am able next winter, I shall certainly get a position in some school in Charleston, not the public ones, I do not like them, but I am more than ever determined to earn my own livelihood and be independent if possible—to have something to make life worth[while], for this aimless, useless existence is dreadful to me. I look forward to Chick's arrival with the children as a great source of interest this summer, for I do not expect to be able to go out much on account of the debility always consequent to my lameness.

. . . Congress, after another debate, has changed our National Motto to *"Deo Vindice"* as more appropriate to our Almighty

May 2
Saturday

Defender, and the field of the flag to pure white, instead of divided by the blue bar. I am sorry for I like the idea of the blue. . . .

May 4
Monday
Isaac went down to the city this morning, taking Joe as his foot-boy & Dudley to be hired at the Government works— thereby effecting a great benefit to the whole household; for both servants were great sources of annoyance. Dudley's insolence, negligence & thefts had indeed become quite insupportable &, Willie being away, mother could not manage. It was a most astounding "coup de main" to him as he considered himself indispensable to us. . . . The "military school" to which he is going will be of essential service in teaching *strict obedience* & good manners, lessons he needed very much. It has amused us very much. . . .

May 8
Friday
. . . Lizzie Burnet came to say goodbye, as they were to leave the next day. She said her father had seen poor Charlotte [Dawson] and did not think she could live more than a few days, as Charlotte herself thinks, though neither her mother nor sisters think her in immediate danger. Mother says she may die at any moment, though her father, who also had liver complaint, lived for years in dreadful health. Charlotte suffers severely all the time and says the only relief she has is when she faints from pain and is unconscious. From what Lizzie said, she must have been dreadfully imprudent, the more surprising, as her mother was always considered an excellent nurse. After being six weeks in bed, the first morning she rose at seven and, though she took an hour to get downstairs, went to breakfast. Next morning she rode three or four miles, and another day twice, while she had a burning fever, which she had constantly, & of which Dr. [Lynch H.] Deas seemed to know nothing. Now he is giving her nothing but brandy or wine, which her mother cannot get. Margaret's [Dawson] arm is in a fearful state, ulcerated to the bone . . . and he is only applying cold poultices, while he fears amputation. He is a very timid, unskilful physician, in whom all the Charlestonians have not the slightest confidence.[9] How I wish the Dawsons would go to the city as their friends wish & have

9 Lynch H. Deas was born in Charleston. He was a graduate of South Carolina College and then took medical courses in Charleston, Philadel-

good medical attendance. It is too dreadful to think of the probability of Margaret's losing her arm at a time too when her assistance is so much needed.

On Tuesday [May 5] Mrs. Griswold Perkins, or Callie, as I have heard her called, sent Carrie a large dish of beautiful roses, of every hue, from snowy white, tea-tinted and every shade of pink & crimson, to the exquisite canary of the Harrisonia, forming the most harmonious blending of beautiful colors and filling the room with their fragrance; on Wednesday [May 6] Charlotte Boykin sent another of exquisite geraniums, and the most superb scarlet cactus and white lily that I have ever seen—in fact, I never saw either before, except the latter in a picture. It is formed of a single petal, with a long golden rod in the center and is indeed a fit sceptre for fairy queen or May queen, as the Camden girls have often borne it. Then that evening cousin Ta [DeSaussure] sent me a beautiful bouquet, the *first I have* received up here so must especially notice it.

. . . Yesterday Callie Perkins again brought another bouquet of rare blossoms for Carrie and invited me to ride, though we were personally unacquainted. However, we had heard much of each other lately, and she felt very sorry for me. Her carriage is only two seated, so she can only ask one at a time, and as her health is delicate, she has to go to ride every day for exercise. She is a fine looking woman with a pleasant face & rather sad expression, appearing older than she really is from her widow's caps. The day was not very pleasant as it commenced to rain later & became quite cold, but I enjoyed the ride very much, and the sight of the beautiful woods, of every variety of shrub & tree, looking so like our low-country forests, and inviting to many as shady nook & dell, then the pretty lanes lined on either side with crab-apple trees, from which however all the blossoms had dropped. I did not know there was anything so pretty so near Camden. She is very fond of Charleston, so we have many feelings in common. She is very sociable and seemed to be as pleased with me as I with her, for she invited me to ride with her in the morning before breakfast, as her mother wishes her to try the effect of the early hours. So I promise myself much plea-

---

phia, and Paris, France. From 1837 until his death in 1883, he practiced medicine in Camden.

sure, as well as benefit to my health, from her acquaintance, for I returned refreshed in mind and body and more reconciled to staying in Camden than I have ever been before. Her mother & herself really feel for the refugees and have already shown it in our short acquaintance—how far a little thoughtfulness, kindness and attention go. She is the only person who has broken the monotony of our lives & ideas by taking us what I call really to ride, to see something of the country, and yet almost every one up here owns a carriage & goes to ride every evening. She took me past the Cornwallis House, as it is called, one of the *lions* of Camden. It was the residence of her great-grandfather, Col. [Joseph] Kershaw, our General's grandfather, during the Revolutionary War, when Cornwallis took possession of it. It is a tolerably large house, in those days considered very fine and elegantly furnished from England. . . . It stands on a slight eminence, with a gently undulating and widely extended space in front—once the lawn and now covered with a beautiful carpet of closely shaven grass, interspersed with clover. Now it stands desolate in the midst of large fields, the unhealthiness of the air in summer gradually compelling the removal of Camden from the vicinity of the Wateree [River] to the more barren but salubrious sand hills. The lawn is the favorite spot for military exercises and three or four years ago, two tournaments took place there.

The news from Virginia is most cheering—decisive victories being gained on Saturday and Sunday at Chancellorsville. . . .

These battles are considered in many respects to be the bloodiest of the war—and our loss is heavy.[10] Gen. Stonewall Jackson's left arm has been amputated, but he is doing well & will soon be able to give the Yanks a few more big scares. . . .

The *Alabama* has been at its old tricks of capturing East Indiamen or Aspinwall steamers and making them pay heavy ransoms for their safety. The London correspondent of the New York *Times* says fourteen more such "Yankee Scarers" are about being launched into the Atlantic for the Emperor of China, alias, the Southern Confederacy, notwithstanding all

10 The Battle of Chancellorsville took place May 1–4, 1863, between 133,868 Union soldiers and 60,892 Confederates. Union losses were 17,278; Confederate losses were 12,821.

the efforts of the Yankee Minister—and the English people with few exceptions are more than ever in favor of the South. The war is pressing too heavily on all classes & the Marquis of Hartington, in a late election speech, said he was out & out Southern & that the South never could be conquered. Vitzelly [Frank Vizitelly] lately went up to Ashley Hall to sketch it; he was also sketching all the principal battle grounds for the London *Illustrated News.*

The New Orleans *Delta* predicts a speedy war between the United States and England & France, & old Mr. Robert Barnwell, who is not an over sanguine man, predicts a speedy recognition of the latter, & peace-blessed peace must soon follow. The victories of the next two months will have immense influence in such happy results. . . .

. . . We were too shocked to learn by the paper that Gen. Earl Van Dorn has been murdered by a Dr. [George B.] Peters; it is dreadful to think of a man who has been unharmed through so many battles, as a brilliant cavalry leader, dying at last by the hands of an assassin.

May 9
Saturday

Stonewall Jackson, too, after passing unhurt through so many of the bloodiest battles, was destined to be wounded by a chance volley and a mistake on the part of his own men. He had already received a ball through the palm of his right hand, and it is said the other wound was received that night when riding around the camp. He and his party were mistaken by our pickets & fired upon, a ball shattering his left arm & compelling the amputation just below the shoulder. . . .

Stonewall Jackson is dead. The mournful tidings are swept over the length and breadth of our land by the electric wires with crushing effect. Every heart is filled with deep sincere grief. We feel as if we had each lost a beloved friend. The Christian Warrior and Hero has gone to his God, leaving a deathless name behind him and an ever-living monument in the hearts of his countrymen. He has left a void which cannot be supplied. When mother came in and told us the sad tiding, we felt as if we had heard of a dreadful defeat. Our hearts sank within us at the blank that was left. He died yesterday from pneumonia, combined with his wounds. When Gen. Lee heard of his wounds, he wrote him a beautiful letter express-

May 11
Monday

ing the deepest regret for his injuries, and saying, if he could have ordered it otherwise, he would have saved him in his own person. To his skill, he ascribed the glorious [Chancellorsville] victory, which, under a kind Providence, we have just won. . . . [Clement L.] Vallandingham's [*sic*] arrest in Cincinnati for speaking against the war has created tremendous excitement in the country around. Hundreds of people flocked to the city and attempted a rescue but failed, when the mob tore down & set fire to one printing office, railroad bridge, a hotel & other buildings. Burnside had to send cannon and troops to quell the disturbance.

Very few or no particulars have reached us respecting Van Dorn's murder except the current reports that it was justifiable, as he had destroyed the conjugal happiness of Dr. [George B.] Peters, who was formerly Senator from Tennessee, & belonging to one of the wealthiest and most respectable families there. He met Van Dorn in the street & shot him dead. It is said not to have been the latter's first offense. However brilliant a man otherwise is, with such a character he cannot be regretted & is no loss to our cause. What a contrast between his death and the noble revered Jackson, whose loss is mourned by each as a personal friend. His body was carried to Richmond, where it was to be embalmed & laid in state & every respect due to such a great and good man paid by a weeping city and nation. . . .

Maria has written to ask me to go down to see them, which I should enjoy very much later in the summer, for it would be useless as well as imprudent to go while my foot is still so weak that I can only walk one or two squares. . . .

May 12
Tuesday
night

. . . Uncle Louis came to see mother today to explain the Confederate War Tax Bill, which has just appeared [on April 24], to her. He says it is one of the most beautiful systems of legislation he has ever seen. Its effects are already practically visible in the great downfall of prices of produce—for all *holders* are taxed 10 percent, on what they own on July 1st, others only 5 percent, the intention being to make the extortioners disgorge their accumulation for the benefit of the public. Consequently the markets are now full, & the supply, together with the immense grain crops everywhere made, had brought wheat flour in one week from *30 odd* dollars a *sack*, to ten, with promise of falling lower still. It is quite time, for meat is so scarce & high & so poor when we buy, that we have had none on table for several days. The ten cent loaves made here are so small, about *four inches* square & *two* thick, that Carrie & I promised to have some hermetically sealed up, like those of Herculaneum & Pompeii, for future generations. The tax bill, besides, falls heaviest on the wealthy, as the greater the amount of Confederate bonds, the heavier percentage has to be paid—as is right—the more property they have, the greater their interest in our ultimate independence.

This evening's paper brings the news of Capt. [George] Cuthbert's death from his wound, which being in the chest, had made me fear it would be fatal—being naturally weak there and inclined to consumption. I am very sorry for his death, but latterly have not felt the same interest in him, as "the boy's" friend & captain of the P.[almetto] G.[uard] as I used to do. My personal acquaintance was very slight, but at one time I felt quite enthusiastic at the mention of his name. However, since he went to Virginia, though he always showed himself a brave and daring man foremost in the fight, yet he did not maintain the discipline nor the distinction once enjoyed by my favorite company, and his men did not feel the same love and enthusiasm for him as at first.

. . . The Quebec *Journal* says news has reached that city that 15 regiments have been ordered from England to Canada & nine vessels loaded with arms, in consequence of [Charles Francis] Adams having notified the English government that if the fleet being built there for the Emperor of China, alias the Southern Confederacy, were allowed to depart, he should consider it as a declaration of war. The debates in Parliament seem chiefly on the American question and are decidedly hot. Mr. [John A.] Roebuck [is] indignant that the government did not assert its dignity by taking immediate notice of Admiral [Charles] Wilkes insolence in regard to the *Peterhoff*—and is for war, which he says the people are ready for.[11] Moreover,

May 14
Thursday

11 The *Peterhoff*, a British merchant ship bound for Mexico, was seized as a blockade runner off the West Indies, February 25, 1863, on order of Admiral Charles Wilkes, the *Trent* affair celebrity. The British claimed the U.S. had no right to stop this ship even though such cargoes often eventually ended up in the Confederacy. A major crisis was averted, however, and later courts accepted the British position.

he says men calling themselves British merchants obtained & received from Adams a safe passport to carry arms to Mexico, to furnish them with means to fight the French, England's allies, while vessels carrying produce were refused it & Yankee spies & informers dodge everywhere, giving all kinds of false information, whereby the *Alexandria*, a small vessel, fit for a mail or packet boat, was seized because perhaps when resold it might be bought by the Confederates. The insolence of the Yankees is fully brought to view. . . .

May 15   It is said that [Stonewall] Jackson had a presentment that he
Friday   would be killed either in the last or one of the great battles of the war—however, he retained his usual calmness and dignity after his wounds. During the amputation he fainted & was unconscious for a few moments. When he recovered, one of his aids asked how he felt. "Very comfortable," he replied. "Order the infantry to the front." At eleven Sunday morning his physician gave up hope & informed him of it, offering stimulants to prolong existence, which he declined. At one, his wife arrived to bid him farewell & soon after his mind began to wander. Among his last words was a reference to his troops. He said, speaking of his Commissary, "tell Mr. [Wells J.] Hawkes to send forward provisions to the men." He died at quarter after three. . . .

Mother received a letter from cousin Willie, this evening *officially* announcing Rutledge's engagement to Emily Ford, saying he also heard various rumors but [had] only known it himself a few days ago. Carrie later received a note from Em, acknowledging it, but saying she had not told her before, because, when she last wrote, everything was not settled. I have no doubt he addressed her at Florence, but matters were not arranged till she went home, so it was not considered a public engagement. . . . Though I had long expected and wished the match, for she suits him admirably and is quite worthy of him, (which I think very high praise of her) still when the fact came upon me at last, I could not help taking a quiet cry. The tears would start involuntarily as I thought how everything would be changed in our family circle when we return to the city. I feel forlorn with so many of "the boys and girls" married or engaged, as well as so many of my other intimate friends. Love & matrimony so completely absorbs all who come within their magic circle that they quite forget & neglect outsiders. It is quite amusing as well as gratifying to hear the remarks made, for Rutledge seems universally known and admired, generally without being personally known. Mrs. [J. B.] Kershaw asked, "Who was the girl fortunate enough to get him; she hoped she was worthy," and Lila Davis said, when in St. John's, she heard a gentleman remark "There was only one man in the army of the Potomac [Army of Northern Virginia] who always looked clean & wore *white shirts*, even the Generals did not. He did not know how he managed it, but soon after a battle, he always was dressed as if just from a drawing room, with a beautifully done up white shirt on." Lila answered, "Lou [Davis] need not tell me who it is, I am sure it is Mr. Rutledge Holmes.". . .

The Crenshaw Woollen Factory & two of the Tredegar Iron Works Finishing shops [in Richmond] have been, the former entirely destroyed, the latter seriously damaged, by an accidental fire arising from the machinery. The Factory is a great loss, as its splendid machinery was new two years ago & cannot be replaced in the South. Only a few pieces of manufactured goods were on hand, but a quantity of raw material. The injuries sustained by the Tredegar works can be repaired in a few weeks, fortunately the loss there not being as great as at first supposed. Both, however, have been working for the government doing immense good, and the loss will be severely felt. *May 16 Saturday*

We hear our gunboats were making preparations a few days ago for another attack on the blockaders, when on calling the *Chicora* roll, one of the crew was missing & could nowhere be found. A day or two before, a man in a small boat had been seen to make his escape to the fleet, and it is now supposed it was probably this man, who of course will betray all our movements, etc., so that the plan has been frustrated. It is indeed dreadful to think how often we find traitors have been among us, and yet how difficult to detect them.

. . . One of the first uses made of our new flag in Richmond was to enwrap the remains of our beloved Jackson, & at Lynchburg [Virginia], a Mrs. Deane had a willow growing *May 19 Tuesday* from a slip brought from Napoleon's tomb. She made a wreath of it mingled with flowers to lay on his coffin as it passed through the city. Just a week before Jackson was wounded, he sat for an admirable photograph, the only one extant, by the request of a Richmond daguerreotypist who sent an artist to him. His life is to appear in a few weeks containing a copy of it. Jackson was twice married—his first wife left no children, but his widow has an infant of five months.

May 21
Thursday

Two long "cards" signed by the various members of Van Dorn's staff have been published in all the papers, vindicating his character from the foul calumny cast on him by his cowardly assassin, who used it to shield his own detestable deed. These gentlemen say Van Dorn had never met Dr. [George B.] Peters' daughter but once, & his acquaintance with his wife was so slight that they could testify to the falsehood of the report. Dr. Peters had been on friendly terms with his victim & shot him in the back of his head, while seated at his office table, writing, having been left alone together a few minutes before by the departure of some of his staff. The murdered man was found dead sitting in his chair, his pen still in hand, while the assassin, who had made every arrangement for instantaneous escape, ran off to the Yankees —surely a strange proceeding for an injured husband. The motives of his vile conduct can be guessed by his having taken the oath of allegiance to Lincoln, two weeks before at Nashville, as testified by a gentleman who had escaped from there, & his having said openly that he had lost all his negroes & property in Arkansas & would soon do something to get them back. And thus to render his treachery yet more acceptable to the Yankees, he murdered a brave & gallant general, whose name they had long held in terror from his brilliant & successful raids. Poor Van Dorn, in spite of the dreadful stain left for a time on his character, I could not help grieving at the fearfully sudden end of one whom I had always admired—and I was proportionably delighted at such a vindication. . . .

May 22
Friday

After our long expectation, Chick [Sidney Pasteur Holmes] and the little ones are at last with us; she looks miserably and is in miserable health. Henry is a very delicate interesting looking child, with clear blue eyes, flaxen hair, & fair complexion, as Carrie has also, only her skin is as clear & white as possible, while he is sunburned. She is very sociable & affectionate, going readily to any stranger, and is as merry a bit of sunshine as ever gladdened anyone's heart; she is the universal pet & plaything, the boys taking as much notice of her as we do. Poor little Henry is a much shyer child on first acquaintance & very soon after he came he got a fall, down the same miserable staircase which so utterly destroyed all my pleasure, rolling down the whole way. Fortunately though, he struck his head, not hurting him very severely, but he was taken sick soon after & quite sick all night and Saturday also. . . .

I received a letter from Rutledge today, dated 14th, same day *May 26* that I wrote to him, announcing his engagement, which took *Tuesday* place just as we thought. He writes Capt. [George] Cuthbert died of pneumonia but was so well when he saw him two days before his death, that he little thought it would be the last time they ever should meet. He is now the only one remaining of the original commissioned officers of the Palmetto Guard, and I do not think there is one left either of the noncommissioned. That company once so proud & brilliant, as brave a set of men as ever marched to battle, is indeed a melancholy wreck, but the halo of glory which encircles the names of its heroic dead can never fade.

[John H.] Morgan is himself again. For months past we have *May 28* heard nothing of him & the silence is at last explained by a *Thursday* letter from one of his men, saying they were placed under Wheeler's command. . . . Though they all admire him very much and would prefer him, if obliged to be under control, yet, from the time they lost their independence of movement, the "esprit de corps" languished, & the men said "we are no longer Morgan's men, but only Wheeler's Third Brigade." Morgan had been for some time petitioning leave to drive the Yankees from the Tennessee border, & the moment freedom of action was once more his, the man obeyed his call with the greatest joy, & the streams being too swollen to allow the artillery to cross, 1500 cavalry dashed through & pursued the enemy 8000 strong, whom they found already retreating, though they had artillery, infantry and cavalry. Our men charged them with a fierce hurrah of joy, and a severe fight ensued, in which they were successful, notwithstanding the great disparity of numbers.[12] Morgan is one of my favorite heroes, & I am always delighted to hear of some new & brilliant exploit. Who can ever properly write a history of this war and enumerate a tithe of the heroes and heroic deeds & deaths of the gallant men who have fallen in the holiest of causes. . . .

For one or two days John has been complaining of sickness & showed on his face that he had been poisoned by touching poison oak or something similar. But today we were horrified to see his face so frightfully swollen that he was unrecognizable & it gradually grows worse. His head is enormous & his eyes completely closed, while he suffers much from pain & the intense flammation. Dan [DeSaussure] was sent for directly & comes twice a day to see him. Yesterday he was very irritable, but today seemed completely subdued. . . .

May 30
Saturday
Most of today has been spent with poor Johnnie bathing his face with cold water & reading or talking to him. He bears it well & seems so grateful for all I can do for him. If I had met him in the street, I should not have known him. . . .

Tonight's paper contains a most beautiful & deserved tribute to our peerless Jackson, strange to say from Henry Ward Beecher, a notorious Abolition & Black Republican preacher. He says Jackson is as much honored & respected in the Yankee army as in ours for his pure, noble and Christian character. . . . No other man has so impressed the imagination of the Yankee soldiery, as Jackson, from the marvellous [*sic*] rapidity of his marches & the terrific thunderbolts he seemed to crush them with. Scarcely a northern paper is received but contains some notice of him, all in the same strain of highest eulogy. Truly amidst the wickedness which disgrace the North, there are still some seeds of virtue left—that they can honor & respect the dead Hero, whom they so feared while living. Well may we be proud of our country which has given

12 On May 17, 1863, the Confederate Congress voted thanks to Morgan for his raiding activities in December, 1862, prior to the Battle of Stones River. His next major raid, the one into Ohio, did not take place until July, 1863. In May he was preparing for the raid.

birth to such truly great and good men as Washington & Jackson. Old Virginia is indeed the Illustrious Mother of Illustrious Heroes.

Tonight's paper also contains an account of the Democratic Meeting held lately in New York City, in regard to the arrest and trial of Vallandigham. The resolutions & speeches are most boldly denunciatory of the government and its despotism of the war, which is pronounced to be cruel, unnecessary and a disgrace. The arrest of Vallandigham, at three o'clock at night in his own house by a company of soldiers who battered down the doors & carried him off from his bed, is denounced, in the most manly terms, as a crime which no king of England has dared commit for 500 years, not occurred in France since the revolution. And indeed the whole affair bears a totally different tone from any former meeting. Mr. James Brooks' speech particularly is worthy of our admiration.[13] He ends by saying that it is time to put a stop to such despotism. If not, they will soon be worse than slaves. They still have the right of petitioning Abraham Lincoln, & it is time for the whole nation to rouse themselves in support of their common rights, &, adds he, if justice is not done, by the Eternal God, I swear to lead an army, if you will trust yourselves to my leadership, to battle to the death for it. May the grain of leaven produce its gradual and destined effect in due time. The court martial first sentenced Vallandigham to imprisonment for two years at the Tortugas or Fort Lafayette— but his Majesty King Abe finally changed it for exile to the South &, a few days ago, he was sent by flag of truce into our lines in Tennessee. But our generals refused to receive King Abe's political prisoner or receive the flag and Mr. V.[allandigham] at his own request, was then left on neutral ground & afterwards received by our generals as a man exiled for having claimed & exercised freedom of speech. His wife is said to have gone deranged.

. . . The petty tyranny of the Yankees in New Orleans is *June 2* equally absurd as disgusting and equals that of the most frightful days of the Reign of Terror in France. Female

13 James Brooks was a Democratic member of Congress from New York and editor of the New York *Daily Express*.

schools entered and searched, because the girls drew seces-
sion flags in their books, & three schoolmistresses, French and
Englishwomen, made to pay fines ranging from $100 to $250.
Young ladies arrested & fined for hurrahing "The Bonnie
Blue Flag" & a negro boy sent to prison & given forty lashes
for hurrahing for Jeff Davis & the red, white & blue.

The report of Mrs. Vallandigham's derangement is false,
she wrote a few days ago to her husband to remain stead-
fast in his principles. Meanwhile, he says he knows it is only
from the generosity of our government that he was received
and permitted to remain & wishes to live in a retired manner
until able to return home. The Ohioans are getting up a petition to Lincoln demanding his unconditional release. Jamie
Davis writes to Lou that the army is under marching orders
& the telegraph announces that Hooker is "changing his base"
so we expect important news soon.

. . . I feel so mortified at the disgraceful character the
Charleston girls have acquired—once considered so modest
and refined & well behaved that a Charleston lady was recognized by her lady like manners anywhere, & now the foreigners say that they have met fast girls, but not equal to those of
Charleston. And those very ones are the ultra fashionables,
who seem to have forgotten alike the dead & the living and
with the grass scarce green on the graves of their brothers,
cousins & other near relatives, have shared in all the gaiety of
the past winter—such as the Rhetts, Alstons, Middletons,
Ropers and all that set of worldly, heartless fashionables. With
a brother and cousin just dead, the [Robert] Barnwell Rhetts
gave & went to balls & are now making themselves conspicuous by the extremes of fashion to which they go. I had always
thought them heartless, as known in former days, but I was
shocked to learn that Mrs. John Ashe Alston, whom we have
always liked & thought so different, has given several parties
since Wash's death, while Helen, with a black ribbon by way of
mourning, goes everywhere. Carrie says it seems as if some
hearts have only been hardened by the war, and I fear bitter
suffering is yet in store for our beloved city. She says the city
is full & she can better tell us who is not there than who is,
and everybody is "dressed to death" as if no war was going
on. . . .

. . . Pemberton seems to be regaining the confidence & esteem he lately lost by the splendid defense of Vicksburg he has made. It is said the last desperate assault of the enemy, in which almost everyone was killed or wounded, was effected by his stratagem of pretending to evacuate the lines, while his guns were so arranged that, as the Yankees rushed in, they were mowed down by hundreds. Much has been written & said in the papers about him—some saying it was treachery, others incapacity, which caused our recent reverses in Miss. It is certainly difficult to obtain the truth & he never has been a favorite of mine; I have always looked for disaster whenever he commanded. However, he has just made a most noble address to his troops, which no one can help admiring, & I trust his character may be completely vindicated. He said: *"You have heard it said that I was incompetent and a traitor and that it is my intention to sell Vicksburg. Follow me and see at what cost I will sell Vicksburg. When every pound of beef, bacon and flour, every grain of corn, every cow, horse, sheep and dog shall have been consumed—when every man shall have perished in the trenches—then, and not till then, will I sell Vicksburg."* This was spoken after the third repulse to the enemy. While Grant is ditching & going to besiege & try to starve the city into a surrender, which he cannot do as it is well provisioned for four or five months. . . .

June 5
Friday

I went "down the street" as the up-country people say, this morning, to try and get my bonnet trimmed, as I should need it if I staid any time in the city; it has not had the trimmings changed since before the Great Fire, & all had been worn one or two seasons before. . . . My "jockey" has not been touched for more than a year and is now quite shabby, so I thought I would have my bonnet neatly trimmed with blue organdy, almost the only material to be had now. . . . Carrie's letter today has completely broken up my plans. . . . Rosa is to be married on the 18th, today week, at St. Philip's church, the wedding to be very private on account of the recent death of Dr. Guerard, but Carrie says Rosa has told her very little of her plans & that little seems very undecided. . . . There is an under current about Rosa's sudden marriage that is not visible. Willie Guerard has nothing in the world to support her on, as he is only a private, unless her father is going to assist them—

June 11
Thursday

and she continue to live there. If she does not, I don't know what will become of his household. It is what I have long thought Mr. Bull ought to do, for she has been a very dutiful daughter & he will not appreciate her fully till she leaves him. But, I do not understand her peculiar reserve to Carrie, with whom she has always been so free hitherto, nor her indecision. . . . As the little boy said "The Blockade don't keep out babies" & the Southern women seem trying to replenish the places of the soldiers who have fallen. . . .

June 12
Friday

Mr. Tom Lee was married Wednesday morning at nine o'clock to Mrs. James Gibbes' daughter Annie of Columbia—all the Lees going over from here. They had a breakfast at Dr. Gibbes', then came over here, & that night Mrs. Markey Lee gave them a grand family dinner, going to table at nine & not leaving it till nearly twelve. Mrs. L[ee] had gone to Charleston and gotten the materials all from Nassau & went to the wedding leaving her servants to prepare everything. She certainly must have splendidly trained old time servants, for in these times especially, they are little short of miracles— so worthless have the majority become. Last night Mrs. Bonney gave them a party & tonight Mrs. Markley Lee gives them a grand reception, from eight to eleven, nearly a hundred persons invited and expected to stay to a handsome supper. Mr. [Tom] Lee was a long, gaunt old bachelor, the walking image of melancholy misery, so I suppose it makes the family rejoicing greater. . . . Maddie Gatewood is to be married on Tuesday, have a reception next day & leave on Friday—& all the young girls here of Eliza's age & younger, are going to give little parties, so Camden is following the universal fashion of gaiety everywhere. But the inhabitants of the *Nunnery* do not expect to participate. Eliza is so quiet in company that, besides being a stranger, she does not receive much notice & consequently does not enjoy parties much. . . .

June 13
Saturday

. . . Bishop [Stephen] Elliott and other ministers are preaching with great effect in the Army of Tennessee; a religious revival has taken place, & many soldiers confirmed, among them Gen. Bragg.

There is something wrong about Van Dorn's death, and I fear it must have been the result of his own conduct. No further notice of it has occurred in the papers and his name is never mentioned—but in the Knoxville *Register* . . . I see a paragraph from the Nashville paper saying Dr. [George B.] Peters had arrived there and said he had not found Van Dorn in criminal intercourse with his wife but refused to give an account of the cause which led to the murder, except before a court of justice. He only says he told Van Dorn he would spare his life to his wife and children (I always understood before he was unmarried) & that he answered he did not care for his wife. But Dr. P.[eters] required him to sign a paper of four articles, which he agreed to do. But at the last interview he had only acknowledged the first fully, the second unsatisfactorily, & refused the others altogether—on which Peters accused him of falsehood & breach of contract. Van D.[orn] ordered him to leave or he would kick him out, when Peters shot him then made his escape carrying off the paper as a witness. But that is only *his* story & I should really like to know the truth of the mystery. . . .

Miss Lucy Fisher, one of Mrs. [Fanny A.] McCandless' teachers, was married this morning at church to Mr. Raumsey. As Mr. [Leslie] McC.[andless] gave her away, there was a general holiday and gathering to the wedding. If Miss Fisher had only got married last autumn, as she expected and I hoped, I would have had her place as teacher which I wanted then. . . . Rev. Robt. Barnwell has been very ill with typhoid fever and is in such a highly excited state, almost crazy from the many distressing deaths and other scenes he has so long been a witness of, that his friends have had to remove him from the position where he has been such a fountain of blessing to our sick & wounded soldiers. I sincerely trust time & care will restore his shattered health and nerves.

June 16
Tuesday

. . . We read a letter today from uncle Henry [Gibbes] to grandmother, which quite relieved us. Grant's army was several days in passing Raymond [Mississippi], as they moved very cautiously expecting to meet Beauregard, whom they much fear, at Jackson [Mississippi]. Grant's orders were "That no private house should be entered, or property destroyed, & that negroes were not to be forced away, but protected if they left their owners." But the rabble, he says, will commit depre-

June 17
Wednesday

dations, and his horses, mules & cattle were carried off, but he saved his milk cows & one team of mules. No personal molestation was offered them, nor as far as he could learn had it really been offered to any one—nor were Allie [Gibbes] or himself compelled "to take the oath." His writing desk was stolen & many minor depredations committed, such as cutting up his buggy harness, etc. so that now he has no way of going about. Neither bacon nor corn were taken, nor were his crops touched—he has planted no cotton but corn entirely; fearing they might get at his wine (an excellent homemade article, which he has been ripening for years) and becoming drunk be made worse, he emptied out 70 gallons, which he could have sold for $700. His negroes all took his advice, save one man, & remained with him. They seem glad to have done so, for a great many who went off are returning, satisfied with the experiment. Those families who run off at the approach of the enemy suffered most losses from them & the negroes. He says he means to remain quietly at home, never mind under what government, for home is home after all— says newspaper accounts from Vicksburg & Port Hudson are correct.

June 20 Saturday Last night the boys went to act in some charades and tableaux gotten up for the benefit of the soldiers and amusement of the young people particularly. John returned with the news of the sudden death of Mr. [Charles H.] Peck & Alester had gone to sit up with the body. Mr. Peck was consumptive & was very ill a day or two ago and better again when he was suddenly seized with a fainting fit and died in a little time. He is no loss as a teacher, for though full of theory & quite ingenious, he was by no means either systematic or practical & besides in such miserable health that he did not do justice to his scholars. . . .

Tonight's paper contains a full account of one of the saddest and most tragical episodes of this eventful war, written by a Northern Surgeon, in the spirit of a gentleman and a Christian and particularly to be appreciated under the circumstances.[14] The papers mentioned a few days [ago] that

14 This account, headlined "Headquarters Post, Franklin Tennessee June 9, 1863," is clipped from the Nashville *Press*, June 11, 1863, and is signed, "W. H. Surgeon Eighty-Fifth Indiana."

Col. [Lawrence] Williams & Lieut [Walter G.] Peters of the Confederate army had been hung in Tennessee by the Yankees as spies, but I had thought nothing more of it till I read this Col. Lawrence Williams of Virginia was a first cousin of Gen. Robt. Lee and had been an officer in the U.S. Army. He was a splendid looking man of over six feet & about thirty years of age, &, the writer says, one of the most accomplished and intellectual men he has ever known—scarcely to be excelled as a talker. He was Inspector General on Bragg's staff and the leader in the daring enterprise which brought his adjutant and himself to such a dreadful doom. Lieut. Peters seemed to be an intelligent refined young man. They passed themselves off as Inspector Generals sent by Rosencrans [William S. Rosecrans] to examine the Yankee fortifications, and so boldly did they carry on their plans, that they nearly succeeded. After minute inspections, they went to Col. [Absolom] Baird & asked for the loan of $50 as they said they had been captured a few days previously by the Confederates & robbed. He lent it to them & Col. Williams gave his note under his assumed name of Col. Orton.

Soon after they left, it flashed upon Baird's mind that they were spies & he called hastily to Col. [Louis D.] Watkins and ordered him to pursue & bring them back. He only had time to take his adjutant with him & ordered him to get his gun ready to shoot them if they refused to stop. Our gallant & daring men were going at full speed, but when overtaken and told by Col. Watkins that Col. Baird begged them to return, as he has something more to communicate, after some refusal saying it would delay them so much, they returned with him perfectly unconscious they were going to an awful death. They were conducted to a tent & [were] perfectly unsuspicious of their being prisoners until one attempted to pass out & found themselves closely guarded. Soon after Col. Baird informed them of his suspicions & wished to search them. It was at first resisted, but on Lieut. Peters' sword was found his name & C.S.A. engraved & Col. Williams had a minute account of all their guns, fortifications, etc.; they then attempted to pass themselves off as persons trying to reach their friends at the North. But, their tale did not hang together well, for so little did they dream of detection, having been so successful, that they had not prepared any tale between them to account for themselves. They seemed as if unable for some time to recover their wits, so astounded were they. Baird telegraphed to Rosecrans about them & received answer that he knew nothing of them & had never given them any pass.

When they found all was discovered, they boldly and manfully confessed it, said they knew death was the penalty & were ready to suffer. They hoped they would die a soldier's death, by the bullet, but they were condemned to the usual fate of spies & met their awful doom as became them—only requesting before the ropes were adjusted that they might be allowed to bid each other farewell & clasped each other in a long close embrace. Companions in life, they were also in death, & one grave held the mortal remains of the gallant spirits whose names will live in history, as [Major John] André's has done, wherever the deeds of this war are told. Col. Williams wore the portrait & a lock of hair of his betrothed, which he requested should be buried with him. Col. Watkins had been an old friend when together in the U.S. army & he [Col. Williams] told the latter it was the only thing which saved him when he overtook them for his hand was on his pistol to shoot him down & escape. He gave his sword & pistols and begged him to use them & his horse also, a noble animal he valued at $5000, & asked him to be kind to it for his sake. The writer says this mournful occurrence had cast a gloom over the whole garrison. Col. W.[illiams] had been well known & admired in the old army, and this is probably the first time that officers of such distinction have ever suffered such a fate. Their names will live in song & story as household words, & the tears of their countrymen will ever keep their memory "green and flourishing as a bay tree," heroes in life and heroes in death.

By the papers I learn the marriage of my old schoolmate Georgia Moore to Mr. F. G. deFontaine, who as *Personne* has long excited deep interest in all readers of the *Courier* & many have been the blessings showered on his head for his letters from the battle fields. . . . It is really amusing to learn how those who are going to housekeeping have to pick up what they want here & there. Isaac has one set of chamber furniture & some for the drawing room, & his sisters & brothers are going to lend them some of the articles of various kinds, left them by their mother. They have plenty of plates, of all kinds, but one cup & five saucers & two tumblers. All of these articles are *very* scarce & *enormously* high, & cousin Willie & Rutledge have given her [Carrie] the only set of *any* kind to be found in the city—a dozen beautiful cut glass tumblers, at $50. We heard there was one common pair here, at five dollars, so she wrote for those & a number of other odds and ends. Going to housekeeping now is certainly "pursuing pleasure through difficulties." Nanna [Hughes] has lent her Sarah, so they are well provided with servants. I am delighted they have been able to get a house, though it is quite far from all of our friends. . . .

It is over a week since I last wrote, & I will have to think how *June 29* the time passed, busily I know. . . . Early in the spring a *Monday* drought was feared & rain constantly prayed for, &, when it did come, it came in torrents, & now a freshet is dreaded. It has rained hard constantly for three weeks past, and daily during the last [week] heavy thunder storms & hail, which have much damaged the standing corn, though the wheat crop is now safe. We, the buyers, are decidedly as much interested as the planters themselves. . . .

Gen. Lee's army has already advanced into Maryland, infantry as well as cavalry. The latter has had a few skirmishes and are giving the Yankees a touch of their own behavior in Pennsylvania, destroying public property of every kind. . . . Everything is encouraging for us there as well as at Vicksburg & Port Hudson, which the enemy continue to bombard without effecting scarcely any damage. At Vicksburg, nobody has been yet killed by it and the ladies go out to witness the magnificent effect of it at night. The city is well provisioned for 60 days, and no fear is felt for the result. The sappers and miners of both parties have reached so near one another, the sound of their pick axes can be heard.

On Friday we were much shocked to learn by the paper the death of Rev. Robert W. Barnwell, who was most emphatically *The Soldier's Friend*, and who fell a martyr to his devotion to them &, on Saturday, we were still more so at the announcement of his wife's leaving four little orphans. But Miss Habersham received letters from some of the Barnwells, giving the melancholy particulars. He had become so completely deranged that he attempted his own life with laudanum and death probably from the effects was a merciful release from a living death in the asylum. Oh insanity is an awful curse, and I think it is almost a crime for any who inherit it to marry. His wife had an infant daughter, the only one, three days old, & unable to stand such repeated shocks, died within twenty-four hours after, and they were buried in the same grave.

July
1
❧
September
25, 1863

Union Attack on Charleston

I came down to Charleston with Rev. S. Elliott; had an exceedingly fatiguing and dull journey as the weather was warm & he got a seat in another car; I did not meet a single acquaintance, most of the passengers being of the "democracy.". . .

July 1
Wednesday

I came to uncle James' where I found James [Holmes] *very sick* with typhoid fever. He came home a week ago but has never been ill. I was invited with others of the family to Mr. Bull's to a musical soiree and went knowing I should meet a room full of celebrities; I found myself almost entirely among strangers, ladies as well as gentlemen & Mr. Bull introduced very few, none to me; consequently I had to go to supper by myself, or rather I followed cousin Willie, whom Mary had persuaded to go. . . . I was therefore placed rather awkwardly. However, I enjoyed myself, for we had delightful singing. . . . [Lieut. Coxall] has besides [singing,] the peculiar accomplishment of whistling, with three fingers in his mouth, keeping admirable time to the duet on the piano and producing quite a pleasing effect. Col. [Ambrosio] Gonzales, who is an enthusiast in music, as I saw by the mere play of his face, played & sang two or three spirited songs, ending with the Marseillaise, to which the others sang the chorus; he has a fine voice & it was really delightful. I recognized him as soon as

July 2
Thursday

he entered by his likeness to Beauregard, of which I had often heard. Our beloved general was also there, so I had a good opportunity of comparing them. I loved to look at Beauregard's quiet modest but determined face, so full of character, but so impenetrable. His square forehead, high cheek bones, dark impressive eyes & closely cut grey hair form a figure, once seen, never to be forgotten. Gonzales is a little taller & with a livelier more sociable face and manner, "the foreigner" can be instantly recognized. Lieut. Col. Delaware Kemper, a Marylander, one of the heroes of Manassas always associated in my mind with Kershaw's regiment to which his battery was attached and whom I have always much admired, was also there. Rutledge knows him well & has often spoken to us of him & told me how he had been mistaken for Beauregard, the guards turning out to salute him. As soon as I saw him, I concluded he must be either Beauregard's son or brother, most probably the latter, as he looked too old for his son, though he seems about thirty. . . . Later I found out who he was and told cousin Willie who introduced himself. I felt quite provoked with Mr. Bull for passing me and introducing him at supper time to Cornelia Davidson, who had just been begging me to take charge of her. Among the other celebrities were Hon. W. Porcher Miles, looking so handsome and dignified, with his bride, a wax doll looking figure, rather fantastic in her style. Dr. Choppin & his wife, Col. Rice, Col. [George W.] Lay of Va., Capt. A. R. Chisolm, & others of Beauregard's staff, and Monsieur St. André the French Consul, good looking and impudent. Rosa looked very prettily, but was quiet & said she knew scarcely anyone, though of course they were introduced to her. After supper, when almost everyone but the singers had gone, Messrs. [Willie] Walker, [Loton] Reid & Cox, played deux temps & waltzes for Sue North & myself. It was very long since I had heard such music and longer since I had danced and I felt exhilerated by both; we were almost the last to leave, and we did not get home till after two. Sue had been all day helping Carrie to move into her house but had taken a cup of tea which kept her awake, and she kept talking to me until nearly four. Of course, I was very tired the next day but felt no other ill effects. In fact it rather did me good. The only thing was I was greatly disappointed in not meeting Capt. [Willie] Earle, whom I knew was in town, & would be invited, but he did not come & Rosa & I conclude his furlough must have been out.

My mornings have been spent resting and reading, (as I feel weary almost all the time); while I feel revived in the afternoon. Friday evening I waited till late for Edward to arrive, then went for Rosa to take a turn on the Battery, but it was too late; I was too tired & sleepy [and] I went to bed. Very soon after, Mr. W. P. Miles & his wife came to pay a visit. I have always admired & respected him so much. Though not a brilliant genius, his clear sound judgement has been a great service to his State and Country, and he is such a perfect gentleman in manners as well as deeds that he is an ornament to society, of whom we may well be proud—everybody trusts him.

I caught sight of Dr. [James] M[orrow] in a complete suit of white, even to his shoes, and I hardly recognized him at first.   *July 3*
  Friday

Miss Ellen Hume, who is also staying here, promenaded with   *July 4*
me on the battery, but I met very few acquaintances—I felt   *Saturday*
quite a stranger—"country come to town." A small fort is   *afternoon*
built at the corner of the Battery, the green turf forming a living wall, & the Calhoun Guard, Capt. Frank Miles, are encamped in the garden. We took tea at cousin Willie's in honor of its being Fourth of July, which we had almost all forgotten.

. . . We went to the Huguenot [Church] which was quite full &   *July 5*
is now the fashionable church from the fine singing of Mrs.   *Sunday*
Peck (certainly not from her husband's milk and water preaching) [and the singing of] Willie Walker, Etta Mills and Loton Reid. Afterwards I spent the evening with Rosa, Mr. Bull walking home with us, and inviting us to another soiree next Thursday. Rosa expects to go soon to Grahamville & he declares he has given up flirting or looking for a wife (grapes being *very* sour indeed) but is going to amuse himself and his friends with these soirees. Sue North, who is a kind of connection, says she will come over & sing for him; she invites the singers & he says he is not going to give handsome supper, nor wine, merely shrimps, crabs, etc. & fruit, the produce of Ashley Hall & corn whiskey for thirsty people.

July 6   . . . There is such a constant flow of relatives coming here,
Monday   passing & repassing through town, that the stage drivers came
to believe it was a boarding house & actually brought an old
lady here a few days ago, much to the amusement of the family.
. . . It is now a standing joke—the Holmes' Hotel—but uncle
James does not like us to go anywhere else. . . .

During the last week I have seen the papers for such a short
time & so irregularly & have felt in such a whirl, after having
been so long immured in the Nunnery, that I cannot write a
particular account, as I would wish, of the operations of our
various armies. However, the sum of the matter is that Lee's
army in various corps have moved into Maryland & Pennsylvania, by various routes, spreading terror and dismay everywhere—the Philadelphians scared to death & fortifying,
while the farmers are driving their cattle northward & moving their property. However, our troops, gradually moving to
Chambersburg, Gettysburg, & Harrisburg [Pennsylvania],
have destroyed public property, bridges, railroads, tunnels,
workshops, machinery, etc. supplying our men fully with
what they need from public stores, but purchasing everything from private persons at old prices, with Confederate
money. Thus our men are well clothed, shod & fed very much
at the expense of the enemy while droves of cattle have been
driven into Va. for safety. Lee's address to his army said that,
if our army retaliated the fearful outrages committed by the
Yankees & which made every Southerner thirst for vengeance
on the foul miscreants, our army would become as thoroughly
demoralized as the Yankees & thereby the very prestige of
victory be lost. So private property is respected and our army
has already called for the respect and admiration of the Yankee People, who say they feel safer with our army than [with]
theirs.

Rutledge wrote that the march had been dreadful, many
cases of sunstroke from the intense heat, and suffocating
dust, & some had died—but the man would drop suddenly as
if shot; just the same account as the Northern papers gave of
Hooker's army in its retreat. Fighting Joe has resigned & I
believe [George G.] Meade has taken his place.[1] . . .

1 Hooker was relieved of command on June 28, 1863, and was replaced
   by Meade.

Cousin John [Holmes] procured us a permit to visit Fort Sumter, but it came so late we were unable to invite a large party, and, as Willie & Maria were engaged to dine with Carrie, everything was uncertain. . . . After waiting some time, Anna [Holmes], Rosa [Bull] Guerard & myself went alone with cousin John; our trip there and back was by no means agreeable as the little high-pressure cotton boats are small and crowded with soldiers & forage, etc. and we had no acquaintance; after various tribulations, we succeeded in landing. . . . We had a pleasant time. I was at first much disappointed in the appearance of the fort expecting to have seen it in the same beautiful order which I heard spoken of last summer, forgetting that the damages of April 7th [1863] necessitated repairs, as well as additional strengthening, so of course, mortar & bricks & sand were still lying about. The workmen were repairing a massive merlon, erected to protect a heavy battery, the upper part of which had been much injured by a 15 inch shell. Just by its side was the 11 inch gun which gave the quietus to the *Keokuk*. Only three guns, heavy ones, are mounted in the second row of casemates, but the fort was bristling with them. The officers took us to visit the bakery where we saw very nice looking large loaves of wheat bread piled up & long flat loaves of corn bread—it really was a tempting display.

We returned home just in time to go to cousin Willie's to tea, quite a pleasant family gathering, and a very nice supper of peaches, cake, bread & butter & biscuits & real hyson tea, which was so strong that several of us, I among others, were kept awake till near daylight—so I amused myself looking out on the moonlit scene before me. . . .

The news yesterday was that Lee had routed the Yankee army and taken 40,000 prisoners, though we scarcely believed the latter item, and a report Vicksburg had fallen—so that we are alternately cheered or depressed.

There seems no doubt that Vicksburg has fallen after all our sanguine hopes and expectations & the constant declaration that the city was well provisioned. Now we learn that the garrison were exhausted with starvation, & [with] mines being sprung, a struggle was useless. The garrison, 17,500 men, are all paroled & allowed to come over into our lines, the officers retaining side arms & baggage. Grant, it seems, had so closely besieged the city intrenching himself in on every side that it was impossible for Johnston to dislodge him or to draw him out, especially with the small force he had, not more than 30,000, while Grant had 100,000.[2] It is a terrible blow to our cause and will prolong the war indefinitely—oh, how much depended on its salvation, but perhaps, as [Episcopal] Bishop [Stephen] Elliott [of Georgia] says, we are not yet prepared for the divine blessings of peace, and we had hoped too much from the grand struggle expected there so long. A letter recently from uncle Henry [Gibbes] says every time the Yankees passed his house, they stole something, and, if Vicksburg fell, he would have to seek another home in the Atlantic.

Lee has certainly gained a victory at Gettysburg Pennsylvania, after two or three days hard fighting, the bloodiest battle of the war, and the loss on both sides dreadful. . . .

. . . A later telegram says Lee was obliged to fall back to Hagerstown [Maryland]. When the gentlemen came home to dinner, they brought news of the arrival of seven Monitors off the bar & Stono[3] and a large fleet of transports off Folly Island. Everything looked so bright three days ago, and now a dark cloud seemed suddenly to have fallen like a pall.

July 10
Friday

Dull & dispirited as we all felt yesterday evening, we thought we might as well go to Mr. Bull's musical soiree & enjoy some good music, even if it were the last time. It was quite different from the first, so few persons, celebrities especially, were there, & everyone seemed so quiet and dispirited. [James Ryder] Randall the Maryland poet was there;[4] he has a fine intellectual face, though not handsome, a very fine broad brow but prominent nose, and a decided likeness to Capt. Zimmerman Davis, though the latter has not such an intellectual cast. Gen. Beauregard was not there, but his brother Capt. [A. N. T.] Beauregard was like the general without

2 At the end of the siege, Grant had 71,000 troops available while the Confederates had about 21,000.
3 A monitor was any shallow-draught warship with large bombardment guns. The most famous was the *Monitor* of *Monitor-Merrimac* fame.
4 Randall was the author of "Maryland, My Maryland."

uniform, a small quiet man and quite modest. He is good
looking and reminded us of Dr. Frank Miles, in fact Rosa
almost spoke to him as the Dr. Though not introduced to me
at supper time, he stepped up & offered his arm, & I was
quite pleased with him. Capt. Wm. Ramsey & Capt. Hill, a
good looking, dandified, conceited Marylander, were also
there—the latter has a good voice, but did not come till after
supper. We had some very good music. . . . We staid after the
elders of our party left & heard the Anvil Chorus sung &
played with the accompaniment of the triangle, & one or two
duets from Trovatore, but the news affected all. . . . We knew
the Mayor, after consultation with Beauregard, would today
issue a proclamation requesting women & children & all non-
combatants to leave immediately. . . . Willie Guerard had just
come &, though I knew more people than at the first & everybody was more sociable, I don't think I enjoyed it as much.

This morning I was awakened about five o'clock by the dull
boom of very heavy guns firing very rapidly from Folly I.
evidently attacking Morris Island. We could see the shells
bursting & occasionally hear their sharp whistle. As I expected to go to Carrie's tomorrow morning before breakfast, I
quietly packed up my clothes. . . . Since breakfast the firing
has only been at intervals. We went on the roof to look & saw
our men had set fire to a house on Morris I. beach, preparing
for an attack, that the enemy might not hide behind it. Everybody is in a state of uncertainty. Uncle James says he won't
tell anyone they must go, but that we had better be prepared.
I don't want to go at all & do not feel the slightest degree of
alarm but do not like to be a burden or cause of anxiety to
any of my friends. . . .

All day yesterday the cannonading was going on, but slower, *July 11*
and every deep boom of these tremendous guns seemed a *Saturday*
death knell, so solemn was the feeling they produced, particularly when the reports of those killed & wounded commenced
to come up. Poor Jamie Bee was the first whose death was
announced, but Yankee prisoners taken today say he is not
dead but desperately wounded. Rumors of every kind were
rife, and the day passed slowly on, leaving almost everyone
very quiet if not depressed. Beauregard had ordered no tele-

grams from the islands to be bulletined for fear of exciting
the people, & most persons augured ill from that, particularly
as we learned two or three of the batteries low down on Morris Island had been abandoned to the enemy. Thursday
morning the Yankees cut down trees on Folly I. unmasking
batteries of very heavy guns which together with Monitors
and boat howitzers which flanked our little battery of nine
guns concentrated a terrific fire of over fifty guns, under
cover of which infantry was landed & the fighting became
desperate, and hand to hand. Our men finally fell back to
Battery Wagner, quite a strong fortification, & which, with
Fort Sumter, kept up constant shelling to prevent the advance
of the enemy. The papers say our loss is nearly 300 killed,
wounded & missing, a number of wounded and exhausted
men, & those who covered our retreat having been captured.
The dead seem to be in small proportion, but most were left
in the hands of the enemy & we cannot learn particulars
except that Capt. Chas. Haskell & Capt. Langdon Cheves
are both really killed. Both were fine officers & Capt. Cheves
especially will be a severe loss to his family as well as his
country. He was a true patriot, shown by deeds not words.
Being over forty, by law he was exempt, but from the beginning of the war he devoted himself to the service of his
country, leaving his plantation & negroes near Savannah &
scarcely even visiting them, while he labored in the engineer
department in the defence [*sic*] of that city & then of this one,
without pay, or at least until lately perhaps. Both officers
exposed themselves in cheering on their men or looking out
and were instantly killed: Capt. Cheves' body was recovered
& buried today in the city. . . .

This morning at daylight the enemy made another attack
with infantry as well as artillery; our men waited for them
lying down, till close upon them, then rose & drove them
back beyond the sand hills, under cover of their boats, with
bayonets, capturing 130 & leaving 95 dead, besides a great
number wounded, our loss being slight. All Saturday cannonading was going on, sometimes slowly then for a few moments
rapidly, then ceasing altogether. Evening closed without even
a report. Anna [Holmes] & I went on the battery for exercises
and to view "*mobocracy*" which turned out in great strength,

utterly regardless of taste & expense. We were almost ashamed to be seen in such a common crowd, but after a while met two or three acquaintances to keep us in countenance. Really, we could not imagine where such people came from; such never used to be seen on the battery. Among the few gentlemen acquaintances, I saw was Dr. [James] M[orrow] who bowed almost to his horse's neck. I wonder when we will meet again to speak.

Saturday evening I learned Alester had arrived with a volunteer corps, & yesterday morning he came to see me—said Friday evening he had gone to a concert given by the Misses Sloman and, while there, the report of fighting having commenced arrived. The boys all got crazy with excitement & determined to come down. He came home between 11 and 12 [and] finding everybody asleep, would not wake mother for fear of *disturbing* her, never reflecting it would disturb her more to wake in the morning & find him gone. So he told Johnnie, &, borrowing $15 from Harry Elliott, started off with Willie Workman, the other boys having drawn back & joined Maj. [J. P.] Thomas at Kingsville without blankets or clothes, except what they had on. . . . If they [had] waited for the midday train, they could have got all they needed, but they feared the fight might be over, so rushed off. But this bombardment will last rather longer than they imagined. . . . Cannonading all day yesterday, just like Saturday, & no news from there. . . .

July 13
Monday

. . . The fighting at Gettysburg was desperate on both sides, for the enemy were on their own soil & besides intrenched on high hills and slopes, up which our men had to charge, and, though great deeds of daring were done by our gallant host & the Yankees driven several times back at various points, still we were not able to drive them entirely from their stronghold. It certainly does not appear to be the great victory at first announced, though a very great battle.

July 15
Wednesday

Our troops on James I. made a reconnaissance & found negro troops to oppose them—scarcely a white officer among them. At the first discharge, they fled pursued by our men who

July 16
Thursday

mowed them down & would have cut them to pieces, but one of our officers put a stop to it, saying he wished some captured to be hung as an example & 16 were taken.[5] Most of the gentlemen think it decidedly a wrong step, as many nice questions will now be involved. If we hang them, will not the Yankees retaliate upon our men. They are fiendish enough to delight in the idea. Yet, it is revolting to our feelings to have them treated as prisoners of war as well as injurious in its effects upon our negroes. However, they were brought to the city barefoot, hatless & coatless & tied in a gang like common runaways.

July 17
Friday
morning

I was much surprised to receive a message from Carrie saying Mary Jane & Hattie [White] & herself had "run the blockade" but expected to leave next day for Summerville & begging me to go to see her. Just as I was about starting, determined to make a great effort to walk so far, "Our good Dr. [Louis De-Saussure]" came in to visit his patients, & said he would drive me up. He is almost the only person who fully understands & appreciates my weakness & debility. The girls arrived soon after I did & most happy were we to meet once more. Dr. White & Sims [White] also came in at different times, so I had quite a pleasant day seeing old friends—Isaac driving me down after tea. By the bye, he has sold his pet horse, Prince, a beautiful animal, $2,000 having been offered him for it, & he now drives a remarkable fine pair of mules, for which he has already been offered $1600.

Lee has recrossed the Potomac, in admirable order, and the army in splendid trim and spirits without loss, though continual skirmishing took place. . . . Lee's move has surprised one half the community & pleased the other—the latter thinking he had gone too far from his base of supplies and communication, particularly as the still frequent heavy rains (which by the bye, are now ruining the fine crops everywhere) made the Potomac almost impassable. It is said that the President ordered the recrossing of the river, much to Lee's anger

5   The black troops (54th Massachusetts Regiment) caught the brunt of the attack, but only gave way grudgingly, thus providing time for other Union troops to form a battle line for the expected attack that never came. See Dudley Cornish, *The Sable Arm* (New York: Longmans, Green, 1956), 151–52.

& mortification, & that he said if it were not for his country he would resign. His retreat from Gettysburg was strategic, to draw Meade's army from the high hills behind which they took refuge.

President Davis has called out all *male residents* of the Confederacy, capable of bearing arms, between 18 & 45. The New York *Herald* of the 14th gives an account of a tremendous riot which took place there in the attempt to enforce the Conscription. . . . Everybody & everything was in a state of excitement, cannon planted in the streets & troops guarding the Post office & Newspaper offices & hotels. Every negro seen by the mob was either murdered or cruelly beaten and altogether a most demoniac scene. I am glad the Yankees are suffering a touch, even though such a faint one, of the horrors they have committed or tried to excite in our midst. . . .

From daylight this morning the enemy was bombarding Battery Wagner furiously; they have over 70 guns concentrated from their various batteries & Monitors & they fired at the rate of 20 shots a minute. It was intended to demoralize our troops, preparatory to the assault, which commenced at dark. I spent a good part of the day with an excellent spy glass watching the [*New*] *Ironsides* and four Monitors: I could see almost every discharge &, when the Yankee shells struck, the earth . . . [sent] up a tall column of sand. I did not feel at all alarmed or excited; I had become so accustomed to the cannonading—but watched everything with intense interest. The [*New*] *Ironsides* lay like a huge leviathan: long, low & black, discharging broadsides, while at her side, but nearer to Morris Island lying between herself & land, was a Monitor whose peculiar black turrets were instantly recognizable, so distinctly defined against the sky are their huge black forms. Our batteries on Morris I. & Sumter slowly replied but with excellent effect; during the morning the Yankee columns were formed for an attack, but our grape and canister drove them back with considerable loss. I could, with a glass, see not only the signalling from our various forts and batteries but from the Yankee observatory on Folly Island, which is high above the trees. I was wishing so much I could read their dispatches & found later that Mr. Westervelt had done so & intercepted Gilmore's [Quincy Adams Gillmore] orders for a general at-

July 18
Saturday

tack on our batteries Saturday night, so our men were ready for them.[6]

Just as we were going to dinner, cousin John's [Holmes] Baltimorean friend from the Marion Artillery, Mr. Jenkins . . . came to get a view of the bombardment; he is a delicate looking, very gentlemanly young man, who quite interested us. Cousin Christopher [Gadsden] & others came later for the same purpose, and the Battery was thronged with spectators; during the afternoon I received a note from Carrie saying the Summerville plan had been necessarily given up . . . so Carrie intended remaining here till obliged to leave, then go to Camden & wished me to come and stay with her. At such a time when everything of interest was concentrated on the Battery & I am not able to walk down there, it really is a sacrifice to friendship to come up into the interior of the town. However, I determined to enjoy a last walk on the Battery, &, with Miss Ellen Ford, promenaded till dark, watching the beautiful effect of the broad flashes of light at every discharge, which illuminated the sky.

On our return, [I] found Gen. [Col. Ambrosio] Gonzales, who had been on the housetop for a long time in cousin Beck's [Holmes] piazza, & I could not help being amused to think how war had leveled ceremony; all were obliged to pass through her chamber, where she was busily writing by a bright gas light. The room was, of course, neatly arranged, but the pavilion down, etc. &, as he was halfway through, some question was asked and a long & interesting conversation ensued which decidedly cheered all parties. He said the reason those lower batteries on Morris I. had not been completed was that, instead of sending their negroes, the planters preferred paying the fines. Consequently instead of the three or four thousand laborers needed, there were only twenty odd at one time, & we did not even have troops enough to build them, for we had sent 10,000 men to Miss. and had only about three regiments here. . . . If the Yankees had dared, they could have taken the city before but now there was no cause for apprehension. . . . Men were not what we

6 Gillmore was commander of the X Corps and the Department of the South between June 12, 1863, and May 1, 1864. He was, therefore, overall commander of the attack on Charleston.

wanted on Morris I., we had plenty now, but heavier guns, which were being rapidly supplied there & on Sullivan's I. If Battery Wagner was taken, the Yankees' troubles would only commence, he said, for it would be a work of time to erect batteries to reduce Sumter & every day was gain to us. He had recommended Beauregard to strengthen the officers' quarters there, the weakest side, by taking away the floors & making a solid wall of compressed cotton on a flooring of wet sand. . . . Battery Bee on Sullivan's I. is as strong as Sumter & heavier guns are being put on Moultrie, so even if Sumter were taken, the city was not necessarily lost. I was really glad I had seen him & was very much pleased with him. Just after, Isaac called for me. . . . Everything seemed to quiet up in Beaufain St. that we all slept as quietly as possible, little dreaming of what a sanguinary engagement was going on almost at our doors.

We learned what a tremendous assault had been made and how gloriously repulsed. About eight Saturday evening, the Yankees advanced in six columns, as Willie Ramsey has since described to me, in perfect line of battle. Our men waited till [they were] within 800 yards, then opened on them with grape & canister, which mowed huge gaps in their ranks; they would waver for a moment, then close up and move steadily on, again to be cut down. Again and again were assaults made, & in the darkness & melie [*sic*] two or three hundred gained a position on the magazine where they planted their flag & held it for more than an hour, it being some little time before they were discovered. A call for volunteers to dislodge them was made & numbers instantly stood forth—and in doing so, we lost the majority of our killed & wounded. . . . After having made other desperate assaults, they were finally driven off. They had expected our men to be completely demoralized by the incessant cannonading, & William White . . . assisting in erecting a mortar battery, says nothing can be more demoralizing for the men [than] to be cooped up all day in the close bomb proofs with this awful neverending roaring and whistling—the nerves kept in such a state of intense excitement. . . . Think of such a battle in the darkness with the roar of artillery mingled with the rattle of musketry. . . . William W[hite] and William R[amsey] have both

July 19
Sunday
morning

given us accounts of the fight & say they had heard of "piles of dead Yankees" & "bodies three deep" but never saw it till now, when they actually would be four deep, one on the other, as they fell forward in every conceivable attitude. It was an awful sight in the ditch below the parapet.

The Yankees sent a flag of truce, seeking the body of Col. [H. S.] Putnam, acting Brigadier, a splendid looking man, grandson of [American Revolutionary War] Gen. Israel Putnam, & requesting to bury their dead. The first request was granted, the latter refused as it was thought they only wanted an opportunity of close inspection, & the answer was we would bury their dead & take care of their wounded, many of whom, however, must have been carried off. We buried 600 among them numerous field officers, as well as captains & lieutenants, & beyond our lines, the enemy buried over 200, among them about 150 negroes. . . . A good many of them were among the 230 wounded brought to the city, many so severely they will certainly die. And a negro had been put alternately with a Yankee in the hospital, much to their disgust, but our surgeons told them as they had put them on an equality they must abide the consequences. Their loss in killed, wounded & prisoners, must be 1500. Col. [Robert Gould] Shaw of Massachusetts was buried with eleven negroes over him.[7] Among the wounded prisoners is a remarkable intelligent negro from Bermuda, educated in the military school there. Having no employment at home & needing support for his mother, he went to New York & Boston to seek it & found large bounties being offered to volunteers. . . . As he had nothing else to provide his mother with, he joined the army & was made a sergeant. He says, when the column to assault was formed, the general rode up to the negro regiment, commanded by Shaw, and told them to charge bravely, remembering if they faltered [that] 10,000 bayonets were behind them. . . . He says they marched with the bayonets almost in their backs. He curses the Yankees fearfully for a set of vile cowards and wretches.

7 Robert Gould Shaw was the commander of the black 54th Massachusetts Regiment. He was perhaps the most famous of the white Union officers leading black troops and personified a threat to the South's racial attitude.

The first thing that greeted my eyes this morning on opening the paper, was our dear Rutledge's name, signing a report of casualties in the S.C. regiments, at the battle of Gettysburg. I knew Kershaw had telegraphed on the third day of the battle to say himself & staff were safe, but nothing particularly had been heard from Rutledge, & I felt sure now cousin Willie had received a letter. Thank God, for his safety, but many of our friends and acquaintances, in the long list, have suffered. . . .

July 20
Monday

. . . A Yankee surgeon & chaplain were captured on Saturday & paroled with 30 other prisoners to attend their wounded. A number of the wounded negroes remained all night on the wharf, our men refusing to move them, & finally making the Yankees do it.

July 21
Tuesday

During the past week I have tried several new trades, as Sarah was suddenly taken & Joe, after losing a pound of tea $12 worth, was afraid to come home & was finally brought back after two days absence. So I turned chamber maid & even laundress, as we found it difficult to procure a washerwoman & besides they charged so extravagantly. Mary Jane & Hattie [White] were part of almost every day with us and Sims [White] constantly. The girls staid with us & while here found our next door neighbors had a quantity of goods taken from the wreck of the *Raccoon* for sale,—the finest French colored cambrics, very wide, which at first they asked $2 for, then reduced to $1.50 & others to $1. according to the injury they received. Many were quite uninjured, & we all made extensive purchases for different friends & the children in the family as well as ourselves, for they also had fine black delaine which they let the girls have at $2, remarkable cheap for these days, when $4 or $5 is the common price. However, they balanced that by asking *$20* a yard for a substantial black silk which we had vainly hoped might be $3 or $5 at least. Friday & Saturday we had many amusing scenes over our various purchases, while the large empty drawing room (a name from courtesy as it contains only two or three pieces of very old furniture & three or four half broken chairs) was festooned with the goods, some to dry mostly, others washed out, dried,

July 29
Wednesday

then pressed round a board while damp, which made them look like fresh goods. . . .

Uncle [Henry Alexander] DeSaussure . . . returned from Sullivan's Island, where he found every vestige of his house & establishment, but his date trees, gone, all the houses from Battery Bee to Fort Moultrie having been taken down & heavy batteries erected in their place. Heavy batteries have also been built on James and Morris Islands & every day there has been cannonading, more or less heavy; a good deal of it was from our mortar batteries shelling the Yankees at the batteries they are erecting on Morris I. We are so accustomed now to the guns we can always tell whether it is a shell or a solid shot & listen for the reports & explosions as coolly as possible. Our casualties are very slight [from] each, sometimes one or two men killed or wounded. . . .

I spent the night at uncle James' & thoroughly enjoyed the glorious moonlight which flooded the broad expanse of our beautiful harbor—but it made me melancholy to think it might be the last time for months that I would fill my heart with the delicious prospect, of which every spot is so dear & frought with thronging memories of the past. . . . Mr. Bull, being one of Beauregard's special aids, whenever any new movement takes place there—he being thoroughly acquainted with every by-path & spot on [*sic*] ground—is an admirable guide & did good service a fortnight ago, when that brush took place on the 16th with the Yankees, & the negroes were captured. . . .

July 31
Friday

Alas [John H.] Morgan, our brave, dashing, brilliant partisan chief, has been captured, after, by the Yankee's own confession, his most brilliant & destructive raid into the very heart of Indiana and Ohio. Oh, how his proud spirit will chafe within his prison walls, particularly as the base foe, with their usual fiendish malignity, have declared that his officers & himself will be kept in close confinement until the Tories & negroes who were captured by [Nathan Bedford] Forrest in their raid on Georgia are exchanged. . . . The past few days have chronicled grievous tidings in the death of the beloved and most useful [William L.] Yancey, who had rendered as important services to the Confederacy with his eloquent pen & still more eloquent tongue, as Morgan has done with his sword.[8]. . . Mother has just lost our coachman, Henry, of typhoid fever. He was a valuable servant, bringing excellent wages & giving no trouble as almost all the others have done.

I walked this afternoon amidst whole streets in ruin to visit our old home; found some soldiers encamped on the spot, so did not go quite to it. But [I] sat for some time on the foundation of Mr. Bull's iron fencing sadly recalling the memories of the past, as I gazed on each familiar point in the beautiful water landscape. The pillars and tall iron steps of Mr. Bull's porch still remained, with vines climbing here & there, bringing vividly to mind our pleasant tableaux & oyster parties & the many, many changes in the merry girls and youths there and then assembled.

August 1
Saturday

Carrie & I lead a very quiet monotonous life; our morning occupied in becoming accomplished chambermaids, laundresses & housekeepers, & trying to train "Joe," who is as slippery as an eel, in the way he should go, (by no means an easy or agreeable task) & occasionally going a little way into King St., for I am still unable to walk even down to the Battery without feeling the effects for several days. I had fondly hoped the rides on horseback I anticipated at Grahamville would fully restore my strength, but there is no prospect of my going there now.

How the past week has flown, bringing with it, however, great and unexpected pleasure for me. Monday morning Mr. Bull stopped here in passing to invite us to spend Tuesday evening at his house to hear some music from Mr. [Willie] Walker and a few other gentlemen. . . . Isaac did not feel like going and thought Carrie had better not, much to my & her own disappointment, & all Tuesday I had been in the most disagreeable frame of mind & body. Feeling very badly, weary, cross, blue, dull & considerably provoked to think I had nothing else to wear but a high neck white cambric very badly done up, the only trimming being a double crimped frill with a nar-

August 8
Saturday

8   William L. Yancey (1814–63) was a leading Southern "fire eater." He was a lawyer in Alabama, a member of the state legislature and the United States House of Representatives during the 1840s, the head of the delegation sent to Europe in 1861 by the Confederate government to seek diplomatic recognition, and a member of the first Confederate Senate.

row black velvet strip between, when I knew everyone would wear something pretty and more suitable and dressy for the evening. However, Isaac drove me down to spend the night with Rosa; very soon after we went downstairs, to my unbounded pleasure and surprise, Capt. [Willie] Earle entered, having just arrived in the city with his battery & come round to pay a visit. He never dreamed of seeing me any more than I of meeting him & the extreme gratification was mutual. I spent the whole evening until after supper with him, recalling the pleasure of last spring and the numerous events which had occurred since our parting. To seeing him was added the prospective pleasure of seeing Jamie and Charlie [Furman]. And altogether, I felt as bright and gay as a young bird. I believed I liked him better than ever, if that could be, when he told me how much he had come to love the low country & Charleston that he wished to live here, if he could persuade a certain fair lady whom he had lately visited thereto. May his fondest hopes be realized, for I believe him fully worthy of the choicest gifts of Heaven. . . . How pleasant it was to have some one who enjoyed talking over the past as much as I did.

The only gentleman musician who came was Mr. [Willie] Walker, & we had very little music; late in the evening Mr. Clarence Dearing, a brother of Gov. Picken's second wife, sang. . . . As a musical soiree, it was a failure. . . . But before Mr. Dearing left, almost everyone was thoroughly disgusted with him. His conceit & perfect self satisfaction were visible at the first glance. He is a tall, stylish looking man, but with a face that won't bear inspection for the expression, however good the features may be. Mother had often told me of his conduct in Virginia, where she met him with his sister, whom she liked very much. But he was by no means admired from his behavior there in a duel & the way he flirted with Rose Freeland, a child of twelve, completely turning her head & making her the talk of the Springs, merely for his amusement. Then a few months ago, he told Maria [Scriven Holmes], who was very slightly acquainted with him, all of his domestic affairs—how, being jilted by one lady, he married another for whom he cared nothing, but he gave her as much money as she wanted & let her have her own way, etc.—all but proving how contemptible he was, respecting neither her nor himself. Moreover he then passed himself off as an un-married man & paid the most assiduous court to a young girl, doing everything but address her, & she did not learn the truth, till after she left. Since, he has been trying the same game, making most of the persons at Mr. Bull's believe he was a widower, but I soon undeceived them & Mr. Earle & Mr. Ashe both said his wife was in Canada. Did he but know the difference between the character with which he entered & that with which he left, I think he would have had lost a little of his conceit; but every one was indignant at his dishonorable behavior. His brother, Major Dearing, is his antithesis. Carrie & Rosa were delighted with him—he was so proud of his wife & so devoted to her.

. . . [Wednesday] afternoon just as I was leaving, I met Mr. Leo Walker, who had just arrived to try to make arrangements to run the blockade with his family to Canada, where he expects to be able to get at some of his means, how I do not know, to maintain them. . . . When he settles them, he will return. He looked so old & careworn, with his hair quite grey & falling long on his neck—such a total change from the handsome, elegant officer, whom I parted with little over a year ago, that I hardly recognized him & felt shocked and saddened. Indeed his face has haunted me continually since. I do not wonder at his care worn air, for I cannot tell how his family get on. Both his wife & himself [were] brought up in every luxury & he never doing a stroke of work, merely an elegant man of leisure & indeed he was one of the most elegant, courteous, refined gentlemen I have ever met—suddenly deprived of every resource, then burnt out & he thrown out of his position by [General R. S.] Ripley's behavior. I cannot see how he has managed to feed & clothe his family. . . .

[Tuesday] morning Dr. White & I commenced at break-fast to discuss what Carrie calls my favorite topic—the Equal-ity of the Sexes—for it always makes me indignant to hear men arrogate to themselves such vast superiority over wom-en, mentally as well as physically. The Dr. agreed with my proposition, then we discussed their various capacities, and I was as surprised as delighted to find what admirable conver-sational powers he possessed, & how intelligent and cultivated & very refined he was. I never have spoken so freely to such a comparative stranger of my thoughts & feelings on many intimate matters, but he drew me on, proving his argument from Bible & Prayer Book in such beautiful style & language & yet with such plain earnest desire of seeking only my own good, that I felt I had gained a friend & a sincere one. And I never received better or more gently administered advice in my life. He spoke as plainly as I did, for I gave him free permission, and very many unpalatable but most wholesome truths were told me. We talked till he had to go out on business, then he renewed the subject after dinner, & time flew so rapidly in a conversation which interested both so much that it was dark before we were roused by Isaac's return with letters.... Again [Wednesday] morning the subject was renewed; this time he brought [Martin F.] Tupper's Proverbial Philosophy to bear its light upon it, revealing to me new beauties & new truths in a book which I have hitherto utterly neglected. But, that is a trifle compared to what I have to thank him for. He has done me more good than he can know. He told me he had been quietly studying my character, and, without intending a compliment, he thought I had an originally fine, noble character, but much warped—that I had a fund of generosity at the depth of my heart, of which I was perhaps myself unconscious, but if I would only let it flow freely forth, I would be astonished at the results myself. It is but seldom I have heard such praise, which I felt came from his heart, & though I fear it is too high, for no one knows my own deep-dyed faults better than I do, I thanked him sincerely for all he had told me & told him I would try to follow his advice. I have never had any subject so closely argued with me step by step, till I knew & acknowledged every word he said was right, even though I knew I was far from doing what I felt was right. He perhaps did not think the study of character was mutual, but he unconsciously revealed the native nobility of his soul, with every word he uttered. He had said my standard of what a man ought to be was too high, but before we parted I felt and told him that I considered him as approaching very near to it. He is a man who *lives* his religion and whose Bible is his daily guide. I never saw the beauty of religion more plainly shown—yet we never once discussed that point, only alluding to it. Until now I had scarcely ever spoken a dozen words to him & had always thought of him as I had heard others speak of him very slightingly as a man who never could get on in the world, & I always fancied he had very little character & less mind. But these, who have spoken thus, know nothing of him, & I felt as if I could "doff my cap" to him with utmost respect & admiration. He is worthy of his mother, though he may not be as brilliant for a man as she was for a woman. I spoke of her as "thoroughly intellectual, & thoroughly practical" & he said he believed I had fully characterized her—but I ought to have added *thoroughly pious.* The Dr. went back home two or three hours ago but will probably return soon. . . .

During the past week the bombardment has gone on as usual, some days day & night, at others almost entirely ceasing, often our batteries alone playing on those of the enemy. . . .

I missed reading [William] Gilmore Simm's late beautiful ode "The City by the Sea" till a few days ago, but I was delighted with it.[9] I never believed he possessed much poetic talent, however prettily he might write as a novelist, but this is really a beautiful, graceful and spirited tribute to our beloved home. Almost every day some spirited and inspiriting little poem or ode by him appears in the [Charleston] *Mercury*, many of them really excellent, particularly his "Beauregard."

August 11
Tuesday

. . . The enemy are as busy at their batteries as we at ours, & an artillery duel is of daily or nightly occurrence generally four or five of our men being killed or wounded. Our men must suffer very much at Fort Wagner, not only from the intense heat and want of good water & plenty of it, but from being obliged to be shut up most of the time in the suffocating bombproofs while shot and shell are rained down upon them. They are relieved every few days, for they become exhausted from want to rest & made sick from the water. Pinckney Lowndes, speaking in his usual flippant style, said if he thought "hell was half as hot and dreadful as Fort Wagner, he would try to be good." The weather is intensely hot everywhere now, & the enemy confess their men suffer fearfully in the trenches. . . .

An extract from a New York paper in today's [Charleston]

9 William Gilmore Simms (1806–70) is usually considered the antebellum South's leading literary light. He wrote in the romantic style, and his works included poetry, biography, novels, and plays. In 1852 he contributed to *The Pro-Slavery Argument.*

Courier severely condemns Burnside for his cruelty and injustice to Morgan & his officers, whom he placed in the Ohio penitentiary & showed his brutality by *shaving their heads* & treating them like convicts, while [Abel D.] Streight's officers for whom they are held as hostages are in the Libby prison at Richmond and treated with kindness as prisoners of war. If our gallant Morgan gets free from their clutches, they will pay dearly for every indignity offered him—but it is just what might be expected from such a creature. . . .

August 17
Monday

Last Friday Isaac came home & told Carrie she must go on Tuesday, so on Saturday he sent us a carriage to go and bid all of our friends goodbye,—for he wanted me to go too. . . . I was very unhappy at the probable prospect of my immediate return to Camden & heard so much sad news on Saturday that I went home very sad. Mrs. [George] I[ngraham] had told us George had seen Frank Harleston's body being carried to his family, he having been killed at Fort Sumter. I was dreadfully shocked & grieved until this morning I learned it was positively untrue—that George had merely heard the report. Then today's paper announced Mary Gadsden's death, &, though prepared for it by Willie's letter, of course I felt shocked. Oh how hard it is to reconcile the mind to death of our friends or acquaintances, even when we know it is inevitable. Poor Harriet Holmes is dying here of dropsy, suffering dreadfully & cannot last but a few days longer. That family have indeed almost drained the bitter cup of affliction —three brothers since the war commenced, all the others desperately ill, & now she, their especial pet, so gentle, amiable, good and affectionate, dying almost by inches. Pretty Sophie Guerard too, after lying ill 80 days with typhoid fever, is now dying of consumption—for there is no possible hope of her recovery.

Carrie & I have been very busy packing since Saturday. I was ready to go with her, as we heard this morning Beauregard was going to issue an order for the women & children to leave as he was determined to defend the city, street by street. But I found it was only the Governor's [M. L. Bonham] recommending them to leave & affording all facilities for them to do so; therefore, I determined to stay a few days longer with Rosa, for I want to enjoy the last of my visit—if it is to be the last—which God grant it may not be.

Today the bombardment was really terrific. There was not a moment's cessation of the daily, heavy roar or the concussion from our own mortar batteries, which made every window rattle. We only remarked it, but continued our packing quietly till Isaac came home during the day and asked if I was not scared by it and ready to go. For, all the Monitors, six or eight I think, the [*New*] *Ironsides*, and a number of wooden frigates had been all morning trying to reduce Fort Sumter to ruins as yet without doing any serious damage, though the land batteries, with their 200 pound Parrott siege guns, had most accurate range. Though no breach had yet been effected, still they made the bricks and sand fly very freely on the southwest face, and it was feared no masonry could stand the mere weight and force of such tremendous missiles. Edwin [White] is at Fort Sumter, so I suppose Isaac learned from him what he told us in confidence that, though every effort was being made to strengthen Sumter with sandbags and cotton bales, yet, as it was feared it must ultimately fall, the heaviest guns were being quietly moved and put into other batteries. Quakers, wooden guns, [were] being put in their places so that when it was found necessary to abandon or blow it up as ought to be done to prevent its occupation by the enemy, the loss will be comparatively slight. . . . The Yankees will have a fearful gauntlet to run before they can reach the city. They have given up the notion of taking Fort Wagner till Sumter falls; as they confess, being of sand, it is almost impregnable, the void occasioned by one shell, being filled by the explosion of another. And though Gilmore [Quincy A. Gillmore] says officially that he only lost 600 odd men from the 10th to the 18th August, the papers confess their loss on the 18th was terrific "probably greater than ever before experienced by the besiegers of such a work." Sumter is so identified with us and our cause that it will be like tearing out our heart-strings should it fall. But now, we feel the safety of our city does not depend on it, as we once thought, and we will not despair. Each day that I stay in Charleston makes me love and cling to it yet more fondly. But all we can do is to hope and trust in the mercy of a righteous God.

I shudder to think of the fate of any of our people, should our city fall, after the awful barbarities committed in Mississippi & vouched for by excellent authority. A party of Yankee officers *hung* a young married lady, in her own house, with a sash taken from off one of them, because she refused to reveal where her husband was. Two more went to a house where an old widow lady, whose name I have forgotten, was visiting—but she belonged to one of the wealthiest and most highly respected families in the state. They heard she had about $40,000, entered her bedroom, took her out of bed, & gave her *500 lashes on her bare back* to make her confess where was the money she did not have. She was so maimed and bruised from their fiendish treatment that she was not expected to recover. Humanity sickens at their demoniacal brutality & far better would it be for South Carolina to become a wilderness and desolation, one vast sepulchre & heap of smoking ruins, than to be cursed for one brief moment with their power to wreak evil.

August 19
Wednesday

. . . Rosa partly expected Mr. [Willie] Guerard & we waited for some time for him to arrive, and, as he did not come, went round to uncle James' to see the bombardment, which had been furious all morning. But the weather was very stormy yesterday, a strong east wind blowing, & all the vessels had drawn off, unable to stand the rough seas, & even the land batteries were quiet for a time. The wind was so furious we could scarcely get round the corner of the battery, but our consolation & hope was it might do some injuries to the enemy. . . .

At supper we commenced a discussion of *A Strange Story* & Victor Hugo's new series *Fantine, Corsette, & Jean Valjean*, the latter works Mr. Earle condemning, and it led to a most delightful literary conversation. I had long been wanting to hear where the quotations "The mill of the Gods grind slowly" & "He whom the Gods would destroy, they first make mad," came from. I concluded from some of the old Greek tragedies, in which he confirmed me, recommending Clytemnestra, Agamemnon & Oedipus Tyrannus for my perusal and promising to send me a little essay he wrote in college on the subject. It was a real treat to listen to such conversation, for I gained instruction as well as great pleasure. . . . Mr. [Willie]

Walker sang & played for us till twenty minutes of *one* and, as Mr. Bull gave both Mr. Earle & himself warm invitations to breakfast, dine or take tea here at any time, Mr. Walker came over this morning. With all his overpowering conceit & presumption, which at times are insufferable, & though I have a very trifling opinion of his character, after Messrs. Hughes and [P. G.] Fitzsimons told us how he literally *sponged* on Mr. Wilson, making his house as free as a hotel yet paying but for one meal a day & at the same time giving himself great airs, yet he can lay aside all that & making [*sic*] himself really pleasant, though I cannot respect him.

... Yesterday there were no casualties at Fort Sumter, strange to say, notwithstanding the furious cannonading, & a few at the other batteries.

As constantly happens, it is over a week since I have had an opportunity to continuing my journal, but the events of each day are indelibly impressed on my mind. Wednesday evening [August 19] Capt. [A. N. T.] Beauregard called to see us, said the General had sent him to try and persuade some ladies to leave & wanted to know when we were going. We told him, in a few days, when Fort Sumter fell—for that was the only danger we anticipated at that time. He said, if only a few days, he thought we might remain, unless any accident should occur—none of us then believing or fearing the city being shelled. Mr. Bull went with Capt. Beauregard afterwards to Mr. [Willie] Walker's musical club, & Rosa & I amused ourselves trying to overlook them from my chamber window. Capt. Shiver, a Prussian officer, sent here by his government as a looker-on, and Capt. Ross, an English officer in the Australian service here for the same purpose, were both there, & Shiver's singing and acting seemed to afford inexpressible amusement to the gentlemen, who were literally convulsed with laughter. Such shouts came from them that it was enough to startle the neighborhood—but the singing sounded to us, though so near, as only so much noise.

Thursday [August] 20th Rosa & I went in the morning to shop as high as Harts, the longest walk I had yet taken &, to my pleasure, found myself so little fatigued that we took a stroll on the Battery near dark. After our morning's walk I read aloud "Tannhausar" a new poem just published and writ-

August 27
Thursday

ten by [Edward Robert Bulwer-Lytton ("Owen Meredith")] a son of [Edward George] Bulwer[-Lytton], the novelist, and a friend whose name I have forgotten, as it is published under assumed names. It is very "Tennysonian" in its style & is a pretty little poem with some beautiful ideas and expressions & several beautiful "pictures" and Wolfram's [von Eschenbach] lyric on Love is as pure as musical. We were indebted to Mr. [Willie] Earle for its perusal, and I tried to get the books he suggested but only procured the tragedies of Aeschylus. I do not know whether it was the influence of the poem or the very peculiar German style of the novel *Charles Auchester* which I had been reading, or the intense stillness of the atmosphere, but I felt as if under a dreamy spell, and I felt as dull and low-spirited as possible—and just wished for Mr. Earle to come and cheer us. For Rosa was as "blue" as I. We were sitting half asleep on the steps, when Mr. Lenan, the French Consul, came to see us, and I was quite agreeably disappointed in him. He is very pleasant and sociable & wanted me to talk French with him, but I could not express myself readily, so I laughingly declined after one or two attempts. He has just learned to speak English since he came to Charleston; we invited him to come & play whist with Mr. Earle to form the quartette but it was the last I saw of him, except as I passed him in the street walking with the captain of the French frigate, the *Grenade*, followed by two of the sailors, the morning I left.

Friday [August] 21st being the day of Fasting, Humiliation and Prayer appointed by the President, I went to St. Philip's very glad once more to sit in the same pew, hear the same music and our own dear Mr. Howe. He gave an excellent and most encouraging sermon, just suited to the occasion from Exodus 14:15.[10] No one could help feeling better, after hearing him, though he strongly denounced the spirit of faultfinding against the President, Generals & prominent men, so prevalent now.

In the afternoon we again walked on the Battery and, to our utter astonishment, passed Willie Heyward limping with a stick & walking very slowly with another gentleman. As it was near dusk, & we did not expect to see him, we did not

10 "Then the Lord said to Moses, 'Why are you crying out to me? Tell the Israelites to go forward.'"

recognize him at first. Indeed he passed me without raising his head, &, only as he passed Rosa, bowed slowly and like an old man & merely saying "Good evening Miss Rosa." We were so taken by surprise, we looked at each other a minute or two without speaking & by that time he was too far gone for us to call him back. We had just been wondering what had become of him, as we had heard nothing of him since he went to Virginia. Willie has just written us that Willie Heyward has written him he commanded the Brooks Artillery at Gettysburg and was soon after seized with inflammatory rheumatism so severely that he is now a cripple & he fears for life. Our Willie has himself been a great sufferer during the last two or three months from some peculiar and painful disease brought by a wetting he got on picket. . . . He has been off duty, that is, active duty, for he assisted the captain with his business but was obliged to ride to camp in a carriage. He writes mother he is slowly improving however.

That evening Mr. Earle came, according to promise, for us to walk on the Battery, to see the bombardment &, cousin Willie coming in just after, went with us (Mr. Earle walking with me). It was a soft, but not brilliant, moonlight night and, though we did not see but one shell burst, I enjoyed it very much. We returned about eleven and found several gentlemen in the drawing room with Mr. Bull playing and singing. Cousin W[illie] left soon after and, as we did not know who were there, we remained in the piazza. One of the gentlemen came & sat by Rosa & commenced talking, & none of us knew who he was. After a time, Rosa guessed it was Capt. Ross, who had been before to see her, but as they had been in the piazza, she did not see his face. I fancied it was [Frank] Vizitelli, to whom I had taken great dislike from what I had heard of him, & after talking to him for some time to relieve Rosa, both of us finally returned to our conversation with Mr. Earle, leaving out Capt. Ross altogether. . . . I was quite provoked with myself when I found afterwards who he was. After they left, Mr. [Willie] Walker, who was with them, returned & sat for some time listening to a very sweet toned violin, delightfully played by some of the Frenchmen, militia, guarding on Moreland's sharf. It was equal to a serenade. It must have been one o'clock when they left. . . .

We slept soundly till next morning. During the night I

heard the fire bells, listened a moment & went to sleep again
—woke at five or a little after, as usual, & not hearing the
usual cannonading, turned over for another nap. An hour or
two later, the maid rushed in saying "Why, Miss Emma, you
not up yet—don't you know the Yankees got in the city last
night, and shelled it, setting a house on fire—some fell near
the battery. . . ." So many startling facts made me spring up &
dress quickly, eager to learn the truth. After breakfast we
went to uncle James' & found them all packing to leave during the day. . . . As Rosa wanted some things from Ashley
Hall, she concluded to go up there—having sent her father
meanwhile to gather the news. All we learned then was that
the Yankees had shelled the city at about three or perhaps
half past two from a new & powerful battery on Black Island
—to the utter astonishment of all the military men who did
not dream the guns from there could reach the city. A dozen
or fifteen incendiary shells had fallen into the city in various
directions. The only one doing any damage fell in Hayne St.
going through the office of the Medical Directory, setting
some loose straw on fire causing the bells to ring. One fell
in Rutledge St. opposite Queen, making a good sized hole
through the plank road, but not exploding. We saw it on our
way to the country. So, all the Yankees did was to scare the
citizens dreadfully.

We learned afterwards that Admiral [Quincy A.] Gillmore
had sent a letter, unsigned however, to Gen. Beauregard,
nine o'clock Friday night, demanding the surrender of Forts
Sumter and Wagner or else he would shell the city—and giving *four* hours time to answer, knowing as he did, that was not
time enough for the answer to reach him. Beauregard was
out on a reconnoisance [*sic*] & Gen. [Thomas] Jordan opened
it, but finding it unsigned, returned it, asking for the official
signature as it could not be recognized without. Before it
could have reached Gillmore, the shelling took place, &, as
Isaac said, they were evidently trying the range of the guns
over different parts of the city. The communication was returned signed showing not only the perfect & most culpable
carelessness & indifference on the part of a commander in
such an important matter, but the utter barbarity of the whole
affair. Beauregard answered by a long and most stinging letter, positively refusing the surrender demanded, but inquir-

ing why he had not also demanded James and Sullivan's islands . . . the forts which had withstood him for over forty days. Now he had turned his guns against a city filled with old men, women, children, and hospitals. He had indeed gained by it an eminence even in this war, etc. . . . [Beauregard demanded] the usual time for the removal of noncombatants granted by all attacking parties, from one to three days. Gillmore answered they had already had *two years* notice, as well as the 40 days bombardment, & would grant no further time but would not shell the city again till eleven o'clock next day. As the communication was received at Battery Wagner at twelve o'clock Saturday night, everybody thought it meant till Monday, Gen. [Johnson] Hagood not having noticed it was dated *three* hours previously. But I am anticipating.

We went to Ashley Hall, which seemed like a minature [*sic*] Paradise in the deep silence & beauty which reigned everywhere. The air was fragrant with the breath of flowers, and there seemed a solemn spell in the atmosphere, broken soon however by a thunder storm & heavy shower, which only added a still more delicious freshness to the air, grass & flowers. We gathered flowers to weave a wreath for Robt. Pringle's coffin and each step around the garden recalled Mr. Earle, Jamie [Furman], Dr. [James] Morrow and the other friends & pleasures of last spring. We had asked Mr. Earle to go with us, but he could not leave the city, & I wrote him a farewell note, returning Tannhausar, still hoping however that Jamie & himself might come to bid us goodbye. We returned home near five, Mr. Bull stopping to get [railroad] tickets for Mary Louisa DeS[aussure] & Emma Ravenel, who were going to Columbia and were to take Becca [Bull] with them. He did not come till dark just in time to carry Becca, then found the cars so crowded he brought her back & told us Col. Del. Kemper & Capt. Carlos Tracey were coming to see us. He went fast asleep on the jongling [joggling] board,[11] while we were nearly so in our arm chairs in the piazza.

The heavy cannonading going on all day had ceased about five, the atmosphere was misty and damp, and the most profound silence reigned everywhere—not even a cricket was

11 A board suspended between two end supports often used for exercise or play.

heard & scarcely a leaf seemed to stir, while we were the only ladies left within more than two squares. We were just remarking on the deep sleep which seemed to have fallen upon all around, when we were roused by the arrival of the gentlemen. I was disappointed, however, when I found they were not Mr. Earle and Jamie [Furman], for Capt. [Carlos] Tracey is tall like the former & Col. [Del] K[emper]'s voice was precisely like J[amie]'s—his slow deliberate way of speaking and rather hoarse voice. However, I was quite glad to meet the gallant hero & hoped to have some conversation with him. But he drew his chair [to] the other side of the piazza, a little distance from Rosa, & too far for me to engage in anything but casual remarks. Capt. Tracey is a tall, goodlooking, elegant gentleman in manners and looks, very intelligent and agreeable, & I enjoyed talking to him, but felt quite provoked, when after supper, we got arranged as before. He told us of the Torpedo boat which had gone out two or three nights before with the hope of blowing up the [*New*] *Ironsides*, which it glided up to, but the engineer unfortunately mistook an order & at the most important moment turned the prow the wrong way. . . . It became entangled in the chains of the [*New*] *Ironsides*, breaking off the torpedo & rousing the Yankees, who hailed her. Capt. [James] Carlin answered it was the *Yankee Cousin*, a tug from Port Royal, on which the Y[ankee] said he did not believe it but would send a boat to her. Our boat immediately glided off & though thirteen shells were fired at her, not one touched her. This is the second failure from nearly the same cause.

He told us also of the *Porpoise*—the cigar shaped boat lately arrived from Mobile.[12] It is 40 feet long & can contain eight or nine men; is worked by machinery & has fins like a fish, which enable it to dive. It can go 20 feet under water, then come up to within 4 feet of the surface and remain one or two hours while it sets off the torpedos attached to it. Col. Kemper said he doubted its success, as it was not a new invention, &, if good, would have been used before. However, it certainly is a wonderful thing, & we hope for its success. It was to go out Saturday night to try and blow up the [*New*]

12 The official name of the *Porpoise* was submarine torpedo boat, *H. L. Hunley*.

Ironsides—for which Trenholm & Co. have offered a reward of $100,000. But I have heard nothing since of it.

They urged us to leave & Isaac had come in the afternoon for the same purpose & uncle James also, but we went to sleep very quietly, determining to wait till Monday & having promised to rouse each other if we heard any shelling. I think I must have woke about three o'clock whether from the shells or from the cold damp mist streaming on me, which chilled me to the bone I do not know. But Mr. Bull called out soon after to Rosa to listen to the shelling. It was a most peculiar fearful sound—the sharp scream or whizz through the air, and they sounded exactly as if coming over the house. I was startled & much excited, but not frightened, but it produced a very solemn feeling, I lay with the windows partly open every moment expecting a shell might burst and kill me and the idea of dying alone, while others were so near, was startling. I wished for Rosa to talk to, for I could not get to sleep, but thought, if she did not seek me, I would not go to her. I must have lain thus at least three quarters of an hour, when Rosa & Becca came down to my room so thoroughly scared they did not know what to do. I had never seen or heard of Rosa's being scared before, except on horseback by a cow, for when other people are excited by danger, she is generally as cool & apparently almost unfeeling as if she had no earthly interest there whatever. But this time she acknowledged she was so scared that her strength had utterly failed her, every limb ached, & she thought if she remained she would have fever. I advised her to get up immediately and pack, for she had not commenced to put up a single article, intending to do so when we returned from church and to go immediately to Grahamville, even if she missed Mr. [Willie] G.[uerard] on the road. For, her father could telegraph to Capt. [G. C.] Heyward & she could go to stay with Willie and Maria, if the other house was not ready. She declared she could not move while the shelling was going on, for she was afraid to go upstairs. Her feelings had been similar to mine. She said she did not feel fit to die, yet every moment expected death.

The boys then came down, & we found it was half past four. They got matches for us, & by five I persuaded Rosa to commence packing while I finished mine, bringing off a quantity of Nassau goods. We sent Dessie [Bull] for stages & persuaded Hallie to accompany Rosa. I left her at six, not finished packing & her room strewn with valuable things she could not carry, while DeS went with Becca, Maum Nancy, and myself to the SC. RR. We found the cars full but not crowded, though at first there was some difficulty in getting our baggage on. . . . [We] had no trouble till we arrived at Columbia, where I had to go, as there is no Sunday train to Camden. However, I left Maum N.[ancy] to hunt for the baggage, though no checks had been given, & I went in the omnibus to uncle Wm's [DeSaussure] where we were warmly received. . . .

I left Monday at midday & met the "indispensable Mr. Rogers," mail agent, hotel keeper, etc. who carries letters between the Brownfields & myself. I had never exchanged a word with him, though I had often seen him, &, as soon as we recognized each other, he came to talk with me & to inquire after Isaac, to whom both he & his wife took a great liking. We had a long and quite a confidential conversation on the subject of the Camden people & their treatment of the refugees. Then I found out he was a North Carolinian, "one of the low rough sort," as he said "who tried to be honest" & certainly no one who looked into his clear blue eyes & open face would doubt the latter part. I knew the proprietors of the De Kalb Hotel had treated him badly about it in the winter, & he told me all about it & their repetition of it—showing how the demon of speculation which is ravaging our country had seized upon them also. I really became quite interested in him & his fortunes.—met the boys at the depot & found aunt Sue & grandmother still here—&, of course, spent all evening telling the news. Monday's paper says the firing, which so alarmed us, was an attempt of the Monitors either to pass Fort Sumter or to cut the piles driven near it, & a general engagement ensued between our batteries & the Yankee fleet and batteries. I suppose it must have been the state of the atmosphere which made it sound as if they were shelling the city. However, Sunday night the city was shelled again. . . . It is indeed wonderful that, with so many hundreds of shot & shell around them daily, so few are wounded & few killed. . . .

. . . Fort Sumter was so much injured by the bombardment on Sunday, the land batteries firing from south to north & the Monitors from east to west, that we have daily expected to hear of its evacuation & being blown up. But cousin Richard [Screven] writes that a celebrated engineer, who has just come on, says it is stronger than ever, for the debris of bricks and sand have formed an almost impenetrable sloping wall, besides the wall of sand bags inside. . . . Cousin Willie writes "though sick, she still bears herself proudly and gallantly, driving back the foe." Hurrah for glorious old Sumter—her brave defenders have made her well worthy of the proud name she bears.

Isaac writes there was a furious storm of wind & rain on Monday, almost equal to that of '56, so there was very little firing. The fleet had to withdraw—but he had been obliged to change his sleeping place for Ann St. as our late home was directly within range of the shells as they came too close for comfort. He says a great many persons from downtown had also moved up town, from the same cause, and were dependent on the hospitality of the citizens of that section to take them in. . . .

I came home to a most distressing scene. Our house being so full, mother had changed sister Fanny's room, giving hers to Carrie & myself, & it roused her to one of the most furious fits of passion she has ever had. In fact, it grows worse & few beyond our own household have known till now what we have had to endure from one who becomes a maniac from passion at times, commencing always from the most trifling things. She became so abusive and violent, striking me & others & threatening worse, that mother sent first for cousin Sarah [Elliott] then for uncle Louis, who had to use force to confine her to her room. He said he had such a case before, in aunt Jane's [DeSaussure] sister, but this was the most distressing case he had ever witnessed. But it was necessary for the welfare of the rest of the family that she should be conquered, & she has been. . . . This morning [she] was released & is very friendly with everyone but myself, because being the only one cool & self possessed, I assisted uncle Louis. Everyone else was much excited, & it made us very anxious for Carrie, for she was particularly angry with her.

Mr. George Trenholm has bought Legaré's Female Academy at Orangeburg & offered it to the City Council to remove the Orphan Children & those who live at the Church Home too. It has been accepted of course, & we hope, when they are

August 29
Friday
[*should*
be 28]

removed, that Uncle may be persuaded to leave also. . . .
. . . We hear daily of refugees everywhere being "sold out"
without knowing where to seek another home, and the extortion, meanness, & speculation of the up-country people in regard to the refugees is dreadful. They take every possible
advantage of their need. Myers, the Charleston Jew, who
bought this house, has sent to tell mother he wants to live in [it]
by Jan. but would like us to *exchange* houses before that. His is
a smaller, dirty, comfortless, mean looking one in the next
street—but he is fixing it up for us. [He] says, however, he
won't turn us out. What is to be the result I don't know, but we
propose facing him with our full battery of ten ladies and see
how he can stand it, when his own family is quite small.

September 3
Wednesday
[should
be 2]

Three weeks ago I wrote this date, then was obliged to lay my
pen aside because I felt so badly. Willie had come up the day
before to try and find a house for his family and a farm to put
his negroes on; he was talking of some place to which I objected
on the score of chill and fever of which I had a horror, and,
while I was speaking, I was seized with a chill, slight however,
but followed by a scorching fever, lasting for hours. Four days
after, it was repeated, and, though I had no further returns, I
was constantly feverish and in fact have been quite sick; Dan
[DeSaussure], who attended me, says I came very near having
jaundice. I was slightly salivated and my strength so much reduced as well as my head so weak and distressed that I have
only sat up all day and gone down to meals during the last three
or four days. I do not recollect having an attack of fever since
the "broken bone" thirteen years ago, when John was a baby,
or to have been in bed from any sickness, for at least ten years,
so this attack has pulled me down considerably. My face has
grown long and thin & white, and the little strength I gained in
town has been quite dissipated. The constant rain of the past
few months has produced great sickness everywhere, & chill
and fever is in almost every yard.

September 23

A month since I left town & what important events have taken
place there. Daily the most furious bombardment was kept up,
each day seeming to increase in fury and for nineteen or twenty days it was most particularly directed to Fort Sumter, the
fleet co-operating vigorously, and trying to pass, after having

succeeded in making it a mass of ruins and disabling every gun. Fortunately very few men were killed or wounded there. Finally the Yankees thought they had completely demolished it and flaming announcements appeared in the Northern papers of its surrender as well as that of Charleston. But though it is in ruins and fourteen times the flag shot down by the fearful tempest of shot and shell which poured into it, it still flaunts a proud defiance to the foe. Finally, Maj. Gen. [Jeremy F.] Gilmer of No. Ca., a celebrated engineer who was sent as Beauregard's second in command, pronounced that it was stronger than ever to *resist attack*, though not to act in the offensive. For though no masonry could withstand the terrific force of those Parrott shot, yet the immense mass of brick and sand, the debris of the walls, had formed an almost impenetrable glacis, within which a sand battery is being erected. . . . The Yankees determined to make a desperate effort to take it and, on the 8th and 9th, about 1000 men in thirty odd barges attacked it at night, thinking they had not to do much more than walk straight into it and expecting to find only a guard of perhaps 100 men. To their utter astonishment and dismay, they were welcomed by volleys of musketry, hand grenades, and *brickbats*, while the neighboring batteries and the gunboats joined in the sport. Our men dashed over the ruins and dragged the astonished Yankees inside by main force, till finally cries of "we surrender" were heard and four barges, three stand of colors, and 102 privates & 13 officers, were captured without a man being hurt on our side, and not one of the enemy having entered the port, except as prisoners of war. Among the latter are Lieut. E. P. Williams, of the *Wissahicon*, commander of the expedition, Lieuts [George] Meade & Porter, sons of Gen. Meade and Admiral Porter. The fight only lasted about half an hour, and the remainder of the boats escaped under cover of the darkness, followed, however, by our balls as parting gifts. From the crashing sounds & the screams and groans heard, as well as empty barges found floating afterwards near Morris I, their loss is supposed to have been very great. . . .

One of the captured flags is said to be the identical "gridiron" carried from Fort Sumter in 1861 and displayed & speechified & prayed over by the Northern mob, till it was almost sanctified in their estimation. Since the "Battle of the

Brickbats"—the enemy have let glorious old Sumter alone. Two or three days before, it had been found necessary to evacuate Forts Wagner & Gregg, after their heroic defense of seven weeks. . . .

Soon after I came up, we learned through extracts from the Northern papers that the reason the city had not been shelled again was that the 300 pound Parrott gun had burst after a few discharges—a portion of the muzzle breaking off and thus much shortening the range of the gun. We hoped so much from our great gun, especially after the great amount of trouble and the delay necessary on account of its enormous size. At last it was placed on White Point Garden, under command of cousin Ormsby Blanding, and at the first discharge it burst, part of the muzzle breaking off and a crack extending along the whole length. Fortunately no one was hurt. I hear that the gun tapers towards the muzzle, which screws on, and that there was a flaw or crack in the gun when it arrived which required [the] Cameron [Foundry] to band it before it was discharged. . . . Moreover, it is said, it was never tried by the maker in England because he said the ammunition necessary was too expensive. I do not know the truth of these rumors, but the fact of the explosion is only too true, occasioning a great and universal disappointment. I do not know whether the other one is to be sent on or not. It was expected that the Monitors would be almost, if not quite, annihilated by the fearfully crushing weight and force of those enormous masses of iron and that our city would be amply defended by it. A Richmond editorial says the explosion was caused by the too great elevation of the gun, that such enormous cannon are only meant to do tremendous execution at short range. But it was understood that this would shoot accurately at five miles, and well between six and seven.

About the time I was taken sick, the *Porpoise* or cigar shaped boat, with four or five men on board, was accidentally sunk [August 30, 1863], & of course the men were drowned. From some recent allusions in the paper, however, very carefully worded, I think and hope it has been recovered. . . .

Willie did not succeed in getting a house for his family & only in getting a man to work his negroes on shares which will barely suffice to feed and clothe them. He returned home two days after I was taken sick. . . . Myers has given us to understand that, if we would pay $1000 for this house, we might still keep it. If not, we have to give him an answer by the first of October, whether we will take the one he is living in, in January, at $500. As there is no other to be had, we will have to take it, though how we are to *cram* into it I cannot imagine—only six rooms & two of them tiny shed rooms. Myers is fixing up the fences & seems to be doing something to the house, but I dread the disagreeabilities of the winter. Cousin Sarah [Elliott] has been "sold out" too . . . so in January they too have to seek another home—where none are to be had. . . .

The papers bring full confirmation of our great victory. Bragg telegraphed yesterday, 24th, to Beauregard that we have captured 7000 prisoners, 40 pieces of artillery, 15,000 stand of small arms & 30 stand of colors and had pushed the enemy to Chattanooga before which our army now is. The battle took place on the banks of the Chickamauga [Georgia] . . . and, curiously enough, it means the "Stream of Death," so called by the Indians because, when many years ago one of their tribes was afflicted with the small-pox, in their agony of sickness, the Indians would run and plunge into this river, hoping to find relief. But of course great numbers died, and the remnant of the tribe, as well as the stream, were called Chickamauga. . . .

September 25
Friday

. . . The battle has been thought on both sides to have been one of the most desperate of the war. The Yankee army was composed of the best fighting materials, far different from those that generally fight in Va., and they were commanded by one of their best and wiliest generals, Rosencrans [*sic*], whom they considered invincible—while Bragg had [so] often fallen back before them that they looked down upon him. With his mere nucleus of an army constantly diminished to reinforce the Western & Virginian armies, he has been compelled since last January to play a grand game of chess, constantly falling back and maneuvering to conceal his weakness, till his own men as well as the majority of other people, unable to understand his movements, were murmuring against him. But now strongly reinforced by Longstreet & Hill, he had an army nearly equal in numbers, though not in artillery, to the enemy's and in the finest spirits eager for the fray & determined to conquer. They say our troops never fought better, a kind of rivalry between Bragg's original army and Longstreet's corps having only added fuel to the flame. Rosecran's whole army was engaged, about 80,000.[13]

But to balance this, Cumberland Gap, one of the strongest natural positions in the world & rendered still stronger by science, has been surrendered [September 10, 1863] to the Yankees either through the treachery, cowardice or incompetency of a Gen. Frazier [John W. Frazer] of Tenn. . . . It is considered one of the most disgraceful events of the war, & the few men who made their escape say it was treachery & that, at any rate, if he wanted to, he could have saved the guns & most of the garrison. . . .

13 Approximately 58,000 Union and 66,000 Confederate soldiers took part in this Confederate victory. Union losses were 16,170, and Confederate casualties were 18,454.

September 26, 1863

✧

October 8, 1864

Bad News from the Battlefields

Rosa Guerard is settled at Grahamville in a log cabin, with Mrs. [G. C.] Heyward and Mrs. Hopson Pinckney—just beyond the confines of the camp. Notwithstanding "the thousand and one crevices" she says are in her room and the many inconveniences, she seems to enjoy herself very much. . . . Willie G.[uerard] can be with her whenever off duty, and the boys from camp go to see her every night. . . . [I] learned Hattie Young no longer intended teaching with Mrs. [Fanny A.] McCandless, so I applied by note & received a very complimentary note saying as soon as she found she needed an assistant she had inquired for me, but heard I had married & gone away.[1] If I could teach Algebra, French & some other high branches, &, if her school opened with 40 scholars, she would give me $600—the same as her other teachers formerly received. I was too unwell to answer her note, till one day cousin Sarah [Elliott] gave me a ride & I went to see her. We had a very pleasant conversation, and she seemed quite pleased with my views of teaching. But I

1 A native of Vermont, Fanny Coleman came to Camden about 1845 to conduct a school for girls. In 1849 she married Leslie McCandless, who in 1837 had migrated from Charleston to teach in Camden. The two conducted academies for boys and girls until the Civil War. Their Civil War activities are described in this diary. After the war, they were estranged, and Mrs. McCandless conducted a school in Atlanta. She died in 1889 and is buried next to her husband in Camden.

told her I could not teach Algebra; I knew nothing of it, having especially disliked it—a branch in which she wished assistance particularly. So nothing was settled, [n]or will be, till she opens school week after next, when she will organize her classes & let me know if she needs my assistance. I walked yesterday evening half way down there, my first walk, so hope to be strong enough if she sends for me.

Grandmother says she never recollects such weather in September before, during her whole life. Almost ever since I have been up here, it has been *cold*; latterly we have found fire in the drawing room comfortable morning and evening—and summer dresses decidedly too thin, though the midday sun was warm. The incessant rains have produced sickness all over the country, principally chill & fever, or intermittent fever. From one end of Camden to the other, it is prevalent—scarcely a yard without two or three down. Several are now sick here. Sue & grandmother [are] in bed today, but none as sick as I was. Everywhere the children are having convulsions. The doctors say they cannot account for it, but it seems a feature of the sickness this year.

October 1 Poor Dan and Sallie [DeSaussure] have had a most crushing blow in the sudden illness and death of little Mary Mansfield, their only child. Sallie has been sick for many days with the same nervous fever and agonizing pains from which Sue is suffering & has scarcely been able to bear the children's noise. . . .

At breakfast time when Mamie was asked what she wanted, she answered "My Mother," the last words she ever spoke. For, she soon after became unconscious & very ill with congestion of the stomach, & though everything Dr. [Lynch H.] Deas & Dan [DeSaussure] could think of was done, she died last evening at eight o'clock. Poor Sallie, in another room unable to hold up her head, had not seen her for a day & after her death had her brought and laid beside her. Dan is utterly crushed by it, while Sallie seems more resigned to God's will. Little Mary was a very intelligent child &, though so young, but three years and a half old, was an interesting companion and as devoted to her parents as they to her. Sallie used to say Mamie was her shadow. A few months ago she was fretful & wanted to get up very early in the morning. Sallie told her no

& threw her arms across her to keep her quiet, & Mary bit her. Sallie then slapped her, and, after crying a little, she crept to her mother, threw her arms around her and said "Mother, I love you more than tongue can tell.". . .

At half past one o'clock last night, our little nephew *Sims White* made his debut on the stage of life, with but short warning previously. . . . Saturday morning a trunk arrived with Isaac's summer clothes & Carrie went busily to work, to overlook, prepare and pack his winter ones to send down on Monday and some ginger cake also. She did not get through till dark, and was as bright and merry as possible, with the exception of a miserable cold and cough she had taken a few days before. She sat with grandmother till nine, then feeling badly went to lie down & called mother, who soon concluded it was not merely her cold. About eleven I went to my chamber &, finding her lying down, asked if she felt badly. She said yes, but scarcely believed what was coming. However, we thought it time for me to decamp from her premises & get them in order; Dr. [Lynch H.] Deas was sent for about twelve, & all was happily over in an hour and a half—remarkably quickly the old ladies say. She has indeed been very fortunate through all her course. The nurse expected had not come, having been very ill, so Nina has had to take her place and I tell her [she] has become quite young & spry since she got that baby in her arms. He is quite a respectable & good looking little fellow: healthy, hearty, & plump, with most vigorous lungs—has plenty of black hair & black lashes, dark eyes we think, and a very small and pretty mouth, notwithstanding the very short curved upper lip like Isaac's & Nanna's [Hughes]. Carrie & himself are both doing very well, Carrie laughing as merrily as any of us to see how perfectly happy little Carrie [Holmes] is over the baby, crowing & clapping her hands with delight & kissing him repeatedly. Henry [Holmes] is equally happy over "my little cousin Sims." I have spent the morning writing letters to the girls as I promised & to tell Hattie [White] of her godson. Today is grandmother's 77th birthday also.

Last Thursday I had an attack of chill & fever just when I thought I was getting quite well & last night another just as I

October 4

October 6
Tuesday

was going to bed & lasting all night. Fortunately they have not reduced my strength, though of course I feel badly & my head [is] distressed. It is quite provoking, as yesterday evening Mrs. [Fanny A.] McCandless sent to ask if I was well enough to go down on Wednesday. She opened school yesterday with between 60 & 70 scholars. I hope, however, to be able to go next week. . . . I got a sweet letter from Rutledge tonight, from before Chattanooga. [He] says he considers our victory complete, though hard work still has to come, as Rosecrans is strongly entrenched & Bragg knows every inch of ground too well to sacrifice his men. . . .

October 17   The last two weeks have flown very rapidly and I am enjoying my first leisure moments to record their events. Carrie's nurse, Annie Baker, quite a respectable & pleasant person, came up when the baby was three days old, & Isaac the next day, while "Big Sims" [White] as Henry [Holmes] called him, arrived on Thursday by the midday train having had a short furlough, shared between the girls, ourselves & Aiken. Just after he came, cousin Sarah [Elliott] lent mother the carriage to transact some business, &, while she was engaged in it, he & I took a ride to see the lions of the town—small enough they are it is true, but the delicious weather repaid us; next morning I determined to enjoy a holiday, in spite of the accumulation of work, and take the exercise I so much needed. Lila & I, with Carrie & Henry [Holmes], therefore, escorted him [Sims White] to the Factory Pond, which was beautiful in its peacefullness, brilliantly reflecting the clear blue sky. . . . Lila & he went by invitation at night to aunt Eliza's but had an "awfully dry time.". . .

Saturday afternoon Maggie Ancrum came over to see me, by my request, to tell me something of Mrs. McCandless' ways & rules. I saw her for the first time and was much pleased. . . . She left me, however, feeling very serious over the prospect of yielding up my long-cherished liberty to the will of another as well as fearing that I might have overrated my capabilities, for until I went on Monday I did not know what I was to teach. In fact the responsibilities I had assumed weighed on me as solemnly almost as if I had been about to "commit matrimony." I walked to church in the morning, the first time I had done so here since last January &, though I rode home, was very much fatigued. However, I came to the conclusion that nothing but regular exercise would restore my long lost strength & Monday morning, I instituted a new order of things by breakfasting at half past seven, then calling for Maggie Ancrum on my way to school. She stood my friend in the rather trying ordeal of meeting sixty odd new faces and being stared at and criticized by them. I found that Mrs. Mc-Candless had persuaded Mrs. Romaré, or "Miss Lucy" as the girls call her, to continue teaching as the school was larger than she anticipated. Mrs. McC.[andless] also continues to open school, and thus I am relieved of much responsibility.

The first day I sat with her, while she heard my classes, to let me get acquainted with them & her mode of teaching. The girls are divided into six classes, which are not however totally distinct as she wished, many of the younger being mingled with the older ones in some studies. However, the 5th belongs particularly to me & consists of girls from 7 & 8 to 11— beginning with Julia Fisher, Frances Oppenheim, Retta Boykin, Charlotte's sister, a handsome, intelligent, merry & ambitious child, Millie McCaa, from Florida, Jamie's niece, who with her elder sister Kate, has remained to go to school. Though not as quick as the three first, she is a dear little creature whose sweet face and soft brown eyes nestled their way into my heart directly. Minnie Rawlinson is a very quiet, well behaved, not very bright, & I think rather timid, girl. Cornelia de Loach, the oldest and decidedly dullest, is very backward, but even out of such poor stuff, I think I shall produce something. But "oh, ye Gods & little fishes," she is the sister-in-law of our horror and my special object of dislike, Capt. [W. L.] DePass, & his sister is in one of my older classes. Indeed I hardly recognize my own identity, surrounded as I often am, by such democratic specimens as Workmans, Wienges, Ammes, Baxley, etc. then a step higher to the Kennedy, Dunlaps, McDowalls, etc., and it is really refreshing to my aristocratic prejudices to come in contact with the Ancrums, Deas, Kershaws, Shannons, Sallie DeSaussure, etc. though I never allow such feelings to be shown. It has taken the whole week for me to get my classes arranged and in train, & for me to get sufficiently acquainted with the names & faces to suit them to each other. I have produced much amusement among them by the frequent mistakes I made, so yesterday I drew up a list, & called the roll to learn how many I daily teach & to my surprise found they were 50 distributed in the various classes.

The daily routine commences with prayers at 8½ & writing till nine in which I superintend also several of the 4th class. . . . The 6th is also shared between Mrs. R.[omaré], Nettie McKain and myself, for they join my class in arithmetic, saying their "tables" etc. & I also hear them read. These little ones generally occupy me till eleven with their reading, history, definitions, grammar and geography. Nettie attends to their sums & compositions. Then comes the class in Racine, composed of ten of the oldest girls, who translate with ease, but, as they only take two pages & learn no grammar, they occupy but a short time. On alternate days, they are joined by ten others and read *Paradise Lost*, but, like most school girls, they do not appreciate its beauties and are only anxious to finish it as soon as they can. It made me feel really sad, recalling as it did our uptown reading club. . . . Next succeeds the 2nd French class, consisting of only Mary & Martha Robinson, who used to go to Madame Logno's where they learned a pretty accent and "glib" way of repeating phrases. They also think, as they have been "through the grammar," they have no further need to learn it. I differ very much in opinion, but they merely translate, learn phrases, verbs, write a few lines of dictation & parse a few lines. After recess I hear Maggie Ancrum's class in [William] Paley's *Moral Philosophy* & a class of twenty in ancient geography. Next week I am also to have 4th class to correct their compositions.

I find teaching the easiest work I ever undertook. I hear that the girls like me & I like them, but I often feel so lonely & homesick even with a roomful of girls. My room is hung with astronomical maps like those which tapestried the walls of "dear old No. 14 Church St." and reminiscences of the happy past are floating around me all the time. Various trifles recall each loved teacher & friends now scattered far and wide, and I miss them so much—and above all—my Dora [Furman]. I feel so little older than the girls I am teaching, grown in height if not in age, that I involuntarily blush in correcting them as if it was an impertinence to do so. I feel the want of companionship & sympathy more than ever, and, though this may fail as a preventative to home & heartsickness, still it gives me regular employment and I feel as if I am no longer entirely wasting my one talent. I generally walk home with some of the girls, & in rainy weather Maggie [Ancrum] gives me a seat. Several times in the morning it has drizzled, so we have ridden. I generally reach home a little before three so weary I can hardly move & after some time devoted to the two Carries and Sims, I spend my afternoons writing letters, seldom being able to finish one. The afternoons are so short and my eyes have been so weakened by my late sickness that I cannot even read the newspapers at night. That is my time for cutting out work, envelopes and other odds and ends. I am getting quite "famous" in the family for making slippers & lamp shades—Confederate accomplishments.

On the last of September, Myers informed mother that he had determined to retain the house he was living in for himself & that she could keep this at $1000 rent—just what I expected he was maneuvering to. As we have no other to go to for none are to be hired or bought, we are obliged to keep it & mother wrote to ask Willie if he would bring up his family to live with us & share the rent. But he meanwhile had procured a farm on Beech Island to which he will move his family & Lieut. [Wilson] Broughton's negroes. So I expect mother will invite aunt Mathewes [Holmes] & cousins Mary and Eliza [Bacot], who are much in need of a pleasant home. Myers has promised to floor the two large basement rooms which will make very comfortable chambers & has already put some repair on the house, much needed. How we all wish now that mother had bought this herself. But we all dreaded so much such a step, as settling us, we feared, for life up here, while our hearts yearned for the low country.

A week ago, I received a very sweet note from Emmie Earle accompanying the essay on the Greek tragedians which Mr. [Willie] Earle wrote & promised me; I appreciate this token of regard & remembrance very much, for it recalled our delightful conversation most vividly. I have not had a moment's time to read it yet but shall enjoy it, if possible, this afternoon. Saturday being my only day of leisure, many things will be crowded into it, & my journal will suffer I know. I miss it so much if I do not write in it.

October 24   This week has flowed on smoothly, quickly, and pleasantly at
Saturday   school; the girls all seem to like me & I am getting my own
little class drilled into my ways. I think they have already improved, and they do not give me much trouble. Ann Kennedy, a very quiet, steady girl of 14 or 15, & Maggie Ancrum,
with one or two older ones, have asked me permission to sit in
my room and I find I command their respect in spite of feeling like a school girl myself, and they have shown me many
agreeable attentions, such as bringing me bouquets or offering me a ride home. I generally walk home with some of
them.

Chick a few days ago received a letter from brother H.[en-
ry] saying she might return to Florida, and she expects to go
next month with Mrs. Kennedy of Camden, who owns a plantation there. Little Carrie has so wound [*sic*] & nestled herself
into my heart that the very idea of her going made me very
sad; it was just after I learned [of] little Rose's [Barnwell]
death, & it made me almost fear to love her too much. For
every child that I pet especially, dies. As soon as I come into
the house I call for Carrie, for I need my sunbeam & though
I spend much of my leisure with our Carrie, petting and playing with Sims, still he cannot take little Carrie's place. . . .

In Virginia, constant cavalry skirmishes are taking place,
sometimes on an extensive scale, & 1200 prisoners have lately
been captured at different times. But, public attention is principally directed to Chattanooga where the President has just
made a visit & reviewed the army. Poor Bragg is so abused in
the papers, I am sorry for him. He has had considerable misunderstanding with several of his generals, Gen. [Leonidas]
Polk for one, whom he relieved of his command for disobedience of orders in not commencing the attack at Chickamauga
on Sunday at daylight, in consequence of which the battle began at ten and darkness came on to prevent the total rout of
Rosecran's army. Forrest, [Daniel H.] Hill & one or two others
are said to have been relieved also. Many people insist they
are only scapegraces for him & hoped the President was
going to relieve him & put Lee or Longstreet over him. I still
have faith in him & trust all will come right, but these
dissensions are most unfortunate in their effect. . . . Mr.
[James M.] Mason has been recalled from England, in consequence of the "systematic rudeness" of Lord John Russell &

has joined Mr. [John] Slidell, while our Government has dismissed every British Consul from the Confederacy in consequence of their unwarrantable assumption of power in regard to foreigners resident here—which has given general satisfaction.[2] Maximilian, Grand duke of Austria, has accepted the crown of Mexico offered him through the power of Napoleon's fleet and army, & I doubt not will prove a good cat's paw in the hands of that far sighted monarch—but a few months will unfold the panorama.[3]

October 31

. . . Willie [Elliott] is not entirely recovered enough to return to cavalry service, and though, of course, very anxious to be married, will not for fear that if he is married & then remains at home, it will be put to that account. . . . Yet if he waits to be married till he is quite well, he will have to return to the army immediately after. Poor fellow, he has really had a hard time. Then the house they are living in has been sold to *three* different people & they cannot find out who is really the owner or whether they will be able to hire it again. They cannot get another to hire, & Mr. [James] Chesnut [Sr.] has offered to loan them his house five miles from Camden & now their horses have been impressed, and, though $1,000 has been given for them, the great difficulty is to replace them. The impressing officer has nearly swept Camden of all the fine horses during the past week; almost every body we know has lost theirs. . . .

(N. B. Scarcely any horses have yet been carried off, and the great excitement has died way as quickly as it was raised. It often amuses me to glance over my journal, and see how many N.B's I ought to add to correct first reports.)[4]

But, Mrs. Bishop [Thomas F.] Davis is going to try to persuade Myers to make an equal exchange of this house for hers, as she wants to be "up in the country" she says; hers is a very nice house, &, if Myers will only consent, we will be much benefited, for it is very near both church & school,

2 On August 4, 1863, Mason was recalled; he gave the British government official notice on September 21, 1863. The issue of British consuls protecting British subjects from service in the Confederate military had long been a problem and one of several leading to the break.

3 Maximilian arrived in Mexico on May 28, 1864.

4 This paragraph was obviously written in later. It is found at the top of a page in the original diary.

besides stores, etc. and, as we have no carriage nor man servant, will be very convenient. I am only afraid Myers will not be accommodating so that will end all our pleasant air castles. Aunt Lizzie Garden has just sold her house and lot for $12,000 to the Catholics, for the Sisters of Mercy—a most admirable bargain for her. . . .

Last Tuesday I went from school to dine at Dan's [DeSaussure], found Sallie better & much cheered by the presence of Douglas & Mac [DeSaussure] & their beautiful blue-eyed baby, a healthy hearty child, much to my surprise, after her dreadful health, but she has a wet nurse this time. Mac was more sociable than she had ever been, & I really enjoyed my visit, especially as cousin Sallie [Boykin] brought me the gratifying information that Mrs. [J. B.] Kershaw & Mrs. Wm. Shannon "were loud in their praise of me & thought me a much better teacher than either Mrs. Mac[andless] or Mrs. Romaré.". . . [They] said that, if I would set up a school on my own account, they would send all their children to me. . . . I am not conceited enough to fancy myself at all superior to Mrs. McC[andless] though there are many things in her system which I do not approve, for I think them injudicious in their effects. Mingling freely with the girls as I do, I have an excellent opportunity of judging.

I have already had to exert my authority very decidedly in two or three cases, conquering the girls immediately, & those too, whom I had learned were considered difficult cases. I only had to show great decision, dignity & firmness &, when they yielded, kindness. . . . Mrs. McC[andless] says my authority shall be upheld whatever course I chose to pursue. I am really quite interested in teaching & in many of my scholars, and it is a peculiar kind of satisfaction to me to conquer difficulties of any kind.

Yesterday there was no school in consequence of the death of little Maggie Kennedy, Ann's sister—a pretty, healthy, hearty looking little child of seven or eight, belonging to the 6th class, who only read to me two or three times before she was taken sick. . . .

November 7
Saturday

The tremendous bombardment of glorious old Sumter has continued steadily since I last wrote, the principal casualty having been the killing of thirteen men by the falling in of

part of the eastern barrack wall from the crushing weight of a
300 lb. Parrot shell. These men had been stationed there to
mount the parapet in case of assault and were instantly killed.
The impression prevails that the enemy are wearing out their
heavy guns from their incessant use, as some are known to
have burst lately, and they must be spending millions of dollars on the ammunition so uselessly wasted at Charleston
alone.

The President [Jefferson Davis] visited our city [Charles-
ton] last week on his way from the west and was most enthusiastically received. What would I not have given to have
witnessed the brilliant courtege of distinguished men who received and escorted him and to have heard his speech. He
visited the fortifications on Sullivan's Island, while the enemy's guns were still "pegging away," as "old Abe" says, at Fort
Sumter, and expressed himself much pleased; he handsomely
complimented the old city & Maj. [Stephen] Elliott and his
garrison particularly. In an address out West, he spoke of [Jo-
seph] Wheeler's late raid in Tennessee as the greatest of the
war. . . .

Quite a severe fight took place before Chattanooga a few
days ago between a considerable force of the enemy, who
tried to flank us, in order to make Bragg withdraw from
Lookout Mt. & a part of our army, who foiled their design,
with considerable loss on both sides. The campaign in Virginia seems ended for the present, for Meade tried to advance to Richmond, thinking our army depleted to fill up
Bragg's, but Lee drove him back in a series of heavy skirmishes, chiefly with our cavalry. He tried to surround Meade
but the latter succeeded in making his escape. Thereupon old
Abe has relieved him as usual from his command,[5] as he has
done Rosecrans, putting [George H.] Thomas in his place
[October 17, 1863]—removing almost the only really skillful
general they have for one whom Gen. Bragg says is "slow and
obstinate." Thomas was under his command during the Mexican war, and he knows him thoroughly. As to Bragg himself, he is one of the worst abused men I know—whether
rightfully or wrongfully, it is impossible to find out. Brother
H.[enry] writes that he is generally unpopular & another

5 Lincoln did not remove Meade; in fact he wired him a "Well Done" on
   November 9, 1863.

commander wished by the army. Uncle Ta [Gibbes], however, is always his staunch defender. The President has publicly freed Gen. [Leonidas] Polk from blame after investigating the matter & put him in command of the Mississippi department, in the place of Gen. [William J.] Hardee, transferred elsewhere.

The days slip by very rapidly and the past week has been so warm it is hard to believe that it is November. The midday sun has been very hot and has prostrated me very much. I reach home aching in every limb. Yesterday I wore a white cambric & found it warm coming home. Today is more seasonable.

November 21 I last wrote a fortnight ago, & on Tuesday & Wednesday it was intensely cold, then moderated immediately, just as it did one year ago, when Carrie was married. Her wedding day passed as quietly as possible, the only notice of it was a letter received a few days later from uncle Ta [Gibbes], written on the 12th, enclosing the note she had written him together with her wedding invitation. He said he had had it ever since in his pocket-book and, as it had passed through two or three hard fought battles, particularly Chickamauga, & several skirmishes . . . he sent them to her to keep with his letter, till Sims was 18. Then [she should] give them to him to show him some of the trials & tribulations our country has passed through at this time, &, if necessary, that it should teach him to protect the country his nearest relatives were now fighting for. . . .

John commenced in October to go to school to Mr. Staudenmeyer, very much against my inclination, for I feared he would learn nothing from him. But there was no other teacher to be had, as mother won't send him to [Leslie] McCandless, after knowing how cruelly he beats his own children & whips the other boys as well as keeping them in often till dark & much later. The gentlemen here hope to get another teacher in January & only took Staudenmeyer as somebody to keep the boys employed until then—knowing in fact nothing of him except that he was an Episcopal minister & was said to be a good classic scholar and mathematician. . . . Carrie's nurse, Annie Baker, told mother he was a bad man & had been turned out of one school & was besides a man of violent temper. She could tell more but did not choose to have such

things come from her. So mother was prepared, but we were
not, for his outrageous treatment of John. Last week, he gave
the boys three pages of arithmetic, at which some demurred,
as too long; he then gave two &, when the lesson was recited,
some questions were at the bottom of the last page which they
had not learned, as the answers were on the next. He sent
them back to their seats to study them & John says the boys
were talking it over among themselves, when he came up,
seized one of the boys & gave him a severe whipping, breaking the cane or ferule on him. [He] then seized him, John
said, by the throat. John said if he had attempted to whip him
as he had done John Adams, he would not have minded it so
much, but he throttled him & pulled him from his seat. Of
course John struggled as was right & natural under such
brutal treatment, & Staudenmeyer knocked him in the back
with his knee, throttled him three times, struck him violently
three times on the ground holding him by the body &
knocked his head against the corner of the wall and desk. . . .
When he came home the marks on his throat were distinct &
his head red, though his thick hair had saved him from
bruises. John said when he released him he could scarcely
speak & felt as if his senses were going. He told him he was
coming home to tell mother how brutally he had been treated,
& he called on all the boys as witnesses.

We, of course, were all so exasperated, we did not know
what to do. I wished myself a man a dozen times, that I might
confront him and, if Willie had been here, he would have
been called to a severe account for it. Mother wrote to ask an
explanation, & he came up to see her. He did not look her in
the face for some time & waited for her to start the subject—a
direct evidence of guilt, for if he had been innocent, he would
have behaved very differently. He is very plausible indeed,
and when he did start, he did not know where to end, declaring John struck at him & tried to throttle him before he
touched him, which bears falsehood on its face. For how was
John to know he intended to whip him more than any other
boy. He gave a long & plausible but, to us, lame self defence,
declaring John must apologize to him before the whole school
for the *"vulgarly rude manner"* in which he had fought him, &
be whipped for his disrespect. He was besides very rude & impertinent in his manner to mother & a day or two after wrote

a very impertinent letter, sending in his bill for the whole session $100. Mother never told us of this till within a day or two, as she knew we would all be roused by it, & she gave it to Dan [DeSaussure], the only person she had to consult. She had previously asked him to make inquiries among the other school boys as to the facts of the case but have [*sic*] not learned much as several had left the room just before it commenced. Frank Bonney came in & said, if he had been larger & had not been afraid, he would have gone to help Johnnie. All agree he was brutally treated. A teacher has full right to whip or keep in a boy for disobedience, disrespect or missed lessons, but not to beat and maltreat him. Besides John is a small boy, & Staudenmeyer a large, strongly built man. He has disgraced himself as a minister & gentleman. Dan showed his letter to several gentlemen & they advised her to take no notice of it, that he has no right to demand payment for nine months and, if he had, he could not claim it till the time had expired.

Since then, we have learned various items about him; he told mother he had been teaching for 30 years, & his wife says he only went to teaching as a livelihood since the war commenced, & various boys have made the same remark as John did some time before this affair—that he knows nothing about teaching, cannot explain a simple sum & cannot control the boys, & that they learn nothing. I also find that long ago Bettie Gatewood told the Ancrums that he was a very bad man & one who did not care how he appeared before ladies. She declined going into particulars, just as Annie did, but left the impression that his moral character was bad. . . . And yet, Mr. [Thomas F.] Davis [Jr.] most unsuspiciously invites him both to read prayers & to preach. Last Sunday, mother & John sat directly in front of him in the first pew & he looked at them steadily for a few moments, then turned away with a sneer on his face. It was as much as I could do to remain in church and I do not think I can stand any more of his preaching. Of all things I loathe a wolf in sheep's clothing in the pulpit. He had a Sunday or two before given us two excellent, practical sermons—one in really beautiful & poetic language, the other ending with a most beautiful hymn, & I had remarked how much he had improved.

Mr. John Elliott preached for us a fortnight ago—from 2

Corinthians, 4:18,[6] as ever an admirable sermon, most beautifully delivered. His oratory is perfect. I shall not readily forget the feelings of almost oppressive awe created by his brief
but intensely thrilling picture of Eternity—"That *waveless,
echoless, shoreless* ocean of eternity." The bare words seem lifeless without his magic voice to thrill them into vivid reality—&
when he referred to "the hoarse surges yet sounding in our
ears," I seemed almost to hear the dread solemnity.

After hearing him, I can understand the magic spell which
bound the listeners to all great orators of ancient as well as
modern times—particularly of Pitt, Fox, Burke, Sheridan
and a host of others, of whom Macauley has written so graphically. . . .

I was much surprised and shocked to learn that cousin Wilmot DeS[aussure], whom I have always liked & respected as
such a sensible man, has made himself as ridiculous as the
Rhetts by his violent tirades against the President, & his popularity & influence have been very much injured by it.

. . . The bombardment of Fort Sumter is still going on, with
occasional digressions to the other batteries or a few shells
thrown into the city without doing any damage worth mentioning. . . .

Mrs. McCandless has showed she approved my teaching &
appreciated my services by handing me a few days ago, in a
handsome and liberal as well as delicate manner, $300. I had
never even asked her definitely what was to be my salary, nor
referred to it at all. It was with a new & peculiar feeling of
independence that I received my earnings, or rather the
"earnest" of future exertions. As I knew mother was short of
funds at present, I lent her most of it, but in January I mean
to lay part out in Confederate Bonds, to accumulate for the
purchase of the watch I have so earnestly desired.

Of course, I have many petty daily annoyances, incidental
to my position and I have sometimes had to reprove the girls
sternly and decidedly, but I have the satisfaction of knowing I
have never lost my temper and that I command the respect of
the girls. I prefer to try to win them to good behavior by gentle but decided treatment & to study by exciting their ambi-

6 "We do not fix our gaze on what is seen but on what is unseen. What is
seen is transitory; what is unseen lasts forever."

tion & interest. The only thing I mind is the continual great weariness & aching in my lower limbs I experience on my return home so that I never have strength or inclination to go out anywhere.

November 22
Sunday

Mother received a letter from cousin Lizzie B[arnwell] two days ago, giving her the sad particulars of her children's deaths. Lydia was a beautiful and interesting child of eleven months, just beginning to talk and walk and was teething; she died after a succession of convulsions. Rose, she says, was also a very pretty child and seemed very womanly and far beyond her years. When she was without servants, Rose would try to help her make up her bed or lay the table or do anything else she could to help her. How well I remember her sweet plaintive blue eyes, which even when a fragile little creature of eighteen months, used to make me fancy, as she lay in my arms, that she saw more than was visible to our eyes. She had a fine memory and had learned to say and sing many little hymns and songs, besides repeating her prayers beautifully. After Lily's death, she would often say, "Mother, you know I have that dreadful cough too, and I am going to die and go to heaven with Lily, then you won't have any little girl here." And often when she thought no one was observing, [she] would kneel down and repeat all her prayers and hymns. Still she did not seem sick till a few days before her death. Cousin L.[izzie] was going into town & took her; she danced with delight at the pleasure of being dressed & riding out but on the way complained of being very sleepy & asked permission to go to sleep, came home sick, & was so but a few days, dying very suddenly in a convulsion. . . .

November 25
Wednesday

I sometimes think my journal will be merely a catalogue of deaths, for almost each day brings us intelligence of the loss of some one in whom we feel interested for their own or their family's sake. Tonight's paper told us of the death of another brave young hero, alike beloved and lamented by all who knew him, Frank Huger Harleston, a loss to his state and city, as well as friends. He had been detailed by Col. [Alfred] Rhett for duty at Fort Sumter. . . .

Yesterday about four o'clock in the morning, while on a

tour of inspection outside of the fort, a parrott shell exploded near him, wounding him so severely that he died a few hours after. He was a young man of fine talents as well as character & bore off the highest honors in the Arsenal as well as Citadel. . . .

Once I wrote almost daily in this, but now I seldom find time to do so more than once a week, & lately for a much longer period. The afternoons are so short that daylight soon fled away minding Sims or Carrie. Alas it will be a long weary time before those pleasures will return, for all are gone, and the house seems forlorn and desolate since the sunshine of our hearts has departed. Isaac came up for Carrie Saturday night at a day's warning & carried her to Summerville to spend the winter with Nanna [Hughes], so that he may run up to see her two or three times a week. Sims had grown so large and pretty, as well as interesting, that we shall miss him terribly as well as the other children. . . .

December 15

The Yankees have been shelling the city [Charleston] constantly, the [shells of] Greek fire being a failure, but the shells of course injuring many houses. Two deserters had gone over to the Yankees & must have given information of the position of Beauregard's headquarters, for they got the range very accurately, & the shells fell thickly around that neighborhood. Still uncle [Henry Alexander] DeS[aussure] refused to move, till Gen. B.[eauregard] sent an aid begging him to move. . . . Aunt was quite sick, and the next night's shelling so terrified her that he consented to leave and moved everything to a house in Judith St. which he found empty & took possession of. It was time, for shells had fallen in the yard & all around them. None have yet gone higher than George St. and cousin Mary [Holmes] says, during the day when it commenced, cousin Sue [Screven] & herself used to walk uptown, out of their way, but at night it was truly terrific to hear the shells whistling all around not knowing where next they would strike. St. Michael's & St. Philip's steeples are principal marks & a short time ago, on Thanksgiving Day, the congregations had to be dismissed on the account. The lower part of the city is almost entirely deserted, all business houses having been removed uptown.

Last Friday, [December 11] about half past nine A.M. a small magazine at Fort Sumter exploded, killing 11 and wounding 41 men. . . . The barracks were set on fire and the fierce rush of wind made its extinguishment for a long time almost impossible, & many of the wounded were severely burned. The Yankees, with their usual barbarity, immediately opened upon the fort with every gun they could bring to bear on it, & everybody we had opened in return. Isaac said it was the grandest concert he had ever heard. Strange to say the enemy's shells did not cause a single casualty. They seem to be getting very weary of their "big job" after five months "pegging away" at our glorious old Fort, which they find "a very hard nut to crack" even with the Monitors & Greek fire. . . .

Last Thursday being appointed as a day of Fasting, Humiliation & Prayer . . . on my return from church I found a most unexpected & delightful surprise in a letter from Dora [Furman] begging me to spend this month with her. Last Christmas she was about to send Charlie [Furman] up for me, when the fire took place, & since then either a full house & her own & her aunt's absence or sickness had obliged her to defer the invitation. It was no excuse for her not writing, but the prospect of once more meeting her almost effaces the past. Holiday commences next week & on Tuesday I will go down to spend two weeks with her; and the Brownfield's being only a half mile off, I shall enjoy double pleasure.

Edward and Sue were both to have gone today, but both had return of fever. However, Sue will go in two or three days, & he as soon as able, reducing our household dreadfully. The house seems so dreary & empty without the merry voices of the children & the sound of their pattering feet.

Three cheers for Morgan, our second [Francis] Marion and terror of the Yankees. He & six of his officers succeeded a few days ago in escaping [November 27] from the penitentiary in Columbus, Ohio, where they were treated like convicts. Capt. [Thomas H.] Hines, one of them, left a note by order of the rest, for the Superintendent, to inform [him] of the fact. Their implements [were] two small pocket knives & time of labor [was] three hours a day for three months. They dug under the walls &, of course, must have had assistance from without. Two, we hear, have since been recaptured.

I feel so young that I cannot realize that today marks the
stadium of my first quarter of a century. I wonder whether
I shall live like grandmother to complete three such eras.

I went down to Stateburg to stay with Dora [Furman]; the
cars were crowded, but I secured a pleasant journey by sharing my seat with Miss Laura Alexander, a very intelligent
pretty N.C. refugee, who used to teach in Mr. [William] Dehon's family, but has latterly been boarding with Mrs. [Mark-
ley] Lee and giving music lessons. We had never met though
we saw each other at church every Sunday & I had heard a
great deal of her. . . . I found Dora awaiting me at Claremont
& was most affectionately welcomed by herself and aunts.
They live seven miles from the depot & we arrived just in
time for dinner. The first thing that caught my eye as I entered the plain rough overseer's house which they had been
compelled to adopt after the destruction of their fine dwelling, was the benevolent countenance of the venerable Dr.
Richard Furman, Dora's grandfather, so universally beloved
and respected.[7] On the opposite wall hung the beautiful portrait of Willie, her uncle Charles' only child, & several other
of the pictures which have been my admiration and study for
years. I was equally delighted to find the portrait, which Dora
had painted of her mother from recollection, had been saved,
& her uncle's very large fine books of engravings—[Hans]
Holbein's portraits, most admirably engraved in colors, Sir
Joshua Reynold's works & the Dresden & Munich Galleries. It
seemed so homelike to be surrounded by silent friends.
 The house burned so rapidly that little was saved beyond
what was in the first story, & a great deal of their clothing,
supplies of every kind, china & glass were destroyed. Their
present contrasted quarters contain only six rooms—a parlor
& dining room in one, Miss Maria & Miss Ann's [Furman]
room, Mr. C.[harles] F.[urman]'s small dormitory, & [there
is] a pantry, with front and back piazza downstairs. Two
small ones [are] above, directly under the rafters & so open
that Miss Ann was very fearful I would get pneumonia, but

7 Richard Furman (1755–1825) was the first president of the Baptist
 State Convention and one of the founders of what is today Furman
 University.

being on their own plantation, they were abundantly supplied with wood and kept blazing fires so that I did not feel the cold there as much as I do here, though they are situated on a hill amidst a succession of other hills and valleys which catches every stray blast of Boreas. Dora calls it Anatok, the Home of the Winds, and they certainly do seem to hold their revels there. In front, the hill rapidly descends to a wooded slope through which a path winds across the fields to Mrs. Brownfield's, whose group of rough log cabins is seen from the back piazza dotting one hill, while the rich brown slopes of many others, interspersed here & there with groves of young pines, added delightful variety to the landscape; far away in the distance stretches what seem to be interminable forests with their blue haze making you almost believe that you gazed on the distant ocean, an illusion still further increased by the gentle murmur of the pines.

Shut up so long as I have been in this flat uninteresting spot, where I felt caged among the trees which so closely shut us out from enjoying either the sunsets or as much of the "blue arch o'erhead" to which I have been accustomed, the natural beauties of the hills and their freedom were much enhanced to my eyes. I grew ten years younger, in the sunshine of love, for I was petted and spoiled to my heart's content & I was happy, so happy, in being with my home friends once more. The Brownfields were only a half mile off, & we saw each other constantly: dining, supping or visiting one another; they are as roughly fixed as any new settlers, for the old dwelling was burnt years ago and they were so anxious to move from their uncle's after their great sickness and sorrow there that they had these hastily put up & no one but Mr. DeLage Sumter saw after it. He only went there once or twice & gave directions so that none of the cabins are connected. You have to go a few steps from one to another. They have had a plenty of annoyance and trouble too, from chimneys tumbling down, roofs leaking, etc. but those have been remedied and above all they have a peaceful, loving household, as happy as they can be after such great afflictions which must ever leave a shadow on their lives. . . . I wished a dozen times that we too lived in a log hut near them. I would not feel our exile half as much. But we have a "demoniacal spirit" which would never let us enjoy peace anywhere. . . .

Miss Maria [Furman] has been in miserable health & Dora also, for the past two years, from dyspepsia, the family complaint. In fact, after Charlie & Jamie [Furman] went into the army, she says she gave up all her horseback rides and walks in which they had always been her companions & felt anxious and interested only for them; her ill health commenced then & was still farther aggravated by repeated colds & wettings received in Greenville, which injured it seriously. But she never complained [n]or let anyone know her daily sufferings, and her stepmother, though once an aunt whom she seemed very fond of, is evidently not one whom she would seek freely as a mother. I have long thought & am now certain that she has made Dora feel that her father's house is not as freely hers as before, yet without being at all unkind—a stepmother in truth. When she told me what she suffered with every breath she drew last winter & spring, I did not wonder she was low spirited & felt no inclination to go out or write— though I told her I forgave her past silence only in hopes of future improvement. She said she constantly wished to write for me to visit her, but the house was almost constantly full & besides having no equipage until recently & she & her aunt both so dreadfully depressed (though she strove to conceal it for Miss M[aria]'s sake) that she could not bear to ask me to go till she could make it pleasanter for me.

Miss M[aria] was so very sick in the spring that they sent for Rev. Samuel F[urman's] son, Dr. John, who lives seventeen miles off. He came up, staid some time & took both cases in hand, then carried them to his own house where he could watch them closer & finally took them to Georgia to visit their relatives there. The restoration of their health commenced then, & they are both now a great deal better. Miss M[aria] [is] on the simplest diet, &, while I was there, Dora was suffering constantly in one way or another from having indulged a little more than usual at table. Living on the plantation, they had abundant supplies of poultry, vegetables, ham & bacon, etc. as well as sorghum, and also had tea & coffee—though the supply of tumblers & cups being much diminished, they had come down to tin tumblers. I never enjoyed the abundant variety of good things without wishing I could share them at home. . . . The days fled only too quickly by. We rose quite early & always took an eggnog before breakfast as tonic, breakfasted late, particularly as it was Christmas & the negroes allowed much liberty. The mornings glided away either reading, talking, walking or riding in the cart or buggy, for Dora has become an excellent "whip" &, though with mules only, drives Miss Maria out constantly to take exercise.

I persuaded Miss Ann [Furman] to cut my hair, the last day of the old year, though it was raining hard & we were going to dine with the Brownfields. It was done under protest at the sacrifice, but my hair had become so broken that I was determined on it. I could not forbear a shout, however, when I first saw myself in the glass I looked so comically ugly. As uncle Ta & aunt Lizzie [Gibbes] told me on my return home, I lost all the good looks I ever had when I cut my hair & pulled out my lashes. Green spectacles now would entitle me to the *outside* at least of an antique blue stocking.

I really envied the B[rownfield]'s their piano, for it adds so much to the cheerfulness of a household & we miss ours so much. They sang & played very sweetly for us, and, after dinner, Caliste [Brownfield] & I took a deux temps for the sake of old times. I turned perfect child again. They are such an industrious set of girls. Mary, Natalie and Fannie [Brownfield] teach the younger ones and read Italian and French together and keep up their music and Mary, Nattie, & Blanche [Brownfield] spin beautifully yarn for their dresses as well as stockings. Sue is a great knitter; I don't know whether she spins too. Blanche cannot be more than ten, & one morning her father told her to try & see how much she could do in one day. She carded till breakfast &, between that & dinner, spun three fine cuts. . . . Without directly saying anything against Mr. [Willie] E[arle], Dora hinted many things, which have made me feel very sad, liking him as much as I do. I felt sure she alluded to him but shrank from inquiring further. I know I cannot expect perfection, but it is a bitter thing to feel the loss of one title of respect or regard of one whom I admire so much. But I will wait and see.

January 1864 I returned home January 2nd 1864, and aunt Lizzie & uncle Ta [Gibbes] [are] here on a week's visit & grandmother & aunt Sue [are] also staying with us. From him I learned many interesting facts about Bragg & his army; he said the defeat at

Missionary Ridge was because our army was so small, not 29,000 men, that they felt that they would be whipped. The President had sent Longstreet to East Tenn., against Bragg's wishes with 20,000, then [Simon B.] Buckner & [Alfred J.] Vaughn, [Jr.], I think it was, were detached with nearly 20,000 more to support him & that not more than 2000 were away on furlough, etc.[8] He said Bragg had offered to be Johnson's [Joseph E. Johnston] chief of staff or to take any position assigned him. He is a glorious old hero and I know will turn "right side up" at last. . . . The weather had been fearfully cold since New Year's day & it grew worse, raining & sleeting, reaching its climax on Friday when we had a sleet storm. It was terrifically cold, such a spell had not been known for 40 years. The sleet lay for three days & it was five & six before it entirely disappeared—then ended in constant rain & today the weather is beautiful.

I went to school through all, save that Friday & last Tuesday, as Mrs. [Lucy] Romaré was not here the first week. We have made many changes in the classes so as not to have them clash, & I have taken the Macauley class of twenty-one girls, giving the Paley to Mrs. McCandless & ancient geography to Mrs. R[omaré]. I felt sure that, if allowed to teach the History as I wished, I could make it an interesting & improving study, while recited as the girls had been accustomed to do, they would learn nothing. For, Macauley never wrote to be studied as a regular school book. His history is a brilliant essay & profound criticism on the manners, customs & morals of the people, as well as the character & motives of its statesmen. I make the girls seek every reference, read the lesson in class, talk it over and explain it, & then they must be prepared to answer any questions on it I put. I have already succeeded in interesting most of the girls, as I make it the foundation for much collateral information. As it is the only recitation they have after recess, I can devote as much time to it as I need.

I have now taken the 5th class entirely under my charge, which they all seem to like as much as I do. I am glad to be rid of the 6th. I have also determined to make the girls speak French in class if possible. Mary Roper, who used to speak it

8   During the battles around Chattanooga (November 23–25, 1863), which included Missionary Ridge, the Confederates had about 64,000 soldiers; the Union about 56,000.

at home altogether when they had a French governess, generally addresses me now in that language. Being as yet obliged to translate my ideas, I do not speak fluently but hope to do so in time, as I find it easier every day. I recently looked over [Victor] Value's *Ollendorff* & found [it] so superior to [J. L.] Jewett's [*Ollendorf's New Method of Learning French*] which I studied, that I took to studying it myself. Next week Lila & Johnnie commence it with me, & I am going to make them talk in French. The Robinsons & Mary R.[oper] are about to review it & commence to translate my favorite *Cinq Mars*—whose author Count Alfred de Vigny died only two or three months ago. His private life was as pure, poetical & beautiful as his literary & social were distinguished. . . .

Willie has just had furlough to remove his negroes & hoped to come to see us & bring his eldest daughter Sallie to stay with us to go to school, but business prevented him. However, she will come later. Brother Henry must be, by this time, once more surrounded by his wife & children; he returned from the Yankee lines about a fortnight ago & has obtained a month's furlough. But as so much of his time has to be spent on the road, he cannot come here, to mother's great disappointment. I never expected him. He was quite sick with dysentery while away & says everyone tells him he lost half his fleshiness, but he is quite well now. . . . They all (13 surgeons, a chaplain, a lady & her children) had a very severe journey after reaching our lines as they found no transportation prepared & the weather dreadful. . . . A Yankee sought him out to enquire after a Northern lady, who has been for a long time teaching in Marion Co. . . . [He] was so delighted to hear of her that he lent brother H[enry] $130 in greenbacks & said he would lend more if he was going to return by way of Ft. Monroe. With that, he furnished himself with a hat, books & a supply of underclothing, which he much needed as he has lost his, & supplied Willie Bull, who is a prisoner, & had lost his baggage, of course. . . .

Gen. Morgan passed through Columbia Christmas & has gone to Richmond where he was enthusiastically greeted. His escape is as wonderful a series of romantic adventures as were those of the Count of Monte Cristo. God certainly seems to have preserved him from the greatest dangers for still more glorious deeds—he says his wife's prayers saved him. Poor

Capt. [Thomas H.] Hines, to whose enterprise & courage the Gen. owed a great deal & who started with him, is feared to be captured or killed, as nothing has been heard of him. Morgan will soon be in the saddle again & then woe to our brutal, merciless foe. Gen. Joe Johnston has taken command of the Army of Tenn. [December 27, 1863], but all is quiet there.

Just before I went to Dora's [Furman] I received a long delightful letter from Lizzie Greene, describing the first few days of doubt & dread after our defeat, as affecting them particularly & enclosing a strip from one of the flags captured [December 13, 1863] by Gen. [Patrick R.] Cleburne when he repulsed the enemy at Ringgold [Georgia]. It was given her by [William J.] Hardee's Medical Inspector, Dr. Bresaycher of St. Louis, whom she describes as one of those rare faces of such exquisite, holy beauty as Raphael would have delighted to paint as a saint. So fair, with beautiful blue eyes, & flowing flaxen hair—showing his German origin in that as well as his name & reminding me directly of the Chevalier Seraphaël, the Child of Music in "Charles Auchester." He is a friend of her brother John [Greene], who is on Hardee's staff of engineers, & she also describes many other prominent officers who[m] she saw constantly. Situated as they are on the borders of debatable ground & so near the army, she has the opportunity of becoming acquainted with "living historical characters.". . .

The Yankees celebrated Christmas by bombarding the city [Charleston] furiously as soon as they found a fire had broken out, most probably set, in Broad St., where it destroyed several offices. They have shelled continually since & the news today is that they have reached John St. Saturday evening's mail brought us the announcement of the birth of Willie's little son named after himself on Thursday 14th, just as he was preparing to leave for camp, so he had the pleasure of seeing him. Sue writes he is a fine large child, but not pretty. . . .

The past ten days have been like those of early spring, very delightful except too warm when returning from school. The afternoons [have been] so delicious & balmy that I pined for the sight and sound of the dashing waves, as we sat with every window open or on the piazza steps. I have always come

January 30
Saturday

[home] however, *very much* fatigued and prostrated so will be glad of the colder weather.

Cousin Beck [Holmes] came to stay with us a week ago.

The Yankees have been shelling the city regularly and ghastly rents and wounds are visible everywhere. The Huguenot Church, uncle [Henry Alexander] D[eSaussure]'s office, cousin Sue's [Screven] home, the Court House, S[outh] C[arolina] Hall, Dan Heyward's & Daniel Ravenel's houses on the Battery & numbers of other well known places have been struck.

. . . Rutledge is expected home on furlough & I should not be surprised if he were married then. Our old friend Peyre Gaillard is a complete paralytic, even in his hands, a mournful victim of the demon of drink—the curse of our land. . . . Willie Bull has returned from imprisonment quite sick & gives sad accounts of the treatment of our wounded by the Yankees. Brother Henry reached home to find little Henry ill with pneumonia.

February 9 . . . A week ago I received a long sweet comforting letter from our dear Rutledge; never did words come more apropos, for I had returned from school so disheartened and disappointed with the girls in my class of Macauley's *Hist. of England*, that I felt really depressed. I think Mrs. McCandless made a great mistake in the selection of that work, for the girls' minds are not prepared for it. Very few have such knowledge of English history to appreciate or even understand Macauley's which is rather an essay on the manners & customs, characters and causes of the great events of the time than a regular history, and never was intended to be studied for the purpose of recitation. I read and enjoyed it exceedingly, finding it as fascinating as a romance; but these girls do not exercise their minds at all & never *think* over what they are studying, nor do they seem to have any ambition to acquire knowledge or ideas. The sole aim of the majority seems merely to get through the lesson as quickly as possible.

February 13 The Macauley class, about whom my thoughts seem to have
Saturday been last occupied, reached their climax—at least I hope so—
this week. On Thursday they gave Mrs. McCandless a specimen of their gross ignorance & miserably learned & recited

lessons & the day before she came in before I had finished, so
she had good opportunity of judging of my difficulties &
their unsatisfactory recitations. Thereupon I gave my opinion
of them to her before their faces, raising a storm & causing
sundry vials of wrath to be emptied on my devoted head. But
as I laughed openly at it & gave them free permission even to
write what they pleased about me in their compositions, it has
blown over. They are all aware of the pains I take to make
their lesson interesting, & now on every alternate Friday, history will be excused & one of the Waverly Novels bearing on
that period will be read. I hope thus to improve & expand
their ideas & give them a taste for literature. I commenced
reading that fascinating set of works when I was eight or nine
years old, & it is astonishing to me to find so few of these
girls of fourteen & sixteen have read any of them.

Mother, sister F[anny] & John left yesterday morning for
Summerville to spend till Wednesday with Carrie and Nanna
[Hughes], then go on to Maria's [Scriven Holmes]; though
John may return after putting them on the Augusta train.
Two nights before they left, mother was arranging her box of
business papers when she came across two or three hundred
old letters which had been saved from the fire. We overlooked
& read many of them, charming epistles from a variety of
relatives. Two delightful ones, gayly brimming with the freshness & hope as well as devoted affection of a youthful fianceé,
from Mrs. [Abbott H.] Brisbane, one written a week or two
before mother's engagement, but when the report of it had
already spread and the other, just before her own marriage,
urging mother to go to Columbia to be her bridesmaid. But
as it took place only a week before mother's, she could not
go. I could not but contrast her letters now so changed in all
save the same devoted love from early girlhood.

Then followed several from our favorite governess, Miss
Harriett Pettit, written to mother in 1844 when she went to
the Virginia Springs with father for his health, leaving us in
charge of aunt Mary [E. Holmes] & Miss P[ettit] who really
acted as kindly & took as much interest in us as if she were a
relative. Edward, a pretty baby of six months, was her especial
pet & darling, often referred to, while Carrie had gone to
spend the summer on the island with cousin Sarah [Elliott]
(how well I remember the Saturday when the Screvens & all

of us children went down there, & Willie, Jamie Fraser, Heber Screven & myself tramped through the hot sand barefooted.) Three pages of one letter were taken up with short letters from Sister F[anny], Sue, and brother H[enry], while Willie had scrawled a line after a long practice on his slate: "I want to see you very much." I used to read a little every day, Miss Pettit said.

I had no idea I was considered "anything remarkable" till a letter from cousin Mary Elizabeth [Holmes] informed me of it; speaking of what she had heard of mother's different children from various members of the family who had just visited her at Boston, she says "I hear Emma is a child of uncommon abilities!!!!" Mother also came across a quarterly account of my scholarship, from Rev. C. W. Howard, dated Oct. 1847, when I was not quite nine years, & it is really quite creditable. Good marks predominate in all the studies & in composition, he said, I was quite creditable & grammar very good indeed. I have no recollection of my compositions, but a vivid one of the grammar . . . and of the spelling class. Mr. H.[oward] ends by saying, "On the whole Emma is a good little girl, her chief defect being an inclination to quickness—Caroline is improving as rapidly as is to be expected from her age—just seven." How well I remember Mr. Howard, & how we loved him & lamented his grievous downfall. I had not heard of him for years, till a day or two ago I saw his name as *Rev. Capt.* C. W. Howard.

February 20
Saturday

Nora Gatewood came to stay with Lila a week ago, & we have kept "Old Maid Hall' very pleasantly. During the morning, Lila initiated her in all the mysteries of a "menage on a war footing" & at night we have read aloud [Richard] Sheridan's famous comedies *School for Scandal*, *The Rivals*, & *The Duenna*, etc. & they have also translated French to me. . . . Yesterday Mrs. McCandless handed me, as sweetener of my toil she said, the second installment of my salary; we omitted several recitations and read to the girls. I exhausted my throat, already sore, in reading to the "very intellectual" Macauley class, *The Fortunes of Nigil*, for two hours, in hopes of interesting them & enlarging their ideas. A few of the girls were really appreciative & listened, and I received "a vote of thanks from a committee of one," Ann Kennedy, while Ellen Deas rewarded me with "Well, now, what's all this been about." A specimen of my daily *pebbles.* . . .

My constant occupation has made me omit a very important & interesting fact: Fan Garden's marriage to Capt. Charlie F[urman] on the 9th of this month at her aunt's in Georgia; Dora & her father went on, & she wrote me Jamie F[urman] could not, as Capt. Earle was "in durance vile," & he had to take command. I should like very much to know the cause. "To make idols and to find them clay"—alas. I have written for Dora, Charlie & Fan to run over & see me for a day or two but fear there is little prospect of that pleasure. If they come, they will find us true to our characters, as dwellers in a Nunnery, for not only are we "quite secure from all visitors" but are keeping Lent strictly, as neither flesh, fish nor fowl are inhabitants of our larder & our bill of fare would suit, I am sure, the most rigorous Catholic: "Peas & rice & potatoes."

The whole army is animated with the brightest & most determined spirit and almost everywhere the soldiers are re-enlisting unanimously, by companies, regiments or brigades for *the war*, (& one body added) even if it lasts 40 years; Congress is trying to remedy the depreciation of the currency by a bill compelling the holders of certain interest notes to fund or pay them into the treasury for taxes before July under the penalty of a tremendous tax on them. . . . A new issue, under proscribed limits, is to be circulated.

*February 26
Friday*

Our Old Maids Hall was invaded, first much to our astonishment by aunt Sue & Mrs. Wm. Jones, the lady with whom she is staying at Longtown, and her two children whom she wished to bring to the dentist. Aunt Sue wanted to see her friends & proposed to spend the night but she declared she could not impose on refugees in that style; however, she finally consented, bringing with her a most generous gift of a large ham, very large homemade loaf, a great treat to us, as we only buy wheat bread now when anyone is sick, eggs, rice & a chicken, besides some nicely spun yarn. She was indeed one of the few who have shown their sympathy with us refugees, in deeds, not sounding words. She said she had not had the opportunity of assisting many refugees but considered it a privilege as well as duty to do so. If there were more like her, the sorrows & hardships of exile would be alleviated. She is an intelligent well educated lady using the choicest language & with the most refined manners. They remained till breakfast Saturday. Half an hour after their arrival came Sue, Sallie [Scriven] & John, having walked from the depot more than a mile, on account of the high charge for omnibus hire.

Sallie is a tall well made girl of thirteen, not exactly pretty, but with a very pleasant face, fair complexion, grey eyes, & soft brown hair. She is certainly a very amiable girl, of good principles, and a fair mind though very backward, so that I have given her very few studies, wishing her to be well grounded first in reading, writing, spelling & arithmetic and [she] has taken up French & dictionary at home with me. . . . The first week must indeed have been a trial to her: so homesick that two or three evenings were spent in tears & then to be stared at & remarked on at school by sixty odd pair of curious eyes. However, she went sturdily & readily to her books to master what at first were difficulties, having been so long from study & taking kindly my numerous corrections of her mistakes in talking as well as spelling.

March 9 It is just seven, a delicious spring morning; I have been up an hour and a half & she [Sallie] is now near me, busily conning her French.

I have lately had much trouble & annoyance from my Macauley class again. Indeed it is the only one which really causes me any consequence, for the girls who sit in my room are a well-behaved set from whom I have never received the slightest mark of disrespect, save once, from one. . . . I believe that I am generally loved & I know am respected by them. I seldom have to speak to them save for studying too loud and am quite satisfied with them. But this class of twenty one of the oldest girls in school do their best, with a few honorable exceptions, to set all authority & rules at defiance. Every mean trick for cheating the teacher seems to be considered lawful. Looking into their books, telling even across the room, studying other lessons, & talking or writing to one another are common practices, which I have broken in some measure. And lately to crown all, several have been very disrespectful, to my astonishment Sallie DeS[aussure] being one of the leaders. The manner of the speeches . . . [are] more so than the words, but done in such a manner that I thought quiet dignity and strict exercise of authority the best way to treat them. They became quite indignant on receiving *failures* for lessons about which they have not one clear consecutive idea and tried the same game I find with Miss Hattie Young, as they are doing with me, only going far beyond with her. But they have made a mistake this time, as they will find later. Hitherto I have treated & called them young ladies, till Mattie Shannon asked me one day why I did so. I told her because I was always treated so, but, as they cannot sustain the character, I shall consider them unruly children.

Mrs. McC[andless] gave them a "scorching" lecture just after, which, had they had any feelings of shame on the subject, ought to have dyed their cheeks at the recollection of their contemptible behavior to Mrs. McC[andless] last summer at examination, which she told me of afterwards. Mary Lyles, as was notorious, had rubbed out some of her marks & been impertinent to Miss Hattie [Young] which created a tumult in the school. . . . The others wanted her expelled, but they themselves had almost all been guilty of the same, though she only had been caught in "flagrant[e] delictu." But, when Mrs. McC[andless] voted her the prize for scholarship, their *virtuous* indignation knew no bounds and they entered into a combination to show it, by rising in a body & leaving the room, as soon as her name was announced. They also voted that she could not receive a single flower, and, on the eventful morning, Miss Hattie was literally imbedded amidst floral offerings of "respect and affection," while Mrs. McC[andless] received but a tiny bouquet from Maggie Dunlap. However, when the obnoxious name was announced, not one had courage enough to be the first to move, but a whisper run through the ranks: "she rubbed out her marks." Thus failed the grand concerted rebellion but not the spirit which animated it, & they are now striving for the mastery, and of course it is a continually protruding thorn. . . .

The Currency question is the principal topic of the day, as the majority of the sellers refuse to take bills of a larger denomination than five because, after the first of April, if not

funded in 4 percent bonds, they will be taxed 33⅓ percent &
$100, 10 percent additional for every month unfunded.[9]
Those of *patriotism* & integrity know this issue to be perfectly
good, but extortioners refuse it or try to make their customers
pay a percentage. It is quite inconvenient, as change is scarce,
& the banks cannot furnish it; there is no agent of the Treasury here, & we have no gentleman to do our business for us.
As Mrs. McC[andless] paid me the other half of my salary
two or three weeks ago, I went over Tuesday afternoon to see
old Mr. [William E.] Johnson & consult him as to what was
best. Neither he nor his wife were at home at first, but his
grand daughter, Nannie [Johnson], one of our scholars, &
Laura Alexander, now staying with Dr. Robert Johnson,
[were there]. We went to the upper story to obtain a pretty
view of the grounds, then sat on the joggling board in the vine
covered piazza, enjoying the delicious freshness of the evening, till they returned. But others came in also, & business
was of course deferred.

To my astonishment & delight, I found Sallie May Ford had
arrived during our absence. We had not met for nearly ten
years & certainly would not have recognized each other. She
has completely captivated me as I doubt not she does every
one who is fortunate enough to know her. She is a half head
shorter than I am, but so *very plump* & with such a huge bust
that she looks still shorter. Her complexion is a charming
mingling of the rose & lily & all her features [are] very pretty,
save her grey eyes which are too full & prominent. She arranges her hair in a peculiar style; heavy front braids & then a
light bunch of short curls besides. On the whole though,
when her face is at rest, you could not call her exactly very
pretty; she reminds you of some portrait of a century ago.
But when her clear joyous laughter rings so merrily & melodi-
ously on the air that it is contagious, she is the most irresistible, bewitching, charming little beauty I know. Then too, her

9 The February 17, 1864, currency law required the exchange of paper
  bills for long-term bonds or new currency. Holders of $100 bills or
  larger had to exchange this money for bonds by April 1 or lose one-
  third value immediately and one-tenth value every month thereafter.
  Money of smaller denominations was to be exchanged for bonds or
  new issue paper currency at the rate of three old dollars to two new
  ones.

noble character makes her as lovable as fascinating. She is what our boys call "a whole souled woman" so amiable, sincere, affectionate, & considerate of others—intelligent, cultivated, active & ingenious in a thousand ways, thoroughly practical, till I believe she can do anything she puts her hands & mind to—independent self-reliant & energetic, to an unusual degree, yet as far as the antipodes from "a strongminded woman" and withal very pious, I believe. She has a fine voice and is altogether such a rosebud & a beam of sunshine that the man who secures her as a companion through life will be fortunate indeed.

She is, besides, one of the Florence Nightingales of the South, and I have no doubt she has gone through greater ordeals in witnessing the sufferings in the hospitals than a hundred women in ordinary life. After the battle of Chickamauga, our wounded soldiers were carried by hundreds to Augusta, where no hospitals were prepared, very few surgeons, and very few Sisters of Charity to dress their wounds. They lay at the depot, covering every spot that could be found for them to rest upon, and but few ladies went forward to assist in the dreadful, yet most necessary, task of dressing their wounds, many of which had not been done for three or four days.

Finally, her brother-in-law, Maj. Clinch, told her she ought to go & help, which she did, accompanied by him, & washed & dressed dreadful wounds. The Catholic & Presbyterian churches were then converted into hospitals & one ward was given to her, which she attended regularly for nearly three months doing surgeon's duty with her own tiny hands, even cutting out *gangrene* from an awful wound. At first, she said she was nearly overpowered by the fearful sights she witnessed and what she had to do; but she has always had great nerve and self possession, as well as presence of mind, and with hints from her father and Dessie [Ford], she became quite successful. . . .

I commenced writing several days ago but was interrupted and during this time a great and overwhelming sorrow has fallen upon uncle John's [DeSaussure] household in the sudden death of aunt Eliza. She has been *very* sick for a long time, a cancer being the root of the disease which sprang from it, but she never kept her bed, always being in her room save when she went out to ride. . . . The funeral took place Saturday morning and the whole family attended. . . .

Old Mrs. [Mary Cox] Chesnut too has gently sunk to rest after a long decline; she was nearly 89 and died Saturday afternoon. Death literally seems to be stalking abroad in Camden.

Yesterday I received a most unexpected letter from Claude Turnbull, from Cokesbury after a year's silence. . . . What a change has the war wrought in her. From the dreamy girl who lived amidst her French, Italian & German books, & seemed bewildered when she descended into every day life, she has become quite practical, sewing busily or knitting for the soldiers & now turned housewife & as busily engaged in making a vegetable garden, with her beloved books, however, by way of companions. . . . There has also been another "On to Richmond" this time led by Col. Ulrich Dahlgreen [*sic*], a fast youth of twenty-one, son of Admiral [John A.] Dahlgreen [*sic*] of the Charleston Blockaders. It was a cavalry raid [February 28–March 4, 1864] & somehow arrived within a few miles of Richmond, but were then met and driven back by about 600 of Hampton's cavalry, the Home Guard, etc. Of course there was much excitement in that city at the time, but very little was said of it in the papers; but papers were found on the body of Dahlgren disclosing a diabolical plot to assassinate President Davis & his whole Cabinet, sack the city & destroy it also I believe. Many of the officers & men of the raiding party were captured, but at first the affair seemed trifling, as skirmishes are of such every-day occurrence.

We certainly have much to cheer us for, besides these advantages, trifling perhaps *if* merely numbers are counted but of great moral weight, the health & spirits of our troops were never better. Then, though the Currency Bill may have & will still occasion some inconvenience and distress, its good effects are already beginning to be seen in the fall of prices in provisions from the immense amount already funded.

Dear old Charleston still receives daily her allotted portion of battering, and "The Gillmore district" is showing ghastly rents in many a once fair & goodly mansion. Portions of two shells have entered uncle James' without, however, doing much damage.

... I received a very long letter ... from Lou Harllee, as lov- *March 19*
ing as in by-gone days though four years had passed since *Saturday*
our correspondence dropped. She, Dora [Furman] and I
[and] perhaps Leonora Shackleford, are the only maiden
members of our class left, & she proposes an Old Maid's
Convention of three to meet at her house. ...

Carolina & the army generally sympathized with our beloved Beauregard in the recent death of his wife at New Orleans
after three years separation. The Yankees, with their usual
brutality, could not let slip the opportunity of publishing the
most insulting remarks upon her as a Southerner & a woman
—which have justly excited the scorn and anger of the world.
The funeral was attended by 60,000 persons, including the
French officers of the *Catinat*, the French, Spanish & Prussian Consuls.

Gen. Bragg was a short time ago [February 24, 1864] appointed as the President's Chief Military Adviser with the consent of Beauregard, Lee, Johnston & others who were his
superiors in rank.

The *Husatonic* [*sic*], one of the iron clad blockaders off
Charleston, was recently blown up by one of our cigar-shaped
torpedo boats, to the consternation of the Yanks. ...

Hard rain almost all day, which Tuesday turned to a furious *March 21*
sleet storm, followed by snow, till it was nearly two inches *Monday*
deep. Wed. the sun rose clear, brilliant & powerful, affording
us a fairy scene for a few hours, but the thaw was the most
rapid I have ever seen. I went to school Thursday for the
first time, & as the next day was Good Friday, holiday was
given, but it poured all day—today, Saturday, clear.

... It seems to me that the world sinks deeper in wickedness *April 15*
every day, & if this war has developed the highest qualities in
one half or one fourth rather, the rest have proved so black at
heart in some way or other, (even those whom formerly we
delighted to honor) that I scarcely know whom to trust and
respect.

I was terribly shocked to learn that Mr. William M. T.[ren-
holm]'s name had become a synonyme [*sic*] for falsehood &
dishonesty since he has been in that fatal quartermaster's department, where the temptations are so great. Dr. John

D.[arby] has sunk down to paying spies to watch Willie Ramsey's most private actions in order to ruin him & caused him to be court martialed upon a long series of infamous charges, of which only one can be proved—the employment of government negroes in cutting wood to sell, while he substituted others, who did not do as well. Beauregard won't allow the sentence to be published, but his friends fear he will be cashiered. Echols is at the bottom of the whole affair but has made Mr. John his cat's paw.

Thursday evening, as we were impatiently waiting for tea, or rather the waiter of corn bread & waffles, for tea is among the almost forgotten relics of the past, we were as surprised as delighted by the very unexpected arrival of Carrie, Sims & "big Sims" [White]. We had not heard from her for nearly three weeks and were just talking of her. When I felt my darling little pet once more in my arms, I forgot weariness & pain & felt as if he imparted some of his superabundant vitality to me. He is a very large fine child, his beautiful blue eyes sparkling as brightly as ever & ever ready for a merry laugh. He is very strong & looks far more like nine than six months old. Sims expected to stay a day, but the change of trains obliged him to return before daylight Friday. Still he has so much of his mother about him that it was refreshing to have seen him even so short a time.

We had another pleasure yesterday afternoon in a visit from "our good doctor" [Louis DeSaussure]. . . . I have been suffering so long from that unceasing aching of the limbs & prostration which had increased during the last two months that the very sight of him did me good. I told him "tanglefoot," alias new corn whiskey, had been recommended to me as the vilest of drinks but best of tonics &, as he approves, I feel sure it will benefit me. I am sure everyone who has ever had the good fortune to be under his charge has showered daily blessings on his head. Lately I have dragged to & from school & spent my afternoons lying down, because I ached from weariness.

Last Tuesday Mrs. Romaré went off suddenly to Richmond to see her husband; she had been expecting the summons for some time, but it & the opportunity followed in so few hours that quite a little excitement was produced in school, which only increased when it was found that Mrs. McC[andless] had engaged Mr. *Goddard Bailey* . . . to take the Spanish & my Racine class, while she & I divided Mrs. R[omaré]'s classes & consolidated the 5th & 6th to diminish the labor. I never had been pleased with the Racine class, for they never studied & indeed had no ambition to improve, so that it afforded me great amusement & satisfaction, which I openly expressed at their discomfiture, when he announced after hearing them translate: "He did not think he would be pleased with them." The next lesson, as I was well assured, was well studied. He is very strict & not only has given them passages to learn by heart but next week will speak entirely in French & make them answer. I am very anxious to be a listener, as well as looker on, but unfortunately am too busy myself. They cannot try with Mr. Bailey any of the disgraceful behavior they have shown to every other new teacher, for he is not only a gentleman but [also] a thoroughly fashionable man of the world. . . . A contemptuous smile or remark will, I think, do more than anything else to sting to exertion. He is a genius, Mrs. McC[andless] says; there's not a topic she has touched upon with which he is not familiar—a master of all the modern languages, music &, in fact, he says he never found anything yet which he could not do by throwing his whole mind upon it. But then, when he had acquired it, he wanted the perseverance to pursue it. He did not add the last, but it was easily gathered from his conversation & life, which I knew, but she did not. He lived a fast life in Va.—spent his own & wife's fortune, then obtained a place in some government office, where defalcation took place to a very large amount just before the breaking out of the war. . . . [The war] prevented particular inquiry, but evidence was strong against him—A very good reason for seeking such a quiet place as Camden. . . .

At school I have made some changes, which are productive of good effects, though I have a great deal more to do. School opens at 8½, when I hear the 2nd French class, then give an hour only to Macauley, when I not only get my whole class together but for better lessons, as the girls are obliged to learn it now at home, & they do not even read it now in class—didn't they look blank when they heard it. Of the 5th class, I have only retained their History, Grammar & Carpenter's spelling. I could not bear to give them up entirely. Then follows 3rd French class of a dozen girls—recess, which I seldom have, Ancient & Modern Geography, Astronomy, just commenced, (all large classes) & Sallie's [Scriven] arithmetic, so I do not expect to be out any day before three. . . .

May I have to thank dear Miss Agnes [Bates], for another literary feast, indebted as I have been to her for so many already. Last summer a translation of Victor Hugo's last novel, *Les Miserables*, made its appearance in spite of the blockade; *Fantine*, the first novel, excited intense interest & was gradually followed by *Cosette, Marius, St. Denis & Jean Val Jean.* Though everyone was talking of this in the lulls between the roar of the cannon & whistling of shells, I did not read it, first, because I was prejudiced against its morality by a criticism from "Sumter," long before it appeared, then by one from Capt. [Willie] Earle. I confess to having tried to procure it in the original, for the sake of the French, but before I heard Mr. E.[arle] speak of it. *Fantine*, only, had appeared then, & I am sure he must have changed his opinion since finishing it. I spoke of it to Miss A.[gnes] &, in her reply, she showed me there was so much more in it than the mere story, then I procured it as soon as I could, &, after I commenced, I never rested till I had "devoured" all. With all its faults, which are glaring & received through the medium of the most ungraceful translation I have ever read, it is a wonderful book—so full of great thoughts, so terse & epigrammatic, so graphic & intensely vivid, that I do not wonder the Parisian workmen & students will go wild over it. It is a *living* epitome of Paris, that equally wonderful concentration of light and darkness. I shall never be satisfied until I own a French copy which I can read & ponder over to my own satisfaction. It is so intensely vivid that I felt as if a witness of the great drama of Waterloo, as well as the minor one of the Barricade of la Chanvrerie & almost held my breath as I *saw* the charge of the 3500 French cuirassiers over the sunken road of Ohain & the deaths of Gavroche & Enjolras. How I could *enjoy* translating it anew, my fingers seem tingling all the time with a desire to correct the awkward, inelegant, unidiomatic expressions with which

it abounds. "The Iliad of all our woes" "Masterly inactivity"—
[John] Randolph of Roanoke.[10]

After a lapse of three weeks, I have to record my first & prob-   *May 7*
ably also last frolic in Camden. Friday evening, April 29th,
Miss [Laura] Alexander gave a Musical Soiree of her scholars
at Mrs. McCandless'. The latter invited Lila & myself to tea to
meet Mr. & Mrs. [Goddard] Bailey before the entertainment
commenced. It was to have taken place the week previous so
we had ample time to anticipate our debut as Nuns, and I
really think we thought oftener of the soiree, than if it had
been a St. Cecilia, & we fully enjoyed it too.[11] I met Mrs.
Bailey for the first time, though we had exchanged visits &
was extremely pleased with her. To great elegance of manner
as well as personal appearance, she unites much sociability &
frankness; she had besides lived much in Charleston, & that
forthwith established a bond between us upon which we
talked freely, &, between the refreshment of heart from that
and of the body from the strong and delicious tea I drank, I
felt exhilarated. . . . Indeed "Emma Holmes was herself
again" & not merely an assistant teacher vegetating in this
dullest of places.

When we entered the front drawing room, we found the
girls assembled & looking so fresh & pretty in evening dress
that many I did not recognize. . . . I found a seat by Lila Davis
& enjoyed the undercurrent of conversation kept up with her,
while the young musicians were singing & playing & really
doing credit to Miss A[lexander]'s instruction. Lila Davis I
have always liked, for besides being very sociable she is quite
intelligent and cultivated. I mingled also among the school
girls & received from Mattie (William) Shannon, quite to my
surprise, (as she had lately been quite offended with me from

10 Miss Holmes's chronology breaks down in May, and the entry dates do
    not always correspond with the actual time of writing. For example,
    under the entry for May 7 she discusses the May 11 death of J. E. B.
    Stuart. Rather than compound the confusion, the entries have been
    left in the order they appear in the diary except for the May, 1864,
    entry, which was taken from the end leaves of Volume III of the diary
    manuscript and included here.
11 The St. Cecilia Society, founded in 1762, held concerts and dinners
    which were highlights of the Charleston social season.

a necessary exercise of authority in school) not only an additional & warmly urged invitation to the approaching May Party, to those already given, but also one to dance the Virginia reel, with which the Soiree ended, and in which Messrs. [Goddard] Bailey and [Leslie] McCandless also joined. We did not reach home till twelve. . . .

Saturday [April 30] we were surprised by the entrance of William White, whose regiment had just arrived on its way to Va. In Columbia the ladies had gotten up an extensive barbecue in honor of the 1st & 2nd regiments, included in Hampton's Legion, who has recently returned from the seat of war & extended their invitation to all the soldiers in the city. The citizens contributed most liberally to afford every delicacy of peace times to the war torn veterans, & the whole affair cost over [$] 40,000. It was held in the extensive grounds of the Female Lunatic Asylum, whose brick walls afforded the privacy necessary; booths were erected in various directions of evergreens & flowers, with patriotic mottoes interwoven, while thousands of tiny battle flags and tobacco pouches, filled, which were afterwards given to the soldiers, were interspersed among the leaves and blossoms. . . . Overhead floated battle flags which had been borne through many a hard fought conflict. . . . The most prominent gentlemen in the city were on the various committees and everything passed off well, though there were about 10,000 persons present. Dr. Palmer gave an eloquent address followed by two or three others. . . .

May 3
Monday
[should
be 2]

Lila and myself attended the May Party or rather Picnic given by the elder school girls in the morning at the old [William] McWillie house. Bessie Goodwyn was queen, thereby rendering her parents very proud and happy; her governess, Cecile Johnson . . . who is only seventeen, was Crowner, while many of the Macauley class were Maids of honor and Flowers etc. . . . Indeed the whole was oddly gotten up; the invitations were given at random, & so peculiarly that we did not know till after our arrival whether we were expected to remain to dinner or the Coronation only. The girls all looked remarkably prettily, their floral ornaments were beautiful, & the throne most tastily arranged. Quite a number of ladies & children went as spectators, & I felt quite provoked that Sallie

[Scriven] had not been invited, but "we refugees never go where we are not invited particularly." To my utter astonishment and almost dismay at first, as we drove up to the house, I saw the piazza filled with soldiers & found Col. [A. D.] Goodwyn had invited them. I had been a Nun so long that it was not until after the Coronation, when I discovered familiar faces among them, that I became quite at my ease again. . . . Between dancing reels & quadrilles, waltzing with Mattie Shannon, talking to Mrs. Bailey & my other lady friends, the day passed very pleasantly. The party broke up about four, as Bessie [Goodwyn] & her mother were very tired, & Col. G.[oodwyn] had given a general invitation to all present (to which his wife added separate ones) to go & finish the frolic by a "war party" at his house—that is dancing without refreshments. We had gone in the morning in Dan's [DeSaussure] carriage & one of uncle J[ohn]'s horses. . . . We had ordered it to return about six but were rather dismayed by the early departure; however, Sallie Stuart, whom we had "chaperoned" all day, had sent a message for her carriage to come and she took us home after waiting with several other girls about an hour. . . .

I put my wits to work to know how we could get there, for the unusual excitement had restored my old vitality & spirits & I "felt in for the frolic." Mother proposed asking for Mary Henry's carriage &, as we felt sure of getting it, we dressed, I in my brown silk and bodice, the only article like party costume that I own, & for Lila, I fixed an impromptu one, of Carrie's pearl colored silk skirt & a white muslin body, one too that we had considered long past service, so much does need sharpen ingenuity. Back came our messenger with the information that one horse was loaned out, so mother sent to our good friend, Mrs. [William E.] Johnson—his [*sic*] coachman was sick & boy out. So, as a last resource, we applied to Mrs. Tom Ancrum & succeeded. William was here & escorted us there at 9½—truly fashionable hours, but others arrived after us. After all, the "Nuns" proved utter wall-flowers. We knew very few gentlemen & none save W.[illiam] W.[hite] came near us. Lila danced with him & became sociable with Bessie [Goodwyn] & the other girls, so I was glad I went. But, during the evening we found Eliza Lee had entirely ignored us & invited the Gatewoods to go home with her, placing both them & us very unpleasantly. . . . After again demeaning myself by asking seats from two of the school girls, Martha Robertson sent us home & I determined this should be the last time I would lower my pride thus.

May 3
Tuesday

I found myself feeling better than I had done for days; the weather was delicious & about eleven I went to spend the morning with Mrs. Perkins, holiday having been given that the girls might recover from their frolic. Thursday last, Mrs. Perkins had taken me to drive up the Mulberry road, where the crab-apples, hawthorne & Cherokee roses were filling the air with their beauty & fragrance; the hawthorne was especially beautiful with its clusters of snowy blossoms, thickly mingled with the dense mass of brilliant green foliage. Of course, I enjoyed the ride, but still more when I discovered how closely our literary tastes coincided, not only our favorite authors being the same, but even the very poems or prose works. The morning passed quickly & agreeably & after a hearty lunch of bread & butter & delicious strong tea, which again seemed to infuse new vitality in my limbs, she started to walk home with me; the air was so balmy we prolonged our walk, then I turned half way back with her, & to my astonishment found it was four when we parted. I returned home to find *dry hominy* the only dinner to be had, but my lunch enabled me to dispense with that. Hominy, cornbread & occasionally a little peas or eggs & still more rarely a scrap of bacon, is our ordinary bill of fare. Still feeling most unusually well, I went to see Mrs. [Goddard] Bailey & her sister Mrs. Colcock, & I believe I spent an hour and a half there, talking about Charleston & Charleston people, a never-ending theme of interest to us refugees—coming away at dark. . . . All these trifling as they are were great variety in my monotonous life.

Returned to school next day & the girls did better than I expected, though their heads are considerably turned. Several had left school, & others, who came to me since to view the constellations, confessed very frankly that they did not study, no news to me certainly, for I have been tortured all the time by the effects. Mrs. Bailey has had another hemorrhage & is very sick. I have taken the greatest fancy for her, and I believe it is mutual. I feel she is & will be a real friend, but her husband will never be anything but an agreeable acquaintance. I don't trust him.

Monday I returned early from school on account of a distressing headache or rather giddiness which necessitated my taking medicine & remaining from school for the first time since I've been teaching. Our sunshine left us yesterday morning when Carrie & Sims [White] returned to Summerville, to our great disappointment. . . . Sims is so handsome, large & strong & so good & playful that he is as general a favorite as his mother; she had just put him in short clothes, which made him as happy as possible, since he can now stand alone by a chair, his great delight.

May 19
Thursday

I cannot understand how anyone can dislike children, I love them devotedly & think the acmé [*sic*] of felicity is such a baby as Sims or little Carrie [Holmes] in one arm, & a book in the other, though the babies seldom allow the book to be read. The dullness of the Nunnery seems to have settled deeper than ever. . . . Last Friday after recess I read "Cristabel & the Ancient Mariner" to the Macauley class, which by the way has dwindled very much. . . .

The news of [Frederick] Steele's & [Nathaniel] Banks' surrender in the Trans-Mississippi department seems fully confirmed. The news from Va. is indeed most encouraging, but the cypress is closely mingled with the laurel, and we mourn the loss of several heroic chieftains, who fell, alas, by one of those heart-rending accidents of battle, by the hands of our own men. The battles occurred in a densely wooded country, well named the Wilderness, which prevented the use of artillery; therefore, the wounds are comparatively slight, & the proportion of wounded to dead among our men very great. . . .

Grant & his proud host of hirelings attacked Lee at the head of the immortal Army of the Potomac [Army of Northern Virginia], on the South side of the Rapidan, & was driven back with terrible loss that day & the next. . . .

May 5
Thursday

. . . Indeed fighting has been & is going on still at so many different points, it is hard to keep up an account of them. . . . But alas [J. E. B.] Stuart has also fallen [May 11, 1864], he

May 7
Saturday

whose name was a terror to the foe. His wound was apparently slight, in the hip, but he died the day after. . . .

June 3   No grand battle at either point yet, but daily skirmishing etc. . . . Gen. [Winfield] Scott says "Beware of Lee on the advance & Johnston on the retreat." The latter has now drawn Sherman 120 miles from his base of supplies & 400 from assistance through a broken mountainous country. . . .

. . . I hope soon to become acquainted with my "predecessor in office.". . . I sent a message to ask Hattie [Young] to come to see me, which she said she would do. I have been longing to know her since I've been teaching the same girls who gave her so much trouble. If I have not succeeded in influencing the elder girls to higher aims & good behavior, I do not think my instruction has proved altogether fruitless among some of the younger ones, who besides seem really fond of me & show it by various attentions & bouquets, etc. altogether wanting among the elder ones. Though, since the May Party, Mattie Wm. Shannon has resumed her early liking for me & been attentive in two or three ways. Last night she sent me one of the largest and most magnificent bouquets that I have ever seen; it was fan shaped, covering a large waiter & composed of the most beautiful roses of all sizes, colors & tints, while the exquisite purity of a lily & the gorgeous scarlet "plumage" of a spring cactus were strikingly contrasted in the centre. . . . The delicate rose colored winter cactus tipped the harmonious blending of so much beauty.

(Darkness compelled me to lay this aside & shows a fine specimen of chirography, the combined efforts of twilight and a miserable pen—a daily thorn in my flesh, for the ink carrodes [*sic*] my finest pens in a few days & it is very difficult & very expensive to supply their place.) . . .

June 8   Each day brings sad tidings from Va. of the death, wounding, capture or missing of some acquaintance or friend, in those daily skirmishes, from which nothing seems gained on either side, while the most precious life blood is poured out like water. . . .

June 10   I have been a week from school, sick with diarrhea, an almost unheard occurrence to me. But, the daily thunder

storms and hot suns have produced general sickness & mine
carried off my remaining mite of strength. And then, we have
nothing on which to regain it, for I have eaten meat but five
or six times in as many weeks—though mother hopes to get
some tomorrow. I expect Dora [Furman] & Fan [Garden Fur-
man] this evening to pay me the long promised visit. . . .

Dora & Fan did come and spent three days with me, but it   *June 18*
rained hard all the time & I was besides sick & suffering so
much that the pleasure of their visit was much marred. Fan is
so extremely thin & sallow that she has lost almost all her
beauty. I am going to stay with them just as soon as school
breaks up. It was a great temptation to go with them, as they
wished, but I thought it my duty to try and return to school,
though I felt sure I should be utterly broken down, as it has
proved. I went back last Wednesday & tried to review the
Macauley class, as they were to be examined on Friday, &
leave. I found they had gained a few ideas at least some, while
others failed entirely. Though Hattie Shannon brought me
home Thursday, I was quite exhausted & had a dreadful
headache which has lasted ever since & prevented me from
attending the examination yesterday. It was the worst I have
had for months, if not years.

Dora declared I ought to note in my journal, as a token of
the extortion of the times, that it only cost them each $1.50 to
come from Stateburg, 20 miles on the cars, while to ride one
mile from the depot here, they were charged $5. apiece. And
as those notes are now taken at one third discount, they paid
$15. to ride up & the same to go back to the cars. As the train
leaves at quarter past three at night, & it was pouring rain, it
was impossible for them to walk.

. . . [J. B.] Kershaw has been made Maj. Gen. . . . When an
officer rises, he can only take his personal staff with him unless he particularly requests it, and, if Kershaw does not do so
for Rutledge, I'll never care more for him.

Lieut. Gen. [Leonidas] Polk was killed on the 14th, while
in the field and in consultation with Gen. Johnston and Hardee, who escaped unhurt from the cannon ball. He was a grand
old hero and an immense loss to church & country.

June 20   . . . Carrie says Sims has two front lower teeth out, & his delight is to hear them strike against anything. Dear little heart, how I long to see him, & little Carrie [Holmes] too, whose hair, Chick writes, is in long ringlets, as Henry's was last year. If it was not for her mother, who is so unwilling for her to leave her again, she would come on to us forthwith.

June 22   With what eagerness and anxiety do we listen daily for the ever welcome shriek of the "ironhorse" which brings us on winged feet, tidings from the great outer world throbbing around us, while, in our dull monotonous life, the mail is the only pulse that appears to beat; then the weary listening for the sound of the hoofs of "Lip's" horse, to know whether we shall send to Mr. [William E.] J[ohnson]'s for letters, & still greater eagerness with which we listen to every sound which seems to announce the return of Mary Ann or Hetty, little imps of darkness, who often tantalize us for a half hour or more. Oh, the blank & disappointment when an empty bag is returned, as occasionally, or only one letter and no paper; we feel as if the very life blood had ceased for an instant; while when we are gladdened with our old friend, the *Courier*, and a handful of letters, (sometimes all for one person) what variety of emotions are then excited by the budget of news they bring, often so opposite in import as happened last night— the death of the aged, as of old aunt Mathewes [Holmes], who was in her ninetieth year & has been bed-ridden many months from a severe fall—the little stranger anticipated in two or three months by Mary Hume H[olmes] a source of happiness to so many—while with poor Annie O'Hear it adds to her overwhelming grief for her husband, whom there can be little doubt was killed in that fatal battle [in Virginia] which has left desolation in so many other Charleston homes—the saddest of sights, a young girl of beauty, talents, refinement & wealth, whose mind is so clouded by melancholy as to be oblivious of the realities of the present, like poor Connie Lamb whose mind has been so deeply affected by the fate of her various brothers, all drunkards; Augustus, burnt to death from spontaneous combustion, George in the Asylum, while his wife is (though her mother was a Middleton and her father D. Heyward Hamilton) a woman of abandoned character, & her eldest brother James was long ago turned out of the house by his father, & whether dead or not, I do not know—that she has fallen into a state of melancholy derangement, the ruin of a character—as Willie Ramsey's, who has utterly disgraced himself, by his dishonesty & peculations in Government affairs. . . .

The first words I heard on returning from school today was *June 24* that our beloved Rutledge was wounded—thank God, not seriously, though painfully in the thigh, on the 19th near Petersburg. This is the first time, after passing through the fearful dangers of three years and a half constant fighting. . . . We have to be very grateful—'twas but last week I received a sweet letter from him. I trust he will be sent home to be nursed into health by loving hands and hearts.

During the last few days, Grant has changed his base from the north to the south of Richmond near Petersburg & daily fighting goes on with comparative small losses on our side, for the enemy has made a series of desperate assaults on the fortifications of Petersburg, always repulsed with tremendous loss. They are sending out numerous raiding parties also, which keep Hampton and his cavalry constantly fighting.

The same grand game of chess is going on in upper Georgia, while [Nathan Bedford] Forrest has given them a checkmate in another part of the board [Brice's Cross Roads, Miss., June 10, 1864], killing & capturing many more men than he carried into battle, besides 250 wagons, heavily laden & other valuables.

A few months ago, some one told me Mary Preston had married Dr. John Darby & gone off to Europe with him, he having gone to procure a false limb for Gen. Hood who is engaged to the younger sister Sallie [Preston]. Tis said the latter's letter of refusal reached him just after the loss of his leg at Missionary Ridge & a short time later she changed her mind; she is now over here with Mrs. James Chesnut [Jr.], dreadfully depressed and anxious as the General is so pressed for time he can only write once a week & then only with a pencil & paper carried in his pocket. . . .

Stateburg—The last few days of my stay at home were so *July 9* busily shared between school, sickness & preparations for my summer trip that my old friend has been neglected (as however has come to be a common thing). Wednesday [June] 29th I examined my little Grammar class, Minnie Shannon gaining 1st honor & Kate McCaa 2nd for general recitations as well as good examinations. All the rest did very well, though at first I feared the whole class was going to break down. . . . Then all the little ones of the 5th & 6th classes, ten, joined in a spelling match. . . . On the whole, my little ones gave me real satisfaction, for I felt not only that they had improved but that they respected & loved me, & had tried to do what I wished. I made them very happy by writing a few words of report and commendation for each one, according to her merit. The Ancient and Modern Geography I had rid myself of the day before.

The afternoon before, Mrs. [Goddard] Bailey had called for me in Mrs. [William L.] Kirkland's landau, and we took the longest and pleasantest drive I've ever had in Camden, past McRea's Mill pond over four miles from the town; the afternoon was slightly clouded, the breeze gentle & the very freedom of riding in an open carriage, without my hat, was invigorating & my spirits rose accordingly. I had just finished enjoying *Hiawatha*, & Henry Bailey was deep in [James Fenimore] Cooper's Indian tales, so that our talk flowed naturally into that channel when she told me Mr. B[ailey] and herself, accompanied by the children, had gone a few summers ago to the Falls of Minnehaha & across Lake Superior—the second lady who had ever travelled in that region, the first having been the wife of Mr. [Henry M.] Rice, a member of Congress from Minnesota, but formerly an Indian trader. They had two old trappers as guides & camped out at night, in true "wild-western" style, though she ended by confessing she was really glad to return once more to civilized life, being naturally very timorous.

We finished the pleasure of our ride by visiting Mrs. McCandless & I learned for the first time how sick and suffering *she* had been from overwork for some time, but most courageously *and womanfully* she concealed it (as her countenance did not show it) & went through all the wearying daily labor. The more I know of her, the more I admire and love her, & feel glad that I have taught if only to have gained such a true and sincere friend.

Poor Mrs. Bailey was obliged to take to her bed again, her ride having been too great an exertion, & I much fear she will always be somewhat on the invalid list, henceforth. On my return home Wednesday, I was so sick all afternoon & next morning that I was only able to get to school by borrowing Mrs. Tom Ancrum's carriage & was then only "patched up" for "immediate use" as I was determined not to fail on that last day. . . . Until Friday afternoon I felt wretchedly, when I made an effort to go to spend my last evening with Callie Perkins. . . . After tea, having been previously refreshed by a rare treat, a tumbler of *lemonade* cool as if iced, then invigorated by their delicious strong tea, I was quite myself again. Callie & I then slipped off to her large and luxurious chamber to enjoy the picture & art talk, & . . . she gave me additional pleasure by playing & singing to the harp. I had often read & heard of it as a grandly melodious instrument, peculiarly fitted for displaying grace & beauty, & had been very much disappointed when for the first time I heard Miss [Betsy] Sloman perform on it at Miss Bates' German Composers. But I found its fulfillment in Callie [Perkins]. As seated on a tall stool, her deep mourning dress fell in heavy folds, contrasting strongly with the white hand on which sparkled a fine diamond, among the chords, while her small close widow's cap gave a peculiar simplicity to her sweet and noble countenance. While she was tuning the instrument, my eye caught one of the well-remembered pictures of dear old Charleston, which almost every house possessed, and, as each familiar spot passed before my gaze, I was not aware she had glided into a tune, until I felt "Home Sweet Home" in the rich sweep of sound. She & her mother then delighted me by singing "Cheer, boys, cheer" one of the most beautiful inspiriting Southern songs which this war has produced. They sang to the piano also, but those two pieces have often haunted me since. I did not leave till eleven & shall ever look back to it as one of the pleasant evenings—the few—of my Camden life. . . .

Sick all day Sunday, till I felt almost like giving up the idea of leaving home, though almost certain [that] change of air was the only efficient remedy. Tuesday [July] 5th Sallie [Scriven] & myself, escorted by John, who went to take her home, left Camden, having for fellow passengers in the omnibus, two Jewish youths & their two negro female servants, one a respectable old "mauma" but the other a girl with whom they seemed on the most familiar & intimate terms, while she took out the worth of her $5 by carrying a live goose. I thought *miscegenation* had already commenced—disgustingly.

Another white female, who kept us waiting a great length of time & who forthwith struck up acquaintance in the freest manner, on reaching depot, & whom I immediately perceived to be one who was trying to pass herself off for a *fine* lady, I found to be the daughter of some woman who used to keep an eating house in the city and is an inveterate opium eater. ... We arrived at Claremont Depot about half past four, & all had to wait for their carriages. ... The "indispensable Mr. Rogers," who carries all my letters and packages there, said the F[urman]'s carriage always came late, as they lived so far off. So I made myself quite easy, enjoying the delicious coolness & freshness of the early morn. About six, Mingo arrived, I of course, concluded for me, but found instead he had brought a letter for me and had expected to go down to town, but the Rosinante which drew his cart had effectually prevented [it].[12]... I proposed to his dismay to ride in the cart, but after mounting in it on my trunk, the old skeleton horse would not budge an inch, till the whip was applied upon which he gave us the immediate benefit of his heels in rather close proximity to my face. So, as there seemed "no go" *there*, I sent to Col. Delage Sumter, two miles off, for his buggy, after opening my trunk & getting a volume of Mrs. [Elizabeth Barrett] Browning's poems to wile away the time. I waited till eight without feeling tired, though I had been so weak & had had but two hours rest, but Mr. Rogers was very polite and attentive, giving me many interesting & instructive agricultural facts in regard to his garden &, by the way, showed me mustard seed for the first time. Then I wrote a note to mother to tell her of my little adventure, which really had done me good. Mr. S.[umter]'s buggy proved a light, open one, drawn by a fat, lazy, remarkably well groomed mule, whose coat was as smooth as satin, & driven by a clean, polite, little tiger; the roads were generally shady & the breeze so pleasant that I was not at all distressed by the heat, though I did not arrive till near ten, Mingo & Risonante having but a

12 Rosinante was Don Quixote's horse, thus any broken-down horse.

few minutes before announced my anticipated arrival. I found I had never written to name the day as I thought, being right sick while writing. . . . We are very quiet & have spent our days in reading aloud Dicken's [*sic*] *Great Expectations* which is very wearisome, rather curious, but with some right witty ideas. . . .

Cousin Beck [Holmes] writes that Rutledge is doing very well indeed; the Dr. says the wound is the most remarkable he ever saw, the ball entering above the knee & ranging up, very near many great arteries, yet never touching one. He was brought on from Va. on a litter, &, when he arrived in Columbia, it was placed on a cart, &, being followed by a carriage & three servants, [he] says he wondered if he was dead & that his funeral. . . . His wound is painful & will keep him several weeks on his back, but his sisters are with him, of course giving unlimited petting, & he has a fine cool room overlooking the whole harbor. Em's [Ford] presence is all that is needed to make him quite happy, & I shall have the happiness of seeing him in a few weeks. . . .

August 2
Summerville

I had no idea I had neglected my old friend so entirely during my visit to Anatok, but the early morning hours were generally occupied in writing letters, or reading, while the day passed reading *Great Expectations* & *The Virginians* to the other girls; one morning Dora [Furman] & I took a delightful ramble of three miles through the woods, a little after five. Sue & Mary B[rownfield] returned on the 19th from their pleasant visit to Mrs. Frederick & spent the next day with us, giving us an account of the letter Mrs. F.[rederick] had just received from her mother Mrs. Lewis, who was a sister of Gen. [John B.] Floyd, telling her of [David] Hunter's late [Shenandoah Valley] raid. . . . Her house had been sacked, & *every thing* carried off—every particle of grain meat or food in every possible shape, inanimate or living, 15 horses, furniture, clothing, bedding, silver—in fact all she owned in the world, save her wedding ring, & an indifferent change of clothing. The house was not only completely stripped, but the walls ripped open & even the ashes barrels & *privies* searched for hidden articles. The family consists of Mr. Lewis, an aged man, his sister & her four little children, his wife & one little child. For two days, these children were vomiting from starvation & she then went to [David] Hunter's headquarters to try & procure some relief. After making her wait an hour, on his toilette, he told her he was glad of it, for that the *women & children were* the *very fiends* of *this war*, sending their husbands, fathers & brothers into the army. He meant to humble the pride of the haughty Virginians to the very dust & that [if] he did not do it that time, he would sweep the earth so clean that it would be incapable of affording nourishment, adding that she would find her house in flames in an hour. It, however, was not burned. A Yankee Colonel carried her a bag of meal, a piece of bacon, & three mattresses & told her with tears in his eyes, that he had never dreamed men could be guilty of such barbarities, that Hunter had *600 released convicts* brought for the very purpose of desolating the country & that he would not stay another day in the army. An Irishman said the same thing and sent her back three pieces of silver. Her negroes recoiled in horror from the atrocities of the Yankees & refused to leave her. The very implements of labor were carried off, and the land [is] indeed a desolation, where it once blossomed like the rose.

They had been spared personal outrage, but higher up, where the negro troops had been let loose, the accounts were awful.

The spirit of the Virginian mother & matron only rose the higher, & she declared she would be willing to lose 10,000 times as much for the cause.

The girls had also seen or heard a letter from Mr. H. A. Middleton's daughter Annie, now Mrs. Hunter of New York, where she has lived since her marriage. She writes that the doctrine of *miscegenation* is publicly preached from three pulpits and openly practised in Broadway where the most elegantly dressed ladies may be seen at all times promenading with a sable companion. Her husband is still kind to her, but she is deserted by all others. One of the latest dances in Yankeedom, she says, is for two females to be harnessed & driven around the room by a man, who whips them as they go. What a fearful picture of degradation and iniquity.

I went to stay with the Brownfields on the 22nd & spent five delightful days with them, going almost every morning to ramble at sunrise through the woods, & over & among the beautiful hills which rolled on every side like huge billows. I had laughed when they said Mrs. Purcell said she did not like to live among the hills, for they struck her with awe—and though I loved them, I still felt awed at their beauty and grandeur. I was never weary of gazing upon them from every point of view; & the Valley of Happiness surrounded by its amphitheatre of stupendous hills, & Evely Hill, crowned with a rich grove of trees interlaced by an almost tropical growth of grape & other graceful vines, will ever remain stereotyped in my memory. The Sunday I spent there was chiefly passed in looking over old letters both in French & English from Mrs. Sumter, some as Natalie Delage, written to Aaron & Theodosia Burr, her adopted father and sister—French letters to her mother from various of the nobility of France & her investiture as one of the Maids of Honor to Queen Isabella of Spain, when after having been taken by pirates on her escape from France to America, was three days after recaptured by the Spaniards & carried to their court, where she remained till the Bourbons were restored to France. Indeed those letters are of inestimable value, but the antique handwriting is so peculiar that it was very difficult for us to read. There was also a lithograph of a letter from Sir Walter Scott to some distinguished New Yorker, thanking him for a copy of Irving's *Knickerbocker*—which had just been published. . . .

The Brownfields call their place Clifton, but Annie Parker calls it Hurricane Hall, for generally there is a strong breeze felt as the house is approached, & in the wide entry of the principal cabin, there is almost always a gale in summer & hurricane in winter. At night, it did not need the slightest imagination to fancy I was on Sullivan's Island, so much did the roaring of the wind resemble that of the sea. It became really cold while I staid there but soon changed again to warm. While there, I received a 12 page letter from Lizzie Greene giving me a sketch of the week preceding & following their sudden flight from their home, where one hour later a battle was raging. Their valuables were already packed, & they saved most of their clothing, silver, some china, a few beds, etc. Their escape was providential, as the battle had commenced. Our line was through their yard and it broke to let the two wagons pass, which contained 20 persons & all they had saved. . . . I could not help almost envying the girls amidst all their danger & wishing I had been there to share it. . . .

Wednesday [July] 27th Dora [Furman], Fan [Garden Furman] & I made up our minds to leave next day, as Edward, who had been at home on sick furlough, was to go down that day. . . . It was a very damp, misty morning, but, after the sun rose, we drove to the "deserted village" of Stateburg, which missed being the capital of the state by one vote. Dr. [William W.] Anderson's fine residence on a hill with a large & pretty lawn & the Norman Gothic Episcopal church near were at the extreme end. Our 16 mile *ride* & the dampness had taken all the starch out of us & we were quite ready for bed. We started earlier Friday & arrived long before the cars; found Mrs. & Bishop [Thomas F.] Davis on board & Miss Ann Stock. . . She said she was not accustomed to travelling without a gentleman & seemed quite helpless, so I took care of her & told her where to get out, etc. I also caught a glimpse of Gen. Hood's very handsome fiancée, Sallie Preston, on the cars with Gen. [James] Chesnut. . . .

I astonished Carrie & Nanna [Hughes] by my unexpected arrival, & I was equally so when I learned Rutledge was to leave on Monday for Pendleton, to be married, though he is just on his crutches. So I went down Saturday to see him & found him bright and well, though thin from his long confinement. He said he had never suffered from his wound since the first day. No day is appointed for his wedding, but he is obliged to be back by the 20th to go before the Medical Board & expects to bring a wife with him. . . . Carrie & Isaac are both very thin, & Sims is also decidedly the worse for the arrival of four teeth and the anticipation of more. He is of course constantly ailing &, when I first saw him, I was shocked at the change in the expression of his face & particularly his beautiful eyes, once such fountains of laughter & now often softened by a plaintive look, as if he already fore-shadowed the sorrows of life. But several days have passed (6th) and he has not only become quite accustomed to but fond of me & is much livelier & very attractive and interesting; [he] delighted to walk with some one's assistance, or holding on to the chairs, & [is] trying to talk, saying Tat for the dog Snap, quite distinctly. For 5 days, Marcus, Patty & Julianne have been sick, so I have taken some practical lessons in housekeeping & minding babies. How thankful I am that I am neither cook nor nurse.

Sunday just after dinner, we girls were sitting in the drawing room, rather in déshabille, when Isaac announced the arrival of Capt. Hayden, his superior officer, to spend the night.[13] The surprise startled me "out of three years growth," but I recovered later and was completely fascinated when I entered into conversation with him. Isaac had sketched him but had not filled out the intellectual portrait as I conceived. His "personelle" is unattractive, for the same two score years which has matured the god-like intellect have left their seal on form & feature. His eyes are a very soft brown but most peculiarly turning inwards, and he is besides extremely nearsighted. But all outward form is forgotten when the rich streams of thought gush forth in the choicest language, fertilizing all who are happy enough to drink of them. He is decidedly the most highly intellectual & richly cultivated mind it has ever been my lot to meet familiarly, a very deep thinker on the grandest subjects, & an equally extensive scholar and traveller. I wish I could remember a tithe of what he said, in his own beautiful language, but it is impressed on my brain as a whole—an evening long to be remembered as an intellectual oasis, & I trust will bear worthy fruit.

In the course of conversation we chanced upon Hugh Miller, & the wonder of Geology—the marvellous revolution of ideas produced by it, the antiquity of the Indian races who left such great works strewn over the continent, principally in Central America & along the Mississippi & Ohio rivers, [Auston H.] Layard's Expedition to Babylon & Nineveh, etc., all subjects upon which I had read & was deeply interested but had never had one to sympathize or talk to me upon them. He did, most delightfully, his language being so choice that it could have been printed just as he uttered them. After conversing some time & giving me much valuable information & many hints in regard to the study of Geology & the best books

13 No definite information on this Confederate officer was discovered. There were a number of officers named Hayden, and the one mentioned so often in this diary may have been John A. Hayden, an engineer. His name appears in Confederate records spelled Hayden and Haydon (a confusion Emma Holmes repeats in the diary).

on the subject, he said with our permission he would enlarge a little on them. . . . He did, connecting them in a most charming little essay on the dispersion & degeneracy of man after the fall as exhibited by the natural history of the world. He showed he was a deep student of the Bible, &, I feel sure, is a Christian. All was traced up to the Supreme Being. Oh, how I enjoyed it all & grieved that, like all other pleasures, that evening must have an end. Isaac says he is a perfect gentleman & likes and admires him very much. He told me his home was on the Potomac, where all his property & his sisters' (who are with him) was destroyed & their negroes carried off. . . . He has [*sic*] been a prisoner in Fort Delaware for seven months. One of his sisters, he said, was familiar with Greek & Latin & several modern languages.

He is operating the Edisto Canal & frequently stops here on his way to & from the city—so I hope to see him again.

August 15 . . . During the past month what a long roll of death have I to
Monday record among friends & acquaintances—some on the battle field, others from wounds, & others again falling from the sickle of the Great Reaper, borne down by disease. . . .

A few days ago, the Yankees sprung a mine under one point of our lines at Petersburg [July 30, 1864] &, during the temporary confusion resulting, threw forward a mass of negro troops inspirited by whiskey to the massacre of our poor lacerated men with the shout "no quarter, Fort Pillow." For a short time that part of our lines was in their hands, but our troops rallied immediately & others coming to their support they were completely recovered, & the negroes, brought for the first time against our veteran army, were terribly punished.[14]

[C. G.] Memminger resigned the Secretaryship of the Treasury a few weeks ago, & Mr. George Trenholm installed to the general satisfaction of the country at large, for his very name was a promise of sound faith, & the Richmond papers say he seems as much at home in his difficult position as if he had been there all his life. The Yankee Secretary [Salmon P.]

14 A 500-foot-long shaft was dug from Union lines to a point twenty feet under a Confederate battery. Here 8,000 pounds of black powder were exploded, resulting in a crater 170 feet long, 60–80 feet wide, and 30 feet deep. The consequent Union assault failed.

Chase resigned about the same time [June 30, 1864] & [William P.] Fessenden of Maine is now the Atlas bending under the terrific load.

On June 19th, Capt. [Raphael] Semmes, having gone with the *Alabama* into Cherbourg, France on the English Channel for repairs, found the Federal *Kearsarge* was waiting outside for him; he challenged [John A.] Winslow &, after leaving all his valuables in the hands of our agent, steamed forth boldly, & the combat commenced as soon as the *Alabama* had reached the legal limit, nine miles from shore. The latter was crowded with spectators, & several vessels were also out to witness the fight between our renowned vessel & its Yankee rival. In one hour & ten minutes, the *Alabama* sunk, the enemy's shot & shell having torn huge holes in its wooden sides through which the water rushed putting out the engine fires. Semmes lowered the flag in token of surrender, but the Yankees fired five shots after. Only two small boats remained uninjured, and the crew made their escape in them & by swimming. (For some time the *Kearsarge* sent no boats to rescue them but allowed the neutral spectators to do so, & Capt. Semmes & about 40 of his officers & crew were saved by the *Deerhound*, a yacht belonging to the firm of Trenholm & Co., & the others saved were taken to the French coast, after which Winslow had the audacity to claim them as prisoners of war; but of course that claim was not allowed.) Thus closed the career of the renowned *Alabama*, but she died game without leaving a trophy to grace the triumph of the enemy, for the captured officers threw their swords into the sea. About twenty-one men were killed & wounded a few, including the surgeon [David Herbert] Llewellyn, going down with the ship. Capt. Semmes was carried to England where he was the hero of the hour, his crew having been almost entirely of Englishmen, & a subscription was immediately set on foot among the Liverpool merchants to replace the sword he flung into the sea, & a vessel put in preparation for him. In a few weeks he expects to be afloat in a finer vessel, the *Rappahannock*, striking greater terror than ever in his dastard foe.

The *Kearsarge* was found by our men to have been ironclad, with chains closely around the bulwarks, but concealed by an outer wooden work, which was partially torn by our shots; her equipment & crew were both greater than ours, &

Winslow pretends our shot did not the least material harm; if so, it may be accounted for by the fact that the *Alabama* had but just returned from a long voyage, which it found had injured the powder & much had to be flung overboard.

In July, Gen. [Jubal] Early made a grand raid into Maryland, threatening Washington & Baltimore very closely, causing intense excitement among the Yankees.[15]. . . The public has not been enlightened as to Lee's full plans in regard to that movement, so whether it carried them out or failed in the principal aim, we know not. But, at any rate, [we] have very substantial proof of their success as a foraging party, for they brought off immense & most valuable plunder in the shape of large droves of cattle, horses & mules, & stores of various kinds, besides making several towns pay heavy ransoms & giving others a touch of their own style of warfare—retaliating by the destruction of private as well as public buildings.

Russia has shown the same "paternal feelings" to the Circassians, as to the Poles, & the remnant of that people, (2 or 300,000 men, women and children) have lately migrated into Turkey, preferring death and the plague or small pox, which awaited them there, to remaining any longer under the Czar.[16] The Sultan has contributed largely from his own private purse to the relief of the sufferers, & every effort has been made for the assistance of the poor exiles.

Thus our sorrows are reproduced at the ends of the earth.

I've learned more since my arrival here of the circumstances of that first battle which left the C.[harleston] L.[ight] Dragoons such an utter wreck. Gen. [Matthew] Calbraith Butler was intoxicated and, when so, perfectly reckless. He called out to the men "You are low-countrymen, are you not, then I'll show you how to fight" or some similar speech—dismounted them & made them double quick two or three miles to the scene of battle when they charged right off.[17] Dr. Jenkins, the Hospital surgeon here, told Maggie P.[urcell] that

15 Early conducted the so-called Washington Raid, actually a series of raids (June 27–August 7, 1864) in the Virginia-Maryland-Pennsylvania region. At one point he came to within five miles of the District of Columbia.
16 The Circassians were people living on the shores of the Black Sea. In 1864 their long resistance to Russian control was crushed.
17 This refers to one of the numerous 1864 battles between Grant and Lee.

his brother, the General, never would double quick his men right into battle, whether it was ordered or not, for it was against his conscience. He knew it injured the men & excited & heated their blood, so that the least wound proved fatal. Tom Lining was the standard bearer & always had a presentiment he would be killed in his first battle; he was told he need not carry the standard in such a battle. He threw it aside & said he would go anyway. He was shot in the leg as they made the first charge & bled to death in less than 10 minutes. These new troops charged boldly forward with head aloft eager for distinction & scorning to seek safety, like the veterans, behind bush & tree. They had been taunted as the kid-gloves, silk stockings & plum cake company, etc. and nobly did they show the true stuff they were made of. . . . The history of this war will be written in letters of blood over every inch of our land, for Capt. Hayden says he sees no prospect of peace & indeed feels sure the Yankees will take Atlanta next week, then come down to Macon [Georgia] & raid through the state. God grant he proves a false prophet.

The Captain came up from town last night, after we had been expecting him two days; I had been reading *Macaria* Miss [Augusta J.] Evans' new novel aloud to the girls & had been wishing for him all day to explain many of the ideas & opinions she either gives herself or quotes & the numerous learned words she uses. I like the book very much but think she has certainly tried to display all her learning in a small space & has only shown herself thoroughly pedantic. He says he met her in Mobile & thinks she is a woman of rather limited learning, taking a few books & studying those deeply, but at any rate she seems to have touched or rather, as Bacon says, only tasted slightly of many others. In *Beaulah*, particularly, she attempted to show her familiarity with German mysticism &, to those who really understood it, she only made an absurd failure; there her aim is, as in *Macaria* (which by the way, means Happiness) is to show how the minds of such peculiarly gifted persons, as her heroines, were led from the sublime faith of their childhood to the utter indifference of the Transcendentalists, by the study of such works, & then purified through suffering. I should not be at all surprised if it was only her own experience written out, nor if, as Capt. H[ayden] thinks, she did not understand what she meant, when she mounted into those closed regions. For Immanuel Kant is her great authority & text, & great minds, he says, after studying him carefully, have written "Nothing, nothing" against page after page. What a mournful record—a long life spent in elaborating—Nothing—

Capt. Hayden also knows Mad. Le Vert & the authoress of *The Initials and Quits* very well. Of the former, he has quite changed my opinion, for he says she really was very much noticed in Europe, even by Queen Victoria. He met her there & knew the facts and that, though she "may have shared largely of the hospitality" of the persons with whom she travelled, parvenus with no recommendation but their wealth & therefore delighted at the eclat of her society, still he feels sure she was not entirely dependent on them. She is very fascinating in manners & conversation, &, though apparently rather egotistical when you first meet her at Mobile where she is the acknowledged Queen of Society, her native good heart soon overshadows that.

The Baroness Tautphoeus was Mary Evans, daughter of a very wealthy Welsh gentleman, who was for a long time mercantile agent of the U.S. & resided for some years in Baltimore. His daughter lived for 13 years in Germany, where she was educated & married & only 24 when she wrote the *Initials.* He says she has no beauty, a thin sharp face being surmounted by thin sandy hair. She has great powers of observation but does not display her talents in conversation. He corresponded with her & urged her to go to Italy & write a similar tale from there descriptive of the inner life of the people, but she fears she would fail in other save German tales.

I had long been wanting to know something definite about Emerson, so often quoted in *Macaria*; he told me his principle doctrine was "that every man contains God in himself and is therefore greater than God, the container being greater than the contained and that every man, of whatsoever capacity, station or condition, was a law unto himself." I said "he showed his ignorance of human nature," & he answered that Emerson knew nothing of that vast & intricate volume & but little of books.

On every subject he touched, I gained new ideas and could have talked on for hours, but Isaac broke us up early by having prayers. I gleaned many particulars of his own history, incidentally, & this morning, speaking of the pleasures of riding on horseback, he said he had never been able to ride or walk until he was twenty-three, from spinal affection, & I noticed also he was slightly deaf on one side. He must indeed have been matured through suffering, but his grand intellect has borne rich fruit. He is an earnest, devout Christian; its spirit breathes through all his knowledge, leading up to God as the Great Source of all, yet without a direct word on the subject of religion. Last night he rebuked me so gently, yet earnestly, for a trifling speech I made. I told him that Saturday evening I drove Carrie out in the buggy, drawn by his old grey, & that Isaac would not trust Sims with us. Isaac said, no, I scarcely wanted to trust you with my wife. I answered gaily that she could jump out, but it made no matter if I broke my neck, for I would not be missed. The Capt. asked, if that was my philosophy, that it was very wrong, for God had placed us here & each would be missed from the appointed sphere. I cannot remember all his words, but their spirit sank into my heart & I felt ashamed of my speech & wished I too was an humble Christian, and that he could be my *"brother Harvey"* to counsel & guide me.[18] He inspires me with the deepest interest, & I feel elevated & purified by his society; his moral influence must be felt wherever he goes. Such characters I've read of, but never met before, & to study him & learn from him is worth to me a hundred books & sermons— for he is a living sermon in himself.

He left this morning, after a most amusing scene in catching & harnessing the old grey—Marcus being still sick & the horse playful. It took the four female servants & the Capt. to head & catch him & Patty & himself to harness up. She used to know how & he knew very little. I told him I was glad there was something he did not know anything more about than we about cooking. He promises to return towards the end of the week, & I shall anticipate it with intense pleasure, for I have a score of things to ask & just to hear him talk is a rare intellectual feast.

And no return of the Captain [Hayden], but instead we have had a week of company & sickness, Marcus, Patty & Julyan

August 17
Wednesday

18 Gabriel Harvey (ca. 1545–1630) was an English critic, who headed a group which met together to condemn all but classical poetry.

[*sic*] being all down at first, & when the latter made their appearance to our great relief, Sarah took her turn, while both babies have been constantly ailing.... During the last two days, Edward [was] dangerously ill with congestion of the lungs, though today he seems decidedly better, & we hope will now recover....

On my journey to Summerville, Miss [Ann] Stock told me that Mrs. Bulow had adopted a baby & named it after Col. Alfred Rhett and then related the earlier passages of her history, which I had never heard. Caroline Ball was engaged to William Middleton, but her mother compelled her to break it off & accept the wealthier Bulow. On the day before the wedding, Mr. M[iddleton] went to see her & claimed her as his promised wife, &, after a short interview, she referred him to her mother. Mr. M.[iddleton] was furious & wretched & vowed he would interfere to prevent the marriage.... Much trouble was anticipated, but his friends persuaded him to keep quiet. Next day, the guests waited so long at the church they feared there was to be no wedding after all. But at last, the bridal party came & she drew her elegant veil closely around her, but the breeze as she entered wafted it closer against her face, disclosing its intense pallor & rigidity, like a corpse several hours old. She pronounced the solemn vows in an unnaturally distinct tone, & her life of sorrow commenced. A worldly mother sacrificed a very handsome daughter upon the alters [*sic*] of Mammon, to a drunken husband who quarreled with the interfering mother-in-law & beat his wife, salving the mortal hurts of mind, body & nature, thus made, with gifts of costly jewelry. I know nothing of Mrs. Bulow's personal characteristics, though my mother & hers were very intimate as young married ladies in the same parish. But after Mrs. Ball became a widow, her conduct altered very much, then changed for the worse, when she married Gamage, another drunkard. I only know Mrs. Bulow as a speaking acquaintance & from report, but anyone can read in those keen black eyes & raven hair & delicately chiselled features, almost Spanish in their style, strong passions & fierce emotions, which, without the control of religion, morality or connubial happiness, have wrecked her life & fame. For years before her husband's death, she had lived away from him, &, when he died, was, I believe, at a Moultrie House hop, the gayest of the gay. . . . And now Mrs. Bulow has openly proclaimed it by the production of this baby, which is nearly a year old, & which she attempts to impose on the public with the most palpable fiction of adoption. . . . An elegant wardrobe was provided, and the mother & grandmother never leave home at the same time now; the latter getting up a night to make all kinds of things for it & these would not be merely for the child of some North Carolina farmer. . . . I cannot help acknowledging the truth of Thackery's [William Thackeray] sketches of society in *The Virginians.* Once I did not believe them or thought at least it was only true of fashionable England but am compelled to allow its painful truth, of ours, also. . . . I sincerely trust such specimens are very rare among the women of the South, whom Mr. [Charles R.] Maturin pronounced "The purest type of womanhood in the world"— and he was an educated Irishman.[19]

Charleston—Ten days ago I came down here on a visit of two days, leaving Summerville at seven on Tuesday morning, & returning Wednesday evening, spending the night here and visiting among my relatives. . . . Wednesday evening Alester came up with Isaac, & I did not know him at first meeting at twilight; he has been sick with country fever off & on six weeks, & is very tall & thin—has a furlough of 30 days, after a year's absence from home. He made me very, very sad by the account of Capt. [Willie] Earle's cruelty to his men, & Gen. [N. G.] E.[vans] & his brothers, drinking.   *September 3*

Can it be that I shall never meet one man whom I can admire intensely & feel deeply interested in, but that some rude blow must crush it all in an instant. "To make idols and to find them clay" has been my lot ever. I almost fear to admire or even like one now very much, for fear of what time may disclose. Dr. [James] M[orrow] I looked upon merely as a very pleasant acquaintance & liked his particular attentions, though I knew he was only flirting. He has proved a sot & libertine, and I do not recognize him any longer when we meet. Benjie [Guerard] fell from what I hoped—but oh, this last stroke has a barbed point; I felt for Capt. Earle a cousinly affection &

19 Charles R. Maturin (1782–1824) was an English playwright and novelist. His *Milesan Chief* (1812) is said to have been imitated by Sir Walter Scott in his *The Bride of Lammermoor.*

felt so interested in his future. Last winter Dora [Furman] gave me the first intimation of this terrible fault, but I hoped, yet dreaded, to receive confirmation. It pains me to hear his name, associated by me with all that is noble, intellectual & attractive, made a byword for brutality. Oh, it is a bitter thought to me that I must tear friend after friend from the niche they occupied as unworthy. I trust Capt. Hayden may retain his high pedestal or I shall lose all the faith in man which a few specimens had inspired me with. Carrie told me he is a Catholic, &, though I felt disappointed, I cannot help admiring him. He never returned as we expected, for he broke the buggy, &, I suppose, we will scarcely meet again.

I came down yesterday and went directly to shop; while in Mrs. Maule's, above George St., a fragment of a time fuse shell whizzed overhead with a loud report & fell into the next yard. The Yankees have only been firing this kind during the last fortnight, & the casualties are becoming serious. The shells will burst in the lower part of town, but the fragments fly over a mile up town, killing or injuring passersby & animals; they do not penetrate houses, but cause loss of life, & it is really dangerous walking out below John St. for the fragments fall in Vanderhorst St. & that portion of the city where I am going to stay & so many of our friends live. Last night one of them set a house on fire &, as soon as our demon foes saw the blaze & knew our firemen were at work, the shells were fired thick & fast, sometimes two or three at one time. I shuddered to hear the dull distant *boom* of the discharge, then watch their flight through the air like meteors; when near, the scream, followed by the sudden deafening report, was terrible. It was kept up all night, & they made my dreams hideous. . . .

October 8   I find not a word has been written here since the day after my arrival in the city, where I staid three weeks, mostly at cousin Willie's. . . . Cousin Willie being unwell, asked me to write off Rutledge's marriage notice for the papers. . . . [He] was so much pleased with my clear round writing that he said, if I would don male attire & go to his office, he would give me $1,000 a year as book-keeper, & adding that he wanted some books written up and, if I would undertake it, a week's work, he would willingly give me $50. I would gladly have done it as a favor, but he would not allow it. So, I went to work with fear & trembling, knowing how particular he was, &, as a good deal was left to my discretion, I was constantly in tribulation, sometimes, quite certain I had made most terrible blunders & affording much amusement to Mary [Hume Holmes], thereby. However, though I did make a good many mistakes at first, as he said he expected, I got through within the time, writing three or four hours a day, &, what was quite pleasant, found he was quite satisfied. The money I forthwith appropriated to purchasing three of Hugh Miller's works, *Popular Geology*, *The Old Red Sandstone* & *Footprints of Creation*, giving $21 for what in former times would not have cost more than $4. I also subscribed to the [Charleston] *Mercury* for a quarter now $10 & intend treating myself also to Gen. [D. F.] Jamieson's late work *Life & Times of Bertrand du Guesclin*, which Mr. Theodore Wagner had printed in England. It is a real pleasure to enjoy once more such beautiful cream tinted ivory paper & excellent type. It is a fine edition & made more interesting by the late and sudden death, of the respected author, of yellow fever in Charleston.

The very day I went down, poor Sallie Bull was taken with typhoid fever & was ill from the first, for she struck the disease in by bathing her neck and arms in cold water for several days previous, when she felt feverish, in order that her father should not perceive it, as she said he always became anxious when anyone was sick. . . . Thursday I went to see her & dined there. Sallie had been quiet all morning & not delirious the night before, so I went home thinking it was a favorable sign, not knowing a change had taken place before I left. . . . I never received a greater shock than when we heard suddenly next morning after breakfast of her death. As it came through servants, we would not believe it till we sent to the Dr.'s to have it confirmed—alas it was indeed too true. . . . After Sallie's death, the Dr. sent Rosa and Becca [Bull] to Columbia on account of yellow fever, which is now raging in the city, & not the common kind more like African coast fever, & even the oldest inhabitants & negroes are falling victims to it. . . . Truly war & pestilence stalk broadcast through our beloved land. Every paper contains the intelligence of the death of some one we know or feel interested in. . . . The roll of death is fearful—the cruel monster is insatiable. . . .

While I was in the city the guerilla [*sic*] hero, Gen. John
Morgan, while on one of his raids, was betrayed by a Mrs.
[Catherine] Williams, a Unionist at whose house he staid, & he
& his staff surrounded. He died [September 4, 1864] as he
lived, a hero, with his arms in his hands. . . . His death did not
excite the public as I had expected, for all minds were so excited about the fall of Atlanta, which after all our hopes, occurred the beginning of September. Of course the outcry was
great against the President & Hood, in regard to the removal
of Johnston, to whom the army was really devoted. . . . Beauregard had lately been placed over the armies of Dick Taylor
& Hood, & [William]Hardee supersedes [Samuel] Jones in
Charleston, so public confidence is restored. Victory ever
seems to follow the standard of Beauregard & the news from
Georgia is already encouraging. Hood's army is entirely in
Sherman's rear, thus cutting off all supplies. Wheeler has
been capturing Rome [Georgia], other towns with garrisons,
tearing up railroads & doing great damage to the enemy's
supply depots. And though Sherman is only 175 miles from
Augusta, his cavalry and transportation are in such dreadful
condition, that he cannot advance. . . .

A few days after I went to Charleston, I called on Capt.
Hayden's sisters living in Mrs. Bishop Gadsden's house; as
soon as they found I was Mr. [Isaac] White's sister, my welcome was very warm. They are *very sociable* & pleasant &,
before I left, we felt almost as if old friends, for they appreciated very highly all Carrie's & Isaac's attention to their brother to whom they are devoted & had heard him speak of us. A
tremendous thunder storm came up, making the heavens
black as midnight, and they wanted me to spend the night,
but I declined & shall not readily forget the run home I had,
through strange streets, only finding my way by the vivid
flashes of lightning & getting in just in time, breathless & hot
to escape the deluge. Alice Haydon, the eldest, appears to be
a little older than I, & Mary a little younger—neither like
their brother having the slightest pretentions to beauty, but
having very pleasant faces. They were very lonely, having
but few acquaintances or friends, though Mrs. [Louis T.] Wigfall was extremely kind, & I went often to see them, dropping
in whenever I went that side to see my relatives & once spending the day there or in fact twice dining with them. They al-

ways met me so warmly it was a pleasure to go. . . . I could realize fully the loneliness of refugees, particularly when their brother was often absent for a fortnight at a time & fragments of time fuses falling all around them till they could not sleep two hours during the night for a week together.

I only saw Capt. H[aydon] for a few minutes one Sunday evening, when I stopped there. He said he wanted to come to see me but would be unable as he had just come down from the country & was about to leave immediately for Columbia on business. I wonder if I will ever meet them again. The girls are so pleased with Charleston from the kindness they have met there that they want to make it their home, if, after the war, anything is left of it. But as the Capt. prophecies the fall of the city by February, there is little prospect of it— and his prophecies unfortunately never have failed. As it is, the shells are going higher day by day & but little space is left for them to reach. I promised to correspond with the girls & wrote soon after my return, inviting them to come & board with us, as Isaac was as anxious as myself about their being exposed to the shells and fever. I have received no answer & think they must have gone to Macphersonville. . . .

Cousin Willie's son & heir, as well as namesake, made his debut Sept. 18th, a moderate sized individual with a very decided mark of character in the shape of a huge nose; always a sign of great men, the papa used to say. The mamma passed the dread ordeal very well & was as bright & gay as ever right after. It rained so hard I could not get there till the mannakin [*sic*] had counted four days, not by "the opening of the flowers" as Timrod says, but by the bursting of the shells. The little fellow has come in stormy times but numerous young companions arrived just before or after to accompany him, and, of course, to suit the times, all are sons. . . .

I hurried home to open school at home, Retta & Sallie Boykin & Frances & Kate Oppenheim having been promised me; Myers has floored the south basement chamber & here I am quietly settled in it, now writing—school room & probably chamber also soon if the Gadsdens & aunt Amelia [Holmes] come up. We feel so anxious about them, we invited them up. If letters had gone right, I would probably have had a very good school. I wrote to tell Mrs. McCandless if she had made no other arrangements I had changed my mind and would resume my duties with her. She answered by return of mail (but the letter never reached me) that she was only to take a small & limited number, & Mr. McC.[andless] would assist her. But, if I would return or advertise, she was sure I would get a good number of the very girls she would not take, & she knew would suit me. Not getting this, I could decide nothing & wrote her a note after waiting nearly three weeks; several notes then passed between her, mother, & myself & I finally left the arrangements to them as I was determined not to lose Rutledge's visit to town. Nothing could repay me for not seeing him; several schools had already sprung up, Miss Hattie Young's being the most patronized, prices being smallest—English 80—French & Latin 60 each. . . . Mrs. Dawson raised her terms to $100, consequently has but 9 or 10—though people know how poor she is & how good her school. Almost all the children were already promised to Hattie Young, so my prospects of increase are small. I had boys offered, but did not want them. . . .

Sallie Boykin is an interesting child of seven, just spelling in three letters & is lower in the scale than I had intended to descend; however, I have already seen visible improvement; Kate is farther advanced, not very studious & quite talkative; they generally occupy me till 12 or half past. I sometimes feel quite impatient at spending so much time for such small remuneration as the ladies arranged my terms from 60 to 80 dollars, the session of nine months—enough to buy me a calico, a muslin & a pair of shoes—nine months labor. Well it is better than nothing.

November 12, 1864

April 7, 1865

A School Teacher and Sherman's Army

S ometimes it seems almost ridiculous to call this a journal & to continue writing in it & I often think of giving it up. I have so little time to write, but again I feel as if I were communicating with one of my old friends, even though at rare intervals. I see it is more than a month since my last date. My school has increased to 5 by the addition of Dr. [Robert] Johnson's little Mary, who though like Nannie in face, does not resemble her in character—is, a quiet, good, studious child, who gives but little trouble, but comes irregularly. Frances Oppenheim has much improved but Kate is a most unsatisfactory scholar—quick, but idle and dreaming. While looking in the book, [she] will miscall letters & spell backwards or wrong over and over till my patience is nearly exhausted. . . . I have kept her repeatedly for one or two hours, but to little purpose—she never seems to mind it. Several times they have not come till quarter to ten & during the past week it was particularly unsatisfactory as they were the only girls at school. Retta and Sallie [Boykin] came back yesterday. I missed my bright interesting little pets very much. They always say "I'll try."

Perhaps I may not teach them many months longer, for Dan [Boykin] came home on a visit two or three days ago & told grandmother that Col. Franklin Pegues, who lives 4 miles from Cheraw, is in want of a teacher & offers a *$100. a month*

& board. He is a wealthy man, with 12 daughters, only one married, & one son three years old. Dan spent the day there & saw them all; was quite pleased with the refinement & luxury shown on every side; the girls are intelligent & agreeable, & he thinks it will be a pleasant position. Col. Pegues asked him to inquire for a teacher for him, & he thought it would suit aunt Sue. But she has engaged for another year at Longtown, so grandmother wrote a note to me, which I received in school, quite unsettling my ideas. I did not think I could accept it in honor, as I felt bound to my school, & had just received the trifling half year's payment. But I went down there in the afternoon, & mother, grandmother & cousin Sallie [Boykin] all advised me to apply for it in justice to myself. For, I could break up at Christmas & return a portion of the money. I thought over the matter & at last concluded to do so, but it was a hard matter for me to break suddenly the ties which bound me here—my darling baby [Sims White] and the delightful friendship with Callie Perkins, which has been drawn much closer since my return home. Seldom does a day or two pass without an exchange of notes, messages or books & papers, or we walk or ride together. I spent a charming literary evening with her a short time ago, & we laid many pleasant plans for reading & walking together. I have never had a friend whose tastes agreed so perfectly with mine, for even Dora & I differ in many things, and, after such a long separation from all such real friendly attentions—such home sociabilities—I have felt them particularly. If I had gone immediately after my return, I would not have minded it so much, now the duty is much harder. But I shall try to think either way—all for the best—both have numerous advantages & disadvantages. Dan [Boykin] leaves today & expects to see Col. Pegues Tuesday &, if not, will write, so I hope to know something definite in ten days at furthest.

Sallie [Furman], Dora's sister, is teaching at home & charges $200 even for beginners and has a very good school, while the Camden people grumbled so loudly over Mrs. McC[andless]'s 300 for advanced scholars. Poor woman, her lot is a hard one. Her husband's naturally violent temper is aggravated by drinking & gambling &, as he dares not show it to the elder girls, he spends it on his own children, rendering their & their mother's lives perfectly miserable & terrifying the younger school girls. In consequence of it & the notes from the parents in consequence, he gave way to temper a few days ago & left the school, refusing to teach again, leaving dismay & confusion behind. But that night, [he] thought better of it & sent a note to the elder girls saying he would meet them as usual next day. He is a most excellent teacher & Sallie DeSaussure's class are much pleased with him, but he treats his own children brutally and, Linnie says, has not spoken to his wife for days; when he wants anything at table, [he] sends his plate by a servant. Her skeleton is as ghastly as ours.

Isaac has paid us two flying visits during the past month, while preparing to be transferred to Columbia as Commissary for the war to Yankee prisoners, at Capt. Haydon's recommendation. He considers him the best Quartermaster & Commissary in the Confederate States—a well earned and deserved compliment. Isaac will be still under the Capt.'s orders. I am so glad for it is pleasant for two such noble men to have fit co-workers. Neither Ike nor Carrie are, however, pleased with the change, as it effectually breaks up all their plans; Carrie will remain with us until perhaps later. . . .

We have also just learned of the death of Bishop [William J.] Boone in China in June when on his way to England for his wife's health. She died & was buried in Egypt. He went on, &, we believe, left his youngest son in London, while Henry is practicing in China. . . . His two others are in New York, one in a counting house, the other studying theology & both imbibbing [*sic*] abolition sentiments, with which uncle John says the Bishop & his wife were also deeply tainted from their long residence abroad—think of it—a Boone and Elliott. . . .

Hood has been outflanking & outwitting Sherman by leaving him at Atlanta & making direct tracks for Tennessee, completely puzzling the Yankees as to his whereabouts but showing his presence by capturing various garrisons in the upper part of Georgia: Dalton, Resaca, etc., & tearing up railroads etc. thus cutting off Sherman's supplies.[1] Beauregard is with Hood & it is forbidden the soldiers to write of the army movements, so we know very little ourselves, except that the men are in excellent spirits, the ranks full & Ho for Tennessee the cry of all.

---

1 Hood took Dalton on October 13, but Sherman held on to Resaca.

. . . [Nathan Bedford] Forrest and his gallant Horse Marines are at the old work of capturing & burning gunboats, transports and other watercraft & thereby supplying Hood's army with clothing, shoes, & blankets at Lincoln's expense.[2]

By the way, the Presidential election took place several days ago, & there seems no doubt from the returns already received that the vulgar, uncouth animal is again chosen to desecrate the office once filled by Washington—the immortal. A prominent Northern politician says it is equivalent to 20 years war. . . . God grant we may be spared that. War there must be, until we "conquer peace," but I trust that great blessing may crown our "altars of sacrifice" long ere such a life time of agony is wrung out.

The myrtle still waves its odorous boughs even amid the cypress wreaths which are strewn on every pathway. Affa Chisolm & Eliza North are engaged—a great pity as they are first cousins, & there has been enough of that in the family. . . . Lizzie Miller writes to me urgently to follow her example &, so I will, when the "right man in the right place" comes across my pathway.

Our dear baby [Sims White] has been sick for three or four days, is cutting six teeth at once, and his short sickness has already weakened him so much he does not care to stand up. . . . He has been hitherto on his feet morning, noon & night, as merry as a cricket & playful as a kitten, & as mischievous. Yesterday evening, I took charge of him while all the rest went to walk, &, with the dear child nestled asleep in my arms with his around my neck, it was very hard to think of going away & leaving him.

Sometime in November, Jimpsey Thurston & Charlie & Ravenel Macbeth were exchanged; the latter had been a prisoner since the capture of Morris Island, July 1863. . . . At Johnson's Island [Sandusky Bay, Lake Erie], whence he was returned, [he was] crowned with the blessings of his fellow sufferers for his unbounded devotion and generosity to them. A prouder laurel could not have been added to his name than their testimony. The Hospital there is entirely managed & all duties done by the prisoners, who selected among themselves those most capable of fulfilling the various

2 West Tennessee Raid, October 16–November 10, 1864.

duties, from the highest to the lowest. Ravenel himself had a severe fit of illness brought on by an attempt to escape, &, when he recovered, offered himself as hospital steward, that position being filled by an incompetent man. . . . Forthwith [he] put himself to regulate the establishment upon a systematic plan &, besides his personal exertions for their comfort, drew largely from his own purse to supply their wants. Many of the returned prisoners have testified their gratitude to him through the papers, giving the public an account of his stewardship & the general management of the hospital in that icebound region, where our brave soldiers from the sunny south necessarily suffered intensely. Capt. Haydon told Carrie that, when he was there, friends (secret societies for their relief) furnished them with books & stationery & other little comforts. . . . Another prisoner told Edward that they used to meet and lecture in turn upon every variety of subject, &, as very many of them were highly educated men, many returned home better informed than when they entered their prison walls. Certainly our poor fellows found means "to extract the jewel from the toad's head" and that "sweet are the uses of Adversity.". . .

William Bell says they are treated brutally; he has often seen the Yankee officer kick right and left among our men, as they [*sic*] walked among them. He always walked out of their way as he saw him coming. Their food was distributed as if they were a parcel of hogs. A barrel of biscuits would be opened & emptied on the ground, where the men had to scramble for them, or, if broth was served, it was ladled in the fastest & most purposely careless manner that the greater part was spilled on the ground or limbs of the men holding their pans or kettles. . . . He has seen a poor wounded man who had crawled between those standing so scalded that his wounded legs were deeply blistered, at which the Yankees laughed heartily. The negro guard would fire upon them for the merest trifle & then pretend they had been trying to escape. This was at Elmira, New York, where at one time were gathered 32,000 men.[3] Numbers died on the voyage home from the crowded state of the transports and the utter

3 The Elmira prison held 10,000 men, but it had buildings for only half that many.

want of common humanity. Certainly the horrors of a slave ship have been out-rivaled by the sufferings of our heroic Southerners. How long, O Lord, how long is our probation through this fearful furnace of affliction and sacrifice to last! On every side we turn, the same barbarity, treachery & falsehood is exhibited by the boasted "most civilized nation of the 19th century."

On the 9th or 10th of November [November 15], Sherman commenced his march to the coast by setting fire to Atlanta & destroying the Gate City almost entirely. A government agent of ours, sent to examine the damages, reports (Dec. 20th) that about 400 houses are left, but the rest is one scene of desolation & destruction—trees cut down everywhere. The progress has been like the commencement—all the barbarities of savage warfare followed in Sherman's wake. Fire, desolation, destruction of all property unremovable—all provisions, cattle & negroes carried away—the rape and consequent death or insanity of many ladies of the best families. Alas what pen can portray the sufferings inflicted by that army of demons, white and black. On they come steadily, for Hood had outflanked Sherman & was in his rear, pushing as steadily for Tennessee. Down they come to Milledgeville [Georgia], whence the Legislature just made their escape. . . .

The Yankees advanced into two corps, one straight upon the road to Augusta, the other down to Macon & Milledgeville [Georgia], raiding parties branching off everywhere & the same story on every side. The Reserves of both Georgia & Carolina were called out, Bragg carried veterans from North Carolina & parts of Hampton's cavalry sent on. Gen. Gustavus W. Smith took command of the Geo. Militia, and [Joseph] Wheeler of the cavalry, which did good service, harassing the enemy on every side. Proclamations were issued calling upon the people to fly to arms, young and old, to remove all provisions & cattle or destroy them, to obstruct every road, & wage guerilla war from every bush and fence. Had this been done, Sherman's course might long ago have been stopped, but the people did not rouse to the danger till too late. Gen. [Birkett D.] Fry—I believe a Georgian—stated that for 100 miles from Atlanta to Sparta, not a hand had been raised to obstruct a single road or fire a single gun, while DeS G[arden] who had gone but a short time before to Columbus, Ga., says he saw hundreds of young men skulking out of the army on every pretense.... He was so disgusted with "the people in the rear" that he said he would not get another furlough for anything. Finally one column was stopped for a time at Oconee Bridge by [Joseph] Wheeler & the militia, but they soon had to fall back to Savannah. The other column went within five miles of Augusta spreading consternation among the citizens. All government property and machinery were removed, and preparations made to defend it, but Sherman left it till he was ready & proceeded onward to Savannah, delaying some time to gather & prepare provisions, for he subsists on the country. His movements seem shrouded generally in mystery or at least but little satisfactory is gained through the papers....

Nov. 30th took place the great battle of Franklin, Tenn. but that must come in its own place. I try to record the prominent incidents of the day, but they crowd upon each other so quickly & I am so seldom able to devote sufficient leisure to them that I often forget the exact dates. I have such a headache now, & the wind is whistling or rather roaring so loudly without that I am quite stupid.... It is the general impression that Savannah will fall. It has been invested for several days by Sherman; the telegraph wires are cut, & the long trestle of the Savannah & C[harleston] R.R. over the river burned, so direct communication is cut off & everybody depends on letter going by private opportunity. Beauregard left Hood soon after Sherman's advance & visited the various points on the coast and is now down with Hardee, we believe. Charlestonians [are] being prepared for a land seige [*sic*] by gathering full stores & ordering that noncombatants shall not be allowed to return, preparatory to ordering the women and children to leave. The people have already been suffering from scarcity of food and fuel, & many box cars are at the depots filled with refugees from Georgia awaiting transportation further inland.

I cannot help believing in Capt. Haydon's prophecy that Savannah, Charleston and Augusta will fall. There seems every probability of it, and he not only prophecied [*sic*] Sherman's advance if Hood did not turn his steps back by the 9th or 10th November, the very time of Sherman's start, but traced his general progress & wrote it out too.

I trust Charleston will become one grand sacrificial altar & funeral pyre before her soil is polluted by Yankee tread. Sherman has sworn to "burn even the very stones of South Carolina and not to restrain his men if he could." With such fearful threats as these & still more fearful example of their being carried out, I shall blush for Charleston, were it left standing. Every spire & housetop should lift its flaming finger to Heaven in supplication to its high tribunal, as well as to proclaim to the world that death is preferable to dishonor. But oh, it will wring tears of blood from every Charlestonian. God grant that this awful trial may be spared us, but I fear the worst.

Hood's army advanced into Tennessee, through Alabama, having long delayed crossing the Tennessee River from the heavy rains and want of supplies. Brother H[enry] writes that what was once an Eden is now one scene of desolation. He does not like Hood and is always regretting Johnston, whom he admired very much. But uncle Ta [Gibbes], who has been first assistant Ordnance officer under Bragg, Johnston & now Hood, says he is worth half a dozen Johnstons, for he never lets his plans be known and, two hours before marching, orders are received, so that he puzzles the enemy greatly. He planned this campaign, & Beauregard approves and allows him to carry it out.

November 30   Hood attacked the enemy in their fortifications, at Franklin, and a tremendous battle was fought, in which brother Henry writes but for darkness we would have utterly routed them. But, it was a fearful sacrifice of general officers. . . . He says the enemy fought desperately, & the battle lasted till midnight. The enemy left an hour after for Nashville where our army are following. . . . At Franklin our loss in general officers was unprecedented. . . . Capt. Carter on [Thomas B.] Smith's staff, [William B.] Bate's division, fell on his father's premises & almost at his door, his skull fractured & six wounds in leg, after two years absence from home. Many another brave Tennessean fell literally fighting for their hearthstones; thousands of them have joined the army & are joining it in its advance, as the people hail our army as their deliverers from Yankee tyranny. In Kentucky they are fleeing into the woods by thousands to avoid conscription & finding their way to our army. Middle Tennessee is a very rich country & perhaps success there will be our salvation here. We have already passed through very many dark trials, & the coming crisis is darkest of all, but with God's help we will hope and conquer.

A few weeks ago [October 7, 1864], the *Florida* Capt. [C. M.] Morris, while lying in the port of Behia on the coast of Brazil & most of the officers on shore resting secure in its being a neutral port, was "cut out" at night by the Yankee war vessel, *Wachusetts* [*sic*], and carried in triumph to Washington, where the officers & men were put in prison. The vessel was soon after sunk, accidentally on purpose, by another vessel running into it, but not before all the valuables, including $12,000 in gold, had been secured. Meantime, Brazil indignantly remonstrates at such a breach of international law & insult to her; France & England talk strongly about it (English merchants & people especially), & communications take place. Brazil demands the restoration of vessel & crew in exact trim as when taken. J. Watson Webb, the Yankee Consul there, writes the most insolent letter to Brazil, disavowing the act as ordered by his government, of whose mercy, etc. he brags in regard to us rebels, while the inferiority of Brazil is covertly & contemptuously sneered under cover of condescension & politeness. What will be the end, it is hard to say, for though the Yankees will back down to the dust, as in the *Trent* case, the *Florida* is not as readily restored as Mason & Slidell, & Brazil is just angry.

Seward has also addressed a very insolent [December 5] letter to [Charles Francis] Adams as an answer to Lord Wharncliffe's request that a committee should be allowed to go to the North & distribute among the prisoners the proceeds of the late Bazaar in Liverpool, refusing point blank. Meantime the Yankee papers insult England more and more every day. The St. Albans raiders or Confederates in Canada have just been released in spite of all the Yankee pleadings.

I have strong doubts whether the enemy will allow to be carried out the arrangement lately entered into between the Commissioners of exchange, to the effect that 1000 bales of cotton were to be sent to New York to be sold by one of our prisoners, an officer appointed for the purpose, & the proceeds invested in clothing & other necessities, which he was to distribute himself among our men. All these [were] to be considered as extras besides what the Yankees were bound to furnish them, the Yankees being allowed to send similar supplies to their men & distributed in the same way. They will get the cotton & then lie as usual & cheat us. We were very much in hopes Willie Gibbes would be exchanged but have heard nothing of him.

. . . When the enemy appeared to threaten Augusta, Lizzie Miller's sister, Mrs. Jonathan Miller, sent her five children with two servants to stay with us, till Sophie would send for them from Liberty Hill. We were quite taken by surprise, but they proved a most interesting and remarkably well behaved set, Bettie, Emmie & Annie, Twiggs, & Norman—the eldest 13, the youngest five, & Minta, their nurse, a perfect mint of comfort—more like a humble companion than servant yet never forgetting her place. She is really pretty & her keen black eyes & straight hair betoken Indian blood. She was dressed as neatly as any of us & was so thoughtful of everything. They staid three days with us. . . .

December 15   Mrs. John. [B.] Mickle called to see me, letters having previously passed between us on the subject and I agreed to go into the country with her to teach her children. Out of her eleven, I am to have eight—six boys and two girls—at $100 a month and board. I will thus be enabled not only to maintain myself but to assist in paying for John's tuition. . . . I expected cousin Lizzie Barnwell to spend Christmas with me and had hoped for Capt. Haydon and Mr. [P. G.] Fitzsimons also, but they went to see their families, & only Isaac came twelve o'clock Saturday night. I had been dreadfully blue & despondent for the day or two previous in consequence of the evacuation of Savannah, its consequent possession by Sherman as a basis of operations, and the probability of the whole state being overrun by our malignant foes, who had sworn to spare neither life nor home to the males, nor honor to the females of Carolina. Uncle Louis paid us a visit on Friday & told us what he thought of the state of the country. He was utterly despondent and made us so, but Isaac cheered us by refuting from official sources many of the rumors and showing we were by no means so reduced for men. It only needed for them to do their duty. Isaac says Savannah is no loss to us in a strategic point of view for it weakened our line, & now as

Grahamville, Pocataligo & those other outposts are gradually given up, we will be able to concentrate our forces around Charleston. He does not think the city will fall or at least without a severe struggle, but the Capt. [Haydon] still considers it doomed. . . . My only wish is, should we be compelled to give it up, let it be only as smoking ruins. But I much fear the thousands still resident there will prevent that.

I am determined, if possible, not to allow myself to give way to such despondency again but to try to hope all for the best and trust in God, and perhaps the loss of all our seaports would after all be the best thing for us by cutting off the supplies of luxuries & throwing the people more than ever on their own resources—by putting a stop to speculation and extortion. There are thousands who do not feel this war, save in the loss of relations & a few luxuries, but who now live in overflowing abundance of necessaries and comforts, and yet they will cry out that they are *starving* and have "nothing to wear."

An example has just been shown by Hattie Shannon's marriage, Dec. 23rd. Just previous, her uncle Sam Shannon brought on his bride, Miss Gyles, of St. Louis, but now of Richmond—a thoroughly fashionable lady, dressed in the latest Parisian fashions and in the greatest extravagance of style. Dinner parties commenced with her & continued with the wedding. Every day there was a party or dinner party for a week. The wedding was very large, and everything in the same elegance and profusion as in peace times. Anna Parker of Charleston, who with her sister Julia waited on her, told me the only thing she missed was champagne. [There were] ice-cream, syllabubs, custards, sugar plums & candy; and this when candy is $30 a pound & common molasses brown sugar $9. I think such extravagance when so many soldiers & houseless refugees are suffering for food is really sinful.

Christmas day, or rather Monday, Grandmother and aunt Sue dined with us; we had such a dinner as we have not had since Carrie was married and, though the fine ham was a recent present from Mrs. [Jonathan] Miller and the turkey one of Isaac's own raising and the rich pudding Lila made was of bread and sorgho [sorghum] yet none of us really enjoyed it when we thought of how hardly our boys might be faring. And Alester afterwards wrote [that] his Christmas dinner had been half done corn-bread; he had been sick for many nights after, with hot fevers, yet without shelter & exposed to very hard rains, protected only by his overcoat and blanket.

December 28
Wednesday

Isaac & I left in a hard rain. I stopped at Claremont for a three days' visit to Dora [Furman], met the Parkers returning home, &, as the carriage had not come for me, they offered me a seat. . . . It was pitch dark & raining & at last the candle went out, &, soon after, the horses missed the path a little and run [*sic*] into the bushes; we waited some time for daylight & then, extricating ourselves readily, arrived without further adventure. I found Fannie B[rownfield] with Dora, & the carriage just starting for me.

The weather continued disagreeable, but I saw all my friends & enjoyed much seeing them, especially Fan [Furman] & her baby and the long confidential talks with Dora. When we will meet again I know not. . . . It seems undoubted that Hood has sustained a severe reverse and is retreating. But it is always hard to get the truth, as the first news is always through Yankee reports in their papers, consequently almost entire falsehoods. Then communication through Geo.[rgia] is slow and interrupted. *This* is certainly the darkest cloud that war has yet spread over our state. With God's help I trust we will weather the storm.

Aunt Lizzie read me a letter Hugh [Garden] had received from Gen. [Edward P.] Alexander, the second officer in rank in the Artillery of the Army of the Potomac [Army of Northern Virginia], recommending his promotion to Major on account of tried bravery and skill on the battlefield & in the command and organization of his company. It was indeed a handsome & well merited compliment. . . .

January 4
1865
Wednesday

I came to Mrs. [John B.] Mickle's ten miles from Camden, among the hills of the Wateree. It was hard to leave my darling baby [Sims White]. He was just 15 months & that morning climbed unassisted into his little buggy, quite a feat of activity & strength.

January 9

Mrs. M[ickle] is a quiet, well educated, kind & considerate lady, whose hands are so well occupied with providing for her little army that I see little of her save at meals & after supper when we sit around the fire and knit. Rebecca & Matilda are

17 & 13, John 16, Joe 15, Willis 14, Belton 10, & Robert & Henry, I believe, 7 & 8. Jamie, Mary & the baby Sarah, very large & uninteresting, are not yet under my jurisdiction. All the children are very quiet, well behaved & respectful in school, neither particularly bright nor dull, but very backward indeed, & John & Willis very timid. Joe, the dullest boy in looks & with a coarse voice, seems to be quickest of the three elder ones, has a decided talent for music & plays very well indeed on the piano. . . . His mother says [he] is quick in all girl's work—spins beautifully. All spend their leisure in the yard, & the boys seldom come into the sitting room after tea. At table, they eat irregularly & leave as soon as done, never talking except to call for what they want. . . . It will be some time before I can draw them out & learn their characters & tastes.

We breakfast at 8½ & dine at 2, so I have a long afternoon, and as by the help of uncle Henry's eye water, I can read by firelight, I read till late at night, generally going to my chamber about nine. My chamber is a south-east one, facing the front, a large one with four windows, from which I enjoy fine views of the sunrise, &, by stepping in the upper piazza enjoy the sunsets also. My maid Levy is exceedingly attentive, as are all the servants, & indeed for the present I and everything I have are the admiration of these country negroes who seldom have a stranger among them.

January 20
Friday
evening

Arrived Mrs. Mickle's youngest sister, lately married, & her husband, Capt. [Solomon] & Mrs. [Harriet] Lorick. He had received a ball in his right cheek, which passed out beyond the ear leaving a deep impression & much affecting the nerves of the eye, & giving him quite a peculiar expression. They left Saturday evening. . . .

January 23
Monday

He [Joe Mickle] has just come and gone after a pleasant little chat. He was a widower & married a few months ago. Mrs. Mickle's sister [was] also [here]. They spent a day and night here a week ago, & I was quite pleased with both. I was invited to dine there last Saturday, but was prevented by the rain which also stopped them and the other married sisters, Mrs. [John] Starke & Mrs. [James] Milling, with their children, from coming over Friday night to some tableaux I arranged for the children. Some had never seen them before, & all were delighted, as well as a score of colored spectators. But I've told them I will not give them any more till they improve. . . . Indeed I have found them strangely ignorant of the commonest facts, ideas, tales, & even articles. Never had heard of *Gulliver's Travels*, nor Munchausen's nor even Jack the Giant Killer, any more than the Hero of the Bean Stalk, beloved memories of my childhood. A mother of pearl paper knife was a curiosity & the Trojan War was an equal revelation. Biblical history they know as little of as of ancient profane records of the mighty past. Yesterday I partly read to John & Rebecca, or made them read, the whole book of Daniel, explaining the prophecies to them & doing my best to interest & persuade them to read & examine for themselves by bringing my various stores of information to bear upon the subject. How thankful I am for having read [Austen H.] Layard's *Expedition to Nineveh & Babylon*. It has been a source of so much pleasure and improvement and has explained so many hitherto obscure passages of the Bible.

Mrs. M.[ickle] does not seem to converse with her children, & either draw out their crude ideas or give them new ones, yet she is quite intelligent & very well educated, & I find her an agreeable companion. I try to draw them toward me by telling them tales or incidents of my life—the sights of city life —etc. & persuading them to read aloud to me occasionally after supper when they've finished their lessons. I have already noticed improvement in many things: I think I have aroused their minds and led them to inquire and think for themselves.

I generally spend my afternoons writing letters, as my correspondence is quite extensive & my epistles usually small volumes. My friends always enjoy them because I write naturally, of what interests me & consequently it pleases them.

I determined to devote a certain time after breakfast every Saturday to this old friend, but company interfered two [weeks]. Last Saturday I was too good for nothing after the tableaux & sitting up till half past twelve Thursday night to finish *Villette*, read for the second time but found most fascinating. This evening George Borrow's *Lavengro*—a most fascinating yet provoking because unfinished biography— chained me to the end. . . . When I opened these pages, my impulse was to cut out the remaining ones and lay the book aside, but the "cacoethes scribendi" seized me, and, in spite of miserable, soft nibbed pens & consequent bad writing, I think I shall continue. Would that the inspiration would lead to something more profitable and enduring than this, but I do not feel within me that uncontrollable impulse to write, without which it would not be worth reading.

Rosa [Bull] Guerard has a son, named Joseph St. Julienne after his uncle; he must be over two weeks old I expect, but I don't think cousin Beck [Holmes] mentioned the date of his arrival. Poor child, everything went wrong as usual. Phoebe, who was to have been her nurse as she had been her mother's, died suddenly shortly before, & another was not sent for till rather late. Cousin Mary [DeSaussure] fortunately went up with cousin Henry [DeSaussure] when sent for & assisted Rosa. . . . She suffered long & much, but without a murmur, and cousin Beck said was very much prostrated; she was sent for when all was over & found Annie Baker as nurse. The baby is a fine hearty, strong little fellow, a fighting character already. . . .

Aunt Amelia [Holmes] has concluded to remain in town, as [James] Conner's Brigade, to the universal joy, has just been allowed to return to their native state to fight on their soil for the first time in four years. They applied for permission to Gen. Lee saying, "In Virginia we have fought like men, at home we will fight like lions." The lines "Back they returned, all that was left, Left of six hundred—Back they came, but not, Not the six hundred" [4] rings in my ears every time I think of the Palmetto Guard, the former pride of our city—both alike in ruins, but undaunted & defiant to their foes. . . . Willie has removed his family to Graham's Turnout, Barnwell, to a rough, unfinished, unglazed house. . . . Having only one wagon, only one mattress, clothing & plates enough to go round . . . the children [were carried] sleeping on pine straw and blankets. The wagon had returned for household articles & negro clothing, but Maria feared the negroes might not go up, as Willie could not be there to make them, & that that part of the country would have already been given up, as our troops were gradually retiring before the enemy.

Sherman has done everything so far to conciliate the Savan-

---

4 Alfred Lord Tennyson, "The Charge of the Light Brigade."

nah people, making every arrangement for the maintenance of public order & ordering everything to go on as usual. He is patting them with his cushioned paw, but the claws will soon appear. A pretended meeting of the citizens—seventeen in reality—was held, putting the city "once more in the Union." Yankee stores are already opened & greenbacks alone current. All their curses loud & deep are heaped upon the doomed City by the Sea—& fearful denunciations of fiendish revenge.

The Virginians gave The Army of the Potomac [Army of Northern Virginia] a grand New Year's dinner. A profusion of all good things was cooked at the Ballard House [Richmond], by an army of cooks, under superintendence of a committee, who packed and saw to the distribution along the lines twenty miles long.

Hood's army, after being repulsed before Nashville by Thomas [December 16, 1864], who had been largely reinforced, retreated without loss across the Tennessee. I have not received letters or papers for ten days, as it rained all Saturday & my last papers were several days old, so I feel perfectly out of the world. The constant rains have produced a great freshet, one of the worst known for 16 years, overflowing many trestles on the Camden & Columbia roads, carrying away a part of the long covered bridge in Camden over the Wateree, cutting off communication and causing much damage and loss everywhere.

The Confederate States have turned over the defence of Columbia to So. Ca., and Isaac, when I last heard from him, was there awaiting orders. I hope he and the Captain [Haydon] will not be separated.

January 26
Thursday

While I was dressing, I received my mail bag with its accumulation of ten days; letters from brother H[enry] gave a dreadful account of the sufferings of Hood's army from the intense cold. The men were ragged & very many shoeless with their feet frost bitten & leaving their tracks in blood, while many sat on the road and *wept* from agony. Brother H.[enry] says he hopes never to suffer again as he did. He was much in want of proper clothing and blankets, and his big toes [were] frost bitten.

The expedition into Tennessee has been indeed a terrible

one, nearly 20 generals & thousands of men killed or wounded; many of the latter were left to the care of the noble Tennessee ladies, who were unbounded in their devotion, but many of our wounded went all the way from Nashville to Corinth, Miss. on crutches to escape Northern prisons. Hood has been relieved, "at his own request," [January 13] but I have not learned his successor; Johnston seems generally desired by the public.

Mr. [James A.] Seddon, Secretary of War, has also resigned,[5] & Gen. [John C.] Breckinridge talked of as his successor. Edward Everett, once of the pretended warmest friends of the South, & greatly admired & respected here—lately a most bitter enemy—died suddenly very recently [January 15]. Aunt Amelia [Holmes] & the children have gone to Athens [Georgia] again (I learned since that uncle A[rthur Holmes] becoming excited at Sherman's threats in regard to the ladies, sent for Anna [Holmes] to go with her mother. . . .)[6]

Uncle Henry Gibbes writes he has another grandchild & sends mother $350 as a Christmas gift. He has shown himself a true brother.

Last but not least of the news was that Hattie White was on a visit to Carrie, & the girls begged me to go down if possible. I was so afraid of being disappointed that I did not ask Mrs. Mickle till the afternoon, when she consented at once, proposing I should leave Friday morning instead of afternoon. . . . Mr. Mickle said, [if] I wished to stay till Sunday, his wife would bring me up; I therefore astonished the family by walking in at twelve on Friday. The weather was bitter cold—thermometer being at 12 deg.—one of the coldest spells for years. Lander's creek was frozen and even the foam from the mill floated congealed like huge water lilies. The carriage broke ice an inch thick on the road, &, in many places, it was deeper.

The girls determined to take advantage of it and enjoy some ice cream. We had much amusement in collecting the materials, finally borrowing eggs & churn. . . . After many quakings & considerable excitement, at half past ten we were regaled with an excellent Confederate article, sorghum &

5 Jefferson Davis did not accept the resignation until February 1.
6 The sentence in parentheses was written on top of a page in the diary manuscript at some time after the original entry.

lemon combined, having produced chocolate cream equal to the palmy days of Mount Vernon Garden, with its fountains, statues, arbors & music—on a tiny scale 'tis true, but all very refreshing and pretty—but now among the reminiscences of the past.

Sims [White] smacked his lips & enjoyed it as much as any and was all the time begging for ice. He has learned many new words & is more engaging than ever. He certainly managed his aunts Hattie [White] & Emmie well Saturday night, for we played hoop & hide till we were tired [of] shouting, & then I trotted round with his plump little legs round my neck. . . .

During service we heard the miserable cracked steamboat bell of our church summoning a congregation & found on coming out that some one certainly was holding service. I could not think of anyone but Staudenmeyer or Dr. [James A.] Young—a blackguard or an extortioner.

I had a pleasant ride with Mrs. Joe Mickle arriving at her house to a three o'clock dinner. . . . By the Bye, a short time ago, I counted 40 blood relations who were or had been in service, several being dead.

February 1
Wednesday

. . . The day was worthy of the opening of spring, as balmy as possible, but I found it enervating & came from school faint and exhausted from my efforts to induct Willis & Matilda [Mickle] into the mysteries of grammar & arithmetic. Dinner revived me somewhat, & I sat up that night till twelve reading Martin Chuzzlenit which is a true mirror held up to hypocrisy & humbug of all kinds, in Yankeedom as well as England. Dickens certainly transcribed some portions from "feeling" experiences of Yankee lion-hunting, boasting, bluster, & ill-breeding. I am really quite indebted to Dora [Furman] & Callie Perkins for my introduction to Thackery [*sic*] and Dickens.

February 5
Saturday
[should
be 4]

Mr. Willis Whitaker, Mrs. M[ickle]'s cousin, dined here. He was a lieutenant in the Texan Brigade, lost his right arm at Gettysburg, and was for fourteen months imprisoned in Fort Delaware, only being released last September. He won my sympathy and high respect by his determined, unconquered, & unconquerable spirit, which he has carried through all the hardships and trials of a soldier's and captive's life. He is quiet, modest but firm & dauntless, and I think worthy of the true definition of man. Small as he is, he bears a great heart. . . . I enjoyed very much talking with a gentleman who was not only intelligent and well educated but one, who having done his duty to his country & who entered into the army *determined* to bear all trials, without murmuring, for liberty, was well qualified to give sound opinions in regard to public matters. If he & I were made enrolling officers, I'm sure the ranks would soon be filled without calling the negroes as Gen. Lee wants & the President too. The latter has been very sick with neuralgia in his right arm but has at last signed Gen. Lee's commission as General in Chief [January 31] & Breckinridge has really become Secretary of War [February 6]. The Virginia Legislature had expressed a wish that all members of the Cabinet be removed, save Mr. [George A.] Trenholm, & some immediately resigned.[7]

February 18

Last week was one of utter failure with all my scholars, till I almost became disgusted & in despair applied the ruler to the younger boys, with a notion it would not be amiss with the elder ones—at least they deserved it as much. Anyway, this week matters have improved. . . .

We heard there had been a fight near Orangeburg, then that Charleston was given up. But I could not, would not, believe such dreadful tidings, but alas, yesterday's letters confirm it. Mother merely wrote it was to be evacuated yesterday & cousin Beck [Holmes], Rosa & the children had come up. The Gadsdens had determined to remain and the DeSaussures were kept by Alexander's illness.

After three years' resistance & hard labor to have to yield at last to stern necessity, for I know nothing else would have compelled the voluntary surrender of the city, for which the enemy have so long thirsted. It can only be because our army is too small to protect both the city and interior. And, of course, the latter is a matter of life & death not only to the state, as the productive part, but to the Confederacy. For, if all our railroads are cut & communication cut off, how is the Army of [Northern] Virginia to be maintained with supplies,

7 Other than Seddon's February 1st resignation as Secretary of War, no other cabinet member resigned during this period.

while the city is comparatively valueless now as a strategical point. For, our army, if there, might easily be hemmed in between the fleet & Sherman & be starved into surrender. It cannot be destroyed as we had so long talked of, for there is no refuge for the thousands still there; no point in the state is safe, & literally they could find neither shelter nor food. Perhaps it is all for the best, and God's hand is in it. Columbia was shelled on Thursday, but the enemy finally driven back several miles. The greater part of Hood's army, after their terrible campaign of suffering, has come to reinforce our army here. Brother H[enry] wrote his command was ordered here. Gen. Lee is coming soon, so we must only hope & trust. Capt. Haydon's prophecy has been fulfilled to the letter—"I give Charleston till February to fall."

Yankee raiding parties are going everywhere, & no one feels safe. Mother writes that so far they have behaved much better than was anticipated from their threats; no houses that were occupied have been burned, nor those where ladies were, molested, though out houses are pillaged. So, she is having corn ground and shelled & put about the house to secure it if possible. It is hard to realize this glorious spring day that deadly strife is around us and that at any moment we may see ourselves surrounded by the brutal foe.

March 4   The past fortnight seems like a fearful dream or nightmare, of which all traces here have passed away, save the vivid recollection. Feb. 18th was Saturday, &, during the morning, came officers, inquiring their road on their way to Charlotte with a train of ordnance or quartermaster's stores from Columbia; then followed the news of that city being in the Yankees' hands, then Winnsboro. Each day brought new rumors. Tuesday Mrs. Joe Mickle announced Lieut. Willis Whitaker's marriage to Lottie June the Friday previous & his own determination to hide in the swamps with wagons of meat & the mules & horses till the enemy had passed, for we heard of them on every side, ravaging & pillaging. Wednesday we were all startled by the cry "The Yankees are here," but they proved only two or three of our men who had killed one Yankee over the river, & captured his companion, who had been guarding a quantity of stolen meat. We were all in a high state of excitement, but I still carried on school amidst constant

false alarms & interruptions. We had all made some preparations for receiving them, by Mrs. M[ickle] burying all her
silver, jewelry, & many other valuables, both barrels and
boxes of lard, molasses and clothing, china, etc.—or rather
the first were buried before they came and the others since,
for they said a worse set would follow. For myself, I put all my
jewelry in a small basket in my pocket, my money & watch in
my bosom carefully concealing the chain, & not wearing a
single ornament; I also filled my mail bag with handkerchiefs
& stockings & a new pair of shoes & wore it under my hoop,
thinking if the house was destroyed, at least I should save
those few. We heard the house of Mrs. Nelson, with whom
aunt Sue stays, had been burned because she made some remark they did not like. It proved a mistake however; only the
uninhabited plantation house was burned.

In the meantime, my distress for home friends in Camden,
where I heard the Yahoos were, was very great. Oh, how I
have suffered for them during these weary days. We knew
Columbia had been nearly destroyed by fire, and my imagination pictured all the horrors to which they would be exposed,
till I felt nearly distracted sometimes. I yearned to be at home
& share all their troubles. I felt as I walked that upper piazza
& sat by myself so many lonely hours without one to sympathize with my griefs, like a prisoner in a dungeon, who at last
is tempted to strike his head against the senseless wall in his
frantic cravings for freedom and home. I felt no *fear* of the
Yahoos but was so intensely excited all the time that my heart
would throb as if suffering from disease at the idea of the
scenes that were to come. I felt as I had done at the sight of
great conflagrations, &, as I expected, when the enemy did
come, I was perfectly calm. Thursday we heard of them at the
plantation two miles off, & school was hastily broken up and
the three elder boys sent into the woods with several men
servants.

That afternoon, I took Dr. [David] Livingston's *Travels in
Africa* & sat composedly to watch for their coming from Mr.
Cook's. Sure enough two did come, followed by two stolen
mules & little negroes, & I quietly announced it to Mrs.
M.[ickle] downstairs. They, however, only stopped at the gate
and asked some questions. But Friday morning soon after
breakfast, they came, a party of five, who asked for break-

fast and, while it was being cooked, they walked about the house and yard, behaving pretty well. I was in the sitting room reading, having first run upstairs, put on my bag & unlocked all my trunks, to save their being broken open. Mrs. M[ickle] sent to ask me to join her in the dining room, where we all remained the rest of the morning. The Yankees, while waiting for breakfast, called for the sideboard keys to get liquor; fortunately but little was there; they called for sugar to make toddy, & when Taylor the houseboy carried the cannister—on his telling them that was all she [Mrs. Mickle] had, took very little. She had buried most of her groceries. The table was laid in the room where we were and, when they finished, one handed $100 in Confederate money to Mrs. M[ickle] as payment, which she said she would have flung back at him if she had dared. But, fearing to suffer from our own imprudence, we all kept perfectly quiet. Whether they stole anything, we could not tell, for before they left another set came pouring in, & the stream was steady for six hours— gradually dying away during the seventh. No place was free from them, save the room we occupied, & not a thing there was touched, though they frequently passed through. Not the smallest box even of children's baby clothes or toys escaped their hands, save the top of my hat box. After the first set left, I tried to persuade one of the maids to go up and get my new toilette comb, a very fine one for which I had recently paid $15 & which I feared they might break if not take, but all were so terrified, none would go; my faithful Liddy was so scared that she was made sick & yet had to wait on the wretches & obey their orders. As soon as they were gone, she "cascaded" freely. Each one tried to get out of their way & keep as much about us as possible.

Down at the plantation they had burned the ginhouse & nearly 80 bales of cotton, much unpacked, only allowing the negroes to carry off a few armfuls. They stole almost all the negroes' meat, Mrs. M[ickle] having sent a good deal to them to save for themselves, & ransacked everything, taking what clothing they wanted. One of the men, a very intelligent negro, said, if he had an opportunity, he would have killed the one who stole his new breeches, but there were too many others by. Two hundred bushels of corn, removed to a house far off, was [*sic*] burned, & they said others would burn the crib, but fortunately so far it is safe.

Up here they called for pillow cases & carried off all the wheat-flour, save a peck the cook stole back from them, almost all the meat, all the turkeys & chickens, filling the carriage with meat. Mr. Cook's [carriage] was laden with chickens &, when the door was opened to put more in, several flew out —all the meal went too—& the cook was kept busy all the time.

Mrs. M[ickle] had left out a few spoons & common knives & forks for daily use, & all save one teaspoon was carried. But, as their pockets were full, some would tumble out & the servants picked up a few old ones.

The house servants all acted admirably. They agreed among themselves to say nothing was buried and, though they tried in every way to bribe, coax or "catch" Taylor admitting the fact, it was of no avail. All persisted that all the silver their mistress had was on the table & had been taken by the first comers. Many persons both white and black were betrayed by being ordered to go straight and get that silver, trunk, money, etc. which they—the Yankees—had seen them bury. The victims, supposing some one had betrayed, would march immediately to the spot. The men, who buried most of Mrs. M[ickle]'s things, took to the woods to avoid this, but Taylor had the keys and went everywhere with them.

The negroes all shared the same fate as ourselves, everything ransacked & whatever was wanted [was] stolen, though the Yankees told them they had come to free them and called them "sis," talking most familiarly. Many of them had hidden their things in the woods, & all were eager to help their mistress save something from the "vile wretches."

During the morning, one walked in & took his seat the other side of the room and commenced speaking of how the soldiers had treated her [Mrs. Mickle]—expressing his disapprobation. . . . On her asking if he could do nothing to prevent it & save her carriage, [he] said, no, he was only a private; she asked where he was from; he said he was an Englishman living in New York,—had entered into this war very foolishly & his term would soon be out, and he did not care which side beat. Finding him thus, I joined in and asked some questions. He said he belonged to the 15th Corps in which he said there were scarcely 9 Yankees, the mass being English, Scotch & Irish, while 100 or 200 were daily arriving in N. York to fill the ranks. Then I hazarded a home thrust "Now, is it a fair fight, when we are single handed," & he frankly confessed it was not.

Later two more *knocked* at the door, came in, & entered into conversation with Mrs. M[ickle]. Finding them well behaved, I fired volley after volley of rebel shot at them. One was from Illinois, the other from Pennsylvania—both young, as indeed are all Sherman's army. The first staid but a short time, the other about three quarters of an hour. Oh, how I enjoyed being able to relieve my bottled wrath and show the spirit which animates the Southern women. I did not forget my character as a lady, but I taunted them with warring on women & children. . . . When they said [General John G.] Foster had Charleston & would certainly burn it, I boasted of being a Charlestonian & said my only regret was that it had not been laid in ashes by our own troops, and that it would have been but for the helpless women & children who had no shelter—that we would never be subdued, for if every man, woman & child were murdered, our blood would rise up & drive them away. Moreover, they showed they never expected to subdue us & our own land, or they would not destroy everything as they did. I laughed at their pretence of "fighting for the old flag and saying, if we had not changed it, they never would have fought us." In fact, I hurled so many keen sarcasms, such home thrusts, that the Pennsylvanian said "I was the best rebel he had met, and that it was such women as I who kept up this war by urging on our brothers and friends." I told him I considered it a high compliment, that I was delighted to find I was able to do so much for my country. He said the war would soon be over, and, in a few months, we would all be in the Union. I answered "Never, the war may last three or four years longer, & we would then stand equal with the United States, & I only hoped he would live to witness such a great consumation."

(Capt. Haydon—should we never meet again I thank you most sincerely for all the firm trust and hope inspired by your great heart and head. You have been a beacon, lighting the way to good deeds and thoughts of "high emprize." Would that there were many such good men. Never can I forget the memorable conversations nor his rebuke. The seed fell on good ground though strewn over the surface with many stumbling stones, & I trust it will yet bear fruit sixty fold. I pray he may be spared through the trials of this war, to witness his country's freedom & glory & be the happiness of his sisters and friends.)

The Yankee was at last so posed that he said he wished he had his "partner" here to answer me, for he could not. I asked him if he had never read French history & looked for retribution, for that they were now drunk with blood and would finally turn upon themselves.

He was the last, and, when he left, I came upstairs and in spite of myself could not help indulging in a hearty laugh. Such chaos was never made by Christian hands. It was truly "confusion worse confounded"—doubly, trebly so. Nothing to the tiniest box of dolls' play things had escaped them, save the top of my hat box—everything that mischief could devise, but fortunately no real damage was done. My ink was emptied on the floor, & my sealing wax, most of my new pens, empty purse, new tooth brush & toilette comb stolen. These last three are real losses, as they cannot be replaced. Some socks I had knit & tooth brushes I had just filled for those at home & the pretty silver headed mother of pearl piercer, aunt B. Holmes gave me & valued for her sake, were also taken. Perhaps as I want them, I shall miss other useful trifles.

From Mrs. M[ickle] they had freely helped themselves to towels, called for pillow cases & carried off thus all her wheat flour save about a peck the cook *stole back.*

We laughed till we cried over the tricks played by the negroes to save their things or to keep the Yankees from talking. One old crippled man, a shoemaker, begged so funnily &, when the creatures were carrying off the blankets, begged them with a tone of terror not to mix them with his, as all the house girls had some catching disease, (on which everyone was hastily thrown, & off they went, making him a present of an old mule.)

Mrs. Tom Mickle, the overseer's wife, stole from them when they left their horses & [had] gone further down the negro quarters. They had first "cleaned" her house, so she returned the compliment & then did not spare her tongue.

They swore to shoot her husband & tried in vain to *bribe* the negroes to betray him. Meantime he was nearby watching them & staying at night sometimes at home sometimes at one of the negro houses.

The servants behaved most faithfully, & that very evening a quantity of things were buried & again Saturday & Sunday, hearing & fearing a worse set. Saturday only one passed & he came in & inquired whether we had been plundered, pretending to be very angry. He was the last, but for many days we were still kept excited, knowing they were at Dr. [John] Milling's plantation three or four miles off.

For two or three nights, I did not undress completely, having no fancy to be caught completely unprepared, & got Liddy to sleep in my room. . . . In the dining room, I "banked" up my desk & journal & some books with the carriage cushions, determined to take my seat there and try to save them. We can readily smile & laugh now, when all is over, but it was serious then. But indeed, after the Yankees really came, I recovered from my "thrills & heart-throbbings" of excitement and could not resist a joke over some of their cool proceedings, even while they were here. The likeness of Dora [Furman] & myself, taken by [George S.] Cook in days of "auld lang syne" & a memento of many happy hours, was found in the yard with the mark of a heel, where some Yankees had ground it under foot, crushing both ambrotype & outer glass of course into fragments—doubtless, with the Nero-like wish that Hydra headed seccession might have been then & there crushed out. I have put it aside as a "relic of barbarity" as well as my tiny copy of [Thomas] Hood's *Poems*, which was stolen by Nicholas Baird from Ohio, & returned next day to my great amusement by one of Mrs. M[ickle]'s "slaves," as he says in the note written inside, ending with his opinion that the Southern ladies are very handsome.

Monday or Tuesday night after we had gone to bed, the servants heard some one knocking at the front door & were so alarmed it was long before they would go to the door; at last they went & found two of our soldiers, who had escaped from the Yankees, or rather said one of their guards had let them off just before reaching Camden. They had been captured at home on furlough, belonged to [Matthew C.] Butler's cavalry, were from Bamberg & had been three weeks prisoners & were now endeavoring to make their way to join the army. They had only got away the Thursday or Friday previous & were perfectly unacquainted with the country. All day they hid in the woods & travelled at night, for fear of being recaptured. They asked for food & guidance. Next night they came back at supper time unable to get on as Yankees swarmed everywhere. They spent the night, & I was especially interested in the youngest, a stripling of 18 or 19, with a true Spartan soul. He had entered Lee's army, when not yet 15, had shared its hard-fought campaigns, was resolved to dare and do all for freedom. He was really modest, seldom speaking unless spoken to & then not with many words but those sternly resolute. His name was Crouch & his companion's Landifer. Both belonged evidently to the "yeomanry" of our land & seemed rather constrained by the society in which they found themselves. Landifer was a man of about 40 & one of the "common herd" in soul and mind, one of those, like Mrs. M.[ickle]—who think there is little use to struggle against such an overwhelming force as Sherman's—that we might as well quietly submit at once. But Crouch is one of the numberless "unknown heroes" of this war, who believes with me that, if a people are only true to themselves & their rights & are willing to lose all rather than liberty, that we will not fail at last to win that priceless boon. I honor any man, however ignorant and humble, who has such sentiments and risks his life for them. It refreshes me to meet such after having had every nerve tingling from Mrs. M[ickle]'s cowardly talk.

The next night they again came to enquire the news & finally spent Friday night here. Just before dark, as I was reading in the sitting room, an enormously fat man was ushered in by Mrs. M[ickle] who remained but a few minutes. I concluded from his remarks to her that he was some overseer who had been "out hiding" & I went on reading. After she left, some few remarks passed between us. Then he drew his chair to the fire near me & commenced giving utterance to such "whipped and cowed" sentiments as completely disgusted & irritated me. And yet, his manner & language showed he was not what I thought. I was mystified but more & more provoked by his speeches, till careless who he was, I administered the lash of sarcasm & contempt very freely. . . . He was equally ignorant of who I was, but I soon informed him I was a

Charlestonian & that I had never encountered such narrow-mindedness & ignorance as since I had been up in the up-country. He took up the cudgels in defence & spoke of having studied medicine in Charleston which mystified me still more, but it did not increase my respect for him, & I know I treated him with the utmost superciliousness. Just before supper, I found out he was Dr. Pickett from Longtown neighborhood, & he found out my name, I suppose. After supper, Mr. Tom Mickle came in & then Crouch & Landifer. Mr. M[ickle] agreed exactly with Dr. P[ickett] & he commenced by asserting President Davis ought to be hung as the fountain head of everything that had failed, or was wrong. Landifer joined in, till I could stand it no longer, & I poured down an avalanche of bottled wrath on them.

I told them this raid & fearful desolation of our state had been brought upon us by the avarice of the people themselves, because their patriotism was in their pockets & they had to thank their own arrant selfishness for it. For, they would not respond to Hampton's & the Governor's [Andrew G. Magrath] call for horses to mount our cavalry, and, because they would not sacrifice a few, the Yankees had now swept the land like locusts—that all those who came here were infantry mounted on stolen mules & horses & that they could never have plundered the country thus if they had no animals. . . . If I had owned animals, if I could not have saved them from their hands, I would have hamstrung or cut the throats of everyone. Such personal sacrifice would have saved the country—that I believed God had sent it as a punishment, because the love of money had swallowed love of country, &, until we were willing to bear such trials as the Netherlanders, we would never succeed—that it was the people at home who grumbled and croaked all the time while they had lost nothing and lived in comfort & luxury and the army more [*sic*] every hardship and trial, cheerfully, and would never consent to yield. Crouch said every word was true and he agreed with me fully and that he knew our army was in want of cavalry. Mrs. M[ickle] said, if the horses had been ordered, they would have been sent, but, as they were only called for, people would not send [them]. There the base spirit which saps the very life blood & palsies the right arm of our generals was clearly revealed. The soul stirring appeal of the governor could not rouse them from their cowardly, selfish, dream of security; they waited till forced, like slaves.

I told them I would not hear the President abused, for he was but man and therefore fallible. Yet the almost unanimous voice of the nation had elected him as the only proper man. . . . Though he might have made great blunders of which I did not consider myself capable of judging, it was not only base and contemptible but absurd to load him with such abuse, first because, as Chief Magistrate, he could not condescend to notice it, and again the fireside generals & politicians found fault with everything, after it had failed and prognosticated nothing but evil, while he bore an Herculanean task upon his shoulders. Moreover, England & France judged as if they were posterity from their distance from the scene of action, &, obtaining their information chiefly from Yankee sources, and yet they gave him unbounded praise.

When Dr. P[ickett] & the rest said there were no men left in the country to have impeded their march, I told him, if all the men who had taken to the woods to save themselves had formed bands & bushwhacked and harassed them at every step, the Yankees would not have walked like masters through the land. Dr. P[ickett] answered, if we had bushwhacked, they would have burned our houses—the coward spirit showing itself everywhere. Crouch said I was right, for they were terribly afraid of bushwhackers. I said every boy capable of bearing a gun ought to turn [out]. Dr. P[ickett] maintained they could not stand it. I told him plenty had gone out & stood it, & it was better they should die in defence of their country than live under Yankee rule. He went on to say he had always been a Conservative & Moderate & opposed to Secession, and believed like Mr. John Mickle, that we ought to have waited for an overt act.

I wished him joy of his Yankee masters & thought he deserved them. The conversation was kept up till eleven. I was much excited for my whole soul revolted from such cowardly ideas. He told me he admired my "spunk," but I feel pretty sure he and all save Crouch considered me bold, conceited and impudent to "talk down" older men thus. But I didn't care for the opinion of such cowards &, when two or three days later, Mr. [John] Starke dined here & said Dr. P.[ickett] had always been Union in his sentiments & strongly favored

[William W.] Boyce's schemes & doctrines, I felt glad of what I said.[8] As we learned that Friday morning the Yankees had burned the ginhouse at Mr. [John] Milling's & gone on, all felt they might now safely cross the river. I trust the soldiers will safely reach their brigade, now only about 1500 strong. We are literally cut off from the rest of the world & do not know where our little army is & what they are doing except being constantly obliged to fall back before Sherman's overwhelming force of 100,000 men. For he won't fight; as soon as he finds our army in front, he swings round one huge corps to outflank us. Crouch said he did that all the time while they were prisoners—marching 50 miles to outflank 10. Thus, Beauregard was compelled to fall back slowly to prevent being surrounded. But our forces were preparing for a final stand at Charlotte.

We *hear* the forces who evacuated Charleston are at Cheraw, and that an attempt of the enemy to cut the road at Florence was repulsed. We know [John G.] Foster and his *negro troops* are in Charleston & shudder for the sufferings of those unhappy enough to be found there. I should feel thankful to know that all my aged relatives there were resting quietly in their graves rather than be exposed to such torture of soul. We know Columbia is more than half destroyed by the fire set by the Yankees & that, they say, over 1000 women & children are accompanying them to go North having lost everything.

From Camden, all that we have learned was by passing negroes, or Mrs. M[ickle]'s, who had been taken by the Yankees to carry their plunder, then allowed to return, till a day or two ago when Mr. Mickle went down. The Yankees staid two days & a night plundering all the time, burning the whole square from the commissary store opposite the hotel, down to Baums [Baum Brothers Merchants], including where "Miss Denie" & Mrs. Crosby lived, [James R.] McKain's drug store, the jail & depots. All the stores were sacked, & negroes invited to help themselves. All Dr. [James A.] Young's stock of books

8 William W. Boyce was a member of the Confederate Congress who, in a September 29, 1864, letter to Jefferson Davis, urged Davis and the Confederacy to respond favorably to the plank of the 1864 Democratic party platform calling for an armistice and peace and return to the Union. This proposal caused an enormous uproar, received wide support in the Confederacy, but was never acted upon.

were pitched in the street. Miss Susan Lang's was the only separate dwelling house burned. The Yankees discovered three barrels of liquor belonging to Oppenheim buried near & became so unruly she said she must leave. They told her, if she did, it would be burnt. The negroes say the Yankees worked the engines to prevent the fire catching the dwellings downtown. The officers of the banks carried all the money, books, and papers out in wagons into the woods, & the whole party was captured, so Confederate money is no longer worth the paper it is on in Camden & scarcely anywhere else, I expect. I hear uncle John's & Mr. William Shannon's houses were very roughly used and that a "bushel" of silver was got at uncle John's, that very little provision was destroyed as they were intent after gold and silver and said they had found more in Camden than in the whole of Geo. they had been through. . . . We hear the Yankees turned off a few miles below Camden & did not go either to uncle John's plantation or Mr. [E. M.] Boykin's. I hope they did not reach the latter's dwelling. The Camden people saved their horses by sending them to the plantations. Mayor [James] Dunlap met the Yankees with the white flag as token of surrender, & we hear his house was but slightly pillaged, & Gen. [J. B.] Kershaw's not at all. Crouch said that, in Columbia, a Yankee told a lady to take off her watch & jewelry &, on her refusing, plunged his bayonet into her side. . . . [He] said he knew "several such crimes had been committed."

Everything I have heard has only increased my anxiety to hear from home.

The week after the raid I kept school irregularly, not requiring any lessons studied save in school. But Saturday morning I called the children to get their lessons marked, &, though I sent three messages, not a boy came to me. That vexed me, for it was the second time the older ones had disobeyed me thus. When their mother came a little after saying I gave the children too long lessons, that it was what she had heard the parents . . . complain of me in Camden—that Willis & Matilda did not understand the long division sums they were doing & I ought to take them out of the book & set sums on the slate instead—etc., etc.—I was really angry and disgusted as I had previously been. This capped the climax, & I answered very sharply & I am sure, if she had had her carriage, I should have gone home forthwith. W[illis] & M[atilda] are incorrigibly dull. Their minds are the rockiest soil I ever attempted to plant; the seed does not live an hour, & no amount of culture seems capable of making it germinate. All I can get from either, is "I don't know," & when I asked M.[a-tilda] why she told her mother she could not do the sums, & me, that she understood them, she answered "she did under-stand them, but that did not make her know how to do them." In grammar & arithmetic, my labor had been alike fruitless— two months work thrown away was very discouraging. I had carried them to verbs and division, &, finding such simple things above the comprehension of 13 & 14, I turned them back to [the] multiplication table & daily compositions, then recommenced from the beginning of each book, explaining freely, & this was all the result. I knew none had too long or too many lessons, for they alternated & their mother con-fessed the boys "did not hurt themselves by study." Yet [she] found fault with me saying three chapters of [Peter] Parley's *History of England*, varying from 8 or 9, to 12 & 15 short para-graphs composed almost entirely of anecdotes, was too much for the elders, & one chapter of his U.S. History [too much] for W[illis] & M.[atilda]. Yet [she] added she was quite satis-fied with their improvement, & I must not expect too much. What satisfaction in such unprofitable labor when the mother weakens my influence by finding fault before the children, as she has done before, & what is the use of trying to make them speak correctly when she says, They *done them* things. I cut every lesson in half & determined I would no longer waste my leisure in the thankless task of trying to interest and expand such clod pates, by reading, showing & describing pictures, & getting books, but would keep myself strictly to my duties.

I felt as if I could not stand this life much longer—every-thing disgusted me. The first month "the new broom swept clean" & everything wore company manners. I looked for the bright side of everything & hoped for the best, but this last month, the flimsy veil has been torn asunder—the Yankees proved a touchstone—by Ithuriel's spear,[9] & their true char-acters were laid bare. Mrs. M[ickle] has proved a narrow-minded selfish woman, her whole heart & mind so wrapped

9 An angel in Milton's *Paradise Lost* who, by means of his sword, caused everything to return to its proper shape.

in her children & *pocket*, as entirely to exclude all higher and nobler thoughts. The petty details of this speck of earth she owns occupies her whole mind. Her patriotism consists in "others doing their duty & bearing the labor & heat of the day, while she enjoys security." She has not been thankful for a single thing saved, but has complained of losing everything, being swept clean, because she has lost a few luxuries & has to economize. As to her faith in God, I have not seen a particle, &, if she is religious, I never saw children more shamefully ignorant of the most well known facts of Bible history. I have proposed to them, if they wished, to read with them an hour every Sunday & explain. They said yes—but I'll see what comes of it. Mrs. M[ickle]'s intellectual capacity has gone down a hundred degrees in my estimation since I found she could not appreciate Shakespeare & had never read half a dozen of his most celebrated plays & not more of the Waverly novels. She spoils every one of her eleven children outrageously; all do just as they please, & occasionally when the boys annoy her at table, she gives them a back-handed slap & tells them "go long from table." When company is here &, when I was considered so, every child is mum, but now they are like so many pigs—everyone grabbing at the nearest dish, quarrelling with those who have got more than they, calling half a dozen times loudly for what they want, &, if a servant does not attend instantly, screwing up a long whining cry immediately. Rebecca is thoroughly selfish & domineering— talks like a sand-hiller & is almost as much wanting in courtesy & refinement of manners at table as the rest, though she has been in Columbia at boarding school. The children wipe their faces & noses in the table cloth, help themselves to butter with their own knives, etc., hogs jowls are brought on table, grinning ghastly with every tooth still projecting. Dogs & cats eat under the table, & the kids often join them. To crown the whole, Mrs. M[ickle] nurses her baby before me & any man, white or black, that happens to be by, etc. Altogether, I am completely deceived in the idea of finding refinement & cleanliness in this house. The boys, elder as well as younger, need fine combs so sadly that I shrink from contact.

Matilda is the only unselfish one among the elder ones, & Robert is the only one who gives me a spark of satisfaction; he is a bright, merry hearted child, & quite intelligent; he is only seven, takes ideas readily & has improved very much, while Patrick Henry (a dreadful misnomer) is an incorrigible dunce. Moreover during the raid, disgusted with the everlasting fretting & quarreling at table which made me glad to leave, even when I had not exchanged a half dozen words with anyone. I took an opportunity in school when alone with Belton, Henry & Robert to try and persuade them to manlier ideas & to believe if they would be patient & ask quietly they would be waited on more readily. All promised to try, but Belton quarrels & cries daily & Henry often, while a glance from me will make Robert remember & be patient, & I have not heard him cry once.

And yet, these children are not bad by nature, but the parents' weakness and indolence has distorted everyone & nearly ruined them. She does not seem to realize the great moral and religious responsibility God has given her; she thinks only of the physical.

March 10
Thursday
[should
be 9]

Just before school, a servant told me my brother was passing in a wagon; I rushed downstairs, supposing it to be Edward or Alester, sick & returning from the army, but to my astonishment, met John, who had been two weeks from home. He had joined the militia just before the Yankees came & had fallen back with them to Flat Rock [N.C.] many miles above this, where some of the boys were captured. He escaped, being at the well, & had staid with some gentleman. The only thing from home he could tell me was that, before he left, he had buried a good deal of the silver & jewelry under the brick pavement of the store room. I persuaded him to stop & take some breakfast, &, as Mrs. M[ickle] said she could not sell me any potatoes as they were rotting, I begged & obtained a few for my darling baby. Next evening I received a message by the returning wagon that "all were well & doing well" and though sadly disappointed in not getting a letter, I felt sufficiently cheered to go over Saturday to dine at Mrs. Joe M[ickle]'s. . . . As it rained a little in the evening, they persuaded me to stay the night & until Sunday afternoon. The ladies are sociable and pleasant, & the children also; they came to meet me and talked freely as I like children to do.

Capt. [Solomon] Lorick was on a visit, & Mr. [John B.]

M[ickle] had just returned from a mule hunt about Sumter where he had seen cousin James B[landing] and Mr. C. Lucas & Dr. Barker from St. John's, who had left home at the approach of Foster's negro troops. Oh, it is anguish indeed to be obliged to fly from home & leave their families exposed to the power of such brutes—far worse than if they were the vilest whites. Those insolent negroes are the bitterest draught the Carolinians have yet had, or I think will have to quaff, from war's ruthless cup.

The above [March 4 entry] has been written at different times during the many lonely dreary hours I spend. Last Sunday [March 5] for the first time in a fortnight, on account of the constant rain & Yankees, I put foot to ground & utterly weary of myself, the house & its inhabitants, I wandered out directly after breakfast through unknown roads that seemed neverending, through rolling pine barrens, where no sound of life were heard, & blazed turpentine trees all that met the eye. I must have walked four miles & spent the rest of the day in my room save for the few minutes devoted to silent meals, when no one spoke to me, & I felt no desire to make the effort to say commonplaces, when my heart was full to overflowing with anguish. During the morning, while reading one of our grand chants & trying to hum the old familiar tune, the dreadful truth suddenly flashed on me & I felt in my heart for the first time that nevermore would we tread the aisles of our loved church nor hear those solemn hymns of praise chanted there. Homeless exiles we are now indeed in the bitterest sense, when our very graves & altars are profaned and ruined by the vilest of hands. We had always "hoped against hope" that the shattered remnant of our city would be preserved, but now I felt what utter destruction, as that of Jerusalem, awaited it, and the thought completely overwhelmed me.

March 11

That night I asked Liddy if she would like me to read the Bible to her at night; she said yes, &, when I had finished, she was very much obliged—the first word of thanks received since I've been here. She is much interested & always glad to hear.

Monday [March 6], Mr. [John] Starke & Mrs. [Harriet]

Lorick dined here. It was refreshing to meet two people who were not "whipped." Mr. [Solomon] L[orick] was on his way home from hiding but was going back to the army. He had been discharged on account of his right hand being severely injured. I walked home with Mrs. L[orick] in the afternoon & spoke to her very freely about the children & my dreariness here—in which she sympathized. For, she said she never could stay more than three days at a time here; it was so lonely. Her sister always was silent, & her many years of ill health had made her more indisposed for exerting herself even to control her children. All saw how she spoiled them. Her father, Dr. [John] Milling, did not allow his children to speak at table unless when spoken to & sent her to school so early that she tried the opposite extreme of which I suffer the fruit. I became so engaged in talking that I walked entirely home with her, without noticing it. In fact, it was a relief to talk & to know some one would appreciate my trials. She wanted me to spend the night, but, as I declined, she sent two maids with me; the moon rose, & I enjoyed my five miles walk very much. The air was deliciously balm & I felt cheered by the company of a young person, who has some spirit, though not intellectual.

March 14
Tuesday

Yesterday I drank a brief but delicious draught of happiness which seemed to give me a new lease on life. Just before school was out, a servant told me, as I thought, that my brother was out at the gate, sick & wanted to see me. I rushed down & met Edward, & before I recovered from my astonishment, saw cousin Willie &, as I withdrew from his embrace, found Willie Guerard near. It was if for the time I was transported to dear old Charleston. All were just from Camden. Willie G[uerard] had been in command of a scouting party including Edward for three weeks; had visited Columbia, Augusta and various other points, then obtained permission to stop in Camden, as he was very unwell. . . . Cousin Willie had started from Charleston just before the evacuation & was about Camden when he learned the Yankees were there, & lingered in the neighborhood till they left. He is on his way to join the Palmetto Guard, now infantry again, & the others to rejoin their company somewhere near Cheraw, where [Joseph] Wheeler gave [Judson] Kilpatrick's men a hard fight and

whipped them taking over 150 prisoners.[10] Gen Joe Johnston
is now in command & Beauregard second—[William J.] Hardee commanding the troops who evacuated the city & near
Cheraw, we believe all our forces are gradually falling back to
Charlotte where a stand is being made. Almost all of Hood's
army are here & all our relatives. Edward says he just missed
brother H[enry] lately, Dr. John Darby says he has been made
full surgeon.

Mother's family fared remarkably well through the fidelity
and good behavior of all the servants,—to my great surprise,
for I did not trust Judy's family. Some few things were buried
&, when the Yankees came, a great deal of the gentlemen's
clothing was given to the servants & concealed by them. Chloe
was active and showed presence of mind, pitching some of the
uniforms, etc. on the top of presses, where there [were] deep
hollows. All the silver forks and spoons on table were taken &
other things which the boys did not enumerate. They were
[there] Friday & Saturday spending the last night dancing in
the kitchen with the servants. The only provisions taken were
what were eaten while there. All seemed to have showed considerable presence of mind. Mary Hume [Holmes] was asleep
when they arrived & got up and put on various articles of
jewelry. [She] sent a silver cup to Nina & never remembered
several bottles of brandy, etc. cousin W[illie] had given her till
they were ransacking her trunk. When remembering she had
put them between it and the wall, as they pulled out the
clothes she threw them behind entirely concealing the bottles.
. . . [As] soon as that set left, [she] had them buried. Some
trunks they did not touch but twice set fire to a large chest in
John's [Holmes] room, destroying it, & twice to the wood
closet; fortunately they were discovered before much damage
was done.

I did not hear a fourth I wanted, for "the boys" came a little
after one & at first only intended remaining a few minutes.
But, I persuaded them to stay to dinner, then informed Mrs.
M.[ickle] who forthwith made preparations for a "company
dinner" a rare treat as clean faces, combed hair, silence &
genteel eating, silver forks, rice & pickles only appear at those

10 This skirmish took place at Monroe's Cross Roads on March 9, 10. It is
    popularly referred to as the the Battle of Kilpatrick's Pants because the
    Union general was so surprised he had to dress before he could respond.

few occasions. Mrs. Joe M[ickle] was here also, & I had so many to inquire about & so much to hear that I could hear but little of each. Rosa must have been staying at uncle John's ever since she came up. Now that I think of it, the Yanks went first in her chamber and took some of her jewelry, a few pieces of silver & her old watch & W.[illie] G.[uerard]'s which were lying in a drawer & cousin Beck's [Holmes] also. Lou [Davis] saved most of the silver by running & hiding it in Rosa's room after it had been searched. Her father's watch was demanded and given up. Uncle DeS . . . asked one man not to take all the silver from an old man who had lost their [*sic*] home, & it was returned as well as a silver cup cousin F[an] begged for. The Yanks did not reach either uncle John's or Mr. Elliott's plantations nor the Boykin settlement. Uncle Louis and cousin Sallie [DeSaussure] lost very little, but the latter broke 27 dozen of wine to prevent their getting it. Grandmother was staying with Mary Henry, who took off her valuable diamond ring & concealed it in her hair. . . . Fearing it might fall out, grandmother lent her one of her caps. The Yankees put their head in, said "Pooh, nothing but old women" & went off, taking only a little meat. Most of her bacon was at her mother's, & they swept her clean.

Mr. Bull set fire to Ashley Hall with his own hands rather than have it desecrated & destroyed by those vile negro-soldiers & went up to Cheraw. . . . In exploding the great Blakely gun on the battery,[11] a piece went through cousin Louis [DeSaussure's] house, & shattered it, & all that square on the Battery was burned by our own men. Truly all our family are indeed homeless. . . . About two thirds of Columbia is destroyed, & very many of our friends lost. . . . The officers of the three [banks] in Camden went in the swamp with all their valuables, & the wagon and party [were] captured. The Y[ankee]s broke open all the stores and told them to help themselves. . . . With the loss of the banks, Confederate money is not worth the paper it is printed on. No one will sell—only barter for provisions. Edward said he had been to Augusta & it was not evacuated then, nor had he heard of its being so since. It was at Aiken [that] Wheeler whipped Kil-

11 The Blakely gun was an English rifled gun which South Carolina imported for coastal defense. Smaller ones were favored by horse batteries.

patrick through the streets, so that the Yankees had no time
to steal, & Wheeler's men, who have been represented as almost as bad, only asked for food needed. . . .

Maria lost heavily of the few things she had carried up with
her—all her stock. No one knows where Emily [Ford] is. She
went to pay Kate Crawford a visit, on her way to Florence, and,
as the C[rawfords] went up to Chester, we hope she is with
them. Every tie of society seems broken, but most people seem
to be drawn nearer by their common misfortunes. In speaking of the fine houses destroyed, we happened to mention
Col. N. Pey's, when cousin Willie remarked it was a signal retribution. For, Rutledge had applied to Rutland, the agent or
children's guardian, to hire it and he drew from his pocket and
read his abruptly rude answer, "that he would make no contract for Confederate money"—that if he did, he would re-
quire $125,000 a quarter, with the right to break the engage-
ment at two days' notice. Had it been occupied by the Holmes,
it would have been saved. Edward says he saw Annie Heyward
who said Lou [Heyward] and herself had been compelled to
leave their residence and walk 16 miles to Augusta, where
they are living in a shanty. Wherever we turn the locusts have
swept. [John G.] Foster's troops have been all through St.
John's, and cousin Martha [DeSaussure] we hear, has lost all
her own and [her] children's clothing. In Columbia they tried
to undermine and blow up the New State House, but, finding
it too massive, contented themselves with destroying the nearly finished marble ornaments, slabs of great size and cost lying
around under sheds and the old State House. . . .

"The boys" left immediately after dinner, and I felt so
cheered by their visit as almost willing to endure a longer
exile here.

But "the fates have decreed otherwise," or rather the mine
was only awaiting a touch of gunpowder. Yesterday morning
I found the little wagon was going to town, and I sent a short
note home. Had the weather been fair and I not so recently
heard from home, I would have gone down, even though
Mrs. M[ickle] did not show any disposition to accommodate
me. School as usual was very unsatisfactory; lesson after lesson missed—Henry stupider than ever over figures. After
writing them daily on the slate and reading them there and in

March 15
Wednesday

the book and learning multiplication tables for days past, he has scarcely read a figure correctly. Or, if he did, a few minutes after, [he] could not tell it. I had striven patiently over and over, day after day, to make him learn to read them, but it was crab progress, worse and worse, all backwards, as he reads and spells. On the other side, Matilda [was] doing simple division in the same style, till my patience was exhausted. I had repeatedly told Henry he was a dunce, which he is, and made him sit down and study again, and, if I was very strict with him, he would then study and give me a good lesson. I told M[atilda] she was a dunce too, for, after so much labor, she did not yet know her multiplication—the reason she could not do her sums. I called Belton to look over his, and he commenced to cry. I felt really provoked and disgusted and told him, if he was my child, I would give him a good switching and thereby put a stop to his everlasting crying. All was faithfully reported to their mother and more added, while causes were left unexplained.

After supper came the crash—just before the wagon had come and brought me long letters from home and a mine of wealth in a large basket of books from Callie Perkins. I was in excellent spirits and had plunged right into one of the books, when Mrs. M[ickle] came in. . . . After some conversation about the Yankee doings, etc. related in my letter, it led the way to the subject I had been thinking of for some time, and had written mother thereon—That unless a portion of my salary was paid in provisions to mother, I would not remain. For, Confederate money is now in Camden, at least, perfectly useless for the necessaries of life, and, therefore, I was really giving away my time without recompense but useless paper. I thought, if my services were useful to her, I ought to be paid accordingly. The answer came as I expected, only with an unanticipated rudely addition. Mother had said lard or peas, in small quantities, would be very acceptable, and I had mentioned them. She said she could spare nothing, for she had just paid very heavily in lard and a cow and calf for two barrels of wheat flour (her character in a nut shell) and she could not supply Mrs. Lyes, her sister, who was needing provisions. She did not know about another year, as if anything could tempt me to remain here so long.

Then she launched out: "you have behaved very improperly in the school room, you have shown your temper there, and you have showed it before me." The children are perfectly disgusted and say there is nothing but "dunce and ignorance" all the time. You've hurt my feelings and called Rebecca dunce which I would never have stood from any teacher, etc. etc." I thought I had good reasons to be angry for the unparalled [*sic*] rudeness of the first part of the speech and the falsity of the last. But, I restrained myself somewhat, for I did not choose to forget myself, if she did, and answered that I was equally disgusted and had long been, and, if she had a carriage, I would return home the next morning—that I had never called Rebecca or the older boys dunces, though I had expressed my surprise at their ignorance of Bible history and many other equally well known facts, etc. I went on to explain the other items of accusation and found from what she said how one sided an account they had given (and she could not help seeing it too). Then she told me how Matilda, though telling me she understood her sums, went to the others and got them to do them for her—a pretty specimen of stupidity and deceit. She informed me Belton and Henry cried every morning and did not want to go to school, that the children did not like me any longer, found fault with the length of the lessons, and picked my whole plan of teaching to pieces. Yet [she] said she was perfectly satisfied with the children's improvement and that I had done my duty. I answered that she seemed a so much better teacher than I and found so much fault that I would leave, particularly as I had long been dissatisfied and found this anything else but an agreeable residence, (I did not enumerate my many causes of disgust) and that moreover the boys had twice openly set my authority at defiance, and she had taken no notice of it. On further talking, I found she knew nothing of Josie's rudeness and disobedience in which John followed just before the Yankee raid. But I told her plainly I intended to leave. She said she could not send me down—my friends would have to provide means. So, I will have to wait sometime longer. Such is the substance of the conversation. Had all other things been pleasant, or even was there refinement—Pooh, I am sick of the whole affair. She has tried to be entertaining since, by always sitting with me after supper and actually then and there and sometimes at table volunteering a few remarks. I would much prefer my book, but do penance by laying it aside, taking up my knitting and forcing myself to talk—oh for a table to write on, not the bed. . . .

March 19 & 20   Read Charlotte Elizabeth's deep spirit-stirring *Judae Captae* & with it Josephus' account of Titus' seige [*sic*] of Jerusalem— the former serving not only as an antidote to the venom of the traitor (whom at first I implicitly believed, never having heard him contradicted until she refuted and exposed his falsity from his own words in regard to the enormities of his country-men) but to lead me to "search the scriptures" more diligently, in regard to the remarkable fulfillment, to the minutest iota, of the events prophecied so many hundreds before as well as of the future restoration of the Jews, whom for a time she al-most makes me love, or at least admire, & reverence their undaunted and surpassing bravery, as well as sympathize most deeply with their anguish over the destruction of their holy city. Perhaps one reason may be because the "city of our love" has fallen also into the hands of a barbarous foe, who threatened its war scarred ruins with the fate of Jerusalem— while the aged men, the matrons & maidens are living and dying in exile, their hearts wrung with anguish, while the flower of our youth lie in unknown graves "on many a gory battle field" or pine, as weary captives in the prisons of their hated foe—tortured—not in the public arena where death could come but once, fearful as it was, but dying ten thousand deaths of bitter agony of heart, for the calamities of their people.

C.[harlotte] E.[lizabeth] bears aloft a beacon whose flash has already illumined many a hitherto dark page. It seems truly lit in the undying "flame of love" kindled towards God's pe-culiar people.[12]

March 21,   I have been reading Hugh S. Legare's Life and writings, or
22 & 23   rather "*living* in his society" and drinking in deep draughts of "nectar."[13] Before I only admired & honored him as one of

12 This entry appears in the end leaves of Volume III of the diary manu-script.
13 Hugh S. Legare (1797–1843) was editor of the *Southern Review* from 1828 until it went out of business in 1832. He was a states' righter and opposed the tariff but fought Calhoun's stand on nullification. He was a

our great men, one of those "intellectual heroes" who will forever stand as one of the grand monuments of our past, inciting us ever to the noblest deeds and thoughts. I have often stood before the elegantly chaste shaft erected to him in our beautiful "City of the Dead" with a reverent awe for the mighty dead, but the spell of his power never touched me till now. "The inner vail of his heart" and soul has been drawn aside and revealed all that was grand & beautiful. I love him for "the love he bore" not only to our beloved home, but to poor Uncle Edward [Holmes], amidst all the fascinations of the highest European society. I did not know until this morning, when I read one of his letters to uncle E.[dward] how very intimate they were, nor how he appreciated his fine qualities of head & heart. Mr. Legare in his fear for the results of Nullification (in which uncle E.[dward] was very prominent) uttered an unconscious prophecy fulfilled, now alas, while his old friend is there lingering out the sad remnant of his life, under negro-rule. "There is no subject that has a thousandth part of the interest this has for me." Dangers are around and above and within and below our poor little State—which may God preserve us from! I ask of Heaven only that the little circle I am intimate with in Charleston should be kept together while I live—in health, harmony and competence, and that, on my return, I may myself be enabled to enjoy the same happiness, in my intercourse with it, with which I have been hitherto blessed. We are (I am quite sure) the *last* of the *race* of South Carolina; I see nothing before us but decay & downfall—but, on that very account I cherish its precious relics the more. My ambition is dead and I think only of *repose* and social enjoyment and usefulness hereafter. Yet my heart sinks within me, often, when I think of what too soon may be, and I say in these touching words "Why should not my contenance be sad, when *the city, the place of my fathers' sepulchres, lieth waste, and her gates are burnt with fire.*" How true, and how melancholy, both as regards the city and the race of intellectual athlete[s]—[John C.] Calhoun, [George] McDuffie, W. C. Preston, [James L.] Petigru, [Thomas Butler] King,

---

member of the South Carolina legislature (1824–30), South Carolina attorney general, U.S. *chargé d'affaires* in Belgium (1832–36), U.S. Congressman for one term, and President Tyler's attorney general and briefly his secretary of state.

[Robert Y.] Hayne, [Stephen] Elliott, [Henry] Grimke, [Henry William] DeSaussure; etc. etc.

In another letter to Mr. Alfred Huger, so long our Postmaster General—and like uncle E.[dward] one of the few of his intimate circle now left (King, Preston & then Petigru having died since this cruel war—at least I think Mr. Preston has died within the past four years) he says—"Stephen Elliott, John Gadsden, & now Grimke is dead—just consider what an irreparable loss for so small a community, in the last five years, and that of men, the oldest of whom was only 58 and the others in what is considered, in Europe, as the very prime of life. The worst of it is that as such persons have never been produced anywhere else in America than in the low country of S.C. so that soil is worn out now and instead of these oaks of the forest, its noble original growth, is sending up, like its old fields left to run to waste, thickets of stunted loblolly pine half choked with broom grass & dog fennel. Take it all together there are few spectacles so affecting as the decay of our poor parish country, which I often think of even at this distance with the fondness of disappointed love; for I have never, since I could form any opinion on such matters, doubted of the immense superiority of Carolina society over all others on the continent, and now feel it more than ever."

These letters were written while Minister at Brussels, where his society was much sought, and he was loved and admired even by royalty. During Leopold's visit to England in 1843, he charged Mr. [Edward] Everett, our Minister, with a particular message to Mr. Legare "that they not only continued to remember and esteem him but sincerely love him." Alas he was cut off, mysteriously in the prime of manhood that very year.

The E. W. J.[ohnson] who wrote the sketch of his life, speaks thus "He now returned to what was ever his favorite habitation—his mother's house in Charleston. To that cultivated city the seat of all his boyish memories, of all those only local attachments which they of a temperament full of mediation and sensibility are sure to retain through life, he repaired, to form, between the studies which he was now to prosecute with increased ardor, the association with many loving and honoring such pursuits, and the occasional relaxation of a society, then (as probably yet) the most genial and elegant that we have ever known, a fresh affection for it, still fonder. It then joined to the intellectual refinement which but one of our cities (*Boston*!!!) possesses in an equal degree, an easy hospitality, a spirit of society, and a gay and graceful amenity of the manners which made it [a] still more charming abode. It was indeed, and we imagine must still be, the best-bred and (in an older sense of the word) the humanest town in all our country. Amidst its circles, Legare found for the first time, a lively congeniality with whatever a scholar's mind might seek for recreation or repose."

... Monday, I wrote mother a very long and full account of the disagreeable past scene [with Mrs. Mickle]. It was a relief to me to communicate it, for it had made me restless and dissatisfied, and I wanted advice whether from the depreciation of the currency it was worth my while to remain under such circumstances. I am not an impartial judge. For, besides not being able here to learn the real state of the currency and its prospects, etc., I am divided by two most contrary feelings— the interest in my own careful labor—though none in the materials (save Robert [Mickle]) and my indignation at the insult and injustice offered me, as well as my strong desire to be once more at home with my baby [Sims White], home friends, and congenial society. I cannot get away for want of an opportunity, and time has softened the first acute stings. I argue constantly with myself what is my duty, is it right for me to cast away this opportunity of doing good, even though I am unappreciated and uncared for, save so far as food and lodging goes. May I not have been expressly guided here as a school of trial for my own great faults of temper and character. Then I think of the Captain's [Haydon] rebuke and words, and [I] long for a draught from his ever-flowing fountain of pureness of heart and great intellect, so encouraging and elevating to mind and heart. If I could only talk to Isaac [White]—he understands my character, and with his generous heart and clear strong judgment, would soon cut the Gordian knot—when shall we meet again.

With the children and Mrs. M[ickle] I preserve my usual calm, cold, rather abstracted, silent manner, rarely speaking to one of the former out of school ... while keeping a strong restraint on not only my natural impatience, but [also] on tongue and eye, by which outward sign might be given of the

March 25
Saturday

feelings within. Each day brings its own trials, but Wednesday was the worst, when Rebecca for the first time—taking the initiative from her mother—was so insolent in manner, during the grammar lesson, that I told her, if she could not behave, she had better leave the room. . . . I saw her (rather than heard) [her] mutter "I won't." I thought another crisis inevitable, peculiarly unpleasant for me as being unable to leave when I wish. But I mastered myself and took no further notice, determined, if the children so dislike and fear me, that they shall respect me. I do my duty conscientiously and thoroughly and that will have to be its own reward.

Thursday night, when I came to bed, Liddy told me of a chance to send letters next day, and I sat up till half past eleven writing, finishing the letter to mother and writing to Callie P[erkins] without any consequent suffering from my eyes. Uncle H[enry]'s "collyrium" has indeed had magical effects, and I am cultivating a growth of eye lashes with as much care and solicitude as Benjie [Guerard] can give his "paint brush" as W[illie] G[uerard] calls it. Last night Rebecca came after supper for me to show her how to write some "notes from mythology" I had given her to do and it was the first time in weeks I've talked to her out of school. This morning [I] reread Dickens' little gem "The Cricket on the Hearth," while so doing, letters were handed me from C[allie] P[erkins] and mother had merely forwarded two from Willie and Alester, both over a month old, but the first direct news from them. . . . Allie wrote from some camp on the N.[orth] E.[ast] R.R. [and] said [that] in the city when the quartermaster's stores were thrown open to the poor people, or rather the N.E. depot where they crowded to get what was flung away, some powder caught on fire, and nearly 500 were killed or wounded. Oh it is fearful to think of the calamities poured out upon our beloved city [Charleston]. The greater part of it was burned when destroying cotton, the flames being so great that one could almost see to read on James Island. George Williams surrendered the city, and the Summervillians did the same, but the Yankees did not take possession for two days after—fearing treachery I suppose.

Callie P[erkins] says all their most valuable silver, clothing, jewelry, etc. had been sent away in different places in the country, fearing a raid only on the town (even the "little old trunk" of relics) and her father went into the woods with all his mules, horses, provisions, etc. and his and his sons' clothing. He was captured and lost all, but was released. Almost everything sent away [was] taken, while all the silver found at the house of course went. She has only two or three trifling articles of jewelry left of all her handsome sets. She was almost sick from terror and excitement, and her mother met an officer at the door and requested they would not disturb her sick daughter. Only one entered and that night three respectable officers slept there and protected them from the intrusion of some drunken creatures. To make her worse, for days, nothing was heard from or of her father, while it was reported her brother was captured, a flood of agony to them who so idolize that only son and brother. Fortunately mother did not hear till John's return, the report of his death, for, as it was, she was wretched about him. Sunday [I] spent reading Charlotte E[lizabeth]'s *Deserter*, every word of which was a keen home-thrust. May the Lord vouch safe me the blessing of his Holy Spirit. I also read *Truth & Falsehood*, an exposé of Roman Catholic methods of proselytism and commenced *Judah's Lion* for the 3rd time.

Monday Mrs. [Harriet] Lorick and Mrs. [Mary] Milling with her very well brought up children spent the day here, the latter and her little ones remaining till Tuesday afternoon. They told me Chatton's house and shop in Camden had been set on fire and destroyed together with the Seminary. . . . Many other attempts at setting fire have been discovered, either just in time or after some damage has been done, both in Camden and the surrounding country, keeping everyone in a constant state of anxiety and alarm. In the town, a strict patrol is kept, all suspicious persons taken up and Mr. [James] Dunlap, we hear, keeps watch alternately at home with his son. It is a terrible state to be in, some of the poor whites as much suspected as the negroes, for they were equally active in using Yankee license to rob. . . . Since the Y[ankee]s left, a good many things have been recovered from both classes by active search.

Dr. [James A.] Young has a few things for sale, but asks $15 for a box of matches, 10 for an indifferent cake of soap, but only 6 for a quire of paper. Dr. [Francis L.] Zemp asks a bushel of corn for a pound of Epsom salts, his mill by "The

Lake of Geneva" was burned, & almost all his large stock of medicines destroyed.

Rebecca [Mickle] arranged a Dutch Doll on Monday night, the best I ever saw, a pillow being dressed and placed in a low chair, with a hideous face marked out with soot & covered by a cap, while R[ebecca] thrust her hands from behind, gloved, to perform all necessary & very expressive pantomime. I was actually asked in with the others to see it.

When anyone dines here, it is refreshing to see the cleanliness & comparative order maintained at table. Mrs. Milling's children are such contrasts to these.

March 27   William Mickle, son of Mr. Joe M[ickle], dined here today, as he did on Saturday—a red-headed youth of nineteen, said to be quite talented, but he has given me no opportunity of judging as he spends most of his time with the boys. I wonder if they've given him their *unvarnished* sketch of me & made him avoid me too—well, no loss to me when I have such fascinating companions as my books. He has been discharged from the army on account of a wound in the ankle, received after only four or five months service.

March 31   ... The Yankees treated the Winnsboro people far worse than the Camden, leaving them so nearly destitute of provisions they had to send to the neighboring district for relief. Several places in town were also set on fire, which so excited cousin E.[lizabeth] that she was removed to the hospital out of danger where she gently sank to rest. Their household were somewhat protected by Gen. [Henry W.] Slocum & his staff staying there.... Hattie W[hite] says her aunt Louisa was "swept clean" both at the town house & plantation, where a year's provision was taken or destroyed. The Yankees were very rude to the girls, stole a quantity of house linen & other things, including some jewelry & silver not buried, &, after ransacking the house, put their bombazine bonnets & nicest articles of dress under piles of clothing, then trampled on them. But the girls held their heads so high & talked so boldly that the wretches left the house in wrathful disgust, vowing vengeance on them.... For many nights, they never even loosed their dresses—when exhausted, flung themselves on the floor, fearing fire. But, she says, so long as hominy & good spirits are left, we can bear all our losses. . . . Our dear minister, Mr. [W. B. W.] Howe, was ordered to leave the city because he would not pray for Lincoln. He is a New Englander by birth but [is] bound heart and soul to the beloved home of his adoption & wife. . . . Cousin W.[ilmot] G. DeS[aussure has] just been up, hunting Gov. [Andrew G. Magrath]— to try and reorganize militia for protection of lower part of the country. Negroes of course everywhere much demoralized. Buck Hall & other "old families" homesteads, redolent with a thousand memories, [are] destroyed.

Mother's letter is long in regard to the subject of my leaving & seems to favor it as I do not find my residence here agreeable. [She] had not yet been able to obtain uncle Louis' advice as I wished. Still I am undecided. I want to go, for there is certainly nothing to compensate me but the gradual improvement of the children. In the fruits of my labor I'm interested, not in them, while their want of soap, water & fine tooth combs almost nauseates me at time, & certainly matters will not improve with warm weather, while the undone food I'm obliged to eat at every meal produces indigestion, constant headache, & lassitude. But I really pity the ignorance of the children, & yet I know they will not reward me for the pains bestowed. They are like logs, which can be shaped, but are incapable of receiving & propagating a grafted idea. Robert is the only one who "takes an idea" & uses it readily.

Then I cannot carry out my plans, because their mother is constantly interfering, so I think I'll let her bear the consequences of her own mismanagement & meddling.

Messrs. [Jacob L.] Shuford & [Claudius H.] Pritchard held service at the little Methodist chapel—the latter preaching a most excellent, thoroughly practical, sermon to the negroes from Jer.[emiah] 8.22 "Is there no balm in Gilead? Is there no physician there? Why then is not the health of the daughter of my people recovered?" drawing all his illustrations from daily life, till as they afterwards said themselves, all were able to understand clearly. And yet . . . [he used] such excellent language as showed him to be far superior in intellect & education to Mr. Shuford, whose rant, snuffle & bald sermon had rather excited my risibilities, the first time. But Mr. P[ritchard] was generally calm & distinct in his delivery. Mr. Shu-

April 2
Sunday
afternoon

ford gave the final prayer, in the usual rant, eliciting numberless groans. I have no doubt that Methodists do a great amount of good among the negroes, judging by the home thrusts he gave them about lying, stealing, cursing, quarreling, etc. and alluding to the Yankees as "sent by the devil" and all the losses, which all should try to bear like Job. "The Lord gave & the Lord hath taken away, blessed be the name of the Lord." I overheard Emily & Penelope discussing the sermon, and all expressed great pleasure, while the former applied it practically. I was as much interested as amused at their theological discussion & biblical knowledge, which proved however that good seed had been sowed and was bearing fruit. Liddy also talked to me about it.

During the morning Rachel, a most respectable old Virginia maumer belonging to the Millings, came up to my chamber to see me. I could not help thinking how much more interest the servants show in me than the whites. She inquired particularly how I was pleased and getting on, for she seemed to have taken a fancy to me the first time she saw me. So, I gave her a slight sketch, at which the old woman shook her head & said it "was not right." She is among the very few who wear the respectable & becoming handkerchief turban, so familiar to low country eyes, and she looked so homelike it did me good to see her. The other negroes at church were all in the most ludicrous & disgustingly tawdry mixture of old finery, aping their betters most nauseatingly—round hats, gloves & even lace veils—the men alone looking respectable. How much better in every way a plain, neat dress for the working classes, as in other countries, & indeed among our country negroes formerly. If I ever own negroes, I shall carry out my father's plan & never allow them to indulge in dress. It is ruin body and soul to them.

Mr. and Mrs. Joe M[ickle] & Mrs. [Harriet] L[orick] came over to church, & I walked half way home with them. The evening was delightful & I in [good] spirits at the prospect of a speedy return home, for Mr. L[orick] took letters down for me. William M[ickle] had staid since Friday afternoon here and the only words I had exchanged with him were good morning & good evening, & none with anyone else saving Mrs. M[ickle], till on the way to church, a few to Rebecca. Such is my interesting life here. What a wonderful transformation soap & water, brushes, & genteel clothes make—I hardly recognized Mrs. M[ickle] & the little boys. The girls I had seen before in "full feather"—R[ebecca] as awkward as a "bear in petticoats" in her trailing black dress. In the morning, she wore an ankle short dress & blue bow! The elder boys walked part of the way with W[illiam Mickle] then turned back to avoid being with me.

When I returned, I got hold of the last Camden *Journal*, a miserable bantling, suddenly grown rich on the decease of its venerable superiors, and appearing as a double sheet containing extracts from a N.Y. paper, *Tribune* I think, of the Yankee reception and doings in our beloved Charleston. Every vein throbbed and nerve tingled over the chuckling avowel of the insults heaped upon the helpless old men, women and children left there. We expected the worst, but oh, my heart bleeds for the relatives and friends compelled to endure the horrors of their accumulated insults. But thank God, the Yankees confess they found but two openly avowed Unionists there—a Daly for one—who kept the shoe store where I dealt so long—while a few sneaking contemptible, drivelling wretches, who, as the Y[ankees] truly said, dare not call their souls their own, pulled their new masters in a corner and tremblingly whispered "they had always been for the Union, but had not dared show it." May such dastards receive their dues. Despicable as is the Yankee, he too despises such loathsome reptiles.

Negroes of course garrison the place & are encouraged to insult their former masters by every petty way malignity can suggest, while a saturnalia reigns among "the colored ladies" who presented several flags & are considered "prettier than those of other cities, save New Orleans." Yankee women are invited to hasten to come and enlighten the young ideas of Africa, no doubt with a similar result to their Beaufort experiment.[14] O Heavens, the mind and heart sickens over the revolting thoughts—miscegenation in truth, & in our city! Meantime, the unhappy remnant of the chivalry of the past

14 Union forces took early control of the Sea Island region of South Carolina and here, while the Civil War was still raging, conducted an experiment in bringing former slaves into freedom. On January 16, 1865, General W. T. Sherman set aside abandoned lands for black settlement. President Andrew Johnson restored the land to the former owners early in Reconstruction, and the experiment collapsed.

are ordered to enroll their names at the provost marshal's and take the oath, displaying the hated Union flag conspicuously about their premises or no protection will be afforded nor passports given. If these orders are complied with, protection from robberies, etc. will be given. Oh, which will these helpless people do—which will they do. Uncle E[dward] is constantly in my mind, poor old man—where uncle James is, I do not know—& "our good doctor's" [Louis DeSaussure] family is there. . . .

The correspondence between Sherman & Hampton—now Lieut. Gen.—in regard to some Y[ankee]s who were caught and hung in Fairfield and Chester, is worthy of both. Sherman says he hears a certain number of his men have been "murdered" & writes to say he concludes it was not by Hampton's orders but warns he will retaliate by a like number, &, as he has 1,000 prisoners, he thinks he "can hold out" as long as Gen. H[ampton] can. The latter hurls his own word murderer in his teeth as true in such a case & informs him *he* will hang *two* for *one*, commencing with *officers*; those men were caught burning private dwellings, & he hoped to God every one such would receive his death from the old men and boys. He goes on to denounce him for firing on Columbia, filled with women & children, without notice, &, after its surrender, laying it in ashes, leaving thousands homeless and starving, while, wherever his army had camped, desolation & defilement worse than death had followed. In the same paper, a letter from a gentleman in Liberty Hill, where they staid a week, corroborates every particular, in one instance, a servant saving her young mistress by taking her place, & another servant's death being caused by their brutality in her advanced pregnancy. I told Liddy of this, & she said that few know what had taken place at Dr. [John] Milling's plantation, because the negroes were so ashamed they could not bear to tell. The wretches staid there a week & gave themselves loose rein in the most indecent manner without the men daring to interfere to save their wives. Thus these wretches have sown hatred among the blacks as well as whites.

April 7   I left Mrs. Mickle's. I had daily watched and waited for some equipage to bring me home, but, none coming, I concluded

mother was unable to procure one. . . . At last, I determined
to ask Mrs. M[ickle] for her little wagon which it was her duty
to have offered before. I rather feared a refusal or excuse of
some kind & anticipated another unpleasant scene, but fortunately she took it quietly, merely saying that perhaps after I
had paid a visit home, I would be willing to return. But that I
as quietly negatived. As the next day was not convenient to
her, I waited till Friday morning. As usual, my breakfast was
undisturbed by a word, & the seven boys trooped off directly after without least notice of me, while the girls took to the
garden only coming as I stepped in to shake hands. The servants had all expressed regret at my leaving, & I think Liddy
& Phillis really were fond of me, both promising to send me
fruit when in season. The weather was doubtful, and it sprinkled on my way down, but I really enjoyed the ride & the
sense of freedom once more.

Of course, my arrival was a great surprise, but I received a
greater one in meeting first cousin John [Holmes] and, as I
stepped indoors, cousin Willie with his arm in a sling, having
received a flesh wound in his right arm at Bentonville [N.C.] a
few days after joining the P[almetto] G[uard]s. He had only
been at home two days. Six Holmes had been in that fight,
and he the only one wounded. Truly God has been good to
our family. Cousin J[ohn] has been sick ever since last August
with chill & fever, typhoid pneumonia, & chill & fever again.
[He] was surgeon in Fort Sumter at the time of the evacuation, &, instead of being blown up, orders were given to put it
in the best order, leaving it cleanly swept, as a monument of
Southern skill, perseverance, industry and endurance, under
the daily bombardment of many months. It had five or six
very heavy guns, some rifled, bearing the channel, which were
of course spiked, & was stronger than in its prime of beauty;
500 men could have held it against 10,000, but alas God has
laid us very low and abased our pride. Every earthly support
has been struck from beneath our trembling feet during the
last few days.

 . . . Sims [White] remembered me & had learned to talk a
great deal during my absence. I sleep with Carrie, & for the
first few nights, I could scarcely sleep from the whirl of mind
produced by the flood of news of friends & acquaintances

which poured on me, besides the idea of being at last able to clasp my little darling, & I lay with one of his hands in mine or my arm over him.

On Sunday at church, I received such warm, pleasant greetings from friends and pupils, that it made me more glad than ever to get home, &, when I met uncle Louis, he expressed such approbation of my letter, which mother had read him, & of my leaving, that I felt quite satisfied. . . . Each day has made me more glad that I did so. Monday morning came rumors of a large body of [John G.] Foster's troops, marching on Sumter, then through Clarendon and Stateburg up here, to destroy the immense quantity of rolling stock & commissary stores and ammunition run up on this road for safety, as the other roads were threatened. We had a few troops scattered about, & breastworks were immediately thrown up at Boykin's mill & various other roads leading here to try to keep them away. Everyone was in a state of painful anxiety from uncertainty & dread of the black troops being let loose on us, and, as we heard all clothing not carried off was destroyed, everywhere persons were trying to conceal it in lofts and out of the way places. We had to borrow a ladder &, through the ceiling of the entry closet, carry boxes and bundles into the unfinished attic. Of course, the servants could not help knowing, & we concluded to keep the little ones away & trust the older ones, so Patty, Louis & Philander, cousin W[illie]'s boy, put the things away we packed. Everything was done so hurriedly & so many changes made that no one knew where to find exactly what they wanted, &, consequently, frequent taking down & putting up occurred, as days passed by. . . . Everywhere was the same tale; burying also going on stealthily, & numberless cute hiding places invented that would have baffled even a Yankee. I am almost afraid to mention what & where, so various are the mischances of this war, and indeed I would not write before, for fear this might be carried off.

Our chief anxiety was about the gentlemen. Each day & almost each hour brought so many various rumors of the proximity of the enemy. Cousin W[illie] was to go to the Hospital for protection, but did not wish to go till absolutely necessary, as he was still sick and helpless. John was to hide in the woods, & cousin John [Holmes] went to stay a day or two at Mary

Henry's with grandmother & cousin Beck [Holmes], Mary having been persuaded to go to her mother's but she feared her house would be burned if left uninhabited. However, hearing the Yankees had left Sumter, he went down with Jamie Blanding, who had brought off his father's mules and horses. We feared they would be caught. One day we would hear we had force enough to keep the enemy away, the next that they were within a few miles of town, the trouble being want of trusty scouts, who would see with their own eyes and tell what they knew & not trust to report. These militia readily took fright. Matters were quiet enough for the girls to dress our church for Easter, which was most tastefully and beautifully done with natural flowers, and we went to church.

Monday the enemy were so near, cousin Willie went to the hospital & sent Philander to ask for a written permission to secrete himself while the Yankees were here, which I gave him & he went off. Then John, who had previously been for two or three days guarding stores across the river, [left]. Late in the afternoon, it was so quiet I had half a mind to go to walk, but seeing a man pass on horseback, I ran to ask the news. "The Yankees are in town & I cant [*sic*] stop." We all dressed to receive them & sat on the front steps to await them but were not insulted by their presence. Soon after, we heard sounds as of knocking down houses and fences, and, when Dudley came in at dark, he said they were all encamped in the park & were cutting fences for fuel. He had been with them since the day before & said orders had been given that not a man should leave camp and picquets [*sic*] been put to keep order. Everything was quiet & so were we, only we resolved not to go to bed, as some might stray in, so we took turns to sit up & watch. But those who took the chairs generally indulged in naps also. We could not imagine how the Yankees could get in without some further notice from the guns of our men, but found afterwards they had divided & some taken a different road from the expected one. It is almost absurd to pretend to write up a journal in such times as these, for each day brings such startling rumors and incidents that the brain is bewildered by the rush of events. We live in a whirl of excitement, and all things are unsettled and uncertain. I will have to try merely to jot down the most remarkable incidents as I remember them.

The Yankees only staid one night here, the 17th, being very much afraid of a surprise from our men & put out strong pickets, barricading some of the streets, etc. One thing which contributed to make them so uneasy was the confidence exhibited, they said, by the ladies who sat at the windows or on the steps to see their entrance. While in Sumter, every house was shut up. The Yankees came in, in splendid order, 14 abreast, singing Methodist hymns, the negro troops last, with their "class leaders" from the city. The whites encamped in the park, the negroes at the lower end of the town & there, where few guards were placed, they committed some gross outrages—violating a young lady at Mrs. Baxley's & behaving so dreadfully that she shrieked for help & guards came & caught one. They also entered the Burnets, pillaging & behaving so insolently that they called for a guard, but they also made their escape. Gen. [Edward E.] Potter made Mr. Markley Lee's his headquarters, &, when an officer came in to announce some disorder, he said, "wherever we go that Massachusetts regiment gives us trouble." And afterwards, when news of the armistice was conveyed to him, he said, if he was sure it meant peace, he would restore all the negroes, for they did not want them, only wanted to starve us out.

A regular camp meeting was held among the negro troops, of course attracting crowds. . . . Tremendous excitement prevailed, as they prayed their cause might prosper & their just freedom be obtained. Great numbers of servants went off from town really crazy from excitement & the parade, as well as the idea of going to Charleston in carriages. Poor deluded creatures, two or three miles from town, their equipages were destroyed, their bundles of clothing having been previously thrown out, & they were marched on, their road traced by broken wagons, dead animals, bundles, drowned infants (15 being found in one pond, thrown by their mothers from exhaustion) & dead women & children. Cousin John [Holmes] had gone to Sumter before they arrived here & said gentlemen . . . had seen these things [and] told of some others he saw himself. At Wright's Bluff, two flat loads of women & children were drowned under circumstances of great barbarity, & they tried to force another load, but they refused, some, taking to the woods, were fired upon & three made their escape to Sumter & told it. Another gentleman says he saw dozens of little negroes all under 12 sitting crying from fright, starvation, & helplessness by the roadside. But, I could fill this book with their fiendish deeds & the heroism & spirit of the Southern women under such calamities as have swept over our land—fragile women, left without a servant, as Mary Boone was, cooking & washing without a murmur. Louis & Joe went off from here, & we believe Mary & several others would have done so, save that they got [started] too late & were turned back by our men. Chloe & Judy do not deny it, but the former said "if she had known in time that her son Thomas was there, she would have gone, but she was carrying cousin Willie's breakfast to the hospital & had a silver spoon, &, if she did go, she did not want to have what belonged to other people." All have behaved very well since, especially Chloe.

The rolling stock had been carried on the tressle [*sic*] work & was there burned by the Yankees. The commissaries knew they could not be saved, for our force was too small to divide, yet let it burn rather than let the citizens have the stores. The grossest mismanagement has existed everywhere in the Commissary & Quartermaster's departments,—our men starving while immense stores were destroyed by the enemy. On the 20th, we heard Lee's army had surrendered [April 9, 1865], being surrounded & starving after constant fighting, only about 20,000 making their escape.[15] It was a crushing blow, and I wept as if I had lost a dearly loved friend, not violently, but as if stunned by the shock. The terms learned later are extremely honorable—officers retaining their side arms & all their private property & to be paroled. . . .

[John B.] Gordon made a speech to his division, which left not a dry eye among his men. As our men filed out to stack their arms, they bitterly cursed the Yankees from the depths of their suffering hearts, yet not one word of insult was returned. Even they were awed by such bravery & heroism as Lee's army had shown, & they were loud in praise of Lee and his men. The Yankees wanted our men to take the oath to fight the French, for a foreign war is staring them in the face, & a few of Lee's men did so but almost everyone is strongly opposed to that; we would rather help the French.

15 According to the parole papers dated April 9, 1865, Lee had a total of 28,231 men under his command when he surrendered.

April
22, 1865
↔
April
7, 1866

Surrender and Reconstruction

April 22
Saturday

News arrived that Lincoln had been assassinated at Ford's Theatre in Washington, (after shooting him, the man sprung out brandishing a dagger exclaiming, "Sic Semper Tyrannus" "Virginia is avenged") and that the same night, April 11th [should be April 14], Seward had been stabbed in several places & his son mortally wounded.

It all seemed so theatric and improbable that for many days we could not believe it till confirmed on official authority. The following Wednesday we were still more confounded & bewildered by hearing that negotiations for peace were arranged between the generals on the terms that we were to go back into the Union on the footing we had previously been, all our rights, privileges, property & negroes as far as possible, on condition we would fight the French.

To go back into the Union!!! No words can describe all the horrors contained in those few words. Our souls recoiled shuddering at the bare idea. What can ever bridge over that fearful abyss of blood, suffering, affliction, desolation, and unsummed anguish stretching through these past four years. The blood of our slain heroes cried aloud against such an end —as if end it could be. Peace on such terms, is war for the rising generation. We could not, we would not believe it. Our Southern blood rose in stronger rebellion than ever and we all determined that, if obliged to submit, never could they *subdue* us. We knew our armies were surrounded by Sherman, Sheridan, [George] Stoneman & Grant, while our men & horses were starving & the officers were winking at the men leaving. An armistice of 40 days had been agreed upon after Lee's surrender, while negotiations were going on.[1] & the surrender of Johnston's army was inevitable. However, though everyone talked about public events, no one tried to speculate on our future, such sudden & unexpected darkness had fallen upon our prospects. Everyone seemed to cast thought aside & while patiently waiting a ray of light, to try to enjoy the present reunion of friends.

[Today] was Eliza's birthday & most unexpectedly Isaac [White] arrived on "Mona" accompanied by a four mule wagon & two servants; cousin Beck [Holmes] & grandmother came in to dine & we had a very pleasant family party—15 grown persons & the two children. Rosa also came in to see us & give an account of their excitement & adventures during the Yankee raid. Though the enemy were within 1½ miles off & on three sides, they never reached them, nor Mr. H. Boykin's plantation, nor Mr. Elliott, & though a fight took place on uncle John's [DeSaussure] plantation, our men pressed them so hard that, though they spent one night there, no negroes were carried off & but little disturbed.

April 25
Tuesday

. . . The Yankees had kept uncle James [Holmes] a prisoner on the flagship on Cooper river because he was persuading everyone there not to take the oath. They kept him two or three weeks & then turned him loose in the city, as they could do nothing with him. But Dr. [Henry] DeS[aussure] had to take it to save his family from starving was the remark, & almost everyone else had taken it. Many persons had gone to the city having lost all on their plantations or fearing to remain unprotected there.

April 26

Cousin Willie & family left with Isaac May 2nd. Edward arrived same day on a mule bringing the confirmation of Johnson's [Johnston] surrender to Sherman on the same terms as Lee and thus all our hopes are blasted by one fell blow. Oh,

End of
May

---

1 No such armistice agreement was made between Lee and Grant.

the bitter flood of anguish and humiliation which each day had brought. Anarchy and chaos seemed to rule everywhere as our ship of State foundered, & I felt as if I could not bear to record the disgrace of my country and my state.

Edward's departure the following Sunday for Maria's [Scriven Holmes] was followed by Alester's arrival that evening, mere skin and bone from chill & fever, having walked over 60 miles and lost all save what was on his back. E[dward] had not been with the main army, been impressing horses in N.C. consequently not directly paroled, and, though Allie was, both talked of going to the Trans-Mississippi, where the President [Jefferson Davis] was trying to make his way with a cavalry guard of 3000 men and a large quantity of specie. I felt as if all hope was not lost when our gentlemen were still willing to endure all rather than yield. But, when Willie & DeS Garden arrived during the next two days and showed how impossible it would be to break their parole or for a handful of men to oppose the whole power of the victory flushed North even if our cavalry who had escaped surrender, could reach the Trans-Miss., when too they showed the corruption that seemed to exist everywhere and the greater as the rank ascended—everybody seeming to consider the breaking up of our government and army, the opportunity for a "grab game" each striving to seize and appropriate what they could of public stores & property, while they in turn were mobbed and robbed by the town & country people—villages sacked in Yankee style by lawless mobs, and every man returning from the army on mule or horse, having to guard his animals & himself with loaded weapons—my heart sunk at the fearful picture & we could not but acknowledge the bitter, humiliating, truth, which our boys openly declared, that we had showed we were incapable of self-government. With all our endurance & heroic courage, our desolations and afflictions, that national lesson has yet to be learned. Oh! God, will future years of oppression as a conquered people chasten and teach us the needful lesson, and shall we ever again be permitted to put it into practice? Alas, the future is very, very dark.

DeS [Garden] & Willie left on Wednesday, the former for Stateburg, & W[illie] of course for home. He had not heard from M[aria] for three months &, fearing the worst, was very low spirited, though determined to go right to the plough to support his family. Instead of brother Henry, DeS brought a letter written in the depths of distress, crushed by our countries [*sic*] wreck, inexpressibly wretched about his family (having heard of a raid there but having received no tidings from Sidney for months & not knowing whether they had suffered) penniless (with the exception of the silver dollar & 10 or 15 cents received by each soldier) on a broken down horse, he had no means of getting home save with the brigade and thus had to pass by us though yearning to meet us after six years separation, & not knowing when we should meet again. Alex Hume came next & then Isaac, but without Capt. Haydon and his sisters as we expected, they having remained in Columbia. About the same time, returned Charlie DeS[aussure], & uncle C[harles Rutledge Holmes]'s son Charles, Harry [DeSaussure] & cousin Louis [DeSaussure], the latter profoundly depressed. As he said, "we only ask the humble privilege of fighting." Though thankful to see all safe, how could we be glad to see them when the cause was so humiliating, heart-rending. And then each day as they came, homeless, penniless, clothesless, with the past an awful quivering wreck, and the future a blank whose gloom was only made deeper by memory of former happiness & peace and the anticipation of greater wrongs and suffering, added another pang. All talked of emigration somewhere beyond Yankee rule. That would be comparatively easy now for single men, but what a living death would exile be, away from all that made life dear, & while their families were left under the hateful tyranny of our foes. For married men, emigration is easy to plan, but hard to carry out. Money is the first needful and who has any or means of transportation. All feel that whatever they might be able to do in the future, for many months at least, they have to sit down passively & wait to learn the course to be pursued towards us. As Carolinians we expect to fare worse than other states. This state of utter passiveness without a thing to do to support themselves & families, compelled idleness & gloom before as well as behind, is dreadful to our gentlemen, a wearing of life out by inches. . . .

Dr. W[hite] [came and] said the Yankees had visited his house in Pinopolis 13 times. The last, his wife was absent, and furniture, clothing, books, doors & windows were broken, torn or carried away, all blankets, quilts, etc. & every particle of meat & poultry [were taken]. But fortunately [they] neither burned the house nor took his corn. [He] says everything is now quiet there, but [there is] much lawlessness on Cooper river. He made our blood almost curdle with grief and horror over the foul murder of Dr. Tom Prioleau, who went to visit his plantation & spent the night, but never woke again; his throat was cut from ear to ear. So beloved & with such a large young family and to be cut off in the very prime of life.

McKenzie Parker was killed at Anderson most wantonly by the Yankees who sacked the town. The villagers did not dream of their being Yankees, thought they were deserters and tories who had committed great outrages at other places. . . . A party of cadets & young men, McK[enzie] among them, said they would go out and see what they could do to stop them. The Y[ankees] ordered them to surrender, & still deceived as to who they were, the boys refused & were fired upon, McK[enzie] dying in a few minutes. The Y[ankee]s expressed great regret, but Rev. John E.[lliott], who witnessed it, said it was a needless murder. Poor McK[enzie], he was such a fine boy in every way, just growing up to assist his mother.

Uncle James has taken the oath at last. He was over a fortnight as prisoner, & [ex-] Gov. [William] Aiken twice went to see him to urge him to yield—at first without effect. But the second time, uncle Edward sent word he was ill, & uncle J[ames] was so agonized at the idea of aunt C[harlotte] being left defenceless among lawless negroes that he yielded, telling the Y[ankee] captain at the time, that he would rather he would shoot him dead. . . . He said he had bitterly regretted it ever since, but perhaps, it has been all for the best, as everyone has to swallow the same nauseously bitter pill. . . . There was a little specie with which uncle James has paid up the taxes on the houses & lots of the various members of the family. Aunt C[harlotte] & himself live in *one* room in his own house with a few old pieces of furniture, drawing rations of a peck of rice or grist apiece a week and bringing it home himself. Our Louis run [*sic*] away from the Y[ankees] & went to him, expressing his regret at leaving home, and asking to be taken to wait on them for his food. Their own servants were in the yard, but doing very little, & he said he intended they should pay rent for their rooms, or move out, as he intended hire of rooms in house & yard to maintain him. He found a therapeutic chair & a few other articles at the Yankee general's next door & claimed them, whereupon they were sent over, & he knows where the old bookcase and books are and thinks he can get them—a single old revolutionary relic.

The Alex G[adsden]s, being burned out, are living in cousin C[harlotte]'s rooms in Aiken Row, Minerva & Maria being devoted to them & actually feeding them for days after the fire. But old Agrippa turned against them, the old, favored family servant, whom they had let go up to the plantation, because he could be more comfortable there. Billy, the boy, formerly so careless & saucy, proved true as steel. He was sent up to Santee to try to get some provisions, but Agrippa refused to let any come & had dug up & distributed all the silver to the other negroes. Billy, by threats of telling the Y[ankee]s and their taking it, made them give up all, & he managed to carry down every piece to his mistress. Such faithfulness "among so faithful few" deserves to be recorded—also that Lizzie's [Gadsden] maid, of similar character, still does all she can for her.... Uncle E[dward]'s Charlotte, the last [person] one would have supposed capable of such thoughtfulness and real delicacy, brought very humbly and respectfully her little boy to Lizzie & asked her to teach him (her only pay scholar) & L.[izzie] says she believes it is really done with a view to help her, knowing now she has lost her property. Her other little scholars are Dr. [Henry] DeS'[aussure] children & other friends, taken as a source of interest & a return of kindness shown her....

On Good Friday [April 14] the Y[ankee]s had a grand Union glorification, "Bob Anderson" returning to raise the old flag over the glorious old fort [Sumter], which he had been compelled to surrender—then a long procession of his colored brethren to a hall where [Henry] Ward Beecher held forth[2]—various other fooleries, ending in a "promiscuous" ball at Mr. William Middleton's fine residence on South Bay—Grace Church, the only Episcopal church open—Rev. *Mercier Greene* officiating, and a promiscuous crowd attending—fit priest for such an assembly—but we excuse him on the score of his utter emptiness and poverty. Late arrivals from the city say the

2 Beecher was pastor of Plymouth Congregational Church in Brooklyn, New York, and a leading abolitionist speaker.

really respectable class of free negroes, whom we used to employ as tailors, boot makers, mantua makers, etc., won't associate at all with the "parvenue free," but have the Orphan House Chapel (the O.H. itself being now for juvenile colored orphans) as a place of worship, Mr. Joseph Seabrook preaching. They are exceedingly respectful to the Charleston gentlemen they meet, taking their hats off & expressing their pleasure at seeing them again, but regret that it is under such circumstances, enquiring about others, etc.

But all Mat. Fuller's native insolence has shown itself fully. James Gibbes & some others were accustomed to employ him to get up club dinners, but discharged him from his frequent intoxication; thereupon, he got a guard [and] caught, tied & beat Mr. G[ibbes] in his own house, severely. Mrs. G[ibbes] who had gone down to consult Dr. [Eli] Geddings, rushed across the street to the Yankee generals at Judge [Mitchell] King's, for assistance, & [she] fell dead on the threshold. What an awful picture of the degradation and ruin of our fair city. And yet, some at least punish negro insolence. An adopted daughter of Mr. Legring wrote him a negro had walked in & informed her he had long been in love with her & had now come to marry her; in her indignation & wrath, she stepped to the window & called a passing Y[ankee] officer, who went in & blew the negroes [*sic*] brains out before her.

An extensive and well planned insurrection was gotten up among the negro troops, who were to destroy the Yankees in the forts, and the other negroes all the white men in the city, intending an African instead of Yankee colony. But it was discovered, and 100 ring leaders hung.

. . . [Moultrie Dwight] found 40 of his father's negroes . . . anxious to get home. He applied to Gen. [John P.] Hatch to know whether he could take them. Hatch told him he not only gave permission but would afford him every facility for removing them, that, after May 15th, no rations would be issued negroes & all not belonging there would have to leave the city.

The gentlemen say the Yankees are like the man who bought the elephant, they don't know what to do with their brethren, since they've made them free.

No white man is allowed to be out in the streets of

Charleston after ten at night. Gen. Lee & his army were treated with greatest respect by the Yankees: Grant would not receive his sword, saying Lee was too brave a man who had been
overpowered by disparity of numbers, not conquered. He
asked Lee how many muskets all told he had had all winter
around Petersburg & Richmond. 32,000 said Lee. If anyone
else had told me so, rejoined Grant, I would have said it was
false, but it is *you* and I believe it. I had 120,000 infantry,
10,000 cavalry & 20,000 artillery.[3] The Yankee officers all
stood bareheaded around Lee, he alone covered, and the
men cheered as loudly for him as for Grant, while our men
laid down their arms, cursing their enemies from the depths
of bitterly wrung hearts, to their faces. The Yankees answered not a word, &, when they afterwards mingled among
our men, they did not utter a single insulting word. They
feared the lion even in chains & never went about singly—
too deeply rooted is Southern hatred. Oh what bitter agony
for the brave men who had fought so long and well to yield to
such a foe after so many deeds of heroic daring. Gen. Lee
went back to his family, *not even paroled*, and is now going to
live on a farm with his family near City Point. We hear his
wife died just before he surrendered. Truly his great heart
must be well nigh crushed by private as well as public afflictions.

And poor President Davis—I grieve for his saddest of fates.
When all here seemed lost, he started for the Trans-
Mississippi with his Cabinet and a large amount of specie
guarded by 3000 cavalry. But after crossing the Savannah,
[he] must have changed his plans, finding them impractical &
dismissed the troops, giving each $25 and then attempted to
make his way with his wife and Mrs. C. C. Clay. At least a
late extract from the Charleston *Courier* says he was captured
with them disguised in female dress.

Andy Johnson, the renegade N. Carolinian & Kentuckian,[4]
now Yankee President, whom for a long time we heard had
been hung by Bob Lincoln & a mob in retaliation of his fath-

3 In the final assault against Petersburg on April 2, a week before Lee
surrendered, there were approximately 63,000 Union soldiers and
19,000 Confederate soldiers involved.
4 Andrew Johnson was from North Carolina and Tennessee.

er's death, is far worse than Lincoln, fiercer and more blood thirsty as renegades always are and talks of the expiatory deaths of Davis and his Cabinet.

President Davis certainly seems to have erred very much to the injury of our cause by his strong prejudices for and against certain generals and other public men, but it is wrong to put the entire failure of our great cause upon his shoulders, when laxity of discipline, corruption, speculation, avarice, desertion & staying at home were the faults of the army and nation. And to think that he and his officers must suffer ignominious deaths! May God guard & protect them in these dark hours of trial.

[Ex-] Gov. [William] Aiken was recently arrested & sent North, after having presided at a "Sympathizing Meeting for the death of Lincoln." For the honor of human nature & our State, I hope it was "under orders." At any rate, among the Vice President's names published, were most of the prominent physicians of the city, Dr. [Henry] DeS[aussure] included. Finding their names to their unbounded surprise, some protested and were informed "they were marked men." Gen. [John P.] Hatch told Moultrie D[wight] that the order was "Arrest Gov. Aiken; if he resists, put him in irons, if strenuously, send him dead or alive"—and that he could not imagine the reason why. Whatever was the accusation, it has been withdrawn and he is at freedom in Washington.

Sherman gave Mrs. Ben Whaley's house to Mrs. Petigru and Mrs. [Henry] King, on account of Mr. [James L.] P.[etigru]'s Union sentiments & Mrs. [Elizabeth C.] Carson, Mr. [George A.] Trenholm's fine mansion in Rutledge Ave. ditto, she having proclaimed in New York her father as a martyr to Unionism. $10,000 was collected by subscription to build him a monument, and meanwhile, she was to have the interest accruing. She was to have been married last Christmas (sale No. 2) to Tileson, an old millionaire of a celebrated firm there.

Several days ago, Judy was so impudent to mother that she ordered her to leave the yard & Hetty soon followed. Mother had the kitchen removed to one of the basement rooms & Chloe cooks, but her maimed thumb is still exceedingly painful & prevents her doing many things. Lila & I determined to commence at once with our household duties, so take it by turn to knead biscuits & churn & attend to the drawing room. Yesterday [May] 28th, I made my first butter, of which I felt rather proud. We succeed right well with our biscuits. Edwin White gave me my first lesson in the art, & Rutledge's Paul, the second. Ann has been sick for several weeks & Mary also, a day or two ago, so I went to work to make up my bed & sweep & dust & have been practicing washing also, preparatory to the coming emancipation. Of course it occupies a good deal of time, but the servants find we are by no means entirely dependent on them. The same time Judy left, Patty tried capers with Carrie, who very quietly ignored her for two or three days, & ironed Sims' clothes & even Isaac's shirts, till Patty, mortified, came and begged her pardon & went to work briskly.

[Gen. Quincy A.] Gillmore has taken [Gov. Andrew G.] Magrath's place & issued an Emancipation Proclamation in Columbia, but we have not yet seen it, nor have any Yankees been here. We hear no vagrants are to be allowed, and owners can make what arrangements they please with their negroes. Our servants are generally respectful and willing to work as well as teach us what we want to learn from them, praising us for our industry and "smartness." We have told them what is coming, & how they will have all their own expenses to pay, & John thinks all will leave save Ann, who is lame, solitary, very dull, slow, timid, and friendless, and who will cling to us for protection. At any rate, like everyone else, we expect to have a great deal thrown upon us at first but will soon get servants. For, though no one has money, they will be glad to be taken for their food, provisions being so scarce. The Canteys have already offered theirs $8 a month, children not provided for, & they talk of refusing, beginning to calculate already the cost of living, never before thought on while master fed and clothed them. Poor deluded fools, I am sorry for them.

We are constantly expecting the Yankees to garrison this town, or at least come over and announce freedom to the negroes, but hear no further rumors of it.

Isaac [saved] two mules & two horses from the general wreck, besides Mona whom he traded off, because he said he was almost mobbed about her & again traded with Edwin

[White] for a very pretty white mare, Kate, a delightful ladies' horse. A few days ago Lila & I took a delicious ride on her & Edwin's grey—a six miles ride, a balmy afternoon, and all dust laid by the constant rain. It made me feel really joyous once more. When Isaac & Capt. H.[aydon] were at Alston, their camp was charged by a mob of men, women & children, *all armed*, who took whatever they wanted from private & public stores, among other items over a dozen mules, four of which belonged to Isaac. He only saved Mona by standing over her with a loaded pistol. She was a magnificent sorrel whom Gen. [Wade] Hampton had offered $400 in gold for, & every officer who saw her wanted her.

Alester has made two or three trips to Longtown trading off mules and horses for a cow and calf forage & future provisions. He is a really working character & tried to set up here as wood merchant but could not make any arrangement either for wood or payment (our old currency of course being dead, & trading alone carried on). John is at school with Mr. [Henry N.] Bruns of Charleston, doing little or nothing. Edward & Willie we have not heard from since they left, only know cousin W[illie]'s family were detained a fortnight in Columbia. Cousin John [Holmes] was very sick just after they left, seriously so, & cousin Beck [Holmes] staid here to nurse him; he is now able to walk out and wanting to go on to Philadelphia to see his family.

Isaac left two days ago with William Bell for Charleston, on horseback, to see whether he can get anything to do. For, Pride and Feelings have to be put aside now; men cannot sit idle forever and let their families want.

Mrs. George Crafts, having lost everything in the low country and in Columbia, went North to her relatives with Sherman's army without leaving even a message for her husband & at first he declared he did not care to see her again, but meant to have his children. But later, his feelings seem much softened towards her, too late however, for a letter came from her aunt in N.Y. to announce her arrival, but saying she was too unwell to write herself. He said he felt sure her sickness must be serious to prevent her from writing to him &, shortly after, her death from typhoid fever, from fatigue, anxiety & probably exposure was announced in a N.Y. paper.

Arrived W.[illiam] W. W.[hite] from Winnsboro to see and *June 2*
consult Isaac about their future, having just missed Edwin *Friday*
[White] also, he having started for Charleston just before
W[illiam] returned from there. He says there is no prospect
of anything being done there now, everything is stagnant
even among the Yankees, who complain loudly of want of
money, even the officers not having been paid off for many
months.

The Yankee Congress meets today month (5th) for an extra
session, and everybody will have to await their action.[5]

W.[illiam] W. W.[hite] is very cheerful and hopeful in his
views of our future. He thinks the Yankees are too cute, with
all their hatred of the Southerners to kill the Goose for the
Golden Egg, and that, in regard to the negroes, they are like
the man who bought the Elephant, then did not know what to
do with it. They have freed the negroes & now don't know
what to do with them, as the negroes think freedom means
freedom from labor & equality with whites, but especially the
former, neither of which ideas suit the Yankee in practice,
however much they may preach about them. The truth is they
hate the negroes and are not only willing for their extermination but assist largely in that mode of abolishing slavery. A
few days ago, William Trenholm, in Columbia, whipped one
of his servants for insolence. The case was reported to Col.
Horton, Yankee Commander, who summoned him to his
office and questioned him thereupon, adding that such punishment was not *legal* now. "But what must I do," answered
Mr. T[renholm], "his insolence was so great I could not put
up with it." "Why, shoot the damned rascal, shoot him." And
thus the philanthropy of their Yankee brethren is displayed
everywhere where the negroes are in their employment:
Whip a man, a fellow being with a soul, degrade by the lash
to the level of a dog—oh no, that is terrible, sinful, lowering
themselves to the footing of a d—d Southern slaveholder—
those monsters of iniquity—but shoot the rascals to be sure
upon the spot, if they disobey the least order. A gentleman
told Alester that he *knew* that was the case about Columbia
and other places where the negroes are working on the rail-

5 Congress did not meet until its regular session in December, 1865.

roads, etc.—that if they gather in knots of three or four to talk, the sentinel has orders to shoot, & the bodies lie there till night before burial.

In Charleston, W.[illiam] W. W.[hite] says he saw an old woman of about 45, with scarcely a tooth left, sitting on the sidewalk wailing loudly & wringing her hands in bitter grief. He stopped to enquire the cause, when a prolonged howl burst forth. "I'm too old to learn to read, and me fingers is to stiff to play the pianny" and again her grief found vent. He kept us convulsed with laughter over similar comic side scenes witnessed during his short stay. He was kept exactly nine months to the day, in prison, leaving Feb. 26th and having fared remarkably well. Kindness begets kindness—and his little attentions to others worse wounded than himself were the means of procuring him afterwards unbounded kindness from their relatives. . . . A Miss Mary White, through Miss Wells, adopted him, and he was not only liberally supplied with suitable clothing of all kinds, but provisions & delicacies in equal proportion, hams, pickles, preserves, pineapple, cheeses, coffee, tea, broma, chocolate, sugar, tobacco, grist, rice, condensed milk, etc. but [also] stationery and books in plenty. These ladies kept up a very constant correspondence, asking him to seek out and inform them of those who were destitute, thus not only making him their almoner, but enabling him through their liberality to assist a great many himself. For, he often had from 15 to 18 daily to share his various meals.

Time never hung heavily on his hands. For, after Desel & Bell, whom he had nursed, (To life, as he is convinced, merely from his attention to washing their wounds frequently & in clean water, for the Yankee nurses seldom did it twice a day & then used the same sponge & water to a dozen, thus planting disease instead of curing wounds, often carrying gangrene direct thus, & seven out of 9 generally died from it of course—May the Lord punish them for their cruelty as he rewards those noble hearted Southern women and Symphthisers [*sic*] for their beneficence and heaven-sent charity) had left, he was made permit-clerk having a comfortable tent with plenty of fire and light and indeed he lacked nothing but freedom, that divine boon to those who use it rightly. All permits for clothing had to come from him and, as only relatives were allowed to send it, when he found a man looking threadbare, he did not examine kindred too closely & issued over 3000 during the four months he held the place. Maj. Colt, the commander, showed himself a humane gentleman & said to him, "I am not inclined to oppress the men, but to do what I can to help them; you are not expected to be acquainted with their genealogy, but we must take what the letters bear on their face." His position not only freed him from all manual labor, but he had a soldier to wait on him, & it besides begot consideration & free access to the hospitals, while others had to procure permits and thus he was enabled to dispense the bounties sent him to advantage. He has had 70 suits at one time to distribute & Mrs. Van B.[?] sent him 50 blankets another. Snow lay three & four, & in some places, five feet deep, from Nov. to end of Feb. when he left. He also nursed Robert Adams to life, after being 108 days in bed with typhoid pneumonia. He himself was three months on crutches, the bone, having been laid bare, of the right knee, for several inches.

That condensed milk is a wonderful discovery made by a Frenchman, who being too poor to carry out his ideas, offered the patent to Mr. W. S. Coates, as he told me, but he thought it a mere catch penny & refused. Some friends of his in West Chester, the rich pasture land of Pa., purchased it and twenty cows to begin with, and have realized immense fortunes.[6] Rich milk has all its watery particles evaporated by heat, like sea salt, leaving nothing but the pure "cacine" which, with some preparation to keep it from souring, & white sugar, forms a rich cream paste, put up in half pint tin cans. A thimble full put in a cup of tea or coffee makes it delightfully rich, sugar being added if desired. If anyone wishes to drink fresh milk alone, a full tablespoonful put in a quart of water, dissolved, then put on the fire and boiled up once, then set aside to cool, has as refreshing a drink as if but a few hours from the cow. With whiskey poured on & sweetened, it made a delightful punch, which was freely distributed to the faint-

6 Several Frenchmen worked on this process, but it was American Gail Borden who in 1856 received a patent and made it commercially successful.

ing exhausted wounded prisoners on their marches, by the Sanitary Commission as well as to their own men. They had everything at their command, while we were struggling against the world.

... Charlie Holmes [came and] says he saw the official announcement of President Davis' arrest and the frock story is only a Yankee clap trap as W.[illiam] W. W.[hite] said, for [P. T.] Barnum was already offering a high price for it. The President was captured in his camp just after rising in the morning. W.[illiam] W. W.[hite] said he heard the Grand Jury in Washington had found a true bill against him & had indicted him for treason, but he did not think they could possibly hang him unless the jury was packed, for there were many prominent & distinguished lawyers who had always been opposed to this war on constitutional grounds. He was sure they would come forward in his defence. A report comes through John Kershaw, who has just returned, that he [Davis] has been released on parole and taking the oath.

How hard it is to get the truth in these days of excitement & no mails. We are entirely dependent on chance passengers for letters, old papers, and reports.

The U.S. Government completely ignores the four years war in resuming its sway & calls for taxes from '61. Gov. [Andrew G.] Magrath has been indicted for treason and carried to Hilton Head for ordering public stores, "after the state had been taken possession of by authorities," to be distributed to soldiers' families to prevent the sacking of towns.

... Dr. Edmund Ravenel's family, with furniture & provisions, were removed to the city to their own house by some of the Yankee Navy who appear to be gentlemen. They consider the army disgraced by association with negroes and won't have anything to do with the army officers. Willie Guerard & Joe Manigault lately went down under Gen. [John P.] Hatch's special order that they should not be molested, tho in officer's dress. But, when at Russell's [they] were arrested by a negro guard, who ignored the order, W.[illie Guerard] believes, because he could not read. ... [They were] marched up to the Citadel, which is now a negro camp, & [were] followed by a constantly increasing negro mob, who though they said nothing, looked very insolently upon them.

Before Lilly [Burroughs] could be married, the Yankees com- *June 7*
pelled uncle Wm. [DeSaussure], Mr. [George A.] Trenholm,
Frank [Trenholm] & Rev. Dr. [Benjamin M.] Palmer, the officiating minister, to take the oath. And then [the Yankees]
crowded into the piazza, peeping in though continually driv-
en away by the gentlemen.

Mr. [James S.][G[ibbes] is as well as usual & he has just returned from a business trip to the North to see his old partner
and arrange matters. He has always worshipped Mammon
most devotedly, and nothing can repel him from its service.

The Yankee Government has just published an order for
all cotton to be brought to certain agents appointed, who after
deducting one fourth of the bale, either in bulk or value, will
mark it "Free," & it can be sold to any purchaser & at any
price the seller chooses, the government rating it at from 35
to 40 cents a pound. Thus, by a direct and heavy tax, better
however than many anticipated, [the government] will commence to indemnify itself for the expenses of the war.

We are indeed a conquered people. Each day brings the *June 10*
dread fact more strongly to view, but none alas more humiliating and painful to every feeling heart than the fate of our
President and great officials. Yesterday's paper contained extracts from a Northern one announcing it [imprisonment],
which made my heart ache as if the tomb had indeed closed
over valued friends. . . . I wept as I pictured [to] myself the
hideous fate to which Yankee malignity had condemned
"those I had delighted to honor." Oh, God, I shudder when I
think of it—a living death, for him who wielded our destinies
for four years. Great as his [Jefferson Davis] errors of judgment have been and much as our failure may have been
owing to his obstinate prejudices for or against certain of our
generals and other officials, still he was a pure minded patriot
whose all was involved in ours. . . . To me, it is [a] dreadful
idea that not only must he bear in his living tomb the consequences of his own misuse of power, but the execrations of
thousands of his countrymen, who lay all the blame of our
fearful failure on his shoulders. If there is anyone I pity &
feel for from the depths of my heart, it is Jefferson Davis. The
Yankees exultantly declare that he is now incarcerated in a

"living Tomb" in Fortress Monroe, from which he will never again come forth alive. C. C. Clay, who with their wives were taken the same time, was imprisoned the same day.[7]

On the twenty-second of May, the doors of the outer world closed on them forever—say their foes in this life—but may Heaven help them in their need. Their rooms had been expressly prepared in the casemates & President Davis occupies the inner one of two, two soldiers always in the same room, guarding, yet never allowed to exchange a single word with their captive, while an officer is always stationed in the outer one, answerable for his safety. Lights are not allowed him, and from such severity, I fear that they intend indeed to cut off every resource even of books and paper and thus leave him to linger out life in the horrible blankness of the tomb—a man in delicate health, blind in one eye, & often suffering dreadfully from the other—to drag out existence thus, & never to learn the fate of those dearest to him. The malignity of such fiends as the Yankees could not invent keener torture to such a nature, but he is a Christian.

Mrs. Davis & Mrs. [C. C.] Clay wre allowed to accompany their husbands as far as Fortress Monroe, parting on the vessel. Mrs. C[lay] was fierce & stormy with wrath & hatred, as I felt sure she would be from what I have always heard of her, a brilliant, very eccentric woman, intense in her feelings & giving free vent to them, while Mrs. Davis, though very much overwhelmed at first, afterwards recovered herself but uttering her indignation in such bitter taunts and sarcasms, as much embarrassed the Yankee officials. President D.[avis] was quite depressed for a few days after their capture, but had recovered his cheerfulness—what will become of his wife & children. His private secretary, Mr. [Burton N.] Harrison, Secretaries [James A.] Seddon & [S. R.] Mallory, & Gen. Lee have already been arrested also & imprisoned for treason, & who else to follow we know not.

It was very singular Mr. [George A.] Trenholm was allowed to take the oath and is unmolested, for Mr. Bull came to see me yesterday [and] said he had seen, the night before, a

7 Clement Comer Clay (1789–1866) was a governor of Alabama and a member of that state's legislature and judiciary. Although an ardent supporter of secession, his role in the war was minor. He was, however, imprisoned, as Emma Holmes indicates here.

copy of a N.Y. paper containing Andy Johnson's proclamation, in which fourteen classes of persons would not be allowed to take the oath, thereby obtaining the protection! of the best!!! and most fatherly government in the world, unless they went in *person* to ask *pardon* from Johnson—on bended knee I suppose, with a rope around their necks.

Among those thus exempt, or excepted rather, from general pardon are all distinguished government officials, all aiders and abetters of our government, all graduates of West Point, all those who had left the U.S. navy or army, all State Senators, & those owning over $20,000 worth of property. So, Mr. Bull is prevented on the two last charges. Mr. [Edward J.] Arthur in Columbia took the oath and, when the Yankees discovered later that he was a State Senator, they revoked it.

Since Isaac left, everything has gone wrong. Marcus, whom he *June 15* thought would never leave him, so indulgent and bountiful a master had he always been to him, went off Sunday with cousin John's [Holmes] boy. And yesterday morning Mary & her two children followed to join Catherine. We had been expecting it & were rather pleased, for we do not want unwilling, careless, neglectful servants about us, &, though the transition state will of course be troublesome, we will soon be able to get others, and better, and at less cost to replace them, for we won't have the children to support. Mother had a talk with Chloe & told her, if she wanted to go, not to sneak away at night as the others had done, disgracing themselves by running away as she had never done, but to come & say she wanted to go—that the reason we had not freed our servants as Mr. [William E.] Johnson & some others had done was because it was not at all certain that they would be freed. For, it depended upon Congress, notwithstanding Andy Johnson's proclamation; that matters might be arranged on a different footing, but negroes still obliged to remain with their masters —that she could not pay her, as she knew, but, if she was willing to remain, she would feed herself & three children as usual. For, plenty of negroes are seeking employment merely for their food. Chloe said she never had run away & never would. She did not approve of such meanness & was quite willing to remain. But if she could, [she] would like to go to Charleston in the autumn when the railroad was finished. She is quick, willing, active & perfectly respectful, & she & Mary Ann really do well. Nina has lately been very discontented & disagreeable, but she too has come all right, pleasant and attentive as usual. Yesterday [she] came in to teach me how to iron gentlemen's collars, my first essay, & was just the Nina of old. Her health is really very bad, & she suffers a great deal when she cannot get her medicine, & she took it into her head that mother could, but would not, procure it & talked and behaved ungratefully. But she succeeded in getting it herself, & it has allayed pain & ill humor. Mother made the same arrangement with her, with the addition that when we had no work for her, she could take it in from others. . . . I suppose Ann, who is still sick, will also settle down, & we can hire an additional washer to do fine dresses, etc. For, mother has hired cousin Beck's [Holmes] Joe on [the] same terms, & he is an excellent servant, willing, respectful, considerate & well trained. Dudley we only employ in the garden & don't know how long he'll stay. We've not seen him since the exodus, as he is hired out for a few days to Thomas, the cooper, to pay for making some tubs, barter & exchange of work being the order of the day. Patty has behaved very well since her late escapade, & Mary Ann & herself carry & bring water, etc. from our chambers, while we make our beds, sweep & dust them ourselves. I was very tired yesterday after my various pieces of manual labor but hope they will drive off headache as medicine won't. I was up at five today & put the chamber in order before dressing, while Lila went to make biscuits— alternating daily. . . .

The long expected Yankee garrison, of 120 Ohio men, arrived yesterday.[8] . . . [They] established themselves very quietly in the public sqaure, by the school house, through which we pass to go down Main St. They are extremely orderly, & we don't anticipate anything but a strict police, for Sue Wilson says the proclamation & their presence made no change in Columbia, & these are some of the same troops. Negroes are not allowed there to be out after a certain hour, just as formerly, & yesterday afternoon, Charlie H[olmes] heard one say to uncle John's Dick (who would not run away but has just been waiting for his friends to give him his freedom) and

8 These troops were two companies of the 25th Ohio Volunteer Regiment.

Mary H[olmes]'s coachman "Do your masters hire you—No, they give us food and clothing—Well he answered, I'm sure that's enough, what more can you expect." In almost every yard, servants are leaving but going to wait on other people for food merely, sometimes with the promise of clothing, passing themselves off as free, much to our amusement. Col. Horton, commandant of Columbia, is very indignant that the citizens "have not shown him more attention, when he is doing all he can to ameliorate their condition."

The Howards, Snowdens & Mr. Richard Walker have just returned from the city where they were not allowed to take the oath, preparatory to trying to produce some business, nor allowed to pay their taxes. The U.S. Government completely ignores the past separation & requires taxes paid up from 1861 &, if not paid within a certain time, additional tax of 10 per cent; if that is not paid within 60 days, property advertised for sale—government agents to purchase—& permission to redeem allowed within another named period. As scarcely anyone has money, property will be sold at a tremendous sacrifice. Mr. [Albert] W[alker] found his large & elegant establishment occupied by his own servants, whom he had left, & who were as humble, respectful & attentive as of old; everything being kept in the neatest and cleanest style. . . . The Courtney's and Conner's fine houses [were] filled with negroes cooking in the drawing rooms. In fact all returned thoroughly disgusted & convinced it was no place for anyone who could stay out, & especially a lady. They confirmed the murder of Dr. Prioleau, but it was William, not Tom, and also of my old friend William Allen, who was chopped to pieces in his barn. . . . It is fearful to think of, for an instant, the foulest demoniac passions of the negro, hitherto so peaceful & happy, roused into being & fierce activity by the devilish Yankees. For, Henry [Ward] Beecher is preaching such treatment to their former owners from Zion church, where Mr. [Thomas] Girardeau used to preach. Truly freedom down in the low country has passed from the Southerner to the negro, & our beloved city has become pandemonium.

It is announced in the paper that President Davis has been placed in irons & removed to a monitor anchored in the stream near Washington. Mr. [George A.] Trenholm is in prison in Charleston, & Mr. [Theodore D.] Wagner has been

& was treated outrageously, we hear. Uncle James writes uncle Edward has been solicited to go on to Washington, on State service, & has accepted. Poor old gentleman—deaf, nearly blind, sick & excessively nervous & irritable, I expect it will kill him outright. A petition has been sent to Andy Johnson by the people (how many I wonder) of the State, praying a citizen of this State might be appointed Provisional Governor, and it is thought [William] Aiken may be placed there. He seems quite in favor with the ex-*tailor* & renegade, Andy Johnson, who has worked in this state & made clothes for Mr. Hamilton Boykin. Truly this revolution has been like a volcanic eruption, sudden and fierce . . . bearing all worthless things to the surface & burying all that made our goodly land fair to the heart & soul, as well as eye, beneath its streams of lava-blood and its ashes of desolation. The very foundations of society are uprooted.

Friday evening I spent with Callie Perkins the first in nearly six months, & very refreshing & pleasant are those quiet sociable talks, ranging from music & literature to cooking & washing & household economy practically being learned. Next morning, I had to put some of those ideas into use, for Ann, poor deluded fool, informed mother she could not wash any longer nor would she remain to finish the ironing. So mother told her she could seek other employment & off she went while we girls went to ironing. . . . Though of course it was fatiguing, standing so long, it was not near as difficult nor as hard work as I fancied. Indeed, since our wardrobes have diminished, so has our washing list. Chloe & Patty both assisted & showed us how to go to work, respectfully & willingly. Cousin Wilmot DeS[aussure] is ploughing, cousin M[artha] cooking, Susie washing, Belle minding the baby, & the boys cutting wood, drawing water, etc.

Saturday cousin John [Holmes] sent down to see [Capt. C. W.] Ferguson, the Yankee Captain here, to take the oath (not having been paroled) that he might get on to see his family. [He] says he felt so ashamed of himself he did not wait to find out the others who went for the same purpose. However, previously [he] had had a long business talk with Ferguson, who seems a determined, sensible, strong headed man, who has no notion of letting negroes play fool here as they do in the city. [He] says they are not free & shall work & behave properly, though on a different footing with their former masters. No negro is allowed to be without settled occupation & employer, every vagrant & loiterer [is] to be brought to him, & he will dispose of them. Owners who apply to get back those who left their premises, have a guard furnished them to arrest & carry them back, as Mr. S. Elliott did to his maids; those who turned servants away are compelled to take them back—as with Col. [A. D.] Goodwyn, but the Yankees are responsible for their behavior or at least will punish them if reported—punishment being gagging, bucking, hanging by the thumb, & shooting—military cruelties, to which whipping is play. In case both master & servant are willing that the latter shall seek employment elsewhere, all control ceases, & a written contract must be drawn up between his new employer & himself. If owners of plantations don't immediately make contracts with their negroes, the crops will be given to the latter, &, on further contumacy, property confiscated & owner treated as one who is trying to embarrass the government.

Indeed the Yankees have a tough job on hand &, having seen a little of the effects of entire freedom in the city, now delude the negroes with the name, while in reality for the first time they will have known what hard labor & suffering is. As no one has money, matters are to go on thus till Jan. when masters will have to pay up to their servant a *third* of the wages due from now. . . . As women used to be hired for $6. & first rate men servants for 10 to 12, they will have an extensive (?) [*sic*] fund to commence life on. In Charleston, white women &, in Columbia, negroes are getting $3.50 a month. Mother sent to [Capt. C. W.] Ferguson to inquire what she had to do about her negroes who went off, as we heard we were obliged to take all back. He said, if she knew where they were, he would send a file of soldiers for them & to teach them they had to work & behave themselves. He has already administered floggings to some & won't let one go, even to Columbia. All ours thought they would get free transportation to the city. Dudley was engaged working at Thomas', the Coopers, & informed him he did not intend working any more for mother. But by yesterday morning (Monday), he had found out the Yankees were his masters, & he walked back here to his work in the garden. We saw Judy & Hetty on Sunday, passing us by quite laughingly but without notice, & we know where all are. Mother is just waiting a few days, for some of the gentlemen to come, & we'll settle matters for them. . . .

. . . [Jamie Davis, Capt. Brown Manning and another officer] went to N.Y. where Mr. C[handler] carried them to stay several days with him, treating them with great kindness & cordiality. Indeed, every where they received great courtesy . . . a great reaction having taken place in N.Y. in favor of the South & against the President's stringent measures, as well as against himself, he having been drunk when he delivered his inaugural address.

The Yankees have indeed fit representatives of their degradation, in Abe Lincoln, the rail splitter & Mississippi Boat Hand, and Andy Johnson, the renegade tailor, who has worked in this state & made clothes often for Mr. Hamilton Boykin.

June 22
Thursday
Alester returned from his wagon trip to Orangeburg to carry Mrs. Sollee & Mrs. Martin, for the first time making some money & that in specie. I really regarded the gold & silver with curiosity, as if they were antique coins or medals. W.[illiam] W. W.[hite] also returned having had the handsomest & most liberal offers from his friends, the Adams, who are unbounded in their gratitude for his nursing Robert for so many months in prison; one gentleman has turned over his entire cotton crop of 40 or 50 bales . . . to purchase goods & open a store in their neighborhood, principally to barter for corn & cotton of the "freedmen" of the surrounding plantations, about 3,000 in number. Wm. [is] only to pay him one third while he lives free from all expenses with Robert A[dams]. Certainly he "cast his bread upon the waters, & it has returned to him after many days" increased an hundred fold. I only wish some of the other gentlemen in the family had an offer one fourth as good. He remained till Saturday waiting for Isaac whom we look for every day, sadly disappointed he does not arrive. Sims [White] talks of him continually, running to the door to see if he is coming, & even when waking at night, will say "mama, papa aint tum" most sadly. He shows new germ of intellect daily.

. . . We have also just heard of Mrs. Barnard Bee's marriage to Mr. Edward Thurston, after three weeks acquaintance—the inconsolable widow & widower—but he is said to be strikingly like Gen. Bee in manners & even somewhat in appearance. Poor Lilly Trenholm has had a short honeymoon & a sad one, for Allie met Frank [Trenholm] in Columbia, who told him she was very ill, while his father is in Charleston jail ordered to pay duty on all goods imported during the war, & taxes on his numerous houses—so that it is thought he will be utterly ruined—his whole property probably not sufficing to pay them. The Yanks are so hard on him because he assisted our Government more than anyone else by his credit in Europe & blockade running.

. . . All under the rank of major are being released. The gen- *June 26* tlemen generally are taking the oath & making contracts with their negroes, all opposition or holding back being worse than useless and the property would then be confiscated for the use of the negroes. But it disgusted me to learn that uncle John [DeSaussure] had sworn he had never entered voluntarily into the war, being always opposed to it, had always opposed it in the Legislature, and had never done anything voluntarily for it. Some parts were undoubtedly true but only the greater shame to him. And for other parts, he talks two ways. He told cousin John [Holmes] he had said so, & I heard him say he would support whatever government was supreme —thus ignoring principle and worshipping Mammon, for he cares only that his property is safe & he is making money. Uncles [Henry Alexander] DeS[aussure] & Louis [DeSaussure] have been deeply mortified & pained by his conduct both as a man & brother since this war [began].

Mother took the oath the last day of June, the provost marshal coming here for the purpose by request. All she had to do was to sign a paper. He told her little negroes must be well whipped, but the grown ones sent either to the military or civil authorities. We have concluded not to take back any of our runaways, for we do not want unwilling, disagreeable servants, who might harass us dreadfully, without resource. As Mrs. Perkin's washer takes all our heavy washing, save fine dresses, we get on very well, though we want a female instead of Joe, & will try to get one. Nina went out several days working with a tailor & then came & had a long talk with mother, saying she wanted to make some regular arrangement about working for us and to know exactly how matters stood. For she said with tears in her eyes & much feeling, she had lived too long with us for there to be any misunderstanding now; we all felt quite gratified, for all are attached to her, & she to us, & we had felt much hurt and [been] provoked by her previous uncivil behavior on one or two occasions. Her sufferings really are great, without her medicine, & when that gives out, she gets cross & dissatisfied till she gets more. She was once more like the Nina of old, who had always petted us & whom we had favored & indulged. I told her I had resolved on taking in some plain work during my leisure this summer & asked her, if she heard of any, to take it for herself & turn it over to me, which she promised to do. . . . I could not help smiling to myself at the revolution of fortune which had made me apply to Keturiah Workman for work—she whom I used to dislike so much & she moving in such a different sphere, but I knew with her many children & few servants, she always wanted help, which she said she would gladly avail herself of had she the wherewithal to pay. As Nanna [Hughes] says, my pride is buried with the Confederacy, or at least all false pride.

June 28 W.[illiam] W. W[hite] returned bringing Sims [White] with
Thursday him. The latter has had an offer as tutor among some of the
[should Longtown connection at aunt Sue's [Gibbes] suggestion. . . .
be 29] Edwin [White] is running a steam saw mill in St. Johns, Edward Porcher & either Prees or Porcher Smith hauling the lumber, getting up at daylight, eating cold breakfast, & working all day. They are fortunate in obtaining employment so soon. Thursday night, the Kennedys, Mathesons & Hailes, united, gave a ball at the latter's house, a hundred & odd persons there—tableaux & dancing, ice cream & hot supper being the order. I cannot understand how people can so soon cast off the memory of this bitter war & rush into gaiety, when the grass is scarce green over the sods that cover their brothers, cousins & uncles. We hear that some Camden youth remarked after a visit home on furlough, "well, 'twill make no matter if we die, we won't be missed, the girls will still dance and be gay.". . .

July 17 [Hattie Grant] . . . was married July 10th at 12 o'clock—with a dinner afterwards at 9 at Mrs. [Mary Chesnut] Reynolds, during one of the most intensely hot spells of weather from which I've ever suffered. It lasted about ten days & was as exhausting to people as utterly destructive to the gardens. For several days past it has been once more made comfortable but frequent thunder storms & showers [occur].

A Committee of gentlemen from Charleston, consisting of uncle Edward [Holmes], Judge [Edward] Frost, Wm. Whaley, [Fred] Richards the tailor, & several men of his standing, lately went on to Washington to request that our state should once more be placed on a civil footing under a governor of our own & be relieved from military despotism. Andy Johnson, whom uncle E[dward] had known in Congress, behaved much better than I expected. He treated them courteously & spoke plainly. He said our State could not be admitted to her rights in Congress till she had proved by her good behavior that she had returned to her duty. . . . Therefore [he] would appoint a Provisional governor. Five names being offered, he finally appointed Ben Perry of Greenville, who, though always a Union man, is, we believe, generally respected & will prove acceptable. He has been long in public life. Andy moreover left the important item of negro suffrage to be determined by the Legislatures of each state, &, of course, there is no longer doubt on that point. Andy said he intended the negro to be free, and, if the Southern people accepted the fact cheerfully & made their arrangements for the new order of things, that every facility would be afforded the country to return to its former prosperity. . . .

Sue & myself are taking in sewing to assist in paying for our washing, etc. It certainly won't be much more than that, for I've always considered seamstresses as a dreadfully ill-paid class & always declared I would never take sewing as my means of livelihood, for it would soon kill me or at least make me feel like committing suicide. For with closest application, a very quick workwoman could barely finish one chemise a day, that is putting really good work upon it. Those we are doing are quite plain, save four rows of cord stitched into the band & three little tucks in the sleeve, & I know it would take me two days of steady work to make one. But as we have very little work of our own, save mending, in which Nina assists, we work together, mother assisting. . . . We lighten our labor by reading aloud *Joseph II*, a delightfully truthful historical novel by Mulback,[9] translated by Mad. Chaudron of Mobile & published 18 months ago. We are to be paid in sugar and soap, at 50 cents a garment. Of course, we should much prefer money, but, that being scarce, barter is the order of the day.

Alester left this morning for the low country with cousin Louis [DeSaussure] on a business trip, but of what kind we do not know, save that it will pay. John has left school, as holiday is given, determined not to return but to try to get work of some kind to do. Uncle Ta [Gibbes]) writes word he has made $60. by making & selling 800 fishing lines & a little also by repairing clocks and watches.

People just up from the city [Charleston] say that there are daily altercations between whites & blacks, in which the latter always suffer, & four or five of them [are] murdered every day—while in Columbia & other places, they are suffering greatly for want of food, for no one will hire those who have children to be fed. Poor wretches, such is Yankee love & philanthropy, but the Southerner will have to harden his heart, lest he become mere pauper-minder. Indeed many of the first families of the land are themselves paupers & cannot afford to hire servants. We are really fortunate with the few who remain with us, for with slight or rather occasional exceptions, they are civil, obedient & willing, & we go on smoothly. Joe is really an excellent servant, &, by his respect for himself as well as us, his care for his own & sister's character, fulfillment of his various duties of a kind he always hitherto disliked, his willingness to oblige, & his straightforward truthful behavior, [he] has won our respect for him. He has been quite worried during the last few days about his sister Chloe's behavior, which was so improper that cousin Louis turned her out of his yard. And now, she is going to town, Joe feared in bad company, and seemed much troubled to know what was his duty—to go & see after her or stay with us, as he had promised cousin John [Holmes].

He generally asks leave to go out but once he did not &, overstaying the few minutes he intended, was not here to

9 Luise Mühlbach was the psuedonym for Klara Mundt (1814–73), a prolific German writer.

hand tea; but he came immediately to apologize to mother & did so again when he was delayed seeing after Chloe. These things are so unusual that I have noticed them particularly.

. . . Mrs. Barnard Bee's example is about to be followed by Mrs. [Francis S.] Bartow—singular—their husbands were killed on the same bloody field [First Bull Run], & they are remarried so near the same time. But both were so lonely & desolate. Mrs. Bartow is to marry Mr. Ephraim Seabrook, already twice married, & the father of several children, neither wife having lived long. Mrs. Bartow tells him she respects, but does not love, for her heart is buried in her husband's grave. She has attracted much interest and sympathy everywhere. She was one of the first ladies we heard of in the Treasury Department & spent several months here during the past winter, & thus we became acquainted with her.

B. F. Perry went on to Washington & saw Andy Johnson. He told him he would not be governor unless all negro troops were removed from the coast. Affairs in the city are dreadful, two insurrections having been found out, one extending far into the country & only known 24 hours before the appointed time. The Yankees will have to use power over the fearful spirit they have raised, for it threatens their existence here as well as ours. *July 21*

Weddings are as numerous as during the war. . . . *July 26*

Isaac, Sims & Mr. [William] Bell left this morning in emigrant style for the low country. Isaac & Mr. B[ell] arrived after ten weeks absence, their letters having miscarried till just before they came up. That time had been spent in hard work. They found on Mr. B[ell]'s plantation nothing but the houses left & one or two negroes who had remained faithful. Three [weeks] were spent in the city trying to recover some of their property from the negroes, succeeding in getting half a dozen chairs of different kinds, a bed & pieces of others, & one or two mattresses, etc. All the handsomest furniture & valuables . . . [had] been stolen by a captain of the navy to furnish a house for himself in town. But naval officers disapprove of such degradation of their character so much, for they have *general-* *August 14* *Monday ly* behaved like gentlemen, that they have court martialed him. Mr. B[ell] has applied to the Secretary of War & perhaps may recover his furniture. Meantime Isaac & himself are going to start a stock farm, on shares, the one having the necessary brain & energy, & the other the land. Their families are to live together on the plantation in winter & at the Barrows in summer.

The place is only 24 miles from Charleston by railroad & 4 from the depot, while it has direct communication by Back River, on which it is situated. It has a steam mill & brick kiln & 5000 acres of fine pasture land, from which they are about to cut wood for sale & thus procure money to start life again with. The future prospects are fair, though the labor, manual labor, is very hard now. . . . As it is just what Isaac has long wished for, I am very glad for his sake, though it almost breaks my heart at the idea of being so entirely separated from my darling boy [Sims White], when we had hoped to be settled near them in the city. . . .

We have just learned that Rutledge is the father of a fine boy, & Mary H.[ume Holmes] will soon follow suit. What a "family tea party" there will be when we meet once more.

Uncle Edward at last accounts had been very ill in Washington & kindly nursed & cared for by old friends. He was very anxious indeed for uncle James to go on to him, but he had no money & could procure none. He mentioned it to some gentlemen & next the firm of B. F. Heriot & Co. sent $125 requesting him to accept it, if it could be of any service, so he immediately went on. Blessings on them for their kind act. . . . Cousin Willie [Holmes] is in business with Ferguson . . . on Northern capital & doing well; &, as he has his aunts, sisters & little cousins, besides his own increasing family to support, he certainly needs all he makes. He has Charlie D[eas] with him, as his aunts have so ruined him by indulgence, that he is insupportable at home, but only needing a firm, strong, kind hand to check & guide him.

DeS Garden came on Saturday & staid till Sunday evening —was very silent & depressed about his future—is seeking a position as teacher of the higher branches, mathematics, engineering, French, etc. for which he is well fitted by education & former experience. Hugh [Garden] is near Charlottesville, Va.

at Judge [John] Robertson's, teaching, and meanwhile studying law under him.[10]

Edward arrived ten days ago & returned today to Willie's to assist him in gathering his miserable crop, which will scarcely pay for the hire of the farm, & the corn borrowed, then remove the family to their own plantation, where the house is not burned & contains Maria's sewing machine, dining table, a sofa & Wilson Broughton's portrait.

August 15

I have just written to Russell proposing to translate the *Life of Bayard*,[11] if he will undertake to have it published, or asking employment as a translator of new French works. Everyone whom I have consulted approves my plan & encourages me, no life of the Chevalier having ever appeared in English that we ever heard of, & all considering [it] a desideratum. Mrs. [Fanny A.] McC[andless] was very much pleased with my idea & DeS [Garden] said it was the best scheme he had heard of yet. It would be a labor of love to me, for I have so long yearned not only to distinguish myself in some way, as a benefactor however small, to the public,—to feel that I had not lived utterly in vain, and that I should leave behind me a single stone to add to the grand fabric of human intellect. Original I know I could not be, for long as I have desired it, I have never felt that "divine afflatus" without which I think, it would be worse than folly to attempt to write; but I feel the "cacoethes scribendi" strong upon me whenever I read & enjoy any fine French book, & I want others to share my enjoyment through my means. I have found my true vocations, teaching & translating, and would rather "stick to my last" than aspire through conceit to what I feel is beyond my powers. And yet, all my friends believe me capable of writing well & easily, even dear Miss Agnes [Bates], whose compliment

---

10 John Robertson (1787–1873) was a congressman, jurist, and author. He played a leading role in attempting to calm seceding states pending the Virginia Peace Convention. When compromise failed, he served as the Virginia governor's agent to invite Lee, Johnston, and other Virginia military officers to stay with their state when it seceded. With the exception of Winfield Scott he was successful in his efforts.

11 Pierre du Terrail seigneur de Bayard (*ca.* 1474–1524) was a French military hero called "le chevalier sans peur et sans reproche" (the knight without fear or blame).

thereon I value exceedingly. Tis strange, too, how many tales I weave in my day dreams, of facts & fiction, of others & myself & have done so from childhood, & yet they are always in fragments. I can feel intensely even in those delicious daydreams, in which surrounded by old friends, I live over past happy scenes or imagine new ones, can feel "their pleased eyes read my face" & hear those soft tones which thrill my every vein. And yet it all vanishes like the fairy mists of the morning when I would attempt to pen them. I can tell a plain story but cannot draw characters or group them, & yet, if only the talent were given, what fine materials lay ready at my hand. Fiction can never equal reality.

Tis very, very strange Isaac has never had an answer from Capt. Haydon, whom, we hear, was again employed in repairing the Greenville road—& not a word from Alice [Haydon], since I sent her package. Must that dream of all manly virtues united, my ideal realized for the first time, save in outward form, to be crushed, like so many others? I will not believe it, or I could no longer trust a man, for never have I met one, in whom I felt more perfect confidence in his truth, sincerity & nobility of soul and mind.

. . . Mary Ann Colburn has disgraced herself by her engagement to a Yankee Lieutenant of the garrison here. The only excuse to be made for her is that her father is Yankee born, & she has so little intellect & so few attractions save her wealth that her society was unsought anywhere. Two of the Brownfields' former negroes have married Yankees—one a light colored mustee had property left her by some white man whose mistress she had been. She says she passed herself off for a Spaniard, & Mercier Green violated the sanctity of Grace Church by performing the ceremony. The other, a man, went north & married a Jewess—the idea is too revolting.

I cannot but hope we will be able to return to the city with the New Year, for the negro troops have already been ordered to leave the state, &, when once more under civil authority, we may hope it will be a respectable & pleasant place to live. People are daily returning, some from here already gone, & others going as soon as the cool weather comes on. And, as all our negroes will be going, we will need white servants. Joe left us last week, and [with] Chloe being sick for two days, we had to try our hands one day for dinner, not wishing to call off Patty from her washing. I succeeded in washing the rice, but not the grist, & Lila undertook the corn bread. But, when a fowl was to be roasted (Mary Ann having picked it & cleaned the pots, John cutting the wood & making the fire) we were compelled to call Patty, for no one knew how to commence. Carrie came down to inspect & learn, so we certainly had cooks enough. But, we didn't spoil the dinner, for it was capital—rice better cooked than for many a day, because put on in *cold* water. To crown the whole, I ran out to the apple & peach trees in dressing gown & without a bonnet, fought the hogs, gathered some fruit in the corner of my dress, & brought in my contribution in triumph. But I don't like cooking or washing. Even the doing up of muslins is great annoyance to me, & I do miss the having [things] all ready prepared to my hand. I generally rise at five or before, though sometimes not till six when very tired, but often rouse servants & household by going to sweep the drawing room.

I have at last discovered what is doubtless in great part the cause of my long continued debility & have commenced to take active tonics, which I trust, with time, will restore me to my former vigor. Now I never feel well. If I could only go to Stateburg for a short visit, it would do me wonderful good, in spirit as well as flesh.

August 18 Friday

. . . By a recent paper we learn that President Davis has lately been allowed to walk for an hour every afternoon on the parapet (his prison has been changed) & Gen. [J. B.] Kershaw, who returned a few days ago, says he is now allowed plenty of the best food and books in abundance. His health is excellent & his eye much improved by his long confinement in a dark room & freedom from use.

Our dear Mr. [W. B. W.] Howe has recently had several hemorrhages from the lungs brought on doubtless by anxiety & excitement in regard to public affairs as well as his very assiduous discharge of his pastoral duties. As he came South for his health, consumption having swept off most of his family, I fear we will never again have the happiness of hearing him in old St. Philip's. His body is too frail for the earnest, energetic, toiling spirit within.

August 22 . . . The negroes are getting worse daily; in every direction we
Tuesday   hear of families being left without a single servant, or those
who stay doing almost nothing. Mary Ann disappeared last
evening, and our hired washer this morning expressed great
dissatisfaction because she had so much water to bring—
though it was distinctly told her when she was engaged. All
have turned fool together. . . .

August 25 Chloe left us after two days' notice, Mary Ann having run
Friday   away just before, so Alester went to cooking & we had a capital dinner, the best okra soup I've tasted for a year or
two, being made with fresh beef instead of bacon; but the effect of good cooking. In the evening, I went to see Callie
Perkins, found as usual a piazza full of visitors but remained
to tea, as she told me she had just decided the day before to
go on to see her husband's mother & sisters in New London,
Conn. & would leave in a few days. Some time ago she told
me they were urging her most affectionately to go & spend
the autumn with them, for, besides being desirous of seeing
her and anxious about her health, Loulie's health is so bad
that she feared they might never meet again, unless she came
now. Callie has often spoken to me of her charming mother &
sisters, particularly Loulie [Perkins], whose likeness she
showed me as an especial privilege, for Callie lets but few
"enter the inner sanctuary" of her heart, & it was a token of
her affection for me to talk thus freely of those so dear to
her. Loulie is brilliantly gifted & has a most intellectual face
with glorious dark eyes which seem to burn through you as
you contemplate them; she also is very reserved but lavished
all her hidden wealth of love on Callie, when she staid with
them as her brother's bride, & there could not be more loving letters written than those urging Callie to go on. Her
parents, too, are so uneasy in regard to her miserable state of
health, the utter debility & slow fever & headaches which
seem to be consuming her away that they finally urged away
all her objections to going on to the *North* & particularly just
at this time.

   I am very glad for Callie's sake, for it is just what she needs
to restore her to health, that greatest of blessings—complete
change of air & scene & the presence of loved ones for whom
her heart has yearned through all her great sorrow. And

though her brother-in-law Joe has lately been promoted to Brig-General for gallantry in the Yankee army, yet Loulie has always been devoted to the Southern cause & admired Beauregard almost as much as we; Maurice [Perkins] is a Prof. of Chemistry in a college [Union College] in Schenectady [N.Y.], & Mrs. Nevins lives three miles from New London. Callie will remain all winter if she finds she can stand the severe cold, from which she always suffers so much, from actual poverty of blood. But what shall I do without her, this dreary winter? I will be doubly bereft when Carrie & the children leave; for a little daughter made her appearance, like Sims quite unexpectedly, Wednesday morning at half past two. All Tuesday she, Carrie, had been busy cutting out Isaac's clothes on the floor; woke up mother at one, when it was concluded 'twas time to make arrangements; doctor & nurse were sent for, but didn't arrive till little Miss Eliza had made her debut. The baby is the counterpart of Sims at the same age & a fine healthy child. She is named after mother &, I expect, will be called Leize, or Lily, I say, though a red one at present. Carrie is remarkably well, notwithstanding suffering much from after-pains. Rosa [Guerard] came with her bouncing boy to see us the same day, &, when I saw Douglas' [DeSaussure] son & namesake born the same day whom Sallie Dan is taking care of while cousin Sallie's [Boykin] Becky acts as foster mother in order to try & keep life in it, 'twas difficult to believe that St. Julien [Guerard] ever could have looked more miserable than the poor little, aged looking, pitable [*sic*] object that little Douglas is—then there's hope for him.

. . . This has been a busy week of hard work, for, as we had no cook, the two boys have taken it by turns, sometimes Patty or Dudley, one day Minda, another night Milly—while all the house work (washing up china, churning, etc.) came on us girls & mother sick as well as Carrie & of course Sims to be minded, as Patty has plenty to do. The little fellow has however behaved remarkably well, is delighted with "my litty shissy" & not at all jealous. Thursday I rested by spending the day with cousin Sallie [Boykin] & sewing for her. Miss Emma Holmes going out for days work at 50 cts—O tempora, O mores!!!!

I am very weary, standing up washing all the breakfast & dinner china, bowls, kettles, pans, silver, etc. & minding Sims, churning, washing stockings, etc.—a most miscellane-

ous list of duties, leaving no time for reading or exercise.
. . . Last night I hemmed an apron in order to gain a little
leisure today, for it has taken me three days to make one for
Lilly DeS[aussure], so little time have I had. It is eight years
since I've sewed at night. Today I was determined to refresh
myself by writing up this & cutting out a spencer [short jack-
et], for which Callie Perkins sent me the fine cross bar
muslin & frilling just after she left. It was part of a night
dress cut out &, as Sherman's men stole the sleeves, they
spoiled the pattern. It not only came most apropos, for all
my dress bodies are splitting, but I appreciated *the degree* of
friendship it indicated, for she would only have sent it to one
she felt intimate with.

Alester had an offer of a wagon & team of six fine mules,
to work on shares, from Mr. Tom Jones of Longtown; [he]
has just returned from arranging terms. As the railroads are
so torn up, all the produce & goods will have to be carried
about the country by wagons.

W. J. Magrath, president of the S.[outh] C.[arolina] R.R.,
has just returned from the North with a two million [dollar]
loan to repair the roads. . . . As the Yankees invented an
instrument to give the Sherman twist to the rails, he has
brought on one they invented to untwist them. Isaac said
that he saw three rails so twisted & interlaced around a
telegraph pole that the ends could not be distinguished.

Gen. [J. B.] Kershaw says much sympathy was expressed
in Boston as well as New York for the South, which many
considered has been very hardly [*sic*] dealt with. And one
young lady with whom he took tea, (& he [was] constantly
invited out) told him that that evening as a crowd of "returned veterans" filled the streets. She stepped into a porch
where were several other ladies, & as they expressed their
sympathy for the maimed & scarred soldiers, she told them
that, instead of pitying them, they had better [pity] the
Southerners who had lost their homes & fortunes & everything by this cruel war. Someone said: why you must be a
Southerner to talk so. "No," she said, "I am not, but I wish
I was. I am proud of a nation who has done such great deeds
& proud that I have the honor of having a Confederate general to take tea with me tonight. And I only wish I knew
all the Confederate prisoners in the city that I might invite

them." Such is the feeling of the Democrats a small minority
& generally among the highest circles of society.

What a busy month has the past been. The week after Leize's *October 1*
birth, Sue had to have a tumor cut from her bosom by uncle
Louis & Dr. [Thomas W.] Salmond, taking chloroform; and,
as she was dreadfully sensitive, irritable & entirely dependent,
cousin Beck [Holmes] came to help mother nurse her; she
was nearly a fortnight in bed & required constant attendance.
Carrie was quite well & bright till the fifth or sixth day,
then came an attack of indigestion, followed by chill & fever,
& she has been sick ever since. During the first two weeks, we
had no cook, so Alester had to cook, though suffering from
immense boils. John had both hands festered & poulticed
from blisters, &, as Minda left, we had no one to call on but
old Molly, who, however, was always willing to help. But Lila
& I were really hard worked, for when we came up stairs, we
had to wait on the sick also, for something was always being
wanted—or Sims to be seen after & put to sleep, as well as
kept indoors & out of noise & mischief.

Since then, we have a constant ebb & flow of servants, some
staying only a few days, others a few hours, some thoroughly
incompetent, others though satisfactory to us, preferring a
plantation life.

. . . All the youths of 21 or 22 are crazy on the matrimonial *October 4*
question. Uncle Henry [Gibbes] says Alester has done the
same foolish thing &, like all of them, want[s] to be married
immediately without a cent in the world or any prospect of
maintenance for themselves much less a family. Charlie
DeSaussure & Ella Reynolds are on the same list, though they
anticipate a long engagement as he is just going to study medicine. He has such a fine mind & great talent for languages
that uncle Louis wanted him to study for a professorship, but
love ruled the point. . . . Ella is between four & five years
older than he, but that seems the fashion, as if the girls were
willing now to take any offer, without regard to suitability. . . .

I wrote to Russell some weeks ago inquiring whether he
would undertake to have published my proposed *Life of
Bayard*. But he said the best translation would be mere
waste paper now on the Southern market, for only school

books were being called for, & the negroes were the only ones who had money to buy. But [he] advised me to write to Harper & Appleton, which I did by Dr. [James A.] Young of this place who went on to New York last week in business connected with the book trade, & who undertook to negotiate the matter for me. So I still hope. Meantime I've just written a second "dun" to Mrs. [John B.] Mickle & have started mantua making, aunt Jane [DeSaussure] being my first patron. We have been making a few pieces of underclothing for the [John M.] Gamewells, (who are just about to go to Brooklyn, as their father, who is a mechanical genius, has gotten work there) & thereupon made a reputation as excellent needle women. . . . Mrs. John Kennedy has just offered us "a month's supply," she says, & then Mrs. [Fanny A.] McCandless expects a box from her relatives, which she will give us to make up. So we have something to keep our heads above water. We have a good washer & cook both to stay in the yard, or at least the latter will soon. She is the wife of Mr. [William E.] Johnson's right hand man, Timbrus, an excellent & most respectable servant, who will be quite an acquisition & protection to the yard, for robbers are "as plenty as blackberries in spring."

Charlestonians are gathering back to their beloved town, but there are no prospects of our speedy return, for rents are enormous, $800 being the lowest being mentioned, so many houses having been destroyed or injured. But we want to move with the New Year into Main St. where we will have near & pleasant neighbors. Here we are lonely &, in case of need, almost without protection when the boys are away, & everybody anticipates trouble from the negroes when the garrisons are withdrawn. As it is, the soldiers are continually getting drunk & creating brawls with the citizens or negroes here, &, because the last paper commented on the late one, it has been suppressed.

October 12 A grand tournament, followed by a fancy ball at Col. [A. D.]
Thursday Goodwyn's house took place here. I was desirous of attending the former, having never witnessed one, that is a regular one, and the weather was so charming that it was very tempting to take a holiday & enjoy a drive together with the gay scene.

But though Lizzie Bailey hired a pair of mules & I borrowed uncle D[an]'s [DeSaussure] carriage, I did not go, as Lila's & Alester's [*sic*] fancy dresses were unfinished &, as Lila had never seen anything of the kind & seldom had an opportunity of enjoying herself, I remained at home to work. Poor Allie was so busy packing furniture & books for cousin Louis [De-Saussure] that he did not get there either. The girls seemed to enjoy the day very much going at half past ten & returning half past three. Jamie Cantey was victor & crowned Lottie Ancrum. Charlie Bonney afforded much amusement as Sancho Panza on a white mule, & Dick Cantey as Don Qui-xote—the latter the absurdest caricature, a stuffed pig in an old militia general's uniform, epaulets, top boots & all, &, though the former [was] suited in style, [he was] an equal caricature in dress.

The ball took place at Col. Goodwyn's. Fortunately the eve-ning was mild & pleasant as we had to walk. Lila went as a Spanish lady in amber colored silk skirt, black velvet bodice, & white body, high comb, & black lace mantilla, fastened by scarlet poppies & cousin Beck's [Holmes] amethyst set. I, as the Duenna, [went] in my only silk—the chocolate brown, with its pretty bodice & trimmings, my flowers & fan trim-mings matching—a large black cross pendant from a tiny necklace, & a tiny ivory rosary being my distinctive signs. My character suited exactly, for I went partly to chaperone Lila & partly for my own amusement as spectator. Allie's dress as a Swiss peasant from its extreme simplicity, white shirt, blue knee pants, black cap & crimson cord & tassels, sash & rib-bons, was quite a relief to the eye after the gorgeous and elab-orate costumes of the Canteys, Richardsons, Murrays & Nel-sons, whose party formed the ball—almost. Most of their dresses had been made for former balls, but considerable taste was displayed in many of the dresses gotten up on the occasion. Highlanders & Scotch lassies abounded—the latter's [*sic*] & indeed most of the girls giving by far too liberal a dis-play of "ankles & ankles continued." But the most perfect & piquant costumes there were those of the Gatewoods & Jen-nie [Gatewood] as Lady Teasdale in brocade & powder, & Nora [Gatewood] as little Bopeep, looked as if they had stepped out of some of [Antoine] Watteau's pictures. But Bettie [Gatewood] was original & bewitching as a Norman peasant with a conecal [*sic*] cap of pink satin curved like a horn at the end, a foot high, trimmed with black lace velvet & gold chains in front & flaps of white lace behind. . . . With her beautiful dimples & sweet smile, I thought her most fascinating. Mr. Theodore Lang—Mrs. Burrell Boykin's brother, a handsome polished & cultivated gentleman—(who sad to think has been but recently released from the Lunatic Asylum—insanity being hereditary in the males & transmitted through the females, though not themselves subject to it) remarked to Meta Deas, who like himself had travelled in Europe, that Bettie was the "counterfeit presentment" of the old Norman Peasants so conspicuous on the Boulevards.

Neither Lila nor I had any acquaintances among the young men there & did not of course expect to dance, having gone as spectators, but I danced two or three "galops" with Bettie [Gatewood], fancy dances having entirely usurped the place of the merry Lancers. Had old Mr. Richard Roper, whom I've always disliked, to take me to supper, but any man was better than none at that crisis, for I was hungry. . . .

We staid to see the "german" dance, said to have 200 figures, & as far as I could judge from the specimens seen, an imitation of the old time graceful Spanish dance, & the Neapolitan Tarentella, as described in Corinne [Jean Coralli Peracini]—but shorn of much their grace & the girls almost all the time in the arms of the gentlemen. Left at half past three, reached home about four, &, as we put away everything before going to bed, it must have been near five before we actually slept; consequently were not up till twelve next day—the first & last time that I'm likely to be guilty of such dissipation. But our dresses did not cost a cent & very little time, while it afforded much amusement & was a break in the monotony of household work. . . .

October 18
Wednesday

I finished & carried home my first work as mantua maker—a black alpaca dress for aunt Jane [DeSaussure], & cape, trimmed with puffs of the same, for which I received $4.50 & much praise for the neatness & good fit. Went & bought myself the long wished for purple calico—really a very pretty one, the ground being true violet shade, with fern palm leaves closely strewn over it. I had sold a pair of Confed. shoes that did not fit & the blank book I bought from Sallie Scriven as a journal & thereby procured the money.

Great annular eclipse of the sun—a very rare phenomenon which however proved quite a disappointment, for we understood it was to be a total eclipse, for three hours, such as many years ago when the cattle & birds went to rest & the negroes gave up working, thinking the day of Judgement had come. Instead it commenced about 8½, almost imperceptibly, unless looking all the time through smoked glass. Gradually a very peculiar wierd blue tint stole over everything, & all the leaf shadows assumed cresent shapes; about half past nine, the climax was reached, the moon completely covering the main body of the sun, which of course being larger, showed a ring (annula) or complete belt of light all around for a few seconds. Then it passed off as gradually on the other side. A total eclipse is formed by the nearness of the moon to the earth, this by its distance.

October 19

Received from Dr. [James A.] Young who has just returned, information of the destruction of my Chateaux D'Espagne in regard to my literary aspirations & hopes of present remuneration. . . . All the publishers say their hands are full of new publications, but school books are keeping them particularly busy, i.e. to supply the educational needs of their free colored brethren. Besides, paper is scarce from the scarcity of cotton & the great drought which has dried up many water powers. Still he advises me to take it up at my leisure.

October 21
Saturday

When I got home, [I] found a sweet letter from Callie [Perkins]—my first—written she said, against Dr.'s orders, for she had scarcely felt strong enough before; that day was feeling better however. She is studying German with Loulie [Perkins], whom she declares is so learned she is sometimes half afraid of her & of course luxuriating in all the petting & endearments she receives & all the new books.

Miss [Dinah Maria] Mulock, our favorite, who, however, is married to Prof. [George L.] Craik, (said to be just the man worthy & suited to the author of *John Halifax* [*Gentleman*], *Woman's thoughts about Women*) has published *Christian's Mis-*

take and Mendelssohn . . . published "Letters from Italy and Switzerland, and also from England and Scotland," particularly charming she says.[12]. . . Jean Ingleton, of Lincolnshire, has created a decided sensation by a new volume of poems. I wonder when I shall enjoy any of these intellectual feasts.

Sunday morning arrived Mr. [William] Bell before breakfast, bearing a letter from Isaac & authority to move his family down, bag and baggage to Charleston. . . . It was a great shock to all of us, Carrie included, for she did not expect to go for a month yet & was unprepared, having been sick, to go to stay among strangers. All day Sunday it filled my mind, & I scarcely dared trust my voice in speaking of it. She went to church in the morning for the first time in months, &, when again to go with us, Heaven alone knows. She tried to insist on remaining till Thursday, but Mr. B[ell] said he had a carriage & wagon with him, & each day's delay had of course to be paid for, while he was at her service to pack, & so she had to make up her mind to go Tuesday. So Monday the boys got up early to kill & salt the hog Isaac had left & then to pack bed & bedding, kitchen utensils & toilette sets, cut glass tumblers, etc.—a little of each making the task more difficult. Sue & I to repair dresses, mother & C.[arrie] to pack, Lila to invite Mr. [Thomas F.] Davis [Jr.] to christen Leize [White] in the afternoon & some friends to be present, while the nurses went to shop. Thus 'twas indeed a busy day.

The christening took place at sunset, mother & Lila, the namesakes being godmothers & cousin Louis [DeSaussure] proxy for Isaac. I felt really disappointed Carrie had not asked me to be godmother, but she said she asked Lila as mother's namesake also. . . . Mr. D[avis] made the service extremely solemn. It was a pleasant, yet sad meeting, for uncle, the old patriarch of the family, and cousin Fan [Garden] went down Tuesday also; it is a sad breaking up to those left behind & makes us very anxious to go where so many branches of our family are regathering. After the guests had left, Mr.

12 Dinah Maria Mulock (1826–87) is most famous for her book *John Halifax Gentleman* (1857), a classic success story which emphasized the role of character in overcoming adversity and gaining success. It indicated that workers themselves could solve the problems they encountered in industry. It was left up to Charles Dickens and others to document the employers' faults.

Bell offered John a place as teamster at $20 a month, a perfect godsend, for he will be thus away from the temptations of the city & directly under Isaac's eye. So he had to be got ready too. I had a long talk with Mr. Bell about him, & I liked him better than I had ever done before. In fact, both Carrie and I commenced to feel real respect for him as a man of some soundness of character & not the mere empty bore we used to consider him. I fear C.[arrie] will find him a pleasanter person to live with than his wife, who has shown herself a wilful [*sic*], spoiled woman. [She is] not at all inclined to economize & yield to the exigencies of the times, save just as long as she cannot have the money to spend.

Well, they went off about eight, & a very sad parting it was, all that was bright & cheering, all our household sunshine then disappearing. We all turned busily to put the house in order, for it seems so desolate & dreary, and we moved grandmother into Carrie's room as more comfortable. But I can't get accustomed to her being here; the impulse is all the time to go & see the baby & sit with Carrie as I've been doing daily. . . .

. . . Aunt Sue left the same day for Longtown & later came Mr. Joe Mickle to see me about my demand for payment at the rate of $500. The M[ickle]s consider [that] quite too much & offered the same proposed by Messrs. [Tom] Jones & Nelson to Aunt Sue, $200; they then asked Messrs. Wm. Shannon & A. Kennedy to decide upon the matter, & they put it down to $250, which I told Mr. M[ickle] I considered a miserable pittance & most decidedly unjust. . . . I would not yield what uncle Louis, Mrs. [Fanny A.] McC[andless] and others considered a just demand. Mr. M[ickle] . . . [wants] to lessen my charge on the plea that educational labor was cheap during the war, as so many persons were offering [themselves] as teachers, and then . . . [he goes] on to value it the same as negro labor. Such narrow mindedness & low standard of ideas & action I never came across before. . . . Mrs. McC[andless], whom I consulted today, says she experienced the same illiberality last year, but that $350 is the lowest rate at which I ought to be paid. I've written to Mr. M[ickle] [that] if I get $100, [I] will gladly use it & wash my hands of them all.

All lands & houses are being returned to their owners & all

October 30

negro troops ordered to be disbanded & all negroes ordered
to go to work or they are to be sent to Africa. And every week
we hear of some other friend going down. I sold my pretty
Gabrielle dress to Patty & went down today to try & purchase
material for a warm cloak with the proceeds; found plenty of
girls out, clustering in Miss Denie's new millinery store, purchasing freely of new finery of all kinds—the colors beautiful,
but style, bold, dashing, extravagant & expensive. Little hats,
or rather boy's caps of straw & felt, are the fashion for the
ladies; bonnets, pressed to form a right angle over each temple, & almost flat against the cheeks, while the fashion plates
show the style of dresses & cloaks as absurd, ugly, & carried to
excess in every way. It really provoked me to see people rushing to buy every new extravagance of fashion, when half have
not paid their debts, & our country is so generally ruined—
laying out all they have on dress, instead of confining themselves to simple things, really needed & suited to the state of
the country. Then to hear Ella Boykin say she was going in a
few days to N.Y. with her father, who is going to sell his cotton, & she would make her purchases there & have her
dresses made up, etc.

Every or almost everybody seems trying to forget the war &
the past four years of agony & bloodshed, but I never can &
rather cherish every memory connected with it. At a newly set
up milliner's I saw a number of familiar photographs, Beauregard, Jeff Davis, Mr. [Edmund] Ruffin, Gov. [Francis W.]
Pickens, Gen. Lee, etc. which swept the present back into the
past with its high sentiments & glorious anticipations and
deeds. Lizzie Burnet came in, & when I called her attention
to the picture of the venerable Edmund Ruffin, which always
recalls father to mind, she exclaimed: the old fool, he shot
himself [on June 18] because Virginia went back into the
Union. It hurt me deeply as well as greatly shocked me to
hear such a dreadful event announced in such flippant language. I had always loved & honored the heroic old man,
who, an aged grandfather fired with zeal for freedom & love
for his native South, buckled on his knapsack & took part in
the actual conflict. He fired the first shot against Fort Sumter,
which opened the deadly struggle. Enrolled among the beloved Palmetto Guard, he seemed closer linked to us. He
shared too in the chase of the flying foe at the first bloody

battle of Manassas, seated on a caisson. No wonder his great enthusiastic wrapt [*sic*] in his country's welfare & freedom broke when all was lost and [it] must have reacted on his worn out frame & excited mind to drive him to such a sad deed.

Since Carrie & our darling prattler left, we have commenced reading aloud at night, to cheer our loneliness, [W. F.] Lynch's *Expedition to the Dead Sea*, which I find quite interesting & fitting in with much of my last winter's reading. As I can now sew at night, I can also gather many odd fragments of time to read or sit up for it, which I've not been able to do this summer. I'm reading [Joseph] Butler's *Analogy [of Religion, Natural and Revealed, to the Constitution and Course of Nature]* a little at a time, principally on Sundays & [John] Cumming's *Church, Before The Flood*, which I like exceedingly. How often I wish I had Isaac here to read certain parts to him, in regard to the alleged discrepancy between Genesis and Geology. Each day I become more attracted to the revelations of that wonderful science.

November 10
Friday

Judge [Thomas J.] Withers died three days ago after about a fortnight's illness of dysentery, while his wife, whom he has been nursing ever since Kate's [Withers] death, is still left, but for how long none can tell. What a broken up family. Accustomed to live in the greatest luxury, they are now so reduced that Randolph, the only son, about nineteen, has been every day cutting & carrying a load of wood to his mother to supply their wants. Mrs. [William L.] Kirkland used to receive from her father [Thomas J. Withers], even after her marriage, $2000 yearly as pin money & now her husband's property is also gone. Since his death, June '64, she has never left the house even to go to church & most of the time has been spent in her chamber. The Judge was a professed infidel & his funeral was as private as possible, Mr. [John] Elliott being the only minister to perform the service. . . . Mr. [Thomas F.] Davis [Jr.] [is] ill of typhoid fever. He was sick some time ago, then better, & the last thing he did was to baptize Leize [White]; [he] was in bed next day & gastric fever has run into typhoid—& great anxiety is felt for the result, for he has no constitution. Mr. [John] E[lliott] is maimed with a sore hand & foot, & the Bishop [Thomas F.] Davis not able to leave the house. The operation lately performed on his eye has proved a failure, & after such excruciating pain, he has lost even his former glimmering of light. Our neighbor, Mrs. Tom Shannon's son, Ben, a young man, when returning intoxicated a few nights ago from a frolic, fell out of the buggy on his head and next day had 125 convulsions, &, we heard, was not expected to live. What an awful death—to pass from life to eternity thus—(later this seems to have been a "canard.")

A letter from Carrie just received gives gloomy prospects for her country life. Mr. [William] Bell cannot recover his furniture, so they don't know exactly what to do. Roughing it would be a trifle, if Mrs. Bell was agreeable, but she has already shown herself a disappointed woman. She was jilted by Warren Nelson & very soon married Mr. Bell, a wealthy planter, who let her do as she pleased, & now she is a spoiled, wilful [sic] woman, by no means disposed to yield with a good grace to circumstances, quite "cranky," given to borrowing from her neighbors & never repaying, & worse than all, is a laudanum taker.

November 12
Sunday

Carrie's wedding day, as brilliantly beautiful as a Sabbath morn as ever dawned, our beloved pastor, Mr. [Thomas F.] Davis [Jr.], passed to his heavenly rest after more than three weeks illness. At one time he seemed so much better [that] Uncle Louis, who was consulting physician, concluded to stop his visits, only continuing at Dr. [Lynch H.] Deas' instance. But in a few hours a sudden & great change for the worse took place & he sank rapidly, unconscious most of the time save when roused. No greater loss could have befallen this community, for besides being a highly talented preacher, he was eminently a true pastor, visiting freely among his flock & sharing their joys & sorrows, making himself everywhere welcome & particularly loved among the refugees. His influence, too, so elevating in its character, was much needed in this community, which seems to think eating & drinking, parties & riding on horses, the highest enjoyments of life. He tried to influence them to higher aims & intellectual pursuits. I had become much drawn towards him during the past summer & liked to go to see him & Mrs. D[avis] who has always been very sociable with us & a great favorite of ours. She was indeed a true help-mate to him. A few evenings before Carrie left, I went to inquire how he was, & he asked me into his snug little study, just my beau ideal of the sanctum of an intellectual, cultivated man—a small south room, lined from floor to ceiling with books. Bruce Davis came in & spoke of the literary club to meet that night for the second time at Gen. [J. B.] Kershaw's, the subject to be discussed being "The future of the South, as influenced by the four years' war & its consequences"—one which deeply interested Mr. D[avis] for he was so anxious for the South to struggle manfully through the present severe ordeal, and rise yet higher in the scale of Christianity, civilization & prosperity, than she had ever been. I staid so late Bruce walked home with me & afterwards Mr. D[avis] went with him to the Club, though so unwell he had to leave early. The following Sunday, three days later, he preached both morning and evening from [?] & Leviticus. His last sermon, on keeping the Sabbath holy & reverencing God's house [was] most solemn & appropriate. He always spoke such plain home truths, unpalatable yet needed, so fearlessly yet affectionately, that they made deep impression on me, & I trust they may yet bear fruit. Monday afternoon Oct. 23rd he baptized Leize [White], his last performance of any sacred office. How little did we dream of his early passing away—his last act the blessing of one of Christ's little lambs. He staid late, conversing with all and taking particularly [*sic*] notice of Sims. He never was out of bed again. What a crushing blow it is to his poor wife & family. It was a most affecting sight at the funeral to see his blind and aged father led in from the vestry room by Bruce [Davis], bereft of his much loved son & coadjutor.

The church was draped in mourning & Mr. [John] Elliott performed the service, a difficult task for him, to restrain his excited & overburdened feelings. . . . The whole Davis family followed their loved one to the grave. Mrs. D[avis] seemed stunned; during the service at the grave, [she] took from her pocket a small book & joined in the beautiful hymn sung (most probably one of his favorites) which he had been collecting for addition to our prayer book.

Mary Hume [Holmes] has a daughter born Oct. 14th, Willie *November 16* not being yet able to walk alone. Cousin W[illie]'s family will move down to the Battery House to join Rutledge & Em in keeping house in the 1st and 2nd floors, as soon as M[ary] can travel. Uncle James' household of seven, aunt C[harlotte], uncle E[dward] & Lizzie G[adsden], coz John, Charlie & cousin B[eck Holmes] live on the 3rd and 4th floors, the latter keeping house, while cousin Willie commands the yard, thus relieving uncle J[ames] & aunt C[harlotte] of all care and trouble.

Cousin John, a few days ago, sent me a ream of fine paper for my translation. His medical practice has much improved, & he has laid by money enough to go on to see his family as soon as well enough, for he has suffered severely from abscesses & carbuncles—poor fellow. His Yankee wife shows herself perfectly indifferent to him, & I doubt not will soon obtain a divorce. Katie Holmes, however, writes him most affectionately.

Uncle Henry [Gibbes] lately sent grandmother $100 a sign he is doing well. . . . The boys & young men are crazy on the subject of marriage now—constant new engagements here. . . . Between the going away of the refugees & the exodus of several families to the west, quite a change has already taken place here. . . .

January 1866 'Tis a farce to call this a journal any longer, for I rarely have leisure to write a word. On the second of Dec. I went down in a returning wagon of Mr. Furman's to see Dora [Furman], considered quite a "daring act" in these unsettled times to ride 15 or 16 miles escorted by negroes only, but Mr. Furman's body servant Joe offered me "the light and airy vehicle."—Staid a month between the Furmans & Brownfields very pleasantly in spite of incessant rain and my being indisposed all the time—had the pleasure of making the acquaintance of "cousin Lydia Baker," aunt Fanny's old friend, & Dr. Charles Taylor, formerly Missionary to China & whom I had been wishing to know ever since I read his book on that country. He is Sallie Dan's uncle, & I learned on my return that he had taken a great fancy to me & would have called, had he known of my return.

I returned [the] 29th. . . . Found mother had engaged rooms at Mrs. Darby's to move next week, but when the day came, she declined renting them. As this was the second uncourteous act in regard to renting houses & none were to be had, mother concluded to remain here & get cousin Louis to hunt for a suitable house for us in the city, that we move as soon as Dr. [Lynch H.] Deas pays her [*sic*] interest.

Callie Perkins has returned so very much improved in health & spirits that it does me good to see her.[13] She introduced me to Loulie [Perkins] who said she had a great mind to write to me & hoped I'd be here when she came here next autumn. I really felt gratified by her interest. . . .

While away, our dear old uncle [Henry Alexander] DeSaussure was called away from all cares & troubles of the times, after a fortnight's illness—he died Dec. 9th.

In the great public world, Earl of Palmerston, so long Premier of England, and Leopold, king of Belgium, are dead. The latter is the father of Charlotte, Empress of Mexico. In December, my friend Capt. [Willie] Earle at last claimed his bride. . . . Matrimony is raging everywhere. Youths from 18 to 20 seem deeply smitten—their only cure wives several years older.

Mr. Bull lately turned off his negroes because they would not work, &, shortly after, the overseer's house, where he & the boys were living, was set on fire at night, & they escaped only with their lives & a little clothing. They then went to the gardener's house, and, another night while preparing for bed, stooped to pick up something just in time to escape a whistling bullet.

Brother H[enry] writes his family are with him in Ocala [Florida] . . . has been there two months—paid expenses & purchased some clothing for his family. Poor Willie has poor prospects—living in a negro house, M[aria] still cooking—Ed & himself going to plant the village lot themselves, as they can't get employment.—Mrs. [John B.] M[ickle] still promising payment—only $75—instead of $100 or $125—but not come yet. Alester guarded cotton, etc. during December—made a little money—guarding again now. Cousin Louis goes to Charleston with his family tomorrow to live in his renovated kitchen & stable & is to seek a house for us. . . .

13 From this point of the diary to its end, Miss Holmes wrote from the very top of each page to the very bottom.

February 7   . . . [I was] made very sad yet very happy by an eighteen page letter from darling Agnes [Bates], written from London, just one month ago, filled with warmest, gushing love for the South "the land of their love" & dear old Charleston "the Jerusalem of their souls." It is a beautiful "crystalization," to use her own word, of the yearning love and sorrow and sympathy for the South and their dear Southern friends amidst all the historic wealth of the Old World where they are self-exiled because they could not endure to live at the North at present & at the South they could do nothing now. Thus they carried the dreams of by-gone years—a residence of many months in Europe—and oh, could I but share my treasure with the other widely scattered friends & pupils, so fondly remembered. I wonder if a lover feels as excited & happy and proud of his letters, as I over mine. I count it one of the greatest blessings of my life to have had the Misses Bates as my teachers & to have won their love—would that I were more worthy of it. Miss A[gnes]' precious letter transports me to another world—a magic world of art & science and beauty and "all things grey with hoary age." And yet, amidst all that splendor & thrilling harmony of the grandest music ever composed by mortal & re-echoing from hundreds of performers amidst the "marble psalm" of York Cathedral and the antique Westminister, "hoary with age and prayers," where they attended the 800th anniversary of dedication, amidst all these, that weary unrest of heart for "a lost home and nationality" is a "minor under-tone" of deepest pathos, which brings the gushing tears to keep green the grave of the dead past.

Oh, my God, when will the dark days end which seem enveloping our stricken land in deeper gloom, day by day. After our national wreck had shrouded it in awful grief & desolation & the gloom of the grave, months of weary despair & waiting for events bade us hope a little. . . . As a nation, while trying to resign ourselves to the fate decreed by the Ruler of the World, we tried to conquer evil destiny by rousing, with all of manhood's energy & woman's faith, to the new and onerous duties laid upon us. For a few brief months the cloud has but lifted to threaten now to over-whelm us. Andrew Johnson, the President, is struggling almost single handed against the ferocious Black Republicans for the rights of the South and the white man. He is trying to restore the Union on the only footing possible—equality of the States & restoration of their privileges in Congress, while retaining their own reserved rights as individual commonwealths. . . . The blood thirsty Radicals, like their predecessors the Republicans of France in 1798, are moving "Hell and Congress" to bring about anarchy by amending the Constitution so as to make the Government an almost unlimited military despotism, holding the South as conquered territory—by granting "universal suffrage" to the negro (who as now [are] the curse that clogs us at every step, I pray may be theirs & prove their destruction). And [the Radicals want] possession forever of all the seaboard for 60 miles in width, the richest & most fruitful & civilized portions of our State, at least. But [John] Sherman amended it to three years & thus it has passed the Senate.[14] The Gas works in Charleston have already been seized by the Government, &, it *is said*, our railroads & banks will soon be, to pay Northern stockholders their losses during the war. . . .

Despair is laying its icy hand on all. Day by day it becomes harder to get money there for the necessaries of life; the little cotton saved has given a galvanized life. . . . No man can tell what a day may bring forth. [Samuel] Laing, as quoted by [Anna C. Johnson] the authoress of *Peasant Life in Germany*, says "Liberty always nestles & springs up to full maturity by ocean side or swift flowing streams" & most truly have the bounding waves of the Atlantic & the sparkling waters of our twin streams, Ashley & Cooper, nursed "the divine spark" in our bosoms. Liberty "sprang full-statued in an hour" from the wave rock "City by the Sea" & then its triumphant [?] was reechoed by every hill & dale of the far inland. Thank God, Charleston is my home. Amidst all her woes, that glorious distinction is hers: she was the Cradle of Secession. . . . I am proud of the honor of claiming her as the "Jerusalem of my love." Liberty is precious, &, though crushed & bleeding under the trampling feet of fanatics & fiends, her very attitude proves that Secession is Right—and though God does not always permit Truth & Justice to triumph at first, for his own wise purpose, yet I do not forget that "The mill of the

14 The 1865 Freedmen's Bureau Act was extended for two more years by a July 16 override of President Johnson's February 19 veto.

Gods wind slowly, but it grinds exceeding small." The Republicans cry aloud for President Davis' life & Capt. Raphael Semmes, our gallant champion on the ocean, was lately arrested when at his own home.

Singular to say many of our most prominent Generals, Lee, Beauregard, Joe Johnston & others, are Presidents, the first of Washington College, Va.—B[eauregard] of the Louisiana R.R. & "uncle Joe" of some [insurance company]. Judah Benjamin has applied to be admitted to the English Bar. [Matthew F.] Maury, [John A.] Magruder & Sterling Price & Jubal Early are in government employ in Mexico, Maximilian being very desirous of settling his empire, after its 40 years of monthly revolutions, with such a valuable body of emigrants.

James L. Orr is now our Governor, having beaten Wade Hampton by a few hundred majority. They are men. Perry [is] but the shadow of them [an] "unclean spirit," a Yankee.

Cousin Louis [DeSaussure] took his family down a week ago and was to seek a home for us, but a letter from Mr. Ingraham yesterday says Dr. [Lynch H.] Deas is entirely unable to pay as he had hoped. So there seems little prospect of our move to the city, as mother so earnestly desires. Money [is] at a low ebb —working giving out. . . . Carrie's life is made as miserable as they [Mr. and Mrs. William Bell] are capable of making it. But she has her devoted husband & blessed children, & Nina who is so devoted—bless her for it—& love can enable one to struggle hopefully amidst all the harassing trials of daily life & the hard labor for a livelihood.

. . . The Misses Sloman are also in England & Miss Betsy [Sloman] has added another verse to Sumter—Sumter in 1865.

February 15   At last I received payment from Mrs. [John B.] Mickle—only $75—after daily expecting it for four months—& uncle Henry Gibbes recently sent mother a present of $100.

February 15 & 16   Thermometer down to 10 deg., vinegar frozen solid into the form of the broken bottle; salt & water, medicine & eggs also frozen. [February 14] *Ash Wednesday* had been warm and pleasant. Saturday [February 17] moderated very much. After dinner, two slight sleet showers of a few minutes each; then bright & pleasant—commenced to rain that night, continued all Sunday [February 18]. Sunday night torrents of rain fell while the wind blew violently—rain till near 10 Monday morning [February 19], clearing up brilliantly and warm with a high March wind, just in time for old Col. [James] Chesnut's funeral. He was 93 &, I believe, [was] "the oldest inhabitant" of Camden. Mrs. [Thomas J.] Withers died a few days before.

Willie writes he has been hauling rails on his shoulders to make a fence. With but three bushels of corn in the house (an old negro one at that) & not a dollar in the world, [he] has contracted with 20 negroes to plant, the Government to furnish provisions to those too poor to buy. But he has not the means to go to Hilton Head to make arrangements or to pay for the freightage. Maria still cooks, but he has made arrangements to send the children to school, & all are well, & he happy in their love in spite of poverty.

We've all had a great shock in the death of the Gallant Gen. *March 1* Ste.[phen] Elliott after a short illness of inflammation of the stomach. When Mr. E[lliott]'s family arrived in the city, they learned his illness & his father went right up. The Yankees put a steamer at his disposal to carry the body & friends to Beaufort. . . . A letter just received from brother H[enry] says Chick gave him a Valentine in the shape of a miniature Tom Pasteur. . . .

. . . In spite of national humiliation & grief & individual sorrow & carking cares, Folly and Frivolity still reign supreme among a certain set, the same who danced before the sod was settled over the bloody graves of their kindred during the war. . . .

On my return from Sallie Dan's, found Alester just arrived —said while he was in Beaufort Mr. [Rev. Stephen] Elliott was very ill with congestion of the lungs. "Sorrows always come in battalions." Poor Willie ([whom] he saw in town) . . . had vainly endeavored to procure funds to carry on planting. His last hope was to try to get a place as Express clerk in Savannah under Gen. W. S. Walker, Superintendent, who had given him a letter of recommendation to Gen. Joe Johnston, Pres. & with whom W.[illie] had been orderly of couriers. Edward expects to become overseer to some one. Cousin Louis is as generous as Mr. B[oykin]; last summer he loaned mother $50. which he has since given her, & on this visit added $100. He has vainly tried to sell our city lot advantageously or get some payments . . . that we might go down to the city . . . but we have to remain here probably for another year. Alester is trying for R.R. Agent at Claremont [N.C.] & we are getting work. I'm getting embroidery as well as dress making.

April 7   What mournful records belong to the past month—the very sudden death of Rev. Stephen Elliott, scarce three weeks after he had laid his beloved son among the graves of his kindred. . . . Old Miss Harriet Pinckney, too, has been gathered to her fathers, full of years & honors. After having dispensed her large fortune most liberally among the poor, in her ninetieth year despoiled of all by the Satanic crew who despoiled "our goodly heritage," she has since been supported by her former pensioners. Old Miss Mary Baker too has gone & our last letter from brother Henry announced the death of his infant son, Tom Pasteur, of spasmodic croup, the day it was a month old. It has been a severe blow to the grieving parents.

Small-pox is raging in our poor old city [Charleston] among the negroes & even very prevalent among the higher classes. . . .

Willie writes a few days ago that, as he could not get funds to carry on planting, he has hired the plantation to Willie Heyward. . . . The latter has evidently set him up in the grocery store he is about starting in Grahamville, from which he is to get half the net profits & hopes to realize a maintenance for his family, which has raised a load from my heart. Hannah, Maria's nurse, is cooking for them, made humble by starvation.

I just returned from [a] three days mantua-making visit to Sallie Dan—have lately made a very pretty morning gown for Sallie Davis & am now making a delaine dress for her mother. We've got our sewing machine working very prettily. . . .

A recent letter from Fannie Gibbes says uncle Henry [Gibbes] has [a] cataract growing on both eyes, but the oculist tells him, as soon as it has formed completely, in two or three weeks, to go back to him to have an operation performed. So there's strong hopes of his recovery. So much blindness in the various branches of our family makes me dread it for myself. Uncle Ta [Gibbes] writes his chain ferry boat is a complete success. [He] has been working a month & in 4½ minutes can carry 4 six-horse wagons & 6 riders over the Savannah river. . . .

Frederica [Fredrika] Bremer is dead & I have just enjoyed her "Bertha" so much.[15]

Last Friday there was a total eclipse of the moon when at the full, & that night mother, Sue, & Lila (who was in bed with a sore throat) sat up till 4 o'clock while I read aloud the whole of *Kate Kennedy* a delightful story of modern life. So natural were the characters and their conversations that we felt personally acquainted with them. I don't know the author.[16]

15 Fredrika Bremer (1801–65) was a Swedish romantic novelist.
16 Half a page is left blank, so more could have been written. Perhaps this indicates that a new journal was begun. However, in the entry for October 18, 1865, Emma Holmes indicated that she sold the book she had meant to use as a diary. No other journal has been discovered. Sometime after this period, Emma Holmes returned to Charleston and spent the rest of her life there, tutoring and teaching. She never married. When she died in 1910, she was buried in the cemetery adjacent to her beloved St. Philip's Church.

Index

CANISIUS COLLEGE LIBRARY

3 5084 00443 8696

Book Shelves
F279.C453 H643 1979
Holmes, Emma, 1838-1910
The diary of Miss Emma
Holmes, 1861-1866

CANISIUS COLLEGE LIBRARY
BUFFALO, NY 14208